THE BEST PLAYS OF 1996–1997

THE OTIS GUERNSEY
BURNS MANTLE
THEATER YEARBOOK

THE BEST PLAYS OF
1996–1997

EDITED BY OTIS L. GUERNSEY JR.

*Illustrated with photographs and
with drawings by* HIRSCHFELD

LIMELIGHT EDITIONS

EDITOR'S NOTE

THE FOOTPRINTS of this, the 78th volume in the *Best Plays* theater yearbook series started by Burns Mantle with the season of 1919–20, are somewhat different in shape from those of its predecessors, but leading in the same direction, with the same goal of purposeful service to the theater community and its affectionate audience.

It has always been a priority of each of the five *Best Plays* editors (Burns Mantle, John Chapman, Louis Kronenberger, Henry Hewes and the undersigned) to follow the theater as closely as possible wherever its imagination and/or caprice might lead; to reflect each season in each volume with as sparkling an image and as thorough a collection of factual data as possible. In the tenure of the present editor since 1964– 65, *Best Plays* has followed the stage's lead with much more frequent recognition— indeed, complete co-equal consideration—of musicals and off-Broadway productions among the ten Best Plays, as they have played a bigger and bigger star part on the New York scene. We have expanded our coverage in pursuit of excellence with Jeffrey Sweet's incomparably perceptive critique of each season. We have mapped the farthest reaches of the tributary theater with Camille Dee's listings of off-off-Broadway and regional theater programs, embellished by Mel Gussow's evaluation of the OOB scene and the American Theater Critics Association's (ATCA's) annual tribute to outstanding new plays across the country. With the dedicated assistance of our regular contributors including Rue E. Canvin (publications, necrology, critics' choices), Jeffrey A. Finn (cast replacements), Sally Dixon Wiener (play synopsis), Michael Grossberg (ATCA citations), Michael Kuchwara (New York Drama Critics Awards), William Schelble (Tony Awards), Henry Hewes (Hall of Fame listings), Thomas T. Foose (historical advisories) and Ralph Newman of the Drama Book Shop, we have maintained our traditional *Best Plays* coverage and increased its facts-and-figures grasp.

With this volume, it's time to make yet another major change, so that we can continue to mirror our volatile theater's history and significance to those who love it. Now, we believe, is the time to change our way of spotlighting the best scripts of the New York theater year. Instead of selecting, independently and unilaterally, ten best plays for a Best Plays section, we will now adhere to the same system of selecting the New York bests as has proved so successful over the past 20 years of presenting ATCA's outstanding cross-country plays. We are adopting consensus in place of individual judgment as our mode of selection. Our featured New York plays will from now on be the major prizewinners, such as but not entirely limited to those chosen by the Tony (selection of the best Broadway offerings, sanctioned by the League of American Theaters and Producers), Lucille Lortel (selection of the best off-Broadway offerings, sanctioned by the League of Off-Broadway Theaters and Producers) New York Drama Critics (qualified esthetic selections made among

vii

Broadway and off-Broadway offerings viewed as a whole) and Pulitzer (qualified esthetic selections made among American playwriting viewed as a whole) award-giving committees. These are to be our featured plays, chosen annually in forms of consensus. We present them with script excerpts in our Prizewinning Plays (formerly Best Plays) section of this volume in exactly the same way and with exactly the same emphasis as with our own personal, unilateral choices in previous volumes. And qualified esthetic selection of a prizewinning play specifically from the regional theater (by ATCA) is prominently featured in another section of our coverage.

Principally, it's our instinct that tells us this is the right change to make at this time. Our reasons, when we reflect on them, are compelling. It has become increasingly more difficult and less appropriate to pick out ten plays for special treatment, to the exclusion of all others. Our New York theater has never been more eclectic, offering entertainments and emotional and intellectual challenges to excite a huge variety of audience tastes. But it is no longer a generally homogeneous dramatic form in which "best" can be usefully evaluated from any one perspective to any very significant esthetic purpose. Our theater has become much too sophisticated for that, ranging from the multi-million-dollar musical spectacle to the piercing solo performance; from *Titanic* to *A Huey P. Newton Story.* At every stage these multiple sizes and shapes of theater offer thrilling experiences to special segments of the audience, though seldom to the audience as a whole. To contemplate them all from a single perspective in the same light of inclusion on an overall "best" list has become an apples v. oranges judgement—difficult to rationalize except as an individual commitment to informed personal esthetic standards.

Best Plays is, essentially, a fact book, and the identification of the best plays of any given season is among its most important facts. If, as in the ATCA selections, we leave the judging to others and let the prizewinners become our Best Plays, so to speak, we continue to perform (perhaps more accurately than ever) our principal function as a comprehensive record of an American theater season.

Also, advanced communication techniques have made playscripts in their entirety much more generally available than in the past. At one time, when the public had access to playscripts only infrequently and in hard covers, the Best Play synopses were an important collection of information for students and theater lovers. Nowadays, almost any play of consequence is easily available in affordable book form, making our synopses less of a novelty. But within our function as a record of achievement over a 12-month period, the winning of a major prize gives each synopsis unique journalistic importance and historical value, restoring much of the stature lost to circumstance. We will continue to present the prizewinners—at least as representative of New York's best plays as any single best list—in all their glory, in traditional *Best Plays* fashion, with excerpts from their texts to place their dramatic style and literary personality on the *Best Plays* permanent record.

The prizegivers don't often overlook any first class candidates. But when, in our judgement, such a rare omission does take place, the *Best Plays* editors won't hesitate to correct it with a special citation of our own—as in the case of 1996–97's excellent *Old Wicked Songs,* which lost out on last year's Pulitzer and was thus ineligible for this year's but is fully honored in these pages.

Jeffrey Sweet has covered the Broadway and off-Broadway scene for this series from 1985–86 through 1995–96 in a series of critical essays so eloquent and well informed that they deserve to be made into a book by themselves. With mutual blessings, he has decided to concentrate on teaching, playwriting (one of his scripts, *American Enterprise*, was cited as a Best Play in 1994) and serving on the management council of the Dramatists Guild, to which he was elected this spring—and contributing to *Best Plays* whatever he can, as with this year's synopsis of the Critics best foreign play award winner, *Skylight*.

Best Plays will continue to offer a factual and judgmental review of Broadway and off-Broadway doings and conjectures on and off stage, in an overview of the season by David Lefkowitz. No newsworthy or esthetic highlight of the theater season has escaped his notice and comment in his report, which begins our 1996–97 coverage. Lefkowitz has his credentials as a theater journalist and enthusiast, including his B.F.A. and M.F.A. in playwriting, film and television from New York University. He edits and publishes his own theater newsletter (*This Month on Stage*), now six years old; and he is a reporter for *Playbill-on-Line*. We welcome his eminently qualified presence on the *Best Plays* team.

We are backing up Lefkowitz's essay with our customary, complete cast-and-credits listings of all shows produced on and off Broadway during the 12 months (June 1, 1996–May 31, 1997) of the season. In these listings, because of increasing instances of musical revivals on the New York scene rearranging the order of the songs or cutting or adding musical numbers to the original score in the refurbished show, we will henceforth include the entire program listing of musical numbers for each musical revival entry. In the past, we have sometimes simply referred to a past *Best Plays* volume for a listing of a revival's musical numbers, but henceforth we will include all of them, every time, as available.

Jonathan Dodd, once of Dodd, Mead & Company, original publishers of the *Best Plays* series, has been supervising editorial detail from the deep historical past, even before the Hewes and Guernsey incumbencies, and he continues to do so with efficiency and enthusiasm. This is the 33d volume to be textually scrutinized by the editor's painstaking wife and the fifth to be published by Melvyn B. Zerman's Limelight Editions. It is the 44th whose readers and editors alike have enjoyed (thanks to the Margo Feiden Galleries) the visions of Al Hirschfeld, who knows and can express in his drawings what actors and actresses really look like in the midst of their performances. This 78th volume in the series is also indebted to the Tony Design Award winners (Stewart Laing for the sets of *Titanic* and Judith Dolan for the costumes of *Candide*) for examples of their outstanding work; to colleagues who helped us acquire the information for the regional critics awards listings—David A. Rosenberg (Connecticut), Caldwell Titcomb (Boston), Joan M. Kaloustian (Chicago) and Rob Stevens (Los Angeles); and to the photographers, examples of whose work, generously supplied by the production offices, illustrate the "look" of the season onstage from Broadway to OOB and from coast to coast, including Richard Anderson, ASF/Scarsbrook, Catherine Ashmore, Coy Butler, Dan Charkin, Susan Cook, Michal Daniel, T. Charles Erickson, Richard Feldman, Sheila Ferrini, James Fry, Maressa Blau Gershowitz, Gerry Goodstein, John Haynes, Martha Holmes,

Ken Howard, Sherman M. Howe Jr., Ken Jacques, Liz Lauren, Joan Marcus, Larry McLeon, Miguel Pagliere, Suzanne Plunkett, Dan Rest, Carol Rosegg, Diane Sobolewski, Martha Swope, Cylla Von Tiedmann, Richard Trigg, Sandy Underwood and David Zeiger.

The hundreds of other people who make it possible to collect the information contained in any *Best Plays* volume cannot be named here but deserve to be thanked and credited by profession as co-authors: the press agents with their prompt, patient and effective response to our requests for material. Behind them and everyone else who has anything to do with the legitimate stage there are first, last and always the playwrights whose persistent and dauntless gift of their time and talent is a bet against overwhelming odds which, if won, pays off more to others than to themselves, in revelation and sheer enjoyment. We thank, hail, and encourage them to continue showing off the flights of their imagination side-by-side with the enduring classics in this oldest and greatest of the dramatic art forms. The playwrights' activities, win or lose, historically or up-to-the-minute, is what *Best Plays* and everything else in the theater is all about.

OTIS L. GUERNSEY Jr.

September 1, 1997

CONTENTS

Drawings by HIRSCHFELD

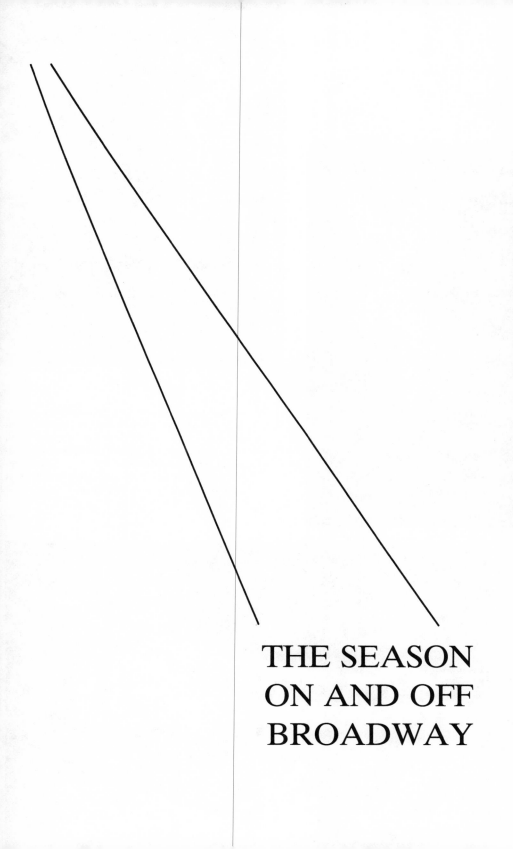

THE SEASON
ON AND OFF
BROADWAY

New Broadway Musicals

Above, Lynn Sterling and Felicia Finley in *The Life; left,* an impression of Robert Cuccioli's dual title role in *Jekyll & Hyde; below,* Captain Smith (John Cunningham), Ismay (David Garrison), designer Andrews (Michael Cerveris), on the gangway and passengers on the dock stare at their great ship with a wild surmise in *Titanic*

BROADWAY AND OFF BROADWAY

By David Lefkowitz

OH, happy season!

For a critic to take a positive, even joyful, stand on the merits of a year of theater can be seen by some as intellectual dishonesty, by others as sacrilege. We are supposed to stand back, even in the best of times, and dissect worrying trends, find the flaws in over-popular hits and wring our hands over fine works that got short shrift. Far be it from me to disregard such time-honored activities in my overview of the 1996–97 New York season, but let it be said, first and foremost, *this has been the best season in years.*

I won't go as far as the League of American Theaters & Producers, who've termed 1996–97 the "Broadway season best ever" because it raked in $499 million (up 14.5 percent from the previous year). And if you asked me to name the great theatrical masterwork penned in the past 12 months, or the innovative, unforgettable musical that sprang to life on a New York stage, I could not. As evidenced by the Pulitzer's vote of no confidence this year, no great work of drama rose to lasting distinction; no musical became the next *My Fair Lady* or *Falsettos*, for that matter.

What New York did get was four new Broadway musicals—of markedly different styles—and a host of straight plays that made off Broadway as adventurous as a day in Disneyworld. If new works by Christopher Durang, Steve Tesich and Craig Lucas failed to win the usual critical rapture, Patrick Marber, John Patrick Shanley, Alan Zweibel, Paula Vogel, David Rabe, David Hare, Leslie Ayvazian, Alfred Uhry, Jonathan Reynolds and Peter Hedges were turning out works of serious entertainment value and dramatic worth.

Fears that increased productivity and competition would have a Darwinian effect on shows, with only the most expensive, honored and well-hyped surviving, had some validity, but no more than in weaker seasons, when one big hit would leave its compadres choking in the dust. If anything, 1996–97 Broadway proved that supply/demand in theater just doesn't fit the mold of high school economics. On Broadway, more product *creates* more demand; a busy season with much to see creates the illusion of success, which in theater, anyway, is almost indistinguishable from the real thing.

The 1996–97 Season on Broadway

PLAYS (3)

Lincoln Center:
  Sex and Longing
  An American Daughter
  THE LAST NIGHT OF
  BALLYHOO

FOREIGN PLAYS IN ENGLISH (3)

SKYLIGHT
Taking Sides
Stanley

MUSICALS (8)

MSG Productions:
  A Christmas Carol
  (return engagement)
  The Wizard of Oz
Juan Darién
Play On!
TITANIC
Steel Pier
The Life
Jekyll & Hyde

REVUE (1)

Dream

SOLO SHOWS (4)

God Said "Ha!"
Men Are From Mars
Mandy Patinkin
Barrymore

FOREIGN-LANGUAGE PRODUCTIONS (2)

Moscow Sovremennik:
  Three Sisters
  Into the Whirlwind

REVIVALS (17)

Roundabout:
  A Thousand Clowns
  Summer and Smoke
  The Rehearsal
  Three Sisters
  London Assurance
Hughie
H.M.S. Pinafore
Chicago
Present Laughter
Grease
Once Upon a Mattress
Annie
*The Young Man From
  Atlanta*
A Doll's House
The Gin Game
The Little Foxes
Candide

SPECIALTIES (6)

Riverdance
  (return engagement)
Radio City Music Hall:
  Christmas Spectacular
  Spring Spectacular
Dreams & Nightmares
Lord of the Dance
King David

Categorized above are all the new productions listed in the Plays Produced on Broadway section of this volume.
Plays listed in CAPITAL LETTERS were major 1996–97 prizewinners.
Plays listed in *italics* were still running on June 1, 1997.

Helping the illusion along was the fruition of the 42nd Street Development Project, a gleam in former Mayor Koch's eye that lay dormant until picking up furious steam in 1995. All at once, the street of peep-shows, fake I.D.s and chop-socky flicks became a Disneyland kaleidoscope of candy-colored shops, family bistros and theaters-in-the-making. A prolific venue for PG-rated fare, the New Victory Theater started the ball rolling in late '95. This season saw the nearby Liberty Theater housing Fiona Shaw's *The Waste Land* and the Selwyn Theater serving as the venue for The Wooster Group's *The Hairy Ape.* Sadly, the 1904 Liberty Theater will most likely become a video game and amusement parlor, but a renovated (yet still rococo) New Amsterdam Theater, now Disney turf, hosted a concert staging of Alan Menken and Tim Rice's poorly received oratorio, *King David*, and will eventually host a live-action version of Disney's *The Lion King.*

Only a few years after the Hellinger Theater became a church for lack of use, Canadian theater entrepreneur Garth Drabinsky was donning a hard hat and giving reporters a mid-construction tour of the Ford Center, a new playhouse on the site of the old Lyric and Apollo Theaters. Soon to be the home of *Ragtime* and other Livent projects, the $30 million, 1,839 seat venue can house epic, tour-conscious musicals generally reserved for caverns like the Gershwin and Majestic. Necessitating the move are the seemingly endless runs of *uber*musicals like *Cats*, *The Phantom of the Opera* and *Les Misérables.* As for using the name of a car company to grace a legit theater, Drabinsky assured reporters Ford paid "substantially more" than a million bucks for the privilege.

By mid-April, 34 of 35 legitimate Broadway theaters were booked, with audiences paying an average ticket price of $47.24 (up 2.5 percent from the previous year). With 10.6 million fannies in the seats, Broadway had its largest audience in 16 years, the second-highest ever. Even the Tonys were up, bouncing back in the ratings and hyped by the presence of host Rosie O'Donnell and the awards' new venue: the enormous Radio City Music Hall. Not only were over 3,000 theater fans able to buy tickets to this usually exclusive event, but musical numbers on the CBS broadcast looked grandly larger than life. Theater zealots attained even greater ecstasy from CBS's deal with PBS, allowing the first hour of the Tony show to be broadcast on public television. This turned the ceremony into a smooth, unhurried, three-hour love-fest, instead of the traffic jam in a hurricane seen in recent years. There was even time for a new award: for orchestrations, an acknowledgment that Broadway's *sound* can be nearly as important as its songs.

A Sly and Sexy Beginning: Chicago

The first part of the season could be summed up in one word: *Chicago*. Mounted in a bare-bones staging evolved from last season's concert version as part of City Center's Encores! series, the Kander & Ebb show that was too cynical for its own time suddenly became the ideal musical for ours: sly, sexy with an ironic wink, and brimming with 20/20 hindsight for an America that watched O.J. Simpson get off while his lawyers became celebrities. The show took Tonys for best revival, director

Chicago

Ann Reinking (Tony-winning ch
eographer) *in center, above* w
James Naughton (Tony-winning b
leading musical actor) and memb
of the company; and *at left in ph*
at left with Bebe Neuwirth (To
winning best leading musical actre
in the John Kander-Fred Ebb-B
Fosse musical, which also collec
Tonys for Walter Bobbie (best m
sical direction), Ken Billington (b
lighting) and best musical revival

(Walter Bobbie), choreographer (Ann Reinking), actress in a musical (Bebe Neuwirth), actor in a musical (James Naughton) and lighting (Ken Billington).

Despite back problems and personal tragedies that kept choreographer and star Ann Reinking out of the show as much as she was in it, *Chicago* stayed the hottest ticket of 1996–97. The show's appeal ran across the board: Joel Grey's return to Broadway (as a memorable Mr. Cellophane), TV star Bebe Neuwirth's perfect Velma, James Naughton's unflappable Billy Flynn, fond memories of Bob Fosse called up by the song "All That Jazz" and by Reinking's Fosse-based choreography, John Kander & Fred Ebb at the height of their ricky-ticky cleverness on tunes like "Class" and "We Both Reached for the Gun," and a small corps of dancers so sexy they wound up on as many magazine covers as the leads.

Early in the run, complaints rippled across the aisles that the show hadn't changed much from its tumultuously received concert staging at Encores!. $75 a ticket was considered a lot of money to pay for no sets and for costumes seemingly cross-pollinated by Victoria's Secret and Danskin. Most audiences were more than happy, though, to tolerate the stripped-down visuals in exchange for stripped-down chorines—and the year's most successful match of tuneful tunes, tart dialogue and stylish razzle-dazzle. Late in the season, the producers of an insipid revival of *Annie* that was, somehow, also nominated for a best revival Tony, took the extraordinary step of admitting (in a letter to Tony voters) that the orphan didn't have a chance against *Chicago*. Instead, the producers begged Tony voters simply to come "with an open mind" and enjoy *Annie* on its own terms.

Those were meager terms indeed, considering the hoopla *Annie* made on its way to New York. It had been 20 years since Charles Strouse, Thomas Meehan and Martin Charnin pocketed a mint from their Depression Era musical. Chastened by the box office failure of *Annie Warbucks* off Broadway and the disastrous train of other *Annie* sequels behind it, Charnin & Co. went back to the drawing board, preferring the safer confines of a revival. Instead of waiting until they discovered a sensational talent who just *had* to be the new Annie, or finding a Miss Hannigan to rival Dorothy Loudon, the creators went for hype over inspiration. In cooperation with Macy's department store, they staged a series of national, open auditions for the new orphan. Hundreds of entrants, some in red wigs and peasant dresses, auditioned for director Charnin, leading to an agonized decision-making process. An ABC-TV documentary on the Annie search captured Charnin on the day he was supposed to announce his choice, telling his creative team, "She's not here." Moments later, however, he changed his mind and picked an 11-year-old Pennsylvanian, Joanna Pacitti, for the coveted role.

Brimming with spunk, projecting well and looking like the comic book orphan, Pacitti seemed a natural. Reports from the road tour said her performance was a bit showy and mechanical, but hey, the role wasn't Desiree Armfeldt.

All was well until Pacitti, only weeks away from opening on Broadway, took a couple of days off to nurse a sore throat. Understudy Brittny Kissinger stepped into the role— and the producers apparently saw what they'd been missing. Pacitti got the ax, which led to her tearful appearances on talk shows and an outpouring of public sympathy for the rejected actress, who wasn't even born when Charnin and Strouse wrote "The sun will come out tomorrow."

Rather than settle back into the obscurity of her father's barber shop (where she'd sung for customers), Pacitti fired off a lawsuit—not against Charnin & Co., but against Macy's for reneging on their "prize." (The still-pending lawsuit charges that the audition was advertised by Macy's as a *contest*, with the winner entitled to play *Annie* on Broadway.) However bland the final product on Broadway, the *Annie* journey had enough twists to keep Agatha Christie bemused: Zappa, the dog playing Sandy, was fired and replaced by *its* understudy. Pacitti then adopted Zappa in real life—and both were chosen to appear together in a summer production of *Annie* in North Carolina. Nell Carter suffered a hernia and then fought with the producers for marketing the show in TV commercials that displayed her name prominently but featured 15-year-old footage of Marcia Lewis as Hannigan. And since children became restive watching the 160-minute musical, Charnin & Co. shaved a few scenes off—including that pessimistic "Herbert Hoover" number and its pesky homeless, proving the destitute are as politically expendable in entertainment as they are in life. Conrad John Schuck (formerly plain old John Schuck) graced *Annie* with his professional Oliver Warbucks, and Raymond Thorne reprised his fine work as FDR. But Nell Carter's clowning proved less than skillful, the orphans were a motley lot and the set had a sawdusty, pack-up-and-tour look.

Replace orphans with courtiers and the same criticism would hold for *Once Upon a Mattress*, another missed opportunity that nonetheless hung on for over half a year until closing the night before the Tony Awards. As critics clamored for Carol Burnett, willowy Sarah Jessica Parker brought sweetness to Princess Winifred, but little vocal oomph or moxie. If the producers wanted to keep Parker's weak points a secret, they weren't helped by lyricist Marshall Barer, who was barred from rehearsals after screaming that Parker was all wrong and that Gerald Gutierrez's direction was putting *Mattress* to sleep.

Even critics weren't that severe, and the show fared well when marketed to younger audiences. For bizarre offstage twists, consider the tale of the Jester. Michael McGrath, lauded for playing Groucho in the American Jewish Theater's popular mounting of *The Cocoanuts*, left that show—much to the producers' ire—to take the Jester role in *Mattress*. In one of those "mutual agreement" spats, *Mattress* bounced McGrath in rehearsals, with the actor returning to *Cocoanuts* just before that show closed out its commercial engagement at the American Place Theater. Taking over as the Jester was David Hibbard, himself the object of controversy in (of all things) *Cats*.

Yes, *Cats* continued at the Winter Garden, on its way to a June 19 record as Broadway's longest running musical. But things in kitty-land got a little hairy when Hibbard, then playing the randy Rum Tum Tugger, got too aggressive with his character's sex appeal. When a New Jersey woman failed to respond to Tugger's gyrating, Elvis-meets-Long-John-Holmes dancing, Hibbard/Tugger turned up the heat, straddled the arms of the patron's seat, and thrust his pelvis in her face. Just a bit of R-rated fun in a G-rated musical, right?

Not for the distraught audience member who sued *Cats* for $6 million for causing her mental anguish and disrupting her sex life. The suit had a dreadful effect—not on Hibbard, but on Harold Prince's production of *Candide* at the end of season. What had been conceived as an audience-friendly, acrobatic, actors-in-the-aisles vaudeville was scaled back to a more traditional proscenium staging. Mere remnants of interactivity remained: Candide squeezing his way across a row of seats; narrator Jim Dale suspended from a birdcage-like box above the audience. Amazingly, this lamentable mounting of Leonard Bernstein's operatic farce scored a number of Tony nominations and glowing reviews, though only Andrea Martin, as the Old Woman, prevailed over Prince's incoherent staging.

If the aforementioned audience member put the fear into Broadway producers, Cameron Mackintosh sent the gooseflesh of actors rippling up and down Shubert Alley. With the ever-popular *Les Misérables* nearing its tenth anniversary, March 12, 1997, Mackintosh flew in with his creative team to give the show a freshening up. What they saw, apparently, were tired performances from long-term cast members, many of whom had grown too old for their roles. The media termed what followed "a bloodbath," as the performers were lined up across the stage and handed letters that detailed their futures in the show. Some performers were terminated, others were asked to re-audition for their roles or for different parts in the show.

Actors' Equity threw a conniption but had little recourse, since the Really Useful Company skated around the rules for firing contracted actors. They paid the casualities off with a sum larger than the performers could have gotten had they challenged the firing, won, and received the standard compensation called for by Equity rules. Sabres were rattled, rules were changed (slightly), and a refurbished cast reopened *Les Misérables* March 12. Hoopla aside, the show still felt like, well, *Les Miz*, an overlong but absolutely sensational evening of musical drama.

None of 1996–97's new musicals reached that kind of glory, but they were as varied a crop as any in the past half-dozen years. *Steel Pier*, *Titanic*, *Jekyll & Hyde* and *The Life* were all brand new works, in music and lyrics, if not story. All but *Jekyll & Hyde* were nominated for best musical Tonys, *Hyde*'s place taken by the novel and superbly designed *Juan Darién*. Two other musicals, *Play On!* and *Dream*, plugged old songs into new stories. Both were essentially ignored for major awards, which wasn't altogether fair, but also spared the industry from the embarrassment of another *Crazy for You* or *Jerome Robbins' Broadway* categorized as a "new" musical.

Juan Darién, though typed as a musical, was really more a specialty item, a puppet-play with ambient sound employing masks, bunraku, marionettes and shadow-play. Its elliptical tale of a young boy (played by a human), more comfortable with jaguars than the cruel hunters and carnival barkers in his town, received critical huzzahs and led to Disney choosing Julie Taymor to stage their *The Lion King* late in 1997. Taymor's ambitious allegory, backed by Elliot Goldenthal's environmental soundscape, had moments of wonder but also outstayed its welcome. Done in shadow-play, the funniest scene in *Juan Darién* showed a tiger swallowing the boy and then evacuating both his boots. Low comedy indeed, but more entertaining than the headache-inducing crucifixion sequence an hour later.

Overworked critics groused that none of the above musicals was a clear triumph. All had book problems; most of the scores had a familiar, warmed-over feeling. Certainly, following the year of *Rent* and *Bring in 'da Noise Bring in 'da Funk*, the absence of a modern, relevant musical with some acknowledgment of the rock/rap era, was keenly felt. Nevertheless, the health of a theater season lies in the wealth of its talent and the quantity of its quality. When *Newsday*'s Linda Winer derides *The Life* for its sexism and vulgarity, while half a dozen others praise it as the best score of the year; when *New York*'s John Simon calls *Titanic* a sinker, while *The New Yorker*'s Nancy Franklin hails the ship; when nearly all the major critics trash *Jekyll & Hyde* but audiences go wild over it; when *Steel Pier* gets dissed as second-rate Kander & Ebb, yet looked like the one to beat for the Tony; that makes for a helluva lot more excitement than, say, sweep-years by *Rent* or *Sunset Boulevard*.

In truth, each of the six *musical* musicals (I thus exclude the sound effects and choral yowling of *Juan Darién*) was worth a trip to the theater. Each had moments to cherish; each merited serious consideration.

Mixing the pastiche-revue concept of *Crazy for You* with the style of what August Wilson had sneeringly dubbed "the chitlin circuit" of black theater, *Play On!* was a huge hit at San Diego's Old Globe Theater before coming to New York. Not only did playwright Cheryl L. West interpolate classic tunes by Duke Ellington into her romantic comedy of 1920s Harlem, she and director Sheldon Epps took as their cue the dress-ups and mix-ups of Shakespeare's *Twelfth Night*. That's a tall order, and the silly results occasionally missed their mark, with the audience remaining distant from the show's two central love stories. At an American Theater Critics Association conference, lead actress Tonya Pinkins said much character material was cut from the text between San Diego and Broadway, leaving performers pushing for emotions that had come more naturally when the script was longer.

Plot did spill out of *Play On!* helter-skelter, and the performances weren't always calibrated to reach a consistent tone. Moment to remember? Andre De Shields and Larry Marshall teaming up for a happy blues, "Rocks in My Bed," that rocked the house. Oddly enough, the specter of August Wilson loomed large even here; the musical number resembled nothing so much as the way characters in *The Piano Lesson* and *Seven Guitars* break into natural, joyous, pulsing song.

Pinkins blamed the quick demise of *Play On!* on the discomfort of New York audiences with black culture—which again brings us to August Wilson. The playwright's public argument with A.R.T. head Robert Brustein was the hottest one-night ticket of the winter. Anna Deavere Smith chaired the debate, which pitted Brustein's multi-culturalism and non-traditional casting against Wilson's call for a more specifically African-American theater. To Wilson, blacks playing traditionally white roles smacks of dishonesty and represents an assimilation that severs American blacks' connection to their African homeland. Yet, contradictorily, Wilson can't abide the so-called "chitlin circuit," a rudimentary, sitcom type of theater (usually gospel musicals) that sell a lot more tickets in the black community than Wilson's plays do. This season's semi-hit, *Born to Sing* (Part 3 of the *Mama, I Want to Sing* trilogy), was an example of the form, though that had more of a cross-over audience than the usual fare at venues like the Beacon and Amsterdam Theaters.

The dance musical *Dream* dispensed with dialogue and built a show out of musical numbers and set pieces. The tunes all have one thing in common: lyrics by Johnny Mercer. He's a name to be reckoned with ("One More for the Road," "Moon River," "Goody, Goody"), but as *Stardust* and *A Grand Night for Singing* demonstrated, a tribute to talent is not enough to hang a musical on. Then again, *Dancin'* and *Noise/Funk* proved choreography *is* enough to fill an evening, and director/choreographer Wayne Cilento had previously managed to turn *The Who's Tommy* from a rock antique into a visual phenomenon. Louise Westergaard and Jack Wrangler (the latter a former adult film star and husband of *Dream* singer Margaret Whiting) conceived the idea of tracing four decades of American life through Mercer's music, but the vision on stage is Cilento's. He starts in a small town straight out of *Oklahoma!*, moves to a posh nightclub, then to a WWII soldiers' cantina, and finishes with a salute to Hollywood's Oscar-time glitz. Missing, despite some marvelous dancing and two dozen songs we all know the first lines to, was a sense of the musical going *somewhere*, rather than just going.

Dream's lead, Lesley Ann Warren, took a critical beating for not being as big a star as the sexpot "character" she played, and the New York *Times* faulted the piece as a whole for having the pre-packaged feel of an Andy Williams TV special. An older, less censorious audience would have likely found much to enjoy in John Pizzarelli's tasty jazz guitar licks and the verve of up-'n'-comer Jessica Molaskey, who gives her all on "Something's Gotta Give." It remains a mystery why Cilento didn't do more with Whiting singing "My Shining Hour" to the servicemen. That she did so in real life, just before the soldiers were shipped off to the Pacific, was a far more moving concept than any on view at the Royale Theater.

Titanic: *Sweeping, Admirable, Inspiring*

Of the *new* new musicals, *Steel Pier* may have been the most classically structured, *Jekyll & Hyde* the most passionate and *The Life* by far the most hummable, but *Titanic* was the most sweeping, admirable and, sometimes, inspiring. Everyone laughed when technical problems beset the musical during previews ("They couldn't get the ship to sink!"), and cast members gritted their teeth to see their songs and characters whittled away to pare the ensemble musical to two and a half hours. Reviewers from the major dailies took librettist Peter Stone to task for trotting on dozens of characters as "types," giving them brief bits of business in the middle, and then expecting audiences to care whether they lived or died after the ship's collision with an iceberg. It's valid criticism; Ida Straus's decision to die with her husband (department store magnate Isidor Straus), rather than save herself in a lifeboat, raises nary a tear when it should devastate.

What the anti-*Titanic*s are missing, however, is an appreciation of the show's scope. Most American theater takes a magnifying glass and holds it over a half-

Candide

[O]n opposite page are examples of [E]dith Dolan's designs for her Tony-[wi]nning costumes for *Candide* char-[ac]ters: *top left,* Gentlemen Mum-[m]ers; *top right,* Pacquette; *bottom [le]ft,* Lady Mummers; *bottom right,* [V]oltaire as Second Gambler

[A]t right wearing Dolan costumes in [a] scene from the musical revival are *[a]t top)* Brent Barrett, *(in middle)* Ja-[so]n Danieley, Harolyn Blackwell, *(at [b]ottom)* Stacey Logan and Jim Dale

dozen strongly detailed characters. *Titanic*'s approach was more sociological—and more grand. Nearly everyone on that ship wants to be somewhere, or someone, else. The Captain had been about to retire but was talked into staying for one last voyage. A meddlesome second class passenger (the delightful Victoria Clark) spends much of the first act doing anything she can to hobnob with the VIPs on the upper deck. Poor passengers on the lower tier simply want to start a new life in America. To Stone and composer/lyricist Maury Yeston, the tragedy of the Titanic is not that a few lovable or fascinating characters got killed in a high seas accident; the tragedy is that hundreds of middle and lower class passengers died because there weren't enough lifeboats on the ship—because storing more lifeboats would have taken up too much space in 1st Class.

Even anti-*Titanic*s were impressed by the show's opening sequence, at ship's boarding. Passengers and crew are briefly introduced, as are the Captain (John Cunningham) and his nemesis, moneyman Ismay (David Garrison), who prefers speed to safety. Though all we see of the ship is a long boarding gangway, the music rises to such majesty, our mind's eye conjures a vessel of monumental splendor.

Nothing in the rest of *Titanic* matches its opening scene, but one doesn't leave the Art Institute of Chicago after viewing Seurat's "Grand Jatte" because everything else on the walls is anti-climactic. Impassioned encounters, clever touches, and an expansive, macro-cosmic perspective inform the entire piece. Stewart Laing's set design could not be more uneven (the crash is laughable: a tiny, model ship sliding across the stage to rumbling sound effects), but his best moments are awesome; the overhead crow's nest; the Robert Wilson-style division of stage space into rectangles, squares and circles. Despite roaring through the Tony Awards with a surprise clinch of most of the major creative awards (best musical, score, book, orchestrations and set), *Titanic* may yet fail on Broadway because of its huge budget, mediocre reviews, and the perception that Yeston's score offers no catchy tunes. In a more equitable universe, however, *Titanic* will find its way to, say, Houston Grand Opera, add an extra half hour of character development to its running time and be far better appreciated as a hybrid opera than as a hybrid musical.

With *Steel Pier*, Kander & Ebb and writer David Thompson actually managed a typical old-fashioned musical—with typical second-act book trouble. *Pier*'s set-up played to the strength of its creative team, notably choreographer Susan Stroman, who evoked the world of Depression Era marathon dancing through a center bandstand, swirling lights, and couples jitterbugging, fox trotting and show-boating on the dance floor. *Pier* panners dismissed the show as a pale copy of the Jane Fonda film *They Shoot Horses, Don't They?*, which took a pitch-dark view of the marathon mentality. In defense of librettist Thompson, dance marathons wouldn't have been as popular and long-lasting if they were always as grimly pathetic as the one depicted in *Horses*. Even dancers who couldn't go the long haul (sometimes weeks) could make money by being sponsored or doing specialty acts, not to mention receiving free room and board. Stroman and Thompson did a commendable job of showing the marathon's glamour and excitement, as well as its desperation: the weary participants sprint like panting dogs around the bandstand; one dancer (Tony-nominated Joel Blum) loses his mind from exhaustion.

Steel Pier also set up a strong central relationship: sweet, disingenuous Rita (Karen Ziemba), a contestant, is actually in cahoots with the guy running the tournament. The fix is in, but she wants to give up the marathon scene, much to the dismay of her dashing but menacing husband (Gregory Harrison), who knows the next marathon can net them $5,000.

Where *Steel Pier* started to splinter was its introduction of a third character, a dashing pilot (Daniel McDonald) who becomes a potential love interest for Rita. That he's actually a dead guy come temporarily back to life is both confusingly and ineffectually handled, and Rita's inner struggle just isn't sufficiently compelling to fill the second act. The nadir comes when the terrific Ziemba must dance 'round and 'round a pole, forced to sing the poor lyrics of "Running in Place." Thus, despite having all the elements of a vintage musical, *Steel Pier* underwhelmed and became less than the sum of its parts. Ziemba and Harrison were fine, though, with Debra Monk a stand-out as straight-talking, coarse, but compassionate fellow dancer, Shelby. The evening's best scene had Monk's Shelby wowing the marathon's spectators (and audiences at the Richard Rodgers Theater) with the raunchy "Everybody's Girl," only to be cheated out of her big moment by a conniving competitor.

If *Steel Pier* lacked a passionate raison d'etre, *Jekyll & Hyde*'s raison d'etre *was* passion. The Leslie Bricusse & Frank Wildhorn musical had spent seven years on the road before reaching Broadway, making more changes and jettisoning more songs than any musical in recent history. Always an "audience show," *J&H* had the reputation of being a critical bete noir, while fans cried buckets over the tragic story and cheered the high-octane cast.

That reputation held in New York, where critics fired poisoned darts at Bricusse's adaptation of the Robert Louis Stevenson novel, saving special arrows for his generic lyrics and the show's perceived kitsch factor. At least New York *Times* scribe Ben Brantley offered a back-handed compliment, writing that the show had a passionate belief in itself not evident in *Titanic* or *Pier*.

Ironically, and not undeservedly, *Jekyll & Hyde* has the best chance of sticking around for two or three years, no matter who won the Tony (*J&H* wasn't even nominated). Bricusse and Wildhorn's musical did have fire in its blood, as well as a captivating matinee idol in Robert Cuccioli, and a voice to shake the rafters in Linda Eder. Her performance, as Lucy the tragic prostitute in love with Jekyll but also drawn to the abusive Hyde, was believable enough, but the real buzz is over her singing, with the "new Streisand" tag actually starting to stick.

Why does it take so long for Jekyll's friends and acquaintances to put two and two together? And why does Jekyll's best friend leave the doctor alone (knowing full well he'll turn into the murderous Hyde) and then run to warn Lucy to leave town, rather than locking Jekyll in his study and calling the police? On an intellectual level, *Jekyll & Hyde* stopped making sense very quickly, but on an emotional level, the show was a grabber all the way. Cuccioli's dashing Jekyll wins women's hearts, while his growling Hyde has the mordant wit of a Sweeney Todd (his victims, besides Lucy, are rich hypocrites who repudiated his experiments). In one scene, Cuccioli, sans special make-up, even gets to flip, line by line, between the doctor and the demon, like a 19th century Sybil. Borderline foolish, it's also the kind of risky, heart-on-the-sleeve gambit that makes *Jekyll & Hyde* a riveting ride. Bricusse remains the weakest lyricist on Broadway, but because the story has real fire, his work here showed improvement over his previous vehicle, *Victor/Victoria*.

That 1996 show continued to pack in audiences, even though the number of missed performances by star Julie Andrews led the production's insurance company to drop her from its policy. Overtaxed and desperate for a month-long vacation, Andrews temporarily left the show in the hands of her good friend Liza Minnelli. Notwithstanding reports of backstage friction between the diminutive diva and *Vic/Vic* co-star Tony Roberts, who balked at Liza's verbal gaffes (e.g., "I'm just an old hooker" instead of "I'm just an old hoofer"), audiences took the frail, pale belter to heart. Andrews returned to the role (well, on and off with understudy Anne

Runolfsson), but only until summer, when the producers will push the show's kitsch factor to a higher level: Andrews's replacement will be Raquel Welch.

Though ineligible for awards, high-profile replacements are big business on Broadway now, with Jerry Lewis's devilish turn in 1995's *Damn Yankees* meriting a whole new opening night. Patti LuPone received raves when she replaced the seemingly irreplaceable Zoe Caldwell in *Master Class*, and when *she* left, Dixie Carter stepped in, with many critics calling her performance the most moving of the three. Faith Prince, excoriated for her last Broadway appearance in *What's Wrong With This Picture?*, won back all her fans and then some as the replacement for Donna Murphy in Christopher Renshaw's acclaimed *The King and I* revival. Meanwhile, rather than close *Defending the Caveman* to begin its road tour, author/star Rob Becker left his solo show in the capable hands of TV's "Commish," Michael Chiklis.

Causing the greatest stir was the replacement for Nathan Lane in *A Funny Thing Happened on the Way to the Forum*. Pundits bandied about a dozen names for the role of Pseudolus, but no one guessed the producers' choice: Whoopi Goldberg. The gender change was not as daunting as one would imagine, since the slave is essentially an asexual role (for example, it is Marcus Lycus who brings out the courtesans; Pseudolus is just an observer). Goldberg turned out to be a revelation. What she lacks in vocal training she makes up for in the sheer joy of clowning. Whereas Lane grimaced in mock pain with every wisecrack, Goldberg, who probably has to work harder technically than Lane did, looked like she was having a ball. Adding to the specialness are occasional scripted wisecracks (Pseudolus points to a handsome Roman and says, "What do I want with one of them white boys? I got one at home," a winking reference to Goldberg's real-life friend Frank Langella) and the subtext gained by having a black woman in a traditionally white male role. Without losing any of its comedy, the great Sondheim song, "Free," takes on tremendous resonance when sung by a black woman playing a slave.

Sunset Boulevard's Elaine Paige, imported from London, was about as good a Glenn Close replacement as one could imagine. She sang with power and skill, and her performance was far more shaded than Betty Buckley's. But Paige's unknown name was a blip to theatergoers, and the show closed, just one more headache in a difficult year for Andrew Lloyd Webber. Not only was his Washington, D.C. tryout of *Whistle Down the Wind* deemed unready for Broadway, his *By Jeeves* stalled regionally as well. When productions of *Sunset Boulevard* around the world started closing, massive layoffs and shut-downs of Really Useful Company offices also ensued. The composer even auctioned off his beloved wine collection. Optimists are hoping Webber's rewrites of *Wind* and his plans for a *Phantom* sequel will bring him back to the top of his game.

At or near the top of *his* game was composer Cy Coleman, who penned so many catchy songs for *The Life*, the first act stretched past a hundred minutes just to fit them all in. Audiences didn't seem to mind, nor were they thrown by Coleman's, David Newman's and Ira Gasman's ludicrous book, which had some grit in its look at 42nd Street, circa 1980, but still felt like Damon Runyon trying to be Melvin Van Peebles. *The Life* follows Queen, a black woman working as a prostitute to support

Fleetwood, her drug addicted boy friend (and personal pimp), and parallels it with the rise of Mary, a seemingly naive, cornfed cutie, making "easy money" in the same world. Just one example of *The Life*'s absurdity: Queen finally dumps her useless boy friend and does so publicly—by accepting a necklace from big bad pimp, Memphis (Chuck Cooper), at the annual Hooker's Ball. Yet when Memphis invites her to his pad after the party, she's shocked—shocked!—at his presumption that she will now be one of his whores. What did she expect, a day-job licking envelopes?

G-rated *The Life* wasn't; brutal moments and coarse humor are, rightfully, part of the landscape here. But the prostitutes, though a less than glamorous bunch, were still too clean-looking and mentally sharp to convince. 1980 may have been pre-AIDS, but it wasn't pre-heroin, pre-amphetamines and pre-syphilis.

Curiously unmoving despite its operatic finish, *The Life* got by—in a big way—on Cy Coleman's score. As of shows of old, we sat through the tolerable but dumb libretto to get to the next hummable number, pretty ballad or show-stopping stomper. When you have Lillias White's marvelous clowning on the bluesy "The Oldest Profession," White and Pamela Isaacs's sunniness on "A Lovely Day To Be Out of Jail," Chuck Cooper's terrifying baritone on "My Way or the Highway," Bellamy Young's sexy take on "Easy Money," and the ensemble's verve on "Why Can't They Leave Us Alone?" and "My Body," who cares that the story makes no sense? (The strange thing is that critics and audiences cared *a lot* when Coleman's *Welcome to the Club*, which had an equally miserable book but similarly catchy songs, folded ignominiously in 1989.) A 1996 concept album of *The Life*'s tunes, sung by Liza Minnelli, Lou Rawls and other guest artists, didn't do the score justice but did feature a near-death George Burns putting his signature rasp to "Easy Money." Much like the show itself—which won the Outer Critics best Broadway musical Award—if you can get past the insanity of it, it's a hoot.

Identify the Creative Contributions?

Though still alive, the symbiotic relationship between writers and directors in the commercial theater could be reaching a crisis point. When Florida's Caldwell Theater essentially copied Joe Mantello's unforgettable staging of *Love! Valour! Compassion!*, the Society of Stage Directors and Choreographers decided to assert the creative contributions of its members. A pending lawsuit charges that a director's contributions to a show should be as protected from plagiarism as the script itself—a position that could prove impossible to enforce. As a second shot across the bow, SSDC then sent a letter to play publishers and licensing organizations, demanding that they cease and desist from publishing stage directions, choreography, ground plans and technical choices not part of the playwright's original script. The question of who contributes what to a production has suddenly gone from a critic's headache to a legal morass bound to get more complicated as these cases multiply and drag on.

If the creative contributions of 1996–97 showed a resurgence of new musicals on Broadway, straight plays again proved few and far between—only three new American and three new foreign plays arrived there this season. After a long stretch of dabbling in cabaret, Christopher Durang returned to the boards with *Sex and Longing*, a scathing satire of American hypocrisy over sexuality, one of the two new American scripts brought to Broadway's Cort Theater by Lincoln Center Theater. With Sigourney Weaver as loping, light-hearted and lascivious Lulu, a sex addict who has to get laid every hour to be happy, the play got off to a rambunctious start. Adding to the fun was Dana Ivey as the sourpuss wife of a drunken, philandering senator. But like *The Life*, which was a decade behind the times in its look at Times Square prostitution, *Sex and Longing*'s corrupt politicians and licentious priests were extremely old news, especially for the man who burned his religious bridges years earlier with *Sister Mary Ignatius*. Weaver and Ivey couldn't save this nasty, over-written work, nor could a clever sequence portraying Congress as a panel of blow-up dolls overcome the feeling that Durang started with a good idea but got stuck trying to out-Durang himself.

Sex and Longing was an obvious and immediate disaster, but the cool reception given the latest work by Durang's friend and perennial Broadway favorite, Wendy Wasserstein, still puzzles. Lauded by *Newsday*'s Linda Winer but dismissed by other major critics as far-fetched and artificial, *An American Daughter*, second of Lincoln Center's Broadway offerings, mustered but one Tony nomination (and win)—for supporting actress Lynne Thigpen. *Daughter* is very much part of the Wasserstein canon; its protagonist is a modern woman who appreciates the stability of domestic life yet yearns, with a degree of ambivalence, for success, respect and, yes, power. Like Heidi and Sara Rosensweig, *Daughter*'s Lyssa Dent Hughes gets swept along in a society where the rules change daily for feminism and women as leaders.

All seems in place for Lyssa (Kate Nelligan) to become the next Surgeon General of the United States, until a soulless television interviewer discovers that she once neglected a jury duty summons. Suddenly, she's cast in the public's mind as a member of the privileged class, above rules that apply to common folk. Sinking her chances utterly are statements she makes, taken out of context, that denigrate middle-American housewives and indirectly chastise the President for not coming to her defense.

With complexity and cleverness, Wasserstein's dramatic satire examines the media's ability to construct "news" out of half-truths, sound-bytes and public opinion polls. She turns on its head the old adage about being able to see ourselves as others see us. In the world of *Daughter*, Lyssa behaves one way, is perceived as another, changes her behavior to fit the perception, is then misperceived, changes again . . . on and on like reflecting-mirrors in a not-fun funhouse. Less convincingly, Wasserstein also puts forth Lyssa's bland marriage (to a somnambulant Peter Riegert) and her unsteady relationship with her respected father (Hal Holbrook), a state senator. We're captivated as Lyssa gives one last interview to salvage her chances for surgeon generalship, yet bored by the meandering father-daughter chat and husband-wife resolution that closes the play.

Kate Nelligan did fine work as a woman aching to stay true to herself while everyone else tries to morph her lifestyle into their version of what the public wants. As Judith, Lyssa's black-Jewish best friend with a suicidal bent, Lynne Thigpen couldn't always walk the character's fine line between absurdity and believable eccentricity, but the problem was with the writing, not the performance. Cotter Smith precisely caught the TV journalist's medium-cool amorality, while Hal Holbrook couldn't have been better cast as the salt-and-pepper-haired senator, whose speech defending Lyssa is a perfect bit of spin-doctoring and characterization.

Whatever *An American Daughter*'s shortcomings, it had more depth and resonance than the year's other drama of political inquisitions, *Taking Sides*. Set in Germany after World War II, Ronald Harwood's play pits a brash, vulgar American major against proud, dignified orchestra conductor, Willhelm Furtwangler. The central question, whether the musician was pro-Hitler, anti-Hitler or somewhere in between, received "Columbo"-style treatment in a diverting but surface-deep exercise. Ed Harris's volatile Major was reason enough to see the play, though Daniel Massey's showy, birdlike Furtwangler detracted from the one-on-one fireworks.

Conversely, David Hare's *Skylight*, which won the Critics Award for best foreign play, burns in the memory precisely because he had such ideal interpreters in Michael Gambon and Lia Williams. Instead of sinking into soap opera or settling for a political debate, Hare's look at a wealthy capitalist visiting his former lover became a harrowing, poignant look at wounded souls. Like Larry the Liquidator in *Other People's Money*, Gambon's charming mogul convincingly defends his business practices, yet learns he can't be both tycoon and white knight. By the same token, Kyra may posit herself as a shining martyr for the underclass, but layers of masochism and guilt pervade her self-denial. Critic John Simon, who'd generally found Hare's plays dry political rants masquerading as drama, wrote that the playwright had turned a corner with 1996's *Racing Demon* and 1997's *Skylight*, putting Hare, finally, on the same playing field, if not the same team, as countryman Tom Stoppard.

Another British drama, *Stanley*, was cause for celebration, not so much for its merit, but because it successfully re-opened the doors of Circle in the Square, at least for the time being, under the leadership of Gregory Mosher and executive producer M. Edgar Rosenblum. Eager to rebuild a theater that never recovered from the calamitous box office failure of 1992's *Anna Karenina*, Mosher offered inexpensive subscriptions (called "memberships") that started with a $37.50 annual fee, plus a mere $10 per ticket charge. Since the annual fee was less than the cost of a normal Broadway ticket, Circle presumably wouldn't have to be locked into a multi-play season. That is, if they had a long-running hit, subscribers wouldn't bristle at paying for a season with only one or two shows in it—a problem that killed Chicago's Candlelight Theater when their Arthur Kopit-Maury Yeston *Phantom* played 54 weeks and alienated their subscriber base.

Shortly after season's end, the Messrs Mosher and Rosenblum resigned their Circle in the Square posts, and it looked as though the organization might never finally re-emerge from its difficulties. For different reasons, after 17 years the off-Broadway Lamb's Theater Company, founded by Carolyn Rossi Copeland, also called it quits, although its space still serves as a home for theater, such as the long-running *Magic on Broadway*. And in October, Circle Repertory Theater, described

BARRYMORE—Christopher Plummer in his Tony-winning performance of the title role in William Luce's play

in the *Times* as "a mainstay of off Broadway for 28 years," went most regrettably out of business, for lack of financial support.

As for Pam Gems's award-winning drama on the life of painter Stanley Spencer, the fine actor Antony Sher invested his selfish artist with zest and zeal, almost making us understand the painter's amoral stance on relationships—to wit, loving one woman at a time just isn't enough. At three hours, *Stanley* became a repetitious exercise of the painter ignoring the woman who loves him and getting dumped on by the lesbian for whom he lusts. Saving the play from pointlessness was its autumnal final scene, with Stanley making a kind of peace with the ghost of his long-suffering spouse (Deborah Findlay). A vivid, sexy Anna Chancellor and a wry Selina Cadell also contributed memorable performances, but the show belonged to director John Caird, who ably turned the difficult Circle space into an artist's playground.

If the Pulitzers were at a loss this year, Tony voters had little trouble choosing a best play, *The Last Night of Ballyhoo*. Alfred Uhry's serious comedy, commissioned for the 1996 Atlanta Olympiad and brought to Broadway with skill by director Ron

Lagomarsino, was the kind of classically commercial work that hasn't taken Tony honors since Neil Simon's *Lost in Yonkers*. Like that masterwork, *Ballyhoo* touches on a dark theme: class-based anti-Semitism within the Jewish community, where German Jews are perceived to have a higher status than their Eastern European counterparts. In the first ten minutes, Uhry unloads traincars full of exposition yet does so in the kind of straightforward, amusing way that used to come naturally to Broadway writers of yesteryear. An hour later, we see the jealousy Lala Levy has for her prettier, more socially accepted cousin, Sunny, and the first act curtain sweeps down with a resounding whoosh of confidence; Uhry knows we won't dare leave without finding out what will happen to Lala, Sunny, Peachy, and the rest of the denizens of this extended 1939 Atlanta family.

Dana Ivey emerged unscathed from *Sex and Longing* to give another acclaimed performance, as the sarcastic but fiercely protective mother of Lala (Jessica Hecht, excellent). Exceptional, too, were Terry Beaver as laconic papa Freitag, Celia Weston as the dazed but sensitive mother of comely Sunny and Stephen Largay as Peachy, the upper-class twit who inadvertently saves the day. A review by Mark Sommers of the Atlanta production of *The Last Night of Ballyhoo* appears in The Season Around the United States section of this volume.

Horton Foote's first Broadway outing in years already came with heavy baggage. Part of the Signature Theater's all-Foote season two years back off Broadway, *The Young Man From Atlanta* got another chance to prove itself after a stunned world said "Huh?" when the domestic piece took the 1995 Pulitzer Prize. A Pulitzer voter told me the choice was more of a cumulative career award for elderly Foote than a specific nod to *Atlanta*, which merely maintained "his career-long level of excellence." Still, the story of Will Kidder, a businessman fired by his company and then thwarted in his attempts to start a new career, should hold an audience, if not electrify it.

Sometimes all it takes is a big stage and some big actors. Robert Falls's production at the Longacre Theater had its longeurs but certainly redeemed a play that was dull as dirt in its 1995 mounting by Signature Theater. Whereas Ralph Waite's Will was a laidback, defeated codger, Rip Torn played him Texas-tall and raring to get back in the saddle. As wife Lily Dale, Shirley Knight's fluttery desperation made us think of Edith Bunker thrust outside the safe world of television. William Biff McGuire scored a Tony nomination as a family friend who brings temporary equilibrium to the household. *The Young Man From Atlanta* stalled in the second act with a leisurely, pointless visit from a former housekeeper, but until then the show was, at the very least, lively enough to make us forgive the Pulitzer pickers. A little. (*Atlanta* became the first post-Tony casualty, though, closing a week after losing to *Ballyhoo*.)

The weightless *Barrymore* marked a considerable improvement for playwright William Luce, which isn't saying much. The author of *Zelda: The Last Flapper* and *Lucifer's Child* had become a master of turning famous historical persons into tedious windbags. That *Barrymore* runs less than two hours, including intermission, shows astonishing restraint on Luce's part. That *Barrymore* stars Christopher Plummer is very good luck. If anyone can lend nobility to John Barrymore's dirty limericks and disconnected reminiscences, it's the artful and agile Plummer. All the same, Nicol Williamson's Barrymore solo the year before, titled *Jack: A Night on the Town*, was far more interesting for the risks it took and the more comprehensive view it offered of The Great Profile's training, marriages and dissolving career.

Play revivals on Broadway this season were a generally underwhelming lot. Financially troubled, the National Actors Theater had high hopes Charles Durning and Julie Harris would set the box office ringing for *The Gin Game*. That hasn't quite happened, though reviews were very good and Harris received her tenth Tony nomination—more than any other actress in Broadway history. D.L. Coburn's two-hander about aging retirees, one a prissy perfectionist, the other a card player with a rage problem, still works as comedy but now feels hollow and familiar as drama. Harris and Durning are pros, but their dialogue work can be sloppy, and we miss the whip-crack exchanges of Hume Cronyn and Jessica Tandy. (Whatever the fortunes of the N.A.T., its artistic director, Tony Randall, had a good year: the 77-year-old actor and his young wife, Heather, gave birth to a baby girl.)

Critics split over Scott Elliott's splashy staging of Noel Coward's *Present Laughter*, some calling it an innovative, go-for-broke farce that took into account Coward's own vanity and homosexuality, others viewing the production as over-heated and under-funny. Star Frank Langella proved a smooth and delicious farceur, though, with Tim Hopper, Caroline Seymour and Allison Janney stand-outs in the uneven ensemble.

Even less assured was a half-English, half-American revival of Jean Anouilh's masterwork at the Roundabout, *The Rehearsal*, directed by Jeremy Sams. Set monotonously against a bleached white drawing room, the story of lies, betrayals and rich people "who break things" had little resonance, even when the story took its harsh, unforgettable twist into tragedy. Roger Rees was a well-spoken, convincingly dissipated Hero; David Threlfall (who looked and sounded strikingly like Monty Python's Eric Idle) amused as the Count, who renounced his game-playing for true love; but Frances Conroy gave a shrill and rushed performance as the manipulating Countess.

Conroy struck out again in the kvetchy *Arts & Leisure* on Playwrights Horizons' 1997 schedule but came through in the later innings with Lincoln Center's revival of *The Little Foxes*. Less a star turn for Stockard Channing's capable Regina than an effective, nicely staged ensemble piece, *Foxes* showcased Conroy's specialty—high-strung helplessness—to memorable effect. Many reviews dismissed Lillian Hellman's 1939 play as creaky melodrama, presumably because to them, strong-willed family members fighting viciously and openly over property somehow lacked sophistication, even when played on John Lee Beatty's opulent, two-level set. To others, the play's stomach-tightening ugliness still worked like strong medicine, with Hellman turning the brilliant trick of making us hate Regina, yet forcing us to root for her because her brothers are so much worse. A crass, menacing Brian Murray; a terrified, pathetic Conroy; and a commanding Kenneth Welsh (as Regina's ailing husband) made *The Little Foxes* a satisfying, properly upsetting evening.

Critics had little use for Scott Ellis's revival of Herb Gardner's *A Thousand Clowns*, calling it a sitcom thoroughly stuck in its time period. Entertaining as it is, the comedy has an unsatisfactory protagonist in Murray Burns. His crabby nonconformity consists of shouting at his neighbors, calling the weather bureau every morning and visiting the Statue of Liberty instead of going to work. Hoo-boy, some rebellion. 1996 audiences, accustomed to corporate downsizing and four-digit layoffs, enjoyed watching Judd Hirsch but were tempted to tell his Murray, "Shut up and get a job." Also unevenly staged, yet better received, was the last show to open during the Tony season, the Roundabout's *London Assurance*. (The Tony season doesn't exactly coincide with the Broadway season. The former ended April 30, the latter May 31.) Few actors are as beloved on Broadway as Brian Bedford, so he had reason to bring tremendous self-assurance to his role in Dion Boucicault's farce. Bedford's smug Sir Courtly chuckled at his own jokes and then waited expectantly for audiences to respond, which they did, surprisingly, with gales of laughter. A little of this went a long way, but the crazy-quilt comedy perked up with the arrival of Helen Carey as a spanking Lady Gay Spanker. Eyes shining, front teeth jutting forward, husky voice bespeaking a lusty nature, Carey rescued *London Assurance* from Joe Dowling's erratic direction and forced Bedford's Courtly to stop showing off and become part of the story.

Our historian, Thomas T. Foose, notes for our added information that "*London Assurance* was that great rarity in New York, a play from the first half of the 19th century. It was Dion Boucicault's first success, at London's Covent Garden March 4, 1841, when the author was about 20. The play came to New York very speedily for those days, and it was seen at the Park October 11, 1841. The Lady Gay Spanker was the very famous actress Charlotte Cushman, who looked something like Marjorie Main and who sometimes played men's parts (in 1845 she played Romeo to her sister's Juliet). *London Assurance* was a huge favorite in New York in the 19th century, with productions almost every season until the last decade."

Al Pacino *was* the story in a sold-out revival of Eugene O'Neill's *Hughie*, a one-act about a down-and-out gambler boring a hotel clerk with his ramblings. The actor not only starred in but directed the hour-long drama, which featured Paul Benedict as the laconic clerk. Audiences clamored, critics fawned, the benefit (for Circle in the Square) raised a bundle, so why grouse that *Hughie* was a dull exercise with a plot that didn't even get going until just before the ending? At $1 a minute, it was the most expensive snob ticket on Broadway.

Most honored of the season's revivals was *A Doll's House*, imported from England on the strength of Janet McTeer's performance as Nora. McTeer's Olivier-Award winning turn netted her a best actress Tony as well, though John Simon and Linda Winer objected to McTeer's girlish housewife, wondering how such a scattered debutante could find the gumption to make Ibsen's world-shaking exit speech. The Nora of the last ten minutes *did* seem too radically different from the Nora of the previous 2:45, but otherwise McTeer and the rest of the cast created a nuanced and detailed world. Overt physical affection between husband (Tony winner Owen Teale) and wife made Torvald's dinosaur values all the more unfortunate. Also strongly conveyed in this mounting was the dual nature of Dr. Rank (John Carlisle), one of literature's most complex villains.

A more black-and-white view of good and evil was shown in *Into the Whirlwind*, performed in Russian with simultaneous English translation by Moscow's Sovremennik Theater for a limited Broadway engagement. Author Eugenia Ginzburg experienced first-hand the terrors of political imprisonment in Stalinist Russia, and an elderly member of the deeply committed cast was actually her cell-mate. Far removed from women-in-prison B-movies, the play had chilling moments (as when a new mother, caught "hoarding" food, watches an officer pour a cup of her saved breast milk on the floor) and a convincing sense of camaraderie. Repetition did lessen the play's effect, as it fell into the typical pattern of torture, reprieve, torture, reprieve. It was far more gripping, however, than Sovremennik's other entry, *Three Sisters*, a lifeless affair (though some critics cheered) weakened by half-baked directorial touches.

Just a few weeks later, off-beat, all-star casting made an all-American mounting of *Three Sisters* at the Roundabout frequently engaging. John Simon called the production a good introduction to Chekhov, acknowledging that the characters and motivations were made clear, as were the author's themes. The sisters themselves were oddly chosen, with Amy Irving most comfortable as self-sacrificing Olga. As Masha, Jeanne Tripplehorn had glamour but not much range; as Irina, Lili Taylor had energy but not much control. Best of the supporting players were Paul Giamatti as neurotic and unhappy Andrei, and Calista Flockhart, cast against type as the ice-veined, manipulative Natasha. The Roundabout also offered a respectable revival of Tennessee Williams's *Summer and Smoke*, starring a wan Mary McDonnell as Alma Winemiller. As the doctor who pushes Alma to the brink of love, Harry Hamlin, though the target of critical brickbats, offered both machismo and brooding angst.

If Jimmy the Greek were still alive, he'd have drooled over the odds of two plays about *Saturday Night Live* comediennes stricken with cancer both arriving in the same season. He'd have lost a bundle. Off-Broadway, Alan Zweibel's *Bunny Bunny* proved a delight, a celebration of Gilda Radner's big-hearted charm in pop colors and zippy vignettes. (So many plaudits were heaped on David Gallo's adorable set design, people overlooked the pleasures of the play itself.) On Broadway, Julia Sweeney served up a quieter piece, joking gently about her years at *SNL* (she played the androgynous "Pat" character), the annoyances of living in New York, her brother's death from cancer, and her own battle with the disease. By steering clear of tear jerking, Sweeney may have undersold the material's emotional impact. It was nice *not* to be overwhelmed by bathos, but audiences accustomed to catharsis in these kinds of evenings went home from *God Said "Ha!"* feeling a tad short-changed.

Surely no one felt shortchanged by *Men Are From Mars, Women Are From Venus*, a two-and-a-half hour seminar by marriage guru John Gray. There was no reason to bring this info-mercial style monologue to Broadway (let alone the enormous Gershwin Theater) except for Gray to sell some books and sign up couples

The 1996–97 Season Off Broadway

PLAYS (29)

Making Porn
Grace & Glorie
Acts of Providence
OLD WICKED SONGS
900 Oneonta
Playwrights Horizons:
  Fit To Be Tied
  Demonology
  Cloud Tectonics
MTC:
  Blues Are Running
  Nine Armenians
  Psychopathia, etc.
  Collected Stories
Cakewalk
The Santaland Diaries
Family Values
Public Theater:
  Golden Child
  Insurrection, etc.
  One Flea Spare
Warp
Second Stage:
  The Red Address
  Sympathetic Magic

In-Betweens
Stonewall Jackson's House
Robbers
Minor Demons
Bunny Bunny
God's Heart
HOW I LEARNED TO
  DRIVE
Bermuda Avenue Triangle

SPECIALTIES (8)

Magic on Broadway
The New Bozena
Late Nite Catechism
The Queen of Bingo
Sharps, Flats &
  Accidentals
Peter and Wendy
The Tokyo Shock Boys
Tap Dogs

MUSICALS (5)

Born to Sing!
Radio Gals
Space Trek
VIOLET
The Green Heart

REVUES (7)

*I Love You, You're
  Perfect,etc.*
When Pigs Fly
Disappearing Act
*Forbidden Broadway
  Strikes Back*
A Brief History, etc.
Capitol Steps
Doctor Doctor

FOREIGN PLAYS
IN ENGLISH (2)

The Steward of
  Christendom
Dealer's Choice

SOLO SHOWS (16)

Aliens in America
"Matty"
Back on the Boulevard
Einstein
Full Gallop
  (return engagement)
Political Animal
The Waste Land
Beat
The Springhill Singing
  Disaster
  (return engagement)
Fyvush Finkel
Neat
My Astonishing Self
A Huey P. Newton Story
Boychik
The Gypsy and the Yellow
  Canary
*Men on the Verge of a His-
  Panic Breakdown*

REVIVALS (21)

Shakespeare Marathon:
  Henry V
  Timon of Athens
  Henry VI (in two parts)
  Antony and Cleopatra
Louisiana Purchase
The Boys in the Band
The Cocoanuts
Valiant Theater:
  Rhinoceros
  A Soldier's Play
  The Tooth of Crime
Roundabout:
  Scapin
  All My Sons
Elektra
New Audience:
  Two Gentlemen of
    Verona
  The Changeling
Encores!:
  Sweet Adeline
  Promises, Promises
  The Boys From
    Syracuse
  The Hairy Ape
  As You Like It

Categorized above are all the new productions listed in the Off Broadway section of this volume.
Plays listed in CAPITAL LETTERS were major 1996–97 prizewinners.
Plays listed in *italics* were still running June 1, 1997.

for his weekend counseling retreats. Grazing the same turf as *Defending the Caveman*, Gray did dispense a few handy tips for keeping a marriage fresh, but a second-act guest panel bombed so precipitously on opening night, he dispensed with the segment for the rest of the week-long run. Instead, he closed the show by having the audience chant, in unison, "I love sex! I love sex!" Chris Durang's Lulu would've been in heaven.

Like John Gray, Spalding Gray idealized his own current marriage—but not before revealing unpleasant truths about the end of his 17-year relationship with another companion. *It's a Slippery Slope* not only showed Gray to be a bit of a cad, but offered a hilarious and poetic account of Gray's travails on America's ski trails. Pam Gems's *Stanley* spent three hours vainly trying to convince us Stanley Spencer's selfishness could be justified because he was a great artist. In 90 minutes, Spalding Gray frankly offered half a dozen examples of his behaving like a complete scoundrel—and we revered him all the more for it. Go figure.

Heads were also scratching over *Dreams & Nightmares*, this time with viewers wondering, "How did he *do* that?" David Copperfield brought his flashy, big budget magic show to Broadway, pulling in record box office grosses and finding a dozen variations on the-body-is-not-where-you-think-it-is illusions. Less grandiose, but often more fun, was an off-Broadway show that went under the half-misleading title, *Magic on Broadway*. Despite little advance publicity, decent reviews and strong marketing to family audiences helped *Magic* become a long-running hit. A smooth pro, illusionist Joseph Gabriel brackets his disappearing birds, swords-through-boxes and mind-reading gimmicks with Benny Hill-style dancers and gentle, Copperfieldian patter. Pushing the evening to must-see status is guest artist Romano Frediani, who bounces tennis balls off drums, juggles with fervor and catches hoops around his neck. Imagine crossing Sam Kinison's insane vigor with the winsome glee of Invisible Circus founder Jean Baptiste Thierree, and you have some idea of the delight Frediani, only 22, invokes in audiences.

Along Came How I Learned to Drive

It had been a numbing dry spell for Paula Vogel, productions of her *Desdemona* and *And Baby Makes Seven* making critics question the promise of her delirious classic *The Baltimore Waltz*. Hushing the complaints with a controlled, mature honesty heretofore unseen in Vogel's work was *How I Learned to Drive*, staged off off Broadway at the Vineyard Theater and then moved to the newly built Century Center Theater for a commercial run. We see the hand that shaped *Waltz* in *Drive*'s vignette style, its frankness about a woman's sexuality and proficiency at using almost vaudevillian laugh breaks to soften the impact of the trepidation lurking around the corner.

Winner of the New York Drama Critics, Lucille Lortel and Outer Critics Awards for best play, *How I Learned to Drive* follows the relationship between teenaged Li'l Bit and her alcoholic Uncle Peck. In Peck, Li'l Bit sees a soothing older man, savvy with the secrets of the world. If indulging his masturbatory needs is a key to

STONEWALL JACKSON'S HOUSE—Katherine Leask *(at top)*, R.E. Rodgers, Starla Benford, Ron Faber and Mimi Bensinger in Jonathan Reynolds's play

understanding that world, so be it. In Li'l Bit, Peck finds a trusting and nubile disciple, too naive to be a tease but too grown-up to be wholly innocent. Only near play's end do we learn that Peck's sexual misbehavior with his niece began, not a year or two before her 18th birthday, but when she was 11.

Throughout *Drive*, we hold our breath waiting for the moment of hell: the scene in which Peck will lose patience and rape the girl, or lose control and beat her up. But Vogel's motive was not sensational ugliness, i.e., the vicious kicks of a *Killer Joe* or sordid "honesty" of, say, *The Life*. Compassion is shown for this very sick man, while Li'l Bit grows into a young woman who can eventually look back at the worst—and best—moments of this relationship, put her foot to the pedal, and speed off into adulthood. Mark Brokaw's direction of *Drive* lets the scenes between Li'l Bit and Peck, played marvelously by Mary-Louise Parker and David Morse, hum with a quiet tension. More raucous looks at Li'l Bit's family—a vulgar bunch, happily spouting risque remarks yet hush-hush about the truth of their daughter's predicament—offer a cheery but not frivolous release.

All over the map in its themes was Jonathan Reynolds's *Stonewall Jackson's House*, certainly the year's nerviest work and sometimes the most dazzling. Scene 1, directed in cartoonish, bad-sitcom style, offers a young black woman showing white tourists around the house of Confederate General Stonewall Jackson. La-Wanda fields questions from a sweet, middle-American couple, as well as complaints from a redneck duo who've read every conceivable book on Stonewall and are fanatically concerned with the furniture's "authenticity." So sick is LaWanda of her life, her job and her cranky tourists, she begs to come home with the gentle retirees—as their *slave*. The debate that ensues, pitting the advantages of slavery (free meals, a settled existence) against its obvious shortcomings, is funny and sharp, but just the beginning.

Reynolds turned the rest of the play on its head. We discover the actress playing LaWanda in this skit is, in fact, the literary manager of a subsidized regional theater. The artistic director and his wife, the company's lead actress, are considering the work for their season. They know the race theme will be controversial but think the comedy will make an important statement about blacks in America. LaWanda vociferously disagrees, calling the play-within-the-play (which was penned by a young white dramatist) insulting to African-Americans' memory of 400 years of slavery.

With arguments that are angry, hilarious and deadly serious, *Stonewall Jackson's House* looks at every aspect of modern black life in America. Like the playwright in his play, author Reynolds is Caucasian, yet the work here is as far removed from *Driving Miss Daisy* condescension as *How I Learned to Drive* is from TV movies about incest. To the play's serious detriment, Reynolds all but jettisons the plot and makes the evening a freewheeling debate. It's too much of a half-digested thing, but one that made us wonder how much better Broadway would be if *Mastergate* and *Angels in America* had been box-office hits instead of just good deeds.

Exhilarating as *Stonewall Jackson's House* could be, the year's most scarifying look at black culture was yet to come. Adventurous New York audiences could watch the performance of the year unfold in the Public Theater's unadorned Lu-Esther Hall. A man, a chair, a cigarette. Well, first no man, just an (overlong) audio collage of soundbytes from the 1960s, heavily favoring black radicals Malcolm X and Huey P. Newton. Then Roger Guenveur Smith, as Newton, took a seat. The man before us was nervous, sucking hard on his cigarette, his voice tremulous, each phrase strongly considered before uttered. Within 20 minutes, this character would be joking, bellowing, wittily goading the audience. In another 20 he was pacing like a tiger around the tiny stage, doing pushups to Bob Dylan's "Ballad of a Thin Man" (the one about Mr. Jones who doesn't know what's happening), and hurling himself back against the chair seat, again and again and again and again, in fits of drug-induced agony. Good performances are a dime a dozen in New York, and great ones can be had for a sawbuck, but Roger Guenveur Smith in *A Huey P. Newton Story* truly made an audience question the line between actor and character. Smith's choice to greet patrons after the performance, no doubt to assure us that he *wasn't* a drugged out, psychotic, former leader of the Black Panthers, wasn't enough to shake the sense that biographical one-person shows had been pushed to a thrilling extreme.

Certainly Spalding Gray's *Slope* and Smith's *Newton* made other solos look like educational exercises, though this year's crop were livelier than usual. Writer-performer Eddy Frierson's *"Matty"* offered a loud, long but often jovial evening with legendary Giants pitcher Christy Mathewson. Donal Donnelly received positive notices for his George Bernard Shaw solo, *My Astonishing Self*. Chubby, Jackie Gleasonish John DiResta (who, I confess, sat in my high school homeroom) caught the media's eye with *Beat*, an uneven look at his career as a police officer on subway and homeless detail.

Appealing in a low-key way was *Boychik*, which studied a man in mourning trying to reconnect with the memory of his Orthodox Jewish father. Though the show had a built-in audience and starred Richard Kline of *Three's Company* fame (he played sleazy friend Larry), *Boychik* came into New York under-funded and succumbed before it could build a paying crowd. Conversely, *Late Nite Catechism*, a long-running Chicago hit, arrived with little hoopla and caught on almost immediately. The acclaim was merited, for Maripat Donovan and co-writer Vicki Quade have managed a delightful hybrid. Though *Catechism* features a strict but joke-cracking nun, it offers neither the fierce apostasy of *Sister Mary Ignatius* nor the nuns-as-penguins pablum of *Nunsense*. Donovan's Sister Mary spins tall tales of saints and martyrs, yet makes clear they're not meant to be taken literally. She also doesn't shy from the hard stuff—wooden rulers as a disciplinary tool, audience questions about abortion—yet always treats Catholicism with loving respect. *Catechism* surely gave lapsed Christians a hankering for the real thing, while giving the rest of us a yen for more Chicago cult hits crossing the Hudson (when, oh when, will *Hellcab* come?).

The season offered other strong solos based on characterization. Most celebrated was Fiona Shaw's *The Waste Land*, captivating as much for its location (the dilapidated midtown Liberty Theater) as for its breathless spectacle of Shaw turning T.S. Eliot's disconnected prose into flashes of real people living in blitz-era England. So effective was the bare bulb swinging over the stage of this austere piece, the Drama Desk nominated *Waste Land* for best lighting. A more traditional character solo was offered by Felix A. Pire concentrating on gay culture in Miami. *Men on the Verge of a His-Panic Breakdown* was a break-out cult hit featuring Pire as a series of homosexual Latin-American men created by author Guillermo Reyes. Funniest was the vignette *ESL: English as a Stressful Language* about an adult education instructor so tortured by his own social status he viciously berates students who'll never reach his level of proper American speech. This sequence featured Reyes's best writing, as did the quieter scene of a restaurateur pleading for his chefs to use authentic ingredients ("Never replace the yucca!"). Other pieces have trouble integrating far-out comic touches into realistic monologues, but Pire proved a 110 percent gung-ho interpreter. He took home an Outer Critics Award for solo performance, beating out Maripat Donovan, Julia Sweeney, and Charlayne Woodard for her solo, *Neat*.

Another off-beat winner was *The Santaland Diaries*, scripted by David Sedaris, co-author of *One Shoe Off* and *The Little Freida Mysteries*. "Santaland" (that is, the extravagant holiday set-up at Macy's department store) is a world where kids make wee-wee in the fake snow, where one gay elf comes on to all the other elves, and where harried shoppers toss dirty diapers into this man-made winter wonderland. Timothy Olyphant's fey performance deflated the material, though even his insipid delivery couldn't kill the show's best laughs or surprising poignancy.

An award-winning West End comedy by Patrick Marber, *Dealer's Choice*, showed the decidedly ungodly side of what Leonard Cohen once termed, "the holy game of poker." Though they can scarcely afford to, employees of a mid-level restaurant take part in a weekly high-stakes poker game with their well-off boss. An examination of the boys' jealousies and empty lives as they lose hundreds of dollars, yet can't say "no" to the weekly game, would be enough for a gritty comedy, but Marber raised the stakes by adding one extra player: Ash, a "friend" of the owner's compulsive gambler son, who turns out to be a loan shark come to collect his debt. Precisely directed by John Tillinger, *Dealer's Choice* was arguably the year's most satisfying all-around production, the mix of English and American actors up to the writing. In off Broadway's other 1996–97 new foreign play, *The Steward of Christendom* at the Brooklyn Academy of Music, Irish actor Donal McCann won unanimous acclaim for playing a former chief of police committed to an insane asylum in Sebastian Barry's elliptical drama.

Nicky Silver could very well have penned the shrewd and delirious *Psychopathia Sexualis*—but he didn't. This farcical look at obsessive personalities kin to Silver's *The Food Chain*, was instead written by John Patrick Shanley, in a major return to form at Manhattan Theater Club. Shanley started the season OOB with a pair of one-acts, *Missing/Kissing*, then came roaring onto the scene with the tale of a groom-to-be confessing to his best friend the one problem that could wreck his wedding night: an argyle sock fetish. Arthur has lived comfortably with this fixation for years, but his narcissistic psychiatrist (Edward Herrmann) reaches the breaking point. He steals the offending footwear, forcing Arthur to go cold turkey. Not only do the one-liners in *Psychopathia Sexualis* land with the crunch of a Monty Python (sockless) foot, Shanley's play also explores the fragility of external behavior—and has a good, nasty laugh at therapists in the bargain. As if providing a wonderful evening of comedy weren't enough, *Psychopathia* also reminded us how frustratingly long the treasurable Edward Herrmann has been typecast as stuffy delegates, malicious advisers and Franklin Roosevelts.

After a tiresome opening sequence, Leslie Ayvazian's familial *Nine Armenians* dove strongly into its central question: how does privileged, well-adjusted Virginia incorporate the tremendous suffering she sees when she visits her family motherland, Armenia, into a "normal" life back in America? Ayvazian overstuffed her drama with obvious metaphors and clan crises, yet the Manhattan Theater Club had a tremendous ace in the hole: Kathleen Chalfant as Grandma, who teaches Virginia the secret of living with suffering. Chalfant's angular body and Grant Wood face worked against any element of pathos in her performance, so when the older woman shared a ritual of sorrow with her granddaughter, the result was doubly heart-rending.

The Blues Are Running, two one-acts by Michael Cristofer, also at MTC, barely hit stride but did introduce Paul Giamatti to the theater scene. He'd later appear (as essentially the same neurotic character) in *Three Sisters* and as radio programmer "Pig Vomit" in the Howard Stern movie *Private Parts*. Oh, and speaking of excretions, the year's worst play was an off-off-Broadway two-hander called *Jasper in Gramercy Park*, with two senior citizens chatting endlessly about the size, shape and consistency of their dog's bowel movements.

Something to Celebrate: Old Wicked Songs

The commercial transfer of *Old Wicked Songs* was something to celebrate. Jon Marans's study of an attentive but secretive voice teacher and a snotty piano prodigy could have served as a textbook on writing a chamber drama. There was humor in the characters' eccentricities, charm in their budding regard for each other, tension in the ugliness that develops between them and sorrow in the revelation, and healing, of the instructor's psychic wounds. Proof of the playwright's brillance comes when instructor Mashkan is about to tell his pupil, Stephen, about the horrors he experienced in concentration camps. Instead of beating us over the head with yet another tale of Nazi atrocities, Marans has the teacher move his mouth silently while we watch the reaction on Stephen's face. Like us, he can respond only in tears. This extraordinary moment is then matched by the last scene, where the Schumann lieder that gave its title to Marans's play becomes a deeply moving coda.

Initially staged OOB by the Barrow Group in 1995, then remounted by Jewish Repertory Theater, Jon Marans's drama also received a West End production this season, the latter starring Bob Hoskins. Off Broadway, the show featured Hal Robinson as Mashkan and Justin Kirk (Michael Stuhlbarg played the role OOB).

Gay themes were interestingly handled by David Ives in *The Red Address*, a strange but compelling drama at Second Stage about a harried, married businessman escaping from the pressures of competition by donning a red dress and high heels. Tremendous pains were taken, by Ives and director Pamela Berlin, to keep the tone of this drama from turning silly. Consequently, *Red Address* sometimes moved slowly and left many critics scratching their heads as to the play's intent. Yet one confrontation, between the protagonist and his second-in-command, was so pointed, so wrenching and so well-structured, it was impossible to dismiss *The Red Address* as mere wing-stretching by the master of one-acts. Ives also offered a program of

A HUEY P. NEWTON STORY—Roger Guenveur Smith as the black activist in a solo performance at The Joseph Papp Public Theater

six new one-acts OOB at Primary Stages, *Mere Mortals*, destined to be raised to full off-Broadway status early in the coming season.

Lanford Wilson's *Sympathetic Magic*, also at Second Stage, hoped to encompass the entire universe. When two young physicists at an observatory discover an anomaly that could effect tremendous changes in scientific thinking, they must contend with an egotistical supervisor whose first thought is towards public relations, his second towards funding of the college sponsoring the research. Faced with looming deadlines and pressure to reveal results too quickly, one physicist must also contend with the unexpected news that his wife is pregnant. Her decision to abort, made without his consultation, sends him into a violent tailspin. Add to this a subplot about her brother—a gay priest—and a gay friend who guides the church choir, and you can see why *Sympathetic Magic* was as frustrating as it was intriguing.

With MTC's vivid 1996 revival of *Blue Window* still lingering in the memory, expectations were high for Craig Lucas to continue his exploration of random events linking people who would otherwise remain solitary in their ecstasies and woes. Certainly Lucas has made a career of turning haphazard twists of fate into something mystical, from the harmless old man stealing a bride's soul in *Prelude to a Kiss* to the dead family members who pop up in the oddest places in *Missing Persons*. With *God's Heart*, alas, Lucas pushes the "what if" quotient past the breaking point. Not only does an Upper West Side mommy-to-be get mixed up with a black look-out for a drug dealer and a hospitalized friend who turns out to be a murderer, Lucas also lards the piece down with sci-fi nonsense about a computer-savvy scientist able to preserve the personality of a dying AIDS victim in purely cyber form. Though *God's Heart* did little to advance the cause of multi-media in commercial theater (as opposed to recent uses in *The Who's Tommy* and *The Monogamist*), even those of us shaking our heads and wondering what Lucas was about when he wrote the play had to admit the three-minute video that encapsulated the AIDS patient's entire life was touchingly done.

Another major disappointment in New York was *One Flea Spare*, which sprang from the Louisville Humana Festival with enough huzzahs to make playwright Naomi Wallace sound like the second coming of Tony Kushner. A look at class distinctions breaking down during the plague years, *Flea* had elements of Pinter in its casual sadism and enough cryptic AIDS metaphors to make the sordid tale "relevant." By most accounts, the Public Theater mounting didn't do the script justice (said text was certainly poetic, but I couldn't make head or tail of its plot or themes).

A cross-Atlantic, modern-dress production of *The Two Gentlemen of Verona*, starring Globe Theater artistic director and wunderkind Mark Rylance, tried hard to be audience friendly but had few workable ideas besides keeping the houselights on throughout (to approximate the Globe's outdoor conditions). More potent off-Broadway revivals were a keenly directed *A Soldier's Play* for Valiant Theater Company and a 50th anniversary staging of *All My Sons* at the Roundabout's Laura Pels space. Miller's vision of suburban America as a facade of picket fences and front porches that hide secrets and mistrusts between neighbors, has become familiar. But his simple tale of a father forced to acknowledge a terrible misjudgment in his past, because it threatens the future of his mentally anguished wife (Linda Stephens) and marriage-minded son (Michael Hayden), hasn't lost its force. John Cullum convincingly took Joe Keller from groggy codger to desperate prevaricator; and, as we all saw in *Wings*, no one plays haunted women like the incomparable Linda Stephens.

The New York *Times* review killed the chances of an off-Broadway piece which many critics considered the year's best musical: *Violet*. A chamber work by Jeanine Tesori and Brian Crawley, *Violet* told of a young Southern girl on a journey in 1964, in company with two servicemen (one black) and the facial scar she received when her father had an accident with his ax. Though the girl finds physical affection with the good ol' boy soldier, it is the black one she loves. Facing Violet, then, are prejudices to overcome from without and within. Producers were lined up to bring the Playwrights Horizons musical to commercial attention when a pan in the *Times* nipped *Violet* in the bud. The New York Drama Critics Circle Award for best musical at least ensured that the piece will be preserved on CD.

Violet notwithstanding, few brand new musicals made their presence felt on the off-Broadway scene. Charles Busch and Rusty Magee's *The Green Heart* was an underappreciated gem, campy yet sweet. Fortune-seeking William (David Andrew MacDonald) marries painfully shy horticulturist Henrietta (Karen Trott) in the hopes of bumping her off and collecting her millions. When those plans go awry, William reconsiders whether killing someone so innately good, and who loves him so much, would be a wise move. Funny subplots abound, with Alison Fraser camping it up *a la* Madeline Kahn as Uta, William's spoiled girlfriend. A lovely title song, and a captivating turn by Karen Trott (especially on the show-stopping "Henrietta's Elegy") should have brought greater success to this generally delightful work.

On a smaller scale, there were laughs to be had at the witty lyrics and better gags of the *Star Trek* parody, *Space Trek*, and even a few gross bellylaughs at the otherwise unendurable *Warp!*. *Radio Gals*, which hoped to be this year's *Cowgirls*, was actually better than *Cowgirls* (how can you not like a show which boasts a song titled, "Edna Jones, the Elephant Girl"?), yet failed quickly at the box office.

Musical revues had better luck off Broadway than new musicals. Most lauded was Howard Crabtree*'s When Pigs Fly*, a sequel-of-sorts to Crabtree's previous revue, *Whoop-Dee-Doo!*, which celebrated gayness in a G-rated, *La Cage* way. A jolly *joie de vivre* and outlandish, rainbow-hued costumes helped make the latter a surprise hit for designer Crabtree, but *When Pigs Fly* was even better. Mark Waldrop's sharp lyrics matched to Dick Gallagher's sprightly tunes matched to cast members dressed as decks of cards, chests of drawers and legendary Broadway characters made the evening soar higher and faster than any animal, pigs included. Pop-eyed, large-framed Stanley Bojarski got the biggest laughs, most notably when he played the artistic director of a Wisconsin community theater announcing the theater's upcoming schedule ("We know you had some problems with this past season. We know you didn't understand *Ruthless*. We know, hey, how many times can you *Paint Your Wagon*? So this season we tried changing the pace with some revues. There was our evening of Frank Loesser's World War II songs: *Brutally Frank*. And then there was our rediscovered Richard Rodgers evening: *You Don't Know Dick*. Hey, they were fun, right?"). Hilarious, too, was Jay Rogers, offering torch songs to those great lovers of culture, Newt Gingrich, Rush Limbaugh and Strom Thurmond. If *Pigs* made it all look so easy, another revue with a gay motif, *Disappearing Act*, showed there's more to the form than lumping together a few nice songs (by Mike Oster) and a hard-working cast. Flat and badly mounted, *Disappearing Act* soon made like its title.

Sadly, Howard Crabtree never saw *When Pigs Fly* take the Outer Critics Circle Award for best off-Broadway musical; he died of complications from AIDS June 28, 1996, days after completing his costume work on the show. It was the second consecutive year that the creative force behind the season's hottest musical died in his prime; last year it was *Rent*'s Jonathan Larson. Another very great loss this year was the death of Broadway's greatest anomaly: a beloved critic. Walter Kerr, who served 15 years at the *Herald Tribune* and 17 at the *Times*, died at age 83.

Forbidden Broadway Strikes Back was a heartening return to form for composer/lyricist Gerard Alessandrini. After a dabbling in movie parodies with *Forbidden*

At Second Stage

ving its programs to full off-
~adway status this season, Second
~e included on its schedule Lan-
~ Wilson's *Sympathetic Magic*
~ *(above in background)* Tanya
~zin, Jeff McCarthy, David Bish-
~and Jordan Mott and *(in fore-
~nd)* Dana Millican and Ellen
~caster; and David Ives's *The Red
~ress* with *(right)* Cady McClain
~ Kevin Anderson

Hollywood because Broadway offered so little to satirize, Alessandrini couldn't re-
sist ribbing the passel of major musical revivals. As with every *FB*, all the cast members proved tremendously versatile, with each specializing in two or three imper-
sonations. Bryan Batt convincingly cavorted as Jerry Lewis, David Hibbard hobbled
happily as American Theater Wing doyenne Isabelle Stevenson, Christine Pedi was
a stitch as Stritch, and Donna English looked and sounded so much like Julie Andrews in her 1960's-era prime, it took a full minute for gasps to ease into laughs.

Charming the hetero crowd was Joe DiPietro's and Jimmy Roberts's *I Love You,
You're Perfect, Now Change*, cute sketches and songs about the singles scene, nup-
tials and parenthood. Song titles such as "Cantata for a First Date," "He Called
Me" and "Marriage Tango" point to a lyrical sophistication a few miles short of

William Finn, but the show struck a chord in audiences so deluged with gay themes they're relieved to be reminded that 90 percent of the time men still date *women*, marry them and make babies. Washington D.C. favorite *Capitol Steps*, a musical sketch group composed entirely of current and former Congressional staffers, offered a buoyant, if surprisingly docile, evening of political satire. Two monologues utilizing spoonerisms for comic effect long outstay their welcome, but a wicked Bob Dole turn, and keen lyric-writing by Bill Strauss, made for capital fun. For pastiche, audiences have been turning to *A Brief History of White Music*, an energetic rendering of a clever idea: since racism dictated that white artists cover blues and soul recordings in the 1950s and 60s, in 1997 why not have three black performers giving an R&B spin to white songs of the same period? The results were an instant hit for the newly reopened Village Gate, moved up to posher digs on West 57th Street.

Considered to have the Midas touch thanks to *Chicago*, Encores! had another smash year of musical stagings in concert form, with a Martin Short *Promises, Promises* the most likely to find future commercial life. Dorothy Loudon brought down the house in *Sweet Adeline*, as did the gorgeously sung and orchestrated number "The Girl Is on His Mind." Similarly rapturous reviews greeted the season's final offering, *The Boys From Syracuse*.

Melodic Irish music was abundant in *Peter and Wendy*, a special Mabou Mines presentation that, though low-key and too long, became an ineffably poignant retelling of the J.M. Barrie fable. In a year of tour de force work by African-American actors (Roger Guenveur Smith in *A Huey P. Newton Story*, Lisa Louise Langford and Starla Benford in *Stonewall Jackson's House*, Lynne Thigpen in *An American Daughter*) Karen Kandel stood alone as the most versatile. The only human on a stage filled with puppets and marionettes, Kandel not only provided all the voices for Peter Pan, Hook, Smee and the rest, but had to play Wendy as both naive adolescent and grown woman, her heart breaking when forced to put away childish things.

Still wondrously child*like*, The Flying Karamazov Brothers returned to New York in *Sharps, Flats & Accidentals*, their juggling as breathtaking as ever, their jokes vastly improved, their gimmicks a delight. Loud, repetitious and grating, Australia's *Tap Dogs* nonetheless staked its claim as this season's *Stomp*, with construction girders and platforms replacing garbage cans and broomsticks as objects of percussive dance. Ireland's *Riverdance* and *Lord of the Dance* also became something of a phenomenon, huge audiences turning out for their crass blend of fine step-dancing, portentous narration, over-amplified Celtic music and endlessly repeated combinations.

Lacking the skill of the Karamazovs, a clown trio in *The New Bozena* tried to scrape by with a few clever gags and characterizations, just not as funny as the creators must have thought they were. The evening was partially redeemed by the final sequence, which had the trio appearing in an Eastern European drama titled *Winter Is the Coldest Season*. Anyone who's seen Czech opera at the Met couldn't help howling at the skewed-angle kitchen and ridiculous family melodrama of the play-within-a-play, especially when lanky Spiv, timid Ramon and hyperactive Revhanavaan incorporated their lunatic novelties into the form's dour conventions.

In a category—nay, a species—all their own were *The Tokyo Shock Boys*, a quartet of Japanese men who had nothing better to do than risk their lives, and dignity, nightly in front of an audience. Oh, they did a lot of time-killing fake stuff, like drumming on an audience member's head, getting the crowd to chant along to the pumped-up music and having a pseudo-swordfight in the dark (the sparks were made by a third member with a cigarette lighter). Killing the show's chances off Broadway was the lack of an overall tone, or sense of build-up, to the various stunts. The quartet were like schoolkids going, "Look at me! Look at me!" though half the time they weren't worth looking at, even though they wore punky haircuts and colorful Japanese costumes.

And yet . . . Gyuzo put a live scorpion in his mouth—yes he did, I saw him. Danna ate handfuls of dry ice and blew white smoke out his nose. He also drank milk and made it shoot out the side of his eye. Other Shock Boy talents included lighting their farts, ingesting dishwashing liquid, and turning one Shock Boy upside down with his head in a metal garbage can, his only company—a lit firecracker.

I've spent this much ink on The Shock Boys in order to lead up to their greatest "trick," one that had even jaded New York jaws dropping and palates tsk-tsking. Gyuzo stuck a toilet plunger to his head. Attached to the end of the plunger was a long rubber string. The other end of that string stopped at Nambu. It wasn't tied around Nambu's neck. It wasn't held between Nambu's teeth. No, the other end of that string was tied around Nambu's testicles, and for the next three minutes both men *engaged in a tug of war*, presumably to see which would detach first, Gyuzo's plunger or Nambu's family jewels. No denying this was a deranged form of entertainment, yet I like to think Samuel Beckett would have appreciated the calculated absurdity of it, William Shakespeare would have cheered its grounding aspect, and the Greeks would have drawn heroic metaphors from the elemental contest. When stripped of its stylistic pretensions, its million dollar budgets, its trappings of sets and costumes, even its addiction to themes and meaning, theater really does come down to, "Hey, look at us!"

And happily, for those who looked this season, there was much to see.

A GRAPHIC GLANCE

1996–97
Drawings
By Hirschfeld

Above, Vanessa Redgrave and David Harewood in the title roles of *Antony and Cleopatra; right,* Al Pacino as Eugene O'Neill's *Hughie*

This Hirschfeld impression of the New York theater season includes *(front row)* Lillias White in *The Life*, Frank Langella in *Present Laughter*, Julie Harris in *The Gin Game*, Christopher Plummer in *Barrymore* and Antony Sher in *Stanley; (middle row)* Michael Gambon and Lia Williams in *Skylight*, David Rasche in *Edmond*, Brian Bedford in *London Assurance* and Janet McTeer in *A Doll's House; (back row)* Fiona Shaw in *The Waste Land*, Rebecca Luker in *The Boys from Syracuse* in the *Encores!* series, David Morse in *How I Learned to Drive*, Michael Hayden and Angie Phillips in *All My Sons*, Bebe Neuwirth in *Chicago* and Donal McCann in *The Steward of Christendom*

Above, Patti LuPone as Maria Callas
in *Master Class; right,* Liza Minnelli
in the title role of *Victor/Victoria; on
opposite page,* Whoopi Goldberg as
Pseudolus in *A Funny Thing Happened on the Way to the Forum*

Mary Louise Wilson as Diana Vreeland in *Full Gallop*

Christopher Plummer in the title role of *Barrymore*

Right, Ed Harris and Daniel Massey in *Taking Sides*

Left, Julie Harris and Charles Durning in *The Gin Game*

Joel Grey, Ann Reinking, Bebe Neuwirth and James Naughton in *Chicago*

pposite page, Bill Irwin in the title role of *Scapin*

Amy Irving, Jeanne Tripplehorn and Lili Taylor in the Roundabout's *Three Sisters*

Kenneth Welsh and Stockard Channing in Lincoln Center's *The Little Foxes*

Harolyn Blackwell, Andrea Martin *(below)*, Jim Dale, Jason Danieley, Arte Johnson and Mal Z. Lawrence in the revival of *Candide*

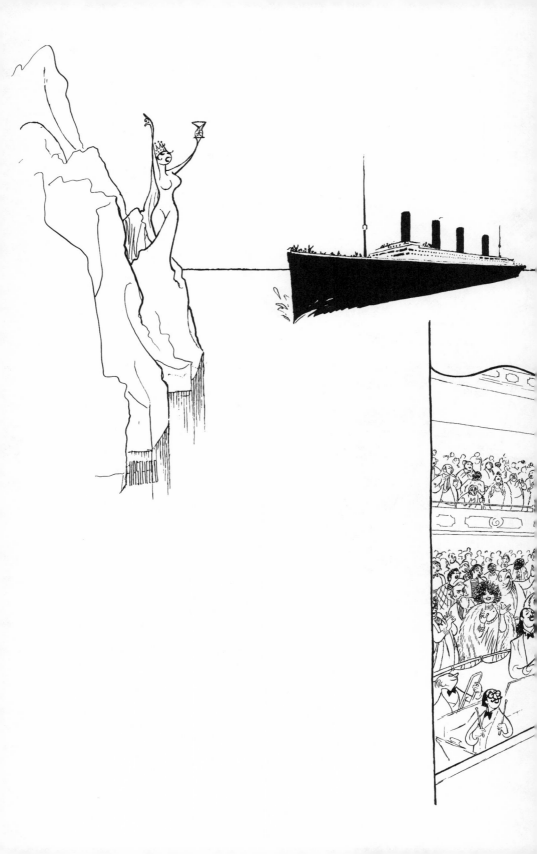

A Pair of Hirschfeld Toasts

On opposite page, a glass is raised to the mighty but ill-fated subject of the musical *Titanic; below,* a standing ovation to the very spirit of the Broadway musical

Frank Langella and Steve Ross in *Present Laughter*

Nell Carter, Sandy and Brittny Kissinger in *Annie*

Wendy Wasserstein, playwrig

Harold Prince, producer-director

Henry Hewes, former drama critic of *The Saturday Review* and recipient of the 1996 Theater Hall of Fame Founders Award, who joked authoritatively, on accepting the Award at a February 3 ceremony, "I'm sorry for every nasty thing I wrote. The fact that I was always right is no excuse."

63

In *Once Upon a Mattress: top row,* Tom Alan Robbins, Lawrence Clayton, Heath Lamberts and David Hibbard; *bottom row,* Mary Lou Rosato, Sarah Jessica Parker, David Aaron Baker and Jane Krakowski

Margaret Whiting in *Dream*

David Copperfield in *Dreams & Nightmares*

Peter Riegert, Kate Nelligan and Hal Holbrook in *An American Daughter*

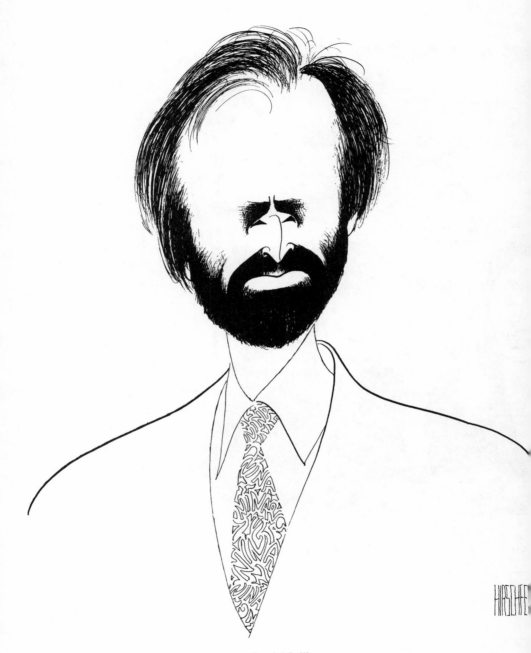

Daniel Sullivan

James Lapine

Robert Goulet on tour in *Man of La Mancha*

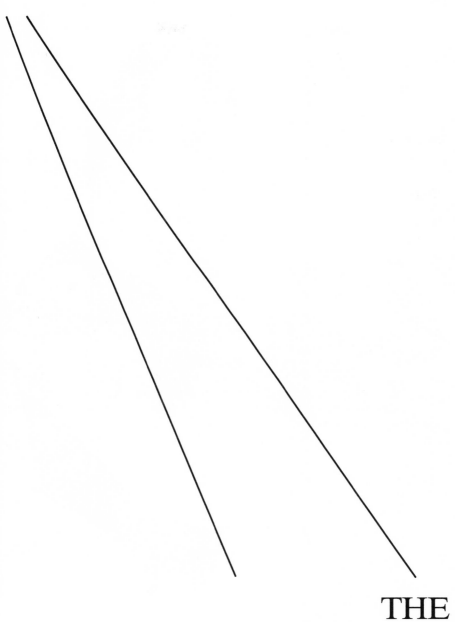

THE
PRIZEWINNING
PLAYS

Here are the details of 1996–97's major prizewinning plays—synopses, biographical sketches of authors and other material. By permission of the playwrights, their representatives, publishers, and others who own the exclusive rights to publish these scripts in full, most of our continuities include substantial quotations from crucial/pivotal scenes in order to provide a permanent reference to style and quality as well as theme, structure and story line.

In the case of such quotations, scenes and lines of dialogue, stage directions and descriptions appear *exactly* as in the stage version or published script unless (in a very few instances, for technical reasons) an abridgement is indicated by five dots (. . . . .). The appearance of three dots (. . .) is the script's own punctuation to denote the timing of a spoken line.

Special Citation

OLD WICKED SONGS

A Play in Two Acts

BY JON MARANS

Cast and credits appear on page 264

JON MARANS was born in 1957 and grew up in Silver Spring, Md., where his father was an organic chemist. After attending the local public schools he went to Duke University, graduating in 1979. With his eye on the musical stage, he studied at Lehman Engel's BMI Musical Theater Workshop, and in the course of his career he has written lyrics for Charles Strouse, Edward Thomas, Dan Levine, Galt MacDermot and other composers. He wrote for The New Carol Burnett Show *on TV and served as a script editor for Michael Douglas's production company at Columbia Pictures.*

Marans's first major recognition as a playwright came in 1986, when he won the Preston Jones New Play Award for his Child Child *at the Chocolate Bayou Theater in Houston. Almost a decade later, on April 25, 1995, his* Old Wicked Songs *opened at the Walnut Street Theater in Philadelphia and began moving into brighter and brighter limelight, as The Barrow Group produced it at Jewish Repertory Theater off off Broadway on November 5, 1995. It was thus eligible—and became a finalist—for last season's Pulitzer Prize, for which, nowadays, some tributary productions are considered, as well as Broadway and off-Broadway shows.* Old Wicked Songs *was then produced by Daryl Roth and Jeffrey Ash in association with Barrow in an open-ended off-Broadway run of 210 performances at the Promenade Theater, rendering it a full-fledged member of the 1996–97 professional theater season in New York, eligible for a whole other set of awards including special* Best Plays *recognition. The author of* Old Wicked Songs *lives in New York City while his outstanding play moves out onto the international stage. It premiered in England at the Bristol Old Vic on October 17, 1996 and went on to major London success at the Gielgud Theater in the West End on November 18, 1996.*

Starting with the season of 1996–97, it is our announced policy to present in synopsis in these pages the major prizewinning scripts instead of a Best Plays *individual selection of the year's outstanding playwriting, for reasons described in detail in this volume's Editor's Note. But this new policy will never prevent us from going out of our way to recognize a major work which, we believe, has been shut out in the normal course of prizegiving for some temporary or technical reason.*

Such a play is Old Wicked Songs. *Ineligible for some of last year's awards because of its OOB status, it nevertheless rose to the top of Pulitzer consideration. It lost out under special circumstances in which all the prizegivers were falling over themselves to get on the bandwagon of* Rent *which, deservedly or not, won everything within its reach including the Pulitzer. The* Best Plays *editors applaud the vigorous dramatic insights and characterizations of* Old Wicked Songs *and are proud to include it here as a special* Best Plays *citation for prizeworthy excellence in the New York professional theater of 1996–97.*

Time: The spring of 1986 continuing through to summer

Place: Professor Mashkan's rehearsal studio in Vienna, Austria

ACT I

Scene 1: Spring afternoon

SYNOPSIS: Professor Josef Mashkan's studio is described as *"old-world Vienna"* in appearance and includes baby grand piano, couch, coffee table, music stand, gramophone and clock permanently set at 5:35. Upstage a window looks out on the city. At right is a hallway leading to a kitchenette and the exit door. As the lights come up on the room, Mashkan, *"a sly, jolly, mercurial Viennese man in his late 50s, nattily attired—including a colorful vest and bow tie,"* is at the piano practicing the first song in the Schumann sequence *Dichterliebe.*

While Mashkan is playing, a young man, Stephen Hoffman, opens the door and watches the professor play. Stephen is *"a 25-year-old prodigy . . . . . somewhat ar-*

rogant, socially awkward, high-energy, light-haired . . . . . dressed conservatively in a jacket, tie and pressed pants." He interrupts the playing with a display of his erudition, identifying the music and adding, "You're playing it in C sharp minor. It was originally written in F sharp minor." Mashkan is understandably annoyed, complaining—in German—of Stephen's rudeness in barging in without knocking.

STEPHEN: The door was unlocked. Isn't this part of the university?
MASHKAN *(in German): I* am part of the university. *This* is my studio!
STEPHEN: Is this 315?
MASHKAN *(in English):* Give me your name.
STEPHEN: Hey, I didn't mean to disturb you—
MASHKAN: I am asking for your name—to report you for lack of manners.
STEPHEN *(getting defensive):* What is this? High school? . . . Stephen. Stephen Hoffman. And now, if you could tell me where 315 is?
MASHKAN *(suddenly nervous):* But today is Wednesday.
STEPHEN: Yeah?
MASHKAN: Stephen Hoffman is not arriving until Friday. Today is Wednesday!
STEPHEN: I took an earlier flight.
     Pause.
MASHKAN *(suddenly enthusiastic):* Well, come in, my boy. This is 315. Come in. I don't know why I snapped at you. Please accept my apology. Uncalled for. Completely uncalled for. Maybe we should start new, because I feel bad about what just occurred, and I really do apolo—well, I can't say that again, can I? . . . So *Gruss Gott.*
     Beat.
STEPHEN: Are you talking to me?
MASHKAN: *Entschuldigung.* I mean . . . excuse me. I thought you knew German.
STEPHEN *(in German):* A little.
MASHKAN: . . . . . And you do not understand *Gruss Gott?*
STEPHEN: *Nein.*
MASHKAN: Ah, curious . . .

Stephen refuses the professor's offer of a cup of coffee, but Mashkan goes to the kitchenette to prepare one anyway. Stephen sits and looks around the room, clearly uncomfortable in such a setting, having been brought up in California (he comments) to appreciate the clean lines of modern architecture.

Observing the headlines of newspapers on the coffee table, Stephen brings up the subject of Kurt Waldheim, asking if Mashkan thinks he's a Nazi. "It's 1986—who cares? . . . What do *you* think?" is Mashkan's reaction from offstage. Stephen replies, "What do I know? I'm a musician. *(To himself.)* Or was." He rises, circles the piano as if it were an enemy. Mashkan enters with the coffee tray, unseen by Stephen, as the young man "*lunges*" at the piano, attacking its keys with "*the opening bars of* 'Im wunderschönen monat Mai,' *playing swiftly and technically perfect, but without emotion.*" Stopping in mid-measure, he exclaims, "Now who the hell is *this*?!" and strikes himself on the side of his head. Mashkan, embarrassed but still unobserved by Stephen, backs out of the room, announces from the kitchenette that he's coming in with the coffee and returns with the tray.

Despite his previous refusal of coffee, Stephen drinks his cup in a single draught and pours another. He explains that he's been roaming around the city by himself for a night and a day. He addresses Mashkan as "Professor Schiller." To Stephen's surprise, Mashkan corrects him. Stephen has come here to study with Schiller and was sent here to what he'd thought was Schiller's studio, not Mashkan's. Mashkan explains: "To study piano accompaniment with Herr Schiller, you must first study singing with me for three months. To understand how the singer feels. These are Professor Schiller's instructions. He must have told you."

Not in so many words, and Stephen is indignant: "I'm not a singer. I play the piano." And it turns out he can't appeal to Schiller, because Schiller's gone to Munich for a few weeks. He wouldn't change his mind anyway, Mashkan assures Stephen, commenting, "When a Jew makes a deal, he sticks to it. Remember *The Merchant of Venice*!", which makes Stephen feel uncomfortable. He decides that this Mashkan arrangement is not for him and heads for the door, but the professor stops him with the remark, "I'll bet you're lousy in bed." Judging from Stephen's reaction, Mashkan may have hit the mark. He's not coming on to Stephen, he's merely stating his firm belief in "a direct correlation between making love to a woman and making love to a piano," and he's just observed Stephen treating a piano brutally.

MASHKAN: . . . . . You almost tried to rape my piano! She must be flirted with, not pounced on. Caress her keys. Let her know she is safe in your arms. Once that is established, *then* you can be wild and passionate. Come, stand here. Let me show you how a seduction is done. First, admire her smooth, shiny skin. *(Running his hands along the piano's keys.)* See her warm, bright smile.

STEPHEN: Half of her teeth are blacked out.

MASHKAN *(amused):* That was funny. I knew you had it in you— somewhere. Come. Smile back at her.

STEPHEN: This is silly.

MASHKAN: What can you lose?

STEPHEN: My dignity.

MASHKAN: Flirt with her. Run your hand through her strings.

Mashkan calls Stephen "Stefan," insisting that that's how it should be in Vienna. He suggests that his pupil prepare himself for gently wooing the baby grand for the next three months, learning to sing the Schumann song cycle *Dichterliebe* to the piano's accompaniment, under the professor's supervision. And Mashkan has bought the score of the *Dichterliebe* as a present for his pupil. He paid 50 schillings for it and will "give" it to Stephen for only 30. Stephen, paying over the money, still insists that all of this will be a waste of both their time. But Mashkan orders that the lessons start the following Tuesday, and it would be very unwise of Stephen not to appear. He reviews what he knows of Stephen's case: Stephen is a talented soloist

OLD WICKED SONGS—Hal Robinson as Professor Josef Mashkan and Justin Kirk as Stephen Hoffman in the play by Jon Marans

who is apparently burned out and hasn't performed in almost a year. Nothing in America has helped him, and, Mashkan continues, "in desperation, you fly all the way to Vienna to study with the famous Professor Schiller. And what does he tell you? You will not study solo pieces—but rather be an accompanist for voice. Very humbling. And further, before you study accompaniment, you must study singing. More humbling. I suppose it might make one feel nervous about one's talent. Make one wonder if he should have been a pianist at all. A scary thought for someone who has dedicated his life to music. Very, very scary. I suppose it might make one a little defensive, a little—arrogant. *Auf Wiedersehen,* Stefan. Until Tuesday."

Mashkan sends Stephen off with a key to his studio, which the professor uses only during the day and where Stephen might need to stay if, say, an opera he was attending ran late and he missed the last train to his dormitory out on the edge of the city. After Stephen goes (without thanking the professor for the key) Mashkan sits, spent, then swallows a pill, shrugs off his feelings and goes back to the piano to practice the first song of the Schumann sequence, *"Im wunderschönen monat Mai."* A recorded version begins, *"perfectly aligned to Mashkan's playing . . . . . louder and louder, gloriously filling the theater . . . . . At the end of every scene throughout the play, different songs from the* Dichterliebe *are heard. These very specific song choices serve two vital purposes. They are integral to the drama of the play, heightening the lead-out of scenes and emotionally aiding the lead-ins to the next scene. Also, they allow the audience to hear these songs in order, thus helping them more deeply to absorb the emotional impact of Schumann's song cycle."*

After about half the first song, a chord interrupts and leads into the next scene.

Scene 2: Tuesday morning the next week

The recorded music stops when Mashkan strikes a chord on the piano and the lights come up. Stephen is standing by the piano, singing "Ah" to each note in a scale Mashkan is playing. While doing so, Stephen manages to get across the information that he reached Professor Schiller by phone and was told to stick it out with Mashkan for three weeks before deciding to quit. He'll do it, but he won't like it.

Mashkan moves the notes higher and higher until Stephen's voice cracks. Stephen is then painstakingly instructed to stand straighter, loosen his tie (which he's never without), breathe from the diaphragm and open his throat wider. Mashkan returns to the piano and plays the song in a rhythm which Stephen finds erratic and hard to follow. Stephen has a pleasant voice, Mashkan allows, but a tempo problem. Stephen claims to have a perfect sense of timing and means to prove it.

STEPHEN: Where's a metronome?

MASHKAN: I don't need one.

STEPHEN *(spotting the clock, heading towards it):* I'll figure it out by the clock.

MASHKAN: That may be a little difficult, since it has not moved for over ten years. The weights—they're unbalanced.

STEPHEN: Clock imitating life?

MASHKAN *(amused):* I should not laugh, since it was directed at me—but it is so rare you make a joke . . . Now please, return to your stand.

> Stephen does. Mashkan begins to play. He starts slowly and then picks up the pace.

STEPHEN: Speeding up.

MASHKAN: It's my solo. I have dramatic license.

STEPHEN: An accompanist is there solely for the singer. Begin again.

MASHKAN: I will not. You missed your cue.

STEPHEN *(briskly):* Not by my count.

MASHKAN *(annoyed, stops playing):* . . . I am not solely a metronome for a singer. I must immerse myself into the song. And if that calls for speeding up a little or slowing down during piano solos, *ist gut.* Art consists of knowing the basic rules and realizing when it is time to deviate from them. You don't want to be just a robot—always sticking to the precise rules, do you Stefan?

STEPHEN *(tightly):* Stephen.

   Beat.

MASHKAN: *(lightly):* Again. From the top.

Stephen obeys, singing correctly until Mashkan hits a wrong note which is sternly identified by Stephen. Mashkan excuses himself lamely but changes the focus of the lesson to the poetic significance of the song's lyrics. Stephen translates flatly, "In the wonderful month of May, when all the trees were blooming . . ." but Mashkan stops him with his own more exuberant interpretation:

  "In the loveliest of months—May
  when the buds are bursting in bloom,
  love rose up in my heart."

Mashkan identifies the verse's sentiment as "manly love *and* feminine love. Manly in its strength. Feminine in its beauty" and likens the city of Vienna itself to the tone of the song, an assembly of exceptionally solid old buildings relieved by the artistry of "the statues, the arches, the molding, the cornices, the facades," each building reaching for the sky at its peak. Stephen still prefers modern "streamlining," which Mashkan believes is reducing architecture to the level of science by cutting away all of its beautiful detail. Likewise (Maskhan continues), when modern music is stripped of passion it becomes mere mathematics. He directs Stephen to sing the song passionately, but Stephen is able only to burlesque it. He feels that while the words are emotionally "hokey," the music contradicts them with melancholy. The song is remembering lost youthful love, Mashkan explains. He plays the tune again, and again he hits what Stephen insists is a wrong note. He orders Stephen to play it himself. "*Stephen circles the piano as he did before and then starts to almost pounce on it. Stephen sits. He breathes and tugs his ears three times—trying to be as subtle as possible doing it—and then begins playing.*" Mashkan wonders why Stephen goes through this breathing and ear-tugging routine. His mother is superstitious and believes in the good luck of threes, Stephen explains.

As Stephen plays and sings, Mashkan identifies the music's emotional changes, sometimes explaining, sometimes singing along with Stephen. The singer is remembering a May of long ago, first sadly, then with love and joy, longing for something which he finally knows he cannot recapture, as the music's sad ending expresses. "*Stephen ends the song noticeably moved. Mashkan's teaching was magical.*" Stephen wants to play the song again, but Mashkan tells him to wait, let his thoughts linger on the moment, recreate it in his mind. But Stephen, disobediently, begins playing again. Mashkan warns him that he'll bring the piano lid down on Stephen's hands unless he stops. Stephen ignores him and keeps playing, "*desperately trying to recreate the feeling*" he has just experienced—and he barely manages to get his fingers out of the way as Mashkan makes good his threat and bangs down the lid.

STEPHEN *(furious):* You could've ended my career!

MASHKAN: I am the teacher, not you. *You* listen to *me!*

STEPHEN: I didn't want to lose it!

MASHKAN: You cannot lose what you do not yet understand! Take a deep breath! Now!

STEPHEN *(angry):* I was giving you a compliment!—

MASHKAN: A deep breath! *(Stephen does, half-heartedly.)* Now close your eyes . . . Close them. *(Stephen does, warily.)* Allow the song to swim about in your brain. Think back. Absorb the feeling of *(Sings.)*

"*Im wunderschönen monat Mai . . .* "

(Spoken.) Words filled with joy accompanied by wistful, melancholy sounds. *(Sings.)*

"*Als alle knospen sprangen . . .* "

Can you hear it? . . . Can you? *(Stephen nods.)* This combination of joy and sadness—this is the core of truly beautiful music. Just as it is the core of drama. Of life. For instance, when you left for Vienna what did your mother say to you?

STEPHEN *(like a bratty kid):* Let Stephen play the song once more!

MASHKAN: That is not what she said.

STEPHEN: She said, "For once, Stephen, go and enjoy yourself." And then she hugged me. And cried.

MASHKAN: She was obviously sad you were leaving—yet still happy you would have this experience. Sadness and joy. When a composer finds both, the result is Mozart. Beethoven. And how do they acquire this perfect combination? Why do some countries give us great composers, while others do not?

Answering his own questions, Mashkan opines that nations like Austria, which has been much oppressed, produce such as Schubert, Brahms and Schumann, while those like England, which hasn't suffered prolonged domination by another power since the days of the Romans, do not give birth either to great music or great singers. Likewise Japan, likewise the United States, Mashkan argues, though he admits Leontyne Price is great, adding, "Of course she is black, and black people have definitely been oppressed."

Stephen puts in his own opinion that the Jews have suffered oppression and nominates Vladimir Horowitz and Leonard Bernstein as possible American greats. Mashkan doesn't agree, but it makes him wonder whether Stephen himself is Jewish. Stephen says that he is not, he is a Protestant.

Stephen takes an offered pastry from Mashkan and is astonished when the professor charges him 20 schillings for it. When the professor hears that his pupil has skipped a Staatsoper performance he had been supposed to attend, he is so angry that he wishes he could take back his pastry. Stephen protests that he was invited by Mashkan to have a pastry, and Mashkan explains: "In Vienna, if you offer something just once, the other person is supposed to say no! Only if the giver persists two more times do you really know he wants you to have it!"

Mashkan returns to the piano, over Stephen's protest that *he* wants to be the one playing the intrument, and goes into "*Im wunderschönen*" again, as the lights fade to black.

Scene 3: Late Wednesday night, two weeks later

The recorded music segues into the second song of the cycle, *"Aus meinen Tranen spriessen,"* as the lights come up part way to a half-lit view of Mashkan, drinking and smoking and apparently going over the notes of this song in his mind. Then, in the darkened studio, a glass of whiskey beside him on the piano, he is playing and singing the third song in the cycle, *"Die Rose, die Lilie, die Taube."* The door opens and Stephen enters, wearing a large green Tyrolean hat and *"exuberantly singing the aria 'Vesti la Giubba' from I Pagliacci."* Stephen thinks he is alone here at the studio and is startled when Mashkan joins him in singing the words to the aria. Each immediately assures the other that he is leaving soon. Mashkan is working late because he feels he needs to practice in order to be an effective teacher (he has no wife to worry that he's coming home late, she has been dead for ten years), and Stephen is here because he went to the opera and missed the last train to his dormitory.

Grudgingly, Stephen admits that he loved "the power and richness behind those voices" in *I Pagliacci* (which Mashkan urges him to call *Der Bajazzo*—the clown—as the Viennese do). During their conversation about opera, Mashkan keeps offering Stephen pastry, and the fourth time he accepts, selects one and forks over 20 schillings. Mashkan goes to the kitchenette to make coffee, while Stephen sits and looks at the pastry box.

STEPHEN *(calling to Mashkan):* You should go to my pastry shop. They only charge sixteen schillings. It's just around the corner. It's called—
    He picks up the box and sees the name of the pastry shop on it.
(He says softly): Tabir.
    MASHKAN *(offstage):* I didn't hear you. What's it called?
    STEPHEN *(calling):* ... That's funny. All of a sudden, it's slipped my mind ... You know, Mashkan, for me the best part of the evening was the end ... The clown, his life in shambles, cries, *"La comedia est finita!"*
    MASHKAN *(offstage):* Sadness and comedy all in one moment.
    STEPHEN *(calling):* And after that the curtain whooshed to the floor—it seemed to fall, it flew down so fast.
    MASHKAN *(reentering, carrying in coffee):* A man is specially trained to bring it down. That is his only task. A wonderful job.
    STEPHEN *(puzzled):* Well, not quite as wonderful as a professor.
    MASHKAN: More lucrative. And stable. It's hard to fire someone from a union job like that.
    STEPHEN: Hard to fire someone with tenure, too.
    MASHKAN: First one must hold a job long enough to get it.
    STEPHEN: ... You don't have tenure?
    MASHKAN *(pouring coffee):* Careful. The coffee is hot. It may burn your tongue.
    STEPHEN *(sipping it):* It's not hot.
    MASHKAN: No? Then maybe I wasn't talking about the coffee.
        They sip.

STEPHEN: . . . When'd you start teaching again?

MASHKAN: Two . . . three weeks ago.

STEPHEN *(suddenly dawning on him):* Am I your only student? That doesn't seem possible. I mean, you're so in control of your life. So . . . strong.

MASHKAN: Ah, strong. Like tonight's coffee. But why is it so strong? Because it has been simmering on the back-burner, slowly evaporating away. In other words, its strength comes from a part of it disappearing. *(Heartfelt.)* A sad strength.

STEPHEN: I like my coffee strong. It gives me a rush . . . Same way I used to feel playing the piano.

MASHKAN: Used to? Ah, so it's the *sitzfleisch* you're currently lacking. *(Stephen looks puzzled.)* It's the ability to keep the seat of the pants sticking to the seat of the chair!

STEPHEN: Hmmmm . . . I'm not so sure I ever really had that . . . My mother has it. She's a painter. Spends hours over the most minute detail—the back of a hand. The shading of a leaf. And loves doing it. My father's a math professor. I'll bet he thinks math is better than sex. I play the piano. And I'm a superb— *(Said derogatorily.)* —technician. *(Going to the piano.)* When I stopped giving concerts a year ago. . . . I was relieved. Sometimes I think the only reason I play is because it came so easily to me. It was a gift.

> *Running his hands over the keys, quickly playing ascending scales with both hands.*

I sat down when I was four and started playing Tchaikovsky's "Waltz in E. Flat."

> *He starts to play the waltz—without breathing or tugging, as he says:*

Everyone thought I was a prodigy. I wasn't. I was a mimic. I listened to the masters and duplicated what they played. Music didn't excite me. Pretending to be someone else—that was the kick.

Stephen demonstrates how he would change his style to fit each composer by changing the tilt of his hat. "It was fun. Uncomplicated," he concludes, but he doesn't want to go on mimicking, "I want to feel something, for once." Mashkan never had any special artist's gift, he admits, "But if these pipes could sing . . . " he adds longingly.

Stephen loved the Staatsoper, and he learns that it was built in 1955 to replicate the one destroyed during World War II. He noticed other effects of that war in the number of handicapped people in the streets or in wheelchairs. Stephen brings up the Jewish population which, he has heard, used to number over 300,000 but now amounts to less than 10,000. "Why does everyone always harp on the Jews?!" Mashkan exclaims, "They are not the only ones who suffered!"

Mashkan offers Stephen another pastry, admitting that he needs to sell him two more to make taxi fare home. Stephen buys three. And then he asks the professor if they can meet a little earlier than usual on Friday, because Stephen will be going to Munich for the weekend. He tactlessly mentions that Professor Schiller will plan his itinerary for him, thus revealing to Mashkan that Stephen has an appointment with Schiller. Mashkan had thought Stephen was getting to like these lessons, but

Stephen is such a strange one that anything is possible, and Mashkan anticipates *sturm und drang* at their Friday meeting. As he exits, Mashkan thanks Stephen for following instructions about attending the opera, and Stephen thanks the professor for making him go.

Alone, Stephen sits at the piano and plays the last few bars of *"Vesti la Giubba,"* as the lights go to black.

Scene 4: Friday afternoon, two days later

The recorded music plays the fourth song of the cycle, *"Wenn ich in deine Augen seh."* Mashkan, at the piano, is getting his expected *sturm und drang* in reality, because outside it is pouring rain and thundering. Stephen enters with a ruined umbrella and his suitcase for the Munich trip. It irritates Mashkan to realize that Stephen has met with Schiller, but his pupil seems ready for a lesson, so Mashkan proceeds to explain that the next song, *"Ich Grolle Nacht,"* requires the accompanist's special attention to the singer's needs to express his anger because he has been deceived. With complete obedience to Mashkan's instructions, Stephen makes an effort to summon up the requisite passion as he sings the lyric to Mashkan's piano accompaniment. It is Mashkan who breaks off, preoccupied with the situation instead of the music. In spite of himself his anger bursts out of him: "This job is all I have! Schiller granted your request, didn't he? . . . . . He has obviously found someone who will do it cheaper—trying to jew me out of a job."

But such is not the case. Schiller doesn't want Stephen to drop this class, because he believes that Mashkan can help him. And Stephen "also made it clear what a wonderful teacher you are." But Schiller agrees that dropping or not dropping it will finally be up to Stephen, who wants to think it over and make the decision on Monday. Meanwhile, there is the Munich adventure, during which, in line with Mashkan's philosophy, he will try to experience both joy and sadness by getting drunk at a beer hall after going to see *The Marriage of Figaro*; and, in contrast, visiting the Dachau concentration camp.

MASHKAN: Do not do that. *Ja*, it's sad, that is true. But we can find other sad things to send you to. *(Trying to be humorous.)* Besides, Dachau is just a bunch of dead Jews.

STEPHEN *(embarrassed to say this):* ... You know that's the ... the kind of remark that can get a teacher fired.

MASHKAN: What?

STEPHEN *(feeling uneasy):* I mean, if you ... I'm Jewish.

MASHKAN *(puzzled):* But I thought you said you were Protestant.

STEPHEN: I lied.

MASHKAN: Why?

STEPHEN: I don't know. Maybe I was just trying on my Christian hat ... I have to get out of here. I can't miss this train. See, I made a deal with my dad. He'd help pay for Vienna if I agreed to visit Dachau. And a deal's a deal. *(Lightly pointed.)* And you know how we Jews love making our deals.

> *Stephen, his suitcase and coat in hand, leaves. Mashkan stands there, stunned. The moment the door slams behind Stephen, we hear recorded music of the last five thundering piano bars of* "Ich grolle nicht." *At the same time, the stage quickly goes dark except for a spotlight on Mashkan. After the final chord of* "Ich grolle nicht" *crashes down—blackout. Curtain.*

ACT II

Scene 1: Tuesday morning, two weeks later

The studio is a mess, with papers and empty coffee cups strewn about. Mashkan, sleeping on the sofa, *"screams and bolts upright"* just before a knocking on the door is heard. He pulls himself together and goes to the door, admitting Stephen dressed informally in white sweat shirt and blue jeans. He hasn't seen Mashkan since returning from Munich. He beats Mashkan to the piano and, without breathing or tugging, plays the right hand part of "Tales From the Vienna Woods" while he tells the professor what he's been doing: exploring Vienna, noting its contradictions ("The Blue Danube isn't blue, it's brown!"), learning that when Vienna was "invaded" by the Germans in 1938, a greater proportion of Austrians than Germans were Nazis.

Mashkan is eager to renew the lessons. Stephen doesn't know what *Dichterliebe (The Poet's Love)* has to do with reality, but when the professor sits at the piano and begins to play "*Ich grolle nicht*," Stephen sings along with him— in English: "I hate you not." Noting that Stephen is determined not to speak German any more, Mashkan informs him that the accepted English translation of the line is "I bear no grudge." Stephen demands his own poetic license. He sings a verse clearly directed at Mashkan:

> "I hate—you not
> Although my heart may break
> Love is forever lost
> Love is forever lost
> I hate you not"

Stephen is portraying a good deal of anger, which Mashkan approves, even though Stephen is letting emotion control the tempo, and Mashkan is having a bit of difficulty keeping in synch.

MASHKAN: Slow down.
STEPHEN *(sings):*
> Where once a heart
> I see there's now a scar
> I see, my love, how truly lost you are

I hate you not
I hate you—not.

MASHKAN *(thrilled):* The translation is loose, but the intent—and the anger: *Gut!* But what happened to that perfect inner metronome?

STEPHEN: I sang with my feelings.

MASHKAN: And completely ignored the beat. It was all you, you, you. What about the piano?

STEPHEN: *You're* supposed to follow *me.*

MASHKAN: But you must be aware of my musicianship, give me my moments, allow us to blend, to become one.

STEPHEN: And what if I don't agree with your interpretation?

MASHKAN: Common ground must exist.

Mashkan offers Stephen a pastry. Stephen, still fueled by anger, takes one and tells the professor, "They only cost sixteen schillings. I shop at the same store. But I'll pay twenty. I don't want you to think I'm cheap." Stephen then proceeds to describe at length, and in detail, his visit to the Dachau camp. Riding out there from Munich on the train, he noticed that it was only 20 minutes from the heart of a city whose citizens regularly protested, "I knew nothing that went on there!" He met a young Jewish woman, Sarah, and together they toured the camp whose green grass, whitewashed buildings and stream with a "quaint little bridge" were a cosmetic contradiction of its horrible purpose. They toured the museum (whose photos were captioned only in German), the crematorium and the Israeli Memorial, "almost completely dark except for a small beam of light shining down from the top." Afterwards they had dinner together and made love far into the night and again the next morning. Stephen began to wonder if he had suddenly become better in bed, and then he realized, "You were right. That combination of sadness and joy. With one emotion heightened, so is the other."

Wandering around Vienna in the past two weeks did nothing to assuage Stephen's anger ("Every time I turned and saw a beautiful bridge or a quaint babbling brook, I broke into a sweat") or his disappointment in the professor for whom he was beginning to develop respect. Stephen drops his Tyrolean hat in front of Mashkan, commenting that it doesn't fit him after all, and prepares to leave. Mashkan stops him by bringing up the subject of Kurt Waldheim and the coming election, which he is sure Waldheim will win. As Mashkan reaches his conclusion that "You can't run a country so heavily Nazi without hiring a few," he rolls up his sleeve so that Stephen—shocked—can see the concentration camp number tattooed on Mashkan's arm.

Silence as he rolls his sleeve back down, covering up the tattoo.

MASHKAN *(drolly):* So you see, Stefan, once again your American mind assumed the obvious—that I was a Nazi. Life is not so clear-cut. There is a mind inside of there. Make it work!

STEPHEN *(confused):* But to say Dachau was just a bunch of dead Jews?

Hal Robinson with Justin Kirk in a scene from *Old Wicked Songs*

MASHKAN *(again lightly):* Disgraceful. And do you know how many times I have heard it said by intelligent Viennese men and women? ... this is why I say anti-Jewish comments first—before anyone else has the chance. My words sting, but not quite as sharply as theirs ... *Ich grolle nicht, und wenn das herz auch bricht*—"I bear no grudge—although my heart may break."

STEPHEN *(not realizing the rudeness of his question):* Where were you sent? I mean, which camp?

MASHKAN *(amused):* Ah, you want to know "my story." No ... each person has but one story in him. Tell it to everyone, and its meaning is cheapened. For next week, practice the eighth song in the *Dichterliebe*. It begins: *Und wüssten's die blumen die kleinen. (Lightly sings the rest:)*

Wie tief verwundent mein herz
Sie würden mit mir weinen
(*Translating*): "If the flowers knew of my grief, they would weep"
STEPHEN: I won't sing it in German.
MASHKAN (*tongue-in-cheek*): And I will not play it in German.
The lights swiftly fade.

Scene 2: Friday afternoon, three days later

A recorded version of "*Und wüssten's die blumen, die kleinen*" is heard, as the lights come part way up on a hazy room and Mashkan, who's been drinking. The music is now coming from the gramophone The lights go down again and then up, showing Mashkan asleep on the couch. This time he doesn't awaken when Stephen knocks and enters. Stephen takes the opportunity to roll up the professor's sleeve and examine the tattooed numbers.

Stephen notices a glass of whiskey and an empty bottle of pills on the table. Alarmed, he shakes Mashkan awake. When he can't make the professor come to the bathroom to vomit whatever he's swallowed, Stephen calls for an ambulance and follows instructions to get Mashkan on his feet and keep him moving. Stephen can't understand why Mashkan is muttering numbers in the mid-40s, it couldn't be the number of pills he's taken, the empty bottle wouldn't hold that many. He loosens Mashkan's tie for easier breathing.

Even in his condition, Mashkan notices that Stephen is now wearing a yarmulke. It is a statement Stephen is making about his pride in his Jewishness, not a sign of any religious conviction. While Stephen is assisting Mashkan, the professor finds an opportunity to snatch the yarmulke off Stephen's head, exclaiming, "If you don't feel it on the inside, don't wear it on the outside!"

Stephen remembers that when he called the ambulance they didn't ask for Mashkan's address. Obviously they've been here before, and Mashkan has tried this before—several times, Mashkan admits it (but he won't tell how many) and maybe that's why some consider him too unstable to hold a job. Stephen hopes it wasn't anything he said that pushed the professor over the edge this time. Mashkan, suffering a spasm, holds out the yarmulke to Stephen "in case you feel the urge to pray for me." (*The lights swiftly fade.*)

Scene 3: Hours later. Night

When the final section of the eighth song finishes, the lights come up revealing Mashkan seated, covered with a blanket, and Stephen entering with a tray of pastries which he's brought as a present. Mashkan's stomach was pumped, and now, Stephen insists, he needs nourishment. Inadvertently, Mashkan asks for coffee in German and then finds it necessary to defend the language as being as much Austria's property as Germany's. And the lyrics of the *Dichterliebe*, Mashkan reminds Stephen, were written by Heinrich Heine, a great Jewish poet.

Stephen is eager for Mashkan to tell him his "story," promising to pass it along to future generations. Mashkan comments, "My secrets . . . . . The words.You have heard them before. Everyone has. They have become commonplace," and then he asks Stephen to help him to stand up so he can look out of the window. But as soon as he's up he manages to escape to the piano bench and begin playing "*Am leuchtenden sommermorgen,*" ordering his pupil to begin a lesson. In this song the singer is strolling in the garden, and the very flowers ask him for forgiveness. Stephen must make this felt in his singing.

MASHKAN: . . . . . Oh, and on this particular bright summer morning, as you walk through the garden, it's a very specific kind of walk. *Wandeln.*

STEPHEN *(matter of fact; he knows it all):* "Wandering."

MASHKAN: Not precisely. It's a little more—specific. *(Standing, demonstrating.)* It's walking without focusing. Seeing, but not really seeing. Hearing without really hearing . . . Think about it while you sing. *(He goes to the piano.)*

STEPHEN: And after that you'll tell me your story?

MASHKAN *(ignoring him as he plays the piano, getting lost in the music):* Concentrate. Seeing without . . . seeing.

STEPHEN *(singing; watching Mashkan getting lost in the music inspires him to do the same):*

One bright shining summer morning

MASHKAN *(surprised):* Good start. Now go deeper inside yourself.

STEPHEN *(more lost in thought, sings):*

Around the garden I walk

MASHKAN *(half to himself, starting to despair):* Yes. Completely isolated. In your own private . . .

STEPHEN *(doing it more, sings):*

The flowers converse in a whisper

MASHKAN *(completely to himself, sadly):* That's it.

STEPHEN *(sings):*

But I refuse

> *Pointedly—to Mashkan.*

To talk!

MASHKAN *(drily):*   . . . Still pushing a little too much—but definitely coming along. Translating songs to English makes you more aware of the meaning. I will use this method on all my English speaking students. If I ever get any.

STEPHEN *(softly):* You will.

Mashkan compares himself in strength to German *lieder.* Stephen, already annoyed because he is not getting Mashkan's "story," is angered by the professor's mentioning favorably anything German. Mashkan begins playing "*Am keuchtenden sommermorgen*" with the comment, "If you understate the grief, we will feel it all the more," and Stephen sings the first couple of lines as the lights fade and the recorded version takes over.

Scene 4: Tuesday morning, June 10, 1986

Newspapers and magazines are spread around the studio. Stephen and Mashkan are looking out the window at the passers-by, speculating on which of them might have voted for Waldheim. Stephen seems now more interested in the music than in politics, although he has resolved that from now on he will speak up against any offensive remark. He's eager to get at the next song, which Mashkan describes to him as alternating sound and silence, the latter being "one of the most difficult things to feel comfortable with. And to allow to grow. Only in silence do we truly listen and comprehend. *(He sits at the piano.)* In the first two verses you sing; then silence; then I play; silence; you sing, and so on. We must truly hear each other in order to have a growing dialogue."

Stephen sings the first verse of the lyrics in English to Mashkan's accompaniment. After he sings the line "I wept while I was dreaming," Mashkan breaks off playing the accompaniment and speaks.

MASHKAN: You asked why I was muttering 43, 44 and 45? Those are the years I remember almost nothing.
> *He plays his accompaniment.*

STEPHEN *(sings, although unsure if he should):*
> I dreamt you were leaving me

MASHKAN: Who wants to remember a starving bunkmate pleading for bread? I turn away. He must not have a face. I do not want a friend. If he dies—*I* must face the loss, not him. *(Lightly.)* Who needs more depression? I am already in a concentration camp.
> *He plays his accompaniment. Stephen is silent, not sure what to do.*

Keep singing! Try to be hopeful.

STEPHEN *(uneasy, sings):*
> When I awoke

MASHKAN: And so I survive. Not because of my courage or compassion, but because I think only of myself.
> *He plays accompaniment.*

STEPHEN *(sings):*
> I was crying

MASHKAN: Perhaps I will never die. For after each attempted suicide, I become more like that boiling coffee on the stove—growing stronger and stronger —and more and more bitter.
> *He plays.*

STEPHEN *(sings):*
> I cried so bitterly

MASHKAN *(sings, the same words but in German, coming from the depths of his
> soul):*
> *Noch lange bitterlich!*
> *He plays cadence after phrase, then speaks:*

And now the music and the lyrics finally come together.

He plays again.

STEPHEN *(heartfelt emotion, sings):*
I wept while I was dreaming
I dreamed you still cared for me
Then I awoke
I was crying
My tears kept flowing free

Mashkan plays accompaniment.

MASHKAN: 1940. We were told to pack whatever we could fit into a suitcase.

STEPHEN *(very uneasy, not sure he wants to hear):* You don't have to tell me—

MASHKAN: Listen . . . It was spring—in the loveliest of months—May. *(Sarcastic.)* *"Im wunderschönen monat Mai"*— *(Recorded music of* "Im wunderschönen monat Mai" *is softly heard.)* When all the buds were bursting in bloom—

As Mashkan leans into Stephen, the lights dim. Mashkan speaks, but no words are heard coming from his mouth. Instead, we only hear the music of the Dichterliebe *growing in volume. Stephen nods, listening carefully to what Mashkan says. As the lights continue to dim, a single beam of light—just like the one described in the Israeli Memorial at Dachau—a single beam of light surrounded by darkness—shines on Stephen. Stephen stands—nodding and listening. Stephen starts to tear up. He tries not to cry. But does. Then sobs.*

The first song of the *Dichterliebe* ends and the lights go to black. Following it, in the darkness, is a recorded version of the cycle's last song, *"Die alten, bösen lieder."*

Coda: A summer morning

Lights come up on the studio, where Mashkan and Stephen are playing and singing the last song of the cycle. As they pause, Stephen remarks that Professor Schiller's studio is nearby, so that he and Mashkan can keep on seeing each other—that is, if Mashkan can find the time. He's expecting a batch of Korean students next week.

Mashkan tells Stephen Vienna's latest joke about "a new disease called Waldheimers. You get old—and forget you were a Nazi." He then offers Stephen a pastry, gratis, which Stephen accepts.

STEPHEN *(serious):* Listen, Mashkan, I just want to say that these last few months—they've meant—

MASHKAN *(interrupting, said quickly):* Ja, Ja, for me too. For me too . . . Sadness and joy.

STEPHEN: And music. Always music. No matter how insolent I was, or belligerent—

MASHKAN: Or pig-headed, or self-absorbed—

STEPHEN: Okay, okay . . . still, I always learned something.

MASHKAN: I am getting a swelled head . . . Please go on.

Mashkan reminds Stephen that seemingly aimless flourishes of Viennese archi-techecture, and of music, are to be valued, not deprecated, because they produce unexpected beauties. The two perform the final song, Mashkan playing the piano and singing the first verse of the English translation of the lyrics:

> The old, wicked songs
> The dreams, wicked and grim,
> Let us bury them!
> Fetch me a large coffin

Stephen sings the next verse, and they alternate singing verses to the end of the song, when they come to a piano solo. Mashkan directs Stephen, "You play."

> *Stephen gingerly approaches the piano and sits down. Stephen caresses the piano now, instead of being rough with her. Just as he's about to play, he breathes and tugs three times. Then Stephen plays.*

MASHKAN *(as Stephen plays):* It is your responsibility during this solo to release us from the sadness we have heard—make us remember the Poet's suffering, but give us a glimmer of hope that this experience will not completely destroy his life. Who knows, perhaps he will learn from it and move to a higher plane. *Verstehst du, Stefan?* Understand?

STEPHEN: Not completely.

MASHKAN: That is good. Question. Always question.

> *As Stephen continues playing the* Andante espressivo *beautifully, Mashkan touches Stephen's head.*

Definitely a hat head. *(Tongue-in-cheek.)* And what a hat it will be.

> *Mashkan listens to Stephen's piano playing, lost in the music. The lights dim.There's a spotlight on Mashkan and on Stephen. As the piece ends, they look at one another. The light goes out on Mashkan. Then on Stephen. Then Vienna. Curtain.*

Critics Award

○○○
○○○
○○○
○○○
○○○
○○○ # SKYLIGHT

A Play in Two Acts

BY DAVID HARE

Cast and credits appear on page 216

DAVID HARE was born at St. Leonard's in Sussex, England on June 5, 1947 and was educated at school there and at Lancing College and then for three years at Cambridge. He has been writing plays since the age of 22. His first full-length work, Slag, *was produced in London at the Royal Court Theater before appearing in its American debut at New York Shakespeare Festival, first in an experimental staging and finally as a full-fledged off-Broadway offering February 21, 1971 for 37 performances, for which its author received an Obie nomination for most promising playwright. His* Knuckle *appeared here as a Phoenix Theater Side Show in 1975 (and off off Broadway at the Hudson Theater in 1981); his* Fanshen *played the regionals in 1976 and OOB in 1977; and his* Teeth 'n' Smiles *was produced in Washington in 1977. And then Hare's* Plenty *moved across the Atlantic after its London production by the National Theater in 1978 to Washington's Arena Stage on April 4, 1980 and a subsequent staging in March 1981 at Chicago's Goodman Theater.* Plenty's *New York debut took place October 21, 1982 off Broadway at the New York Shakespeare Festival Public Theater for 45 performances, after which Joseph Papp moved it to Broadway for an extended run of 92 performances. It was named a Best Play of its season, and the New York Drama Critics Circle voted it the year's best foreign play.*

American production of Hare's plays has continued with A Map of the World *(1985) amd* The Knife *(1987, a musical for which Hare wrote the book) at the Public*

Theater; The Secret Rapture *(1989, produced on Broadway by the Shuberts and Joseph Papp);* Pravda *(1989 at the Tyrone Guthrie Theater in Minneapolis, co-authored with Howard Brenton);* Racing Demon *(last season at Lincoln Center, a close runner-up for the Critics Award for best foreign play); and now* Skylight, *beginning September 19, 1996 for Hare's longest Broadway run of 116 performances and running away with the Critics Award for best foreign play on the first ballot.*

The list of Hare's playscripts includes The Great Exhibition, Brassneck *with Howard Brenton,* The Bay at Nice, Wrecked Eggs, Murmuring Judges, The Absence of War *and adaptations of Pirandello's* The Rules of the Game, *Brecht's* Galileo *and* Mother Courage and Her Children *and Chekhov's* Ivanov, *all produced in England. Hare is also the author of seven original screen plays and has won numerous awards for his works on both stage and screen. He has just directed Wallace Shawn's movie* The Designated Mourner *starring Mike Nichols and Miranda Robinson, and he is looking forward to the production of his next play,* Amy's View, *by the National Theater.*

The following synopsis of Skylight *was prepared by Jeffrey Sweet.*

Time: The present

Place: A flat in Northwest London

ACT I

Scene 1

SYNOPSIS: The curtain rises on a shabby apartment on the second story of a building in northwest London. A much-used kitchen area and a plentitude of books give some clues to its occupant, Kyra Hollis, a thirtyish woman who enters the apartment. That it is cold outside is evident by the heavy overcoat she wears. That it is cold inside is evident by the fact that she doesn't take it off as she busies herself, beginning to draw a bath in the offstage bathroom and making preparations for a spaghetti dinner.

She has neglected to close her front door, and Edward Sergeant, 18, enters as she is offstage. When she returns, she is startled to see him. Startled but pleased. "Well, will you give me a kiss?" she says. He tells her he happened to be in the neighborhood when he realized she lived close by, so he succumbed to the impulse to visit. She turns off the bath and turns on an electric heater. And, with humor, she prompts him to come to the point. And he does: his father.

Edward tells her that his mother, Alice, died of cancer about a year ago. Kyra hadn't heard. She hasn't been in touch with his father, Tom Sergeant. And Edward confesses that he didn't "happen" to be in the neighborhood. He thinks Kyra can help his father. Tom has changed since Alice's death. Edward confesses that he's nervous about this visit, and Kyra, offering him some tea, assures him that he's doing fine. "I don't really know the whole history. I mean, between Dad and you," says Edward. He describes the strained, silent dinners he has with his father in their house in Wimbledon. Kyra is a little startled to hear that Edward is now living in the country.

EDWARD: I know. Well, that doesn't help. The sense of all that sort of *nature*, trees and flowers, sort of flapping around. He did it for Mum, to give her some peace at the end. But now it just seems pointless and spooky. Me, I get on a bus and head for the street.
>   *Kyra brings mugs and teabags.*
I keep saying, Dad, you're not dead, you're fifty. It's too early for lupins. Jesus! What I liked about Dad, he was sort of ageless. I think that's why he was such a success. All ages, all types. He knew how to reach them. But now he's in this kind of hideous green fortress.
KYRA: Does he talk to you? About what he feels?
EDWARD: You know Dad. He's not what you might call "emotionally available." But also . . . let's face it . . . well, I can be quite a shit. *(He faces Kyra directly.)* Have you read Freud?
KYRA: Some.
EDWARD: I read some recently. I told Dad everything had to come out. That you pay a price. Is that true?
KYRA: I don't know.
EDWARD: For everything you repress there's a price to be paid.
KYRA: You told him that?
EDWARD: Yes.
KYRA: And how did he take it?

Edward reports that he and his father had a big fight and that Edward seems to have left home, staying with a girl with whom he works selling hot dogs outside football grounds—not exactly a girl friend. She lets him sleep with her, and he appreciates that. He complains a bit about his father—that under the charm there's something a bit threatening about him. And he suspects Tom's something of a sexist, too. And when you add to this his current mood, it's a pretty oppressive mix.

EDWARD: . . . . . There's always this doom. This heaviness. He comes home every night. Wham! He lands on the sofa. You feel the springs go. One night he actually destroyed a whole sofa. He cracked a sofa, he landed so hard! . . . . . Guess his response? Guess his response to it! Next day he just bought a whole new sofa! A new sofa!
KYRA: Well, that seems fair enough.
EDWARD: No, you're wrong. It's an attitude, Kyra. It's all *Yellow Pages*. Whatever. Leaves on the roof? *Yellow Pages!* The lavatory's blocked? *Yellow Pages!* That's how he lives. He even orders in meals. It's absurd! He flicks through. Pizza!

Chinese! It's *Citizen Kane!* Only with *Yellow Pages.* I said to him, Dad, for God's sake get real. Not everything in life is in *Yellow Pages.*

> *Kyra is just drinking her tea.*

KYRA: Isn't it grief?

EDWARD: Yes, of course

KYRA: He's grieving.

EDWARD: He's sitting there alone in this bloody great house. Like some stupid animal. Licking his pain. *(He turns towards her, more tentative as he talks of his mother.)* Mum . . . of course, I mean, everyone said to me . . . Alice wasn't as clever as him. People assumed she was some sort of dumb ex-model. But she kept Dad moving. Now he just sits there. *(He is vehement, trying to drive his pain away.)* I say for Christ's sake, it's been almost a year. And three years' illness. We knew it was coming. It's been a long time. Let it out, for fuck's sake. Because, I tell you, otherwise . . . it's driving us both bloody mad.

Edward tells Kyra that his sister Hilary is at university, and, after a year of selling hot dogs and knocking about, he expects to go, too, and study something or other. Edward is conscious that, coming from an affluent background, he has more options than do the students from the slums Kyra teaches. But, in a way, he envies her students and envies Kyra, too.

EDWARD: . . . . . I mean, I think in a way you're so lucky, living like this.

KYRA: Well, thank you.

EDWARD: I'm not being rude. I mean it. In this kind of place. *(He pauses for a second.)* Dad said . . .

KYRA: What? What did Dad say?

EDWARD: I suppose he hinted . . . he was implying . . . in a way he was saying that you made a choice.

> *Kyra looks at him a moment, then gets up to take the tea things out.*

Look, whenever I mention it, he always says it's none of my business. He gets really angry. He says very little. I mean, I've been trying to get him to talk about you. Shit, that's what I mean, for fuck's sake. After all, it's my life as well. We saw you for years. Well, didn't we?

KYRA: Yes. Yes, you did.

EDWARD: Until just a few years ago. They were great times. Then you vanished. Why?

KYRA: Think. Just think. It's probably the first thing you think of. And it's the reason.

Edward explodes with the anger of the abandoned. He can't blame his mother for leaving—she died, after all. But Kyra simply disappeared without a word to him. And there's stuff he doesn't understand. Why, for instance, his parents seemed to get along better when Kyra was there. "That's often true. Of a couple," Kyra replies. "They need a catalyst. A third person there, it helps them to talk." When Edward presses her for details, Kyra finally loses her cool. He seems to want to judge something. If he has an appetite for that, he should become a lawyer. But he should refrain from putting people's private lives on trial. Her vehemence makes them both smile a little. As pleased as she has been to see him, she suggests that she needs some time to tend to her students' homework.

Before Edward leaves, he wants to know if Kyra misses anything from his father's world. "I miss a good breakfast," she replies. "Toast wrapped in napkins. Croissants. And really hot coffee from a silver pot. Scrambled eggs. I never have those. And I do miss them more than I'd have thought possible." Edward suggests that perhaps she misses his father, too. She doesn't confirm or deny. She kisses him. She tells him she hopes to see him again. He heads for the door, then blurts out, "Kyra, I wish you would bloody well help." He disappears, leaving Kyra a bit shaken. Then she goes offstage and we hear the sound of the bath running again.

Scene 2

Not much later, an insistently-ringing doorbell draws Kyra, wrapped in a towel, from her bath. She looks out the window to see who is responsible for the din and tosses down a key. She collects jeans and some sweaters, unlocks her front door to admit the guest who will soon arrive, then disappears into the bathroom to dress. The guest is Edward's father, Tom, a large, well-dressed man approaching 50. He is looking around the room when Kyra returns, dressed.

The two instantly indulge in verbal sparring, but it is evident that Tom is very concerned about her feelings about him. (It is also evident that Tom doesn't know Edward has preceded him.) He thought of calling, but he was afraid she might hang up. "I suppose I thought perhaps you hated me," he says. Kyra replies, "Yes. If you'd rung then you'd have found out." Tom gruffly confesses that it's been difficult for him. Alice's death and all. He reports that Alice died bravely, spending her days looking at birds through the skylight he built for her over her bed in the house in Wimbledon. He asks Kyra if she is "still at that same place," meaning the slum school where she teaches. Kyra says that she is. Some people in the area—some police and a fellow teacher who was given such a hard time she had to leave—have trouble dealing with the kids and the neighborhood, but she seems to be O.K. "Some people are victims," she comments. "I walk in perfect peace to and from school. I'm not a mark, that's the difference."

Edward still hasn't taken off his coat. If she wants, he'll have "this really good bloke" who does jobs for him in his restaurants come and put in central heating. Unless she'd rather be cold. No, she'd rather be warm. "Warm, but not indebted." He asks her to go out with him to dinner. She prefers to cook her spaghetti. She asks him about business.

One gets the impression that he's pleased to be given a cue to complain. He went public with his restaurants and is now encumbered with a chairman of the board and an overpaid management guru who wanders in for four hours a week and pretends to listen.

SKYLIGHT—Lia Williams as Kyra Hollis with Christian Camargo as Edward Sergeant *(left)* and Michael Gambon as Tom Sergeant *(right)* in the play by David Hare

TOM: . . . . . It was how I was always told you could get women into bed. By doing something called "listening to their problems." It's a contemptible tactic.

KYRA: You wouldn't do it?

TOM: No. Of course not. You know me, Kyra. I wouldn't stoop to it. Listening's halfway to begging. Either they want you or else they don't.

> *Kyra smiles as she goes to get a chopping board with which she comes back.*

But this bloke . . . he does it all the time in the business. "How interesting. Really? Is that what you think?" Then he does what he'd planned in the first place. It's called consultation. Buttering you up and then ignoring you.

KYRA *(setting down the board):* I can imagine.

TOM: Oh yes, that's how things go nowadays . . .

KYRA: Is there no way you can get rid of him?

TOM: No. It's the price I paid for floating the company. It made me millions, I can hardly complain. I offered you shares, remember? I never knew why you refused.

> *Kyra flashes a look at him to suggest he knows perfectly well why she refused.*

When we went public they jumped thirty-fold. You could have had the house in the West Indies. Like me.

KYRA: Oh, really?

TOM: Well maybe not quite. But at least you could have moved up in the world.

Kyra ignores this, choosing to go on chopping the onions.

Banks and lawyers! That's all I see. So perhaps you did well. Perhaps it wasn't so stupid. Coming here.

KYRA: It wasn't stupid.

TOM: No.

> *She has spoken with such quiet firmness that he looks up. Then he moves away, implicitly accepting what she's just said, but happy to resume his stories.*

And the stories continue. Tom cites a confrontation with another backer of a potential business who acknowledged that Tom takes risks he (the backer) doesn't. He quotes the backer as adding. "But . . . . . has it occurred to you that this may be the reason finally why it's *you* who always has to come grovelling to *me*?" When Kyra questions the complete veracity of the quote, Tom is offended. Why does Kyra doubt him? Alice did, too. If he says a thing is so, it's *so.*

Tom remembers the old days fondly. Remembers actually physically counting the restaurant's take at night with Kyra. Then, he had to succumb to the urge to expand. Though there were four or five lovely years when you could just go into a bank with a good idea and walk out with pots of money. The banks would capitalize vision then. Now? Well, Tom figures, she can imagine from what's in the newspapers—

Actually, Kyra tells him, she can't. She doesn't read the papers any more. He's appalled. He can't imagine not wanting to be in touch with what's going on. She says the news just makes her angry, so she reads classic novels, and she watches only old films. "Those you like because they're romantic," he says. "They have something we don't," says Kyra. And to change the subject, she asks him about Edward.

Tom is off on another rant. Edward is 18, spending money, mocking the achievements that made the money that he's spending. "He called me a brainless animal," says Tom, " . . . . . just doing business without asking why." What Edward, from his disdainful perch, doesn't seem to appreciate is that Tom has actually gotten things *done.* That has to be worth something. Not that Edward has any kind of an answer for this point. The boy doesn't seem to be capable of connecting his mind to his mouth to any constructive purpose. But as a teacher Kyra has to know what's going on. "Language belongs to the past. This is the world of Super-Mario. Bang! Splat! Spit out your venom and go."

Tom remembers the talking he and Kyra used to do when they were together. As for Edward, Tom can't take the boy's rancor seriously, and no, he insists (without convincing), it doesn't particularly bother him. And, rather uneasy, he asks if she's allowing him to stay. Just for dinner. In reply, she puts two plates onto the table. He thanks her, then starts to give her advice how to cook the meal.

They get to talking about Kyra's first night at the restaurant. She walked in looking for a job waiting tables. Alice hired her. Then 45 minutes later, there was a medical emergency with one of the children that required Alice to go to the hospital; and, on a hunch, she gave Kyra the job of supervising the restaurant that night. And Kyra did fine. Sitting in the deserted restaurant in the early hours of morning, she felt that this was indeed where she belonged. At four in the morning, Alice returned to the restaurant with Tom in tow. The three had brandy and coffee together. Tom remembers thinking, " . . . . . this is the strangest night of my life. This girl I'd never met before, bringing brandy and coffee. It's as if she's been with us the whole of our lives."

As he remembers it, Kyra even stayed in their house for some of the early days. And Kyra remembers thinking that being with them in that house became desperately important to her. Though she remembers incurring Tom's wrath when she took off for a time to go to university. Tom didn't see the point of it. He told her that higher education was only a way of postponing real life. But she knew that when she was finished, there was a home waiting for her, and she did indeed return to the restaurant when she came back to London.

Kyra remembers, too, that Tom showed a jealous streak at the thought she was having a normal sex life. Somehow, a nude painted of her by an artist boy friend fell off the wall when Tom saw it. Tom had lectured her about it, had told her she was like a daughter in their family. Tom interrupts. He never used the word "daughter," but Kyra insists he did. And she remembers, listening to the lecture, she thought, "Here we go . . . . . This is only going to be a matter of time."

For a moment, their closeness is palpable. Then Tom breaks the mood with more talk of business, of the drive to expand. When Alice was ailing, Tom could only react by redoubling his efforts, building his restaurant empire. He wished Kyra had been with him then. He missed her professionally. "I kind of missed you in person as well."

> *Kyra looks at him a moment, just non-committal as she works. Tom is serious.*

TOM: . . . . . I really did, Kyra. I never . . . I've never got used to it. Ever.

KYRA: What, missed me so badly, it's taken you three years to get back in touch?
> *It is said lightly, Kyra not wanting the atmosphere to darken, but he at once starts to protest strongly.*

TOM: Now, look . . .

KYRA: I mean, come on, let's be serious . . . .

TOM: You think I haven't wanted to? My God, you think I haven't wanted to call? To pick up the telephone? You think I haven't wanted to jump in the car and bust my way through that bloody door?

KYRA: But then why didn't you?

TOM: Kyra, why do you think?
> *They both know a bridge is about to be crossed even before it happens.*
Because I knew once I saw you, then I'd be finished. I knew I'd never be able to leave.

He is so clearly speaking from the heart that Kyra cannot say anything. So instead she turns and goes back to her pasta.

KYRA: O.K., well, I must say, that's an answer . . .

TOM: You see.

KYRA: What?

TOM: I'm getting better. Well, aren't I?

KYRA: Getting better at what?

TOM: Talking about my feelings. You always told me I had no gift for that stuff.

KYRA *(frowns, puzzled at this):* As far as I remember, we had no need for it. We had no need to discuss our feelings at all. Or rather, I didn't. I could always tell what you were feeling. It never had to be said. You'd wander about the office in Chelsea. Later we'd go home to work. We'd sit in the kitchen with Alice. I'd spend the evening reading to your kids.

There is a moment's silence. Tom is serious, low, when he speaks.

TOM: I could never understand it. I still don't. You never felt the slightest sense of betrayal.

KYRA: There we are. I always felt profoundly at peace. *(She waits a moment, wanting to be precise.)* I don't know why, it still seems true to me: if you have a love, which for any reason you can't talk about, your heart is with someone you can't admit—not to a single soul except for the person involved—then for me, well, I have to say, that's love at its purest. For as long as it lasts, it's this astonishing achievement. Because it's always a relationship founded on trust.

TOM: It seems mad to me.

KYRA: I know. You didn't feel that. I knew you never understood it. Why I was able to go on seeing Alice. Why we were always at ease. Why I loved her so much. But I did. It's a fact. There it is. The three of us. It gave me a feeling of calm . . . . . You were the person I fell in love with. And as it happened, you arrived with a wife.

Kyra asks him to grate cheese for her. He, of course, doesn't consider what she's handed him to be cheese. If she wants cheese, he has "this really great bloke" who can get her good stuff. She is amused at his summoning up another "great bloke." Tom decides he's going to ask his driver, Frank, to go get some kind of decent take-out. Kyra realizes that Frank is sitting downstairs, waiting in the car. "You leave him down there?" she says indignantly. Tom tells her that waiting is any driver's main job, and it is a bit condescending of her to rush to the defense of a man who is perfectly content to be doing his job and who doesn't feel injured in the slightest. "People . . . . . want to be treated . . . respected like adults for the job they are paid for, and not looked down on as if they were chronically disabled, as if they somehow needed *help* all the time. I mean, yes, this was the craziness! This was the whole trouble with business and you! You looked down—always!—on the way we did things. The way things are done. You could never accept the nature of business. I mean, finally that's why you had to leave."

This is news to Kyra. She rather thought that her leaving had something to do with Alice finding out that Kyra was sleeping with Tom. She always said she would if Alice ever found out, and she was as good as her word. It was an abrupt exit, so abrupt she didn't say goodbye to the others in the restaurant. But she felt she had no choice. "You have something worked out in your own mind. Then something changes. The balance is gone. You no longer believe your own story. And that, I'm afraid, is the moment to leave."

As Tom begins to grate the cheese, Kyra switches the subject to the new house he's in. Tom tells her he and Alice moved there very shortly after they got the news about Alice's illness. He tells how lying there, looking through the skylight, Alice developed a mystical frame of mind that was difficult for him. He doesn't like people who brag about their "spiritual" side. He thinks it's a kind of one-upsmanship. He does, however, approve of religion. There are rules, structure, history. But Alice drifted off into spirituality, and Tom never felt he could reach her. "What you're saying is the two of you never got straight," says Kyra. "No," says Tom.

Kyra suggests that his guilt got in the way. Tom doesn't care for the word, but there's something to it. What made it more maddening was that Alice didn't give him hell for his infidelity. She withdrew, took up artsy interests and started gardening. She would claim she thought they were always a bit mismatched and then go on to say that perhaps Kyra was really the person he should have ended up with. Alice praising Kyra made it even harder for him.

Since Alice has died, Tom is coping all right, he insists, though he wasn't too keen to be visited by someone from some local support group, a woman who came by to be professionally sympathetic in his hour of grief. He didn't want her help. "You suffer," says Tom. "That's what you do. There are no short cuts. There are no easy ways. And I have been doing my share of suffering."

Kyra says, yes, so she's heard. Tom picks up on this. Heard? Kyra tells him that Edward stopped by earlier in the evening to express his concern about his father. Tom fumes at the idea that Edward stuck his nose in. Kyra tells Tom to stop being willfully obtuse. She tells Tom that he's making Edward's life miserable because of the guilt he feels over Alice. Tom says he isn't impressed with Kyra's analysis of the family dynamic, but Kyra rams on. She tells him that she hasn't believed the lies he's been telling about how well he's managing: "And me, I'm standing here, nodding, smiling, agreeing like some ape . . . and thinking, is this man lying to me deliberately? Or does he not even notice? Or is he so used to lying to himself? It's all right for me. I'm fine. You can tell me anything. Any old story. I'm lucky because I've moved on. But Edward is young. He needs his father. He deserves honesty. He deserves not to be treated like dirt."

A little shocked at the directness of her attack, Tom concedes that there is some truth there. Unable to face Alice, he raced around the world on business. And he could guess the opinion people had of him, being absent from his sick wife's bedside so much. Not that Edward behaved all that well either. Tom came home one time to find him and a gang of friends bombed and stoned and God knows what.

TOM: . . . . . I remember screaming. "What the hell are you doing? Don't you know your mother is lying up there?" I was so angry. I felt this anger, I never got over it. Every day this fury that you had walked out. Walked out and left me to handle this thing. I did try to use it. I used your memory. I kept saying, look, I must behave well. I must try. Because who knows? If I behave well, I still have a chance here.

KYRA: A chance?

TOM: Yes.

KYRA: What sort of chance?

TOM: I think you know what I mean. I kept on saying, if I behave well, if I get through this, then maybe Kyra is going to come back.

> *Kyra stands stunned, understanding how deep his feeling is. He goes on haltingly.*

Sitting by the bed. Just awful. Looking at Alice, propped up on the pillows, her eyes liquid, cut off . . . I'd think, oh shit, if Kyra were with us, if Kyra were here . . . *(He stops a moment and shakes his head.)* Jesus, why weren't you? "If Kyra were here, she'd know what to do."

> *Kyra stands absolutely taken aback, as if not knowing what to think about his shocking devotion to her. He knows how much this has affected her.*

You told me, you said, always be honest. Look life in the eye. Be courageous. Don't be afraid. But you ran and left us.

KYRA: Yes. I had to.

TOM: You did what you said people never should do.

KYRA: I had no alternative. I had to get out of Alice's way. I had to make a new life of my own.

TOM: And this is it, Kyra? This is the life that you made? Will you tell me, will you tell me, please, Kyra, what exactly are you doing here?

Stunned by his outburst, after a second Kyra tells him to go down and send Frank away. Tom does indeed go downstairs to perform this errand. Kyra mechanically puts food on the table, getting lost in the task of cutting bread. Tom returns. They embrace. She holds him desperately, crying and shaking with grief. He runs his hand through her hair over and over and tells her, "Kyra, Kyra, I'm back." *Curtain.*

ACT II

Scene 1

At 2:30 in the morning, having thrown on pants and a shirt, Tom emerges from the bedroom to find Kyra in the main room eating the food they never got around to and working on the copybooks of her students. Tom jokes about moving in with her. Underneath the jokes, one can sense that he is hoping for some sign that more of a commitment will be forthcoming from her. It will soon be end of term, he notes. Maybe she'd like to go to a nice warm island for a holiday with him. He knows that resolving the bigger things can't be that simple, of course. "For God's sake, I'm not totally insensitive," he says. "I don't think, 'One fuck and everything's solved . . . ' "

Kyra wonders why it took Tom so long to make contact again. He says that partially it was that he tried to pretend he didn't need her so much. Besides, he has been very busy with the reorganization of his business, though the thought has crossed his mind to retire with a woman he could worship. She doesn't like the word "worship": "When a man says he worships you, he's building a scaffold. It's a matter of time till he claims that you've let him down."

She tells him of a group of women she meets after work on Fridays. She finds she's learned to enjoy listening to people. And what she has gleaned from this listening is the great courage most people muster in order to manage. People who think the "mass" do nothing but vegetate in front of the TV should hear some of what she hears on her morning bus ride across town to school. People are smarter than some give them credit for being.

From here she segues into the world of the school where she works. Yes, it's hard, and yes, there are the odd incidents of violence and hooliganism, but it's possible to do something meaningful there. She doesn't approach her classes naively, though. By her own account, she's gotten tougher. She has had to learn how to offer the proper balance of reassurance and security on one hand and intellectual challenge on the other. With a determined cheerfulness, she tells Tom that she's actually one of the older teachers. The young ones, the ones fresh out of college, do it for a few years, marry and then move to less rigorous trials.

Kyra tells him that early on she had her moments of doubt. She had a confrontation with a student who spat on her and called her names so vile that she went home in tears. "Then I thought, right, this is it. No more crying. From today I learn certain skills—survival skills if you like. I master certain techniques, if for no other purpose that in the years ahead . . . maybe even after I've finished, perhaps . . . I can say, right, it was a job, and I bloody well did it. I learned how you have to survive." She has come to think that her years with Tom in his restaurant, as lovely as they were, were a dream, something removed from the realities of the way life is really lived in England today.

Tom presses her. Does she have friends, does she have a social life? She says she's mostly too tired to have much, but yes, she does get together with others. It was a friend who found her this apartment. Tom jokes, "You call that an act of friendship?" Kyra says she doesn't much mind the cold; she'd learned to live with it growing up with her father, a man who taught economy by keeping the heat down. Her father died recently. As Tom remembers, her father had a fair amount of money. Kyra replies that her father was very fond of cats and most of the estate went to an animal charity. Tom is outraged for her, but she refuses to express anger. Tom wants to know what her plans are. "Tom, I don't expect this to make any sense to you. But I'm planning to go on just as I am." Tom responds by saying that "an idea of the future" seems to him to be important. She insists she does have an idea of the future, and it consists of doing a job she believes in.

Tom begins to talk of Alice, how he first saw her picture in a magazine in which she was modeling. He courted her with red roses. She'd resisted, saying that she couldn't be bought. But that's something she never understood about Tom—he gave not to get something, but for the sheer pleasure of the giving. Like the room Tom

Michael Gambon and Lia Williams in a scene from *Skylight*

built for Alice to be ill in, Kyra suggests. Tom confirms this. "I preferred it that she should be happy. What's wrong with that? I wanted her to die in a place that she liked." He started giving her roses again, but, one week before she died, Alice asked him to stop. "She said, 'It isn't the same.' She said, 'The flowers were when you loved me. You and I were really in love.' She said, 'Now I don't want them.'" Relating this, he is almost overwhelmed by his grief. The one thing Alice had to hold over him was the fact that he had betrayed her with Kyra. She wouldn't forgive. She wouldn't relent. She went to her death refusing to offer him that comfort. "She used her death as a way of punishing me." These days, he comes home from a hard day of work, but he can get no rest. He takes walks in the middle of the night, tries to get drunk, but there's no relief. He keeps wrestling with the hopeful thought that "something must come of all this." And he's grown more certain that what must come of all this must involve Kyra.

TOM: . . . . . I suppose I feel: what happens now? Do we just leave it? Just leave it completely? And if we did, isn't that like admitting our guilt?
KYRA: Tom . . .
TOM: No, look, isn't that like saying we did behave shabbily? And, oh it was just an affair! And then when she found out, it was over? Doesn't that seem to you wrong?
> *Kyra looks at him, then frowns, moving away a little. She is decisive, trying to be as serious as he was.*
KYRA: Tom, you know there's something which you do have to deal with. There is this whole world I'm now in. It's a world with quite different values. The people,

the *thinking* is different . . . it's not at all like the world which you know. *(Tom looks at her, saying nothing.)* I mean, if we ever . . . if we . . . what I'm saying . . . if we can work out a way of keeping in touch . . . then you have to know I've made certain decisions. And these are decisions you have to respect.

TOM: Why, I mean, yes.

KYRA: Good.

TOM: Surely. I'm not a complete idiot.

KYRA: No.

TOM: You're saying you've made an informed and serious choice.

> *A note of mischief is beginning to be detectable. Kyra looks at him suspiciously.*

You've chosen to live in near-Arctic conditions somewhere off the North Circular. No, really. Why should I have any problem with that? *(He is beginning to get into his swing, exaggeratedly gesturing round the room now as he pours himself more scotch.)* I promise. I'm deeply impressed with it. I assure you, it gives me no problem at all. Put a bucket in the corner to shit in, and you can take hostages and tell them this is Beirut!

Kyra defends her flat. It's very reasonable, and it's not very different from the way a great many people live. Tom has no right to look down on them. Tom retorts, "I do have to say to you, Kyra, in one thing you're different from everyone else in this part of town. You're the only person who has fought so hard to get into it, when everyone else is desperate to get out!" He also notes that, though she teaches in a slum on one side of the town, she has chosen to live in an entirely different slum and spends a good deal of time commuting between these two depressing points. It seems to him that she's punishing herself. And romanticizing the "ordinary folk," as well, as if they tapped into some great reservoir of common wisdom. She replies that one of the reasons she's working in the slum is because people like him systematically look down on the underprivileged and assume that they are capable of nothing.

Tom is amused at her self-portrait as one of the reborn. He thinks that it goes deeper than her sense of mission. He returns to the theme of her apparent desire to punish herself.

TOM: I mean, I've been listening, I've been listening to this stuff you've been telling me—the bus! The school! Even the kind of place you choose to live in—and I'm thinking, my God, my dear old friend Kyra's joined some obscure religious order. The Kensal Rise chapter! She's performing an act of contrition. *(He suddenly laughs, the next thought striking him.)* You say to me, Lord goodness, everything's psychological. I can't be happy because I've not come to terms with things that I've done. But you—you're like Page One. A textbook Freudian study! Your whole fucking life is an act of denial! It's so bloody clear. You know what it's called? Throwing Teddy in the corner! You're running so fast you don't even know you're in flight.

KYRA: Running?

TOM: Yes. Of course. Yes, it's obvious.

KYRA: I suppose you couldn't tell me. I'm running from what?

TOM: Do I need to say?

> *His look, half-modest, half-arrogant infuriates her as much as his answer, and she turns away exasperated.*

KYRA: Oh honestly, this really ... I mean this is contemptible! Why do men always think it's all about them?

TOM: Because in this case it is!

> *But Kyra never even reaches the kitchen before turning on him again.*

KYRA: I'll say this for you. You always understood procedure. You've always known the order in which things should be done. You fuck me first. *Then* you criticize my lifestyle......

TOM: Now Kyra ...

KYRA: Doing it the other way round, of course, would be a terrible tactical mistake.

Tom insists that she's wasting her talents on people who are at the bottom. Kyra insists that what galls him is she's using her talents where he doesn't approve. She is tired of these comments about her—that she has buried herself away in the slums because of some psychological or sexual problem or other. Who cares why she's doing it? "If I didn't do it, it wouldn't get done." That seems to her to be the important thing. Passionately, Kyra continues: "I'm tired of these sophistries. I'm tired of these right-wing fuckers. They wouldn't lift a finger themselves. They work contentedly in offices and banks. Yet now they sit pontificating in Parliament, in papers, impugning our motives, questioning our judgements. And why? Because they themselves need to feel better by putting down everyone whose work is so much harder than theirs. *(She stands, nodding.)* You only have to say the words 'social worker' ... 'probation officer' ... 'counsellor' ... for everyone in this country to sneer. Do you know what social workers do? Every day? They try and clear out society's drains. They clear out the rubbish. They do what no one else is doing, what no one else is willing to do. And for that, oh Christ, do we thank them? No, we take our own rotten consciences, wipe them all over the social worker's face, and say 'if ...' FUCK! 'If *I* did the job, then of course if I did it ... oh no, excuse me, I wouldn't do it like that ...' " *(She turns, suddenly aggressive.)* "Well I say, 'OK, then, fucking do it, journalist. Politician, talk to the addicts. Hold families together. Stop the kids from stealing in the streets. Deal with couples who beat each other up. You fucking try it, why not? Since you're so full of advice. Sure, come and join us. This work is one big casino. By all means. Anyone can play. But there's only one rule. You can't play for nothing. You have to buy some chips to sit at the table. And if you won't play with your own time ... with your own effort ... then I'm sorry. Fuck off!' "

Tom grants much of what she has said. But is she happy? Kyra insists that it isn't about happiness. Tom says that she's made much of the cold and misery of her childhood with her father. What has she done but voluntarily create a new version of that misery in which to live? The fact is, the only time she lived a happy life—surrounded by friends and a family worth the name—was when she lived in Tom and Alice's world.

Kyra says that this is indeed what Tom would like to believe is true. He would like to imagine that she has no happiness away from him. She's noticed him sniffing around, looking for some evidence that a man has been here, acting as if he had rights of ownership. What has he been doing but complaining about how his rights have been abused? He felt he had the right to be forgiven by Alice. Why? As he sat by her deathbed, wasn't he still fantasizing about someone else? Doesn't it occur to him that the "balance of sympathy" might lie elsewhere?

Tom says she has no right to judge. Kyra wasn't there. She bailed out. She abandoned them. But Kyra draws a parallel between his being hurt that Alice never forgave him and the business class in general being hurt because nobody expresses any appreciation of their "creating wealth." She continues, "Suddenly this new disease! Self-pity! Self-pity of the rich! No longer do they simply accumulate. Now they want people to line up and thank them as well." One of the things she finds attractive about the people Tom and his ilk disdain is that they don't walk around with a sense of entitlement. They don't whine about how unappreciated they are. They just go about their jobs and do what is necessary. One of the things that first attracted her to him was that he knew, deep down, that doing the hard work of survival was harder than running a bank or being in government or managing a company. He came from a working class world. Now she thinks he's forgotten.

So, Tom responds, because he's rich now, he isn't entitled to feelings? He thinks she has gotten so wound up by her ideology that she's not seeing people as people any more, only symbols. And she looks on him as a symbol of something that obviously enrages her, though he isn't sure what.

For Tom, it all comes back to the personal. And now they talk about Alice's discovery that he and Kyra were sleeping together. When that happened, convinced that the marriage was over (Alice herself didn't much care to continue), Tom had proposed to Kyra. And what did she do? She ran. The fiction was that she did it for Alice and for the children. But really it was because she was terrified. She professes this great love for the people, but she can't seem to manage loving and committing to one person. The idea of it scares her. "You love the people because you don't have to go home with them. You love them because you don't have to commit." She's built her life on denial, on escape, on an avoidance of what she can't handle.

So, that's finally it, Kyra says. He got what he came for. "You wanted me to say I never loved you enough. Well, plainly, in your view, I didn't. So that's the end of it. Isn't it?" Now he should go. She has copybooks to mark.

Infuriated, Tom begins to hurl her books around. The explosion of fury shakes them both. He returns to the bedroom to finish dressing. She gets a glass of water, then calls a car service to pick him up and take him back to Wimbledon.

As they wait, they go over the end of their relationship. It revolved around some letters she wrote to him when she was on holiday. Love letters. Letters that he was supposed to have been careful enough not to allow to be seen by anyone else. Except he had indeed been careless, and Alice had happened upon them and it was all over. Tom admits he was remiss. Kyra thinks it wasn't an accident. She thinks he wanted them to be discovered. This was the one thing she had asked him not to do, the secret she had asked him to keep, and he had done it anyway.

KYRA: We had six years of happiness. And it was you who had to spoil it. With you, when something is right, it's never enough. You don't value happiness. You don't even realize. Because you always want more. *(She is beginning to be upset by what she is saying. He knows it is true.)* It's part of the restlessness, it's part of your boyishness. You say that you knew that I loved and valued your family. You knew how much you were loved. But that can't be true. Well, can it? Because if you had realized, why would you have thrown it away? *(She looks at him, completely sincere.)* I love you, for God's sake. I still love you. I loved you more than anyone on earth. But I'll never trust you, after what happened. That's what Alice said. You'll never grow up. There is no peace in you. I know this. For me there is no comfort. There's no sense of rest. The energy's wonderful. Oh God, I tell you the energy's what everyone needs. But with the energy comes the restlessness. And I can't live that way.

TOM *(serious now, pleading, unflinching):* You wanted a family. You say what you loved was family. I'm happy to start a family again.

KYRA: No. It's too late. And you know it.

TOM: Do I? Yes, I suppose that I do.

> *The doorbell rings. She turns and looks to it. They are both standing, some ways between them. Tom does not move.*

The point is, I lived a long time next to cancer. Apart from anything, it fucks up your brain. You start thinking things are deliberate. That everything's some kind of judgement. And once you think that, you might as well die.

Yes, he came wanting forgiveness, and he wanted some of what they had back. He apologizes for the mess he's made. She says it's O.K. He kisses her on the cheek and heads for the door. As a final shot, he suggests she should come to one of his restaurants. "There are one or two which are really not bad. I promise you, you know, on a good night, it's almost as nice as eating at home." With that, he's gone. She turns off the light and the ineffectual heater.

Scene 2

Cold morning light spills over the wreckage left over from last night. There's a racket of banging and ringing at the front door. Kyra, pulling on clothes, comes out of the bedroom and goes down the stairs to see who's making such a noise. She returns to the main room with Edward, who is carrying a large styrofoam box that appears to be quite heavy. Last night she said that what she missed most of all was breakfast. Well, O.K., that's what he's brought.

With the help of a friend who works in the kitchen at the Ritz, he's smuggled out a first-rate breakfast as well as a generous helping of the Ritz's silverware and linens. And with great grace, Edward puts together a very impressive table—melon, fresh-squeezed orange juice, croissants, coffee, scrambled eggs. *"Kyra is suddenly overwhelmed and throws her arms around Edward, holding him close, the tears pouring down her cheeks."* She releases him, and he adds a rose to the table.

Kyra's afraid she's going to have to eat quickly. There's this student she has to meet. Kid comes from a hideous home, and it means extra work for her, but there's something about him. She tells Edward, "I mean, to be a teacher, the only thing you really have going for you . . . there's only one thing that makes the whole thing make sense, and this is finding one really good pupil . . . . . You set yourself some personal target, a private target, only you know it—no one else—that's where you find satisfaction. And you hope to move on from there . . . . . And that is it, that's being a teacher. One private target, and that is enough."

Kyra has been retrieving the scattered books and is now on the floor, lost in her own thoughts. Pretending to be a waiter, Edward moves behind a chair and invites her to sit. She accepts the invitation. They sit opposite each other and begin to enjoy a good breakfast. *"The table looks incongruously perfect in its strange setting."* The lights fade. *Curtain.*

Tony Award

THE LAST NIGHT OF BALLYHOO

A Play in Two Acts

BY ALFRED UHRY

Cast and credits appear on pages 232–233

ALFRED UHRY was born in Atlanta in 1936. His father was a furniture dealer and by avocation an artist whose paintings are now hung in museums. Uhry can't remember when he didn't write—he didn't care much for the novel he wrote at age 9, so he immediately switched to writing for the theater, partly inspired by family visits to see such shows as South Pacific *and* Kiss Me, Kate. *At Brown University, from which he graduated in 1958, he won the competition to write the book and lyrics for the varsity shows (Robert Waldman wrote the music). His first New York production of record, a 1968 Broadway musical version of* East of Eden *entitled* Here's Where I Belong, *written with Waldman and Alex Gordon, closed after only 1 performance, but Uhry was taken under the broad wing of Frank Loesser, and soon his work was appearing on all three TV networks and on various stages. For the latter, his work has included* The Robber Bridegroom *(music by Waldman, 1974 OOB at St. Clements, 1975 on Broadway for 15 performances by the Acting Company, winning Tony and Drama*

Desk nominations, and returning to Broadway the following season for 145 more performances); lyrics for the musical Swing *at Kennedy Center in 1980; a new adaptation of* Little Johnny Jones *on Broadway (but again for only 1 performance) in 1982;* America's Sweetheart *at the Hartford Stage Company in 1985, and five reconstructions of period musicals for the Goodspeed Opera House.*

Uhry's Driving Miss Daisy, *his first non-musical play, opened off Broadway at Playwrights Horizons April 15, 1987, collected the 1987 Pulitzer Prize, was cited as a Best Play of its season and remained for 1,195 performances. In its Southeastern debut at Atlanta's Alliance Studio Theater it ran for 20 months and then toured Russia and China. Uhry's* The Last Night of Ballyhoo *also premiered in Atlanta, July 20, 1996, winning a 1996 ATCA Citation before coming on to Broadway February 27, 1997 and collecting the 1997 Tony Award for the best play of the season. A review by Michael Sommers of its prizewinning Atlanta production appears in the introduction to* The Season Around the United States *section of this volume.*

Uhry wrote the screen play for the movie version of his Driving Miss Daisy, *winning a Writers Guild Award and an Oscar. His other screen credits include* Mystic Pizza *and* Rich in Love. *He is married, with four daughters, and lives in New York City where he has been active in Dramatists Guild affairs as a member of its council and an advisor to its Young Playwrights Festival.*

The following synopsis of The Last Night of Ballyhoo *was prepared by Sally Dixon Wiener.*

Time: December, 1939

Place: Atlanta, Georgia

ACT I

Scene 1

SYNOPSIS: *"Lights up on Adolph Freitag's ugly house on Habersham Road. We see a portion of the living room, a hall with stairs leading to the bedroom floor, and a portion of the dining room beyond the hall. The house is vaguely Spanish: stucco with a tile roof, Moorish archways, wrought iron railings, etc. The furnishings are many and heavy. Lala Levy is decorating a Christmas tree in a corner of the living room, surrounded by cardboard boxes of ornaments, a few strings of Christmas tree lights strung across the furniture. Lala is an unsure, awkward young woman, dressed in unbecoming clothes. There is a desperate air about her. Reba Freitag, her aunt, is seated on sofa, knitting. She is in her late 40s, a pretty, vague woman, not quite in synch with everybody else."* It is the middle of December, late in the day.

As Lala decorates she is singing "The First Noel." Reba had forgotten that Lala's singing voice was so sweet. *"Beulah (Boo) Levy enters from the kitchen, an apron over her sensible house dress. She is a serious woman, about 50 or so. She carries a lace tablecloth."* Boo demands to know where the treetop star has come from (Lala bought it at Rich's) and insists her daughter take it down: "Jewish Christmas trees don't have stars." If there's a star, Lala may as well get a manger scene for the lawn, and then everyone passing by will assume "we're a bunch of Jewish fools pretending we're Christian." Reba agrees. Boo believes a tree is a festive decoration, like pumpkins and Valentine hearts. It's an American holiday.

It's the night of the premiere of *Gone With the Wind*, and Lala reminds them that Clark Gable's in town and they should be celebrating Atlanta's moment in history. Boo thinks Lala should put her mind on getting a date for Ballyhoo, less than two weeks away. She wants Lala to call Sylvan Weil in Lake Charles. "A Louisiana Weil! Finest family in the South," Lala parrots her mother. Lala doesn't want to call Sylvan. He was all Lala talked about after Edith Asher's wedding, Boo claims. They're only acquaintances, Lala insists, and he isn't the romantic type.

Lala insists she's going to town to participate in all the excitement of the premiere. She must, because she's writing a novel, she announces. If it's made into a movie she needs to see what a premiere is like.

BOO: Your novel does not exist and the Weil boy does.

REBA: Your mama has a point.

BOO: You didn't listen to me up at the University of Michigan, and look what happened! You got yourself so humiliated.

LALA: That wasn't my fault.

REBA: It was that awful sorority.

BOO: The fault does not lie with Sigma Delta Tau. You didn't prepare for rush week.

LALA: Mama!

BOO: I told you to prepare some peppy and interesting topics to discuss, but of course you paid me no mind, and look what happened. You were rejected.

LALA: I was accepted into A E Phi.

REBA: That's true.

BOO: Hah! A E Phi! Nobody but *the other kind* belongs to A E Phi, and the whole world knows it.

LALA: I don't want to talk about it any more.

BOO: You'd better. You keep making the same mistakes over and over! Your place in society sits there waiting for you, and you do nothing about it.

LALA: Guess what, Mama? We're Jews. We have no place in society.

BOO: We most certainly do! Maybe not right up there at the tip top with the best set of Christians, but we come mighty close. After all, your Great Grandma's Cousin Clemmie was—

Here Lala joins in, and they say the next sentence together.

BOO and LALA: The first white child born in Atlanta!

LALA: God knows I've had that information drilled into my skull enough times.

BOO: Then why hasn't it sunk in? Why won't you use your connections and your birthright to make something of yourself instead of mooning over nonsense like tree trimming and movie premieres?

LALA: Only you would manage to ruin Christmas and *Gone With the Wind* in one fell swoop.

She rushes out of the room and up the stairs.

Boo is distressed because Lala is the only unmarried girl in her set. She blames it on the red measles that Lala got at the start of kindergarten. When she was able to go back to school, "all the popular children had formed their attachments." She just never caught up, despite Lala's or Boo's efforts. Boo realizes Lala's unpopular. Reba feels she scares people off. But Reba admits her daughter doesn't have a Ballyhoo date, either.

Boo feels God is laughing at the joke he's played on her: Reba has a daughter, Sunny, "bloomin' like a rose" at Wellesley, while Boo has one, Lala, who crawled home in disgrace from the University of Michigan in the middle of her first semester, embarrassing Boo. Lala claimed she was homesick, Reba recalls. And luckily people believed it, Boo replies.

Adolph Freitag arrives home, notices the star and likes it, even if Boo disapproves. *"He is a man in his middle 40s, soft body, hard mind—a pillar of the business community, double-breasted suit, white-on-white monogrammed shirt. He carries a briefcase and the evening paper."* He announces he's asked someone from the office home for supper. Boo isn't pleased, as Louisa, the cook, is out sick.

Joe Farkas arrives. Adolph introduces him to Reba, his sister-in-law (Mrs. Freitag) and Boo, his sister (Mrs. Levy). Joe is *"a vigorous young man in his late 20s. He has a New York accent."*

On learning that Joe has been working for the Dixie Bedding Corporation for several weeks, Boo is resentful at not having been told. Adolph explains that Joe will be traveling some and taking care of some things here. Boo concedes her brother must think well of Joe, finally is persuaded to call him by his first name, but wants to know what part of New York he's from. He's from Eastern Parkway. When Reba wonders if he might know her cousin who lives on Madison Avenue, Boo points out that Eastern Parkway is in Brooklyn. Joe doesn't know her, of course.

Boo calls Reba into the kitchen. Alone with the newspaper Adolph and Joe confess to each other they've never read *Gone With the Wind*. Joe also confesses his mother's not too happy about him living at the YMCA. Lala comes downstairs, dressed to go to town, and Adolph introduces Joe to her. Adolph asks if she's going to the premiere alone. Lala assures him she has two dates. He tells her Joe's a fan of *Gone With the Wind* too. He's teasing, Joe tells Lala. Lala suggests they have supper here and then go downtown together to see the celebrities—her dates can date each other, she shrugs.

As the food is put on the table, Lala admits to never having met a Farkas before, wondering if it's a New York City name. He supposes it is, so Lala assumes he must be acquainted with "the smart supper clubs in Manhattan." It seems he's never been to one. Lala reveals she will possibly be going to New York soon—to meet with publishers about her novel. "Oh, my God!" Boo sighs. Adolph suggests they eat, and Reba lifts her water glass in a toast: "Welcome to Atlanta, Joe!"

Scene 2

"It is an hour later. Dinner is over. Reba is making trips on and offstage from the dining room, clearing the table. Lala and Joe are in the living room. Adolph is back in his easy chair with the newspaper, fast asleep." Lala is telling Joe the first sentence of her novel: "From where she sat atop the weathered buckboard wagon, Ropa (short for Europa) Ragsdale could see the charred and twisted remains of her beloved plantation." Now she has to think of a name for the plantation, something very Protestant, and suddenly comes up with Habersham Hall—after the name of the street she lives on, Joe realizes. Lala makes a point of assuring him their address is "about the best" in town. Many Junior League members live here, and her family is the only Jewish one, except for a house beyond Paces Ferry, where the neighborhood begins to run down.

Reba mentions Sunny's name. Joe is confused when told Sunny is Reba's daughter. Reba is pointing upward—"That kind of sunny." It seems she was born in a storm, and they certainly couldn't call her Cloudy!

Boo comes into the living room, complaining that their cook Louisa had better return to work. Joe could have helped, he and his brothers were drying dishes at an early age, and they cook, too—old country staples, from Russia, Poland and Hungary. Boo finds this interesting. Her brother Adolph never enters the kitchen except for nocturnal ice box raiding.

Joe wonders why Sunny isn't there. She's at Wellesley, he's told. "She got the brains. I got the moxie," Lala explains. Joe remarks that he's heard Lala went to college, too. This upsets Lala, and Boo intervenes, explaining that Lala missed the social life in Atlanta so much, she came home. They were pleased to have her back.

REBA: Tell me, Joe, will you be going up to your home for Christmas?

JOE: No ma'am. My boss . . . . . keeps me hoppin' too much for that. But it's okay. My family doesn't celebrate Christmas.

BOO: I see.

JOE: I'll be home for Pesach, though.

LALA: Pesach?

JOE: Passover.

BOO: You remember, Lala. That time we went to the Seder supper with one of Daddy's business acquaintances. I believe their name was Lipzin. They lived over on Boulevard or somewhere. You were in the sixth grade. It was very interesting.

LALA: I was in the fifth grade, and I spilled a glass of red wine all over the tablecloth.

JOE: Right. One of us does that almost every year. Part of the ritual.

LALA: You have to sit through one of those boring things every single year? One night of all that ish-kabibble was enough to last me the rest of my life.

BOO: Now, Lala. Be tolerant.

JOE: I sit through two every year. First night at Aunt Sadie's. Second night at home.

LALA: Poor baby!

JOE: Are you kidding? I wouldn't miss either one of 'em for anything in the world.

REBA: Now, they have those in the spring, don't they?

JOE: Yes ma'am. That's right. March or April.

LALA: Good. Then you'll be here for Ballyhoo.

BOO: Lala!

Joe wonders what Ballyhoo is. "The young people come from all over the South," Reba explains. Joe likens it to a convention, but it's not like that, not about business. The agenda is hay rides, weenie roasts, parties and, on the last night, a dance. Reba claims it was started in Macon right after the war, when it was decided to get everyone together at Christmas time in Atlanta, but Boo insists it started in Gulfport after Nathan Solomon's 95th birthday party. Boo wakes up Adolph to confirm her version, asking him to tell Joe how Ballyhoo started. Adolph looks at her, wondering, "What the hell would he care about a stupid thing like that?" Lala implies maybe he would. Especially if he plans on going.

Joe remarks on how late it's getting. Lala figures the movie isn't even over yet, and they have lots of time to go downtown and then meet her crowd somewhere. But Joe is catching a train early the next morning and must call it a night. Boo agrees: Mr. Farkas has the Dixie Bedding business to deal with and should leave. After the thank yous and the goodnights, Lala tells the others to stop staring at her and goes upstairs. Boo turns to her brother: "Adolph, that kike you hired has no manners."

Scene 3

"In the dark we hear the voice of a Train Conductor: 'Baltimore. The stop is Baltimore. Baltimore coming up!' " It is five days later, and the lights rise on a sleeping compartment on the Crescent Limited. Sunny Freitag, 20, *"attractive, shy,"* is alone reading a book, when there is a knock on her door and Joe Farkas enters, inquiring if she's Sunny Freitag. Her Uncle Adolph wanted him to look in on her and see if she needed anything. She doesn't, but thanks him and begins reading again—Upton Sinclair's *The Profits of Religion.* "The glorious unwashed masses and the beauty of the working class. You really enjoy reading this stuff?" Joe asks. Yes, Eugene V. Debs as well, she asserts. But she's not a communist. She's majoring in sociology. Joe explains that he works for her uncle, whom he calls Mr. A., not in Baltimore—he's just here on business—but in Atlanta. He doesn't sound like Atlanta, Sunny remarks. It boggles her mind that a college junior like herself whose

grade average is A minus is still regarded as an infant who can't even take the train home alone. Why the minus?, Joe wonders. Trouble with zoology, she explains, asking about his average. He didn't go to college. He did attend art school, but only for a few weeks before his father died and he'd had to go to work.

Joe is curious as to whether Sunny has a lot of things lined up for the Christmas vacation. "A lot of work," Sunny indicates. Does that mean she won't go to "this Ballyhoo thing?" Sunny asks if her uncle told him about that. It was Lala, Joe admits.

JOE: I think she wants me to take her.

SUNNY: Oh. And?

JOE: I pretty well side-stepped the issue.

SUNNY: You were smart.

JOE: How's that?

SUNNY: Ballyhoo is asinine.

JOE: Yeah? Why?

SUNNY: Oh, you know, a lot of dressed up Jews dancing around wishing they could kiss their elbows and turn into Episcopalians.

JOE: Sounds pretty terrible.

SUNNY: It is.

JOE: Wanna go with me?

CONDUCTOR *(offstage):* All aboard! All aboard.

JOE: Word is I'm a good dancer.

SUNNY: I'm not.

JOE: Baloney. I gotta get to work. Think it over.

He smiles, leaves. She looks after him.

Scene 4

"The Freitag house. It's 8 o'clock the following morning. A pile of wrapped presents is under the tree, which is now minus its star. The remains of breakfast are on the dining room table where Adolph sits with his coffee going over some paperwork. Reba, in a housecoat, is cleaning up. Boo comes in from outdoors, carrying the morning paper which she hands to Adolph. She appears to be agitated." When Boo went down the driveway to get the *Constitution,* she saw Louisa go up the Arkwrights' driveway. She asked her if she weren't going up the wrong driveway, and Louisa said no, it's the right driveway, she is working for the Arkwrights. Reba doesn't understand. "She quit!" Boo explains, after Boo asked her if she knew anything about the pocket change that was disappearing from Adolph's bureau. As she left, Louisa promised to return the red umbrella she had borrowed from Reba, but in Boo's opinion Reba will never see it again. And she's afraid Louisa will bad-mouth them to the Arkwrights and, more importantly, to other servants on the Peachtree trolley whom Boo might want to employ as a replacement.

They'll find someone after New Year's, Reba assumes, but Boo complains about their having to do all the work in the meantime. Adolph is going with Reba to meet Sunny's train and wonders if she's ready to go. She's all dressed except for her dress, she assures him as she goes upstairs.

THE LAST NIGHT OF BALLYHOO—Terry
Beaver as Adolph Freitag in the play by Alfred Uhry

Adolph is disturbed about Hitler in Poland. Boo thinks his concern should be for his family. She doesn't know why Adolph's meeting Sunny. He doesn't have to, he wants to, he announces. He never meets Lala, Boo pouts. He would, he tells her, if she went anywhere.

BOO: Sunny isn't a direct pipeline to the Lord Almighty, you know.
ADOLPH: Who said she was?
BOO: That's how you treat her.
ADOLPH: For God's sake, Beulah! Maybe you forgot how Simon looked after us all when Papa died.
BOO: He had to. He was the oldest.
ADOLPH: Maybe he had to support Mama, but he didn't have to put me all the way through Tech, and Lord knows he didn't have to buy you that trousseau you raised such hell over and all that damn sterling silver. That's when he was just getting Dixie Bedding started, and I know for a fact he didn't have two nickels to rub

together. He must've borrowed and squeezed and cut all kinds of corners. I know he worried himself sick over his obligations to all of us, and I know that's what landed him in Oakland Cemetery a good twenty-five years ahead of schedule, and I'll be God damned if I have to justify myself to you if I feel like meeting his daughter at the train when she comes home from college.

BOO: You get yourself so worked up. You'll be laying out there right beside Simon if you don't look out.

Adolph calls upstairs to Reba to hurry up. Boo urges him to calm down, but he wants to be there on time, if she doesn't mind. Boo reminds him that Lala's father, DeWald, is every bit as dead and gone as Sunny's father, Simon, and reminds Adolph that he never gave DeWald a real chance to succeed in the business. For that matter, Boo goes on, Adolph and Simon never gave Boo herself a chance to take part in Dixie Bedding either, though Boo got better arithmetic grades in school than either of the men. Adolph protests that they tried DeWald everywhere, in the factory, in the front office, in sales. Maybe DeWald wasn't as smart as all the Freitags, Boo admits, "but he was a good man. And it was a shame how you two did him."

Reba appears and goes off with Adolph, who returns briefly. "DeWald had beautiful table manners," he concedes to Boo before going off again.

The telephone rings. It's Sylvan Weil, and Boo's tone of voice becomes more friendly. She asks about his Aunt Ethel and wonders if she still has the limp she had as a girl. Boo calls sweetly to Lala to come to the telephone. "It's the Weil boy," she says, *sotto voce.* Lala takes the phone, and she and the boy (who is called "Peachy") have a brief round of banter. Then she hangs up. He is coming to Atlanta the day after Christmas. But did he ask Lala to Ballyhoo? Boo wants to know. He only said he and his parents were coming for the Zacharias's golden wedding anniversary. That would be his great uncle, Boo calculates, wondering if the boy has that same ugly red hair. He does, Lala reports. It could be worse, Boo shrugs, but he didn't mention Ballyhoo? It would be good for Lala to be seen with a Weil, Boo argues. She can do better than him, Lala insists—she may have different plans. She doesn't, Boo informs her. Ferdy Nachman's mother told Boo yesterday that Ferdy's taking Carol Strauss to Ballyhoo. Boo picks up the telephone. She's calling Peachy's Aunt Ethel, despite Lala's plea that Boo hasn't seen her in 30 years.

Scene 5

"11 o'clock that night. Sunny and Adolph are playing gin at a card table. Reba sits nearby, knitting . . . . . There is a feeling of warmth in the room." Sunny is adding up points, and Adolph writes the figure down. Sunny confesses she liked it when he used to let her win. He didn't, he insists. He wonders if Wellesley is making her stupid, since she's losing. Reba asks if that's possible. Higher education can lead to insanity, Reba believes, recalling what happened to Viola Feigenbaum, one of seven sisters, "One more hideous than the next," but Viola was "the least hideous" and

the smartest. She went to Peabody Normal, in Nashville, taking teacher training. Then she went crazy on the train. An hour after the train left the station she took off all her clothes and ran up and down the day coach. They had to roll her in a tablecloth and take her off the train, Reba continues.

Sunny is curious as to what became of Viola. Reba says she got married and went to Louisville and that her husband and his family never knew about that train incident. Sunny can't believe they didn't hear about it on the "Southern Jewish grapevine." Reba confesses they were the other kind. "Other kind of what?" Sunny asks. Reba believes Sunny knows what she means, but Sunny is not teasing her mother. She really wants to know.

REBA: East of the Elbe.
SUNNY: What?
REBA: That's how Grandma used to explain it.
SUNNY: What's the Elbe?
REBA: Well, I believe it's a river somewhere.
ADOLPH: Separates Germany from Czechoslovakia.
REBA: Yes. And west of it is us and east of it is the other kind.
SUNNY: But why are they the other kind?
REBA: Well—they just are.
SUNNY: How can you tell?
REBA: The way they look.
SUNNY: That's preposterous. Are you saying you could pick a hundred Jews off the street at random and tell who's what kind just by looking at them?
ADOLPH: Sure. The German Jews would be the ugly ones. I mean the men. And, of course, the Feigenbaum sisters.
SUNNY: It's a lot of mumbo jumbo, and you both know it. And don't tell me they talk louder. Nobody talks louder than Aunt Boo.
ADOLPH: That's for sure.
SUNNY: And don't tell me they act peculiar, either, because—
REBA: Now don't you say one word about your cousin Lala. She does the best she can!
SUNNY: I rest my case. Gin.

Sunny confides that she misses her uncle when she's away. He asks about school. It's all right, except for the freezing cold botany field trips. Reba goes upstairs, and Adolph reminisces about a day 20 years ago when he'd gone into Sunny's father's office to talk about an ad. Simon had put something he'd been looking at underneath some folders, very furtively. Later, when Simon had gone to the bank, Adolph went into his office again to see what it was. He'd been reading catalogs from Smith, Vassar and Wellesley, researching schools for Sunny when she was six months old. "Wouldn't he be tickled tonight?" Adolph remarks.

They are still playing cards when Lala and Boo come in. They've been to *Gone With the Wind* again. Sunny asks how it was. Just the same, Boo claims, but Lala believes you can't absorb a masterpiece in a single viewing. She could see it a thousand times. It seems Lala has swiped a photo from the movie theater lobby. Boo sees it as a crime, but Sunny thinks they won't miss "one silly photograph."

There's a car in the driveway. Boo thinks it might be the police, but it's Joe. He'd seen the lights on and has some figures from Washington for Adolph. He asks Sunny how their pal Upton Sinclair is, and notes she got home safely. It's explained to Lala that Uncle Adolph had sent Joe to check on Sunny on the train. Lala wonders if Joe's seen *Gone With the Wind* yet—"It's a dream!" "Dreams don't last four hours," in Boo's opinion. She also thinks it's late to have company in the house. Joe is about to go, when Adolph insists he can't be sent off without something to eat. Lala volunteers to make coffee. Boo goes upstairs, remarking that coffee this late can give people gas.

Adolph apologizes for his sister's unpleasantness and chats with Joe briefly, mentioning that he'd been a traveling man himself once. He goes upstairs, leaving Sunny and Joe alone in the living room. Sunny wants to ask Joe something—how did he get to Atlanta? It seems he was selling mattresses at Macy's Herald Square, was offered a job as assistant bedding buyer in the D.C. store, and then the store across the street wanted him to assistant-manage. That chain was taken over by Dixie Bedding, and when her uncle came to check on them he hired Joe to work for him.

Joe wants to ask Sunny something, too: "Are you people really Jewish?" " 'Fraid so," she admits. "A hundred per cent all the way back—on both sides." He supposes she means she's afraid she's Jewish. Only an expression, she shrugs, asking to change the subject.

Joe admires the Christmas tree, wondering if it's a family tradition. She's always had Christmas trees, Sunny states. He's only trying to learn the local customs, Joe assures her. Everyone Sunny knows has a tree, but that does not mean they're not Jewish. Just that they don't want to be, Joe counters. Not much to do about it— whether she wants to be or not, she is. Joe suggests she could anglicize her name. "Sunny Friday. Sounds like a weather report," she remarks. "Or a striptease artist," Joe thinks. Even calling herself Sunny O'Houlihan, people would still know, she claims: "It hurts sometimes." Joe says he knows, but Sunny doesn't think so. She assumes he grew up in a Jewish neighborhood and didn't feel different, but she grew up on Habersham Road. "Only two Jewish mailboxes," Joe quotes Lala.

SUNNY: That's all we wanted—to be like everybody else.
JOE: And you are.
SUNNY: Oh no. No we're not.
JOE: Whaddaya mean?
SUNNY: The summer between sixth and seventh grade my best friend was Vennie Alice Sizemore. And one day she took me swimming at the Venetian Club Pool. Her parents were members. So we were with a whole bunch of kids from our class, and the boys were splashing us, and we were all shrieking—you know—and pretending we hated it, when this man in a shirt and tie came over and squatted down by the side of the pool, and he said, "Which one is Sunny Freitag?" And I said I was, and he said I had to get out of the water. And Vennie Alice asked him why

and he said Jews weren't allowed to swim in the Venetian pool. And all the kids got very quiet and none of them would look at me.

JOE: What did you do?

SUNNY: I got out of the pool and phoned Daddy at his office. When he came to get me all the color was drained out of his lips. I remember that.

JOE: And Vennie Alice?

SUNNY: Oh, her mother called up Mama and apologized. We stayed friends— sort of. Neither of us ever mentioned it again, but it was always there. So believe me, I know I can't hide being Jewish.

JOE: Yeah, so how come you try to camouflage it so much?

SUNNY: Oh, stop it! You think being Jewish means you have to run around in one of those little skull caps and a long white beard?

JOE: Not in your case.

SUNNY: I'm serious!

JOE: Well, I guess I think being Jewish means being Jewish.

Sunny talks to Joe about the comparative religions course she's just taken with a professor who believes that every faith is pretty much the same "with different window dressings." Sunny agrees with her and doesn't believe that what a person's religion is matters very much in today's world. It matters to some who are important, Joe insists: "Like Hitler." Sunny regards Hitler as an aberration. Joe suggests they drop it. It's his first date with her. He doesn't choose to use the time talking about Hitler. It isn't a date, Sunny points out. It would be if they went to the White Castle up in Buckhead, he urges, if she's hungry. "A little," she admits, but she shouldn't go because her mother wouldn't know where she was. He's probably more accustomed to girls who—"Who what?" he wonders. "Take more chances," Sunny replies.

He asks if going out the next night would be too big a gamble. "And maybe a movie first," she agrees. "Not *Gone With the Wind*," Joe stipulates. It will be a good date, and the second will be better—Ballyhoo, he reminds her: "We made a deal."

Lala comes in to say the coffee pot boiled over, but Joe should leave anyway. "Y'all made a deal?" Lala asks. Joe's asked her to Ballyhoo, Sunny tells Lala. Facetiously, Joe feels they should be aware of the fact that he isn't as Jewish as they are—he has royal Russian blood: "There's a story in the family about my great-grandfather and the Czarina's grand niece, or was it my great-grandmother and the Czar's third cousin?"

When Joe's gone, Lala is angry, calling Joe aggressive. She "wouldn't be seen at Ballyhoo with him." "A decision you won't have to make," Sunny remarks. Sunny's been back less than a day and already lording it over her, Lala says. "Poor Miss Wellesley. It must be exhausting to have to deal with us piddling little inferiors." And Lala goes on.

LALA: Remember your daddy's funeral?

SUNNY: What?

LALA: Uncle Simon's funeral—all those flowers and all those people—seven hundred I think the newspaper said. Mayor Hartsfield and that congressman and I don't know who all. Remember?

SUNNY: Of course. What about it?

LALA: Remember what I wore?

SUNNY: What you wore?

LALA: Yes.

SUNNY: What is wrong with you, Lala?

LALA: You don't remember. Why should you? Well, I remember what you wore to mine.

SUNNY: What?

LALA: My daddy's funeral. Three months later. Remember? That sad little biddy chapel with hardly anybody in it. And those pathetic gladiolas in back of the coffin. It was like a mockery of what your daddy had. And you wore an adorable navy blue suit. Brand new, so were the shoes. The soles weren't even scuffed.

SUNNY: Why would you remember a thing like that?

LALA: Because you wanted everybody to look at you!

SUNNY: I did not!

LALA: Nobody wears a whole new outfit unless they want to be looked at! That was supposed to be my tragedy! You already had yours and you had to have mine too!

SUNNY: That is a terrible thing to say!

LALA: But it's true, and you know it.

SUNNY: I know no such thing.

LALA: Oh come on, Sunny. You've always gotten all the attention. Even from God!

SUNNY: What?

LALA: He didn't give you one Jewish feature, and look at me!

SUNNY: That's absurd.

LALA: Look at my hair! Look at my skin! Look at my eyes! Listen to my voice! I try, and I try, and no matter what I do it shows, and there's just nothing I can do about it.

Lala shouldn't be so hard on herself, Sunny feels. But Lala claims Sunny makes it worse, back for one day and getting invited to Ballyhoo. Why does Lala care about Ballyhoo? Sunny asks. Sunny cares as much as she does, Lala believes. Sunny insists she thinks "it's a joke." Lala asks her why she's going, then. If Lala wants her to stay home, she will, Sunny retorts, then changes her mind: "No. That's crazy! I want to go." Lala calls her a hypocrite. Sunny calls Lala a wet blanket: "No wonder nobody wants to take you to Ballyhoo." But somebody does, Lala tells her, somebody from one of the finest families in the South! Sunny will see when Sunny comes "crawlin' to Ballyhoo with a New York Yid tryin' to suck up to his boss," and Lala will come in with someone who belongs there—"a Louisiana Weil!" *Curtain.*

ACT II

Scene 1

"The next morning, Boo is at her desk doing the accounting. Sunny is studying. Reba and Lala are also on stage." Boo is arguing with Lala about calling Peachy Weil. Lala won't and suggests Boo call Peachy's aunt again. Reba reports Boo already did—at 6:15 a.m. (Boo's hollering woke her up.) When Boo says she'll call him if Lala won't, Lala does. The family cook says Peachy and his parents have left for Atlanta. They'll just have to wait, Lala tells Boo. But Boo calls the cook and asks her to see if Peachy's tuxedo is in his closet. "You're pretty brainy," Sunny compliments Boo. "If I were running the Dixie Bedding Company we'd all be rich by now," Boo replies. Reba is puzzled. She thought they *were* rich.

It turns out the tuxedo is not in Peachy's closet, nor are his patent leather dancing shoes. Boo and Lala are ecstatic, taking this as proof positive that Peachy's taking Lala to Ballyhoo. Then Boo wonders what Lala will wear. Lala wants Boo to go shopping with her ("It's gonna cost Uncle Adolph an arm and two legs"), but Boo hasn't finished her accounts and has a pot roast to fix. Reba could do the pot roast, Lala reasons. Boo doesn't think much of Reba's pot roast, but agrees—if Reba will stay away from the garlic. They leave.

Reba won't stay from the garlic, she assures Sunny: "Garlic makes a pot roast." As they neaten up the living room, Reba tells Sunny how much she admires her, she has so much sense, and Sunny didn't inherit it from her. "Who says I didn't?" Sunny asks. If there'd been a Ballyhoo in her day, Reba goes on, she'd probably have acted just like Lala, and here Sunny is, happy to stay home and study for finals and not paying any mind to the "whole silly rigamarole."

SUNNY: Mama?
REBA: Yes?
SUNNY: I am going to Ballyhoo.
REBA: You are! How nice! With who?
SUNNY: With Joe.
REBA: That good-looking boy who works for Adolph?
SUNNY: Yes.
REBA: Well, that's fine! And what are you gonna wear?
SUNNY: I was thinking maybe the blue velvet I wore in David and Virginia's wedding.
REBA: Yes. It's put away in the cedar closet.
SUNNY: I'll go get it out.
        She starts out of the room.
REBA: You know, I wore blue the first time I went dancin' with your daddy.
SUNNY: Oh, Mama!
REBA: Well, go on up and air out that dress. You wouldn't want to go to Ballyhoo smellin' like a mothball.

Sunny goes upstairs. Reba continues with her cleaning.
(*To herself.*) She is a little bit like me! Thank the Lord!

Scene 2

"That night, Adolph is asleep in the living room, the evening paper in his lap."
Boo calls to Adolph and then to Reba, who's in the kitchen, "We're ready." Lala
appears on the staircase in her new formal—*"Very GWTW with a hoop skirt so wide
she can barely get down the stairs. The price tag still hangs from the dress. Like all of
Lala's outfits, this one isn't quite becoming."* Lala wants to know what her uncle
thinks. He calls her Scarlet O'Goldberg, but after a glance from Boo assures her
she'll be the belle of the ball. And she won't have anybody being fresh with her—
they can't get anywhere close to her. Suppose she can't dance in it, Lala worries.
Reba assures her it's a dancing dress. Lala asks Adolph to dance when Boo and
Reba begin humming "The Pink Lady Waltz."

Sunny and Joe come in, and Sunny compliments Lala on her dress, Lala thanks
her. Joe and Sunny begin dancing, too, and Joe, despite being a good dancer, somehow manages to step on Lala's dress and tear it. Lala screams, and Boo manages
vituperatively to blame not only Joe, but everybody else for not letting Lala "have
her joy for five minutes." Boo and Lala go upstairs, followed by Reba, who tries to
comfort them, saying it's a small rip and can be repaired.

Joe apologizes to Adolph. He can pay for the dress, he tells Adolph. "That's good
because I can't," Adolph remarks sarcastically. He tells Joe to forget it. Sunny apologizes for Boo's dramatics. "She's the Jewish Tallulah Bankhead," Adolph sums her
up. Reba calls to Sunny to come upstairs.

Joe is all too aware that Adolph's sister doesn't like him. "I'm too Jewish," he
tells Adolph. "You are?" Adolph asks and confesses he's not his sister's keeper.
Well, actually he is, but he isn't responsible for her thinking. Back in his neighborhood, Joe recalls, Jews are proud of being Jewish and "always trying to claim everybody . . . . . ball players, movie stars . . . . . who is and who's part." Joe has a great
aunt who swears Franklin Roosevelt's real family name is Rosenfeld.

Adolph has given Ballyhoo tickets to Sunny. Joe insists that he pay for them
himself, or he won't go. Adolph informs Joe they were complimentary. Joe asks
why.

ADOLPH: I'm a past president of the club. They send me free tickets to everything
that goes on there.
JOE: The club?
ADOLPH: Standard Club.
JOE: Country club, right?
ADOLPH: Well, it would be if it was in the country. Right now it's a town club
with delusions of grandeur.
JOE: Sounds pretty spiffy.
ADOLPH: I wouldn't say that.
JOE: Jews only?

Celia Weston as Reba Freitag, Jessica Hecht as Lala Levy and Dana Ivey as Boo Levy in a scene from *The Last Night of Ballyhoo*

ADOLPH: You bet.

JOE: No Christians allowed?

ADOLPH: Technically, but the truth is none of 'em would wanna come anyway. They've got clubs of their own, which they won't let us near.

JOE: So this is where all the Jews go.

ADOLPH: Oh no. We're restricted too.

JOE: What do you mean?

Adolph looks uncomfortable.

ADOLPH: Um, I mean membership is restricted to the well padded. As you can clearly see by the girth of the ex-president. Also well padded in the monetary sense, of course.

JOE: I guess I'm a long way from joining, hunh?

ADOLPH: Who knows?

JOE: Still, I pay my way to this dance or I don't go.

Adolph doesn't know the value of the tickets, but Joe takes out two bills and hands them to him, saying he thinks this should cover it. "And then some," Adolph believes. Sunny, coming downstairs, wonders if her uncle is bribing Joe to take her out. Adolph explains Joe's insistence on paying for the Ballyhoo tickets.

The "great ball gown tragedy" is over, Sunny reports, thanks to her mother. Joe asks Sunny to tell Lala he is sorry. Sunny already did, and Lala has forgiven Joe. "I'm such a klutz," Joe admits. Sunny doesn't know what that means, but Adolph thinks it means clumsy. Sunny asks if that's Yiddish and is impressed that Adolph knows some Yiddish. He only knows a few words, it seems.

Joe takes his departure, saying goodnight to Adolph and " 'night, Sunshine" to Sunny. When he's gone, Adolph asks if that's what people call her—Sunshine. Only Joe, she says, he is imaginative, and a good dancer and has beautiful hands. And he is "very bright" for someone who never went to college.

Adolph reminds her he was sold on Joe before she was. He knows it isn't his business, also that it could put Boo in Piedmont Hospital, but he believes Sunny should "hold on to this boy." They don't come any finer. She agrees. Adolph also feels that her father would approve.

Sunny wants to know whether her uncle was ever in love. He was, it seems. Sunny asks what her name was, and Adolph has to admit he never knew. She was someone who rode the same Chatahoochee Avenue trolley every morning. He admired her beauty but never spoke to her. She once gave him the tiniest of smiles, which she also gave to everyone else. And once they exchanged gestures signaling that it was an unusually hot day. After that, Adolph expected they might soon fall into conversation.

ADOLPH: But then, a couple of days later, I got on the streetcar, and she wasn't there. And she was never there again.

SUNNY: What happened to her?

ADOLPH: I have no idea. I asked the motorman, but he didn't even know who I was talking about. Imagine that! A beautiful girl like her—getting on and off his car every single day, and he never even noticed.

SUNNY: And there never was anybody else?

ADOLPH: Not really. I went with some girls, and I suppose I could've married one of 'em, but in the back of my mind I was waiting for somebody like the girl on the streetcar.

SUNNY: She was the love of your life.

ADOLPH: Yah. And you know why?

SUNNY: Why?

ADOLPH: I never saw her for more than twenty minutes at a time, and I had no dealings with her whatsoever.

SUNNY: Stop it. You'd make somebody a wonderful husband.

ADOLPH: Just what I need—another female to live in this house!

Lights fade.

Scene 3

"11 a.m. Christmas Day. The dining room table is set for cake and coffee—with the good silver and china. A home-made coffee cake sits on a cake pedestal in the center of the table. All that remains of the Christmas presents are ribbons, paper and discarded boxes. Boo is putting the living room in order. Reba is standing in the open front door, speaking to someone outside. She holds a red umbrella and a small wrapped gift." Reba is thanking Louisa for returning her umbrella and for the gift she's brought, telling her not to be a stranger—and to wish the Arkwrights a Merry Christmas. She closes the door and unwraps the jar of watermelon pickles Louisa's put up for them. Reba thinks that's sweet of her. She reads the card aloud: "Happy Holiday to you and Mr. Adolph and both the girls." She believes Louisa must have meant Boo, too. Boo claims not to care, and she hates watermelon pickles anyway. What's on her mind is that the Weil boy is about to appear, and she wants the place tidied up. The Weils are notoriously neat, it seems. And she wants everyone out of the way to give Lala and Peachy privacy. Reba hopes Boo won't have a stroke before he appears.

Adolph comes downstairs wearing the hand-knit argyle sweater Reba made him for Christmas. He doesn't have to wear it, Reba says. It's hard for him to convince her he loves it. He picks at the coffee cake and Boo snaps at him.

Peachy arrives. *"He is in his middle 20s—self-important, with bright red hair."* He introduces himself to Adolph and tells him his cousin says Adolph's a worse golfer than he is. Adolph asks if Peachy plays. "Varsity at Tulane three years running," Peachy answers. He admires the "Chanukah bush" and Reba tells him Lala decorated it. "You the mother?" he asks her. She explains she's Lala's aunt, by marriage. Boo chats with him briefly, mentioning his Aunt Josephine and Uncle Ike: "Imagine—married fifty years!" Peachy's reply is, "To one of those two? No, thanks!"

Lala comes downstairs. Her opening gambit is something about "lettin' all kinds trash into decent people's homes." "Hey," Peachy greets her. That's what the horses—and the asses—are fed, Lala remarks. Boo is upset. Peachy asks if Lala's "always this sassy," and Lala claims some things he says are "downright terrible."

Boo offers Peachy coffee cake. He asks if it contains nuts. It does. Pecans. He's allergic to nuts and would die from a pecan. Adolph helps himself to a big piece.

When the others go off, Lala asks Peachy if he really would die? He asks, "What do you think?", makes faces at her, and she laughs. It just came out of his mouth, he admits, but a roommate of his did have an allergy to nuts. There was peanut butter in a chocolate cake, and he didn't know and died at the dinner table. "Really?" Lala asks. Again he asks, "What do you think?" She tells him to go "right this minute," but he can't. He has come over because he has to tell her that he can't take her to Ballyhoo. He has to take his cousin from Columbus. His family is forcing him to. His mother was sure Lala'd understand. Even when he admits his cousin is "a nifty little dancer," Lala is staying in control and trying to be a good sport about it.

PEACHY: Listen. I hate to do this, but I have to ask you something, okay? I don't know anybody else to ask.
LALA: All right.
PEACHY: Should I buy her a white orchid or a purple orchid?
LALA: What color is her dress?
PEACHY: How the hell would I know?
LALA: Then I guess white.
PEACHY: White. Thanks.
LALA: Unless she's wearing black. Then purple.
PEACHY: Oh, I'm pretty sure she won't be wearing black.
LALA: Why?
PEACHY: She's nine years old.
LALA: What?
PEACHY: I swear. My cousin Sally is nine years old.
LALA: Your family is making you take a nine-year-old to Ballyhoo?
PEACHY: What do you think?
LALA: I—I—
PEACHY: Hah hah!
LALA: You're terrible!
PEACHY: Be ready at nine tomorrow night.
LALA: Nine?
PEACHY: Because I'll be here at ten.
        He goes to closet for coat and starts to leave.
What color you wearing?
LALA: Not black.
PEACHY: Then I'll be sure to get purple.
LALA: You're terrible.
PEACHY: You said it! Bye, Sassyass!

Peachy's gone when Boo comes on from the kitchen to offer him something else. Assured that everything's all right about Ballyhoo, she remaks on what "a lovely boy" he is.

Scene 4

"The next night, December 26, Peachy and Joe sit side by side on the sofa. Peachy is wearing a tuxedo, holds an orchid corsage in a box. Joe has on a dark suit, no flowers. Adolph is sitting in his customary chair, reading the evening paper. Silence. Joe breaks it," asking Adolph about the war news. Not good, he tells Joe. Joe has relatives in Poland and in Russia. Adolph says they should hope for the best. "Let's hope they can dodge bullets," Peachy tosses off. "Excuse me?" Joe asks. This mess isn't his fault, Peachy shrugs, and it isn't his problem. It is Europe's, and they have to solve it themselves. It would depend on where one's family is, Adolph opines. Peachy's has been in Louisiana for a century and a half, he wants it known.

Joe goes to greet Sunny as she comes downstairs. *"She is dressed simply, but well. She looks great."* Joe tells her she looks terrific, and she thanks him. He apologizes about not wearing a tuxedo, he hadn't known, and also about the flowers. She's not perturbed.

As Lala's about to descend, Peachy picks up the corsage box. Lala swoops down and strikes a pose at the bottom of the steps. He teases her, asking why she hasn't dressed up for the party. He gives her the corsage—two white orchids. Lala is thrilled.

Reba tells Sunny she won't wait up, which Sunny knows means she will, and Reba excuses herself and goes upstairs. Sunny and Joe leave.

As Boo is pinning on Lala's corsage, Peachy says Dorothy Stein, who's married to his cousin Tony, says "hey." Lala can't seem to remember who she is and asks what her unmarried name was. Peachy doesn't know, but she was in Lala's dorm at Michigan. Lala, upset, asks if she was Dorothy Wolf, from Shaker Heights. That's her—and was Lala in her sorority "or something?" Peachy asks. Lala passes out. Peachy is shocked, but Boo claims it's overexcitement and Lala's not having eaten dinner. She assures him Lala'll be fine and suggests he go out and warm up the car. Lala's evening wrap is very light. He leaves.

Lala tells Boo she isn't going. She explains that Dotty Wolf rushed Sigma Delta Tau when she did, but Dotty got in. It was four years ago, Boo points out. She won't have forgotten, Lala states. Maybe she'll be kind, Boo suggests. "Never in this world," Lala surmises, again refusing to go.

BOO: You've made some very bad decisions about your life. Don't let this be another one.

LALA: Mama! I won't go to Ballyhoo and have people laugh at me!

BOO: If they're gonna laugh at you, they'll do it whether you go or not. At least show a little backbone, for God's sake! We're not weak people! Now you get yourself up and go on out to that car!

LALA: I can't!

BOO: You have to!

LALA: No!

BOO: Well, I guess you're right. Dotty Wolf probably does remember, and she probably will tell. And everybody you know will be sayin' "Lala Levy didn't get into Sigma Delta Tau at Michigan. What an awful pill she is!"

LALA: Mama!

BOO: And then they'll say "Not only that. She had a fit and fell down on the floor in front of the Weil boy, and she acted so crazy she couldn't go to the last night of Ballyhoo."

LALA: You are just hateful!

BOO: And pretty soon it'll be "Lala Levy? I don't believe she's been out of that house on Habersham Road for —why it must be twenty years now." Do you see any other possibilities, Daughter?

No answer.

Well, go on upstairs and work on that radio script. I'm sorry. It's a novel this week, isn't it? Just leave the dress on my bed, Sugar. I'll take it back to Rich's tomorrow.

Boo goes into the dining room. In the hall, Lala gets herself together and exits through the front door.

Adolph comes into the dining room from the kitchen, clearing his throat. Boo had thought he'd gone to bed. She wonders if she should have allowed Lala to stay home, but she's unsure of how many more opportunities Lala will have. This one was lucky. Adolph agrees.

Boo asks Adolph if he ever considers how odd it is that the two of them ended up together. He admits he has. Boo never would have imagined something like this when they were small. He hadn't either. "I thought we were gonna be happy when we grew up," she confides, "what do you think happened?" Adolph honestly doesn't know, he confesses.

Scene 5

"In the darkness, we hear Jerome Kern's 'All the Things You Are' played by a dance orchestra." The lights come up on a corner of the Standard Club, where Sunny and Lala enter on their way to the ladies room, leaving Peachy and Joe to chat while waiting for their return. Peachy wonders how Joe likes the Standard Club, in comparison to the Progressive Club. Joe likes the Standard all right but has never been to the Progressive. Peachy thinks Joe is kidding.

PEACHY: I thought that's where you people went.

JOE: Us people.

PEACHY: The Other Kind.

JOE: Other kind?

PEACHY: Yeah. You know. Russian. Orthodox. The Other Kind.

JOE: Wait a sec. Let me get this straight. So the—whaddayacallit—Progressive Club is where me and the rest of The Other Kind belong . . .

PEACHY: Thass right.

JOE: And this one—The Standard Club—?

PEACHY: Us. German Jews.

JOE: German Jews only?

PEACHY: Well, they're startin' to let in a few others because they need the initiation fees. But they try to only take the ones that are toilet trained. At least that's the way Uncle Ike puts it.

JOE: Sunny knows all this, right?

PEACHY: Knows it? Her uncle's the goddamn past president! So you got nothin' to worry about. You'll be treated like a prince tonight.

Joe says to hell with it and goes off. Sunny, returning from the ladies room, calls out after him, bewildered.

Scene 6

"The Freitag house, several hours later . . . . . is dark, except for a table lamp in the hall. Sunny enters through the front door," as Adolph, in his bathrobe, enters from the kitchen, carrying a dish of fried chicken, surprised to see Sunny. He'd thought she was going to breakfast after the dance. All Sunny knows is, when she came out of the ladies room Joe was gone, and she asked Harold Lillienthal to drive her home.

Joe arrives and tells the others he went for a drive: "Seemed like the best thing to do." Coolly, Joe and Sunny bid each other good night and start to exit in their separate directions. Adolph stops them and advises them to have a discussion, then exits upstairs.

Sunny asks Joe what happened—she thought they were having a good time. They were, Joe admits, and she is a good dancer. But she should have told him that his type of person is not welcome at the Standard Club. She doesn't run it, she snaps. But she took him there, Joe accuses. Sunny declares that she wanted to dance with him and didn't think it would make such a difference. When Joe asks her if she's planning to go swimming at the Venetian Club any time soon, she claims it's not the same thing. Joe thinks it is and doesn't like to be where he's not wanted. He's wanted, Sunny argues, because nowadays anyone can join the Standard Club—making Joe wonder whether that should make him feel any better.

If he'd said something, she could have explained about the "other kind" business. Having grown up with it doesn't necessarily mean she believes it. She regards Joe and herself as equals. "Spoken like a true Wellesley girl" he rages, "you make me sick!" And he makes her sick, Sunny fights back. It's not all about how Joe felt, it's also about how she felt, having everybody in the club looking for him. She'd never been so embarrassed. Where she comes from, men don't desert girls. Joe apologizes, but very sarcastically.

SUNNY: You think this is funny? Of course you do. How could you know any better?

JOE: Wait a minute. How could I know any better?

SUNNY: No! Wait! I—

JOE: Thank you very much. Yeah. Okay. I get it.

SUNNY: We were brought up differently. That's all I mean.

JOE: I know what you mean. You smell like a rose and I smell like a salami sandwich.

SUNNY: I didn't say that. You're not listening to what I'm trying to—

JOE: I'm listening real good, and you know what I hear? Jew hater talk—clear as a bell! Oh yeah, I been hearing that garbage all my life, but damned if I thought I'd ever hear it coming out of a Jewish girl.

SUNNY: How dare you! Storming into this house in the middle of the night and swearing and yelling and accusing me of all kinds of absurd—

JOE: Right! Whyn't you just call me a kike and get it over with?

SUNNY: I think it is over.

As Joe goes to the door he says something in Yiddish. Sunny doesn't know what he's saying. He translates: "Thanks for nothing."

Joe leaves and Sunny goes upstairs. Adolph comes down and goes into the living room. The doorbell rings: Lala has come home, and Adolph lets her in the front door. She is in a fine state of agitation and calls for her mother. Boo, in a robe, rushes down, followed by Reba. Lala is crying, and Boo hugs her, asking if it was the Wolf girl from Michigan. That wasn't it. It's that Peachy has proposed.

Boo begins to cry also, then asks "Are you sure?" Peachy comes in and informs everybody, "We've been talking about it since Thanksgiving"—not he and Lala, but "Mother and Daddy and me." His daddy approves because they know "what they're gettin' here, all the way back on both sides," and his mother told him he can have Lala if he wants her. In fact, she was going to get Grandma Zacharias's engagement ring out for him to bring, but he thought he'd wait in case "somebody better turned up at Ballyhoo."

"This is the best part," Lala announces: Peachy says he might consider moving here and working at the Dixie Bedding Corporation. Boo is thrilled, and asks Adolph if he isn't. "What do you think?" Adolph replies.

Scene 7

"In the dark we hear a Train Conductor's voice: 'The station is Wilmington. Wilmington Delaware coming up. This station is Wilmington.' *Lights up on the sleeping compartment. It is one week later, January 3. Sunny is on her way back to college. She is reading a book. A knock on the door."* It is Joe. They greet each other with a noncommittal "Hi." He wonders if she's still reading Upton Sinclair. She is. Sunny wishes him a Happy New Year and Joe reciprocates. It seems he's in the area looking at a bed springs factory. Sunny assumes Uncle Adolph told him to check in on her. Joe lets her think so, then admits he lied. The factory is in West Virginia, and he got up at 3:30 A.M. and drove here, not wanting to miss the train. Sunny's glad he didn't.

What Joe said "about Jew hater talk" couldn't be true, Sunny declares, because it would be as if she were hating herself. It's ignorance, she explains, this big hole where the Judaism isn't. But she does know some Yiddish, something that was said at dinner at her suitemate's house in Chestnut Hill: "Shabot Shallim—something like that." Joe informs her that it's not Yiddish, but Hebrew. It's the Friday night blessing.

Sunny apologizes for taking him to Ballyhoo. She ought to have known better and is sorry. Joe's sorry that he acted badly, too. She doesn't blame him. They confess to missing each other, and end up embracing, then kissing. They are both crying.

CONDUCTOR *(offstage):* All aboard! All aboard!

SUNNY: Oh no!

JOE: Don't worry. This is only the beginning.

SUNNY: Of what?

JOE: Who knows, Sunshine? We got the whole future to choose from.

SUNNY: Yes!

JOE: So think of something really good, and we'll just make it happen.

SUNNY: Okay.

JOE: What did you think of?

> *Lights up on the Freitag house. The Christmas tree is gone. The dining room table is set for dinner. Adolph, Boo, Reba, Lala and Peachy are already seated. Sunny and Joe join them. Sunny lights the Sabbath candles.*

SUNNY: Baruch ata Adonai. Eloheinu melech olam, asher kideshanu bemitsovotav, vetsivanue lehadlik neir shel Shabat. Shabat Shalom.

Each in turn repeats "Shabat Shalom." *"The candles shine."* Curtain.

Critics, Lortel Awards

OOO
OOO
OOO
OOO
OOO
OOO **VIOLET**

A Musical in Two Acts

BOOK AND LYRICS BY **BRIAN CRAWLEY**

MUSIC BY **JEANINE TESORI**

BASED ON *THE UGLIEST PILGRIM* BY **DORIS BETTS**

Cast and credits appear on pages 269–270

BRIAN CRAWLEY (book and lyrics) was born in Iowa City on September 1, 1962 and grew up in Cincinnati, where his father was a vice president of Procter & Gamble. After high school he went on to Yale. He was already testing himself as a writer, mostly in the realm of poetry. But after graduation in 1984 he turned toward the stage and studied at the American Conservatory Theater in San Francisco. He credits the influence of Arthur Ballet, educator and onetime director of the Office for Advanced Drama Research, for guidance in his playwriting career, which has taken off this season with major awards for his his first New York production of record, the musical Violet. *It was presented off Broadway by Playwrights Horizons March 11, 1997 for 32 performances and won not only the Lucille Lortel Award for best off-Broadway musical of the year but also the New York Drama Critics Circle Award for best musical in competition with all those big new Broadway shows that flooded into town at the end of the season.*

Experimental New York venues like West Bank Cafe, Alice's Fourth Floor and Home for Contemporary Theater and Arts have seen some of Crawley's other material, and Crawley has appeared in person at a Tribeca club sponsored by the musical magazine Fast Folk. *His immediate future includes two more musicals:* Fire, Earth, Water, Air *with his* Violet *collaborator, Jeanine Tesori, and* Playing at Love *with Jenny Giering. He lives in White Plains with his wife, Kathy, and son, Max.*

JEANINE TESORI (music) is the daughter of a physician. She was born in 1961 in Manhasset, L.I. and educated there at the Paul D. Schreiber High School. Her innate love of music led her to begin writing it at a very early age, but in high school she became preoccupied with sports and abandoned composition for a time. She gravitated back to it at about 16 years of age, however, and when she moved on to college at Barnard she majored in music, doing some conducting from junior year onward and graduating with a B.A. in 1983.

Tesori contributed the dance music for Broadway's The Secret Garden *(1991), the 1995 revival of* How to Succeed in Business Without Really Trying *and this season's* Dream. *On November 3, 1994 the Goodspeed Opera House in East Haddam, Conn. produced the musical* Starcrossed: The Trial of Galileo, *with music by Tesori and book and lyrics by Keith Levenson and Alexa Junge, under Martin Charnin's direction. Her collaborator on her first major New York production,* Violet, *was Brian Crawley, and her off-Broadway producer was Playwrights Horizons, which presented the show March 11, 1997 for a modest run of 32 performances. It was vividly remembered by the prizegivers, however, who awarded it the Drama Critics and Lortel Awards as the best musical of the 1996-97 season.*

Tesori's works have also included the incidental music for Orpheus Descending *at the Alley Theater in Houston and the score for the Emmy Award-winning TV documentary* China; Walls and Bridges. *She conducted the orchestras of* The Secret Garden, *the original Broadway production of* Tommy, A Sondheim Evening *at Louisiana Symphony,* Frida *at Brooklyn Academy of Music and the first European production of* Tommy *in Frankfurt, Germany. She has taken part in numerous recordings. In addition to* Fire, Earth, Water, Air *(another musical with Crawley), in immediate prospect are conducting and arranging the music in* Make Someone Happy *by David Ives and Phyllis Newman and writing a new musical in collaboration with Tina Landau. Tesori is a member of the Dramatists Guild and ASCAP (from which she has received an award in each of the past seven years), is married and lives in Manhattan.*

Time: Early September, 1954

ACT I

Spruce Pine, North Carolina to King's Point, Tennessee

SYNOPSIS: In a small town in the Blue Ridge Mountains, Violet, 25 years old, is checking a bus schedule, while Young Vi—Violet at age 13—is gathering kindling wood *"to the percussive sound of wood being chopped. The two are in separate domains, not watching one another."*

YOUNG VI *(sings):*
>   Mama, why's a man have eyes?
>   If I tell you, don't you tell—
>   So he can try you on for size
>   There's honey in the bushes, Lord
>   And water in the well

VIOLET *(sings):*
>   A battered nose and a pimpled chin—
>   Uneven eyes to take it in. . . . .

YOUNG VI *(sings):*
>   Mama, why's a man have hands?
>   If I tell you, don't you tell—
>   Go ask your beau, he understands
>   There's honey in the bushes, Lord
>   And water in the well

VIOLET *(sings):*
>   I have to start the Preacher on the scar
>   That cuts a rainbow clear across my cheek

YOUNG VI *(sings):*
>   There's honey in the bushes, Lord
>   And water in the . . .

FATHER *(offstage):* Violet, watch out!
>   *Young Vi straightens, her mouth open wide, terrified by something we
>   can't see. Violet stiffens.*

At the bus station a young man asks Violet where she is going, but she pointedly ignores him, and he wanders off. *"Perhaps, when Violet turns, a shaft of sunlight cuts across her face."* It is terribly scarred, as we can tell from the reaction of the play's characters to this disfigurement, but its details are left to the imagination, not materialized in the actress's makeup.

A Bus Driver announces the imminent departure of the bus to Memphis via Nashville. Violet and an Old Lady pick up their luggage and prepare to board. Violet drops a book she is carrying, and the Old Lady—on Violet's "good" side—picks it up, noticing that it is called *The Baltimore Catechism* and that its margins are full of notes. Taking back the book, Violet explains she is not a Catholic and that the book was her mother's.

The Bus Driver is taking tickets on Violet's "bad" side and is visibly startled at the sight of her scar. In the song "Surprised," Violet asserts that he'll be surprised when she comes home next week with a new, healed face. As she takes a seat in the bus, Violet *"exchanges a look with a black soldier, Flick, she has noticed sneaking a drink,"* and the Old Lady sits next to her.

OLD LADY: You going far?

VIOLET: Tulsa, Oklahoma.

OLD LADY: I never been there. I hear the trees give out. *(Sees the scar.)* Oh! My goodness. *(Covers.)* Course my mailman Vincent Finzer was born with a cleft palate, and he couldn't *be* any sweeter.

VIOLET: I wasn't born with this scar. It took an axe blade to split my face in two.

The Old Lady is on the way to visit a son and grandchildren in Nashville and talks about her family (eight children). The bus passengers begin humming, then all of them sing "Left my troubles all behind me/Back there when I climbed on board," followed by individual thoughts about their destinations in "On My Way." Violet's thoughts are of the kind of features she'd like to have in her new face.

As the bus crosses the North Carolina Border, the singing continues, and then all at once Young Vi is seen running down a mountain path where she meets her Father coming the other way. She is clearly upset because the Elam brothers had waited until Father was away from home and then came up to pester her. He comforts her by giving her a quarter to go to the movies. *"She throws her arms around him"* in gratitude and goes on her way.

At Kingsport, Tennessee, the bus pauses at a rest stop, and the passengers get out. To avoid being joined at a table by the Old Lady, Violet takes a seat at the grill beside the black sergeant, Flick, who is shuffling cards. Seated next to him is Monty, a white paratrooper corporal, both soldiers headed to Fort Smith. A Waiter approaches and suggests that Violet might prefer to sit in a booth.

WAITER: You might be more comfortable there. Problem with putting a nigger in uniform is, he comes to think he's just as good as anybody else.
> *Flick stiffens; Monty looks up at the Waiter and waits for Violet's answer.*

VIOLET: You mean him? *(Pause.)* Why, we're traveling together.
> *The Waiter snorts, slaps down a plate in front of Violet, with a toothpick-speared sandwich and chips. Flick turns around in his seat and looks Violet full in the face.*

(Snaps.) Don't think that means anything, mister.
> *Flick shrugs and turns back around.*

I know what that must be like for you people.

MONTY: Last year he coulda been thrown in jail for sitting here. But you know what that's like.

FLICK *(stands up and grabs his duffel):* Come on, Monty. Let's grab a table.

MONTY: Trouble with putting a waiter in an apron is, he starts to think he's cute.
    Monty slugs his beer, then slaps down the empty bottle on the counter, in imitation of the pissy Waiter. He follows Flick to a table in the back.

FLICK: Don't buy any more of his beers. I've got some hootch on the bus.
    Flick begins to deal out the cards . . . . . Violet picks up the top slice of bread, stares at the chicken, pushes a few potato chips around.

VIOLET *(calls over):* By the way. I wouldn't play with him. He's a mechanic. It's a way to cheat on the deal.
    Flick and Monty look at one another, then at her.
One-handed grip; the mechanic's grip. It's the middle finger. He can second-deal and bottom-deal. He can buckle the top card with his thumb and peep.

MONTY: Ain't she sweet.

FLICK: Lady, what is it you want? To play?
    Violet comes over to their table.

VIOLET: I get mad if I'm cheated.

FLICK: And mean when you're mad. *(Laughs.)* I'm Grady Fliggins, and they call me Flick.
    Flick leans over with mock formality to shake her hand. She cuts the deck he offers against a possibly stacked shuffle, pulling out a center third and and restacking the deck three times. Flick grins.

VIOLET: And I'm Violet Karl. Spruce Pine.

MONTY: Monty Harrill. From near to Raleigh. You gon' eat that sandwich?

VIOLET *(pushes it toward him):* Chickens I got at home. Why don't we play straight draw poker.

In Spruce Pine, Father looks over the groceries and money Young Vi has brought home and sees that, as usual, she's been short-changed. She's had only the very beginnings of schooling in arithmetic. Father insists she sit down with him and learn to play poker, using money she had earned herself—after all it was her father's $3.18 she let the grocer take from her. As Father shuffles, his instruction takes the form of a song lyric in "Luck of the Draw": "You got your royal flush, your straight flush, your four-of-a-kind/A full house, a flush, 'n' a straight, 'n' a three-of-a-kind/Two pair, one pair, and no pair at all/But high cards never won a pot, that I can recall."

As the song continues, they play a hand, Father showing Young Vi how to draw to a pair of queens and how to bet, winning 11 cents from her with three of a kind. He wins the next hand too, commenting in song, "Some say things happen by design/ By demand, decree or law/I say most things fall in line/ By the luck of the draw." He has won 36 cents from her, but Young Vi is getting to like the game and insists on dealing the next hand. *"Flick, Monty and Violet have also been playing; now their games overlap,"* and so does their participation in the "Luck of the Draw" lyrics. After drawing only one card, both Violet and Young Vi bet a dime. Called, they

VIOLET—Michael McElroy as Flick and Lauren Ward
as Violet in the Brian Crawley-Jeanine Tesori musical

show their hands. Each has a royal flush, Young Vi asking, "Is that good?", Violet
declaring "By the luck of the draw." They rake in their winnings.

Kingsport to Nashville, Tennessee

The Bus Driver herds the passengers aboard. Violet evaluates her companions'
poker skills: Flick is "so good he doesn't have to cheat," but Monty has several ways
of telegraphing what he's holding. She tells the men she used to play poker with her
father and drink with him, too, after age 15. She explains how she happens to be on
this trip: "It's a pilgrimage. I'm going to see this television Preacher in Tulsa, the
one that heals? And I'm coming home pretty. With this face, I think that counts as
healing. I'll even trade if he says to . . . I'd take somebody's weak eyes or deaf ears."
Flick laughs at this.

VIOLET: I don't know what you think is so funny.
MONTY: We don't think it's funny.
VIOLET: How come you're both laughing at me then.
MONTY: I'm not laughing.
FLICK: Listen. I'll take that face on, and a game leg besides, if your Preacher
makes me a warrant officer.
    Flick winks. Both Monty and Flick start to laugh at the idea.
VIOLET: Don't be ridiculous.
FLICK: Okay. You and me swap faces then. That's my final offer.
VIOLET: But what do I want with colored skin? No offense, but I want people to
think I'm pretty.

But Flick is offended, and he gets up and goes back to the bus bathroom. Well, you said you'd swap it off! What's wrong if I don't want it any more'n you? *(Pause.)* His drink and his cards, and I hurt Flick's feelings. I oughta be the expert in hurt feelings.

Questioned by Monty, Violet reveals that Father is now dead. He left her some money which helped pay for this trip. Monty suggests that Violet would be better off seeing a doctor, as the Preacher may be a fake. But Violet has had enough of doctors—the last one she consulted in Charlotte on her 18th birthday said that she and her father had waited too long, it was too late to help her. But for the Preacher, it's never too late.

MONTY: Don't suppose you got a man back home.
VIOLET: Nope. All on my lonesome.
MONTY: Explains a lot. If you had a man, he wouldn't let you make a trip like this.
VIOLET: How would you know?
MONTY *(sings "Question & Answer"):*
    Someone sure has had some troubles;
    A girl on a mountain alone
    Nothing but her chores to do
    No one near worth talkin' to
    Feeling sorry for herself for being on her own
VIOLET *(sings):*
    You have all of the answers
    To the stupidest questions
    But the truth is never so pat—
    Try and wrap your mind around that . . . . .
MONTY *(sings):*
    You think you know the answers
    But you don't know the questions
    Bet the truth would knock your ass flat—
    Try and wrap your mind around that

    Things get pretty wicked out there
    Tulsa jus' ain't like your farm
    Best be careful now, ya hear?
    Ugly, everywhere you look
    What you ought to cultivate's a healthy dose of fear

Monty suggests that if Violet really believes the Preacher can help her, she should ask him to change her into a man while he's at it. She accepts his kidding good-naturedly until he grabs her catechism. An envelope stuffed with papers falls out, and Monty waves it at Violet, intimating it might be full of love letters. Now angry, Violet demands her property back.

The scene shifts to the attic in the Karls' house, where Young Vi, wearing one of her mother's old hats, is reading the catechism. It was her mother's book, full of notations her mother made that Father feels are unsuitable for a young girl. Violet has been forbidden to read this book until she's 16. When she hears Father tramping up the attic stairs looking for her, she tries—unsuccessfully—to hide it.

> *She shyly produces the book.*

YOUNG VI: It's only a catechism.

FATHER: It's what she wrote inside that worries me.

YOUNG VI: You never told me she was religious.

FATHER: Your mama was so mindful of heaven, she was no earthly good.

YOUNG VI: Is it true she had the choice of any boy in the five counties hereabouts?

FATHER: Is that what she says?

> *He opens the book and flips though its pages.*

YOUNG VI: I s'pose she liked best the boys who had done some traveling.

FATHER: You're the expert.

YOUNG VI: Why don't you like me asking no questions?

FATHER: *Any* questions.

YOUNG VI: *You* don't talk proper.

FATHER: And because I don't, people think I'm stupid. I hate to see you take after me there.

YOUNG VI: I'm nothing like you. Sometimes I wonder if I'm even yours.

FATHER: You're mine, all right. Fulla questions.

> *Offers her his hand.*

I'm feelin' lucky tonight. I got a quarter says you can't win a single hand.

YOUNG VI: You're on.

In the Nashville bus station, the voice of a new Bus Driver annouces the departure in 15 minutes of the bus to Memphis. The soldiers are playing cards. The Old Lady comes over to say goodbye to Violet and invites her to spend the night with her here instead of going on to Memphis. She's worried that the two soldiers might try to take advantage of Violet. "Next week, when I'm pretty, I hope I'll have that problem," Violet tells her, refusing the invitation to stay over. Monty makes a remark the Old Lady resents, and she takes a swipe at him with her purse before exiting.

Violet upbraids Monty for being rude to the Old Lady. Monty then aims his mockery at Flick, who pulls rank ("You better watch your mouth, Corporal"). Flick invites Monty outside to settle the matter, but Violet cools them down. Still retaliating, Flick reveals to Violet that Monty's full name is Montgomery, which Monty earnestly hopes Violet will not now start using.

Violet muses on the change she hopes will take place in her appearance in Tulsa. The soldiers want to know what Violet hopes for. She tells them in "All to Pieces."

VIOLET *(sings):*
> If I had gypsy hair
> And a face to match it
> No traces anywhere
> Of a wayward hatchet
> I could be Cyd Charisse
> Shooting on location
> In some far-off and tiny nation
>
> Oh, with lips like those
> I'd look almost shameless
> Oh, but add the nose.
> Now I'm pure and blameless
> If Cyd Charisse isn't, that's how it goes
> I love 'er all, I love 'er all
> I love 'er ah—ah—all to pieces! . . . . .

Violet continues explaining in song that a touch of Brigitte Bardot's mystery would also be appropriate. She picks up a copy of *Time* with Ursula Andress on the cover. Monty suggests she ask the Preacher for Ursula Andress's legs. Violet reacts angrily, "What's the matter with my legs?" and then continues to list (in song) the parts of Elke Sommers, Judy Garland, Grace Kelly, Rita Hayworth and others that she'd like to include in her new appearance.

> *Monty and Flick, unnoticed by Violet, turn to the sports column in* Time.

VIOLET *(sings):*
> I could shine like a moonbeam
> On the silk of a ball gown
> I could be someone lovely
> Turning heads on her first night in town
> In town
> All I need is someone
> To wonder, who is she
> To ask how to meet me

MONTY: St Louis? Nah.

VIOLET *(sings):*
> To love me all to pieces

MONTY: They're eight games out with thirty to go . . . . .

> *Past and present interleave, as Young Vi runs on singing to herself, gathering split kindling into a pile. From a new vantage point we can see her father chopping wood in time to her song.*

VIOLET: You know what, Monty? Both of you. Drop dead!

YOUNG VI *(sings):*
> There's honey in the bushes, Lord
> And water in the well

Violet shakes her head and leaves the two men to board the bus.
YOUNG VI *(sings):*
Mama, why's a man have hands?
If I tell you, don't you tell—
Go ask your beau, he understands
There's honey in the bushes, Lord,
And water in the . . .
FATHER: Violet, watch out!
Young Vi straightens, her mouth open wide, terrified.

Nashville to Memphis, Tennessee

The scene changes to a chapel, where the TV Evangelist is holding a session in the process of being broadcast.Young Vi is not only part of the congregation but also in a state of hysteria, as the Preacher concentrates his attention on her scar. She pulls herself together and explains that it was done by an axe blade when she was 13, and she's eagerly ready for God's healing touch. After the Preacher puts his hands on her face, Young Vi collapses into the arms of Virgil, an assistant, and the Preacher shouts that now she is healed: "Praise the Lord, for He has *healed* thee of thy scar! Go forth now, go forth and *shout!*" He confronts the TV camera, stretches out his fingers and suggests that his TV audience match their fingers to his on the TV screen and feel the divine power . . .

In the bus, Flick rouses the apparently sleeping Violet with a whisper, wanting to show her the river they're crossing. She sits up and tells him she's been day-dreaming. Flick hopes that some day Violet will come visit the seashore and watch the men work the nets and make chowder afterwards. Violet tells Flick, "I never knew a negro to talk to before; we don't see too many in the mountains," and she is curious about him. He's a "two-rocker sergeant" (he tells her), and he likes the Army because it gives him status and authority. He and Monty may be sent to Vietnam, Flick admits, but he knew the risk he was taking when he joined the Army, and he wonders whether Violet has considered the risk in her own adventure: that the Preacher may be a fraud. Trying to heal herself at home by touching the Preacher's fingers on the TV screen was ineffective in her case, Violet explains.

VIOLET: I told myself this wouldn't be hard. People in Spruce Pine are used to me. I forget what it's like to see me for the first time. It's what I liked about you, the way you looked at me, like you'd seen worse things.
FLICK: So what do you need with this Preacher? You came this far without him.
VIOLET: But what if I can be to the Preacher what Goliath was to David, a need so giant I will drive him into action? So giant that God could be invented on the spot.
FLICK: Violet, let me tell you something. You gotta do what you gotta do, but in the end you do it alone. You choose your road, then you walk it, one step at a time.
(Sings "Let It Sing"):

Raise your foot, now that's the way
You'll be movin' on today
Raise the other, put it down
Now you're headed into town
Whoa boy, you got left, right
Oh, boy ain't that right . . . . .

Two kinds of people in this world,
Some say yes and some say no
Time to say what side you're on;
Eeny meeny miny mo

Say yes, and your adventures start
Not always as expected
Say no, you stay apart,
But you stay protected . . . . .

There's precious little, really, folks like us control—
You can make your music from the simplest thing
And you're the one has got to tend your soul;
You got to give it room and let it, let it sing
You got to give it room and let it sing . . . . .

Memphis

As the bus arrives at Memphis, Monty seems a bit jealous of the intimacy between Violet and Flick. Memphis is the end of the line for this bus, and the bus for Tulsa doesn't leave until the next day. The soldiers invite Violet to join them in an evening of fun, staying overnight at a boarding house Flick knows well. "No thank you. I don't think that would be right," Violet answers. She intends to seek a bed with some Memphis cousins she's never met.

Monty goes off to find Violet a taxi, while Flick stays to help her with her suitcase. A man dressed in a mechanic's uniform approaches, joined by his friend Rufus, who has a knife. They expresses resentment at seeing a black soldier and a white woman together, particularly when the soldier is wearing symbols of rank: "They don't make you jack shit in Tennessee." Violet tries to attack the Mechanic, but is held back by Flick. Monty comes back and joyfully enters the fight that ensues. The Mechanic picks up a crowbar but is disarmed by Flick, who then chases him away. Monty takes Rufus's knife away from him but is doubled over by a punch in the stomach, enabling Rufus to grab Violet's purse and suitcase and run off with them.

The address of Violet's cousin was in the suitcase, along with a dress of her mother's she was going to wear in Tulsa, so now she has to remain under Flick and Monty's wing—a miracle, Monty calls it. Soon the men are watching a black Landlady usher Violet into a room with a bed and the sound of a blues guitar solo coming in through the window. Flick goes down the hall with the Landlady.

MONTY: After tonight, you'll have sump'n real to write in that book of yours. Sump'n to remember.

VIOLET: So many things you can't remember, even by writing them down. Everything that happens gets in the way.

Hearing raised voices out in the hall, Violet and Monty fall silent.

LANDLADY: Whatsamatter, you crazy? Bringing those two here? This ain't New York City. Anyone finds out about that gal, there's gonna be trouble.

FLICK: Almeta, come on. Her suitcase was stolen.

LANDLADY: She could lose five suitcases and have a dozen scars, and she'd still be white. I got a business to consider.

Flick pulls a twenty dollar bill out of his wallet.

All right. Y'all can stay the night, but don't ever bring them back here again. And if you leave the premises? Use the exit on the alley.

VIOLET: Maybe this was a bad idea.

MONTY: Naaah—we'll go get drunker than my old cousin, draw some dirty pictures in your book. You come on down the hall and get drunk enough to drive a tractor, all right?

Monty departs, and Violet takes off her dress, lies down on the bed and falls fast asleep. As she does so, Young Vi and Father appear, Young Vi showing her father that her scar has been miraculously removed, while a Radio Singer accompanies their scene with "Who'll Be the One (If Not Me)." The Old Lady enters, drinking bourbon. Young Vi introduces the Old Lady to her father, and the old folks dance to the Radio Singer's tune: "Who's gonna glove/Your delicate hand/Who's gonna bounce/You on his-a knee/Who's gonna know/The lay 'a the land/Who'll be the one/ If not me."

Father disappears, and Monty appears to dance with the Old Lady and Young Vi. The Old Lady leaves, and then Young Vi leaves, disappointed because Monty won't dance with her again. At this moment, *"Violet jolts awake. Monty is reading her book and doesn't see her. She considers speaking but instead lies down and pretends to be asleep."* Monty leafs over the pages of Violet's book and sorts out his thoughts about her in "You're Different."

MONTE *(sings):*
..... Ever since you
Sat with him 'n'
Me, well Flick ain't the same
You never act like other women
And he acts like he's tame
You're a pain in the ass
You got no kinda class
And a tongue with a nasty aim
But there's something about you ...

You're different, that's what
Good lookin'? You're anything but
Annoying as hell at the start . . .
Course I know that scar must reach to your heart. . . . .

You're different, that's it,
And more than I care to admit—
There's somethin' you got goin' for you
Means that there's no way I can ignore you
You're different, that's all

Flick comes in with a Coke and a flask. Violet pretends to wake up and is handed a spiked drink. She gets dressed, and their night on the town begins as they enter a dance hall where a Music Hall Singer is presenting the song number "Lonely Stranger/Anyone Would Do." The three dance showily, but "*there is little touching involved, as that would spell trouble for Flick.*" When Flick takes time out to fetch drinks, "*Monty takes Violet in his arms for some slower dancing . . . . . Monty's hands start to wander a bit; Violet is surprised but does nothing to stop him. When Flick returns, he sees this, catching Violet's eye, not Monty's. Resigned, Flick sets down the beers and turns to leave the two alone. Violet lets go of Monty and runs to follow Flick.*"

MUSIC HALL SINGER *(sings):*
    Some day . . .
    Lonely stranger
    No stranger to what's in my heart
    Am I in danger
    In danger, lettin' this start
HOTEL SINGER *(sings):*
    How'd I get to be so blue?
    Seems I don't have anyone
    When right now anyone would do

At the hotel, Flick and Violet pause outside the door to her room, Violet making a point of mentioning that it has no lock. When Flick reaches out and touches her scar tenderly, she doesn't flinch, but the Landlady appears, interrupting them. They bid each other good night and part.

Monty returns to the hotel and goes right into Violet's room, bumping into a chair in the dark and waking her up. Her reaction is, "What? Where's Flick?", but when Monty puts his hand in Violet's lap, "*She pulls him down to her, and as they kiss the lights fade.*"

It's the last day of high school, in Spruce Pine, and Billy Dean is following Young Vi home which, he emphasizes, "Means I *like* you, I wanna *get* with you," even though he's only recently been calling her names like "Freak-Face."

Monty and Violet are sitting up, talking in her bed. Monty is half asleep.

MONTY: What do you think, Viii-lut? Black leather pants, jacket—tools stuck all over my body with duct tape—

VIOLET *(derisive):* The secret life of boys.

MONTY: C'mon, Viii-lut. One day I'll come through Spruce Pine flat out, throw you up behind me on my cycle! We'll lean all the way through them mountains. Would you like that? Take you through cricks and ditches . . . You can jes' holler and hang on. *(He yawns.)*

BILLY DEAN: Look, they found out I never done it. They axed me, when you get with a girl, and you hit the bump? Does it go off to the left, or the right? And I didn't know.

YOUNG VI: Billy Dean, why didn't you just answer? You had even odds of getting it right.

He still doesn't get it. She laughs at him.

How much are you getting for this?

BILLY DEAN: C'mon, Violet.

YOUNG VI: *How much.*

BILLY DEAN: Five dollars. We could split it.

YOUNG VI: I don't want the money. I want you to be gentle.

BILLY DEAN *(quick, eager):* I'll be gentle.

YOUNG VI: And Billy Dean, here's a tip—there isn't any bump.

In the hotel bedroom, Monty observes to Violet, "I wasn't the first, was I?" and goes to sleep dreaming of his motorcycle and leaning against Violet in the bed.

VIOLET *(sings "Lay Down Your Head"):*
Lay down your head and sleep, sleep
I'll be your pillow, soft and deep
Leave me your troubles, I will keep
Your days gone by, your days gone by

Lay down your head and dream, dream
You're much gentler than you seem
Is there a chance you might redeem
My days gone by, my days gone by. . . . .

As the Music Hall Singer and two Hotel Singers join in repeating some of "Lonely Stranger" and "Anyone Would Do," *"Flick is back out on the street, zipping up his jacket against the night air, sipping from his flask."* Curtain.

Lauren Ward and Michael Park (as Monty) in a scene from *Violet*

ACT II

Memphis to Fort Smith, Arkansas

The bus pulls into Fort Smith late at night with the passengers drowsy and the Bus Driver singing "Lonely Stranger." The soldiers get off here, while Violet goes on to Tulsa. Monty (whom Violet irritates by calling him "Montgomery") goes to buy Violet candy and soda—as he has been doing at every stop all day. Flick comes over to Violet's seat, writes his address on the back of a gum wrapper and gives it to Violet. In her turn, Violet tears a piece of paper out of her book, intending to write "This is the day which the Lord hath made" on it but changing her mind. She writes something else and hands it over to Flick.

FLICK *(reading):* You wish you'd stayed in the mountains?
VIOLET: Almost. Though I never would've met Monty then.
FLICK *(looks away, rises):* Right. Best of luck to you now.
VIOLET: Or you! Flick, I meant you too. I didn't mean . . .
FLICK: All this candy 'n' shit, 'scuse my French, know why Monty's buying it? Cuz he thinks that's easier'n talking to you. There's a man you can count on.
VIOLET: What do you know about it?
FLICK: I know a plain girl when I see one, with dreams don't make no sense.
VIOLET: Maybe not to you.
FLICK: Don't you get it? You're just a piece of ass to him. And an easy on that.

VIOLET: What gives you the right to be jealous?

FLICK: What makes you think I am?

VIOLET: You heard me say I left the door unlocked.

FLICK: Last I heard, it *couldn't* lock.

VIOLET: What did you expect, an invitation?

FLICK: Forget it. I don't go for sloppy seconds anyhow.

VIOLET: Sure seemed like you were ready to go last night.

FLICK *(sings "Hard to Say Goodbye")*:
Don't worry
Don't sweat it
Go do somethin' wrong, then move along
Cuz it won't weigh on your mind
If you don't let it
It isn't hard to say

I'm so sorry
I meant better
Hell, it's nothin' new you put me through
Take your time now to spell out just why
In your first letter
It isn't hard to say goodbye . . . . .

VIOLET *(sings)*:
You know what really bothers you?
Monty had the nerve to do
What you were only
Dreaming of
Monty's just a boy, Flick, I know that
But I don't regret it
I'll remember forever
I did something fine

FLICK *(sings)*:
Monty's not the point
Isn't now, never was
But you can't ever get enough
Of a thing you don't need
What your mind doesn't heed
Your heart does

Two kinds of people in this world
Some say yes and some say no . . . . .

If I was smart I'd go back home
But I don't give a damn
And I'll tell you why
I'm miles and miles from who I am
So for once I'm not afraid or shy
Goodbye

I'm gonna miss you Flick, a lot
I wish you felt the same as I
Goodbye

Violet disappears to the bus bathroom, as Monty comes back with his gifts. "Set her down gentle," Flick warns Monty, emphasizing that Violet is only a passing fancy for Monty. Monty doesn't disagree and disgusts Flick by reminding himself selfishly, "Least I won't be with her when it hits." Monty apologizes and admits there are times when he could promise Violet anything. He asks for Flick's help in parting from her. The two soldiers begin the song number "Promise Me, Violet" by assuring each other they have each other's phone number and will keep in touch. Violet joins them in the song, telling Monty, "You got my number so call me/Expect to hear from me soon/Some night you're drunk and you're lonely/Under the spell of the moon." The soldiers begin to depart, but Monty returns and continues the song, appealing to Violet to come to this bus station on her return trip Sunday, any time of the day, he'll be waiting for her.

MONTY *(sings):*
  Promise me, Viii-lut
  Why won't you face me
  All I want is you
  You're not some beauty
  That don't concern me

  I'll be here for you
  I'll be waiting
  By the roadside
  Make my lonesome dream come
    true
FLICK *(sings):*
  I've been waiting, for a lifetime
  For someone simply
  To look and see me
  The way that I see you

FLICK *(sings):*
  Should I speak up—
  Or let her go—
  Am I just caught up in a dream—

Violet informs Monty decisively (still in the song) that she's not coming back on this route. Monty offers to buy her ticket back here, but she declines. She is certain that Monty is only trying to extend a one-night stand into a two-nighter. He argues that he's the best thing that ever happened to her, but Violet is onto him: "Too bad you open your mouth, boy/You look too good to be true." Monty swears he'll be here on Sunday, as the Passengers join in the song.

Tulsa, Oklahoma—Hope and Glory Building

The Passengers take over the singing, as the scene changes to the Preacher's chapel in Tulsa—"*half stage set, half Art Nouveau temple (a relic of Tulsa's oil boom style)*." The Passengers become a choir with the rhythmic, hand-clapping number

"Raise Me Up." The Preacher joins them in invoking divine power to raise them up and let them fly like angels.

The Preacher addresses his congregation on the subject of healing. A woman who could not walk is now dancing, and soon, "Every cane will be broken, I believe every wheelchair will be abandoned, I believe every stretcher will be overturned!"

The Preacher directs the choir to resume singing, and he harangues the congregation, shouting "Glory!" and raising his hands—a cue for a spotlight to be concentrated on him. But the lighting cue is missed, and the Preacher mistakes Violet for the errant lightboard operator and tries to fire her. When she makes him understand she is not an employee but one of those who have come to be healed, the Preacher explains that tomorrow night is healing night—the night of his TV show—and puts her in his assistant Virgil's hands.

In Spruce Pine, Father is helping an obviously injured Young Vi—a quilt pressed to her cheek—down the mountain in search of help, singing "God Almighty, show your mercy/God Almighty, please forgive" in the song number "Down the Mountain." He picks up Young Vi to carry her across a stream. At the same time, Violet shows Virgil her envelope full of slips of paper, explaining that these are "The Bible verses which must speak for me." Virgil gives her no encouragement, so she walks out on him.

In Spruce Pine, Father is glad to see a light on in the doctor's house. He prepares to kick the doctor's door open, while Violet, in Tulsa, flings open the door to the chapel, approaches the altar (not knowing that the Preacher is watching her from one of the back pews, where he has been praying) and reprises "Raise Me Up" as she makes an offering to the Lord of her scraps of paper with their Bible quotations.

When Violet quotes one of them aloud—" 'The crooked shall be made straight': Isaiah"—the Preacher startles her by responding, "He was talking about a valley, not a scar." Violet begs for his help, quoting some of her other Biblical gems. He claims to be exhausted and asks her to come back some other time.

VIOLET: I can't, not tonight. I came from North Carolina on a Greyhound Bus!

PREACHER: What do people think, I'm a healing jukebox? Drop a quarter in and watch me go? Come to the service tomorrow, sister, like ever-body else.

VIOLET: Well which is it, a service, or a *show*. Call it an act and you could take it to Vegas.

PREACHER: Let me tell you something, Miss Hoity-Toity. I started out preaching from the back of a flat-bed truck. I faced the doubtful. I faced the Klan. Sister, I was on *fire* for the Lord. I could feel his power *burning* in my fingers. And most everybody who came got their miracle.

VIOLET: Why can't I have one too? . . . . .

PREACHER: Truth is, sister, the fire's gone out. Been out for some time.

VIOLET: You dirty thief! You have stolen years of my life!

PREACHER: Once I had ever-thing scripted, the Almighty started missing his cues. Even if I wanted to heal you, I couldn't. Sometimes, what with the service and all the trimmings, people get so excited they heal themselves. Maybe Vegas isn't such a bad idea.

The Preacher insists Violet doesn't really need healing—after all, her wound healed long ago. She prevents him from leaving and orders him "Look at Me" in song.

VIOLET *(sings):*
　　Look at me
　　No one will look at me
　　No one will dare to spend
　　The time it takes to
　　Look at me—
　　To really look at me
　　What did I do to make
　　You angry at me
　　My God
　　This is so hard

　　Look at me
　　Look at me
　　Can you imagine
　　What it's like when people
　　Look at me . . . . .

The Preacher has disappeared, but Violet continues to address God, beating her book against a pew until it comes apart and she can throw the pieces up in the air. She prays in song to be blessed with something, anything that will relieve her shame.

Violet's father has taken the place of the Preacher. Young Vi enters and joins him. They talk to each other, as Violet continues her song.

FATHER:
I'm not the one who up and decides one
day the woodshed is the place to play.

VIOLET *(sings):*

YOUNG VI:
I'm not the one who doesn't check to see
his blade is loose!

Don't shudder
Look elsewhere
Act distant,
Embarrassed

FATHER:
It wasn't loose! The shim came out, damn
it. A man can't be expected to check the shim
every time he uses his axe.

You better
Be careful
Cuz I won't
Accept this
Not this time
I'm almost there

YOUNG VI:
I bet you check it now.

VIOLET *(sings):*
> God, I just want you to apologize

Father is willing to admit to Violet that the accident was all his fault, and he would make any amends, but this doesn't help to get back the twelve years of Violet's painful exposure to jeering boys and pitying grownups. Father pleads that he too has been viciously mocked with doggerel that has been going the gossip rounds: "Father Karl was chopping wood—chopped his daughter pretty good. Don't let Father Karl see *you*—he might chop your face in two."

Furthermore, Violet insists, Father carelessly took her to an incompetent doctor who sewed her up "like a pair of old shoes," and then Father waited for years until it was too late to repair the damage to her face. Violet speculates that Father may have done this on purpose, so that no boy would take her away and she would have to remain at home with him. This makes Father so angry that he has to control himself to prevent hitting her. He sings "That's What I Could Do," reminding her that he did what he could to raise and take care of her.

> *He places both hands gently on her cheeks, across her scar, then removes them.*

FATHER *(sings):*
> Forgive me
> You're my only star
> Look how bright,
> Look how strong,
> Look how beautiful you are
>
> I raised you stronger, child, than me
> Which you'll always be
> That's what I could do . . . . .

Father steps back and admires Violet. She asks excitedly, "Do I have a miracle?" She raises her hand to her face but decides not to touch it, instead asking her father how she looks.

> *There is a great whirring sound, and all the Bible quotes on the altar are borne mysteriously into the air, then scattered. When they have settled, the Father has disappeared.*

VIOLET *(sings):*
> Lucky my miracle turned out so gentle
> Maybe the best ones appear accidental
> I don't dare to check it in the mirror
> Give him time, to get the features clearer
> But by the soldier's base

Wait and see
When I show my brand-new face . . . . .

Tulsa to Fort Smith, Arkansas

Violet is returning on a bus whose passengers include a Creepy Guy who is handing out religious pamphlets, another Old Lady, a former midway barker named Earl and a multiple divorcee named Mabel. Their conversation consists mostly of minor quarrels, and they do not comment on Violet's looks one way or the other.

Violet wonders aloud whether Monty will meet her and whether he'll recognize her. She decides that if he shows by his reaction that her face is still scarred, she'll tell the Driver not to let him on the bus.

The Driver announces that they're approaching Fort Smith. The Old Lady takes out a compact to freshen her makeup and offers it to Violet, who turns away, explaining, "It's your mirror I'm avoiding. I don't want to jinx my miracle. You see, before I went to Tulsa, my entire cheek was covered by a great big scar. Clear across my nose." The Old Lady observes, "I'm not sure what to make of that, dear," and Violet goes on, "I know it's hard to believe, seeing me now. But when I step off the bus, my healing will be complete." She can't see either of the soldiers through the bus window, but she joins the Driver and other Passengers in getting off.

> *Monty, in the dress uniform of the Green Berets, spots Violet. One of the glass panels of the station walls is a door, and it opens to reveal Flick.*
> MONTY: Viii-lut, there you are . . . I wasn't sure which bus you'd be on.
> VIOLET: Monty? *(Excited.)* It was all I could do not to sneak a look before I got here. Well? What do you think?
> MONTY: I tried to tell you what would happen, But you didn't wanna hear it.
> VIOLET: Oh!
> *Her hand flies to her cheek. She takes off running. The sun makes a funhouse mirror of the glass door Flick holds open, and in it Violet sees her own image reflected . . . . . She stares at herself, too stunned to speak. When the glass door closes, the spell is broken.*

Violet begs both the soldiers to go away, but Monty invites her to come to San Francisco with him—he's on his way to Vietnam. Violet has a twinge of alarm that Flick too may be on his way to war, but Flick reassures her, "Not me." Monty shows Violet a toy ring he's brought as an indication of his intention to buy her a real one in California. When Monty sees that Violet isn't going to accept his offer, he tells her he's going to miss her and goes on his way, admonished by Violet, "You be careful." As Monty moves away, Young Vi appears.

> FLICK: Vi-oh-LETTE—maybe you still feel a hundred miles from who you are.
> VIOLET: I've got to get back on the bus.

YOUNG VI *(sings):*
   Don't pull back—
   FLICK: YOUNG VI *(sings):*
But I know who you are. And I know   Don't shudder
where you belong.   Look elsewhere
   VIOLET:
All alone on the side of some goddamn   Give me the wings
mountain.   Of an angel
   FLICK:
No, Vi-oh-LETTE, you belong with me.   I'm almost there

Violet pulls away when Flick tries to approach her. In a reprise of "Promise Me, Violet," he assures her that she has indeed been transformed by this experience, as he too has changed, so that now, "Sweet Jesus, look at me/I can't begin to find/The words to tell you/How I love you."

   FLICK *(sings):*
All I want is you   VIOLET *(sings):*
I've been waiting—   I've been waiting—
Scared to lose you—   Afraid to lose—
Scared my plan would fall through—   How do I know you'll never leave?
I've been waiting, for a lifetime   But maybe you're the one I'm waiting for
For someone simply   The first one to simply
To look and see me   . . . See me
   VIOLET *(sings):*
   The way that I see you
         Violet turns away from Flick in confusion.
   YOUNG VI *(sings):*
   Mama, why's a man have eyes?
   If I tell you, don't you tell
   VIOLET: Flick. What do you see when you look at me?
   YOUNG VI *(sings):*
   Mama, why's a man have hands?
   If I tell you, don't you tell—
         Flick reaches out to caress and kiss Violet's face.
   Go ask your beau, he understands
   There's honey in the bushes, Lord
   And water in the well
   FLICK *(sings "Bring Me to Light"):*
   If I ask you to be with me by and by
   Will you meet me tonight, love
   If it's too dark to see with the naked eye
   Will you bring me to light
   FLICK and VIOLET *(sing):*
   If I happen to stagger and fall behind

Will you help me to fight, love
Will you help me to walk, will you ease my mind

"Will you bring me to light?" echo all the other characters—including Monty—
as they join the chorus one by one, finally asking in song, "If I tell you my heart has
been opened wide/If I tell you I'm frightened/If I show you the darkness/I hold
inside/Will you bring me to light?"

    Curtain.

Tony Award

○○○
○○○
○○○
○○○
○○○
○○○ **TITANIC**

A Musical in Two Acts

STORY AND BOOK BY **PETER STONE**

MUSIC AND LYRICS BY **MAURY YESTON**

Cast and credits appear on pages 240–242

PETER STONE (story and book) was born February 27, 1930 in Los Angeles, the son of the late movie producer and writer John Stone. He took his B.A. degree at Bard (which also granted him a D.Litt. in 1951) and his M.F.A. at Yale Drama School in 1953. He began his writing career in France, where he contributed to all media. His musical theater credits begin with Friend of the Family *(1958), but his first work for Broadway was the book for a musical version of Jean-Paul Sartre's* Kean *in 1961. There followed the books of* Skyscraper *(1965),* 1776 *(a Best Play of 1968–69 and winner of the Critics and Tony Awards for best musical),* Two by Two *(1970),* Sugar *(1972),* Woman of the Year *(1981, Tony for best book),* My One and Only *(a Best Play of 1982–83),* Grand Hotel *(a Best Play of 1989–90, for which Stone was widely credited with an assist on the Luther Davis book of the musical for which Maury Yeston contributed additional music and lyrics) and* The Will Rogers Follies *(1991, Critics and Tony Awards for best musical). Now there is* Titanic, *which opened on Broadway April 23 and sailed on into the summer after embellishing Stone's distinguished record further with the 1997 Tony Awards for best musical and best book.*

157

Stone is also credited with one straight Broadway play, an adaptation of Erich Maria Remarque's Full Circle *(1973), and contribution to an off-Broadway program of sketches,* Straws in the Wind, *at American Place in 1975. He may be the only person ever to win a dramatist's Grand Slam: a Tony, an Oscar (for best original 1964 screen play,* Father Goose*) and an Emmy (for an episode of CBS's* The Defenders *in 1963). He has also won an Edgar (Mystery Writers of America Award) for his screen play* Charade, *a Christopher Award for his movie adaptation of his own* 1776 *and various other accolades for his stage musicals, his movies (which include* The Taking of Pelham 1-2-3, Mirage, Arabesque, Sweet Charity, Skin Game, Who's Killing the Great Chefs of Europe? *and* Just Cause*) and his many TV scripts.*

Stone's contribution to the contemporary theater has included leadership of his profession as president of the Dramatists Guild, the national society of playwrights, composers and lyricists, since 1981. He is married and lives in New York City.

MAURY YESTON (music and lyrics) was born October 23, 1945 in Jersey City, N.J. He received his B.A. at Yale in 1967 and his M.A. at Clare College, Cambridge, England in 1972. In 1974 he received his Ph.D. at Yale and joined its music faculty as Associate Professor of Music Theory. From 1976 to 1982 Yeston served as Yale's Director of Undergraduate Studies in Music and then moved on to the BMI Music Theater Workshop and a theater career as a composer and lyricist.

It was as a Yale undergraduate that Yeston started writing music, contributing to college shows and composing Movement for Cellos and Orchestra *which was given its premiere performance by the Norwalk Symphony Orchestra with Yo Yo Ma as guest artist. He had written a children's musical based on* Alice in Wonderland *and produced at the Long Wharf Theater in New Haven in 1970, but his first credit in the New York theater was the incidental music for the Best Play* Cloud 9 *off Broadway in 1981. He had begun writing songs for a musical in 1973 in Lehman Engel's BMI Workshop, and they later were included in his music and lyrics for the Broadway musical and Best Play* Nine *which opened May 9, 1982, ran for 739 performances and won Yeston the Tony and Drama Desk Awards for the best score of a musical. He was previously associated with Peter Stone in another Best Play, contributing additional music and lyrics to the Robert Wright–George Forrest score of* Grand Hotel: The Musical *which opened on Broadway November 12, 1989 and ran for 1,077 performances. This season's* Titanic *won him the personal accolade of the Tony for best score (for which Jonathan Tunick also won the Tony for best orchestration).*

Yeston's many other activities have included the score for the musical Phantom, *with book by Arthur Kopit, produced in regional theater; the authorship of two text-books,* The Stratification of Musical Rhythm *(1975) and* Readings in Schenker Analysis *(1977); the score for the movie* Ripe Strawberries; *the albums* Goya: A Life in Song *and* December Songs; *and a musical in Japanese,* Nukata No Okime, *produced in Tokyo. He has received two BMI Awards, in 1982 and 1989. He now presides over the BMI Workshop and teaches at Yale occasionally. He is married, with two sons, and lives in Woodbridge, Conn.*

Time: Between April 10 and 15, 1912

PROLOGUE

Harland & Wolff, Shipbuilders

SYNOPSIS: Thomas Andrews, ship designer, enters in front of the show curtain, which depicts an architect's drawing of the great steamship Titanic. He carries a rolled-up set of blueprints and sings "In Every Age."

ANDREWS *(sings):*

    In every age mankind attempts
    To fabricate great works
    At once magnificent
    And impossible . . .

    On desert sands, from mountains of stone
    A pyramid!
    From flying buttresses alone
    A wall of light!
    A chapel ceiling
    Screaming one man's ecstasy!
    One man's ecstasy . . . . .

In song, Andrews cites other miracles like Stonehenge and the Parthenon. He looks over a model of Titanic and describes it.

ANDREWS *(sings):*

    A floating city!
    Floating city!
    A human metropolis . . .
    A complete civilization!
    Sleek!
    And fast!
    At once a poem
    And the perfection
    Of physical engineering . . . . . *(Exits.)*

ACT I

Scene 1: Southampton: The "Ocean Dock"

It is 6 a.m. on Wedesday, April 10, and a long "White Star Line" gangway reaches upward to the offstage floating colossus commanding the awed attention of human beings dwarfed in comparison to the looming ship they are coming here to board. First on the scene are members of the crew: a stoker, Frederick Barrett, 24, a radioman, Harold Bride, 24, and a lookout, Frederick Fleet, 25, saying goodbye to their girl friends. Barrett sings "How Did They Build Titanic?" and answers his own question, "Near a thousand feet in length/Huge beyond past endeavor/Strong beyond mortal strength/Forty-six thousand tons of steel/Eleven stories high."

The three men stare at Titanic in wonder and are joined by other crewmen as they sing "There She Is": "Tow'ring high/Broad and grand/Ship of dreams."

At 8 a.m. Capt. Edward J. Smith, *"a grey-bearded officer who, though speaking with a quiet voice, radiates authority and confidence,"* arrives on the scene and greets the other arriving officers. A stevedore and others recite the ship's Loading Inventory, which includes 7,000 heads of fresh lettuce and 36,000 oranges. There are more and more arrivals of crew members and more recitation of inventory ("122,000 pounds of meat, poultry and fish . . . . . 55,000 china dishes"), and at 10 a.m J. Bruce Ismay, *"late 40s, chairman of the White Star Line, fastidiously dressed, with dark hair and a full mustache,"* and Andrews join the Captain on the gangway. In song, they express their pride in Titanic as "The largest moving object in the world!"

Capt. Smith orders 3rd Officer Herbert J. Pitman to begin boarding 3rd Class passengers, among them "the three Kates"—*"young Irish girls"*—and Jim Farrell, *"a handsome Irishman."*

KATE MURPHEY: Holy Mother of God! Is that a ship or a mountain?

KATE McGOWAN: It looks long enough so a body could *walk* to America! I'm Katherine McGowan, but everybody calls me Kate.

KATE MULLINS: I'm Kate, too. Kate Mullins.

KATE MURPHEY: And I'm Kate three! Kate Murphey—

They squeal and hug one another.

KATE MULLINS: It must be fate, then!

KATE McGOWAN: It's not fate. It's Irish.

KATE MULLINS: You travellin' alone?

KATE McGOWAN: Not me. I've got a feller. See that good-lookin' one up ahead? *(She indicates Jim Farrell.)* I'm plannin' to marry him.

KATE MURPHEY: When's that gonna be?

KATE McGOWAN: Soon as I meet him.

And "Get me aboard," sings Kate McGowan, introducing the song "I Must Get on That Ship." She is joined by the other Kates, 3rd Class passengers and then the 2nd Class passengers—*"professionals, shopkeepers, etc."*— being herded aboard by Pitman. This group includes Edgar and Alice Beane, *"middle-aged Americans with middle-west accents"* and Charles Clarke with Caroline Neville, *"young, British, he's middle-class, she's an aristocrat."* "I Must Get on That Ship," sing the 2nd Class passengers.

TITANIC—David Garrison as J. Bruce Ismay, Michael Cerveris as Thomas Andrews and John Cunningham as Capt. E.J. Smith singing pridefully about "The largest moving object in the world" in a scene from the musical with story and book by Peter Stone and music and lyrics by Maury Yeston

ALICE BEANE *(sings):*
    The finest people will attend
    The best among them we'll befriend
    They'll stand right next to us
    Be at my fingertip . . .
ALL *(sing):*
    Great heads of state and millionaires
    Who run the world's affairs
    Will all be there
    I must get on that ship!

    For the maiden voyage!
    For the maiden voyage!
    Get us all aboard!

Now it is the turn of the lst Class passengers to board and be directed to their luxurious accommodations by Pitman and the senior lst Class steward, Henry Etches, 50. Alice Beane watches their stately entrance with great interest, recognizing and identifiying them one by one in "The lst Class Roster"—the Astors, the Wideners, Benjamin Guggenheim, the Thayers. Alice gossips to her husband Edgar about each of them as they enter.

The Strauses—Isidor and Ida, both in their late 60s—are next to enter.

PITMAN: Mr. and Mrs. Isidor Straus may proceed to Parlour Suite B-55—

ALICE BEANE *(sings):*

Aren't they modest?
You'd never think by looking at them
That he and his brother own Macy's Department Store
Own Macy's Department Store
Outright!
And he was a close advisor
To President Grover Cleveland
And served in the House of Representatives
Two full terms!
And that's his wife of forty years, named Ida
Sad! She hasn't been well
So the two of them have been wintering
On the French Riviera
French Riviera . . .

A blast from the ship's horn and Pitman's cry of "All ashore who are going ashore!" signal Titanic's departure. Capt. Smith gives orders to cast off the lines, as the gangway is lowered.

Scene 2: Aboard R.M.S. Titanic

At noon, all are assembled at the Poop Deck on the stern. The voices of the company join the celebratory sound of Titanic's horn and the higher-pitched whistles of the tugboats, singing "Godspeed Titanic": "Sail on, sail on/Great ship Titanic!/ Cross the open sea/Pray the journey's sound/Till your port be found/Fortune's winds/Sing Godspeed to thee . . . . . "

Scene 3: The Dock

An American, Frank Carlson, carrying two large valises, runs on and sees that the great ship has left without him. He has told everyone back in Poughkeepsie that he's coming home on the maiden voyage of Titanic and will be very much embarrassed to have been left behind: "If that isn't the story of my entire goddam life—"

Scene 4: The bridge & Boiler Room #6

At 5 p.m., Capt. Smith is on the bridge, accompanied by Officers Murdoch, Lightoller and Boxhall. Quartermaster Hitchens is at the helm. The Captain gives orders for the ship to proceed at 19 knots. Murdoch goes to the telephone and orders the boiler rooms, "Maintain 68 revolutions of the wing propellors."

Ismay comes onto the bridge, followed by Steward Etches bringing champagne and glasses. The Captain informs them he permits no alcohol on his bridge, and

Ismay's reaction is, "Technically speaking, E.J., it could be considered *my* bridge." But the steward, opening the bottle, tactfully pretends that it's flat and takes it away, apologizing to the Captain.

ISMAY: . . . . . With or without champagne, I want to toast our ship: The Royal Mail Steamer Titanic—nearly a quarter of a mile in length, she's bigger, grander and safer than any ship in history, the greatest achievement in transatlantic navigation since that very first crossing four hundred and twenty years ago.

Andrews enters with his set of plans in hand, as always.

Ah, Andrews, there you are! Just in time. I was just congratulating the three of us on our magnificent contribution to the twentieth century. *(Raising his empty glass.) Progress*, gentlemen! I give you *progress*.

CAPT. SMITH: I trust you'll excuse us, Mr. Ismay. We have our duties—

ISMAY: Tell me, E.J.—what's our present speed?

CAPT. SMITH: Nineteen knots, Mr. Ismay.

ISMAY: Really, I would have expected us to be going faster, now that we've cleared land. Tell me, Andrews—I understand that twenty-two knots would be necessary in order to make a six-day crossing. In your expert opinion, is Titanic capable of that speed? *(As Andrews glances at Smith.)* Come, come, Andrews, you're the one who built the thing—*are* we capable of twenty-two knots?

ANDREWS: Capable. Yes, sir, I'm sure we are. Possibly a bit more if pushed— twenty-three perhaps—but—

ISMAY: *Excellent*, sir! I'm very pleased to hear it!

ANDREWS: *But*—for a maiden voyage it is customary to proceed prudently.

ISMAY: It's the maiden voyage that creates *news*, dammit! And I intend for this one to create a *legend*! So answer me straight, Andrews—when can we expect to run at full speed?

ANDREWS: When the Captain orders it, sir.

ISMAY: Then we must persuade him to do so, mustn't we?

CAPT. SMITH *(a beat):* In point of fact, Mr. Ismay, I was about to give the order when you walked in. Mr Murdoch—increase speed to twenty knots.

MURDOCH: Twenty knots, aye, aye, sir. *(He picks up the telephone.)* Increase steam, Mr. Bell—give us seventy-one revolutions.

ISMAY: Twenty knots. Well, it's a start, I suppose. Carry on, gentlemen— *(He turns and goes.)*

CAPT. SMITH: Watch your compass, Mr. Hitchens—you're drifting off course.

HITCHENS: I don't think so, sir—

CAPT. SMITH: Don't argue with me, man! If I say you're off course then you're bloody well off course!

Down in Boiler Room #6 on the Orlop Deck, the stokers (including Frederick Barrett) and Chief Engineeer Joseph Bell have received their orders from the bridge. Barrett expresses his opinion that it's too soon to increase Titanic's speed that much. Andrews, who is down there inspecting the machinery, has no comment.

Bell reminds Barrett that it's Captain's orders. Barrett goes on to sing about coal from the mine where "The dust of coal in the air is black/And a trickle of sweat runs down your back" to the boiler where "Coal it is that makes the steam/That runs the machines that run the world" in "Barrett's Song," as the stokers begin shoveling and Andrews exits.

Up on the bridge, Capt. Smith is seen entertaining a lady passenger, Mme. Aubert. Barrett reminds himself of life in the coal mines of Leicestershire and Nottingham, and the dream that "If you got above the ground/You'd save your soul/Some way"—escape as far from the mine pit as possible by going to sea.

BARRETT *(sings):*
But, born to the coal, there's no place for you
Elsewhere
You trade a life of dank and gloom
To shovel in the boiler room
But now you're seven decks below
A lady's dainty feet . . .

And nothing has changed
There's nothing a miner can do
The pit and your mates
Turned into the hold and the crew
And the screws are turning at seventy-two . . .

Faster and faster we watch as we gain evermore
Seventy-three, and too soon it is seventy-four . . .

For a record speed I believe we strive!
For the maiden trip, that's too hard to drive
If you push her faster than seventy five!

That is the truth
I swear!

Scene 5: The Saloon ("D)" Deck

From a 2nd Class promenade on "D" Deck, Alice Beane and her husband Edgar are walking past a line of portholes. Peering through one of them, Alice is getting a view of the lst Class Dining Saloon and its inhabitants. She wishes she could "rub elbows" with such people and believes they'd be impressed with her husband's extensive knowledge of the hardware business. But Edgar is sure that 2nd Class passengers like themselves won't be allowed anywhere near the lst Class facilities and passengers. Alice is determined that she'll manage it somehow.

The Beanes stroll off, and Charles Clarke and Caroline Neville come on. She also looks through the porthole at all the rich Americans, "Jabbering about all those things my father lives for: international banking, venture capital, cornering the market." Charles doesn't know, all his father ever had was "a market on the corner."

CAROLINE: Oh, Charles, I love it when you become sarcastic. It makes me feel like we're a real married couple.

CHARLES: You know perfectly well we'd have separate cabins if I could have afforded them.

CAROLINE: But separate cabins would have meant separate beds.

CHARLES: Yes, well, we had to make do with what we had, didn't we? *(They start off.)* You don't suppose we'll burn in hell for it, do you?

CAROLINE: Stop worrying, darling—in America it's not a sin at all.

CHARLES: What isn't?

CAROLINE: Saving money.

They laugh, and he kisses her lightly as they go.

They are replaced by two of the 1st Class stewards, Etches and Andrew Latimer, Etches coaching his companion (in song) about the care and feeding of the millionaires gathering for dinner. Etches knows exactly how to cater to each one of them, because he's served them all before on other ships of this line: "Mr. Astor takes his toast dry/Mrs. Straus likes the grouse/With the sauce on the side/And the Wideners love kidney pie/Bring it hot, if it's not/They'll be fit to be tied," and so forth. He is proud (Etches finishes) to serve these demanding passengers "With our especial form of care."

Scene 6: The 1st Class Dining Saloon

On the other side of the porthole, 1st Class passengers are summoned by a page striking a triangle for dinner in the area of the Captain's Table, with two smaller tables near it: John Jacob and Madeleine Astor, Benjamin Guggenheim and Mme. Aubert, John and Marion Thayer, George and Eleanor Widener, Ida and Isidor Straus and Mrs. Charlotte Drake Cardoza, together with a retired British major decked out in all his many medals, Ismay and others. The waiting staff serves them champagne, as they sing "What a Remarkable Age This Is!".

1ST CLASS PASSENGERS *(sing):*
    We're sailing aboard the greatest ship
    That ever sailed the seas
    The hull and keel imperviously
    Stronger by degrees!
THEIR WIVES *(sing):*
    Magnificent crystal chandeliers
    Parquet in all the floors

ETCHES *(sings):*
    The ceiling is Jacobean
    A decor their world adores . . . . .
ALL *(sing):*
    If it could be put in a phrase . . . it's
    "What a remarkable age this is!"
MEN *(sing):*
    A fellow's invented see-through film
    He calls it "Cellophane!"
ALL *(sing):*
    Another has built a parachute
    For jumping out of an airplane!

    Remarkable things flow endlessly
    From out the human brain!
    Indeed
    And what a remarkable age this is! . . . . .
ETCHES *(addressing his staff, sings):*
    Keep the Captain's table pristine
    Here we seat the elite whom we happily serve
    Here they dine on fine French cuisine
    It's the creme de la creme's
    Exclusive preserve!

    Giving deference to their preferences is *our* chief art
    We play a part
    In a perfectly working machine

    You should ever be aware
    This is a privilege great and rare
    A special burden that we bear
    In our respective lives!

As Capt. Smith enters, a bellboy annouces the dinner for Thursday, April 11. Bandmaster Wallace Hartley's three-piece string ensemble begins playing. Capt. Smith sits at one end of the Captain's Table and Ismay at the other, with the Astors, Thayers, Wideners, Guggenheim and friend and the Major.

MAJOR: Never forgot my last tour in India during the Tirah campaign of ninety-seven, to reopen the Khyber Pass when we were ambushed by eight thousand crazed, godless savages who attacked without . . .

ISMAY *(interrupting):* E.J.! Have you ever had so many distinguished Americans in your charge at one time? You know most of them, I'm sure. And, of course, everyone knows the Major—

CAPT. SMITH: Of course. Welcome aboard. Mr. Guggenheim, you're becoming quite a regular on the Atlantic run.

BENJ. GUGGENHEIM: In point of fact, this is my thirty-fourth crossing.

ISMAY: E.J.! You haven't told us how many miles we covered yesterday.

CAPT. SMITH: Four hundred eighty-four, Mr. Ismay.

ISMAY: Are you pleased with that?

CAPT. SMITH: Yes, sir, I am. It's better than I expected for the first day.

ISMAY: In that case, I'm sure we'll do even better *today.*

> *1st Officer Murdoch has entered and now approaches Capt. Smith. The music stops.*

MURDOCH: Begging your pardon, Captain—Mr. Hitchens has requested his course.

CAPT. SMITH: Tell Mr Hitchens to set course at west northwest, two-nine-two degrees.

MURDOCH: That's the northern track, sir.

CAPT. SMITH: I'm well aware of that, Mr. Murdoch. *(With a glance at Ismay.)* It will save us both coal and time. At least three hours.

ISMAY: Three hours! Oh, well done, E.J.!

The triangle is sounded again, announcing dinner for Friday, April 12, and the music resumes. An anecdote of the Major's is again interrupted by Ismay's question about mileage, which for this period was 519. This time it's Radioman Bride who enters the illustrious precincts of the 1st Class Dining Saloon and approaches the Captain with a message from the Furness Liner Rappahannock, reporting an iceberg . . . but before Bride can read any more of this message aloud, Capt. Smith takes the paper from him.

A bellboy announces the dinner seating for Saturday, April 13. At the Captain's table, the guests are making small talk when 2nd Officer Lightoller comes in to confirm the Captain's orders for the present speed of the ship—21 knots. Ismay isn't content with this. He's promised the New York arrival before nightfall on Tuesday. This annoys the Captain, who feels it's too soon to make any such prediction. He excuses himself, claiming duties on the bridge. The passengers take up their song about this remarkable age and their remarkable Captain.

Scene 7: The bridge

Murdoch is in command, with Lightoller at the helm, when the Captain comes onto the bridge. Murdoch reports that the temperature of the water is dropping (it is now 34 degrees fahrenheit), and there is a warning from Coronian of a large iceberg directly in their path. But it is 600 miles away, Capt. Smith observes, and they'll keep a sharp lookout. And the Captain orders the speed increased to 22 knots—78 revolutions of the wing propellors—to keep Ismay out of their hair.

Murdoch and Smith discuss their careers. Murdoch received his Master's papers at 25, youngest in the history of the line, but isn't sure he's yet ready to take on a captain's very heavy responsibilities. Smith has seen 43 years of service with White Star and wanted to retire but agreed to see Titanic through its maiden voyage, much to his wife's displeasure.

The Captain leaves the running of the ship to Murdoch. Murdoch considers what it's like "To Be a Captain" in song: "Yours to set course/Yours to command/You hold their souls/In the palm of your hand."

Scene 8: The Middle ("F") Deck; The 3rd Class Commissary

In the modest dining accommodations of 3rd Class, the three Kates and Farrell are seated with other passengers of various nationalities (played by the same actors as the 1st Class passengers and grouped here in the same positions). The 3d Class Steward instructs them not to take food to their cabins below, "It encourages the rats." Kate McGowan and Jim Farrell have indeed made each other's acquaintance and are locked in conversation.

FARRELL: I hear there's gonna be some music later on—maybe you and me could try out a dance or two.

KATE McGOWAN: Me dance? Not on your life. It's too much like work.

FARRELL: Work? You call *that* work? It's a funny thing, Kate, but this is the first and only time in me whole life I've passed four entire days in a row doin' no work at all. It isn't natural, I tell you. It makes me feel positively sinful,

KATE McGOWAN: Don't get *too* attached to it, m' boy-o, for it won't be lasting much longer. And that goes for all that fine, rich food they keep pushin' under our noses, *and* three times a day, too. Sure and me entire family could live a week off just what I been leavin' on me plate. And all of it for free!

FARRELL: *Free*? Are you daft, then? Why do you suppose they charged us every bit of sixty shillings for our passage? What'd I need with all this fine cloth on the table and electrical lights?

KATE McGOWAN: Well, Jim Farrell, I'm gonna have fine cloth, electrical lights *and* a whole lot more when I get to America. *Includin'* me own personal bathtub. I'm gonna rise straight to the top, I will, just like cream! *(Sings "Lady's Maid.")*

      I aspire to heights of glory
In the new world, *that* can be
In that grandest nation, I'll stand tall
Reach my very highest hopes
Of all . . .
I'm aimin' to have a real profession, I am!

KATE MULLINS: Me, too!

KATE MURPHEY: Me three!

KATE McGOWAN *(sings):*
I want to be a lady's maid!
Lady's maid in America
In America the streets are paved with gold

KATE MURPHEY *(sings):*
   I want to be a governess
   Governess in America
   In America it's better I am told
KATE MULLINS *(sings):*
   I want to be a sewing girl
   Sewing girl in America
   In America I'll sew till I am old . . .

Other 3rd Class men and women join in the song, looking forward to new lives and ambitions as a shopkeeper, a constable, an engineer, even a millionaire. Kate McGowan, singing to herself, reveals that she has a special reason to look for a brighter future: "Better place for me and you/Better land to start anew/Better land for the baby/That I/Hold."

Scene 9: The bridge

Murdoch is at the helm, Andrews is taking notes on some of the intruments and Lightoller is present. Ismay enters and hears from Andrews that there have been a few little problems with the ship—weak water pressure, crew's quarters overheating. What Ismay really wants to know is, why aren't they going faster?

ANDREWS: We're doing 22 knots, Mr. Ismay. That's better than any White Star ship's ever managed.

ISMAY: Answer me straight, Andrews: you chaps at Harland and Wolff built the Cunard ship, too—was Titanic *intentionally* designed to run slower?

ANDREWS: I really must protest the implication, sir. When your father ran the line he demanded safety and comfort *before* speed. Cunard may get the passengers there a little faster, yes. But White Star gives 'em a far better ride.

ISMAY: It's a new world, Andrews. These days people want speed above everything else. Americans would gladly lose their dinner over the rail if it means arriving in New York a day sooner.

   Capt. Smith has entered.

CAPT. SMITH: Mr. Ismay—is there something you wanted?

ISMAY: E.J.! I was wondering if you're now able to predict with any certainty our landing in New York by Tuesday afternoon.

CAPT. SMITH: I can only say it's still possible.

ISMAY: *Possible?!* But it's *imperative,* dammit! If we have to stand off until Wednesday morning our return to England will be delayed a full twenty-four hours! Titanic *must* be known as a six-day ship, E.J.—even the bloody *krauts* can do it! And if second-rate tubs like Deutschland and Kaiser Wilhelm can turn around in a fortnight, then so, by God, will *we!*

   This outburst creates an awkward silence.

CAPT. SMITH *(finally):* I'm sure we'll do everything we can, Mr. Ismay.

ISMAY *(his smile returns):* Splendid. That's all one can ask, isn't it?
> *As he turns and goes, the sound of telegraphic transmission is heard, the dots and dashes of the ship's wireless.*

Scene 10: The Radio Room

In *"a small, cluttered cabin"* full of Marconi equipment, Radioman Bride is busy at his transmissions when Stoker Barrett enters and asks how much it would cost to send a message to his girl Darlene in England. He is told that the minimum rate is two pounds fourpence—more than twice what they pay Barrett for working a round trip on the Titanic—but Bride will send it for nothing, as a favor. Barrett gives the radioman Darlene's full name and address, then dictates "The Proposal" of marriage in song while Bride taps it out.

BARRETT *(sings):*
> . . . . . Be thee well
> May the Lord who watches all watch over thee
> May God's heaven be your blanket as you softly sleep
> Marry Me
> When you're finally in my arms you'll plainly see
> This devoted sailor's heart and soul
> Are yours to keep!

"Yours-to-keep," echoes Bride, finishing the transmission and then reflecting on his situation in his own song, "The Night Was Alive." As a young man, he was shy and lonely until he found his calling.

BRIDE *(sings):*
> Then I found Marconi's telegraph
> It could span the planet's width by half
> Fifty yards, two thousand miles
> The same!
> Touch the spark . . . sound the tone
>
> And the night was alive
> With a thousand voices
> Fighting to be heard
> And each and every one of them
> Connected to me . . .
>
> And my life came alive
> With a thousand voices
> Tapping out each word
> Like a thousand people
> Joined with a single heartbeat

Tapping out our dit dit-dah-dit dah-dit . . . . .

Bride and Barrett repeat parts of their songs as a duet. Then the Radioman reports to Barrett, "Message received." The sound of hymn singing is heard as the lights fade on the scene.

Scene 11: The Boat Deck: 1st Class Promenade

The hymn is a recessional for the Sunday morning services, after which Capt. Smith leads a group of 1st Class passengers onto the Boat Deck where Hartley and his band provide a lively tune, "Doing the Latest Rag."

HARTLEY *(sings):*
　. . . . . I love the cool of the breeze
　Feel the rhythm of the song in your knees
　Promenading along at your ease
　Like a feather in the air
HARTLEY & BAND *(sing):*
　Is that a hint of a chill?
　When you're dancing out of doors it's a thrill
　Keeps you hardy and healthier still
　Take a partner if you dare

　Everyone is bursting with emotion
　Dancing as we cross the mighty ocean
　Moving to the rhythm of
　The latest rag!

Professional dancers perform and then show their steps to the passengers participating in the singing and dancing. Among them is Alice Beane, who has managed to steal her way into 1st Class but is being pursued by Etches trying to send her back to 2nd Class where she belongs.

ALL *(sing in split chorus):*

Out on the well-deck	Dance with me, please
Ship's personnel deck	Feel the rhythm of the song
Feel all the ocean spray	In your knees
	Promenading along
Upper hotel deck	At your ease
Oh, what a swell deck!	Like a feather in the air
Kick all your troubles away	Is that a
The port parallel deck	Hint of a chill?
It's "la plus belle deck"	When you're dancing
	Out of doors

All of the rest, passé	It's a thrill!
	Keeps you hardy
Great demoiselle deck	And healthier still
Watch all the girls	Take a partner if you
Sashay!	Dare!

Scene 12: "A" Deck

As the scene changes from 1st to 2nd Class, all exit except Alice Beane, at the rail, joined by her husband Edward. She sings "I Have Danced" to her skeptical spouse, exclaiming, "It was oh, such a dream come true!" She wishes Edward could expand his business and make enough money so that they could visit all the grand hotels and posh resorts. "Why don't you just calm down and enjoy what we have, Alice?" Edward suggests—but Alice has had a taste of elegance and now yearns for more.

Scene 13: The bridge; then the Promenade ("B") Deck, the Saloon (D") Deck, the Middle ("F") Deck; the 1st Class Smoke Room & the crow's nest

On the bridge, Hitchens is at the helm, with Murdoch and Lightoller. Capt. Smith enters and orders the speed increased to 23 knots. Lightoller shows the Captain a message from Mesaba reporting a large iceberg at 42 degrees (a French Liner, La Touraine, has reported it at 41 degrees, but they dismiss this as an error in radio transmission). Murdoch orders the increase, with the wing propellors at 81 revolutions.

In 1st Class, the Strauses, at the rail, are discussing a message Isidor has just sent to his son Jesse, giving him permission to expand Macy's toward becoming "the largest retail store in the world."

In 2nd Class, Etches is having a cigarette. Beane, "clearly very depressed," introduces himself as the husband of the woman who crashed the 1st Class tea dance. Tactfully, Etches responds, "Ah. Yes, quite so, sir. And a charming woman she is."

In 3rd Class, Kate McGowan tells Jim Farrell of "a friend of mine—a very dear friend. It seems she left home because she'd made a mistake. A mistake she couldn't get rid of." Farrell's response is a noncommittal, "She shoulda been more careful."

In 1st Class, Straus tells his wife he may run for Congress again—he really liked it there. In 2nd Class, Beane is ruefully admitting to Etches that his wife wants more from life than he can give her. In 3rd Class, Kate is telling Farrell that of course her "friend" knows who the father was, and she continues, "So tell me, Jim Farrell, could a decent feller care for a woman who already has a bit of family?"

In the 1st Class Smoke Room, the men are smoking cigars and playing cards. George Widener's partner is J.H. Rogers, "*a bespectacled American in his 40s.*" The room's decor includes the model of the Titanic seen in the Prologue. The Major begins another anecdote, and the others have heard it so many times, they cry out in unison, "*—crazed, godless savages!*" in just the right place. Thayer tells them of reports that there are professional card sharps among them. Rogers agrees, commenting, "I've even heard talk that the notorious Jay Yates is aboard . . . . . I'd give you ten to one he's here somewhere."

Five bells (10:30 p.m.) sound in the crow's nest, where Frederick Fleet is on lookout, singing "No Moon."

FLEET *(sings):*
   No moon
   No wind
   Nothing to spy things by
   No wave
   No swell
   No line where sea meets sky
   Stillness
   Darkness
   Can't see a thing, says I
   No reflection
   Not a shadow
   Not a glint of light
   Meets the eye . . . . .

In 1st Class, the Strauses are beginning to feel the increasing cold. In 3rd Class, Kate McGowan invites Farrell to put his arm around her to protect her from the cold (which he does). On the bridge, at 11 p.m., Capt. Smith remarks on the change in the weather, with the ocean down to 31 degrees and the air to 33, in a flat calm. Those on the bridge and Fleet in the crow's nest sing in counterpoint.

FLEET *(sings):*	SMITH & OFFICERS *(sing):*
. . . And we go sailing	See how calm it is
Sailing	
	Smooth as polished glass
Ever westward on the sea	Ah, the open sea
	Feel the bite in the air
. . . We go sailing	
Sailing	
	Smooth as polished glass
	Ah, the open sea

Ever on
Go we . . .

CAPT. SMITH: Good night, gentlemen. I'll be just inside. Keep a sharp watch. The naked eye, that's something you can depend on. *(He goes.)*

LIGHTOLLER *(picks up the telephone):* Crow's nest, this is the bridge. Keep an eye peeled for ice.

On the 2nd Class Deck, Charles Clarke tells Caroline Neville that the first thing he's going to do when he reaches America—after they get married—is look for a job as a sports writer.

Samples of Stewart Laing's Tony Award-winning scene designs for *Titanic* appear on these pages: *above,* the show curtain on which the ship's length is compared with the height of the Statue of Liberty; *above on opposite page,* the model of the great ship as it appears in motion in the final scene of Act I; *below,* a design suggesting an upper deck, looking toward the bow

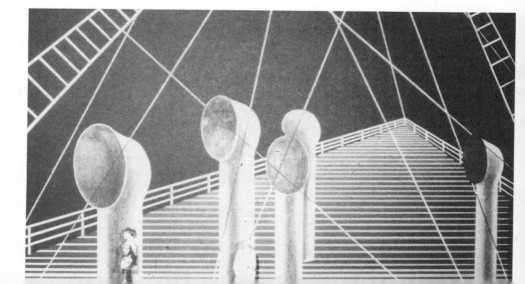

Mrs. Cardoza enters the 1st Class Smoke Room, startling its male inhabitants, particularly the Major, by her presence in this sanctuary off limits to women. She exhibits every intention of remaining, and she asks bandleader Hartley about a new song she's heard of, called "Autumn."

HARTLEY *(sings):*
  Autumn
  Shall we all meet in the autumn?
  Golden and glowing by autumn
  Shall we still be best of friends?
  Best of friends . . .

MRS. CARDOZA: Gentlemen—let me introduce myself—

ASTOR: Mrs. Charlotte Cardoza. I know who you are, Madam. Recently widowed with a *considerably* generous inheritance.

MRS. CARDOZA: And I know about you, Mr. Astor. Recently married to a *considerably* younger wife.

ASTOR: You seem to enjoy shocking people, Madam. I have heard you described as a "modern woman" by people who don't mean it as a compliment.

MRS. CARDOZA: And I've heard you described as "the world's greatest monument to unearned income."

HARTLEY *(sings):*
  . . . Let breezes blow
  And turn cold
  As we continue growing old
  This autumn

Love newly found
May yet last

MRS. CARDOZA: So what do you say, gentlemen? I happen to play an excellent game of auction bridge—may I join you?

MAJOR: Where's your sense of occasion, Madam? I understand you've just lost your husband.

MRS. CARDOZA: Yes. But not at cards.

As the Major leaves in disgust, Astor offers her his place at the table and, smiling, she sits.

On the 3rd Class Deck, Kate McGowan asks Farrell to marry her when they get to America. Farrell accepts, commenting, "Chances are you wouldn't take a 'no,' anyway."

Members of Titanic's staff join Fleet in singing "No Moon" in counterpoint to the passengers singing "Autumn." The number then wanders into excerpts from other songs.

FLEET *(sings):*	BRIDE *(sings):*	BARRETT *(sings):*
No moon	The night was alive	The screws were turning
No wind	With a thousand voices	At eighty-one
No moon	Night was alive	The screws were turning
No wind	With a thousand voices	At eighty-one

ANDREWS *(sings):*

At once a poem
And the perfection
Of physical engineering

In the crow's nest "11:38 p.m." is displayed. Fleet sees something straight ahead.

FLEET: Dear Mother of God—

He rings the brass bell three times—DING! DING! DING!—then cranks the telephone.

Iceberg right ahead!

Murdoch, Lightoller & Hitchens . . . . . are on the bridge. They will remain remarkably calm.

MURDOCH: Thank you. Quartermaster, hard a'starboard.

HITCHENS *(turning the wheel):* Hard a'starboard. The helm's hard over, sir.

MURDOCH *(peers through the binoculars):* Full astern.

LIGHTOLLER: Full astern, sir—

HITCHENS: The bow's reacting, Mr. Murdoch—two degrees to port.

MURDOCH: The distance, Mr. Fleet—

FLEET: A quarter mile—maybe a little less—

HITCHENS: —nine degrees—ten, eleven, a full point—

MURDOCH *(to himself):* Turn—turn—

HITCHENS: Jesus, Mary and Joseph. Look at the size of it—

LIGHTOLLER: Looks like the Rock of bloody Gibraltar—
HITCHENS: It's going to pass a'starboard, sir—
MURDOCH: Yes, all right, I think we're going to miss it.
    Blackout.

The collision: A tableau

> *Titanic, looking quite small and insignificant under a starlit but moonless sky, sails across the dark, smooth-as-glass sea. As she continues off, there's a loud, ominous scraping sound; it lasts for a full eight seconds. Curtain.*

ACT II

Scene 1: 1st, 2nd and 3rd Class corridors & the bridge

Guggenheim comes out of his stateroom into the 1st Class corridor, pulling on his dressing gown. He has noticed that the engines have stopped, and he rouses the Wideners next door. Etches comes in calling, "Wake up, wake up," telling Mrs. Astor it probably isn't much of a crises, but he's following orders to arouse the sleeping passengers.

On the bridge, Murdoch is at the helm but appears to be in shock, as Lightoller reports to him that at 11:40 p.m. they grazed an iceberg below the water-line on the starboard side. Murdoch hopes against hope that "If we only grazed it, it couldn't be that bad." Capt. Smith enters and is told what happened. As a precaution, Lightoller has begun to alert the passengers. "I want them on deck and wearing life preservers," the Captain orders, "At the very least they could use a drill. We've never had one, have we?"

In the lst Class corridor, Etches and stewards are knocking on cabin doors and directing their occupants—in the song "Wake Up, Wake Up"—to proceed at once to the Grand Salon, dressed warmly, with their life preservers.

PASSENGERS *(sing):*
Almost midnight
Strange commotion
In the corridor

ETCHES & STEWARDS *(sing):*
Wake up! Wake up! Wake up!
Wake up! Wake up!

Engine noise
Appears much quieter
Than it was before

Wake up! Wake up! Wake up!
Wake up! Wake up!

Can there be some incident
Some accident

ALL *(sing):*
    The Captain can't ignore? . . .

On the bridge, the Captain receives information that the boiler rooms are taking in water. Murdoch is still in shock, gripping the helm, while Capt. Smith issues orders to close the watertight doors, work the pumps and relay the ship's position to the radio room. The Captain tries to bring Murdoch back to his full sense by ordering him, "Let go of the helm, we're dead in the water!"

At 11:53 on "D" Deck, a bellboy with a megaphone is singing out, "Second Class passengers/Proceed to the First Class Salon/Please bring your life preservers/And await further instructions." The 2nd Class passengers express their confusion and apprehension.

2ND CLASS PASSENGERS *(sing):*
    . . . . . What's happened?
    Do *you* know?
    It seems the ship is stopping

    A rumor
    A rumor
    I vaguely heard a rumor

    An impact
    Slight impact
    It seems the ship is stopping

1ST COUPLE *(sing):*	2ND COUPLE *(sing):*
Can there be	Is there an incident
Some incident	Is there an—
Some—	

ALL *(sing):*
    —Accident the Captain can't ignore?

The 2nd Class Steward tells Clarke that the paint has been scratched by an iceberg, and they're pausing to make repairs. Nevertheless, all 2nd Class passengers must go to the 1st Class Grand Salon as soon as possible, as ordered.

On the Bridge, Ismay arrives, protesting the stopping of the ship. Captain Smith tells him they've struck an iceberg and they've halted to assess the damage. "In the meantime, Captain, I see no need to alarm the passengers," Ismay concludes.

At 11:56 p.m. on "F" Deck, the 3rd Class stewards, "*a less refined lot*," are banging on the cabin doors and ordering, in song, "Third Class passengers/Fore and abaft of the Well Deck/Please find your life preservers/And await further instructions." Here the passengers are also expressing their confusion and alarm, but in several languages. Farrell wants to go see what's going on above but is rudely admonished, "You'll wait down here like you're told!"

On the bridge, Andrews enters and makes his damage report to the Captain.

ANDREWS *(reading from his notebook):* There's a gash three hundred feet long below the water-line on her starboard side—there's water in the forepeak—in number one and two holds—in the mail room—and in three of the boiler rooms. In all, six of the sixteen compartments have been breached.

ISMAY: But that's all right. You assured us those compartments are watertight.

ANDREWS: She was designed to stay afloat with any three flooded. Perhaps even four. But certainly not six.

ISMAY: Andrews—what are you saying?

ANDREWS: Titanic is sinking, Mr. Ismay.

ISMAY: Nonsense! God Himself couldn't sink this ship!

CAPT. SMITH: How long has she got, Mr. Andrews?

ANDREWS *(a beat):* An hour and a half, Captain. Two at most.

There is total silence. Lights fade.

Scene 2: The 1st Class Grand Salon

Lightoller encounters Etches and whispers to him the true condition of the ship. 1st Class passengers are gathering, singing "Dressed in Your Pajamas in the Grand Salon," with Etches participating in the song and answering passengers' questions with reassuring fabrications. 2nd Class passengers are gathering here also, impressed by their 1st Class surroundings. Etches continues his solicitous attentions to his clients, and the stewards continue their reassuring patter, but uneasy confusion is still the mood of the moment, as voices weave into song.

ALL PASSENGERS *(sing):*		ETCHES & STEWARDS *(sing):*	
Dressed in your pajamas		Mr. Astor, please	
In the Grand Salon		Your lifebelt	
Feels to be bizarre		Mr. Guggenheim, please	
In the extreme		Put it on now	
How the lights burn		It's a mere formality	
Ev'ry crystal bright		There is no cause for	
As a star		Concern	

STEWARDS:	1ST GROUP:	2ND GROUP:	3RD GROUP:
We'll be on			
Our way!	Strange		
	And quite		
	Disorienting	We'll be on	
	Being here!	Our way!	Strange and
A minor delay			Quite
	Disorienting		
			Being
Now!	Recently		
	Awakened in a	A minor delay	Here!
A simple pre-	Daze!	Now	Recently
			Awakened in a

-caution!	Ev'ry light is Burning	A simple Precaution	Daze!
A moment of	With intensity!		Ev'ry light is Burning with
Rest!	Ev'rything Surrounded by a Haze!	A moment of	Intensity!
We'll be on Our Way!		Rest!	We'll be on Our Way!
	Strange and Quite disor- -ienting	We'll be on Our	
We hardly	Being here!	Way! Need	Strange and Quite disor- -ienting
Stay	Recently Awakened in a	We hardly Need	Being here!
Now	Daze	Stay now!	Recently Awakened in a
Any minute Now!			Daze!
	Any minute!		
Any minute Now		Any minute Now!	Any minute!
Any minute Now!		Any minute Now!	

ALL *(sing):*
    We'll be on our way!
    We'll be on our way! . . . . .
        Lights fade.

Scene 3: "E" Deck: A stairwell

"*From below, looking up the stairwell,*" at 12:10 a.m., the three Kates appear. Kate McGowan is the first to sing out in "The Staircase."

KATE McGOWAN *(sings):*
    . . . . . It's blocked up here, we can't get through
    What the hell are we supposed to do?
    Jim Farrell, where've you gotten to?
FARRELL *(entering, sings):*
    Over here, Kate! Look here, Kate!
    There's water runnin on the floor!
    See it comin' underneath the door!

And I think behind it there's lots more! . . .
It's two foot deep in the men's dormitory. The boat's sinking!
KATE MURPHEY: What're we supposed to do, then—drown with all them other rats?
KATE McGOWAN: Don't be daft. *(Sings.)*
    There's lifeboats!
    They're up there!
    I've seen 'em in a snapshot!

Stoker Barrett comes in and warns the Kates that the ship is going down and they'd better get up to the lifeboats. They don't see how it's possible, but Barrett will show them the way he found to sneak up to the radio room just the other day.

Scene 4: The Boat Deck

At 12:16 a.m., some of the 1st Class passengers are going to the lifeboats, the women expressing concerns, the men trying to be reassuring. Rogers asks Mrs. Cardoza to tell his sister in Ohio that he—Jay Yates, the notorious card sharp—was aboard the Titanic. Mrs. Cardoza is surprised to learn that Rogers is Yates under an assumed name, because she won from him. "Our game was interrupted," Rogers-Yates points out.

Capt. Smith comes in followed by Andrews, who stops him and calls the Captain's attention to the disastrous shortage of lifeboats: there are only 20, which will carry no more than 1,000 of the 2,200 passengers aboard—they would need 54 lifeboats to take care of everyone. "*I* didn't design this ship, Mr. Andrews," is the Captain's terse comment. Andrews replies, "And *I* didn't instruct the management on the number of boats . . . . . Well over half of us are going to die in approximately ninety minutes."

Capt. Smith hopes for a rescue ship, and he is on his way to the Radio Room to assess the situation. Lightoller comes in to report.

LIGHTOLLER: Captain—all 1st and 2nd Class passengers are proceeding to the Boat Deck as ordered. The 3rd Class have been assembled on the Well Deck, awaiting instructions.
ANDREWS: Captain, I don't think the passengers and crew fully comprehend their predicament yet. You'll have to tell them, of course—
CAPT. SMITH *(again stops):* Tell them what, Mr. Andrews? That more than twelve hundred of them are already dead? I think not, sir. There would be general panic! They'll kill each other in order to survive!
LIGHTOLLER: Awaiting instructions, Captain—
CAPT. SMITH: What? I want you up top, in charge of loading the boats.
LIGHTOLLER: The 3rd Class passengers, sir—they're all down below—
CAPT. SMITH: That's not your concern, Mr. Lightoller! Carry on—
LIGHTOLLER: Yes, sir— *(He goes.)*

ANDREWS: Captain, are you taking it upon yourself to decide who lives and who dies? I'd remind you that while you *are* the Captain, you were not hired to play God.

CAPT. SMITH: Then let it be God who decides.

ANDREWS: It would appear that God is already leaning toward the 1st Class.

CAPT. SMITH: How so?

ANDREWS: They're closest to the lifeboats, aren't they?

CAPT. SMITH: Then perhaps He'll even the score by sending us a ship. *(He goes, followed by Andrews.)*

Scene 5: The Radio Room

Radioman Bride is sending out a continuous "Titanic C-Q-D—situation critical," when the Captain and Andrews arrive. Bride reports that there are several ships in the area, the nearest being California, ten miles away but unresponsive to Titanic's signal—probably their one radioman has signed off for the night. The next nearest is Carpathia, 58 miles away and coming to them at full speed—more than four hours away. Ismay comes in, hoping that something can be done to save the ship. Bride tries out a new distress call—S-O-S—while the others fling reproaches at each other in the form of the song "The Blame."

ISMAY *(sings):*
    Possibly a ship will come
    Possibly we'll all be saved
ANDREWS *(sings):*
    Dammit, sir, *listen*!
    We're hem'rhaging fast!
    It's our *hull* that's been staved!
ISMAY *(sings):*
    Couldn't you design it right?
    Whoever heard of steel that rips?
ANDREWS *(sings):*
    Ismay, I'm just in the business of building
    It's God who sinks ships! . . .
ISMAY *(sings):*
    There stands the Captain
    Who sailed us straight into disaster!
ANDREWS *(sings):*
    Oh, now it's the Captain's turn
    Pray, who urged him to go faster? . . .
        No answer.
    Why then, *thank* you, Mr. Ismay
    For your contribution
    Now please pray for some

In the Radio Room of their sinking ship, Ismay *(left)*, Capt. Smith *(center)* and Andrews *(right,* with Martin Moran as Radioman Bride) confront each other accusingly in the musical number "The Blame"

Miraculous solution!
Your timing is perfect!
Now help us, please
If you can!
CAPT. SMITH *(sings):*
Who called for speed and to break every record?
Who had to keep all the millionaires happy?
ISMAY *(sings):*
How *dare* you, Smith?!
I will not stand here indicted!

Who ignored warnings of icebergs when sighted?
>   *He turns to Andrews.*
Who, sir, refused to extend up the bulkheads?
ANDREWS *(sings):*
>   *You*, sir! To give the First Class
>   Bigger staterooms!
CAPT. SMITH *(sings):*
>   *Who* undermined the position of Captain?
ISMAY *(sings):*
>   And *who* took a course too far north for the season?
CAPT. SMITH *(sings):*
>   And who kept insisting
>   We land ever sooner? . . .

"*Who did it*?" they ask each other, continuing in song until finally Capt. Smith sings quietly to himself, "There's only one Captain/And I was in charge . . . /This is my ship/No one else's . . . "

Scene 6: At the lifeboats

1st and 2nd Class passengers are in line for the boats, along with Farrell and the Kates, who have made it up from 3rd Class. Lightoller orders the men to stand aside and let the women and children get into the boats. In the song "Getting in the Lifeboat," Mrs. Thayer urges her young son to come along with her, as Thayer, remaining behind, hugs his son and promises to join him the next morning. When her turn comes, Ida Straus refuses to get into the boat, insisting on remaining with her husband. Alice Beane is impressed by being next to Mrs. Astor as they get into the boat, but at the moment of parting her only thought is an apologetic "I love you, Edgar."

Murdoch, helping Lightoller load the last of the lifeboats, must assign two oarsmen to it. One of them is Fleet. Barrett is nearby but has never rowed a boat, and Jim Farrell speaks up, "I can row, sir! I was a fisherman by trade." He is ordered into the lifeboat with the Kates, calling "Sorry, mate," to Barrett, who wishes Farrell good luck.

In the midst of this activity there are heard strains reprised from "I Must Get on That Ship," "Lady's Maid," "The Night was Alive" and Barrett's "The Proposal," sung to a photo of his girl friend Darlene. His song becomes "We'll Meet Tomorrow," in which he is joined by others, as the officers give the final order, "Lower away!"

COMPANY *(sings):*
>   We'll meet tomorrow
>   We will find a path
>   And reach tomorrow, past this day of wrath

We'll be together once again
Cling to your hope and prayers till then . . .
BARRETT *(to the photo, sings):*
I'll hold thee closely
As I say goodbye
And keep your image
In my memory's eye
And all this love of ours will soar
Come dawn or danger
We'll meet tomorrow
And have each other evermore . . . . .
CHARLES CLARKE *(sings):*
Come say you love me
As I kiss your eyes
Let one brief moment
Make eternal ties . . .
FULL COMPANY *(sings):*
If tomorrow is not in store
Let this embracing
Replace forever
Keep us together
Evermore

Scene 7: Portholes

The lifeboats have gone. On the Boat Deck—now markedly tilted, as the ship is going down—outside the radio room, there is a row of portholes. Behind one, the four millionaires—Guggenheim, Thayer, Astor and Widener—are discussing the voyage. Astor felt there were too many climbers aboard: "Lately I've noticed that anyone with a few million dollars considers himself rich." Guggenheim quotes Balzac, "Behind every great fortune lies a great crime" and suggests they confess theirs to each other. *"He is met with total silence. Then the lights go out."*

Behind another porthole are Beane, Rogers, Barrett and Clarke. Rogers suggests a game of two-handed stud, and Beane accepts. Barrett and Clarke were looking forward to their marriages, now fated not to take place, and Barrett tries to make the best of it: "At least we're not making any widows, are we?" Clarke suggests a drink, as the lights go out.

Behind another porthole, Capt. Smith receives reports from a bellboy that all 20 lifeboats have been launched; from Etches that all the 1st Class women except one are safely away but most of the men are still on board; and from Murdoch that Ismay jumped into one of the lifeboats. "More than anything else the man wanted a legend," Capt. Smith remembers. "Well, now, by God, he's got one."

Murdoch takes this opportunity to shoulder the blame for the disaster: "Captain—I want you to understand that I take full responsibility. I was on the bridge at the time of the—if I were a fit master I'd have rammed the iceberg head on. We'd have staved the bow, perhaps lost a few people, but the ship would have survived." The Captain is sure that Murdoch did what he thought best at the time, but Murdoch still feels that he has let the Captain down. He and the Captain depart, leaving Etches alone to reprise a portion of "To Be a Captain," as the ship's horn sounds and the lights go to black.

Scene 8: The Upper Promenade ("A") Deck

The Strauses are at the rail, where *"the tilting of the deck has now increased perilously."* Etches, ever the attentive Steward, brings in a tray with glasses and the ship's last bottle of the Cristal 1898 champagne.

IDA STRAUS: My goodness. It would be a shame to open it.

ETCHES *(opens the bottle and fills the glasses):* All things considered, Madam, it would be a shame not to.

ISIDOR STRAUS: Won't you have a glass with us, Mr. Etches?

ETCHES: Later perhaps, sir. I still have my regular people to attend. May I say it's been a great pleasure over the years serving you both? *(He goes.)*

ISIDOR STRAUS *(hands her a glass of champagne):* To us.

IDA STRAUS: Who else?

　　　　They touch glasses and drink.

You know? You're still a pretty good-looking fella.

ISIDOR STRAUS: I'd have to be, to keep such a beautiful wife. *(Sings "Still.")*
　　Still
　　The way I love you
　　Still
　　Lives in my heart

IDA STRAUS *(sings):*
　　After all of the years
　　We've been together

BOTH *(sing):*
　　Holding our love
　　Still . . .

ISIDOR STRAUS *(sings):*
　　The way you move me
　　Still
　　Feels as it did
　　When you first became mine
　　Whispered the words

BOTH *(sing):*
　　"I will" . . .

　　I loved you then
　　And I love you
　　Still . . . . .

Isidor Straus wraps his champagne glass in his handkerchief, places it on the sloping deck and crushes it under his foot, with a final "Still!"

Scene 9: The 1st Class Smoke Room & the deck above

At 2:16 a.m., the 1st Class Smoke Room *"now reflects the severe tilt of the ship."* Andrews is alone there, his life preserver slung over a chair, a brandy snifter in hand, studying plans spread over the card table. On the deck above, Capt. Smith calls out through a megaphone, *"I declare this vessel lost! From now on it's every man for himself!,"* then he exits. Andrews expresses his thoughts in the song, "Mr. Andrews' Vision." Titanic is sinking because the bulkheads stopped a deck too low, he now believes—the intruding water rose up and overflowed them into all the supposedly watertight compartments. Furiously, he erases and redraws parts of the plans.

A bellboy's entrance, coming in and asking if Andrews isn't going to try to save himself, brings the designer back to his senses. As the bellboy runs off, Andrews picks up the scale model of Titanic and stares at it, manipulating it.

ANDREWS *(Cassandra-like, he now sees the future; sings):*
    The ship will start to plunge beneath the surface
    The water lapping at our feet
    Down sinks the bow, up flies the stern
    To the sky . . . . .
    The panicked people in retreat
    A thousand strong, they'll climb up
    Toward the aft deck
    They'll cling there desperately, like bees
    To a hive!
    There they'll hold fast
    Doomed to the last
    Lost and abandoned and all
    Still alive . . .
        *The room and the deck above now start a slow increase of the tilt, until
        it is almost too precipitous to stand. The stranded passengers (most of
        them 3rd Class) and crew are seen struggling as they attempt the steep
        climb to the stern of the ship.*
    A few of them will hang there
    From the railings
    As, one by one, they'll drop away!
    More than two-hundred-fifty feet
    They will fall
    And after that, I cannot say
    I will not say!

    The rest, in swarms, will overrun the boat deck
    They'll lose all sense of right and wrong

It will be every man for himself, all right!
The weak thrown in with all the strong!

First Class and Third and Second
Will mean nothing!
And sheer humanity alone will prevail
One single class
Brute, harsh and crass
That's what will come of the world that set sail
The veil of madness once again descends.
Autumn . . .
Shall we all meet in the autumn?
Shall we all meet in the autumn?
The piano now rolls toward him, trapping and crushing him against a bulkhead.

Scene 10: The aftermath

Aboard Carpathia, the survivors, wrapped in blankets, are standing in a line, going over and over the tragedy, its causes and consequences.

LIGHTOLLER: One moment the ship was there—and the next, she was gone.

MADELEINE ASTOR: There were over a thousand poor souls swimming in the freezing water.

FARRELL: We wanted to go back for 'em, of course, to pick 'em up. But we couldn't do it, could we?

MRS. CARDOZA: They'd've swamped us, of course—then no one could have survived—

ALICE BEANE: The sound they made was deafening—like an entire foorball stadium was out there in the dark somewhere.

CAROLINE NEVILLE: Then, after a half hour, it just stopped—

KATE McGOWAN: I'm ashamed to say, I was relieved—you couldn't stand listenin' to it any longer.

BRIDE: I'll hear those voices for the rest of my life.

ISMAY: Why shouldn't I have taken that place in the lifeboat? It would have gone empty.

Lightoller figured there were 450 empty places in the lifeboats. Fleet wishes he'd seen the iceberg sooner, and Etches wishes they hadn't kept going faster and faster. Bride stayed with his telegraph key to the last but never got a response from the California. Caroline Neville saw hundreds of deck chairs afloat on a sea filled with ice. Mrs. Cardoza heard the musicians playing "Autumn" until the very end. Lightoller, continuing to do his arithmetic, calculates that since there were only 711 survivors, 1,517 perished. Among them (Etches remembers) were the 50 bellboys, none more than 15 years old and none of whom survived. And, Etches finishes, "In a matter of only a few minutes, the largest moving object on earth had totally disappeared."

The survivors reprise the song "In Every Age" as they pass the model of Titanic from hand to hand down the line. The offstage voices of the rest of the company join the survivors in the song, becoming the finale as the group of survivors falls silent, and *"only the voices, offstage, are heard."*

VOICES *(sing):*
    Floating city! . . . . .

    At once a poem
    And the perfection
    Of physical engineering . . .

    Sail on, sail on
    Great ship Titanic
    Cross the open sea
    Pray the journey's sound
    Till your port be found
    Fortune's winds
    Sing Godspeed to thee

    Fortune's winds
    Sing Godspeed
    To thee
        Curtain.

Critics, Lortel Awards

○○○
○○○
○○○
○○○
○○○
○○○ # HOW I LEARNED TO DRIVE

A Full Length Play in One Act

BY PAULA VOGEL

Cast and credits appear on page 291

PAULA VOGEL was born in 1951 in Washingon, D.C., where her father was in the advertising business. She graduated from Catholic University in 1974 and went on for graduate studies to Cornell, where she served for a time on the faculty of the department of theater arts. In love with the theater, she wanted to be a part of it and turned to playwriting after finding no success as an actress and believing in those days that no woman could establish herself in a career as a director. Ms. Vogel's first two plays of record in the New York theater were produced by Circle Repertory: The Baltimore Waltz *February 11, 1992 for 39 performances, winning a playwriting Obie (it was also produced in April of that year at the Alley Theater in Houston) and* And Baby Makes Seven *the following season on April 27 for 22 performances.*

Ms. Vogel's How I Learned to Drive *came onto the stage on tiptoe and took over the spotlight and the fanfare at the highest level. It was produced by the Vineyard Theater, opening as an off-off-Broadway offering March 16, 1997 (a couple of weeks too late to be eligible for this year's Pulitzer), moving to full off-Broadway status May 6 and soon sweeping the Lucille Lortel (best off-Broadway play), New York Drama Critics Circle (best play regardless of category) and Drama Desk (best play) Awards.*

A new Vogel play, The Mineola Twins, *was produced this spring at Trinity Repertory in Providence, R.I., where she resides. Her plays have been produced in several regional theaters and nations, and the list of her stage works includes* Hot and Throbbing, Desdemona *and* The Oldest Profession. *Some of them have been published in an anthology entitled* The Baltimore Waltz and Other Plays. *In addition to the New York prizes, Ms. Vogel has won awards and fellowships from AT&T New Plays, the Fund for New American Plays, the McKnight, the Rockefeller Foundation's Bellagio Center and the National Endowment for the Arts. She is also a member of New Dramatists.*

SYNOPSIS: A Voice announces, as the house lights dim . . .

VOICE: Safety First—You and Driver Education

. . . and this Voice will continue to make such annoucements which become the titles of scenes as the play progresses. The sound of a car ignition signals the arrival onstage of Little (Li'l) Bit stepping into a spotlight. She will be given a driving lesson (Li'l Bit tells us) on a warm summer evening in a parking lot under a Maryland moon. It's 1969 and she is 17, sitting with a married man, Peck, in the front seat of a Buick Riviera. *"The two sit facing directly front. They do not touch. Their bodies remain passive. Only their facial expressions emote,"* as they discuss the attractive smell of Li'l Bit's hair and her shampoo. Peck wants to show her a thing or two. She warns him not to go too far. Peck promises, "I'm not gonna do anything you don't want me to do." He hasn't had a drink all week and feels he should be rewarded for good behavior.

PECK: Just let me undo you. I'll do you back up.
LI'L BIT: All right. But be quick about it.
    Peck pantomimes undoing Li'l Bit's brassiere with one hand.
You know, that's amazing. The way you can undo the hooks through my blouse with one hand.
PECK: Years of practice.
LI'L BIT: You would make an incredible brain surgeon with that dexterity.
PECK: I'll bet Clyde—what's the name of the boy taking you to the Prom?
LI'L BIT: Claude Souders.
PECK: Claude Souders. I'll bet it takes him two hands, lights on, and you helping him on to get to first base.
LI'L BIT: Maybe.
    Beat.
PECK: Can I . . . kiss them? Please?
LI'L BIT: I don't know.
PECK: Don't make a grown man beg.
LI'L BIT: Just one kiss.
PECK: I'm going to lift your blouse.
LI'L BIT: It's a little cold.
    Peck laughs gently.

PECK: That's not why you're shivering.
>*They sit, perfectly still, for a long moment of silence. Peck makes gentle,*
>*concentric circles with his thumbs in the air in front of him.*
How does that feel?
>*Li'l Bit closes her eyes, carefully keeps her voice calm.*
LI'L BIT: It's . . . okay . . .
>*Sacred music, organ music or boys' choir, swells beneath the following.*
PECK: I tell you, you can keep all the cathedrals of Europe. Just give me a second
with these—these celestial orbs—
>*Peck bows his head as if praying. But he is kissing her nipple. Li'l Bit,*
>*eyes still closed, rears back her head on the leather Buick car seat.*
LI'L BIT: Uncle Peck—we've got to go. I've got graduation rehearsal at school
tomorrow morning. And you should get on home to Aunt Mary—
PECK: —All right, Li'l Bit.
LI'L BIT: —*Don't* call me that no more. (*Calmer.*) Any more. I'm a big girl now,
Uncle Peck. As you know.
>*Li'l Bit pantomimes refastening her bra behind her back.*
PECK: That you are. Going on eighteen. Kittens will turn into cats. (*Sighs.*) —I
live all week long for these few minutes with you—you know that?
LI'L BIT: I'll drive.

VOICE (*cutting in*): Idling in the Neutral Gear

The music changes to the sound of a car's engine. Li'l Bit, in her 30s, comes
forward to talk about the curious nicknames in which her family indulges—never
anything usual like Junior or Bubba. A trio of actors listed as "Male Greek Chorus,"
"Female Greek Chorus" and "Teen-Age Greek Chorus" play all the characters
except Li'l Bit and Peck, and here the "Female Greek Chorus" appears as Li'l Bit's
Mother, explaining that they looked between the baby's legs when she was born and
noticed there "just a little bit"—hence her nickname. Peck remembers when he
could hold the baby Li'l Bit in just one hand. Li'l Bit comments, "Even with my
family backgound, I was sixteen or so before I realized that pedophilia did not mean
people who loved to bicycle."

VOICE (*intruding*): Driving in First Gear

Li'l Bit remembers a typical dinner in 1969 with her family, with her mother
(Female Greek Chorus) and her grandmother (Teenage Greek Chorus) commenting on the extraordinary size and development of Li'l Bit's breasts. Uncle Peck is
trying to change the subject when Li'l Bit's grandfather (Male Greek Chorus) chimes
in with, "If Li'l Bit gets any bigger, we're gonna haveta buy her a wheelbarrow to
carry in front of her—" Li'l Bit is annoyed by this invasion of her privacy, and when
her grandfather pursues it with "Five minutes before Li'l Bit turns the corner, her
tits turn first," she starts to leave the table. Peck manages to calm her down and
persuades her to stay and finish the meal.

Li'l Bit is looking forward to college in the coming fall, where she hopes to improve herself and her prospects by reading and studying such wondrous things as the works of Shakespeare. Grandfather ridicules the notion that anything she might learn in college would be of any help to her in fulfilling her destiny, which is to "lie on her back in the dark." Li'l Bit, furious, explodes: "You're getting old, Big Papa ... You are going to die—very, very soon. Maybe even *tonight*. And when you get to heaven, God's going to be a beautiful black woman in a long white robe. She's gonna look at your chart and say: uh-oh. Fornication. Dog-ugly mean with blood relatives. Oh. Uh-oh. Voted for George Wallace. Well, one last chance: if you can name the play, all will be forgiven—and then she'll quote, 'The quality of mercy is not strained.' Your answer?—oh, too bad—'Merchant of Venice,' Act Four, Scene Three—and then she'll send your ass to fry in hell with all the other crackers."

Li'l Bit marches out. Grandfather's reaction is to ask for Li'l Bit's uneaten dish of gumbo.

Aunt Mary (Female Greek Chorus) urges her husband Peck to go after Li'l Bit, who has moved to another part of the stage and is in tears. Peck approaches her cautiously and reminds her that he's only an in-law, so her overflowing resentment of her family shouldn't include him. Peck hands her his handkerchief to wipe away her tears, and then "*Without her seeing he reverently puts it back.*" He reminds her that her grandfather is in fact going to die soon and is a member of her family.

PECK: Family is ... family.

LI'L BIT: Grown-ups are always saying that. Family.

PECK: Well, when you get a little older, you'll see what we're saying.

LI'L BIT: Uh-huh. So family is another acquired taste. Like French kissing?

PECK: Come again?

LI'L BIT: You know, at first it really grosses you out, but in time you grow to like it?

PECK: Girl, you are ... a handful.

LI'L BIT: Uncle Peck—you have the keys to your car?

PECK: Where do you want to go?

LI'L BIT: Just up the road.

PECK: I'll come with you.

LI'L BIT: No—please? I just need to—to drive for a little bit. Alone.
      Peck tosses her the keys.

PECK: When can I see you alone again?

LI'L BIT: Tonight.
      Li'l Bit crosses to center stage while lights dim around her.

VOICE *(directs):* Shifting Forward From First to Second Gear

Li'l Bit remembers that when she was expelled from college in 1970, it was rumored that indiscreet relations with men were the cause. But the real reason leading to her downfall was that she took to drinking a fifth of Canadian V.O. a day. Then she became almost a vagrant, sleeping in friends' homes, cruising through the nights in her 1965 Mustang, contented as long as she had sufficient gas for her car and whiskey for herself.

VOICE *(announces):*   You and the Reverse Gear

Going back in remembered time to 1968, Li'l Bit is having dinner alone with Peck in a restaurant on the Eastern Shore. They are celebrating her passing her test for a driver's license on the first try, followed by her "first legal, long-distance drive." Peck suggests Li'l Bit have a cocktail, while promising not to have anything alcoholic himself. Li'l Bit reminds Peck she hasn't yet reached the legal drinking age. Peck assures her that like a lot of places back where he came from in South Carolina, the Eastern Shore is "very understanding if gentlemen wish to escort attractive young ladies who might want a before-dinner cocktail."

As Li'l Bit agrees that she might have just one, her mother appears in a spotlight and recites the rules of social drinking: a lady may get tipsy but never sloppy, must line her stomach with bread and lots of butter, must sip slowly, must never mix drinks or choose anything with sugar or an umbrella or fruit but drink like a man— "straight up or on the rocks, with plenty of water in between."

Obedient to her mother's rules, Li'l Bit asks their waiter (Male Greek Chorus) whether there's any sugar in a martini. Learning there is none, she orders it. The waiter does a double-take but gets a communicative look from Peck, who orders an iced tea. In anticipation of a large tip, the waiter brings the requested drink which Li'l Bit instantly turns into an empty martini glass.

Li'l Bit wonders why Peck left South Carolina. It was to serve with the Marines in the Pacific Theater, he informs her—and clearly, he doesn't want to talk further about it. And he has no intention of going back to South Carolina to live: "I think it's better if my mother doesn't have a daily reminder of her disappointment" that, like his father before him, Peck never amounted to anything.

After the waiter serves Li'l Bit another martini, she observes that the floor in this very old inn is radically slanted. And her mother again appears, obviously more than a little tipsy and adding to her list of rules: don't risk being slipped a Mickey Finn by leaving a drink unattended, make frequent use of the ladies' room if she finds she's had too many, "Don't be shy or embarrassed. In the very best of establishments, there's always one or two debutantes crouched in the corner stalls, their beaded purses tossed willy-nilly, sounding like cats in heat, heaving up the contents of their stomachs."

As the waiter escorts her reeling mother off, Li'l Bit requests another martini, which the waiter at first refuses and then serves after significant gestures from Peck. Li'l Bit is becoming sloppily sentimental, assuring Peck that he is an important person and (in spite of Peck's obvious distaste for this subject) that his mother must love him. When the waiter brings the check, Peck rewards him handsomely, telling him to keep the change and assuring him that, intoxicated as Li'l Bit obviously is, they do not need his further assistance.

HOW I LEARNED TO DRIVE—David Morse as Peck
and Mary-Louise Parker as Li'l Bit in Paula Vogel's play

Mother wanders drunkenly back onto the scene and is again intercepted and removed by the waiter, as she issues one final rule of alcoholic conduct: "As a last resort, when going out for an evening on the town, be sure to wear a skin-tight girdle, so tight that only a surgical knife or acetylene torch can get it off you—so that if you do pass out in the arms of your escort, he'll end up with rubber burns on his fingers before he can steal your virtue."

VOICE: Vehicle Failure

Peck maneuvers the stumbling Lil Bit to the car and gets her into the front seat. She is somewhat surpised that he seems to be taking her home instead of upstairs at the inn, though she is aware the latter would be wrong.

LI'L BIT: It's not nice to Aunt Mary.

PECK: You let me be the judge of what's nice and not nice to my wife.
> *Beat.*

LI'L BIT: Now you're mad.

PECK: I'm not mad. It's just that I thought you . . . understood me, Lil Bit. I think you're the only one who does.

LI'L BIT: Someone will get hurt.

PECK: Have I forced you to do anything?
> *There is a long pause, as Li'l Bit tries to get sober enough to think this through.*

LI'L BIT: . . . I guess not.

PECK: We are just enjoying each other's company. I've told you, nothing is going to happen between us until you want it to. Do you know that?

LI'L BIT: Yes.

PECK: Nothing is going to happen until you want it to.
> *A second more, with Peck staring ahead at the river at the wheel of his car.*

(Softly.) Do you want something to happen?
> *Peck reaches over and strokes her face, very gently. Li'l Bit softens, reaches for him and buries her head in his neck. Then she kisses him. Then she moves away, dizzy again.*

LI'L BIT: —I don't know.
> *Peck smiles; this has been good news for him—it hasn't been a no.*

PECK: Then I'll wait. I'm a very patient man. I've been waiting for a long time. I don't mind waiting.

LI'L BIT: Someone is going to get hurt.

PECK: No one is going to get hurt.

Li'l Bit becomes very sleepy, and Peck covers her with a lap robe from the back seat. She rests on his shoulder as Peck "turns the ignition key." Then he leaves the sleeping Li'l Bit in the car and strolls downstage.

VOICE: Idling in the Neutral Gear

Peck admits that he has, in fact, been visiting his home in South Carolina a couple of times a year—not so much to see his mother and family, but to enjoy the fishing in the swampy tidewater inlet he loves. He remembers going after pompano one day with his little Cousin B.B. (Teenage Greek Chorus) under a spectacular sky, taking along a beer-and-crabmeat picnic.

PECK: . . . . . I can taste that pompano now, sauteed with some pecans and butter, a little bourbon—now—let it lie on the bottom—now, reel, jerk, reel, jerk—look—look at your line. There's something calling, all right. Okay, tip the rod up—not too sharp—hook it—all right, now easy, reel and then rest—let it play. And reel—play it out, that's right—really good! I can't believe it! It's a pompano—good work!

Way to go! You are an official fisherman now. Pompano are hard to catch. We are going to have a delicious little—

What? Well, I don't know how much pain a fish feels—you can't think of that. Oh, no, don't cry, come on now, it's just a fish—the other guys are going to see you —no, no, you're just real sensitive, and I think that's wonderful at your age—look, do you want me to cut it free? You do?

Okay, hand me those pliers—look, I'm cutting the hook, okay? And we're just going to drop it in—no, I'm not mad. It's just for fun, okay? There—it's going to swim back to its lady friend and tell her what a terrible day it had, and she's going to stroke him with her fins, and then they'll do something alone together that will make them both feel good and sleepy— *(Peck bends down, very earnest.)* I don't want you to feel ashamed about crying, I'm not going to tell anyone, okay? I can keep secrets. You know, men cry all the time. They just don't tell anybody, and they don't let anybody catch them. There's nothing you could do that would make me feel ashamed of you. Do you know that, B.B.? Bobbie—*Robert.* Okay. *(Peck straightens up, smiles.)* Do you want to pack up and call it a day? I tell you what— I think I can still remember—there's a really neat tree house where I used to stay for days—I think it's still here—it was the last time I looked. But it's a secret place— you can't tell anybody we've gone there—least of all your mom or your sisters— this is something special just between you and me? Sound good? We'll climb up there and have a beer and some crab salad—okay, Bobby?

Then it's Li'il Bit's turn to consult her memories of the past, like sitting at the kitchen table with her mother and grandmother in a freewheeling discussion of men, women and sex. "Men only want one thing," Mother asserts ("What is it they want?" asks Li'l Bit, wide-eyed), "So Don't Give It to Them," Mother continues, in words that are obviously capitalized. Grandmother complains of her husband being a bull. She was married at 14, a legal age in those days, and claims never to have experienced orgasm.

Grandfather comes in and boasts, "I picked your grandmother out of that herd of sisters just like a lion chooses the gazelle—the plump, slow, flaky gazelle dawdling at the edge of the herd—your sisters were too smart and too fast and too scrawny." He makes his escape before Grandmother can get after him with a broom. She tells her daughter, "Yes, sir, your father is ruled by only two bosses! Mr. Gut and Mr. Peter! And sometimes, first thing in the morning, Mr. Sphincter Muscle! . . . . . Men are bulls!", she concludes, and Mother adds, "They'd still be crouched on their haunches over a fire in a cave if we hadn't cleaned them up."

LI'L BIT: And just about then, Big Papa would shuffle in with—
GRANDFATHER: What are you all cackling about in here?
GRANDMOTHER: Stay out of the kitchen! This is just for girls!
GRANDFATHER *(as he leaves):* Lucy, you'd better not be filling Mama's head with sex! Every time you and Mary come over and start in about sex, when I ask a simple question like "What time is dinner going to be ready?", Mama snaps my head off!

GRANDMOTHER: Dinner will be ready when I'm good and ready! Stay out of this kitchen!

VOICE: When Making a Left Turn, You Must Downshift While Going Forward

In 1979 (Li'l Bit recalls, stepping forward and addressing the audience) she met a young man on the bus to upstate New York, where she was teaching a class and working on her thesis. He was a student, a senior, "appealing in an odd way." All at once, she could see in her mind's eye, like watching a play, how the evening would go when they arrived at their common destination—dinner together, a walk home, then inviting him up to her room: "Dramaturgically speaking, after the faltering and slightly comical 'first act,' there was the very briefest of intermissions, and an extremely capable and forceful and *sustained* second act. And after the second act climax and a gentle denouement—before the post-play discussion—I lay on my back in the dark and I thought about you, Uncle Peck. Oh: oh—this is the allure. Being older. Being the first. Being the translator, the teacher, the epicure, the already jaded. This is how the giver gets taken."

Li'l Bit, as a 15-year-old, "*gawky and quiet as the gazelle at the edge of the herd,*" then steps in to another family discussion of men, women and sex. She asks her mother and grandmother whether it hurts to lose one's virginity. Only "like a pinch," her mother reassures her, annoying Grandmother, who wants Li'l Bit to believe that it's agony, expecially if done before marriage. Mother exclaims, "I'm going to tell her the truth! Unlike you, you left me and Mary completely in the dark with fairy tales and told us to go to the Priest! What does an eighty-year-old priest know about love-making with girls!"

Mother refuses to scare Li'l Bit with old wives' tales about evil and sin, but advises her that it's very, very important to make sure that the man she accepts in her bed really loves her. Grandmother comments, "If she stops and thinks before she takes her knickers off, maybe someone in this family will finish high school!" Li'l Bit braces herself against the Mother-Grandmother argument she knows is coming. If Grandmother and Big Papa had informed and helped her, Mother argues reproachfully, she wouldn't have been forced to marry Li'l Bit's no-good father. But Mother received no sympathy from her parents, let alone help. Li'l Bit can't bear to listen to these recriminations one more time and is happily relieved when the Chorus members launch into a refrain from a motown song.

VOICE: Before You Drive

The Voice elaborates on this lesson: "Always check under your car for obstructions—broken bottles, fallen tree branches and the bodies of small children. Each year hundreds of children are crushed beneath the wheels of unwary drivers in their own driveways. Look beneath the car and look up and down the street to spot any children who might be innocent targets of a moving vehicle. Children depend on *you* to watch them."

VOICE: You and the Reverse Gear

In 1967, Peck orders Li'l Bit into the driver's seat and begins a lesson by asking her, "What's the most important thing to have control of inside the car?" Li'l Bit responds, "That's easy. The radio" and turns it on. Peck turns it off, demanding all of Li'l Bit's total attention, and runs through an adjustment of the car's features: the distance of the seat from the pedals, the side and rear view mirrors, the steering wheel, the manual gear shift ("Once you learn manual, you can drive anything"). Instructed always to keep both hands on the wheel, Li'l Bit asks coquettishly, "If I put my hands on the wheel—how do I defend myself?" Peck reminds her sharply that driving a car is serious business, "When you are driving, your life is in your own two hands. Understand?", and he would never touch her while she's doing it.

PECK: I don't have any sons. You're the nearest to a son I'll ever have—and I want to give you something. Something that really matters to me. There's something about driving—when you're in control of the car, just you and the machine and the road—that nobody can take from you. A power. I feel more myself in my car than anywhere else. And that's what I want to give to you. There's a lot of assholes out there. Crazy men, arrogant idiots, drunks, angry kids, geezers who are blind—and you have to be ready for them. I want to teach you to drive like a man.

LI'L BIT: What does that mean?

PECK: Men are taught to drive with confidence—with aggression. The road belongs to them. They drive defensively—always looking out for the other guy. Women tend to be polite—to hesitate. And that can be fatal. You're going to learn to think what the other guy is going to do before he does it. If there's an accident, and ten cars pile up, and people get killed, you're the one who's gonna steer though it, put your foot on the gas if you have to, and be the only one to walk away. I don't know how long you or I are going to live, but we're for damned sure not going to die in a car. So if you're going to drive with me, I want you to take this very seriously.

LI'L BIT: I will, Uncle Peck. I want you to teach me to drive.

PECK: Good. You're going to pass your test on the first try. Perfect score. Before the next four weeks are over, you're going to know this baby inside and out. Treat her with respect.

LI'L BIT: Why is it a "she"?

PECK: Good question. It doesn't have to be a "she"—but when you close your eyes and think of someone who responds to your touch—someone who performs just for you and gives you what you ask for—I guess I always see a "she." You can call her what you like.

LI'L BIT *(to us):* I closed my eyes—and decided not to change the gender.

VOICE: You and the Reverse Gear

It is 1966, and Li'l Bit's schoolmates are giving her a hard time because of the conspicuous development of her breasts. *("Throughout the following, there is occa-*

sional rhythmic beeping, like a transmitter signalling. Li'l Bit is aware of it but can't figure out where it is coming from. No one else seems to hear it.")

A group of youngsters (Male, Female and Teenage Greek Chorus) pretends that one of them, Jerome (Male Greek Chorus), is having a violent allergy attack. Alarmed, Li'l Bit offers to get the school nurse and asks what is causing the attack. "Foam rubber!" exclaims Jerome, enraging Li'l Bit by plunging his hand into her bosom.

There is the sound of running water, and Li'l Bit and the women Chorus members pretend to be draped only in towels, preparing to take a shower. The two others induce Li'l Bit to take off her towel and get under the shower first. Observing that Li'l Bit's phenomenal breasts are *not* foam rubber, the two are gleeful because they've won a bet from Jerome.

Standing against the wall at the Sock Hop, Li'l Bit is self-conscious, feeling herself the object of scrutiny which a companion (Female Greek Chorus) actually envies. Peck is one of those watching her, but from another part of the stage, *"in a strange light,"* where he is setting up a camera.

Greg (Male Greek Chorus, *"ardent, sincere and socially inept . . . . . intent on only one thing"*) comes over and asks Li'l Bit to dance. Graciously, she refuses, confiding to her companion that Greg is too short, his head comes to an awkward level, particularly in the fast numbers where "he can watch me—you know—jiggle." Again Greg asks her to dance, and again Li'l Bit refuses, beginning to notice Peck.

FEMALE GREEK CHORUS: You know, you should take it as a compliment that the guys want to watch you jiggle. They're guys. That's what they're supposed to do.

LI'L BIT: I guess you're right. Sometimes I feel like these alien life forces, these two mounds of flesh, have grafted themselves onto my chest, and they're using me until they can "propagate" and take over the world, and they'll just keep growing, with a mind of their own, until I collapse under their weight and they suck all the nourishment out of my body and I finally just waste away while they get bigger and bigger and—

Li'l Bit's classmates are just staring at her in disbelief.

FEMALE GREEK CHORUS: You are the strangest girl I have ever met.

Li'l Bit's trying to joke but feels on the verge of tears.

LI'L BIT: Or maybe someone's implanted radio transmitters in my chest at a frequency I can't hear, that girls can't detect, but they're sending out these signals to men who get mesmerized, like sirens, calling them to dash themselves on these "rocks."

Greg once again asks her to dance, and once again Li'l Bit refuses politely. Now an invisible magnetism seems to draw Li'l Bit away from Greg and the Sock Hop toward Peck. *"As Li'l Bit talks to us, she continues to change and prepare for the coming session. She should be wearing a tight tank top or a sheer blouse and very tight pants."* She remarks that every man's home includes some room or area that is his sanctuary, his den—"Here he keeps his secrets: a violin or saxophone, drum

Mary-Louise Parker with Michael Showalter (as Male Greek Chorus)
in a scene from *How I Learned to Drive*, directed by Mark Brokaw

set or dark room, and the stacks of *Playboy*." In Peck's house his private place was
the basement.

VOICE: You and the Reverse Gear

A year earlier, in 1965, Li'l Bit, at 13, is nervously getting ready for a photo shoot
with Peck. "*As in the driving lesson, he is all competency and concentration,*" as he
prepares his Leica on its tripod. He assures Li'l Bit that they won't be interrupted
down here in the basement. Aunt Mary has gone to a theater performance, and she
wouldn't come down here anyway.

Li'l Bit reminds Peck that she's posing for him under certain strict conditions,
one of which is "No frontal nudity." Peck is astonished that she would even know
of such an expression, but he keeps his cool, turns on a tape and instructs Li'l Bit
just to enjoy the music and react to it almost like dancing. "But nothing showing,"
Li'l Bit states. Peck agrees, " 'Nothing showing. Just a peek.' *He holds her by the
shoulder, looking at her critically. Then he unbuttons her blouse to the midpoint and
runs his hands over the flesh of her exposed sternum, arranging the fabric, just touch-*

ing her. Deliberately. Calmly. Asexually. Lil Bit quiets, sits perfectly still and closes her eyes."

Peck is going to keep giving instructions but tells Li'l Bit to consider him a disembodied voice and move about as though reacting alone in front of her mirror. "*Li'l Bit closes her eyes. At first selfconscious, she gets more into the music and begins to sway: we hear the camera start to whir.*" Peck keeps shooting as he tells her she's beautiful (the boys in school don't think so, Li'l Bit interposes).

LI'L BIT: I think Aunt Mary is beautiful.

PECK *(stands still):* My wife is a very beautiful woman. Her beauty doesn't cancel yours out.

More casually; he returns to the camera.

All the women in your family are beautiful. In fact, I think all women are. You're not listening to the music.

Peck shoots some more film in silence.

All right. Turn your head to the left. Good. Now take the back of your right hand and put it on your right cheek—your elbow angled up—now slowly, slowly, stroke your cheek, draw back your hair with the back of your hand—good. One hand above and behind your head; stretch your body; smile—*(Another pose.)* Li'l Bit. I want you to think of something that makes you laugh.

LI'L BIT: I can't think of anything.

PECK: Okay. Think of Big Papa chasing Grandma around the living room.

Li'l Bit lifts her head and laughs. Click.

Good. Both hands behind your head. Great! Hold that—*(From behind his camera.)* You're doing great work. If we keep this up, in five years we'll have a really professional portfolio—

Li'l Bit stops.

LI'L BIT: What do you mean, in five years?

PECK: You can't submit work to *Playboy* until you're 18.

Peck continues to shoot; he knows he's made a mistake.

LI'L BIT: —Wait a minute. You're joking, aren't you, Uncle Peck?

PECK: Heck no. You can't get into *Playboy* unless you're the very best. And you are the very best.

LI'L BIT: I would never do that!

Peck stops shooting. He turns off the music.

PECK: Why? There's nothing wrong with *Playboy*—it's a very classy maga—

LI'L BIT *(more upset):* But I thought you said I should go to college!

PECK: Wait—Lil Bit—it's nothing like that. Very respectable women model for *Playboy*—actresses with major careers—women in college—there's an Ivy League issue every—

LI'L BIT: —I'm never doing anything like that! You'd show other people these—other *men*—these—what I'm doing—why would you do that?! Any *boy* around here could just pick up, just go into the Stop & Go and *buy*—Why would you ever want to—to share—

PECK: Whoa, whoa. Just stop a second and listen to me. Li'l Bit. Listen. There's nothing wrong in what we're doing. I'm very proud of you. I think you have a wonderful body and an even more wonderful mind. And of course I want other people to *appreciate* it. It's not anything shameful.

LI'L BIT *(hurt):* But this is something—that I'm only doing for you. This is some-thing—that you said was just between us.

PECK: It is. And if that's how you feel five years from now, it will remain that way. Okay? I know you're not going to do anything you don't feel like doing. *(He walks back to the camera.)* Do you want to stop now? I've got just a few more shots on this roll—

LI'L BIT: I don't want anyone seeing this.

PECK: I swear to you. No one will. I'll treasure this—that you're doing this only for me.

Li'l Bit, still shaken, sits on the stool. She closes her eyes.

Li'l Bit? Open your eyes and look at me. *(Li'l Bit shakes her head no.)* Come on. Just open your eyes, honey.

LI'L BIT: If I look at you—if I look at the camera: you're gonna know what I'm thinking. You'll see right through me—

PECK: —No, I won't. I want you to look at me. All right, then. I just want you to listen. Li'l Bit. *(She waits.)* I love you.

Li'l Bit opens her eyes, startled. Peck captures the shot.

(Softly.) Do you know that? *(Li'l Bit nods her head yes.)* I have loved you every day since the day you were born.

LI'L BIT: Yes.

Li'l Bit and Peck just look at each other. Beat. Beneath the shot of herself on the screen, Li'l Bit, still looking at her uncle, begins to unbutton her blouse.

VOICE: Implied Consent

The Voice goes on to explain, "As an individual operating a motor vehicle in the State of Maryland, you must abide by 'Implied Consent.' If you do not consent to take the Blood Alcohol Content test, there may be severe penalties: a suspension of license, a fine, community service and a possible *jail* sentence."

VOICE: Idling in the Neutral Gear

Aunt Mary comes down center to praise her husband Peck, "a good man" who does the dishes at home and is borrowed by everyone in the neighborhood for heavy lifting and other taxing chores. He works hard and never talks of his troubles, not even of the leftover nightmares from his service in World War II: "We don't talk about it. I know he's having a bad spell because he comes looking for me in the house and just hangs around me until it passes . . . . .

"I'm not a fool. I know what's going on. I wish you could feel how hard Peck fights against it—he's swimming against the tide, and what he needs is to see me on the shore, believing in him, knowing he won't go under, he won't give up." Li'l Bit is "a sly one" who thinks her hold on Peck is a secret. But when the girl goes away to college, Aunt Mary will get her husband back to "sit in the kitchen while I bake, or beside me on the sofa when I sew in the evenings. I'm a very patient woman. But I'd like my husband back. I am counting the days."

VOICE: You and the Reverse Gear

On Christmas 1964, Li'l Bit wanders into the kitchen to watch Peck, who is doing the dishes, in aid of women who've been on their feet all day. The men in Li'l Bit's family don't do dishes, she observes, and she admires her uncle for it. She had noticed earlier that Big Papa may have hurt Peck's feelings, but whatever happened, Peck has brushed it off.

Li'l Bit asks Peck not to have anything more to drink tonight and wonders why he drinks so much. He doesn't overdo it, he contends, but he is the kind of person with a fire not in the belly like Wall Streeters or in the head like scientists, but in the heart, where drinking can help. Li'l Bit has noticed that talking with her once in a while also helps Peck, but they don't get to see each other that often.

LI'L BIT: I could make a deal with you, Uncle Peck.

PECK: I'm listening,

LI'L BIT: We could meet and talk—once a week. You could just store up whatever's bothering you during the week—and then we could talk.

PECK: Would you like that?

LI'L BIT: As long as you don't drink. I'd meet you somewhere for lunch or for a walk—on the weekends—as long as you stop drinking. And we could talk about whatever you want.

PECK: You would do that for me?

LI'L BIT: I don't think I'd want Mom to know. Or Aunt Mary. I wouldn't want them to think—

PECK: —No. It would just be us talking.

LI'L BIT: I'll tell Mom I'm going to a girl friend's. To study. Mom doesn't get home until six, so you can call me after school and tell me where to meet you.

PECK: You get home at four?

LI'L BIT: We can meet once a week. But only in public. You've got to let me— draw the line. And once it's drawn, you mustn't cross it.

PECK: Understood.

LI'L BIT: Would that help?

PECK (very moved): Yes. Very much.

LI'L BIT: I'm going to join the others in the living room now. (Turns to go.)

PECK: Merry Christmas, Li'l Bit.

Li'l Bit bestows a very warm smile on him.

LI'L BIT: Merry Christmas, Uncle Peck.

VOICE: Shifting Forward From Second to Third Gear

In 1969, Chorus individuals read a series of affectionate notes from Peck to Li'l Bit, who is away at college. From September to November they count down the number of passing days. Along with the notes, he has been sending her candy, perfume and other presents. She didn't come home for Thanksgiving as planned, and she has been absent from her dorm room (studying in the library?) and hard to get in touch with. Finally, there's a note from Li'l Bit to Uncle Peck: "Don't come up next weekend for my birthday. I will not be here—"

VOICE: Shifting Forward From Third to Fourth Gear

In a Philadelphia hotel room on December 10, Li'l Bit paces angrily while Peck sits on the bed. There's champagne for her and ginger ale for him. Li'l Bit reproaches him for sending her notes and presents and for the countdown (which was leading to this very date, her 18th birthday, when she becomes a consenting adult). But it was Li'l Bit who chose this hotel room instead of a restaurant for their meeting— because, she says, she didn't want to speak of these matters in public.

It's a conversation she's reluctant to pursue, however. She delays by asking for a drink of champagne, which she downs quickly and holds her glass out for another. As she does so, she persuades Peck to have a glass of champagne himself—"It's not polite to let a lady drink alone"—and Peck complies, sipping tentatively.

Li'l Bit has found the school work difficult and fears she may be flunking (she admits, as she pours herself another glass), but her response is a harsh "No" when Peck suggests she might take a break and come home for a while. Peck has bought himself a Cadillac El Dorado, expecting that Li'l Bit might enjoy driving it. He confesses that he has missed her even more than he thought he would.

LI'L BIT: Uncle Peck—I've been thinking a lot about this—and I came here to-night to tell you that—I'm not doing very well. I'm getting very confused—I can't concentrate on my work—and now that I'm away—I've been going over and over it in my mind—and I don't want us to "see" each other any more. Other than with the rest of the family.

PECK *(quiet):* Are you seeing other men?

LI'L BIT *(getting agitated):* I—no, that's not the reason—I—well, yes. I am seeing other—listen, it's not really anybody's business!

PECK: Are you in love with anyone else?

LI'L BIT: That's not what this is about.

PECK: Li'l Bit—you're scared. Your mother and your grandparents have filled your head with all kinds of nonsense about men—I hear them working on you all the time—and you're scared. It won't hurt you—if the man you go to bed with really loves you.

    Li'l Bit is scared. She starts to tremble.

And I've loved you since the day I held you in my hand. And I think everyone's just gotten you frightened to death about something that is just like breathing.

LI'L BIT: Oh, my god— *(She takes a breath.)* I can't see you any more, Uncle Peck.

PECK *(downs the rest of his champagne):* Li'l Bit? Listen, listen. Open your eyes and look at me. Come on. Just open your eyes, honey. All right, then I just want you to listen. Li'l Bit—I'm going to ask you just this once. Of your own free will. Just lie down on the bed with me—our clothes on—just lie down with me, a man and a woman—and let's—hold one another. Nothing else. Before you say anything else. I want the chance to—hold you. Because sometimes the body knows things that the mind isn't listening to . . . and after I've held you, then I want you to tell me what you feel.

LI'L BIT: You'll just . . . hold me?

PECK: Yes. And then you can tell me what you're feeling.

LI'L BIT *(half wanting to run, half wanting to get it over with, half wanting to be held by him):* Yes. All right. Just hold. Nothing else.

> *Peck lies down on the bed and holds his arms out to her. Li'l Bit lies beside him, putting her head on his chest. He looks as if he's trying to soak her into his pores by osmosis. He strokes her hair, and she lies very still.*

Male Greek Chorus enters Li'l Bit's thoughts, stating, "Recipe for a Southern boy." He is followed in her imagination by Aunt Mary, and Li'l Bit joins them in listing the personal details adding up to their vision of the ideal Southern youth: steel blue eyes, a suggestion of army and/or fishing skiff in his walk, "a curl of Elvis on his forehead," a wide leather belt and neatly pressed khakis, "his heart beating Dixie," etc. Li'l Bit leans over Peck and comes close to kissing him but resists and gets off the bed.

Peck asks her what she felt. Li'l Bit lies to him, telling him she felt nothing. Peck shocks Li'l Bit by then asking her to marry him, producing a ring he has brought for the occasion. Such a suggestion is "Way Over the Line," Li'l Bit tells him in capitalized words and orders him home to Aunt Mary. "*Peck lies down on the bed for a moment, trying to absorb the terrible news. For a moment, he almost curls into the fetal position.*" Then he pulls himself together and rises, in control of himself.

LI'L BIT: Are you all right?
> *With a discipline that comes from being told that boys don't cry, Peck stands upright.*
PECK: I'm fine. I just think—I need a real drink.
> *The Male Greek Chorus has become a bartender—at a small counter, he is lining up shots for Peck. As Li'l Bit narrates, we see Peck sitting, carefully and calmly downing shot glasses.*
LI'L BIT *(to us):* I never saw him again. I stayed away from Christmas and Thanksgiving for years after. It took my uncle seven years to drink himself to death. First he lost his job, then his wife and finally his driver's license. He retreated to his house and had his bottles delivered.

Peck stands and puts his hands in front of him—almost like Superman flying.

One night he tried to go downstairs to the basement—and he flew down the steep basement stairs. My aunt came by weekly to put food on the porch—and she noticed the mail and the papers stacked up, uncollected. They found him at the bottom of the stairs. Just steps away from his dark room. Now that I'm old enough, there are some questions I would have liked to have asked him. Who did it to you, Uncle Peck? How old were you? Were you eleven?

As Peck is seen taking up his usual station in the driver's seat of his car, Li'l Bit sees him in her memory as a kind of Flying Dutchman, doomed to wander the back roads of Carolina in his 1956 Chevy until he meets a young girl who will love him of her own free will and set him free.

VOICE: You and the Reverse Gear

In the summer of 1962 Li'l Bit, 11 years old, is being told that she can't go to the beach with Uncle Peck, driving for seven hours in the car with him, because her mother doesn't like the way Peck looks at her. Li'l Bit assures her mother she can handle her uncle and persuades her mother to let her go.

After Li'l Bit goes to the car, Teenage Greek Chorus speaks all of her lines in her conversation with Peck. They're making such good time that they've been able to take a scenic back road. Peck suggests that Li'l Bit might like to try to drive the car, here where there's no traffic. Li'l Bit protests that she can't reach the pedals. Peck suggests she can sit in his lap and steer.

Li'l Bit moves into Peck's lap. She leans against him, closing her eyes.

PECK: You're just a little thing, aren't you? Okay—now think of the wheel as a big clock—I want you to put your right hand on the clock where three o'clock would be; and your left hand on the nine—

Li'l Bit puts one hand to Peck's face, to stroke him.

TEENAGE GREEK CHORUS: Am I doing it right?

PECK: That's right. Now, whatever you do, don't let go of the wheel. You tell me whether to go faster or slower—

TEENAGE GREEK CHORUS: Not so fast, Uncle Peck!

PECK: Li'l Bit—I need you to watch the road—

Peck puts his hands on Li'l Bit's breasts. She relaxes against him, silent, accepting his touch.

TEENAGE GREEK CHORUS: Uncle Peck—what are you doing?

PECK: Keep driving.

He slips his hands under her blouse.

TEENAGE GREEK CHORUS: Uncle Peck—please don't do this—

PECK: Just a moment longer—

Peck tenses against Li'l Bit.

TEENAGE GREEK CHORUS *(trying not to cry):* This isn't happening.
>   *Peck tenses more sharply. He buries his face in Li'l Bit's neck and moans*
>   *softly. Teenage Greek Chorus exits, and Li'l Bit steps out of the car. Peck,*
>   *too, disappears.*

VOICE: Driving in Today's World

Li'l Bit reflects: "That was the last day I lived in my body. I retreated above the neck, and I've lived inside the 'fire' in my head ever since." At 35, she finds things like family and forgiveness of increasing importance. She still won't do anything that jiggles like dancing or jogging, but driving fills her with great pleasure, and today the gas tank is full, in preparation for a 500-mile jaunt. She goes to her car and begins the various chores of preparing to drive, as she was taught: check under the car, lock the doors, adjust the various facilities including the most important one to her—the radio.

LI'L BIT: I fasten my seat belt. Adjust the seat. Then I check the right side mirror—check the left side.
>   *She does.*
Finally, I adjust the rear view mirror.
>   *As Li'l Bit adjusts the rear view mirror, a faint light strikes the spirit of*
>   *Uncle Peck, who is sitting in the back seat of the car. She sees him in the*
>   *mirror. She smiles at him, and he nods at her. They are happy to be going*
>   *for a long drive together. Li'l Bit slips the car into first gear.*
(To us.) And then—I floor it.
>   *Sound of a car taking off. Blackout. Curtain.*

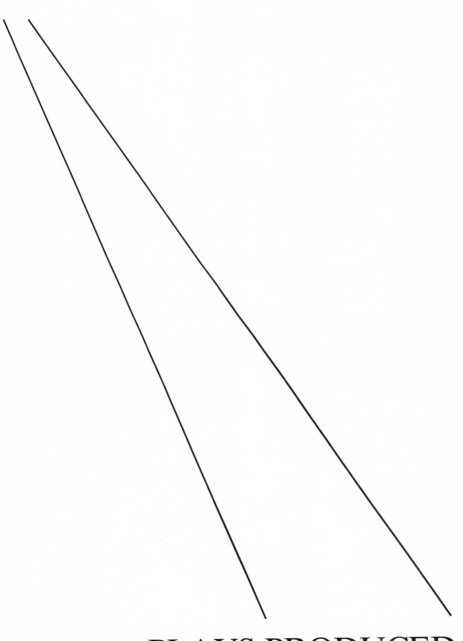

PLAYS PRODUCED
IN NEW YORK

PLAYS PRODUCED
ON BROADWAY

Figures in parentheses following a play's title give number of performances. These figures do not include previews or extra non-profit performances. In the case of a transfer, the off-Broadway run is noted but not added to the figure in parentheses.

Plays marked with an asterisk (*) were still in a projected run June 1, 1997. Their number of performances is figured through May 31, 1997.

In a listing of a show's numbers—dances, sketches, musical scenes, etc.—the titles of songs are identified wherever possible by their appearance in quotation marks (").

HOLDOVERS FROM PREVIOUS SEASONS

Broadway shows which were running on June 1, 1996 are listed below. More detailed information about them appears in previous *Best Plays* volumes of the years in which they opened. Important cast changes since opening night are recorded in the Cast Replacements section of this volume.

***Cats** (6,116). Musical based on *Old Possum's Book of Practical Cats* by T.S. Eliot; music by Andrew Lloyd Webber; additional lyrics by Trevor Nunn and Richard Stilgoe. Opened October 7, 1982.

***Les Miserables** (4,195). Musical based on the novel by Victor Hugo; book by Alain Boublil and Claude-Michel Schönberg; music by Claude-Michel Schönberg; lyrics by Herbert Kretzmer; original French text by Alain Boublil and Jean-Marc Natel; additional material by James Fenton. Opened March 12, 1987.

***The Phantom of the Opera** (3,902). Musical adapted from the novel by Gaston Leroux; book by Richard Stilgoe and Andrew Lloyd Webber; music by Andrew Lloyd Webber; lyrics by Charles Hart; additional lyrics by Richard Stilgoe. Opened January 26, 1988.

***Miss Saigon** (2,556). Musical with book by Alain Boublil and Claude-Michel Schönberg; music by Claude-Michel Schönberg; lyrics by Richard Maltby Jr. and Alain Boublil; additional material by Richard Maltby Jr. Opened April 11, 1991.

***Beauty and the Beast** (1,312). Musical with book by Linda Woolverton; music by Alan Menken; lyrics by Howard Ashman and Tim Rice. Opened April 18, 1994.

***Grease** (1,213). Revival of the musical with book, music and lyrics by Jim Jacobs and Warren Casey. Opened May 11, 1994. Note: A touring production of *Grease* visited the City Center for 6 performances 11/29/96-12/1/96; see its entry in the Plays Produced on Broadway section of this volume.

Show Boat (949). Revival of the musical based on the novel by Edna Ferber; book and lyrics by Oscar Hammerstein II; music by Jerome Kern. Opened October 2, 1994. (Closed January 5, 1997)

Sunset Boulevard (977). Musical based on the Billy Wilder film; book and lyrics by Don Black and Christopher Hampton; music by Andrew Lloyd Webber. Opened November 17, 1994. (Closed March 22, 1997)

*Smokey Joe's Cafe (932). Musical revue with words and music by Jerry Leiber and Mike Stoller. Opened March 2, 1995.

How to Succeed in Business Without Really Trying (548). Revival of the musical based on the book by Shepherd Mead; book by Abe Burrows, Jack Weinstock and Willie Gilbert; music and lyrics by Frank Loesser. Opened March 23, 1995. (Closed July 14, 1996)

*Defending the Caveman (653). Solo performance by Rob Becker; written by Rob Becker. Opened March 26, 1995.

Moon Over Buffalo (308). By Ken Ludwig. Opened October 1, 1995. (Closed June 30, 1996)

*Victor/Victoria (669). Musical with book by Blake Edwards; music by Henry Mancini; lyrics by Leslie Bricusse; additional musical material by Frank Wildhorn. Opened October 25, 1995.

*Master Class (573). By Terrence McNally. Opened November 5, 1995.

Love Thy Neighbor (225). Solo performance by Jackie Mason; created and written by Jackie Mason. Opened March 24, 1996. (Closed January 5, 1997)

State Fair (102). Musical based on the screen play by Oscar Hammerstein II and the novel by Phil Stong; book by Tom Briggs and Louis Mattioli; music by Richard Rodgers; lyrics by Oscar Hammerstein II. Opened March 27, 1996. (Closed June 30, 1996)

Seven Guitars (187). By August Wilson. Opened March 28, 1996. (Closed September 8, 1996)

*The King and I (476). Revival of the musical based on the novel *Anna and the King of Siam* by Margaret Landon; book and lyrics by Oscar Hammerstein II; music by Richard Rodgers. Opened April 11, 1996.

*A Funny Thing Happened on the Way to the Forum (468). Revival of the musical with book by Burt Shevelove and Larry Gelbart; music and lyrics by Stephen Sondheim. Opened April 18, 1996.

Lincoln Center Theater. A Delicate Balance (186). Revival of the play by Edward Albee. Opened April 21, 1996. (Closed September 29, 1996)

*Bring in 'da Noise Bring in 'da Funk (450). Transfer from off Broadway of the musical performance piece based on an idea by Savion Glover and George C. Wolfe; conceived by George C . Wolfe; choreography by Savion Glover; book by Reg E. Gaines; music by Daryl Waters, Zane Mark and Ann Duquesnay. Opened November 15, 1995 off Broadway where it played 85 performances through January 28, 1996; transferred to Broadway April 25, 1996.

Big (193). Musical based on the movie by Gary Ross and Anne Spielberg; book by John Weidman; music by David Shire; lyrics by Richard Maltby Jr. Opened April 28, 1996. (Closed October 13, 1996)

*Rent (454). Transfer from off Broadway of the musical with book, music and lyrics by Jonathan Larson. Opened off off Broadway January 26, 1996 and off Broadway February 13, 1996 where it played 56 performances through March 31, 1996; transferred to Broadway April 29, 1996.

Buried Child (71). Revival of the play by Sam Shepard. Opened April 30, 1996. (Closed June 30, 1996)

An Ideal Husband (309). Revival of the play by Oscar Wilde. Opened May 1, 1996. (Closed January 26, 1997)

Circle in the Square. Tartuffe: Born Again (29). Revival of the play by Molière; adapted by Freyda Thomas. Opened May 30, 1996. (Closed June 23, 1996)

PLAYS PRODUCED JUNE 1, 1996–MAY 31, 1997

Roundabout Theater Company. 1995-96 season concluded with **A Thousand Clowns** (32). Revival of the play by Herb Gardner. Opened July 14, 1996. (Closed August 14, 1996) Produced by Roundabout Theater Company, Todd Haimes artistic director, Ellen Richard general manager, Gene Feist founding director, at Criterion Center Stage Right.

Nick Burns	Dov Tiffenbach	Sandra Markowitz	Marin Hinkle
Murray Burns	Judd Hirsch	Arnold Burns	David Margulies
Albert Amundson	Jim Fyfe	Leo Herman	John Procaccino

Understudies: Mr. Hirsch—John Procaccino; Miss Hinkle—Jackie Apodaca; Messrs. Fyfe, Procaccino—Jason Huber.

Directed by Scott Ellis; scenery, Henry Dunn, Ben Edwards; costumes, Jennifer von Mayrhauser; lighting, Rui Rita; sound, Richard Dunning; casting, Pat McCorkle; production stage manager, Jay Adler; stage manager, Charles Kindl; press, Boneau/Bryan-Brown, Adrian Bryan-Brown, Erin Dunn.

Time: Early April, 1962. Act I: Murray Burns's apartment, 8:30 in the morning. Act II, Scene 1: Murray Burns's apartment, 8 o'clock the following morning. Scene 2: Arnold Burns's office, later that afternoon. Scene 3: Murray Burns's apartment, early that evening. Act III: Murray Burns's apartment, half an hour later.

A Thousand Clowns was first produced on Broadway April 5, 1962 for 428 performances and was named a Best Play of its season. This is its first major New York revival of record.

*Roundabout Theater Company. 1996-97 schedule of five revivals. **Summer and Smoke** (53). By Tennessee Williams. Opened August 16, 1996; see note. (Closed October 20, 1996) **The Rehearsal** (56). By Jean Anouilh; translated by Jeremy Sams. Opened November 21, 1996; see note. (Closed January 10, 1997) **Three Sisters** (a.k.a. The Three Sisters) (61). By Anton Chekhov; translated by Lanford Wilson. Opened January 22, 1997; see note. (Closed April 6, 1997) ***London Assurance** (53). By Dion L. Boucicault. Opened April 16, 1997; see note. And *1776*, scheduled to open 7/16/97. Produced by Roundabout Theater Company, Todd Haimes artistic director, Ellen Richard general manager, Gene Feist founding director, at Criterion Center Stage Right.

SUMMER AND SMOKE

Young Alma	Nathalie Paulding	Dr. Buchanan	James Pritchett
Young John	Chad Aaron	Alma Winemiller	Mary McDonnell
Rev. Winemiller	Ken Jenkins	Rosa Gonzales	Lisa Leguillou
Mrs. Winemiller	Roberta Maxwell	Nellie Ewell	Hayley Sparks
John Buchanan Jr.	Harry Hamlin	Mrs. Bassett	Celia Weston
Pearl; Rosemary	Elizabeth Zambetti	Roger Doremus	Adam LeFevre
Dusty; Vernon; Archie Kramer	Todd Weeks	Papa Gonzales	Emilio Del Pozo

Citizens of Glorious Hill: Carlo D'Amore, Geoffrey Dawe, Todd Lawson, Will McCormack, David Reilly.

Understudies: Messrs. Jenkins, Pritchett, Del Pozo—Bernie McInerney; Miss McDonnell—Rebecca Finnegan; Messrs. Hamlin, LeFevre—Geoffrey Dawe; Mr. Weeks—Todd Lawson; Misses Zambetti, Leguillou, Sparks—Jessica Ferrarone; Miss Paulding—Karina LaGravinese; Mr. Aaron—Jesse Eisenberg.

LONDON ASSURANCE—Brian Bedford as Sir Harcourt Courtly and Helen Carey as Lady Gay Spanker, both Tony-nominated performances, in the Roundabout's revival of Dion Boucicault's play

Directed by David Warren; scenery, Derek McLane; costumes, Martin Pakledinaz; lighting, Brian MacDevitt; original music and sound, John Gromada; casting, Pat McCorkle; production stage manager, Roy Harris; stage manager, Julie Baldauff; press, Boneau/Bryan-Brown, Erin Dunn, Paula Mallino.

Time: The turn of the century through 1916. Place: Glorious Hill, Miss. Part I, A Summer—Prologue; The fountain. Scene 1: The same. Scene 2: The Rectory interior and the Doctor's office. Scene 3: The Rectory interior. Scene 4: The Doctor's office. Scene 5: The Rectory interior. Scene 6: Outside Moon Lake Casino. Part II, A Winter—Scene 7: The Rectory and the Doctor's office. Scene 8: The Doctor's office. Scene 9: The Rectory and the Doctor's office. Scene 10: The fountain. Scene 11: The Doctor's office. Scene 12: The fountain.

The last major New York revival of *Summer and Smoke* took place on Broadway 11/23/76 for 24 performances in a version rewritten by Tennessee Williams and retitled *Eccentricities of a Nightingale*. The last major New York production under its original title, in an earlier (1951-52) version, was by the Roundabout off Broadway 9/16/75 for 64 performances.

THE REHEARSAL

The Countess	Frances Conroy	Hero	Roger Rees
Damiens	Nicholas Kepros	Villebosse	Frederick Weller
The Count	David Threlfall	Lucile	Anna Gunn
Hortensia	Kathryn Meisle		

Valets: Jeffrey Cox, Clay Hopper, Douglas Mercer.

Understudies: Misses Conroy, Meisle—Nance Williamson; Messrs. Rees, Kepros, Threlfall—Terry Layman; Mr. Threlfall—Tom Bloom; Miss Gunn—Mary Francis Miller; Mr. Weller—Jeffrey Cox.

Directed by Nicholas Martin; scenery, Robert Brill; costumes, Michael Krass; lighting, Kenneth Posner; sound, Aural Fixation; casting, Jim Carnahan; production stage manager, Jay Adler.

Time: 1950, over three days. Place: France. The play was presented in two parts.

The first major New York productions of this Anouilh play (*La Répétition, ou l'Amour Puni*) took place off Broadway in the season of 1951-52 and on Broadway 11/27/52 for 4 performances. Its last major New York revival took place on Broadway as *The Rehearsal* in the Pamela Hansford Johnson-Kitty Black adaptation 9/23/63 for 110 performances. It was named a Best Play of 1963-64.

THREE SISTERS

Andrei Prozorov	Paul Giamatti	Chebutykin	Jerry Stiller
Olga	Amy Irving	Fedotik	Robert Bogue
Masha	Jeanne Tripplehorn	Rodez	Justin Theroux
Irina	Lili Taylor	Ferapont	Ben Hammer
Natalya Ivanovna	Calista Flockhart	Anfisa	Betty Miller
Kulygin	David Marshall Grant	Maid	Keira Naughton
Vershinin	David Strathairn	Soldiers	Matthew Lawler, Saxon Palmer
Baron Tuzenbach	Eric Stoltz	Musicians	Gennady Gutkin, Gab Hegedus
Solyony	Billy Crudup		

Standby: Misses Irving, Tripplehorn—Diane Fratantoni. Understudies: Messrs. Giamatti, Grant—Matthew Lawler; Misses Flockhart, Taylor—Keira Naughton; Mr. Strathairn—Robert Bogue; Messrs. Stoltz, Crudup—Justin Theroux; Messrs. Stiller, Hammer—Mitchell McGuire; Miss Miller—Jane Cronin; Messrs. Bogue, Theroux—Saxon Palmer; Miss Naughton, Others—Jeroen Kuiper.

Directed by Scott Elliott; scenery, Derek McLane; costumes, Theoni V. Aldredge; lighting, Peter Kaczorowski; sound, Raymond D. Schilke; casting, Jim Carnahan; production stage manager, Lori M. Doyle; stage manager, Alex Lyu Volckhausen.

Time: The turn of the century. Place: In and around Prozorov's house in a Russian provincial town. Act I: Early May, midday. Act II: The following February, evening. Act III: Two years later, early morning. Act IV: The following autumn, midday. The play was presented in three parts with the intermissions following Acts II and III.

The most recent major New York presentation of *Three Sisters* was November 7, 1996 for 5 performances in the Russian language by the visiting Moscow Theater Sovremennik. Its last major English-language production in New York was by Manhattan Theater Club in the Jean-Claude van Itallie translation 11/30/82 for 48 performances.

LONDON ASSURANCE

Cool	John Horton	Grace Harkaway	Kathryn Meisle
Martin	Robert Neill	Pert	Rita Pietropinto
Charles Courtly	Rainn Wilson	Mark Meddle	John Christopher Jones
Richard Dazzle	Christopher Evan Welch	James	Matthew Schneck
Sir Harcourt Courtly	Brian Bedford	Lady Gay Spanker	Helen Carey
Max Harkaway	David Schramm	Mr. Adolphus Spanker	Ken Jennings
Mr. Solomon Isaacs	Andrew Weems		

Understudies: Messrs. Jennings, Welch, Jones—Andrew Weems; Mr. Wilson—Robert Neill; Messrs. Neill, Weems—Matthew Schneck; Misses Meisle, Pietropinto—Victoria Beavan.

Directed by Joe Dowling; scenery, Derek McLane; costumes, Catherine Zuber; lighting, Blake Burba; sound, Mark Bennett; casting, Pat McCorkle production stage manager, Jay Adler.

Time: 1841. Place: London and Gloucestershire. Act I: An anteroom in Sir Harcourt Courtly's house in Belgrave Square, morning. Act II: The lawn before Oak Hall, a fine Elizabethan mansion, a few days later, early afternoon. Act III: The same, the next evening. Act IV: A drawing room in Oak Hall, later that night. Act V: The same, 11 p.m. the following night. The play was presented in two parts.

The last major New York revival of *London Assurance* took place on Broadway 12/5/74 for 46 performances in the Royal Shakespeare Company production.

Note: Press date for *Summer and Smoke* was 9/5/96, for *The Rehearsal* was 10/31/96; for *Three Sisters* was 2/13/97, for *London Assurance* was 4/30/97.

Circle in the Square. 1995-96 season concluded with **Hughie** (56). Revival of the play by Eugene O'Neill. Opened August 22, 1996. (Closed November 2, 1996) Produced by Circle in the Square, Theodore Mann and Josephine Abady co-artistic directors, in association with the Long Wharf Theater, Arvin Brown artistic director, M. Edgar Rosenblum executive director, at Circle in the Square Theater.

A Night Clerk .... Paul Benedict
"Erie" Smith .... Al Pacino

Directed by Al Pacino; scenery, David Gallo; costumes, Candice Donnelly; lighting, Donald Holder; casting, Rosalie Joseph; production stage manager, Jack Gianino; press, Jeffrey Richards Associates, Roger Bean, Irene Gandy.

Time: The summer of 1928. Place: The lobby of a small hotel on a West Side street in midtown New York. The play was presented without intermission.

The last major New York revival of *Hughie* took place on Broadway 2/11/75 for 31 performances with Ben Gazzara as "Erie" Smith.

Skylight (116). By David Hare. Produced by Robert Fox, Roger Berlind, Joan Cullman, Scott Rudin, The Shubert Organization and Capital Cities/ABC, in the Royal National Theater production, at the Royale Theater. Opened September 19, 1996. (Closed December 29, 1996)

Kyra Hollis .... Lia Williams   Tom Sergeant .... Michael Gambon
Edward Sergeant .... Christian Camargo

Understudies: Miss Williams—Sarah Knowlton; Mr. Camargo—Michael Hall.

Directed by Richard Eyre; scenery and costumes, John Gunter; lighting, Paul Gallo, Michael Lincoln; sound, Freya Edwards; production stage manager, Susie Cordon; press, Boneau/Bryan-Brown, Adrian Bryan-Brown, Bob Fennell.

Time: The present. Place: A flat in Northwest London. The play was presented in two parts.

Lovers trying to connect across unbridgeable emotional and intellectual differences. Winner of the New York Drama Critics Circle Award for best 1996-97 foreign play; see the Prizewinning Plays section of this volume.

H.M.S. Pinafore, or The Lass That Loved a Sailor (9). Revival of the operetta with libretto by W.S. Gilbert; music by Arthur Sullivan. Produced by New York City Opera, Paul Kellogg general and artistic director, Sherwin M. Goldman executive producer, George Manahan music director, at the New York State Theater. Opened in repertory September 20, 1996. (Closed November 9, 1996)

Capt. Corcoran .... Victor Benedetti   Ralph Rackstraw .... George Dyer
Bill Bobstay .... James Bobick   Josephine .... Barbara Shirvis
Bob Becket .... Don Yule   Sir Joseph Porter, K.C.B. .... James Billings
Little Buttercup .... Diana Daniele   Cousin Hebe .... Angela Horn
Dick Deadeye .... Joseph McKee

Directed by James Billings; conductor, John McGlinn; choreography, Jessica Redel; scenery, Michael Anania; costumes, Joseph A. Citarella; lighting, Jeff Davis; chorus master, Joseph Colaneri; assistant director, Albert Sherman; musical preparation, Steven Mosteller; press, Susan Woelzl, Bettina Altman-Abrams.

Place: Quarterdeck of the H.M.S. Pinafore off Portsmouth, England. Act I: Noon. Act II: Night.

The last major New York revival of *H.M.S. Pinafore* was by Light Opera of Manhattan 11/3/82 for 36 performances.

Note: In addition to its new production of *H.M.S. Pinafore*, New York City Opera presented repertory productions of two other theater musicals this season, as follows: *Brigadoon* 11/13/96 for 14 performances and *The Mikado* 3/8/97 for 6 performances.

Riverdance (21). Return engagement of the dance and music revue with music by Bill Whelan;

poetry by Theo Dorgan. Produced by Abhann Productions Ltd., Moya Doherty producer, at Radio City Music Hall. Opened October 2, 1996. (Closed October 20, 1996)

Narrator	John Cavanagh	Solo Singers	Katie McMahon,
Solo Dancers	Colin Dunne, Eileen Martin,		Morgan Crowley
	Maria Pagés		

Others: Tarik Winston, Eileen Ivers, Ivan Thomas, Daniel B. Wooten, Herbin Van Cayseele.

Riverdance Irish Dance Troupe: Sarah Barry, Dearbhail Bates, Natalie Biggs, Lorna Bradley, Martin Brennan, Rachel Byrne, Yzanne Cloonan, Andrea Curley (assistant dance captain), Jo Ellen Forsyth, Fiona Gallagher, Susan Ginnety, Deirdre Goulding, Paula Goulding, Conor Hayes, Miceál Hopkins, Donnacha Howard, Kellie Hughes, Ciara Kennedy, Sinéad Lightley, Eileen Martin, Stephen McAteer, Sorcha McCaul; Kevin McCormack (dance captain), Jonathan McMorrow, Aoibheann O'Brien, Niamh O'Brien, Cormac Ó Sé, Ursula Quigley, Joan Rafter, Pat Roddy, Sheila Ryan, Anthony Savage, Glenn Simpson, Claire Usher, J.R. Vancheri, Raymond Walls, Leanda Ward.

Moscow Folk Ballet Company: Svetlana Kossoroukova, Ilia Stretsov, Tatiana Nedostop, Marina Taranda, Iouri Oustiougov, Serguei Iakoubov, Iouri Shishkine, Olena Krutsenko.

The Riverdance Singers: Derek Byrne, Patrick Connolly, Jennifer Curran, Tony Davoren, Maire Lang, Kay Lynch, Lorraine Nolan, Cathal Synnott (choirmaster).

Drummers: Abraham Doron, Vinny Ozborne, Andrew Reilly, Derek Tallon.

The Riverdance Orchestra: Noel Eccles musical direction, percussion; Eoghan O'Neill musical direction, bass guitar; Eileen Ivers fiddle; Brian O'Brien uileann pipes, low whistles; Kenneth Edge soprano and alto saxophones; Nikola Parov gadulka, kaval, gaida; Éilís Egan accordion; Des Moore electric and acoustic guitars; Desi Reynolds drums, percussion; Jim Higgins bodhrán, darrabukkas. dunbeg, ouda; Pete Whinnett keyboards.

Understudy: Mr. Dunne—Pat Roddy.

Choreography: Reel Around the Sun, Thunderstorm—Michael Flatley; Women of Ireland—Jean Butler; Shivna, Russian Dervish—Moscow Folk Ballet Company; Firedance—Maria Pagés; American Wake—Michael Flatley, Paula Nic Cionnath; Trading Tips—Colin Dunne, Tarik Winston; Andalucia—Maria Pagés, Colin Dunne; Heartland—Michael Flatley, Colin Dunne, Jean Butler.

Directed by John McColgan; scenery and painted images, Robert Ballagh; costumes, Jen Kelly; lighting, Rupert Murray; sound, Michael O'Gorman; projection design, Chris Slingsby; orchestrations, Nick Ingman, Bill Whelan; executive producer, Julian Erskine; stage manager, Sara Smith; press, Merle Frimark.

Extravaganza featuring Irish step dancers as well as choral and solo songs and dances by European performers. A foreign show previously produced in Dublin and London and at the Music Hall 4/13/96 for 8 performances.

SCENES, DANCES AND MUSICAL NUMBERS, ACT I: Introduction. Scene l: Reel Around the Sun (Corona, The Chronos Reel, Reel Around the Sun). Scene 2: "The Heart's Cry." Scene 3: Women of Ireland (The Countess Cathleen, Women of the Sidhe). Scene 4: "Caoineadh Chú Chulainn" (Lament). Scene 5: Thunderstorm. Scene 6: "Shivna." Scene 7: Firedance. Scene 8: Slip Into Spring—The Harvest. Scene 9: Riverdance ("Cloudsong," Dance of the Riverwoman, Earthrise, Riverdance).

ACT II: Introduction. Scene 10: American Wake (Nova Scotia Set, "Lift the Wings"). Scene 11: I—"Heal Their Hearts—Freedom," II—Trading Tips, III—Morning in Macedonia (The Russian Dervish), IV—Oscail an Doras (Open the Door), V—Heartbeat of the World—Andalucia. Scene 12: "Home and the Heartland." Scene 13: Riverdance International.

*Lincoln Center Theater. Schedule of four programs (see note). Sex and Longing (45). By Christopher Durang. Opened October 10, 1996. (Closed November 17, 1996) Juan Darién (49). By Julie Taymor and Elliot Goldenthal; music and original lyrics by Elliot Goldenthal; based on a tale by Horacio Quiroga; produced in association with Music-Theater Group, Lyn Austin and Diane Wondisford producers. Opened November 24, 1996. (Closed January 5, 1997) *An American Daughter (56). By Wendy Wasserstein. Opened April 13, 1997. *The Little Foxes (40). Revival of the play by Lillian Hellman. Opened April 27, 1997. Produced by Lincoln Center Theater under the direction of Andre Bishop and Bernard Gersten, Sex and Longing and An American Daughter at the Cort Theater; Juan Darién and The Little Foxes at the Vivian Beaumont Theater.

SEX AND LONGING

Lulu .... Sigourney Weaver	Rev. Davidson .... Peter Michael Goetz
Justin .... Jay Goede	Bridget McCrea .... Dana Ivey
Sen. Harry McCrea .... Guy Boyd	Policeman; Jack; Special Witness ...... Eric Thal

Understudies: Miss Weaver—Felicity LaFortune; Messrs. Goede, Thal—Bill Dawes; Messrs. Boyd, Goetz—Michael Arkin; Miss Ivey—Cynthia Darlow.

Directed by Garland Wright; scenery, John Arnone; costumes, Susan Hilferty; lighting, Brian MacDevitt; sound, John Gromada; casting, Daniel Swee; stage manager, Dianne Trulock; press, Philip Rinaldi, Miller Wright.

Place: In and around Lulu's apartment; in and around the Senate. The play was presented in three parts.

Sexually active roommates come to grips with the religious right and other social phenomena.

JUAN DARIEN

Plague Victims; Schoolchildren;	Juan (Boy) .... Daniel Hodd
Circus Tigers .... Company	Drunken Couple .... Kristofer Batho,
Mother (Dancer); Old Woman ... Ariel Ashwell	Andrea Kane
Mother (Vocalist) ...... Andrea Frierson Toney	Senor Toledo .... Martin Santangelo
Hunter .... Kristofer Batho	Circus Barker; Street Singer .... David Toney
Mr. Bones; Schoolteacher .... Bruce Turk	Green Dwarf ... Andrea Kane, Sophia Salguero
Shadows .... Stephen Kaplin, Company	Maria Posa .... Sophia Salguero
Juan (Puppet) .. Kristofer Batho, Andrea Kane,	Ballad of Return Soloist .. Irma-Estel LaGuerre
Barbara Pollitt	

Musicians: Richard Cordova conductor; Richard Martinez, Bruce Williamson keyboards; Geoffrey Gordon, Valerie Naranjo percussion; Svetoslav J. Slavov violin; Susan Rawcliffe didjeridu, wind instruments; John C. Thomas trumpet, didjeridu; Ray Stewart tuba.

Understudies: Mr. Hodd—Khalid Rivera; Misses Ashwell, Salguero—Andrea Kane; Miss Toney—Irma-Estel LaGuerre; Messrs. Batho, Turk, Toney—Tom Flynn; Mr. Santangelo—Kristofer Batho.

Directed by Julie Taymor; scenery and costumes, G.W. Mercier, Julie Taymor; lighting, Donald Holder; sound, Tony Meola; puppetry and masks, Julie Taymor; casting, Jay Binder; stage manager, Jeff Lee; press, Philip Rinaldi, Miller Wright.

Subtitled A Carnival Mass, an orphaned jaguar cub, nurtured by a human mother whose baby has died of the plague, turns into a human child but reverts to the jungle after the mother dies.The play was presented without intermission.

AN AMERICAN DAUGHTER

Lyssa Dent Hughes .... Kate Nelligan	Timber Tucker .... Cotter Smith
Quincy Quince .... Elizabeth Marvel	Sen. Alan Hughes .... Hal Holbrook
Judith B. Kaufman .... Lynne Thigpen	Charlotte "Chubby" Hughes ...... Penny Fuller
Walter Abrahmson .... Peter Riegert	Jimmy .... Andrew Dolan
Morrow McCarthy .... Bruce Norris	Billy Robbins .... Peter Benson

Television Crew: Drew Barr, Denise Burse, Ron Parady, Alison Tatlock.

Voices: Television and Radio Personalities: Michael Kinsley, Charlie Rose, Peter Schweitzer, Susan Stamberg, Russ Titelman, Sarah Wallace; The Boys—Erich Bergen.

Understudies: Misses Nelligan, Fuller—Lee Bryant; Miss Marvel—Alison Tatlock; Miss Thigpen—Denise Burse; Messrs. Reigert, Smith—Andrew Dolan; Messrs. Norris, Benson, Dolan—Drew Barr; Mr. Holbrook—Ron Parady.

Directed by Daniel Sullivan; scenery, John Lee Beatty; costumes, Jane Greenwood; lighting, Pat Collins; sound, Scott Lehrer, Donna Riley; casting, Daniel Swee; stage manager, Roy Harris.

Time: Act I, the present. Act II, one week later. Place: A Georgetown living room, Washington, D.C.

Woman nominee for surgeon general comes under intense Washington media scrutiny.

THE LITTLE FOXES

Regina Giddens	Stockard Channing	Leo Hubbard	Frederick Weller
Addie	Ethel Ayler	William Marshall	Richard E. Council
Cal	Charles Turner	Benjamin Hubbard	Brian Murray
Birdie Hubbard	Frances Conroy	Alexandra Giddens	Jennifer Dundas
Oscar Hubbard	Brian Kerwin	Horace Giddens	Kenneth Welsh

Understudies: Miss Ayler—Marjorie Johnson; Mr. Turner—Allie Woods; Misses Conroy, Channing—Jennifer Harmon; Messrs. Kerwin, Welsh—Daniel Ahearn; Mr. Weller—Aaron Harpold; Messrs. Council, Murray—Jack Davidson; Miss Dundas—Stina Nielsen.

Directed by Jack O'Brien; scenery, John Lee Beatty; costumes, Jane Greenwood; lighting, Kenneth Posner; sound, Aural Fixation; original score, Bob James; casting, Daniel Swee; stage manager, Jeff Lee.

Time: Act I, the spring of 1900, evening. Act II, a week later, early morning. Act III, two weeks later, late afternoon. Place: The living room of the Giddens house in a small town in Alabama.

The last major New York revival of *The Little Foxes* took place 10/9/92 for 4 performances in its musical version, *Regina*; and 5/7/81 in its straight-play version on Broadway for 126 performances.

Note: Lincoln Center Theater also presented *It's a Slippery Slope*, solo performance by Spalding Gray, written by Spalding Gray, on Sunday and Monday evenings at the Vivian Beaumont Theater, for 17 performances 11/10/96-1/6/97.

Taking Sides (85). By Ronald Harwood. Produced by Alexander H. Cohen, Max Cooper and Duncan C. Weldon at the Brooks Atkinson Theater. Opened October 17, 1996. (Closed December 29, 1996)

Maj. Steve Arnold	Ed Harris	Helmuth Rode	Norbert Weisser
Emmi Straube	Elizabeth Marvel	Tamara Sachs	Ann Dowd
Lt. David Wills	Michael Stuhlbarg	Wilhelm Furtwangler	Daniel Massey

Standbys: Mr. Massey—Richard Clarke; Messrs. Harris, Weisser—Mark La Mura. Understudies: Misses Marvel, Dowd—Vera Farmiga; Mr. Stuhlbarg—Tony Gillan.

Directed by David Jones; scenery, David Jenkins; costumes, Theoni V. Aldredge; lighting, Howell Binkley; sound, Peter Fitzgerald; co-producer, Hildy Parks; casting, Meg Simon, Janet Foster; production stage manager, Bob Borod; stage manager, David Sugarman; press, David Rothenberg Associates, David Gersten.

Time: 1946. Place: Maj. Arnold's office in the American Zone of occupied Berlin. Act I: February, morning. Act II, Scene 1: April, night. Scene 2: July, morning.

A noted conductor, who insists that art has no politics, is interrogated about his pro-Nazi sympathies. A foreign play previously produced in London.

Moscow Theater Sovremennik. Schedule of two programs in the Russian language with simultaneous English translation provided by Erika Warmbrunn. **Three Sisters** (5). Revival of the play by Anton Chekhov. Opened November 7, 1996. (Closed November 13, 1996) **Into the Whirlwind** (3). Adapted by Aleksandr Getman from the memoirs of Eugenia Ginzburg. Opened November 15, 1996. (Closed November 16, 1996) Produced by Marina and Rina Kovalyov in the Sovremennik Theater production, Galina Volchek artistic director, at the Lunt-Fontanne Theater.

THREE SISTERS

Prozorov	Boris Ovcharenko	Tuzenbach	Valery Shalnykh
Natalia Ivanova	Yelena Yakovleva	Solyony	Mikhail Zhigalov
Olga	Galina Petrova	Chebutykin	Igor Kvasha
Masha	Marina Neyolova, Olga Drozdova	Fedotik	Avangard Leontiev
Irina	Ekaterina Semyonova	Rode	Alexei Kutuzov
Kulygin	Gennady Frolov	Ferapont	Rogwold Sukhoverko
Vershinin	Valentin Gaft	Anfisa	Galina Sokolova

LINCOLN CENTER THEATER PRODUCTIONS—
Above, Martin Santangelo, Daniel Hodd and Bruce Turk in
the Tony-nominated Julie Taymor-Elliot Goldenthal musical *Juan Darién,* presented in association with Music-Theater
Group at the Vivian Beaumont Theater; *below,* Peter Riegert, Kate Nelligan and Hal Holbrook in Wendy Wasserstein's *An American Daughter* at the Cort Theater

Maskers, Victims of Fire, Soldiers: Company.

Directed by Galina Volchek; production design, Pyotr Kirillov, Vyacheslav Zaitsev; costumes, Vyacheslav Zaitsev; music, Moisey Vainberg; assistant director, Galina Sokolova; production stage manager, Joe Valentino.

The last major New York revival of *Three Sisters* was by Manhattan Theater Club off Broadway 11/30/82 for 48 performances in the English version by Jean-Claude van Itallie.

INTO THE WHIRLWIND

Eugenia Ginzburg .... Marina Neyolova,	Tamara .... Elena Kozelkova
Yelena Yakovleva	Fisa .... Nina Doroshina
Prisoners:	Lilia Eats .... Elena Millioti
Derkovskaya .... Galina Sokolova	Paulina Myasnikova ...... Paulina Myasnikova
Little Anya .... Lyudmila Krylova	Witnesses:
Big Anya .... Galina Petrova	Kozlova .... Ekaterina Semenova
Lidia Georgievna .... Tatyana Biziaeva	Volodya .... Alexey Kutuzov
Ira .... Inna Timofeeva	Investigators:
Nina .... Tatyana Ryasnyaskaya	Livanov .... Gennady Frolov
Zina Abramova .... Liya Akhedzhakova	Tsarevsky .... Mikhail Zhigalov
Katya Shirokova .... Maria Sitko	Elshin .... Alexander Kakhun
Karolla .... Olga Drozdova	Bikchentayev .... Vasiliy Mishchenko
Milda .... Liliya Tolmacheva	Court Chairman .... Vladimir Zemlyanikin
Vanda .... Marina Khazova	Court Secretary .... Vladislav Fedchenko
Greta Kestner .... Tamara Degtyariova	Elderly Guard .... Alexander Berda
Clara .... Marina Feoktistova	Young Guard .... Maxim Razuvaev
Annenkova .... Natalia Katasheva	Deputy Chief of Prison ...... Viktor Tulchinsky
Viktoria .... Tatyana Koretskaya	Satrapiuk .... Sergei Garmash
Grandma Nastia .... Alla Pokrovskaya	Prison Physician .... Ruslan Kovalevsky

Prisoners, Watchers, Guards: Company.

Directed by Vladimir Poglazov; production design, Mikhail Frenkel; assistant director, Olga Sultanova; production stage manager, Joe Valentino; stage manager, Olga Sultanova; press, Denise Robert Public Relations, Raisa Chernina, Arthur Cantor.

American premiere of a Russian play adapted in 1989 from the memoirs (first published in 1967) of a victim of Soviet oppression who spent 18 years in the gulags. This play has long been performed in Moscow as part of the Sovremennik troupe's repertory.

Radio City Music Hall. Schedule of two programs. **Radio City Christmas Spectacular** (195). Spectacle including *The Living Nativity* pageant; originally conceived by Robert F. Jani. Opened November 7, 1996. (Closed January 5, 1997) **Radio City Spring Spectacular** (18). Spectacle including *The Glory of Easter* pageant; originally produced by Leon Leonidoff. Opened March 28, 1997. (Closed April 6, 1997) Produced by Radio City Productions, James A. McManus president, Howard Kolins executive producer, Penny DiCamillo producer/director of Rockettes, at Radio City Music Hall.

RADIO CITY CHRISTMAS SPECTACULAR

Santa Claus; Narrator ..... Charles Edward Hall	Thinker .... Kristoffer Elinder
Mrs. Claus .... Deborah Bradshaw,	Tannenbaum .... Joanne Palenzuela
Melanie Vaughan	Bartholomew .... Ernie Lee
Clara .... Ann Brown, Melisssa Hough	Thumbs .... Leslie Stump-Vanderpool
Young Boy ..... Kyle Hershek, Reed Van Dyke	Swings .... Steve Babiar, Marty Klebba
Elves:	
Tinker .... Michael J. Gilden	

Skaters: Laurie Welch & Randy Coyne, Maradith Meyer & Patrick Hancock.

Rockettes: Abby Arauz, Leslie Barlow, Dottie Belle, Kiki Bennett, Linda Bloom, Tara Bradley, Christine Brooks, Dani Brownlee, Elizabeth Charney, Jennifer Clippinger, Cathy Cohen, Renee Collins,

Lillian Colon, Helen Conklin, Alison Court, Laurie Crochet, Kathy Dacey, Susan DeCesare, Dottie Earle Deluca, Prudence Gray Demmler, MaryLee Dewitt, Joanne DiMauro, Susanne Doris, Deanna Fiscus-Ford, Juliet Fisher, Toni Georgiana, Eileen Grace, Leslie Guy, Susan Heart, Cheryl Hebert, Vicki Hickerson, Ginny Hounsell, Stephanie James, Donna Kapral, Debby Kole, Anne Kulakowski, Judy Little, Mary Frances McCatty, Julie MacDonald, Anne Mason, Lori Mello, Carol Toman Paracat, Kerri Pearsall, Renee Perry Lancaster, Kerri Quinn, Michelle Robinson, Kimberly Rokosny, Louise Ruck, Laureen Repp Russell, Lainie Sakakura, Mary Ellen Scilla, Jane Sonderman, Alyssa Stec, Leslie Stroud, Lynn Sullivan (Rockette Captain), Elizabeth Stover Surgil, Cindy Tennier, Karyn Tomzak, Rachel Tucker, Kristin Tudor, Angela Vaillancourt, Rhonda Watson, Leigh-Anne Wencker, Darlene Wendy, Marilyn Westlake, Michelle Whitcomb, Elaine Winslow, Beth Woods, Eileen Woods, Deborah Yates.

Ensemble: Barbara Angeline, James Allen Baker, Alan Bennett, Linda Bowen, Maureen Brown, Michael Clowers, Kelly Cole, John Dietrich, Carolyn Doherty, Madeleine Ehlert, Tim Fournier, Robert Fowler, Ivy Fox, Edgard Gallardo, Kevin Gaudin, Cynthia Goerig, James Register Harris, Selena Harris, Lesley Jennings, Tom Kosis, Deborah Leamy, Troy Magino, Marty McDonough, Corinne McFadden, Heather McFadden, Michael McGowan, Hannah Meadows, Stephanie Michels, Mayumi Miguel, Joan Mirabella, Brad Musgrove, Mark Myers, Jim Osorno, Sean Palmer, Wendy Piper, Keenah Reid, Tim Santos, Joni Schenck, John Scott, Stephen Seale, Michael Serapiglia, Michael Susko, Kathleen Swanson, Bill Szobody, Owen Taylor, Susan Taylor, Jim Testa, David Underwood, Derrick Yanford.

Radio City Orchestra: David Chase conductor; Henry Aronson assistant conductor; Mary L. Rowell concertmaster; Andrea Andros, Carmine DeLeo, Michael Gillette, Nannette Levi, Susan Lorentsen, Samuel Marder, Holly Ovenden violin; Barbara H. Vaccaro, Richard Spencer viola; Frank Levy, Sarah Carter cello; Dean Crandall bass; Kenneth Emery flute; Gerard J. Niewood, Richard Oatts, John M. Cippola, Joshua Siegel, Kenneth Arzberger reeds; Russell Rizner, Nancy Schallert, French horn; Richard Raffio, Hollis Burridge, Dave Rodgers trumpet; John D. Schnupp, Thomas B. Olcott, Mark Johansen trombone; Andrew Rogers tuba; Howard Joines, drums; Mario DeCiutiis, Maya Gunji percussion; Anthony Cesarano guitar; Susanna Nason, Henry Aronson piano; Jeanne Maier harp; George Wesner, Fred Davies organ.

Directed and choreographed by Robert Longbottom; musical direction and vocal arrangements, David Chase; lighting, Ken Billington, Jason Kantrowitz; original orchestrations, Elman Anderson, Douglas Besterman, Michael Gibson, Don Harper, Arthur Harris, Phillip J. Lang, Dick Lieb, Don Pippin, Danny Troob, Jonathan Tunick, Jim Tyler; dance music arrangements, David Chase, Peter Howard, Mark Hummel, Marvin Laird; "Silent Night" arrangement by Percy Faith; associate producer, Steve Kelley; production stage manager, John Bonanni; first assistant stage managers, Robin R. Corbett, Tom Aberger; stage managers, Kathy J. Faul, Doug Fogel, Janet Friedman, Carey Lawless, Joseph Onorato, Nichola Taylor; press, Steven Henderson.

Original music—"Santa's Gonna Rock and Roll" and "I Can't Wait Till Christmas Day" music by Henry Krieger, lyrics by Bill Russell, arrangements by Bryan Louiselle; "What Do You Want for Christmas" music by Larry Grossman, lyrics by Hal Hackady; "Christmas in New York" by Billy Butt; "Christmas Is the Best Time of Year" music and lyrics by Paul Johnson.

64th edition of Radio City Music Hall's Christmas show, starring the Rockettes and including the traditional Nativity pageant, presented without intermission.

SCENES AND MUSICAL NUMBERS: Overture—Radio City Orchestra (arrangement, Don Pippin).

Prelude, Flight Over New York—(film score arrangement, Bryan Louiselle).

Scene 1: Santa's Gonna Rock and Roll—Santa, Rockettes (choreography, Robert Longbottom; scenery, Michael Hotopp; costumes, Gregg Barnes; Rockette dance arrangement, Peter Howard).

Scene 2: *The Nutcracker*, A Little Girl's Dream—choreography, Robert Longbottom; scenery, Michael Hotopp.

Scene 3: The Parade of the Wooden Soldiers—Rockettes (restaged by Violet Holmes; choreography, Russell Markert; scenery, Charles Lisanby; costumes, Vincente Minnelli).

Scene 4: Here Comes Santa Claus (new scene)—Santa (choreography, Robert Longbottom; scenery, Michael Hotopp; costumes, Gregg Barnes; dance music arrangement, David Chase).

Scene 5: Christmas in New York—Rockettes, Radio City Orchestra, Company (choreography, Marianne Selbert; Rockette choreography, Violet Holmes; scenery, Charles Lisanby; gowns and Rockette costumes, Pete Menefee; ice skating coach, Jo Jo Starbuck).

Scene 6: Ice Skating in the Plaza.

Scene 7: Santa & Mrs. Claus in Concert—(choreography, Robert Longbottom; scenery, Michael Hotopp; costumes, Gregg Barnes; dance music arrangement, David Chase).

Scene 8: Carol of the Bells—Rockettes, Company (choreography, Scott Salmon; scenery, Charles Lisanby; costumes, Pete Menefee).

Scene 9: Santa's Toy Fantasy—Santa, Mrs. Claus, Elves (choreography, Scott Salmon, Linda Haberman; scenery, Charles Lisanby; costumes, Pete Menefee; Elves costumes, Gregg Barnes).

Scene 10: The Living Nativity With One Solitary Life—"Silent Night," "O Little Town of Bethlehem," "The First Noel," "We Three Kings," "O Come All Ye Faithful," "Hark, the Herald Angels Sing" (restaged by Linda Lemac; scenery, Charles Lisanby; costumes, Frank Spencer).

Jubilant, "Joy to the World"—Organ, Company.

RADIO CITY SPRING SPECTACULAR

Rabbit .... Dennis Callahan

Rockettes: Kiki Bennett, Elizabeth Charney, Lillian Colon, Alison Court, Kelly Croteau, Kim Culp, Susanne Doris, Rebecca Downing (Rockette Captain), Anne Gaertner, Eileen Grace, Prudence Gray Demmler, Susan Heart, Cheryl Hebert Cutlip, Vicki Hickerson, Ginny Hounsell, Stephanie James, Debby Kole, LuAnn Leonard, Judy Little, Michele Lynch, Setsuko Maruhashi, Anne Mason, Mary Frances McCatty, Patrice McConachie, Lori Mello, Carol Toman Paracat, Kerri Pearsall, Renee Perry Lancaster, Laureen Repp Russell, Rachael Sellars, Leslie Stroud, Karyn Tomzak, Rachel Tucker, Kristin Tudor, Rhonda Watson, Darlene Wendy, Beth Woods, Eileen Woods.

Brackney's Madcap Mutts: Tom Brackney, Bonnie Brackney.

Errol Manoff's Fantasy Factory: Geoffrey Bennett, Robert Johnson, Errol Manoff, Shawn Martin, Educardo Vinals, Alejandro Zucchi.

Ensemble: Todd Anderson, Barbara Angeline, Alan Bennett, Christine Brooks, Michael Clowers, Kyle Craig, Lea Carmen Dellecave, Mark Esposito, Lisa Gadja, Kevin Gaudin, Peter Gregus, Jennifer Hampton, Paige Harman, Cornell Ivey, Shawnda James, Brian Marcum, Corinne McFadden, Carol Lee Meadows, Mark Myers, Ginger Norman, Kerri Quinn, Keenah Reid, Gregory Reuter, Vincent Sandoval, Scott Spahr, Darius Williams.

Radio City Orchestra: Marvin Laird conductor; Mary L. Rowell concertmaster; Andrea Andros, Eric De Gioia, Carmine DeLeo, Michael Gillette, Nannette Levi, Susan Lorentsen, Samuel Marder, Holly Ovenden violin; Barbara H. Vaccaro, Richard Spencer viola; Alessandro Benetello, Sarah Carter cello; Dean Crandall bass; Kenneth Emery flute; John M. Cippola, Gerard J. Niewood, Barry Nudelman, Joshua Siegel, Charles Wilson reeds; Russell Rizner, Lisa Pike, French horn; Richard Raffio, Dave Rogers, Bill Rohdin trumpet; John D. Schnupp, Thomas B. Olcott, Mark Johansen trombone; Andrew Rogers tuba; Marty Fischer drums; Jim Theobald, Dan Haskins percussion; Al Cohen, Kevin Kuhn guitar; Jeanne Maier harp; Susanna Nason piano; Robert Wendel 2d keyboard; George Wesner organ.

Director and choreographer, Linda Haberman; original production directed and choreographed by Scott Salmon; musical direction and vocal arrangements, Marvin Laird; scenery, Michael Hotopp, Eduardo Sicangco; costumes, Frank Krenz, Bob Mackie, Pete Menefee, Eduardo Sicangco, Jose Lengson; Gershwin sets and costumes, Erté; lighting, Ken Billington, Jason Kantrowitz; orchestrations, Michael Gibson, Dick Lieb, Glenn Osser, Jim Tyler; dance music arrangements, Mark Hummel, Marvin Laird; senior Rockette choreographer and "Dancing in Diamonds" staging, Violet Holmes; Glory of Easter restaging, Linda Lemac, vocal solo recording, Marilyn Horne; assistant choreographers, Dennis Callahan, Rebecca Downing; scenic supervisor, John Farrell; associate lighting designer, Laura Manteuffel; associate producer, Steve Kelley; production stage manager, John Bonanni; lst assistant stage manager, Robin R. Corbett; stage managers, Tom Aberger, Bruce Hoover, Joseph Onorato.

Original Music Credit: "Put a Little Spring in Your Step," music and lyrics by Jeffrey Ernstoff. Special Music Credits: "On the Sunny Side of the Street" and "Rockettes April Showers," dance music by Mark Hummel; "Put on Your Sunday Clothes," music and lyrics by Jerry Herman; "La Cage aux Folles," music by Jerry Herman, arranged by Gordon Lowry Harrell; "Dancing in Diamonds" and "There Are No Girls Like Showgirls," music by Don Pippin, lyrics by Sammy Cahn; "Encore," music by Stan Lebowsky, lyrics by Fred Tobias, arranged by Tom Bahler, orchestrated by Robert Freedman.

The Music Hall's annual spring revue starring the Rockettes and featuring the Easter pageant produced annually from 1933 to 1979 and revived in 1990, presented without intermission. ACT I, Prologue—The Glory of Easter pageant. Overture—Radio City Orchestra. Scene 1: Pure Imagination—Rabbit. Scene 2: "Put a Little Spring in Your Step"—Singers, Dancers, Rockettes in Happy Feet. Scene 3: "On the Sunny Side of the Street"—Rabbit. Scene 4: Errol Manoff's Fantasy Factory. Scene 5: Rockettes April Showers. Scene 6: With Gershwin—Singers, Dancers, Radio City Orchestra, Rockettes (music and lyrics by George and Ira Gershwin).

ACT 2, Entr'acte. Scene 1: Rockettes Easter Parade—Rabbit, Rockettes, Scene 2: Easter Yeggs. Scene 3: Brackney's Madcap Mutts. Scene 4: "Dancing in Diamonds"—Rockettes. Scene 5: Yesteryear, Easter Morning in the 1880s—Company.

*Chicago (226). Revival of the musical based on the play by Maurine Dallas Watkins; book by Fred Ebb and Bob Fosse; music by John Kander; lyrics by Fred Ebb; original production directed and choreographed by Bob Fosse. Produced by Barry and Fran Weissler in association with Kardana Productions, Inc. at the Richard Rodgers Theater. Opened November 14, 1996.

Velma Kelly	Bebe Neuwirth	Mona	Caitlin Carter
Roxie Hart	Ann Reinking	Matron "Mama" Morton	Marcia Lewis
Fred Casely	Michael Berresse	Billy Flynn	James Naughton
Sgt. Fogarty	Michael Kubala	Mary Sunshine	D. Sabella
Amos Hart	Joel Grey	Go-to-Hell-Kitty	Leigh Zimmerman
Liz	Denise Faye	Harry	Rocker Verastique
Annie	Mamie Duncan-Gibbs	Aaron	David Warren-Gibson
June	Mary Ann Lamb	Judge	Jim Borstelmann
Hunyak	Tina Paul	Martin Harrison	Bruce Anthony Davis
		Court Clerk	John Mineo

Orchestra: Rob Fisher conductor; Jeffrey Saver assistant conductor, piano, accordion; Seymour Red Press, Kenneth Hitchcock, Richard Centalonza woodwinds; John Frosk, Darryl Shaw trumpet; David Bargeron, Bruce Bonuissuto trombone; Leslie Stifelman piano; Jay Berliner banjo; Ronald Raffio bass, tuba; Marilyn Reynolds violin; Ronald Zito drums, percussion.

Standbys: Misses Reinking, Neuwirth—Nancy Hess. Understudies: Mr. Grey—John Mineo; Miss Lewis—Mamie Duncan-Gibbs; Mr. Naughton—Michael Berresse; D. Sabella—J. Loeffenholtz; Others—Mindy Cooper, Luis Perez.

Directed by Walter Bobbie; musical direction, Rob Fisher; choreography, Ann Reinking in the style of Bob Fosse; scenery, John Lee Beatty; costumes, William Ivey Long; lighting, Ken Billington; sound, Scott Lehrer; original orchestration, Ralph Burns; dance music arrangements, Peter Howard; script adaptation, David Thompson; musical coordinator, Seymour Red Press; associate producer, Alecia Parker; presented in association with Pace Theatrical Group; casting, Jay Binder; production stage manager, Clifford Schwartz; stage manager, Terrence J. Witter; press, The Pete Sanders Group, Helene Davis, Glenna Freedman.

Time: The late 1920s. Place: Chicago.

The last major New York revival of the musical *Chicago* took place off Broadway last season under Walter Bobbie's direction 5/2/96 for 4 performances in the City Center's Encores! series. The present revival is based on that production. An orchestral number "Chicago After Midnight" in the original production is not included here. The Roxie Hart-Velma Kelly number "Hot Honey Rag" in this production is not listed in the original production but was choreographed by Bob Fosse.

ACT I

"All That Jazz"	Velma, Company
"Funny Honey"	Roxie
"Cell Block Tango"	Velma, Girls
"When You're Good to Mama"	Matron
"Tap Dance"	Roxie, Amos, Boys
"All I Care About"	Billy, Girls
"A Little Bit of Good"	Mary Sunshine
"We Both Reached for the Gun"	Billy, Roxy, Mary Sunshine, Company
"Roxie"	Roxie, Boys
"I Can't Do It Alone"	Velma
"My Own Best Friend"	Roxie, Velma

ACT II

Entr'acte	Orchestra
"I Know a Girl"	Velma

PRESENT LAUGHTER—Jeff Weiss and Frank Langella
in a scene from the revival of the play by Noel Coward

"Me and My Baby" .... Roxie, Boys
"Mister Cellophane" .... Amos
"When Velma Takes the Stand" .... Velma, Boys
"Razzle Dazzle" .... Billy, Company
"Class" .... Velma, Matron
"Nowadays" .... Roxie, Velma
"Hot Honey Rag" .... Roxie, Velma
Finale .... Company

Present Laughter (175). Revival of the play by Noel Coward. Produced by David Richenthal and Anita Waxman in association with Jujamcyn Theaters at the Walter Kerr Theater. Opened November 18, 1996. (Closed April 20, 1997)

Daphne Stillington	Kellie Overbey	Roland Maule	Tim Hopper
Miss Erikson	Margaret Sophie Stein	Henry Lyppiatt	Jeff Weiss
Fred	Steve Ross	Morris Dixon	David Cale
Monica Reed	Lisa Emery	Joanna Lyppiatt	Caroline Seymour
Garry Essendine	Frank Langella	Lady Saltburn	Judith Roberts
Liz Essendine	Allison Janney		

Understudies: Mr. Langella—David Cale, John Wojda; Misses Janney, Overbey, Seymour—Gayton Scott, Orlagh Cassidy; Miss Emery—Susan Pellegrino, Orlagh Cassidy; Messrs. Weiss, Cale, Hopper—John Wojda, K.L. Marks; Misses Stein, Roberts—Gayton Scott, Susan Pellegrino; Mr. Ross—K.L. Marks, John Wojda; Miss Roberts—Susan Pellegrino.

Directed by Scott Elliott; scenery, Derek McLane; costumes, Ann Roth; lighting, Brian MacDevitt; sound, Raymond D. Schilke; casting, Bernard Telsey; production stage manager, Barnaby Harris; stage manager, John Harmon; press, Jeffrey Richards Associates, Irene Gandy, Mark Cannistraro, Roger Bean.

Time: Spring 1939. Place: Garry Essendine's studio in London. Act I: Morning. Act II, Scene 1: Evening, three days later. Scene 2: The next morning. Act III: Evening, a week later.

The last major New York revival of *Present Laughter* was by Circle in the Square on Broadway 7/15/82 for 180 performances.

God Said "Ha!" (21). Solo performance by Julia Sweeney; written by Julia Sweeney. Produced by James B. Freydberg & John Steingart, Gavin Polone, Georgia Frontiere, F.O.J. Productions, Caralyn Fuld and Lifetime Television at the Lyceum Theater. Opened November 19, 1996. (Closed December 8, 1996)

Directed by Beth Milles; scenery, Michael McGarty; lighting, Russell H. Champa; costumes, Connie Martin; sound, John Shivers; co-producers, Pachyderm Entertainment, On the Fly Entertainment; producing associates, Michelle Leslie, Ralph Sevush; production stage manager, Franklin Keysar; press, Boneau/Bryan-Brown, Jackie Green.

Miss Sweeney as a daughter telling stories about her family's idiosyncrasies and emotions, as parents and children are brought together in battle against cancer. The play was presented without intermission.

*****Madison Square Garden Productions**. Schedule of two programs. **A Christmas Carol** (90). Return engagement of the musical based on the story by Charles Dickens; book by Mike Ockrent and Lynn Ahrens; music by Alan Menken; lyrics by Lynn Ahrens. Executive producers, Michael David, Edward Strong and Sherman Warner of Dodger Productions. Opened November 22, 1996. (Closed January 5, 1997) *****The Wizard of Oz** (29). Musical based on the story by L. Frank Baum; adapted by Robert Johanson; music by Harold Arlen, lyrics by E.Y. Harburg from the M-G-M motion picture; background music by Herbert Stothart. Opened May 15, 1997. Produced by Madison Square Garden Productions, Tim Hawkins producer, at the Madison Square Garden Theater.

A CHRISTMAS CAROL

Beadle .... David Lowenstein	Scrooge at 8;
Mr. Smythe .... James Judy	Ignorance .... Zachary Stefan Petkanas,
Grace Smythe ..... Jennifer Blain, Cara Horner	Evan Silverberg
Scrooge .... Tony Randall	Fan at 6; Want .... Gemini Quintos,
Cratchit .... Nick Corley	Diana Mary Rice
Old Joe; Mr. Hawkins .... Don Mayo	Scrooge's Father;
Mrs. Cratchit .... Robin Baxter	Undertaker .... Michael X. Martin
Tiny Tim .... Matthew Ballinger,	Scrooge at 12 .. Matthew Hoffman, Christopher
Pierce Cravens	Mark Petrizzo
Poulterer; Judge .... Michael H. Ingram	Fan at 10 .... Eliza Atkins Clark,
Sandwichboard Man; Ghost of	Elizabeth Lundberg
Christmas Present .... Ben Vereen	Fezziwig .... Ray Friedeck
Jonathon .... Jason Fuchs, Evan J. Newman	Scrooge at 18 .... Michael Moore
Lamplighter .... Ken Jennings	Young Marley; Undertaker .... Ken Barnett
Blind Hag; Scrooge's Mother ...... Joan Barber	Mrs. Fezziwig .... Joy Hermalyn
Fred .... Greg Zerkle	Emily .... Emily Skinner
Mrs. Mops .... Corinne Melancon	Fiddler .... Brad Bradley
Ghost of Jacob Marley .... Paul Kandel	Sally .... Whitney Webster
Ghost of Christmas Past .... Ken Jennings	Ghost of Christmas Future ... Valentina Kozlova

Charity Men: Michael H. Ingram, Keith Byron Kirk, Seth Malkin.

Street Urchins: Matthew Hoffman, Christopher Mark Petrizzo, Zachary Stefan Petkanas, Gemini Quintos, Diana Mary Rice, Evan Silverberg.

Lights of Christmas Past: Matthew Baker, Christopher F. Davis, Sean Thomas Morrissey, David Rosales.

The Cratchit Children: Eliza Atkins Clark, Matthew Hoffman, Elizabeth Lundberg, Sean Thomas Morrissey, Christopher Mark Petrizzo.

Business Men, Gifts, Ghosts, People of London: Matthew Baker, Joan Barber, Ken Barnett, Robin Baxter, Leslie Bell, Carol Bentley, Brad Bradley, Betsy Chang, Candy Cook, Rosa Curry, Christopher F. Davis, Ray Friedeck, Peter Gregus, Jeffrey Hankinson, Joy Hermalyn, Michael H. Ingram, James Judy, Louisa Kendrick, Carrie Kenneally, Keith Byron Kirk, David Lowenstein, Jason Ma, Seth Malkin, Donna Lee Marshall, Michael X. Martin, Dana Lynn Mauro, Don Mayo, Elizabeth Mills, Corinne Melancon, Michael Moore, Sean Thomas Morrissey, Adam Pelty, Gail Pennington, Angela Piccinni, Pamela Remler, Samuel Reni, David Rosales, Emily Skinner, Whitney Webster, Greg Zerkle.

Swings: Rachel Black, Rob Donohoe, Jesse Adam Eisenberg, Nicholas Gould, Dana Leigh Jackson, Don Johanson, Robin Lewis, Grace Ann Pisani, Jordan Siwek, Lindsay Sperber, Cynthia Thole, Brandon Uranowitz, Jeff Williams.

Angels: Bergen Beach School, P.S. 26 Chorus, Terrill Middle School, P.S. 250 Concert Chorale.

Red Children's Cast: Jennifer Balin, Pierce Cravens, Jason Fuchs, Matthew Hoffman, Elizabeth Lundberg, Grace Ann Pisani, Gemini Quintos, Evan Silverberg, Jordan Siwek.

Green Children's Cast: Matthew Ballinger, Eliza Atkins Clark, Nicholas Gould, Cara Horner, Evan Jay Newman, Zachary Stefan Petkanas, Christopher Mark Petrizzo, Diana Mary Rice, Lindsay Sperber, Brandon Uranowitz.

Orchestra: Paul Gemignani conductor; Mark C. Mitchell associate conductor; Aloysia Friedman concertmaster; Karl Kawahara, Ann Labin, Sebu Serinian violin; Clay Ruede cello; Charles Bergeron bass; David Weiss, Kenneth Dybisz, Alva Hunt, Daniel Wieloszynski, John Winder woodwinds; Stu Sataloff, Phil Granger, Dominic Derasse trumpet; Ronald Sell, French horn; Phil Sasson, Dean Plank trombone; Nick Archer, Mark C. Mitchell keyboards; Jennifer Hoult harp; Michael Berkowitz drums; Glenn Rhian percussion.

Directed by Mike Ockrent; choreography, Susan Stroman; musical direction, Paul Gemignani; scenery, Tony Walton; costumes, William Ivey Long; lighting, Jules Fisher, Peggy Eisenhauer; sound, Tony Meola; projections, Wendall K. Harrington; flying, Foy; orchestrations, Michael Starobin, Douglas Besterman; dance arrangements and incidental music, Glen Kelly; associate director, Steven Zweigbaum; associate choreographer, Chris Peterson; casting, Julie Hughes, Barry Moss; production stage manager, Steven Zweigbaum; stage manager, Rolt Smith; press, Cathy Del Priore.

Time 1880. Place: London. The play was presented without intermission.

This is the third annual production of this *A Christmas Carol*, whose list of scenes and musical numbers has differed slightly with each presentation.

SCENES AND MUSICAL NUMBERS

Scene 1: The Royal Exchange
 "A Jolly Good Time" .... Charity Men, Smythe Family, Business Men, Wives, Children
 "Nothing to Do With Me" .... Scrooge, Cratchit
Scene 2: The street
 "You Mean More to Me" .... Cratchit, Tiny Tim
 "Street Song (Nothing to Do With Me)" .... People of London, Scrooge, Fred, Jonathon,
                                          Sandwichboard Man, Lamplighter, Blind Hag, Grace Smythe
Scene 3: Scrooge's house
 "Link by Link" .... Marley's Ghost, Scrooge, Ghosts
Scene 4: Scrooge's bedchamber
 "The Lights of Long Ago" .... Ghost of Christmas Past
Scene 5: The law courts
 "God Bless Us, Everyone" .... Scrooge's Mother, Fan at 6
Scene 6: The factory
 "A Place Called Home" .... Scrooge at 12, Fan at 6, Scrooge
Scene 7: Fezziwig's Banking House
 "Mr. Fezziwig's Annual Christmas Ball" .... Fezziwig, Mrs. Fezziwig, Guests
 "A Place Called Home" (Reprise) .... Emily, Scrooge at 18, Scrooge
Scene 8: Scrooge and Marley's
 "The Lights of Long Ago" (Part II) .... Scrooge at 18, Young Marley, Emily,
                                                                    People From Scrooge's Past
Scene 9: A starry night
 "Abundance and Charity" .... Ghost of Christmas Present, Scrooge, Christmas Gifts
Scene 10: All Over London
 "Christmas Together" .... Tiny Tim, The Cratchits, Ghost of Christmas Present, Fred, Sally,
                                                                    Scrooge, People of London
Scene 11: The graveyard
 "Dancing on Your Grave" .... Ghost of Christmas Future, Monks, Business Men, Mrs. Mops,
                                                            Undertakers, Old Joe, Cratchit
 "Yesterday, Tomorrow and Today" .... Scrooge, Angels, Children of London
Scene 12: Scrooge's bedchamber
 "London Town Carol' .... Jonathon

Scene 13: The street, Christmas Day
"Nothing to Do With Me" (Reprise) .... Scrooge
"Christmas Together" (Reprise) .... People of London
"God Bless Us, Everyone" (Finale) .... Company

THE WIZARD OF OZ

Dorothy Gale .... Jessica Grové
Aunt Em; Glinda .... Judith McCauley
Uncle Henry; Winkie
  General .... Roger Preston Smith
Hunk; Scarecrow .... Lara Teeter
Hickory; Tinman .... Michael Gruber
Zeke; Cowardly Lion .... Ken Page
Almira Gulch; Wicked Witch
  of the West .... Roseanne

Prof. Marvel; Wizard of Oz .... Gerry Vichi
Toto .... Plenty
Mayor of Munchkinland .... Louis Carry
Barristers .... Wendy Coates,
                                   Jonas Moscartolo
Coroner .... Derrick McGinty
Nikko .... Martin Klebba

Munchkins, Crows, Apple Trees, Poppies, Citizens of Oz, Flying Monkeys, Winkies: Vivian B. Ba-yubay, Maggie Keenan Bolger, Patrick Boyd, Kai Braithwaite, Lindsy Canuel, Casey Colgan, Christine DeVito, Chantele M. Doucette, Peter William Dunn, Danielle Lee Greaves, Gail Cook Howell, Heidi Karol Johnson, Martin Klebba, Benjamin E. Lear, Don Mayo, M. Kathryn Quinlan, Gemini Quintos, D.J. Salisbury, Dana Scarborough, Samantha Sensale, Evan Silverberg, Andrea Szucs, Christopher Trousdale, Wendy Watts. Swings: Lenny Daniel, Jamie Waggoner.

Orchestra: Jeff Rizzo conductor; Maggie Torre associate conductor; Rick Dolan concertmaster; Heidi Modr, Peter Martin Weimar violin; Maxine Roach viola; Eliana Mendoza cello; Joseph Bongiorno bass; Svjetlana Kabalan flute; Lynne Cohen oboe; Mark Thrasher, Eddie Salkin, Don McGeen wood-winds; Julie Pilant, Kelly Dent horn; Rich Raffio, Liesel Whitaker trumpet; Mike Christenson trombone; Richard Rosenzweig drums; Lou Oddo percussion; Nina Kellman harp; Maggie Torre, Madelyn Rubin-stein keyboards.

Understudies: Mr. Gruber—Patrick Boyd; Mr. Teeter—Casey Colgan; Mr. Smith—Lenny Daniel; Roseanne—Danielle Lee Greaves; Miss McCauley—Gail Cook Howell; Mr. Page—Don Mayo; Miss Grové—M. Kathryn Quinlan; Mr. Vichi—Don Mayo, Roger Preston Smith.

Directed by Robert Johanson; choreography, James Rocco; musical direction, Jeff Rizzo; scenery, Michael Anania; costumes, Gregg Barnes; Winkie costumes, A.T. Jones & Sons; lighting, Tim Hunter; sound, David R. Paterson; dance and vocal arrangements, Peter Howard; orchestrations, Larry Wilcox; music coordinator, John Miller; animals, William Berloni; flying, Foy; associate choreographer, Donna Drake; casting, Julie Hughes, Barry Moss; production stage manager, Lora K. Powell; stage manager, Regina S. Guggenheim.

This version of *The Wizard of Oz* had been adapted from the screen play for the Royal Shakespeare Company by John Kane and previously produced at the Paper Mill Playhouse. The play was presented without intermission.

MUSICAL NUMBERS

Scene 1: The Gales' farm in Kansas
"Over the Rainbow" .... Dorothy
Scene 2: Professor Marvel's wagon
Scene 3:The Gales' farm
  The Cyclone
Scene 4: Munchkinland
"Come Out, Come Out" .... Glinda, Dorothy, Munchkins
"Ding Dong the Witch Is Dead!" .... Glinda, Mayor, Barristers, Coroner, Munchkins
"Follow the Yellow Brick Road" .... Dorothy, Munchkins
Scene 5: A cornfield
"If I Only Had a Brain" .... Scarecrow, Dorothy, Crows
"We're Off to See the Wizard" .... Dorothy, Scarecrow
Scene 6: An apple orchard
"If I Only Had a Heart" .... Tinman, Dorothy, Scarecrow, Apple Trees
"We're Off to See the Wizard" .... Dorothy, Scarecrow, Tinman
Scene 7: A wild forest
"Lions, Tigers and Bears" .... Dorothy, Scarecrow, Tinman

"If I Only Had the Nerve/We're Off to
    See the Wizard" .... Cowardly Lion, Dorothy,Tinman, Scarecrow
Scene 8: A field of poppies
    "Poppies/Optimistic Voices" ...... Glinda, Dorothy, Scarecrow, Tinman, Cowardly Lion, Wicked
    Witch, Poppies
Scene 9: Outside the gates of the Emerald City
    "Optimistic Voices" .... Female Chorus
Scene 10: Inside the Emerald City
    "Merry Old Land of Oz" .... Dorothy, Scarecrow, Tinman, Cowardly Lion, Guard, Citizens of Oz
    "King of the Forest" .... Cowardly Lion, Dorothy, Tinman, Scarecrow
Scene 11: The Wizard's chamber
Scene 12: The haunted forest
    "March of the Winkies" .... Winkies
Scene 13: Inside the Witch's castle
    "Ding Dong the Witch Is Dead!" (Reprise) .... Winkies, Dorothy, Cowardly Lion,
    Scarecrow, Tinman
Scene 14: The Wizard's chamber
Scene 15: Inside the Emerald City
    "Over the Rainbow" (Reprise) .... Glinda
Scene 16: The Gales' farm in Kansas
    Finale .... Company

Grease (6). Limited return engagement of the Tommy Tune production of the musical with book, music and lyrics by Jim Jacobs and Warren Casey. Produced by Barry & Fran Weissler and Jujamcyn Theaters at the City Center. Opened November 29, 1996. (Closed December 1, 1996)

Vince Fontaine	Don Most	Roger	David Josefsberg
Miss Lynch	Sally Struthers	Jan	Farah Alvin
Sonny	Stephen Gnojewski	Danny Zuko	Adrian Zmed
Kenickie	Steve Geyer	Eugene Florczyk	Christopher Youngsman
Frenchy	Alisa Klein	Patty Simcox	Stephanie Seeley
Doody	Roy Chicas	Sandy Dumbrowski	Christiane Noll
Betty Rizzo	Tracy Nelson	Cha-Cha Digregorio	Lori Lynch
Marty	Cathy Trien	Teen Angel	Lee Truesdale

The Heartbeats: Denise Boccanfuso, Stefani Rae, Joelle Letta. The Dream Mooners: Shannon Bailey, Stefani Rae. The Four Straight A's: Shannon Bailey, Christopher Youngsman, Alan Jenkins, Daniel Pawlus.

Ensemble: Shannon Bailey, Denise Boccanfuso, Ashton Byrum, Scot Fedderly, Alan Jenkins, Michelle Kittrell, Joelle Letta, Daniel Pawlus, Stefani Rae, Mary Ruvolo.

Swings: Ginger Norman, Thomas Scott, Timothy Edward Smith.

The High School Band: John Samorian conductor; Kelsey Halbert assistant conductor, keyboards; Jim O'Donnell guitar; Dan Gross drums.

Directed and choreographed by Jeff Calhoun; musical direction, John Samorian; scenery, John Arnone; costumes, Willa Kim; lighting, Howell Binkley; sound, Tom Morse; hair design, Patrik D. Moreton; associate choreographer, Jerry Mitchell; dance supervisor, Patti D'Beck; musical supervision and vocal and dance arrangements, John McDaniel; orchestrations, Steve Margoshes; presented in association with Pace Theatrical Group and TV Asahi; associate producer, Alecia Parker; casting, Stuart Howard, Amy Schecter; production stage manager, L.A. Lavin; stage managers, Jill B. Gounder, Gary Mickelson; press, The Pete Sanders Group, Anita Dloniak.

The Broadway company of the Tommy Tune production of *Grease*, which opened 5/11/94, was still going strong at the Eugene O'Neill Theater when this touring company of the same production made a special Thanksgiving visit to the City Center and then continued its road tour.

ACT I

Scene 1: Rydell High
    "Alma Mater" .... Miss Lynch, Company
    "We Go Together" .... Pink Ladies, Burger Palace Boys

Scene 2: Cafeteria
"Summer Nights" .... Sandy, Danny, Pink Ladies, Burger Palace Boys
Scene 3: School hallway
"Those Magic Changes" .... Doody, Company
Scene 4: Marty's bathroom
"Freddy, My Love" .... Marty, Pink Ladies
Scene 5: Street corner
"Greased Lightnin' " .... Kenickie, Burger Palace Boys
"Greased Lightnin' " (Reprise) .... Rizzo, Burger Palace Boys
Scene 6: Bleachers
"Rydell Fight Song" .... Sandy, Patty, Cheerleading Squad
Scene 7: School yard
"Mooning" .... Roger, Jan
"Look at Me, I'm Sandra Dee" .... Rizzo
Scene 8: The lockers
"Since I Don't Have You" .... Sandy
"We Go Together" .... Company

ACT II

Scene 1: Rydell High boy's gym
"Shakin' at the High School Hop" .... The Four Straight A's
"It's Raining on Prom Night" .... Sandy, The Four Straight A's
"Born to Hand Jive" .... Eugene, Miss Lynch, Company
Scene 2: Outside the Burger Palace
"Beauty School Dropout" .... Teen Angel, Frenchy, Choir
Scene 3: Twi-light Drive-in
"Alone at the Drive-in Movie" .... Danny
Scene 4: Rizzo's rec room
"Rock 'n' Roll Party Queen" .... Doody, Kenickie
"There Are Worse Things I Could Do" .... Rizzo
"Look at Me, I'm Sandra Dee" (Reprise) .... Sandy, Rizzo
"Grease" Finale .... Company

Dreams & Nightmares (54). Magic show created and performed by David Copperfield; adapted by David Ives. Produced by Magicworks Entertainment and Pace Theatrical Group at the Martin Beck Theater. Opened December 5, 1996. (Closed December 29, 1996)

With K.L. Steers, Holly Raye, Wesley Fine.
Visual artistic director, Eiko Ishioka; additional lighting, Robert Wierzel; creative advisor, Francis Ford Coppola; magic consultant, Chris Kenner; illusion manager, Tim Merrell; special effects, Rene Nadeau; sound, Glenn T. Labay; stage manager, J. Stan Jakubiec Jr.; press, Richard Kornberg & Associates, Rick Miramontez, Don Summa.
The magician David Copperfield starring in "an intimate evening of grand illusion."

Once Upon a Mattress (187). Revival of the musical with book by Jay Thompson, Marshall Barer and Dean Fuller; music by Mary Rodgers; lyrics by Marshall Barer. Produced by Dodger Productions and Joop Van Den Ende at the Broadhurst Theater. Opened December 19, 1997. (Closed May 31, 1997)

King Sextimus	Heath Lamberts	The Nightingale of	
Queen Aggravain	Mary Lou Rosato	Samarkand	Ann Brown
Prince Dauntless	David Aaron Baker	The Royal Cellist	Laura Bontrager
Winnifred	Sarah Jessica Parker	The Royal Ballet	Arte Phillips, Pascale Faye
Sir Harry	Lewis Cleale	Minstrel	Lawrence Clayton
Lady Larken	Jane Krakowski	Player Queen	David Jennings
Jester	David Hibbard	Player Prince	David Elder
Master Merton	Tom Alan Robbins	Player Princess	Bob Walton

Other Players: Arte Phillips, Nick Cokas, Stephen Reed.

Knights, Lords, Ladies: Nick Cokas, David Elder, David Jennings, Sebastian LaCause, Jason Opsahl, Arte Phillips, Stephen Reed, Bob Walton, Ann Brown, Maria Calabrese, Thursday Farrar, Pascale Faye, Janet Metz, Tina Ou, Aixa M. Rosario Medina, Jennifer Smith.

Orchestra: Eric Stern conductor; Todd Ellison associate conductor; Michael Roth concertmaster; Edward Joffe, Rick Heckman, Roger Rosenberg woodwinds; Joe Mosello, Glenn Drewes trumpet; Keith O'Quinn trombone; Liuh-Wen Ting viola; Daniel D. Miller, Laura Bontrager cello; Richard Sarpola bass; John Meyers drums, percussion; Todd Ellison, Adam Ben-David keyboards.

Standbys and Understudies: Miss Parker—Janet Metz; Mr. Lamberts—Tom Alan Robbins; Miss Rosato—Jennifer Smith; Messrs. Baker, Hibbard—Bob Walton; Mr. Cleale—David Elder; Miss Krakowski—Ann Brown; Mr. Robbins—Stephen Reed; Mr. Clayton—Jason Opsahl; Swings—Pamela Gold, Thomas Titone.

Directed by Gerald Gutierrez; choreography, Liza Gennaro; musical direction and vocal arrangements, Eric Stern; scenery, John Lee Beatty; costumes, Jane Greenwood; lighting, Pat Collins; sound, Tom Morse; orchestrations, Bruce Coughlin; dance arrangements, Tom Fay; incidental music arrangements, Eric Stern; music coordinator, John Miller; executive producer, Dodger Management Group; casting, Jay Binder; production stage manager, Steven Beckler; stage manager, Brian Meister; press, Boneau/Bryan-Brown, Adrian Bryan-Brown, Susanne Tighe.

Time: Spring 1428. Place: In and about the castle. The play was presented in two parts.

Once Upon a Mattress was first produced by the Phoenix Theater 5/11/59 for 460 performances. It was revived off Broadway by Equity Theater in the 1966-67 season for 14 performances.

ACT I

Overture

"Many Moons Ago" .... Minstrel, Players
"An Opening for a Princess" .... Dauntless, Lady Larken, Knights, Ladies
"In a Little While" .... Lady Larken, Sir Harry
"Shy" .... Winnifred, Knights
"The Minstrel, the Jester and I" .... King, Minstrel, Jester
"Sensitivity" .... Queen
"Swamps of Home" .... Winnifred, Dauntless, Ladies
"Normandy" .... Minstrel, Jester, King, Lady Larken
"Spanish Panic" .... Queen, Winnifred, Dauntless, Knights, Ladies
"Song of Love" .... Dauntless, Winnifred, Knights, Ladies

ACT II

Entr'acte

"Quiet" .... Entire Court
"Goodnight, Sweet Princess" .... Dauntless
"Happily Ever After" .... Winnifred
"Man to Man Talk" .... King, Dauntless
"Very Soft Shoes" .... Jester
"Yesterday I Loved You" .... Sir Harry, Lady Larken
"Lullaby" .... The Nightingale of Samarkand
Finale .... Entire Court

Men Are From Mars, Women Are From Venus (8). Solo performance by John Gray; written by John Gray; based on his book. Produced by Skylar Communications at the Gershwin Theater. Opened January 27, 1997. (Closed February 1, 1997)

Scenery, Denise Stansfield; lighting. Eric Todd; sound, Joseph Light; production supervisor, Marty Hom; press, Susan Blond.

Advice and comment on the relationships between men and women. The show was presented in two parts.

Stanley (74). By Pam Gems. Produced by Circle in the Square, Gregory Mosher producing director, M. Edgar Rosenblum executive producer, in the Royal National Theater production,

STANLEY—Antony Sher *(right)* as the painter Stanley Spencer with Anna Chancellor in the Tony-nominated Royal National Theater production of the play by Pam Gems

Richard Eyre director, at Circle in the Square. Opened February 20, 1997. (Closed April 27, 1997)

Hilda	Deborah Findlay	Dorothy	Selina Cadell
Stanley	Antony Sher	Dudley	Peter Maloney
Henry	Barton Tinapp	Elsie	Alison Larkin
Gwen	Barbara Garrick	Mrs. Carline	Victoria Boothby
Patricia	Anna Chancellor	Brian	Jase Blankfort
Augustus John	Ken Kliban	Tim	Chad Aaron

Others: Company.

Andrew Lippa piano, keyboards.

Directed by John Caird; scenery and costumes, Tim Hatley; lighting, Peter Mumford; sound, Freya Edwards; music, J.S. Bach, arranged by Ilona Sekacz; casting, Hopkins, Smith & Barden, Pat DiStefano; production stage manager, R. Wade Jackson; stage manager, Deirdre McCrane; press, Bill Evans & Associates, Michael S. Borowski, Jim Randolph, Terry M. Lilly.

Time: 1920–1959. Place: The village of Cookham in Berkshire and at Hampstead in London. The play was presented in two parts.

Love in various forms and dreams of glory among the artists of the period, with particular focus on the life and work of Stanley Spencer. A foreign play previously produced by Royal National Theater in London.

*The Last Night of Ballyhoo (107). By Alfred Uhry. Produced by Jane Harmon, Nina Keneally and Liz Oliver at the Helen Hayes Theater. Opened February 27, 1997.

Lala Levy .... Jessica Hecht	Joe Farkas .... Paul Rudd
Reba Freitag .... Celia Weston	Sunny Freitag .... Arija Bareikis
Boo Levy .... Dana Ivey	Peachy Weil .... Stephen Largay
Adolph Freitag .... Terry Beaver	

Standbys: Misses Hecht, Bareikis—Mandy Fox; Messrs. Rudd, Largay—Robert Gomes; Mr. Beaver—Philip LeStrange; Misses Weston, Ivey—Peggity Price.

Directed by Ron Lagomarsino; scenery, John Lee Beatty; costumes, Jane Greenwood; lighting, Kenneth Posner; sound, Tony Meola; incidental music, Robert Waldman; casting, Jay Binder; production stage manager, Franklin Keysar; stage manager, Bob E. Gasper; press, Boneau/Bryan-Brown.

Time: December 1939. Place: Atlanta, Georgia, Adolph Freitag's house, at the Standard Club and aboard the Crescent Limited. The play was presented in two parts.

Friction and abrasion within an Atlanta Jewish family at the time of the world premiere of the movie *Gone With the Wind*. Previously produced in regional theater by the Alliance Theater, Atlanta. Winner of the 1996–97 Tony Award for best play; see the Prizewinning Plays section of this volume.

Mandy Patinkin in Concert (15). Solo performance by Mandy Patinkin. Produced by Dodger Endemol Theatricals at the Lyceum Theater. Opened March 1, 1997. (Closed March 22, 1997)

Piano: Paul Ford.

Director, Eric Cornwell; sound consultant, Otts Munderloh; sound associate, Mary McGregor; press, Boneau/Bryan-Brown, Chris Boneau.

Limited engagement of a benefit concert, presented without intermission.

Lord of the Dance (12). Dance musical created by Michael Flatley; choreographed by Michael Flatley; original music by Ronan Hardiman. Produced by Michael Flatley for Unicorn Ltd., Derek MacKillop for John Reid Enterprises Ltd. and Harvey Goldsmith at Radio City Music Hall. Opened March 4, 1997. (Closed March 17, 1997)

Lord of the Dance .... Michael Flatley	Morrighan .... Gillian Norris
Saoirse .... Bernadette Flynn	The Little Spirit .... Helen Egan
Don Dorcha .... Daire Nolan	Erin .... Anne Buckley

Principal Dancers: Bernadette Flynn, Daire Nolan, Gillian Norris.

Clan of the Celts, Warlords, Warriors, Girls of Ireland (The Lord of the Dance Troupe): Desmond Bailey, Steven Brunning, Declan Burke, John Carey, Linda Cawte, Donal Conlan, Kerrie Connolly, James Devine, Michael Donellan, Denise Flynn, Mark Gilley, Caroline Greene, Catriona Hale, Fiona Harold, Kathleen Keady, Kellyann Leathem, Dearbhla Lennon, Tony Lundon, Patrick Lundon, Karen McCamphill, Derek Moran, Chelsea Muldoon, Jim Murrihy, Areleen Ni Bhaoill, Cian Nolan, Paul Noonan, Sharon O'Brien, Damien O'Kane, Colleen Roberts, Mary Ann Schade-Lynch, Conor Smith, Dawn Tiernan.

The Lord of the Dance Orchestra: Anne Dudley conductor; Dave Keary orchestra leader, electric and acoustic guitars, bouzouki; Gerard Fahey pipes, low whistle, bouzouki, flute, saxophone; Liam O'Connor accordion; Gary Sullivan percussion, drums; Eamonn Byrne bass guitar; Paul Drennan string synthesizers, kurzwell, sound effects; Malread Nesbitt, Cora Smyth violin; Anne Buckley solo soprano.

Director, Arlene Phillips; musical direction, Ronan Hardiman; orchestration, Anne Dudley; additional choreography, Marie Duffy-Messenger; show design, Jonathan Park; costumes, Sue Blane; lighting, Patrick Woodroffe; stage manager, Sue Banner; press, Steve Henderson.

Conflict between good and evil, dramatized in dance and flavored with Celtic folklore and rock music. A foreign (Irish) production.

ACT I, Scene 1: Cry of the Celts—Spirit, Lord of the Dance, The Clan, Erin. Scene 2: Erin the Goddess. Scene 3: Celtic Dream—Saoirse, Girls. Scene 4: The Warriors—Don Dorcha, Warriors. Scene 5: Gypsy—Morrighan. Scene 6: Strings of Fire—Violins. Scene 7: Breakout—Saoirse, Girls. Scene 8: Warlords: Lord of the Dance, Warlords—Lord of the Dance, The Clan.

ACT II, Scene 1: Dangerous Game—Spirit, Don Dorcha, Warriors. Scene 2, Hell's Kitchen—Lord of the Dance, Don Dorcha, Warlords, Warriors. Scene 3: Fiery Nights. Scene 4: The Lament—Violins. Scene 5: Siamsa—The Clan. Scene 6: She Moves Through the Fair—Erin. Scene 7: Stolen Kiss—Saoirse, Lord of the Dance, Morrighan. Scene 8: Nightmare—Lord of the Dance, Don Dorcha, Warriors. Scene

9: The Duel—Lord of the Dance, Don Dorcha. Scene 10: Victory—Lord of the Dance, The Clan. Scene 11: Planet Ireland.

Play On! (61). Musical conceived by Sheldon Epps; book by Cheryl L. West; with the songs of Duke Ellington. Produced by Mitchell Maxwell, Eric Nederlander, Thomas Hall, Hal Luftig, Bruce Lucker, Mike Skipper and Victoria Maxwell in association with Kery Davis and Alan J. Schuster at the Brooks Atkinson Theater. Opened March 20, 1997. (Closed May 11, 1997)

Vy	Cheryl Freeman	CC	Crystal Allen
Jester	Andre De Shields	Duke	Carl Anderson
Sweets	Larry Marshall	Rev	Lawrence Hamilton
Miss Mary	Yvette Cason	Lady Liv	Tonya Pinkins

Denizens of Harlem: Ronald "Cadet" Bastine, Jacquelyn Bird, Wendee Lee Curtis, Byron Easley, Alan H. Green, Frantz G. Hall, Gil P., Lacy Darryl Phillips, Lisa Scialabba, Erica Vaughn, Karen Callaway Williams.

Musicians: J. Leonard Oxley conductor; George Caldwell assistant conductor, piano; Jerome Richardson, William Easley, Jimmy Cosier reeds; Earl Gardner, Virgil Jones, Stanton Davis trumpet; Britt Woodman trombone; Ben Brownz bass; Brian Grice percussion.

Understudies: Miss Pinkins—Angela Robinson; Misses Freeman, Cason—Stacie Precia, Angela Robinson; Mr. Anderson—Alan H. Green, William Wesley; Mr. Hamilton—Alan H. Green, Frantz G. Hall; Mr. Marshall—Alan H. Green, Gil P.; Mr. De Shields—Bryan S. Haynes, Lacy Darryl Phillips; Miss Allen—Wendee Lee Curtis; Swings—Germaine Goodson, Bryan S. Haynes, Stacie Precia, William Wesley.

Directed by Sheldon Epps; choreography, Mercedes Ellington; musical direction, J. Leonard Oxley; musical supervision, arrangements and orchestrations, Luther Henderson; scenery, James Leonard Joy; costume design, Marianna Elliott; lighting, Jeff Davis; sound, Jeff Ladman; creative consultants, Louis Johnson, Frankie Manning; musical coordinator, William Meade; associate producers, Leon Memoli, David Levy, Nancy Eichorn, Louis F. Raizin, James L. Simon, Fred H. Krones; casting, Pat McCorkle, Tim Sutton; production stage manager, Robert Mark Kalfin; stage managers, Lurie Horns Pfeffer, Jimmy Lee Smith, Matthew Aaron Stern; press, Richard Kornberg Associates, Jim Byk, Rick Miramontez, Don Summa.

Time: The swingin' 40s. Place: The magical kingdom of Harlem.

Shakespeare's *Twelfth Night* loosely translated into a 20th century Harlem vehicle for Ellington's music. Originally produced by the Old Globe Theater, San Diego.

ACT I

Scene 1: Grand Central Station
   "Take the 'A' Train" .... Vy, Ensemble
Scene 2: 125th Street
   "Drop Me Off in Harlem" .... Vy , Denizens of Harlem
   "I've Got To Be a Rug Cutter" .... Jester, Vy, Cotton Club Dancers
Scene 3: The Duke's apartment
   "I Let a Song Go Out of My Heart" .... Duke
Scene 4: The Cotton Club
   "C Jam Blues" .... Cotton Club Dancers
   "Mood Indigo" .... Lady Liv
Scene 5: Lady Liv's dressing room
   "Don't Get Around Much Anymore" .... Vy, Lady Liv
   "Don't You Know I Care" .... Rev
Scene 6: The Cotton Club
   "It Don't Mean a Thing" .... Jester, Miss Mary, Sweets, Rev
Scene 7: The Duke's studio
   "I Got It Bad and That Ain't Good" .... Duke, Vy
   "Hit Me With a Hot Note and Watch Me Bounce" .... Vy, Duke, Duke's Band
Scene 8: The Cotton Club
Scene 9: Alley outside of the Cotton Club
   "I'm Just a Lucky So and So" .... Jester, Cotton Club Dancers

Scene 10: The Cotton Club
"Everything But You" .... Lady Liv, Vy
"Solitude" .... Vy, Duke, Lady Liv, Rev

ACT II

Scene 1: The Cotton Club
"Black Butterfly" .... Lady Liv's Escorts
"I Ain't Got Nothin' But the Blues" .... Lady Liv
Scene 2: Lady Liv's dressing room
Scene 3: The Cotton Club
"I'm Beginning to See the Light" .... Rev, Cotton Club Dancers
"I Got It Bad and That Ain't Good" (Reprise) .... Rev
Scene 4: Outside of the Cotton Club
"I Didn't Know About You" .... Vy
Scene 5: The Cotton Club
"Rocks in My Bed" .... Sweets, Jester
Scene 6: Lady Liv's apartment
"Something to Live For" .... Rev, Lady Liv
Scene 7: Outside of the Cotton Club
"Love You Madly" .... Miss Mary, Sweets
Scene 8: The Duke's apartment
"Prelude to a Kiss" .... Vy, Duke
Scene 9: 125th Street
"In a Mellow Tone" .... Vy, Duke, Lady Liv, Rev, Denizens of Harlem

*__Barrymore__ (79). By William Luce. Produced by Livent (U.S.) Inc., Garth H. Drabinsky chairman, at the Music Box. Opened March 25, 1997.

John Barrymore .... Christopher Plummer
Frank .... Michael Mastro

Understudy: Mr. Mastro—Jim Semmelman.
Directed by Gene Saks; scenery and costumes, Santo Loquasto; lighting, Natasha Katz; casting, Beth Russell, Arnold J. Mungioli; production stage manager, Susan Konynenburg; stage manager, Jim Semmelman; press, Mary Bryant.
Time: A month before John Barrymore's death. Act I: The spring of 1942. Act II: Later the same evening.
Virtually a solo performance by Plummer as the famous actor in decline, telling stories to an offstage stagehand and planning a production of _Richard III_. Previously produced at the Stratford, Canada, Festival.

*__Annie__ (78). Revival of the musical based on Harold Gray's comic strip _Little Orphan Annie_; book by Thomas Meehan; music by Charles Strouse; lyrics by Martin Charnin. Produced by Timothy Childs & Rodger Hess and Jujamcyn Theaters in association with Terri B. Childs and Al Nocciolino at the Martin Beck Theater. Opened March 26, 1997.

Annie .... Brittny Kissinger	Apple Seller; Fred McCracken;
Molly .... Christiana Anbri	Ickes .... Brad Wills
Pepper .... Cassidy Ladden	Dog Catcher; Fred; Jimmy Johnson;
Duffy .... Mekenzie Rosen-Stone	Howe .... Tom Treadwell
July .... Casey Tuma	Dog Catcher; Cecille; A Star To Be;
Tessie .... Lyndsey Watkins	Ronnie Boylan .... Sutton Foster
Kate .... Melissa O'Malley	Sandy .... Cindy Lou
Miss Hannigan .... Nell Carter	Lt. Ward; Hull; Justice Brandeis ... Drew Taylor
Bundles McClosky; Sgt Thayer;	Sophie, the Kettle; Mrs. Pugh;
Sound Effects Man;	Perkins .... Barbara Tirrell
Honor Guard .... Michael E. Gold	Grace Farrell .... Colleen Dunn

Drake; Bert Healy;
Morganthau .... MichaelJohn McGann
Mrs. Greer;
Bonnie Boylan .... Elizabeth Richmond
Annette; Connie Boylan .... Kelley Swaim
Oliver Warbucks .... Conrad John Schuck

Rooster Hannigan .... Jim Ryan
Lily .... Karen Byers-Blackwell
Oxydent "Hour of Smiles"
Producer .... Jennifer L. Neuland
H.V. Kaltenborn's Voice .... Bryan Young
F.D.R. .... Raymond Thorne

Hooverville-ites, Warbucks' Staff, New Yorkers: Sutton Foster, Michael E. Gold, Michael John McGann, Jennifer L. Neuland, Elizabeth Richmond, Kelley Swaim, Drew Taylor, Barbara Tirrell, Tom Treadwell, Brad Wills.

Understudies: Miss Kissinger—Alexandra Kiesman; Mr. Schuck—Drew Taylor; Miss Dunn—Kelley Swaim, Christy Tarr; Miss Carter—Barbara Tirrell; Mr. Thorne—Tom Treadwell; Mr. Ryan—Michael E. Gold; Miss Byers-Blackwell—Jennifer L. Neuland, Christy Tarr; Miss Anbri—Mekenzie Rosen-Stone; Miss O'Malley—Casey Tuma; Misses Watkins, Ladden, Rosen-Stone, Tuma—Alexandra Kiesman; Sandy—Zappa; Swings—J.B. Adams, Christy Tarr.

Orchestra: Keith Levenson conductor; Anne Shuttlesworth associate conductor, keyboard; Blair Lawhead violin; Marison Espada cello; Donald Downs, Craig Johnson trumpet; Joseph Petrizzo tenor trombone; Alan Ralph tuba; Vincent Della Rocca, Timothy Ries, Donald Haviland saxophones; Ray Kilday bass; Marco Granados flute; Ed Hamilton guitar; Mark Mule drums; Christine Cadarette keyboard.

Directed by Martin Charnin; choreography, Peter Gennaro; musical direction and supervision, Keith Levenson; scenery, Kenneth Foy; costumes, Theoni V. Aldredge; lighting, Ken Billington; sound, T. Richard Fitzgerald; musical coordinator, John Monaco; associate producers, Tamar Climan, Herb Goldsmith; casting, Stuart Howard, Amy Schecter; production stage manager, Bryan Young; stage manager, Jeffrey M. Markowitz; press, Peter Cromarty.

Time: Act I, December 11-19, 1933. Act II, December 21-25, 1933.

Annie was first produced on Broadway 4/21/77 for 2,377 performances, was designated a Best Play of its season and won the Critics and Tony Awards for best musical. A sequel *Annie 2: Miss Hannigan's Revenge* was produced out of town 1/4/90 but closed prior to its New York opening. This, *Annie's* first major New York revival, was originally produced by Goodspeed Opera House.

ACT I

Scene 1: The New York Municipal Orphanage (Girls Annex), St. Marks Place
  "Maybe" .... Annie
  "It's the Hard-Knock Life" .... Annie, Orphans
  "It's the Hard-Knock Life" (Reprise) .... Orphans
Scene 2: Lower Broadway
  "Tomorrow" .... Annie
Scene 3: A Hooverville near the East 10th Street Gas Works
  "We'd Like to Thank You" .... Hooverville-ites
Scene 4: The Orphanage
  "Little Girls" .... Miss Hannigan
Scene 5: The Warbucks Mansion at Fifth Avenue and 82nd Street
  "I Think I'm Gonna Like It Here" .... Grace, Annie, Drake, Cecille, Annette, Mrs. Pugh,
                                                                                                 Other Servants
Scene 6: From Fifth Avenue to Times Square
  "N.Y.C." .... Warbucks, Grace, Annie, Star To Be, New Yorkers
Scene 7: The Orphanage
  "You Make Me Happy" .... Miss Hannigan, Grace
  "Easy Street" .... Miss Hannigan, Rooster, Lily
Scene 8: Warbucks' study
  "You Won't Be an Orphan for Long" .... Grace, Drake, Mrs. Pugh, Cecille, Annette,
                                                                                                 Servants, Warbucks

ACT II

Scene 1: The NBC Radio Studio at 30 Rockefeller Center
  "You're Never Fully Dressed Without a Smile" .... Bert Healy, The Boylan Sisters,
                                                                                     The Hour of Smiles Family

THE YOUNG MAN FROM ATLANTA: Rip Torn and Shirley Knight in a scene from the revival of the Pulitzer Prizewinning play by Horton Foote

Scene 2: The Orphanage
Scene 3: Washington: The White House
Scene 4: The Gallery at the Warbucks Mansion
Scene 5: The east ballroom of the Warbucks Mansion

*The Young Man From Atlanta (79). Revival of the play by Horton Foote. Produced by David Richenthal, Anita Waxman and Jujamcyn Theaters in association with the Goodman Theater and Robert Cole at the Longacre Theater. Opened March 27, 1996.

Will Kidder .... Rip Torn	Pete Davenport .... William Biff McGuire
Tom Jackson .... Marcus Giamatti	Clara .... Jacqueline Williams
Miss Lacey .... Pat Nesbit	Carson .... Kevin Bresnahan
Ted Cleveland Jr. .... Stephen Trovillion	Etta Doris Meneffree .... Beatrice Winde
Lily Dale Kidder .... Shirley Knight	

Directed by Robert Falls; scenery, Thomas Lynch; costumes, David C. Woolard; lighting, James F. Ingalls; original music and sound, Richard Woodbury; associate producer, Joan Levy Finkelstein; casting, Bernard Telsey; production stage manager, Susie Cordon; stage manager, John Handy; press, Jeffrey Richards Associates, Irene Gandy, Roger Bean.

Time: Spring 1950. Place: Houston, Tex. Act I, Scene 1: Will Kidder's office, a weekday afternoon. Scene 2: The Kidder residence, that evening after dinner. Scene 3: The Kidder residence, one week later. Act II, Scene 1: The Kidder residence, the following day. Scene 2: The Kidder residence, later the same day. Scene 3: The Kidder residence, later the same day.

The Young Man From Atlanta was first produced by Signature Theater Company in an off-off-Broadway engagement limited to 24 performances 1/27/95, when it won a Best Plays citation and the Pulitzer Prize. This production, originally mounted by the Goodman Theater in Chicago, is its first New York revival.

*A Doll's House (63). Revival of the play by Henrik Ibsen; new version by Frank McGuinness. Produced by Bill Kenwright in association with Thelma Holt at the Belasco Theater. Opened April 2, 1997.

Nora Helmer	Janet McTeer	Anne-Marie	Robin Howard
Torvald Helmer	Owen Teale	Helene	Rose Stockton
Kristine Linde	Jan Maxwell	Messenger	John Ottavino
Nils Krogstad	Peter Gowen	Bobby and Ivan	Liam Aiken, Paul Tiesler
Dr. Rank	John Carlisle		

Understudies: Misses McTeer, Maxwell—Rose Stockton; Messrs. Teale, Gowen—John Ottavino; Messrs. Carlisle, Ottavino—Kent Broadhurst.

Directed by Anthony Page; scenery and costumes, Deirdre Clancy; lighting, Peter Mumford; sound, Scott Myers, John Owens; music, Jason Carr; U.S. casting, Pat McCorkle; production stage manager, Sally J. Jacobs; stage manager, Tom Santopietro; press, Philip Rinaldi, Barbara Carroll.

Time: 1879. Place: The Helmers' living room in a small Norwegian town. Act I: Christmas Eve, morning. Act II: Christmas Day, late afternoon. Act III: the day after Christmas, night. The play was presented in two parts with the intermission following Act I.

The last major New York revival of *A Doll's House* was by the Acting Company off Broadway 5/15/95 for 3 performances.

*Dream (69). Musical revue based on the lyrics of Johnny Mercer; conceived by Louise Westergaard and Jack Wrangler; music by various authors; see listing below. Produced by Louise Westergaard, Mark Schwartz, Bob Cuillo, Roger Dean, Obie Bailey, Stephen O'Neil and Abraham Salaman at the Royale Theater. Opened April 3, 1997.

Brooks Ashmanskas	Susan Misner
Todd Bailey	Jessica Molaskey
Jonathan Dokuchitz	Kevyn Morrow
Angelo Fraboni	John Pizzarelli
Amy Heggins	Darcie Roberts
Jennifer Lamberts	Timothy Edward Smith
Nancy Lemenager	Lesley Ann Warren
Charles McGowan	Margaret Whiting

Orchestra: Bryan Louiselle conductor; Grant Sturiale associate conductor, piano; Robert Millikan, Larry Lunetta, Jon Owens trumpet; John Fedchock, Rock Ciccarone, George Gesslein trombone; Andrew Sterman, Daniel M. Block, Scott Shacter, Dennis C. Anderson, Robert Eldridge reeds; Katie Dennis, Javier Gandara, French horn; Nancy Brennand harp; Peter Donovan bass; Robbie Kirshoff guitar; Tony Tedesco drums; Ed Shea percussion;

The John Pizzarelli Trio: John Pizzarelli guitar, banjo; Ray Kennedy piano; Martin Pizzarelli bass.

Standbys: Miss Warren—Jane Summerhays; Miss Whiting—Denise Lor. Understudies/Swings: Jeffry Denman, Jody Ripplinger, Bill Szobody, Deborah Yates.

Directed by Wayne Cilento; choreography, Wayne Cilento; musical direction and vocal arrangements, Bryan Louiselle; scenery, David Mitchell; costumes, Ann Hould-Ward; lighting, Ken Billington;

sound, Peter Fitzgerald; musical supervision and vocal arrangements, Don Pippin; dance music arrangements, Jeanine Tesori; orchestrations, Dick Lieb; assistant musical supervisor, Jan Rosenberg; musical coordinator, Mel Rodnon; Mercer visualization, Jack Wrangler; assistant choreographers, Travey Langran, Alko Nakasone; dance supervisor, Jerome Vivona; associate producers, Nicole Michele Cuillo, Nancy La Vista, L. Michael Post, Elisa Sterling; casting, Julie Hughes, Barry Moss; production stage manager, Diane DiVita; stage manager, Tripp Phillips; press, Susan L. Schulman.

Collection of 42 of the hundreds of songs for which Johnny Mercer wrote the words for movies, Broadway shows and recordings as one of the major lyric artists of the century. Previously produced at Tennessee Repertory Theater.

MUSICAL NUMBERS

ACT I, Scene 1—Savannah, the Age of Innocence: "Dream" (music by Johnny Mercer)—Darcie Roberts, Jessica Molaskey, Nancy Lemenager, Company; "Lazybones" (music by Hoagy Carmichael)—Amy Heggins, Kevyn Morrow, John Pizzarelli, Company; "On Behalf of the Traveling Salesmen" (music by Walter Donaldson)—Brooks Ashmanskas, Timothy Edward Smith; "Pardon My Southern Accent" (music by Matt Malneck)—Lesley Ann Warren; "You Must Have Been a Beautiful Baby" (music by Harry Warren)—Charles McGowan, Darcie Roberts; "Have You Got Any Castles, Baby?" (music by Richard Whiting)—Jonathan Dokuchitz, Warren, Company; "Goody, Goody" (music by Matt Malneck)—Warren, Company; "Skylark" (music by Hoagy Carmichael)—Molaskey; "The Dixieland Band" (music by Bernie Hanighen)—Pizzarelli, Company.

Scene 2, Magnificent Obsession—The Age of Decadence: "I Had Myself a True Love/I Wonder What Became of Me" (music by Harold Arlen)—Warren, Roberts; "Jamboree Jones Jive" (music by Johnny Mercer)—John Pizzarelli Trio, Company; "Fools Rush In" (music by Rube Bloom)—John Pizzarelli Trio, Company; "Come Rain or Come Shine" (music by Harold Arlen)—Ashmanskas; "Out of This World" (music by Harold Arlen)—Roberts; "I Remember You" (music by Victor Schertzinger)—Molaskey; "Blues in the Night" (music by Harold Arlen)—Warren; "One for My Baby" (music by Harold Arlen)—Margaret Whiting.

Scene 3, Rainbow Room: "You Were Never Lovelier" (music by Jerome Kern)—Pizzarelli; "Satin Doll" (music by Billy Strayhorn and Duke Ellington)—Susan Misner, Men; "I'm Old Fashioned" (music by Jerome Kern)—Roberts, Dokuchitz; "Dearly Beloved" (music by Jerome Kern)—Dokuchitz, Roberts; "This Time the Dream's on Me" (music by Harold Arlen)—Pizzarreli, Warren, Whiting; "Something's Gotta Give" (music by Johnny Mercer)—Molaskey; "Too Marvelous for Words" (music by Richard Whiting)—McGowan, Company.

ACT II, Scene 1, Hollywood Canteen: "I Thought About You" (music by James Van Heusen)—Pizzarelli; "And the Angels Sing" (music by Ziggy Elman)—Orchestra; "The Fleet's In" (music by Victor Schertzinger)—Men; "G.I. Jive" (music by Johnny Mercer)—Warren, Molaskey, Lemenager; "I'm Doin' It for Defense" (music by Harold Arlen)—Roberts; "Tangerine" (music by Victor Schertzinger)—Ashmanskas, Company; "Day In-Day Out" (music by Rube Bloom)—Whiting; "Jeepers Creepers" (music by Harry Warren)—John Pizzarelli Trio; "That Old Black Magic" (music by Harold Arlen)—Warren; "Laura" (music by David Raksin)—Dokuchitz; "You Go Your Way" (music by Johnny Mercer)—Company; "My Shining Hour" (music by Harold Arlen)—Whiting, Company.

Scene 2, Academy Awards: "Hooray for Hollywood" (music by Richard Whiting)—Ashmanskas, Angelo Fraboni, Morrow, Smith; "Accentuate the Positive" (music by Harold Arlen)—Ashmanskas, Fraboni, Morrow, Smith, Lemenager; "In the Cool, Cool, Cool of the Evening" (music by Hoagy Carmichael)—Whiting, John Pizzarelli Trio; "Charade/The Days of Wine and Roses" (music by Henry Mancini)—Dokuchitz, Molaskey, Company; "Moon River" (music by Henry Mancini)—Warren; "On the Atchison, Topeka and the Santa Fe" (music by Harry Warren)—Company.

*The Gin Game (48). Revival of the play by D.L. Coburn. Produced by National Actors Theater, Tony Randall founder and artistic director, Manny Kladitis executive producer, at the Lyceum Theater. Opened April 20, 1997.

Fonsia Dorsey .... Julie Harris
Weller Martin .... Charles Durning

Standbys: Miss Harris—Natalie Norwick; Mr. Durning—Tom Troupe.

Directed by Charles Nelson Reilly; scenery, James Noone; costumes, Noel Taylor; lighting, Kirk Bookman; sound, Richard Fitzgerald; production stage manager, Mitchell Erickson; press, Springer/Chicoine Associates, Gary Springer, Candi Adams.

Time: The present. Act I, Scene 1: Sunday afternoon, visitor's day. Scene 2: Sunday afternoon, one week later. Act II, Scene 1: The following evening, shortly after dinner. Scene 2: The following Sunday afternoon.

The Gin Game was first produced on Broadway 10/6/77 for 517 performances and was named a Best Play of its season and won the Pulitzer Prize. This is its first major New York revival.

***Titanic** (45). Musical with story and book by Peter Stone; music and lyrics by Maury Yeston. Produced by Dodger Endemol Theatricals, Richard S. Pechter and the John F. Kennedy Center for the Performing Arts at the Lunt-Fontanne Theater. Opened April 23, 1997.

Officers & Crew of R.M.S. Titanic:
Capt. E.J. Smith .... John Cunningham
1st Officer William Murdoch   David Costabile
2d Officer Charles Lightoller .... John Bolton
3d Officer
  Herbert J. Pitman .... Matthew Bennett
Frederick Barrett,
  Stoker .... Brian d'Arcy James
Harold Bride, Radioman .... Martin Moran
Henry Etches,
  1st Class Steward .... Allan Corduner
Frederick Fleet, Lookout .... David Elder
Quartermaster Robert Hichens;
  Bandsman Bricoux ...... Adam Alexi-Malle
4th Officer Joseph Boxhall;
  Bandsman Taylor .... Andy Taylor
Chief Engineer Joseph Bell; Wallace Hartley,
  Orchestra Leader .... Ted Sperling
Stewardess Robinson .... Michele Ragusa
Stewardess Hutchinson .... Stephanie Park
Bellboy .... Mara Stephens
Passengers aboard the R.M.S. Titanic
1st Class:
J. Bruce Ismay .... David Garrison
Thomas Andrews .... Michael Cerveris
Isidor Straus .... Larry Keith
Ida Straus .... Alma Cuervo
J.J. Astor .... William Youmans
Madeline Astor .... Lisa Datz
Benjamin Guggenheim .... Joseph Kolinski
Mme. Aubert .... Kimberly Hester
John B. Thayer .... Michael Mulheren

Marion Thayer .... Robin Irwin
George Widener .... Henry Stram
Eleanor Widener .... Jody Gelb
Charlotte Cardoza .... Becky Ann Baker
J.H. Rogers .... Andy Taylor
The Major .... Matthew Bennett
Edith Corse Evans .... Mindy Cooper
  Also David Elder, Erin Hill, Theresa
McCarthy, Charles McAteer, Jennifer Piech,
Clarke Thorell.
2d Class:
Charles Clarke .... Don Stephenson
Caroline Neville .... Judith Blazer
Edgar Beane .... Bill Buell
Alice Beane .... Victoria Clark
  Also John Bolton, Mindy Cooper, David
Costabile, David Elder.
3d Class:
Kate McGowen .... Jennifer Piech
Kate Murphey .... Theresa McCarthy
Kate Mullins .... Erin Hill
Jim Farrell .... Clarke Thorell
  Also Adam Alexi-Malle, Becky Ann Baker,
Matthew Bennett, Mindy Cooper, Alma
Cuervo, Lisa Datz, Jody Gelb, Kimberly Hester,
Robin Irwin, Larry Keith, Joseph Kolinski,
Michael Mulheren, Charles McAteer, Ted
Sperling, Mara Stephens, Henry Stram, Andy
Taylor, William Youmans.
On Shore:
Frank Carlson .... Henry Stram

Orchestra: Kevin Stites conductor; Matthew Sklar associate conductor, keyboard; Nicholas Archer assistant conductor, keyboard; John Miller music coordinator; Joel Pitchon concertmaster; Les Scott, David Kossoff, Steve Kenyon, John J. Moses, John Campo woodwinds; Brian O'Flaherty, Wayne J. DuMaine trumpet; Theresa MacDonnell, Michael Ishii, French horn; Keith O'Quinn, Jeff Nelson trombones; Charles Descarfino, Dave Ratajczak percussion; Carol Zeavin, Naomi Katz, Xin Zhou, Andrea Schultz, Avril Brown violin; Kenneth Burward- Hoy, Sally Shumway viola; Eugene Briskin, Sarah Seiver cello; Gregg August bass; Onstage Trio—Ted Sperling, Adam Alexi-Malle violin, Andy Taylor cello, double bass.

Understudies (listed by role): Barrett—Drew McVety, Andy Taylor; Bride—John Bolton, Drew McVety; Fleet—Jonathan Brody; Bell, Hartley—Jonathan Brody, Peter Kapetan; Murdoch—John Bolton, Peter Kapetan; Lightoller—Jonathan Brody, Andy Taylor; Hichens—Jonathan Brody, Drew McVety; Boxhall, Rogers—John Jellison, Drew McVety; Pitman, Major, Mr. Straus—John Jellison; Capt. Smith—John Jellison, Joseph Kolinski; Ismay—Matthew Bennett, David Costabile, Peter Kapetan; Andrews—Matthew Bennett, Joseph Kolinski; Farrell—Drew McVety, Jonathan Brody; Charles Clarke—Andy Taylor; Mr. Beane, Mr. Astor—John Jellison, Peter Kapetan; Mr. Widener—Jonathan

Brody, John Jellison; Mr. Thayer, Mr. Guggenheim—Jonathan Brody, John Jellison, Peter Kapetan; Mr. Etches—David Costabile, Henry Stram; Kate McGowen—Lisa Datz, Theresa McCarthy; Kate Mullins, Kate Murphey, Mme. Aubert, Mrs. Astor—Melissa Bell; Mrs. Widener, Mrs. Thayer, Mrs. Cardoza—Kay Walbye; Mrs. Beane, Mrs. Straus—Jody Gelb, Kay Walbye; Swings—Melissa Bell, Kay Walbye, Jonathan Brody, John Jellison, Drew McVety.

Directed by Richard Jones; choreography, Lynne Taylor-Corbett; musical supervision and direction, Kevin Stites; scenery and costumes, Stewart Laing; lighting, Paul Gallo; sound, Steve Canyon Kennedy; orchestrations, Jonathan Tunick; action coordinator, Rick Sordelet; executive producer, Dodger Management Group; casting, Julie Hughes, Barry Moss; production stage manager, Susan Green; stage manager, Richard Hester; press, Boneau /Bryan-Brown, Adrian Bryan-Brown, Susanne Tighe, Amy Jacobs.

Time: Between April 10 and 15, 1912. Act I, Prologue: Harland & Wolff, Shipbuilders. Scene 1: Southampton, the "Ocean Dock." Scene 2: Aboard R.M.S. Titanic, the stern. Scene 3: The Dock. Scene 4: The Bridge and Boiler Room # 6. Scene 5: The Saloon ("D") Deck. Scene 6: The 1st Class Dining Saloon. Scene 7: The Bridge. Scene 8: The Middle ("F") Deck; the 3d Class Commissary. Scene 9: The Bridge. Scene 10: The Radio Room. Scene 11: The Boat Deck; 1st Class Promenade. Scene 12: "A" Deck. Scene 13: The Bridge; then the Promenade ("B") Deck, the Saloon ("D") Deck, the Middle ("F") Deck, the 1st Class Smoke Room, the Crow's Nest.

Act II, Scene 1: The 1st, 2d and 3d Class corridors and the Bridge. Scene 2: The 1st Class Grand Salon. Scene 3: "E" Deck, a stairwell. Scene 4: The Boat Deck. Scene 5: The Radio Room. Scene 6: At the lifeboats; Scene 7: Portholes. Scene 8: The Upper Promenade ("A") Deck. Scene 9: The 1st Class Smoke Room. Scene 10: The aftermath.

A memoir of the notorious maritime tragedy presented in the form of a musical, with all characters and events based on fact. Winner of the 1996–97 Tony Award for best musical; see the Prizewinning Plays section of this volume.

ACT I

Prologue
"In Every Age" .... Andrews
The Launching
"How Did They Build Titanic?" .... Barrett
"There She Is" .... Barrett, Bride, Fleet
"Loading Inventory" .... Smith, Stevedores, Ship's Personnel
"The Largest Moving Object" .... Ismay, Smith, Andrews
"I Must Get on That Ship" .... Pitman, 2d and 3d Class Passengers
The 1st Class Roster .... Pitman, Mrs. Beane
"Godspeed Titanic" .... Company
"Barrett's Song" .... Barrett
"What a Remarkable Age This Is!" .... Etches's Staff, 1st Class Diners
"To Be a Captain" .... Murdoch
"Lady's Maid" .... The Kates, Steerage
"The Proposal" .... Barrett
"The Night Was Alive" .... Bride
"Hymn" .... Company
"Doing the Latest Rag" .... Hartley, Bandsmen Bricoux and Taylor, Company
"I Have Danced" .... Alice & Edgar Beane
"No Moon" .... Fleet, Company
"Autumn" .... Hartley

ACT II

"Wake Up, Wake Up!" .... Etches, Stewards, Company
"Dressed in Your Pajamas in the Grand Salon" .... Company
"The Staircase" .... The Kates, Farrell
"The Blame" .... Ismay, Andrews, Smith
To the Lifeboats
"Getting in the Lifeboat" .... Mr. & Mrs. Thayer
"I Must Get on That Ship" (Reprise) .... Murdoch, Lightoller, Steward, Bellboy, Passengers
"Lady's Maid" (Reprise) .... Jim Farrell
"Canons" .... Company

"The Proposal" (Reprise) .... Barrett
"The Night Was Alive" (Reprise) .... Bride
"We'll Meet Tomorrow" .... Barrett, Bride, Clarke, Company
"Still" .... Isador & Ida Straus
"To Be a Captain" (Reprise) .... Etches
"Mr. Andrews' Vision" .... Andrews
"In Every Age" (Reprise) .... Company
Finale .... Company

*Steel Pier (44). Musical conceived by Scott Ellis, Susan Stroman and David Thompson; book by David Thompson; music and lyrics by John Kander and Fred Ebb. Produced by Roger Berlind at the Richard Rodgers Theater. Opened April 24, 1997.

Bill Kelly .... Daniel McDonald
Rita Racine .... Karen Ziemba
Shelby Stevens .... Debra Monk
Mick Hamilton .... Gregory Harrison
Mr. Walker .... Ronn Carroll
Buddy Becker .... Joel Blum
Bette Becker .... Valerie Wright
Johnny Adel .... Timothy Warmen
Dora Foster .... Alison Bevan
Happy McGuire .... Jim Newman
Precious McGuire .... Kristin Chenoweth
Luke Adams .... John C. Havens
Corky .... Casey Nicholaw
Dr. Johnson .... John MacInnis
Sonny .... Gregory Mitchell
Preacher .... Adam Pelty
Steel Pier Marathon Couples:
Couple #39 .... Karen Ziemba,
                              Daniel McDonald
Couple #32 .... Debra Monk, John C. Havens
Couple #17 .... Valerie Wright, Joel Blum
Couple #4 ... Kristin Chenoweth, Jim Newman
Couple #26   Alison Bevan, Timothy Warmen
Couple #46 .... JoAnn M. Hunter,
                              Gregory Mitchell

Couple # 8 .... Dana Lynn Mauro,
                              Andy Blankenbuehler
Couple #50 .... Elizabeth Mills, Jack Hayes
Couple #56 .... Leigh-Anne Wencker,
                              Robert Fowler
Couple #44 .... Ida Gilliams, Adam Pelty
Couple #51 .... Sarah Solie Shannon,
                              Casey Nicholaw
Couple #54 .... Mary Illes, Brad Bradley
Couple #3 .... Rosa Curry, John MacInnis
Couple #18 .... Leigh-Anne Wencker,
                              Jack Hayes
Couple #41 ...... Ida Gilliams, John MacInnis
Couple #11 ...... Rosa Curry, Robert Fowler
Couple #30 ...... Elizabeth Mills, Adam Pelty
Couple #25 .... Kristin Chenoweth,
                              Gregory Mitchell
Couple #19 .... Mary Illes, Casey Nicholaw
Couple #14 .... Leigh-Anne Wencker,
                              Brad Bradley
Couple #40 ...... Ida Gilliams, Robert Fowler
Couple #55 .... Sarah Solie Shannon,
                              Brad Bradley
Couple #34 .... Rosa Curry, Jack Hayes
Couple #29 ..... Mary Illes, Timothy Warmen

Mick's Picks: Mary Illes, Rosa Curry, Sarah Solie Shannon. The Flying Dunlaps: Leigh-Anne Wencker, Jack Hayes, JoAnn M. Hunter, Robert Fowler, John MacInnis.

Orchestra: David Loud conductor; James Moore associate conductor, keyboard; Alexander Vselensky concertmaster; Jeff Kievit, Christian Jaudes, Richard Kelley trumpet; Charles Gordon tenor trombone; Earl McIntyre bass trombone, tuba; Roger Wendt, Anita Miller, French horn; Robert Renino bass; Greg Utzig guitar, banjo; Antony Geralis keyboard; Bruce Doctor drums; Christopher Cardona, Paul Woodiel violin; Susan Follari, Jill Jaffe viola, violin; Jennifer Langham cello; Lawrence Feldman, William Shadel, Andy Drelles, Ken Berger woodwinds.

Standbys: Messrs. Harrison, McDonald—Brian Sutherland; Misses Ziemba, Monk—Cady Huffman. Understudies: Mr. Harrison—Timothy Warmen; Mr. McDonald—Jim Newman; Mr. Blum—Brad Bradley, Adam Pelty; Mr. Warmen—Julio Agustin, Gregory Mitchell; Mr. Havens—Casey Nicholaw, Adam Pelty; Mr. Newman—John MacInnis, Scott Taylor; Mr. Carroll—Brad Badley, Casey Nicholaw; Miss Ziemba—Valerie Wright; Miss Monk—Alison Bevan; Miss Chenoweth—Mary Illes, Sarah Solie Shannon; Miss Bevan—Angelique Ilo, Leigh-Anne Wencker; Miss Wright—Leslie Bell, JoAnn M. Hunter; Swings—Julio Agustin, Leslie Bell, Angelique Ilo, Scott Taylor.

Directed by Scott Ellis; choreography, Susan Stroman; musical direction and vocal arrangements, David Loud; scenery, Tony Walton; costumes, William Ivey Long; lighting, Peter Kaczorowski; sound, Tony Meola; orchestrations, Michael Gibson; dance and incidental music arrangements, Glen Kelly; projections, Wendall K. Harrington; musical coordinator, John Monaco; associate choreographer, Chris

Peterson; associate producer, Pace Theatrical Group; casting, Johnson-Liff Associates; production stage manager, Beverley Randolph; stage manager, Frank Lombardi; press, Boneau/Bryan-Brown, Chris Boneau, Michael Hartman, Jackie Green.

Time: August 1933. Place: Steel Pier, Atlantic City.

Marathon dancing and romance in the Depression era.

ACT I

Prelude

Scene 1: The beach/the boardwalk

"Willing to Ride" .... Rita

Scene 2: The Steel Pier Ballroom

"Everybody Dance" .... Mick, Mick's Picks, Company

"Second Chance" .... Bill

Scene 3: Mick Hamilton's office

Scene 4: The rest stations

Scene 5: The Steel Pier Ballroom

"Montage I" .... Company

Scene 6: Behind the bandstand

"A Powerful Thing" .... Mick, Company

Scene 7: The Steel Pier Ballroom

"Dance With Me/The Last Girl" .... Mick, Rita, Bill, Company

"Montage II" .... Company

Scene 8: Mick Hamilton's office

Scene 9: The Steel Pier Ballroom

"Everybody's Girl" .... Shelby

Scene 10: The diving horse tank

"Wet" .... Rita, Bill

Scene 11: The Steel Pier Ballroom/The Trenton Air Show

"Lovebird" .... Rita

"Everybody Dance" (Reprise) .... Mick, Company

ACT II

Entr'acte

Scene 1: The rest stations

"Leave the World Behind" .... Bill, Rita, Company

Scene 2: A corridor near the dance floor

Scene 3: The Steel Pier Ballroom

"Montage III" .... Company

Scene 4: Outside the Steel Pier Ballroom

"Somebody Older" .... Shelby

Scene 5: The rooftop of the ballroom

"Running in Place" .... Rita

Scene 6: The Steel Pier Ballroom

"Two Little Words" .... Precious, Mick's Picks, Company

"First You Dream" .... Bill, Rita

Scene 7: The women's rest station

Scene 8: The Steel Pier Ballroom

"Steel Pier" .... Mick, Rita, Rick's Picks

Scene 9: The women's rest station/Outside the Steel Pier

"Steel Pier" (Reprise) .... Company

The Life (42). Musical based on an original idea by Ira Gasman; book by David Newman, Ira Gasman and Cy Coleman; lyrics by Ira Gasman; music by Cy Coleman. Produced by Roger Berlind, Martin Richards, Cy Coleman and Sam Crothers at the Ethel Barrymore Theater. Opened April 26, 1997.

Jojo .... Sam Harris	Chichi .... Sharon Wilkins
Carmen .... Lynn Sterling	Frenchie .... Katy Grenfell

Tracy; Street Evangelist .... Judine Richard
Bobby; Cop .... Mark Bove
Oddjob; Shoeshine ...... Michael Gregory Gong
Silky; Street Evangelist;
    Enrique .... Rudy Roberson
Slick; Street Evangelist;
    Shatellia .... Mark Anthony Taylor
Memphis .... Chuck Cooper
April .... Felicia Finley

Snickers .... Gordon Joseph Weiss
Lacy .... Vernel Bagneris
Queen .... Pamela Isaacs
Sonja .... Lillias White
Fleetwood .... Kevin Ramsey
Mary .... Bellamy Young
Doll House Dancer .... Stephanie Michels
Lou .... Rich Hebert

Ensemble: Mark Bove, Felicia Finley, Chris Ghelfi, Michael Gregory Gong, Katy Grenfell, Stephanie Michels, Judine Richard, Rudy Roberson, Lynn Sterling, Mark Anthony Taylor, Sharon Wilkins.

Orchestra: Gordon Lowry Harrell conductor; Joseph Baker associate conductor, keyboard; David Spinozza guitar; Warren Odze drums; Gary Haase bass; Mark Berman keyboard; Dave Yee percussion; Gregory Gisbert, Hollis Burridge trumpet; Mike Migliore, Tom Christensen, Dale Kleps woodwinds.

Understudies: Miss Isaacs—Kimberly Hawthorne, Tracy Nicole Chapman; Miss White—Sharon Wilkins; Messrs. Ramsey, Cooper, Roberson—James Stovall; Messrs. Harris, Hebert, Weiss—Michael Brian; Mr. Bagneris—Rudy Roberson; Miss Young—Felicia Finley, Stephanie Michels; Swing—Tracy Nicole Chapman.

Directed by Michael Blakemore; choreography, Joey McKneely; musical direction, Gordon Lowry Harrell; scenery, Robin Wagner; costumes, Martin Pakledinaz; lighting, Richard Pilbrow; sound, Peter Fitzgerald; orchestrations, Don Sebesky, Harold Wheeler; dance and vocal arrangements, Cy Coleman, Doug Katsaros; music coordinator, John Miller; fight staging, B.H. Barry; associate producer, Frank Tarsia; casting, Julie Hughes, Barry Moss; stage manager, Ara Marx; press, The Jacksina Company, Judy Jacksina.

Time: Then. Place: Around 42d Street.

Love and melodrama among those who worked the streets of the Times Square area, circa 1980s. Previously produced off off Broadway at the Westbeth Theater Center, Arnold Engelman producing director.

ACT I

"Check It Out!" .... Company
"Use What You Got" .... Jojo, Company
"A Lovely Day To Be Out of Jail" .... Queen, Sonja
"A Piece of the Action" .... Fleetwood
"The Oldest Profession" .... Sonja
"Don't Take Much" .... Memphis
"Go Home" .... Queen, Mary
"You Can't Get to Heaven" .... Queen, Sonja, Street Evangelists
"My Body" .... Frenchie, Chichi, Tracy, Carmen, Sonja, Queen, April
"Why Don't They Leave Us Alone" ... Oddjob, Bobby, Silky, Slick, Snickers, April, Carmen, Chichi, Frenchie, Queen, Sonja, Tracy
"Easy Money" .... Mary, Jojo, Fleetwood
"He's No Good" .... Queen
"I'm Leaving You" .... Queen
"The Hooker's Ball" .... Lacy, Company

ACT II

"Step Right Up" .... Enrique, Slick, Oddjob, Bobby
"Mr. Greed" .... Jojo, Bobby, Enrique, Oddjob, Slick
"My Way or the Highway" .... Memphis, Queen
"People Magazine" .... Lou, Mary
"We Had a Dream" .... Queen
"Use What You Got" (Reprise) .... Mary, Lou, Jojo
" 'Someday' Is for Suckers" .... Sonja, Frenchie, April, Shatellia, Carmen, Chichi
"My Friend" .... Queen, Sonja
"We Gotta Go" .... Fleetwood, Queen
"Check It Out!" (Reprise) .... Company

KING DAVID—The Company in a scene from the Alan Menken–Tim Rice concert musical which reopened the restored and refurbished New Amsterdam Theater under the management of Walt Disney Theatrical Productions

*Jekyll & Hyde** (39). Musical based on the novella *The Strange Case of Dr. Jekyll and Mr. Hyde* by Robert Louis Stevenson; conceived by Steve Cuden and Frank Wildhorn; book and lyrics by Leslie Bricusse; music by Frank Wildhorn. Produced by Pace Theatrical Group and Fox Theatricals in association with Jerry Frankel, Magicworks Entertainment and The Landmark Entertainment Group at the Plymouth Theater. Opened April 28, 1997.

John Utterson .... George Merritt	Attendant; Jack; Under Footman; Doorman;
Sir Danvers Carew .... Barrie Ingham	Curate; Tough .... Charles E. Wallace
Dr. Henry Jekyll; Edward	Nurse; Alice; Housemaid; Whore;
Hyde .... Robert Cuccioli (evening perfs.)	Bridesmaid; .... Emily Scott Skinner
Robert Evan (matinees)	Nurse; Bet; Housemaid; Young Girl;
Old Man; Davey; Manservant at Sir Danvers's;	Bridesmaid .... Jodi Stevens
Mr. Bisset; Maitre d'Hotel; Priest	Kate .... Leah Hocking
at Wedding .... David Chaney	Molly .... Molly Scott Pesce
Mental Patient; Ned; Tough .... David Koch	Polly; Whore .... Bonnie Schon
Mental Patient; Bill; Newsboy;	Mike; Groom .... John Treacy Egan
Choir Boy; Groom; Tough .... Bill E. Dietrich	Mr. Simon
Doctor; Lord G; Poole .... Donald Grody	Stride .... Raymond Jaramillo McLeod
Attendant; Albert; 1st Gentleman;	Rupert; Sir Douglas; Policeman;
Priest at Funeral .... Frank Mastrone	Barrow Boy .... Michael Ingram

Rt. Hon. Archibald Proops; 2d Gentleman;	Gen. Lord Glossop;
Sir Peter; Barrow Boy .... Brad Oscar	Siegfried; Policeman;
Lord Savage;	Barrow Boy .... Geoffrey Blaisdell
The Spider .... Martin Van Treuren	Emma Carew .... Christiane Noll
Lady Beaconsfield;	Lucy; Boy Soprano .... Linda Eder
Guinevere .... Emily Zacharias	

Orchestra: Jason Howland conductor; Ron Melrose associate conductor, keyboard; Jan Rosenberg assistant conductor, keyboard; Dale Stuckenbruck concertmaster; Nam Sook Lee violin; Debra Shufelt viola; Ted Mook cello; David Finck bass; Robert Bush, Matt Dine, Paul Garment woodwinds; R.J. Kelley horn; Herb Besson trombone; James Saporito, Randall Hicks percussion; Adam Cohen keyboard.

Understudies: Messrs. Cuccioli, Evan—Frank Mastrone, Bill E. Dietrich; Misses Eder, Noll—Leah Hocking, Emily Scott Skinner, Jodi Stevens; Mr. Merritt—Geoffrey Blaisdell; Mr. Ingham—Martin Van Treuren, Donald Grody; Miss Zacharias—Bonnie Schon; Mr. Grody—Brad Oscar, Geoffrey Blaisdell; Messrs. Blaisdell, Ingram—John Treacy Egan; Mr. Van Treuren—Frank Mastrone; Mr. Oscar—Bill E. Dietrich; Mr. McLeod—David Koch; Swings—Paul Hadobas, Rebecca Spencer.

Directed by Robin Phillips; choreography, Joey Pizzi; musical direction, Jason Howland; scenery, Robin Phillips; costumes, Ann Curtis; lighting, Beverly Emmons; sound, Karl Richardson, Scott Stauffer; orchestrations, Kim Scharnberg; musical supervision, Jeremy Roberts; musical coordinator, John Miller; vocal arrangements, Jason Howland, Ron Melrose; special effects, Gregory Meeh; fight coordinator, J. Allen Suddeth; executive producer, Gary Gunas; associate producer, Bill Young; casting, Julie Hughes, Barry Moss; production stage manager, Maureen F. Gibson; stage manager, David Hyslop; press, Richard Kornberg & Associates, Rick Miramontez, Don Summa, Jim Byk.

Musical version of Stevenson's melodrama of good and evil in conflict within the same person, previously produced developmentally by the Alley Theater, the 5th Avenue Musical Theater and Theater Under the Stars, and on a national tour.

ACT I

Scene 1: A London street
Scene 2: The violent ward, St. Jude's Hospital
"Lost in the Darkness" .... Dr. Jekyll
Scene 3: A London square
"Facade" .... Ensemble
Scene 4: St. Jude's Hospital
"Jekyll's Plea" .... Dr. Jekyll, Board of Governors
Scene 5: The sidewalk, Regent's Park
"Facade" (Reprise) .... Ensemble
Scene 6: Sir Danvers Carew's home, Regent's Park
"Emma's Reasons" .... Simon Stride, Emma
"Take Me as I Am" .... Dr. Jekyll, Emma
"Letting Go" .... Sir Danvers, Emma
Scene 7: Dock side, London's East End
"Facade" (Reprise) .... Ensemble
Scene 8: Backstage at The Red Rat
"No One Knows Who I Am" .... Lucy
Scene 9: The Red Rat
"Good 'n' Evil" .... Lucy
Scene 10: Harley Street
Scene 11: Dr. Jekyll's consulting room
"This Is the Moment" .... Dr. Jekyll
Scene 12: Dr. Jekyll's laboratory
Scene 13: The East End
"Alive" .... Hyde
Scene 14: Harley Street
Scene 15: Dr. Jekyll's consulting room; the Carew house
"His Work, and Nothing More" .... Dr. Jekyll, John Utterson, Sir Danvers, Emma
Scene 16: Dr. Jekyll's consulting room
"Someone Like You" .... Lucy

Scene 17: The Embankment, Westminster
"Alive" (Reprise) .... Hyde, Ensemble

ACT II

Scene 1: A London street; outside the cathedral; a pharmacy; Harley Street; supper club entrance in the
    West End; Platform at Victoria Station
"Murder, Murder" .... Newsboy, Ensemble
Scene 2: Dr. Jekyll's laboratory
"Once Upon a Dream" .... Emma
"Obsession" .... Dr. Jekyll
Scene 3: The Carew house; the river bank
"In His Eyes" .... Lucy, Emma
Scene 4: The bridge, London's East End
"Dangerous Game" .... Hyde, Lucy
Scene 5: Dr. Jekyll's laboratory
"The Way Back" .... Dr. Jekyll
Scene 6: Lucy's room, above The Red Rat
"A New Life" .... Lucy
"Sympathy, Tenderness" .... Hyde
Scene 7: Dr. Jekyll's laboratory
"Lost in Darkness" (Reprise) .... Dr. Jekyll
"Confrontation" .... Dr. Jekyll, Hyde
Scene 8: Westminster
"Facade" (Reprise) .... Ensemble
Scene 9: St Anne's Church, Westminster
"Dear Lord and Father of Mankind" .... Boy Soprano

***Candide** (39). Revival of the musical adapted from Voltaire; book by Hugh Wheeler; music
by Leonard Bernstein; lyrics by Richard Wilbur; additional lyrics by Stephen Sondheim and
John Latouche. Produced by Livent (US) Inc., Garth H. Drabinsky chairman, at the Gershwin
Theater. Opened April 29, 1997.

Voltaire; Dr. Pangloss; Businessman; Governor;
  2d Gambler (Police Chief); Sage .... Jim Dale
Candide .... Jason Danieley
Paquette .... Stacey Logan
Baroness Von Thunder .... Julie Johnson
Baron Von Thunder; Grand Inquisitor;
  Columbo; Pasha-Prefect
  of Constantinople .... Mal Z. Lawrence
Cunegonde .... Harolyn Blackwell
Cunegonde
  (certain performances) .... Glenda Balkan

Maximilian .... Brent Barrett
Hugo; Radu; Don Issachar; Judge Gomez;
  Father Bernard; Turhan Bey .... Arte Johnson
Old Lady .... Andrea Martin
2d Bulgarian Soldier .... Paul Harman
Heresy Agent .... David Girolmo
Governor's Aide .... Allen Hidalgo
Sheep One .... Nanne Puritz
Sheep Two .... D'Vorah Bailey
Lion .... Seth Malkin

Candide Ensemble: D'Vorah Bailey, Mary Kate Boulware, Diana Brownstone, Alvin Crawford,
Christopher F. Davis, Sherrita Duran, Deanna Dys, David Girolmo, Paul Harman, Joy Hermalyn, Allen
Hidalgo, Wendy Hilliard, Elizabeth Jiminez, Julie Johnson, Ken Krugman, Chad Larget, Shannon Lewis,
Seth Malkin, Andrew Pacho, Nanne Puritz, Owen Taylor, Eric van Hoven. Swings: Matthew Aibel,
Rachel Coloff, Joseph P. McDonnell, Starla Pace.

    Orchestra: Eric Stern conductor; Paul Hostetter associate conductor, percussion; Erica Kiesewetter
concertmaster; Elizabeth Lim, Aloysia Friedmann, Elizabeth Chang, John Connelly, Laura Frautschi
violin; Sarah Adams, Shelley Holland-Moritz viola; Adam Grabois, Roger Shell cello; Judith Sugarman
bass; Brian Miller, Laura Conwesser flute; Steven Hartman, Meryl Abt clarinet; Robert Ingliss oboe;
Jeffrey Marchand bassoon; Carl Albach, John Dent trumpet; Chris Komer, Leise Anschuetz Paer,
French horn; Dick Clark, Ken Finn trombone; Marcus Rojas tuba; Grace Paradise harp; James Preiss,
Tom Partington percussion.

    Understudies: Mr. Dale—Mal Z. Lawrence, Paul Harman; Mr. Danieley—Chad Larget, Eric van
Hoven; Misses Blackwell, Balkan—Nanne Puritz, Mary Kate Boulware; Miss Martin—Julie Johnson,

Joy Hermalyn; Miss Logan—Nanne Puritz, Shannon Lewis; Mr. Barrett—Ken Krugman, Seth Malkin; Messrs. Johnson, Lawrence—Paul Harman, David Girolmo; Miss Johnson—Joy Hermalyn, Rachel Coloff; Mr. Malkin—Alvin Crawford, Joseph P. McDonnell; Misses Puritz, Bailey—Mary Kate Boulware, Diana Brownstone, Rachel Coloff; Messrs. Harman, Girolmo—Matthew Aibel.

Directed by Harold Prince; choreography, Patricia Birch; musical supervision and direction, Eric Stern; scenery, Clarke Dunham; costumes, Judith Dolan; lighting, Ken Billington; sound, Jonathan Deans; orchestrations, Leonard Bernstein, Hershy Kay; music continuity and additional orchestrations, John Mauceri; music coordinator, John Miller; assistant to Harold Prince, Arthur Masella; casting, Beth Russell, Arnold J. Mungioli; stage manager, Bonnie Panson; press, Mary Bryant.

The last major New York theater revival of *Candide* was by Chelsea Theater Center under Harold Prince's direction at the Brooklyn Academy of Music 12/11/73 for 48 performances, moving to Broadway 3/10/74 for 740 performances. The present production was based on three earlier versions of the musical.

ACT I

Overture
"Life Is Happiness Indeed" .... Voltaire, Candide, Cunegonde, Maximilian, Paquette
"Best of All Possible Worlds" .... Pangloss, Candide, Cunegonde, Maximilian, Paquette, Ensemble
"Oh Happy We" .... Candide, Cunegonde
"It Must Be So" .... Candide
"Westphalian Chorale" .... Ensemble
"Glitter and Be Gay" .... Cunegonde
"Auto-da-fe" .... Company
"Candide's Lament" .... Candide
"You Were Dead You Know" .... Candide, Cunegonde
"I Am Easily Assimilated" .... Old Lady, Dons, Company
"Quartet Finale" .... Candide, Cunegonde, Business Man, Old Lady, Ensemble

ACT II

"Ballad of the New World" .... Candide, Ensemble
"My Love" .... Governor, Maximilian
"Allelulia" .... Ensemble
"Sheep Song" .... Sheep, Lion, Paquette
"Bon Voyage" .... Governor, Ensemble
"Quiet" .... Old Lady, Candide, Paquette
"Best of All Possible Worlds" (Reprise) .... Candide, Paquette, Old Lady, Sheep
"What's the Use" .... Pasha-Prefect, Turhan Bey, Police Chief, Ensemble
"You Were Dead You Know" (Reprise) .... Candide, Cunegonde
"Make Our Garden Grow" .... Company

King David (5). Concert version of a musical with book and lyrics by Tim Rice; music by Alan Menken. Produced by Walt Disney Theatrical Productions and Andre Djaoui at the New Amsterdam Theater. Opened May 15, 1997. (Closed May 23, 1997)

David	Marcus Lovett	Abner	Timothy Shew
Bathsheba	Alice Ripley	Jonathan	Roger Bart
Young Solomon	Daniel James Hodd	Michal	Judy Kuhn
Joab	Stephen Bogardus	Goliath	Bill Nolte
Samuel	Peter Samuel	Young Absolom	Dylan Lovett
Saul	Martin Vidnovic	Absalom	Anthony Galde
Agag	Timothy Robert Blevins	Uriah	Peter C. Ermides
Jesse	Michael Goz	Abishag	Kimberly JaJuan

Ensemble: Mark Agnes, Joan Barber, Stephanie Bast, Robin Baxter, Kristen Behrendt, Timothy Robert Blevins, Benjamin Brecher, Timothy Breese, Kirsti Carnahan, Nick Cavarra, Philip A. Chaffin, Michael DeVries, Peter C. Ermides, Hunter Foster, Ray Friedeck, Anthony Galde, Michael Goz, Ellen Hoffman, Kimberly JaJuan, James Javore, Keith Byron Kirk, Ann Kittredge, David Lowenstein, Barbara Marineau, Donna Lee Marshall, Michael X. Martin, Karen Murphy, Bill Nolte, Ilysia Pierce, Ron Sharpe, Timothy Shew, Rachel Ulanet, Andrew Varela, Melanie Vaughan, Sally Wilfert, Laurie Williamson.

Orchestra: Michael Kosarin conductor; Belinda Whitney-Barratt concertmaster; Karl Kawahara, Robert Zubrycki, Mary Whitaker, James Tsao, Lorra Baylis, Susan Lorentsen, Eric DeGlola, Ashley Horne, Britt Swenson, Quing Guo, Lisa Matricardi violin; Crystal Garner, Liuh-Wen Ting, Alfred Brown, Richard Spencer, Louis Day, Susan Dubois viola; Caryl Paisner, Eileen M. Folson, Chungsum Kim, Deborah Assael, Maureen McDermot cello; William Sloat, Jacqui Danilow, Anthony Morris bass; Helen Campo flute; Vicki Bodner oboe; Kim Laskowski bassoon; Edward Joffe, Daniel Wieloszynski, Alva Hunt, Ken Hitchcock, Frank Santagata woodwinds; Byron Stripling, Joe Mosello, Alex Holton trumpet; Jim Pugh, Larry Farrell trombone; Paul Faulise bass bone; Jeff Lang, Larry DiBello, Katie Dennis, Peter Gordon horns; Benjamin Herman, Daniel Haskins, James Musto percussion; Tommy Igoe drums; Ted Baker, Brian Besterman keyboards; Vincent Fay electric bass; Jack Cavari, Scott Kuney guitar; Stacey Shames harp.

Understudies: Marcus Lovett—Peter C. Ermides; Miss Ripley—Kristen Behrendt; Mr. Hodd, Dylan Lovett—Dominick Carbone; Messrs. Bogardus, Samuel—Michael DeVries; Mr. Vidnovic—Michael X. Martin; Mr. Bart—Hunter Foster; Miss Kuhn—Rachel Ulanet; Mr. Nolte—Michael Goz; Mr. Galde— Timothy Robert Blevins, Hunter Foster.

Directed by Mike Ockrent; musical direction, vocal and incidental music arrangements, Michael Kosarin; scenery, Tony Walton; costumes, William Ivey Long; lighting, David Agress; sound, Jonathan Deans; orchestrations, Douglas Besterman; music coordinator, John Miller; co-producer, Ritza B. Barath; casting, Jay Binder; production stage manager, Alan Hall; stage managers, Jim Woolley, Karen Potosnak; press, Boneau/Bryan-Brown, Chris Boneau, Patty Onagan, Miguel Tuason.

The Biblical story of David presented as an oratorio on the occasion of the reopening of the refurbished New Amsterdam Theater under Disney management.

ACT I

1. Prologue .... David, Bathsheba, Solomon, Joab, Chorus
2. Samuel
   "Israel and Saul" .... Joab, Samuel, Saul, Chorus
   "Samuel Confronts Saul" .... Saul, Samuel, Agag, Chorus
   "Samuel Anoints David" .... Joab, Samuel, Jesse, David, Chorus
3. Saul
   "The Enemy Within" .... Saul, Chorus
   "There Is a View . . ." .... Joab, Abner, Saul, Chorus
   "Psalm 8" .... David
   "Genius From Bethlehem" .... Saul, David, Abner, Joab, Jonathan, Michal
4. Goliath
   "The Valley of Elah" .... Goliath, Abner, Joab, David, Saul, Soldiers
   "Goliath of Gath" .... Goliath, David, Joab, Soldiers, Chorus
   "Sheer Perfection" .... Joab, Saul, David, Michal
5. Jonathan
   "Saul Has Slain His Thousands" .... Joab, Chorus
   "You Have It All" .... Saul, Jonathan, David
   "Psalm 23" .... Saul, David
   "You Have It All/Sheer Perfection" (Reprises) .... Jonathan, Joab, Michal, David
6. Exile
   "Hunted Partridge on the Hill" .... Joab, Saul, Michal, David, Men
   "The Death of Saul" .... Saul, Jonathan, Ghost of Samuel, Chorus
   "How Are the Mighty Fallen" .... David, Chorus

ACT II

7. David the King
   "This New Jerusalem" .... David, Absolom, Voice of Jonathan, Joab, Chorus
   "David & Michal" .... David, Joab, Michal
   "The Ark Brought to Jerusalem" .... David, Chorus
   "Never Again" .... Michal, David
8. Bathsheba
   "How Wonderful the Peace" .... Absolom, Joab, David, Chorus
   "Off Limits" .... Bathsheba, David, Joab

"Warm Spring Night" .... David
"When in Love" .... Bathsheba
"Uriah's Fate Sealed" .... David, Joab, Bathsheba, Chorus
"Atonement" .... David, Ghosts of Saul & Samuel, Bathsheba, Chorus
9. Absolom
"The Caravan Moves On" .... Joab, Absolom, David, Ghosts of Saul & Samuel, Men
"Death of Absolom" .... Joab, Absolom
"Absolom My Absolom" .... David
10. David's Final Days
"Solomon" .... Solomon, Joab, David, Bathsheba
"David's Final Hours" ...... Michal, David, Joab, Bathsheba, Voices of Goliath, Saul, Jonathan &
Samuel, Chorus
"The Long Long Day" .... David
"The New Jerusalem" (Reprise) .... Solomon, Company

CLOSED PRIOR TO BROADWAY OPENING

Productions mounted by New York producers for Broadway presentation, but which closed after tryout performances, are listed below.

Applause. Revival of the musical based on the film *All About Eve* and the original story by Mary Orr; book by Betty Comden and Adolph Green; music by Charles Strouse; lyrics by Lee Adams. Produced by Barry & Fran Weissler in association with Kardana Productions. Opened in tryout October 22, 1996 at the Tampa Bay Performing Arts Center. (Closed November 10, 1996 at the Morris A. Mechanic Theater, Baltimore)

Margo Channing	Stefanie Powers	Bill Sampson	John Dossett
Eve Harrington	Kate Jennings Grant	Howard Benedict	Nick Wyman
Duane Fox	Darrell Carey	Peter	Jay Russell
Buzz Richards; Tony Announcer	Stuart Zagnit	Bert	Bill Ullman
Karen Richards	Janet Aldrich	Stan Harding	Denis Jones

Others: Belle Callaway, Bruce Moore, Lynne Morrissey, Mark Arvin, Gregory Butler, Marc Calamia, Deirdre Goodwin, Jenny Lynn Suckling, Lisa Mandel, Sharon Moore, David Parker, Stepp Stewart.
Directed by Gene Saks; choreography, Ann Reinking; music supervision and vocal arrangements, John McDaniel; scenery, Michael Anania; costumes, Robert Mackintosh, Thomas Starzewski; lighting, Howell Binkley; sound, Peter Jay Fitzgerald; orchestrations, Bruce Coughlin; dance music arrangements, Irwin Fisch, Bruno Casolari, Charles Strouse, Ian Herman; associate producer, Alecia Parker.
Applause was first produced on Broadway 3/30/70 for 896 performances and was named a Best Play of its season and won the Tony for best musical. It has never had a major New York revival.

MUSICAL NUMBERS: "Applause," "Broadway Babble," "Think How It's Gonna Be," "But Alive," "The Best Night of My Life," "Who's That Girl?", "Fasten Your Seatbelts," "Welcome to the Theater," "Inner Thoughts," "Good Friends," "She Killed Them!", "One of a Kind," "One Halloween," "I Don't Want to Grow Old."

Whistle Down the Wind. Musical based on the novel by Mary Hayley Bell and the 1961 film produced by Richard Attenborough; book by Patricia Knop; music by Andrew Lloyd Webber; lyrics by Jim Steinman. Produced by The Really Useful Company at the National Theater, Washington, D.C. Opened December 12, 1996. (Closed February 9, 1997)

Swallow	Irene Molloy	Boone	Timothy Nolen
Brat	Abbi Hutcherson	Minister	Allen Fitzpatrick
Poor Baby	Cameron Bowen	Edward	Chuck Cooper
Aunt Dot	Candy Buckley	Earl	David Lloyd Watson

Rod	Timothy Shew	Amos	Steve Scott Springer
Sheriff Cookridge	Mike Hartman	The Man	Davis Gaines
Candy	Lacey Hornkohl	Preacher	Ray Walker

Others: Adinah Alexander, Johnetta Alston, Dave Clemmons, Georgia Creighton, Emily Rabon Hall, Melody Kay, Wayne W. Pretlow, John Sawyer, Bob Stillman, Laurie Williamson, Wysandria Woolsey, Sasha Allen, Alex Bowen, Graham Bowen, Gina DeStefano, Rori Godsey, Scott Irby-Ranniar, Clarence Leggett, Julia McIlvaine.

Directed by Harold Prince; choreography, Joey McKneely; musical direction, Patrick Vaccariello; scenery, Andrew Jackness; costumes, Florence Klotz; lighting, Howell Binkley; sound, Martin Levan; projection design, Wendall K. Harrington; musical supervision, Michael Reed; orchestrations, David Cullen, Andrew Lloyd Webber.

Lousiana children discover a strange man in their barn and believe he is heaven-sent. The play was presented in two parts.

MUSICAL NUMBERS: "Vaults of Heaven," "Spider," "Grownups Kill Me," "Whistle Down the Wind," "The Vow," "Safe Haven," "Tire Tracks and Broken Hearts," "If Only," "Cold," "When Children Rule the World," "Annie Christmas," "No Matter What," "A Kiss Is a Terrible Thing to Waste," "Wrestle With the Devil," "Nature of the Beast."

PLAYS PRODUCED OFF BROADWAY

Some distinctions between off-Broadway and Broadway productions at one end of the scale and off-off-Broadway productions at the other are blurred in the New York theater of the 1990s. For the purposes of *Best Plays* listing, the term "off Broadway" signifies a show which opened for general audiences in a mid-Manhattan theater seating 499 or fewer and 1) employed an Equity cast, 2) planned a regular schedule of 8 performances a week in an open-ended run (7 a week for solo shows) and 3) offered itself to public comment by critics after a designated opening performance.

Occasional exceptions of inclusion (never of exclusion) are made to take in visiting troupes, borderline cases and nonqualifying productions which readers might expect to find in this list because they appear under an off-Broadway heading in other major sources of record.

Figures in parentheses following a play's title give number of performances. These numbers do not include previews or extra non-profit performances.

Plays marked with an asterisk (*) were still in a projected run on June 1, 1997. Their number of performances is figured from opening night through May 31, 1997.

Certain programs of off-Broadway companies are exceptions to our rule of counting the number of performances from the date of the press coverage. When the official opening takes place late in the run of a play's regularly-priced public or subscription performances (after previews) we sometimes count the first performance of record, not the press date, as opening night—and in any such case in the listing we note the variance and give the press date.

In a listing of a show's numbers—dances, sketches, musical scenes, etc.—the titles of songs are identified wherever possible by their appearance in quotation marks (").

HOLDOVERS FROM PREVIOUS SEASONS

Off-Broadway shows which were running on June 1, 1996 are listed below. More detailed information about them appears in previous *Best Plays* volumes of appropriate date. Important cast changes since opening night are recorded in the Cast Replacements section of this volume.

***The Fantasticks** (15,356; longest continuous run of record in the American theater). Musical suggested by the play *Les Romanesques* by Edmond Rostand; book and lyrics by Tom Jones; music by Harvey Schmidt. Opened May 3, 1960.

***Perfect Crime** (4,169). By Warren Manzi. Opened October 16, 1987.

***Tony 'n' Tina's Wedding** (3,281). By Artificial Intelligence. Opened February 6, 1988.

***Tubes** (2,478). Performance piece by and with Blue Man Group. Opened November 17, 1991.

***Stomp** (1,362). Percussion performance piece created by Luke Cresswell and Steve Mc-Nicholas. Opened February 27, 1994.

The Food Chain (332). By Nicky Silver. Opened August 24, 1995. (Closed June 9, 1996)

***Grandma Sylvia's Funeral** (902). Transfer from off off Broadway of the environmental theater piece conceived by Glenn Wein and Amy Lord Blumsack; created by Glenn Wein, Amy Lord Blumsack and the original company. Opened October 4, 1995.

Mrs. Klein (280). By Nicholas Wright. Opened October 24, 1995. (Closed June 29, 1996)

Manhattan Theater Club. Valley Song (96). By Athol Fugard. Opened December 12, 1995. (Closed June 23, 1996) **By the Sea by the Sea by the Beautiful Sea** (38). Program of three one-act plays: *Dawn* by Joe Pintauro, *Day* by Lanford Wilson and *Dusk* by Terrence McNally. Opened May 30, 1996. (Closed June 30, 1996)

Lincoln Center Theater. A Fair Country (153). By Jon Robin Baitz. Opened February 19, 1996. (Closed June 30, 1996)

Bein' With Behan (78). Solo performance by Michael L. Kavanaugh; written by Michael L. Kavanaugh. Opened March 10, 1996. (Closed June 9, 1996)

Forbidden Hollywood (225). Revue created and written by Gerard Alessandrini. Opened March 10, 1996. (Closed September 1, 1996)

Take It Easy (113). Musical with book, music and lyrics by Raymond Fox. Opened March 21, 1996. (Closed June 30, 1996)

Cowgirls (319). Musical conceived by Mary Murfitt; book by Betsy Howie; music and lyrics by Mary Murfitt. Opened April 1, 1996. (Closed January 5, 1997)

Papa (78). Solo performance by Len Cariou; written by John deGroot. Opened May 5, 1996. (Closed July 13, 1996)

Playwrights Horizons. Arts & Leisure (25). By Steve Tesich. Opened May 19, 1996. (Closed June 9, 1996)

Curtains (64). By Stephen Bill. Opened May 21, 1996. (Closed July 16, 1996)

Second Stage. Dark Rapture (29). By Eric Overmyer. Opened May 23, 1996. (Closed June 16, 1996)

PLAYS PRODUCED JUNE 1, 1996–MAY 31, 1997

***Making Porn** (395). By Ronnie Larsen. Produced by Caryn Horwitz at the Actor's Playhouse. Opened June 12, 1996.

With Rex Chandler (as Jack Hawk), J. Bixby Elliot, Ginny Godfrey, Rob Jones, Ronnie Larsen, Steve Sanders.

Directed by Ronnie Larsen; press, Caryn Horwitz.

Chandler portraying a straight man who has become a porn star in a play about the gay pornography industry. Previously produced in eight U.S. cities.

Johnny Hanson replaced Rex Chandler and Joanna Keylock replaced Ginny Godfrey 10/1/96. Blue Blake replaced Johnny Hanson 11/22/96. Ryan Idol replaced Blue Blake 12/17/96. Sonny Markham replaced Ryan Idol 4/1/97.

The Joseph Papp Public Theater/New York Shakespeare Festival Shakespeare Marathon. Schedule of four revivals of plays by William Shakespeare. **Henry V** (25), opened June 18, 1996; see note (closed July 14, 1996) and **Timon of Athens** (24), opened August 6, 1996; see note (closed September 1 , 1996). Produced by The Joseph Papp Public Theater/New York Shakespeare Festival, George C. Wolfe producer, Rosemarie Tichler artistic producer, Joey Parnes executive producer, Laurie Beckelman executive director, with the cooperation of the City of New York, Rudolph W. Giuliani Mayor, Peter F. Vallone Speaker of the City Council, Schuyler Chapin Commissioner of Cultural Affairs, Henry J. Stern Commissioner of Parks and Recreation, at the Delacorte Theater in Central Park.

Also **Henry VI, Parts l, 2** and **3**. Presented in two parts entitled **The Edged Sword** (31; opened November 12, 1996) and **Black Storm** (21; opened November 23, 1996), in repertory. (Repertory closed January 5, 1997) **Antony and Cleopatra** (46). Opened February 18, 1997; see note. (Closed April 5, 1997) Produced by The Joseph Papp Public Theater/New York Shakespeare Festival, George C. Wolfe producer, Rosemarie Tichler artistic producer, *Henry VI* at Martinson Hall, *Antony and Cleopatra* at the Anspacher Theater.

ALL PLAYS: Margaret M. Lioi senior director of external affairs; Wiley Hausam and Bonnie Metzgar associate producers; Brian Kulick artistic associate; casting, Jordan Thaler, Heidi Griffiths; press, Carol R. Fineman, Thomas V. Naro, Bill Coyle.

HENRY V

Chorus .... Company	Capt. Gower .... Michael Gaston
King Henry V .... Andre Braugher	Capt. Fluellen .... Kenneth L. Marks
Duke of Gloucester .... Danyon Davis	Alexander Court .... William Robert Doyle
Duke of Exeter .... John Woodson	Cpl. Nym .... Jerry Mayer
Duke of York .... Douglass Stewart	Lt. Bardolph .... Jarlath Conroy
Earl of Warwick .... Michael C. Hall	Mistress Quickly;
Archbishop of Canterbury;	Queen Isabel .... Kathleen Chalfant
Ensign Pistol .... Jeff Weiss	Boy .... Torquil Campbell
Bishop of Ely;	English Herald .... Adam Soham Larmer
Monsieur Le Fer .... David Costabile	King Charles VI .... George Morfogen
Earl of Cambridge;	Dauphin Louis .... Teagle F. Bougere
Duke of Orleans .... Christian Camargo	Katharine .... Elizabeth Marvel
Lord Scroop of Masham;	Alice .... Kristine Nielsen
John Bates .... Lance Reddick	Duke of Berri .... Benim Foster
Sir Thomas Grey;	Constable of France .... Daniel Oreskes
Michael Williams .... Gus Rogerson	Montjoy .... Henry Stram
Sir Thomas Erpingham;	
Gov. of Harfleur .... Yusef Bulos	

Citizens of Harfleur, English Soldiers, French Soldiers, Attendants, Clerics —Louise J. Andrews, William Robert Doyle, Benim Foster, T.J. Kenneally, Adam Soham Larmer, Michael Neeley, Daniel Pearce, Robert Ramirez, Mary Randle, Douglass Stewart.

Directed by Douglas Hughes; scenery, Neil Patel; costumes, Paul Tazewell; lighting, Brian Mac-Devitt; original music, sound effects and musician, David Van Tieghem; fight direction, Rick Sordelet; production stage manager, Buzz Cohen.

Place: England and France. The play was presented in two parts.

The last major New York revival of *Henry V* was by New York Shakespeare Festival at the Delacorte 6/22/84 for 27 performances.

TIMON OF ATHENS

Painter	Peter McRobbie	Servilius	Mark H. Dold
Poet	Teagle F. Bougere	Alcibiades	Jack Stehlin
Merchant	Yusef Bulos	Lucius	Geoffrey Owens
Jeweler	Matthew Saldivar	Lucullus	Boris McGiver
Timon	Michael Cumpsty	Ventidius	Francis Jue
Flavius	Henry Stram	Sempronius	Herb Foster
Old Athenian	Jerry Mayer	Timandra	Susan Pilar
Lucilius	Sean Patrick Thomas	Caphis	Michael C. Hall
Apemantus	Sam Tsoutsouvas		

Creditors: Michael C. Hall, Francis Jue, Robert Ramirez, Matthew Saldivar. Senators: Teagle F. Bougere, Peter McRobbie, Robert Ramirez, Matthew Saldivar. Bandits: Francis Jue, Jerry Mayer, Robert Ramirez. Servants: Michael C. Hall, Robert Ramirez, Matthew Saldivar, Adam Soham Larmer. Soldier: Michael C. Hall.

Understudies: Messrs. Owens, McGiver, Bougere—Mark H. Dold; Messrs. Cumpsty, Dold—Michael C. Hall; Messrs. Stehlin, Hall, Tsoutsouvas—Adam Soham Larmer; Messrs. Foster, Bulos, Mayer, Saldivar—Robert Ramirez; Messrs. Thomas, McRobbie—Matthew Saldivar; Messrs. Stram, Jue—Sean Patrick Thomas.

Directed by Brian Kulick; scenery and costumes, Mark Wendland; lighting, Mimi Jordan Sherin; original music, Mark Bennett; choreography, Naomi Goldberg; production stage manager, James Latus.

Place: Athens and surrounding wilderness. The play was presented in two parts.

The last major New York revival of *Timon of Athens* was by National Actors Theater on Broadway 11/4/93 for 37 performances.

HENRY VI
PART I: THE EDGED SWORD

Duke of Bedford, Richard Plantagenet (later Duke of York), Messenger—Steven Skybell.
Duke of Gloucester, Soldier, Messenger—Patrick Morris.
Earl of Salisbury, Lawyer, Messenger—Mark Kenneth Smaltz.
Cardinal Winchester, Duke of Alencon—Walker Jones.
Messenger, Vernon, Watchman, Margaret (later Queen Margaret)—Angie Phillips.
Messenger, Lord Talbot, John Hume, Post, Murderer, Jack Cade—Boris McGiver.
Messenger, Earl of Warwick, Duchess of Gloucester—Fanni Green.
Dauphin Charles of France, Earl of Suffolk (later Duke of Suffolk)— Graham Winton.
Bastard of Orleans, King Henry VI—Tom Nelis.
Joan of Arc, Duke of Somerset, Margery Jourdain—Jan Leslie Harding.

HENRY VI
PART II: BLACK STORM

King Henry VI—Tom Nelis.
Duke of York, Sir Humphrey Stafford, 1st Keeper, Lady Bona, Post— Steven Skybell.
Jack Cade, George (later Duke of Clarence)—Boris McGiver.
Stafford's Brother, Old Clifford, Edward Prince of Wales—Patrick Morris.
Lord Say, Duke of Somerset, Earl of Rutland, Messenger, Lady Grey (later Queen Elizabeth), Post—Jan Leslie Harding.
Young Clifford, 2d Keeper, King Louis IX of France—Mark Kenneth Smaltz.
Queen Margaret—Angie Phillips.
Earl of Warwick—Fanni Green.
Edward (later King Edward IV)—Walker Jones.
Richard (later Duke of Gloucester)—Graham Winton

BOTH PLAYS: Musician—Mark Dresser or Glen Moore; directed by Karen Coonrod; scenery, P.K. Wish; costumes, Constance Hoffman; lighting, Kevin Adams; sound, Darron L. West; original music, Glen Moore; production stage manager, Erica Schwartz.

HENRY VI—Fanni Green (Warwick), Mark Kenneth Smaltz (Salisbury), Jan Lesile Harding (Somerset) and Tom Nelis (King Henry VI) in the Shakespeare Marathon revival at The Joseph Papp Public Theater

The last major New York revival of *Henry VI* was by New York Shakespeare Festival at the Delacorte in two parts 6/23/70 for 18 performances and 6/24/70 for 17 performances. Each of the two parts of the present production (which was developed by Karen Coonrod, John Dias and Henry Israeli as part of the Public Theater's LuEsther Lab and artists-in-residence program) was presented with one intermission.

ANTONY AND CLEOPATRA

Veteran of the Civil Wars	Enobarbus .... Alex Allen Morris
(49-40 BC) .... Don Campbell	Eros .... Teagle F. Bougere
Ventidius .... Peter Francis James	Octavius Caesar .... Carrie Preston
Antony .... David Harewood	Lepidus; Dolabella .... Sam Tsoutsouvas
Cleopatra .... Vanessa Redgrave	Agrippa .... Steven Skybell
Charmian .... Fanni Green	Octavia .... Nancy Hower
Iras .... Jennifer Wiltsie	Sextus Pompeius; Decretas ...... Boris McGiver
Alexas; Unknown Soldier .... George Causil	Menas .... Ben Shenkman
Mardian .... Jason Ma	Schoolmaster;
Maecenas .... Julio Monge	Unknown Soldier .... Avery Glymph

Music and Songs—Company.

Directed by Vanessa Redgrave; scenery, John Arnone; costumes, Ann Hould-Ward; lighting, Rui Rita; sound, J.R.Conklin; composer, Mark Bennett; musical direction, Christopher Drobny; production stage manager, James Latus.

Time: February, 40 BC to August 1, 30 BC. Place: From Alexandria in Egypt to Rome and the Bay of Naples; to Parthia (Iran); to Athens and Patras in Greece; to the seaport in the Bay of Actium (today's Albania); to Alexandria. The play was presented in two parts.

The last major New York revival of record of *Antony and Cleopatra* was by New York Shakespeare Festival 6/13/63 for 63 performances.

Note: Press date for *Henry V* was 6/30/96, for *Timon of Athens* was 8/25/96, for *Antony and Cleopatra* was 3/13/97.

Note: The Joseph Papp Public Theater's Shakespeare Marathon presentation of all Shakespeare's 36 plays, which began under the late Joseph Papp's direction, comes to an end with this season's productions and, finally, with the forthcoming revival of *Henry VIII,* to open at the Delacorte 6/13/97. The Public's Marathon has taken place as follows: 1987-88 season, *A Midsummer Night's Dream, Julius Caesar, Romeo and Juliet*; 1988-89 season, *Much Ado About Nothing, King John, Coriolanus, Love's Labor's Lost, The Winter's Tale, Cymbeline*; 1989-90 season, *Twelfth Night, Titus Andronicus, Macbeth, Hamlet*; 1990-91 season, *The Taming of the Shrew, Richard III, Henry IV, Part 1* and *Part 2*; 1991-92 season, *Othello* and *Pericles, Prince of Tyre*; 1992-93 season, *As You Like It, The Comedy of Errors*; 1993-94 season, *Measure for Measure, All's Well That Ends Well, Richard II*; 1994-95 season, *The Merry Wives of Windsor, Two Gentlemen of Verona, The Merchant of Venice*; 1995-96 season, *The Tempest, Troilus and Cressida, King Lear.*

Louisiana Purchase (4). Concert presentation of the musical based on a story by B.G. DeSylva; book by Morrie Ryskind; music and lyrics by Irving Berlin. Produced by Carnegie Hall at Weill Recital Hall. Opened June 19, 1996. (Closed June 23, 1996)

Sam Liebowitz;		Beatrice	Debbie Gravitte
Dean Manning	Merwin Goldsmith	Lee Davis	James Ludwig
Col. Davis Sr.	John Wylie	Emmy-Lou	Alet Oury
Col. Davis Jr.	Michael Marotta	Marina Van Linden	Judy Blazer
Capt. Whitfield	Rick Crom	Mme. Yvonne Bordelaise	Taina Elg
Jimmy Taylor	Michael McGrath	Sen. Oliver P. Loganberry	George S. Irving

Ensemble: Kim Lindsay, Keith Byron Kirk, Peter Eldridge, Lauren Kinham, Darmon Meader, Kim Nazarian, Jamie Baer, Peter Flynn.

With the Carnegie Hall Theater Orchestra.

Directed by Scott Baron; musical direction, Rob Fisher; orchestrations, Robert Russell Bennett.

Louisiana Purchase was first produced on Broadway 5/28/40 for 444 performances. This is its first major New York revival of record.

MUSICAL NUMBERS, ACT I: Overture, Apologia, "Sex Marches On," "Louisiana Purchase," "It's a Lovely Day Tomorrow," "I'd Love To Be Shot From a Cannon With You," "It'll Come to You," "Louisiana Purchase" (Reprise), "Outside of That I Love You," "You're Lonely and I'm Lonely," "Dance With Me (Tonight at the Mardi Gras)," Finale.

ACT II: Entr'acte, "Wild About You," "Latins Know How," What Chance Have I With Love?", "The Lord Done Fixed Up My Soul," "Fools Fall in Love/Old Man's Darling-Young Man's Slave," "You Can't Brush Me Off," "Finale Ultimo."

Grace & Glorie (134). By Tom Ziegler. Produced by Edgar Lansbury, Everett King and Dennis J. Grimaldi at the Laura Pels Theater. Opened July 16, 1996. (Closed November 10, 1996)

Grace Stiles	Estelle Parsons
Gloria Whitmore	Lucie Arnaz

Directed by Gloria Muzio; scenery, Edward Gianfrancesco; costumes, Robert Mackintosh; lighting, Brian Nason; sound, John Gromada; associate producer, Ashley/Bernstein; production stage manager, Alan Fox; stage manager, Cathy B. Blaser; press, Jeffrey Richards Associates, Irene Gandy.

Time: One recent fall. Place: Grace's cottage located in the Blue Ridge Mountains of Virginia. Act I, Scene 1: A Monday afternoon. Scene 2: Early the next morning. Scene 3: Late the following Friday. Act II, Scene 1: Late Saturday morning. Scene 2: Early evening that same day.

Well-educated hospice volunteer and an elderly mountain woman terminally ill from cancer take care of each other. Previously presented at the Dorset, Vt. Theater Festival.

Acts of Providence (31). Program of two one act plays by Edward Allan Baker: *Dead Man's Apartment* and *Dolores*. Produced by Cindy Webster and the New American Stage Company at St. Peter's Church. Opened July 17, 1996. (Closed August 11, 1996)

BOTH PLAYS: Directed by Ron Stetson; scenery, Edward Gianfrancesco; lighting, Jeff Segal; press, Shirley Herz Associates, Miller Wright.

DEAD MAN'S APARTMENT: With Ilene Kristen, Alexandra Lee, David McConeghey, Michael Cambden Richards. Comedy, a man's lunch break in company with a mistress who wants him to marry her.

DOLORES: With Amelia Campbell, Fiona Gallegher. Two sisters drawn together as victims of domestic violence.

Second Stage Theater. Schedule of five programs. **Aliens in America** (13). Solo performance by Sandra Tsing Loh; written by Sandra Tsing Loh. Opened July 19, 1996. (Closed July 28, 1996) **Tooth of Crime (Second Dance)** (24). By Sam Shepard; music and lyrics by T Bone Burnett; co-produced with the Signature Theater Company, James Houghton artistic director, Thomas C. Proehl managing director, Elliot Fox associate director, in association with Lucille Lortel. Opened December 23, 1996. (Closed January 12, 1997) **The Red Address** (24). By David Ives. Opened January 13, 1997. (Closed February 2, 1997) **Sympathetic Magic** (38). By Lanford Wilson. Opened April 16, 1997. (Closed May 18, 1997) And *Something Blue* by Michaela Murphy scheduled to open 6/11/97. Produced by Second Stage Theater, Carole Rothman artistic director, Suzanne Schwartz Davidson producing director, Carol Fishman associate producer, *Aliens in America, The Red Address, Sympathetic Magic* and *Something Blue* at the Second Stage Theater, *Tooth of Crime (Second Dance)* at the Lucille Lortel Theater.

ALIENS IN AMERICA

Directed by Steve Kaplan; scenery, Lauren Helpern; lighting, Traci Klainer-McDonnell; sound, Aural Fixation; production stage manager, Delicia Turner; press, Richard Kornberg & Associates, Don Summa, Rick Miramontez.

Excerpts from the life experience of Miss Loh, a writer-performer with a German mother and Chinese father, growing up in Southern California and venturing to Ethiopia on a family holiday. The play was presented without intermission.

TOOTH OF CRIME (SECOND DANCE)

Hoss	Vincent D'Onofrio	Chaser	Jesse Lenat
Becky	Rebecca Wisocky	Doc	Paul Butler
Meera	Sturgis Warner	Crow	Kirk Acevedo
Ruido Ran	Jeffrey Anders Ware	Ref	Michael Deep

Musicians: Jagoda percussionist; J.D. Foster bassist, multi-instrumentalist; Chris Cochrane guitarist.

Directed by Bill Hart; scenery, E. David Cosier; costumes, Teresa Snider-Stein; lighting, Anne Militello; score and sound design, David Van Tieghem; video design, Kevin Cunningham, Wild Kind; musical direction, Loren Toolajian; production stage managers, Ruth Kreshka, James FitzSimmons; press, Richard Kornberg (Second Stage), James L.L. Morrison (Signature).

Rock star is confronted in musical rivalry by an intrusive gypsy, in rewritten version of Shepard's 1972 play which premiered as *The Tooth of Crime* at the Open Space Theater in London and off Broadway 3/7/73.

THE RED ADDRESS

E.G. Triplett	Kevin Anderson	Driver	Jon DeVries
Dick	Ned Eisenberg	Lady	Cady McClain
Ann; Waitress; Prostitute	Welker White	Soldier; Maitre d'	Josh Hopkins

Directed by Pamela Berlin; scenery, Christine Jones; costumes, David C. Woolard; lighting, Donald Holder; sound, John Kilgore; production stage manager, Susan Whelan; stage manager, Thea Bradshaw Gilles.

Revised version of a play staged in 1988 at New Dramatists, a psychological mystery centering on a business executive's eccentric romance with his beautiful wife. The play was presented without intermission.

SYMPATHETIC MAGIC

Ian Anderson .... David Bishins	Pauly Scott .... David Pittu
Don Walker .... Jeff McCarthy	Susan Olmsted .... Dana Millican
Barbara De Biers .... Ellen Lancaster	Liz Barnard .... Tanya Berezin
Carl Conklin White .... Herb Foster	Mickey Picco .... Jordan Mott

Directed by Marshall W. Mason; scenery, John Lee Beatty; costumes, Laura Crow; lighting, Dennis Parichy; sound, Chuck London; original music, Peter Kater; fight staging, B.H. Barry; casting, Johnson-Liff Associates; production stage manager, Denise Yaney; stage manager, Karen Potosnak.

Place: San Francisco and the Bay Area. The play was presented in two parts.

The universe examined from the viewpoint of characters in the arts, religion and science.

*I Love You, You're Perfect, Now Change (347). Musical revue with book and lyrics by Joe DiPietro; music by Jimmy Roberts. Produced by James Hammerstein, Bernie Kukoff and Jonathan Pollard at the Westside Theater Upstairs. Opened August 1, 1996.

Jordan Leeds   Jennifer Simard
Robert Roznowski   Melissa Weil

Violinist: Jacqui Carrasco.

Standbys: Messrs. Leeds, Roznowski—Thomas Michael Allen; Misses Simard, Weil—Jill Geddes.

Directed by Joel Bishoff; musical direction, Tom Fay; scenery, Neil Peter Jampolis; costumes, Candice Donnelly; lighting, Mary Louise Geiger; sound, Duncan Edwards; production supervisor, Matthew G. Marholin; vocal and instrumental arrangements, Jimmy Roberts; associate producer, Matt Garfield; press, Bill Evans & Associates, Jim Randolph.

From dating to in-laws, aspects of the modern mating game viewed in a comedy perspective. Previously produced in regional theater at the Long Wharf Theater, New Haven, Conn.

ACT I

"Cantata for a First Date" .... Company
"A Stud and a Babe" .... Robert Roznowski, Jennifer Simard
"Single Man Drought" .... Simard, Melissa Weil
"Why? Cause I'm a Guy" .... Roznowski, Jordan Leeds
"Tear Jerk" .... Leeds, Weil
"I Will Be Loved Tonight" .... Simard
"Hey There, Single Guy/Gal" .... Leeds, Simard
"He Called Me" .... Simard, Company
"Wedding Vows" .... Company

ACT II

"Always a Bridesmaid" .... Weil
"The Baby Song" .... Leeds
"Marriage Tango" .... Roznowski, Weil
"On the Highway of Love" .... Leeds, Company
"Waiting Trio" .... Weil, Roznowski, Simard
"Shouldn't I Be Less in Love With You?" .... Roznowski
"I Can Live With That" .... Leeds, Weil
"I Love You, You're Perfect, Now Change" .... Company

The Boys in the Band (88). Transfer from off off Broadway of the revival of the play by Mart Crowley. Produced by Kardana Productions, Steven M. Levy, Dennis J. Grimaldi, WPA Productions, Charles Hollerith Jr. and Randall L. Wreghitt, by special arrangement with Lucille Lortel, in the WPA Theater production, Kyle Renick artistic director, at the Lucille Lortel Theater. Opened August 6, 1996. (Closed October 20, 1996)

Michael	David Drake	Bernard	William Christian
Donald	Christopher Sieber	Alan	Robert Bogue
Emory	James Lecesne	Cowboy	Scott Decker
Hank	David Bishins	Harold	David Greenspan
Larry	Sean McDermott		

Directed by Kenneth Elliott; scenery, James Noone; costumes, Suzy Benzinger; lighting, Phil Monat; sound, John Kilgore; associate producer, Adam Weinstock; casting, Johnson-Liff Associates; production stage manager, Chris De Camillis; stage manager, Christina Massie; press, Jeffrey Richards Associates, Irene Gandy, Mark Cannistraro.

Time: May 1968. Place: The East 50s, New York City. The play was presented in two parts.

The Boys in the Band was first produced off Broadway 4/15/68 for 1,000 performances and was named a Best Play of its season. This, its first major New York revival, was originally produced 6/20/96 at WPA Theater.

Born to Sing! (134). Musical with book and lyrics by Vy Higginsen and Ken Wydro; music by W. Naylor. Produced by Vy Higginsen & Ken Wydro and Mitchell Maxwell & Alan J. Schuster in association with SuperVision Productions and Workin' Man Theatricals at the Union Square Theater. Opened August 8, 1996. (Closed December 1, 1996)

Doris Winter	Lisa Fischer	Samantha Summers	Stacy Francis
Mama Winter	Kellie D. Evans	Minister of Music	Charles Stewart
Dottie Winter	Tanya Blount	Auditioner	Charles Perry

Narrator: Jessica Care Moore, Debora Rath, Shari Headley, Samantha Davis alternating. Harris Sisters: Anita Wells, Anissia Bunton, Kim Summerson. Four Guys: Pierre Cook, Tyrone Flower, Richard Hartley and Damon Horton & Ronnie McLeod alternating.

Choir: Sopranos—Anissia Bunton, Dawn Green, Sheila Slappy, Kim Summerson; altos—Robin Cunningham, Lorraine Moore, Anita Wells; tenors— Pierre Cook, Tyrone Flower, Richard Hartley, Damon Horton, Ronnie Mcleod, Charles Perry; alternates—Marilyn Davis, Linda Fennell, Gerald Latham.

Orchestra: W. Naylor conductor, Michele McKoy assistant conductor, keyboard; Kevin McKoy keyboard; Janine Gowers, Miguel Bramwell drums.

Understudies: Miss Fischer—Sheila Slappy; Miss Evans—Lorraine Moore; Miss Blount—Dawn Green; Miss Francis—Kim Summerson.

Directed by Ken Wydro; musical supervision, W. Naylor; scenery, Mike Fish; costume supervision, Carlos Falchi, Malissa Drayton; lighting, Marshall Williams; sound, DonJuan Holder; stage movement, Charles Stewart; co-producers, Kery Davis, Victoria Maxwell; associate producer, Lesley Mazzotta; production stage manager, Leopold M. John; stage manager, Marlon Campbell; press, Keith Sherman & Associates, Jim Byk, Kevin Rehac.

Continuing the story begun in *Mama, I Want to Sing* (1983) and continued in its *Part II* (1990), "Doris Winter" is now a gospel superstar recruiting members of a choir for a world tour.

ACT I

Scene 1: On stage
"Lead Us On" .... Mama Winter
Scene 2: Audition hall
"Interpretations" .... Auditioner
"Lord Keep Us Day by Day" .... Harris Sisters
"Sweeping Through the City" .... Mama Winter, Girls
"Blessed Assurance" .... Samantha Summers

I LOVE YOU, YOU'RE PERFECT, NOW CHANGE—Jennifer Simard, Melissa Weil, Jordan Leeds and Robert Roznowski in a scene from the revue with book and lyrics by Joe DiPietro and music by Jimmy Roberts

"Is My Living in Vain" .... Four Guys
"Blessed Assurance" (Reprise) .... Dottie Winter
"Narration/Poem" .... Narrator
Scene 3: The Winter residence
   "Give the Child a Break" .... Mama Winter, Doris Winter
Scene 4: Press conference, Mt. Calvary Church.
   "And the Winner Is" .... Doris Winter, Ensemble
Scene 5: The Winter residence
   "Your Time Will Come" .... Doris Winter, Dottie Winter
Scene 6: Church/Whole Truth rehearsal studio
   "Born to Sing" .... Samantha Summers, Ensemble

ACT II

Scene 1:Tokyo concert hall
   "Harmony" .... Doris Winter, Ensemble
Scene 2: Hotel room—Tokyo
   "Who Needs Who?" .... Samantha Summers, Doris Winter, Mama Winter, Ensemble
Scene 3: Public performance—Istanbul
   "Lord Keep Us Day by Day" (Reprise) .... Harris Sisters
Scene 4: Onstage
   "Take a Stand" .... Mama Winter, Dottie Winter, Doris Winter
Scene 5: Venice
   "The Sky's the Limit" .... Samantha Summers, Ensemble
Scene 6: On stage
   "Who You Gonna Blame?" .... Samantha Summers, Dottie Winter

Scene 7: Backstage—Cairo
"Center Peace" .... Mama Winter, Ensemble
Scene 8: Backstage—Berlin
"Attention Must Be Paid" .... Doris Winter, Dottie Winter
Scene 9: Backstage—Paris
"Poem" .... Narrator
"Face to Face" .... Mama Winter, Doris Winter, Dottie Winter, Samantha Summers
Scene 10: Grand Finale—London
"Take the High Way" .... Dottie Winter, Ensemble
Encore
"Lead Us On" (Reprise) .... Mama Winter, Ensemble

*When Pigs Fly (334). Musical revue conceived by Howard Crabtree and Mark Waldrop; sketches and lyrics by Mark Waldrop; music by Dick Gallagher. Produced by Gail Homer Seay, Peter Hauser and Jane M. Abernethy in association with Marc Howard Segan at the Douglas Fairbanks Theater. Opened August 14, 1996.

Stanley Bojarski
John Treacy Egan
David Pevsner

Jay Rogers
Michael West ("Howard")

Understudy: Keith Cromwell.
Directed by Mark Waldrop; musical direction, Philip Fortenberry; scenery and lighting, Peter Hauser; sound, Rob Gorton; associate director, Phillip George; production stage manager, Glynn David Turner; press, Tony Origlio Publicity, Michael Cullen.
In the context of a man named Howard putting on an extravagant show under many difficulties, an assortment of revue numbers dealing with sundry aspects of modern American life and times.

MUSICAL NUMBERS, ACT I: "When Pigs Fly"—"Howard," Company; "You've Got to Stay in the Game"—John Treacy Egan, Stanley Bojarski, David Pevsner, "Howard"; "Torch #1"—Jay Rogers; "Light in the Loafers"—Pevsner, Egan; Coming Attractions With Carol Ann: "Coming Attraction 1"—Egan, Rogers, Pevsner, "Howard"; "Coming Attraction #2"—"Howard," Angel Voices; "Coming Attraction #3"—Bojarski, Egan, Rogers; "Not All Man"—Pevsner, "Howard"; "Torch #2"—Rogers; "A Patriotic Finale"—Egan, Company.
ACT II: "Wear Your Vanity With Pride"—Company; "Hawaiian Wedding Day"—"Howard"; "Shaft of Love"—Rogers, Egan, Bojarski,"Howard"; "Sam & Me"—Pevsner; "Bigger Is Better"—Egan, "Howard"; "Torch #3"—Rogers; "Laughing Matters"—Rogers; "Over the Top/When Pigs Fly" (Reprise)— "Howard," Company.

The Cocoanuts (165). Transfer from off off Broadway of the revival of the musical with book by George S. Kaufman; music and lyrics by Irving Berlin; adapted by Richard Sabellico. Produced by Raymond J. Greenwald, Ltd. in the American Jewish Theater production, Stanley Brechner artistic director, at the American Place Theater. Opened August 15, 1996. (Closed January 5, 1997)

Jamison .... Michael Waldron
Eddie the Bellboy .... Brad Bradley
Robert Adams .... Alec Timerman
Mrs. Potter .... Celia Tackaberry
Penelope Martyn .... Laurie Gamache
Polly Potter .... Becky Watson

Harvey Yates .... Michael Berresse
Henry W. Schlemmer
  (Groucho) .... Michael McGrath
Willie the Shill (Chico) .... Peter Slutsker
Silent Sam (Harpo) .... Robert Sapoff
Hennessey .... Richard Ziman

Orchestra: C. Lynne Shankel piano; David Kirshenbaum 2d piano; Joe Mowatt percussion.
Understudies: Misses Tackaberry, Watson—Andrea Bianchi; Messrs. Waldron, McGrath, Slutsker, Sapoff—Frank Moran; Mr. Ziman—Michael Waldron; Messrs. Berresse, Timerman, Bradley—Craig Waletzko.
Directed and choreographed by Richard Sabellico; musical direction, C. Lynne Shankel; scenery, Jeff Modereger; costumes, Jonathan Bixby; lighting, Herrick Goldman; vocal and dance arrangements,

C. Lynne Shankel; executive producer, Stanley Brechner; casting, Stuart Howard, Amy Schecter; production stage manager, Jason Brouillard; stage manager, Peter Asplund; press, Jeffrey Richards Associates, Irene Gandy, Roger Bean.

Time: 1925. Place: In and around the Cocoanut Hotel in Cocoanut Beach, Florida. The play was presented in two parts.

Originally, the show had the Marx Brothers acting in a musical; now, it has actors playing them acting in the show first produced 12/7/25 for 377 performances. This adaptation, previously produced 5/12/96 off off Broadway by American Jewish Theater, is its first major New York revival of record.

ACT I

"Florida by the Sea" .... Company
"A Little Bungalow" .... Robert, Polly
*"Pack Up Your Sins and Go to the Devil" .... Penelope, Harvey
"We Should Care" .... Robert, Polly
"Florida by the Sea" (Reprise) .... Company
"Always" .... Robert, Polly

ACT II

"Five O'Clock Tea" .... Mrs. Potter, Bellboy
"Tango Melody" .... Schlemmer, Mrs. Potter
*"When My Dreams Come True" .... Robert, Polly
*"Shaking the Blues Away" .... Penelope, Harvey
"The Tale of a Shirt" .... Company
"Always" (Reprise) .... Company
*Songs interpolated into this production.

Disappearing Act (39). Musical revue with words and music by Mike Oster. Produced by Jeff Bannon and Phyllis Miriam in association with Bosco, Ltd., Shawn Churchman, Norman Kurtz, Steven M. Levy and Adam Weinstock at the 47th Street Theater. Opened September 4, 1996. (Closed October 6, 1996)

    Jamie MacKenzie   Branch Woodman
    Michael McElroy

Keyboards: Ron Roy.

Directed by Mark Frawley; choreography and vocal arrangements, Mark Frawley; music direction and arrangements, Ron Roy; scenery, Bill Clarke; costumes, Gregg Barnes; lighting, Tim Hunter; sound, Jim Van Bergen; production stage manager, Brian Rardin; press, the Pete Sanders Group, Michael Hartman, Glenna Freedman.

Songs and sketches about the gay life.

MUSICAL NUMBERS, ACT I: "Fear and Self-Loathing"—Company; "They Say"—Company; "Men Who Like Their Men" (additional lyrics by Jeff Bannon, Mark Frawley and Jamie MacKenzie)— Branch Woodman with Michael McElroy and Jamie MacKenzie; "Gentrification"—McElroy, MacKenzie; "Just Go Shopping"—Woodman with McElroy and MacKenzie; "I Had to Laugh" —MacKenzie; "A Secret"—Company; "Children Are a Blessing"—Woodman, McElroy; "A Friendly Vacation"—Company; "Let Me In"—Woodman; "Something's Wrong With This Picture"—Company; "Rants and Raves"— Woodman, MacKenzie; "I Slept With a Zombie"—McElroy with Woodman and MacKenzie; "The Ride Home"—MacKenzie; "Looks Like It Might Rain"— Woodman; "The Dance Floor"—Company.

ACT II: "All Tied Up on the Line"—Company; "In Here"—MacKenzie; "Dear Diary"—Company; "What Do Ya Know"—McElroy; "Fruits of Domestic Bliss"—Woodman, MacKenzie; "Old Flame"—Company; "In Our Community"— Company; "Ounce of Prevention"—McElroy with Woodman; "An Ordinary Day"—MacKenzie; "Trio for Three Buddies"—Company; "Faded Levi Jacket"— Woodman; "They Say" (Reprise)—Company; "Disappearing Act" (additional lyrics by Jeff Bannon, Mark Frawley and Jamie MacKenzie)—Company.

"Matty" (95). Solo performance by Eddy Frierson; written by Eddy Frierson; based on the life and writings of Christy Mathewson. Produced by Black Bags Three Productions in association with Edmund Gaynes and the Mathewson Foundation at the Lamb's Downstairs. Opened September 4, 1996. (Closed December 1, 1996)

Directed by Kerrigan Mahan; scenery, Robert Smith; costumes, Suzan Kay Frierson; lighting, Lawrence Oberman; stage manager, Tiffany Yelton; press, David Rothenberg Associates.

Subtitled An Evening With Christy Mathewson, a stage portrait of the great New York Giants baseball pitcher.

Old Wicked Songs (210). By Jon Marans. Produced by Daryl Roth and Jeffrey Ash in association with The Barrow Group at the Promenade Theater. Opened September 5, 1996. (Closed March 9, 1997)

Prof. Joseph Mashkan .... Hal Robinson
Stephen Hoffman .... Justin Kirk

Standbys: Mr. Robinson—Mitchell Greenberg; Mr. Kirk—Mark Boyett.

Directed by Seth Barrish; scenery and costumes, Markas Henry; lighting, Howard Werner; sound, Red Ramona; associate producers, Frank Basile, Darci Carlton, Elsa Haft, Val Sherman; casting, Pat McCorkle; production stage manager, D.C. Rosenberg; stage manager, Charlotte Volage; press, Shirley Herz, Sam Rudy.

Time: Beginning in the spring of 1986 and continuing through to summer. Place: Prof. Mashkan's rehearsal studio in Vienna, Austria. Act I, Scene 1: Spring afternoon, 1986. Scene 2: Tuesday morning, the next week. Scene 3: Late Wednesday night, two weeks later. Scene 4: Friday afternoon, two days later. Act II, Scene 1: Tuesday morning, two weeks later. Scene 2: Friday afternoon, three days later. Scene 3: Hours later, night. Scene 4: Tuesday morning, June 10, 1986. Coda: A summer morning.

Young, talented, egotistical American pianist and his elderly, tolerant Viennese teacher are brought into conflict, but finally together, over Schumann's song cycle "Dichterliebe" and attitudes toward the Nazi treatment of the Jews. Previously produced off off Broadway last season by Daryl Roth and The Barrow Group at Jewish Repertory Theater. A Best Plays Special 1996–97 Citation; see the Prizewinning Plays section of this volume.

Back on the Boulevard (24). Musical solo performance by Liliane Montevecchi. Produced by Lucille Lortel at the Martin R. Kaufman Theater. Opened September 11, 1996. (Closed September 28, 1996)

Violinist: Michael Nicholas.

Musical direction, Dick Gallagher; scenery, Michael Anania; lighting, F. Mitchell Dana; stage manager, Ed Baldi; press, Susan Chicoine, Gary Springer.

A cabaret style solo revue previously produced in London.

MUSICAL NUMBERS, ACT I: "Paris Canaille," "Sweet Beginnings," "Bruxelles," "Le Dernier Pierrot," "Le Temas," "Never Do Anything Twice," "Tico Tico," "It Might as Well Be Spring," "Autumn Leaves," "I've Got You Under My Skin," "La Vie en Rose," "My Man," "You Don't Know Paree," "I Love Paris," "Ballet Barre."

ACT II: "Je Cherche un Millionaire," "Formidable," "Just a Gigolo," "Boulevard of Broken Dreams," "Bridge of Caulaincourt," "Hey Jacques," "Irma la Douce," "Fangled Tango," "But Beautiful," "Ne Me Quitte Pas," "I Don't Want to Know," "Follies Bergere," "Bonsoir."

900 Oneonta (8). By David Beaird. Produced by Circle Repertory Theater, Austin Pendleton artistic director, Andrew Chipok managing director, at Circle Repertory Theater. Opened September 15, 1996. (Closed September 22, 1996)

Dandy	Leland Crooke	Morely	Sam Groom
Carrie	Venida Evans	Gitlo	Jon Cryer
Burning Jewel	Missi Pyle	Persia	Hallie Foote

Woodrow	Devon Abner	Tiger	Garret Dillahunt
Fr. Bourette	Barry McEvoy	Palace	Michelle Hurd
Beauty	Mikel Sarah Lambert		

Directed by David Beaird; scenery, Shawn Motley; costumes, Laurie Churba; lighting, John Lewis; sound, Jason Fox; stage manager, Francys Olivia Burch; press, Jeffrey Richards Associates, Irene Gandy, Roger Bean.

Time: 1980. Place: Bastrop, La. The play was presented in two parts.

Shady doings of an individually and collectively disfunctional Louisiana family. Previously produced in London.

Einstein (54). Solo performance by John Crowther; written by Willard Simms. Produced by Pearl Productions in association with Edmund Gaynes at the American Jewish Theater. Opened September 19, 1996. (Closed November 10, 1996)

Directed by John Crowther; scenery, Eric Warren; adapted for the American Jewish Theater by Robert L. Smith; costumes, Il Creativo Productions; lighting, Lawrence Oberman; sound, Chuck Estes; stage manager, D. Mark Lyons; press, David Rothenberg Associates.

Character sketch of Einstein at age 67 in 1946.

*Full Gallop (277). Return engagement of the solo performance by Mary Louise Wilson; written by Mark Hampton and Mary Louise Wilson. Produced by David Stone, Amy Nederlander-Case and Barry & Fran Weissler in the Manhattan Theater Club production at the Westside Theater. Opened September 24, 1996.

Directed by Nicholas Martin; scenery, James Noone; costumes, Michael Krass; lighting, David F. Segal; sound, Bruce Ellman; associate producer, Edwin Schloss; production stage manager, Ira Mont; press, The Pete Sanders Group, Glenna Freedman.

Time: 1971. Place: Diana Vreeland's Park Avenue apartment. The play was presented in two parts.

Mary Louise Wilson as the late Diana Vreeland, renowned former editor of *Vogue*, at the time when she had just been fired from that post. Previously produced in regional theater at the Old Globe Theater, San Diego and off Broadway in this production 10/18/95 for 39 performances.

Elektra (6). By Sophocles; translated in the modern Greek language by Yorgos Heimonas and performed with English supertitles; produced by ICM Artists in association with Kritas Productions in the National Theater of Greece production at the City Center. Opened September 25, 1996. (Closed September 29, 1996)

Elektra	Lydia Koniordou	Chrysothemis	Tania Papadopoulou
Orestes	Miltos Dimoulis	Aegisthus	Stefanos Kyriakidis
Pylades	Yorgos Karamichos	Tutor	Alexandros Mylonas
Clytemnestra	Aspasia Papathanasiou		

Directed by Lydia Koniordou in association with Dimitris Economou; scenery and costumes, Dionysus Fotopoulos; lighting, Alekos Yiannaros; choreography, Apostolia Papadamaki; music, Takis Farazis; press, Jeffrey Richards Associates.

The last major New York revival of this Sophocles play took place on Broadway in the Piraikon Theatron of Greece production 9/7/64 for 8 performances. The play was presented without intermission.

*Magic on Broadway (318). Magic revue performed by Joseph Gabriel. Produced by Catco Inc. and Skyline Entertainment Inc. at the Lamb's Theater. Opened September 29, 1996.

Magic Assistants: Lucy Gabriel, Vincent Giordano. Juggler: Romano Frediani. Dancers: Heather Rochelle Harmon, Melanie Doskocil, Kathleen Grimaldi, Karen Mascari, Victoria Whitten.

Choreography, Tiger Martina; lighting, Gregory Cohen; sound, Robert Cotnoir; executive producer, Donald Spector; producers, Mary Rodas, Dee Snyder; production stage manager, Kelley Kirkpatrick; press, Richard Rubenstein, Alan Locher.

Magic show starring Joseph Gabriel, with embellishments, presented in two parts.

Radio Gals (40). Musical with book, music and lyrics by Mike Craver and Mark Hardwick. Produced by Elliot Martin and Ron Shapiro in association with Lee Mimms and Amick Byram at the John Houseman Theater. Opened October 1, 1996. (Closed November 3, 1996)

Hazel C. Hunt	Carole Cook	Rennabelle	Klea Blackhurst
Miss Mabel Swindle	M. Rice	Gladys Fritts	Rosemary Loar
Miss Azilee Swindle	P.M. Craver	O.B. Abbott	Matthew Bennett
America	Emily Mikesell		

Understudies: Misses Cook, Loar—Melissa Hart; Messrs. Craver, Bennett—Sean McCourt; Mr. Rice—John Ogden; Misses Mikesell, Blackhurst —Jessica Wright.

"The Hazelnuts": "Mabel Swindle" piano, trombone; "Azilee Swindle" bass, tuba, guitar, ukelele, xylophone, piano; "America" fiddle, flute, clarinet, saxophone ukelele, xylophone; "Rennabelle" drums, trumpet, bass, ukelele xylophone; "O.B. Abbott" accordian, trombone, ukelele; "Gladys Fritts" theremin, dishpan, spoons, ukelele; "Hazel C. Hunt" ukelele, birdwhistle, dishpan and spoons, tambourine.

Directed and choreographed by Marcia Milgrom Dodge; scenery, Narelle Sissons; costumes, Michael Krass; lighting, Joshua Starbuck; sound, Tom Morse; musical supervision, Christopher Drobny; musical arrangements, Mark Hardwick with Klea Blackhurst, Mike Craver and Emily Mikesell; associate producer, Marjorie Martin; production stage manager, Daniel Munson; press, Jeffrey Richards Associates, Irene Gandy, Roger Bean, Mark Cannistraro.

Time: A warm day in May in the late 1920s, well before "The Crash." Place: The home of Hazel C. Hunt in Cedar Ridge, Ark.

Early days of radio when it could be a home industry with bureaucrats seeking to prevent it from intruding anywhere it pleased on the broadcasting band. Previously produced in regional theater by Arkansas Repertory.

ACT I

"The Wedding of the Flowers"	Hazel
"Sunrise Melody"	Hazel, America, Rennabelle, Azilee
"Aviatrix Love Song"	America
"Horehound Compound I"	The Hazelnuts
"If Stars Could Talk"	Gladys, Rennabelle, America
"When It's Sweetpea Time in Georgia"	Azilee
"Dear Mr. Gershwin"	Rennabelle
"The Tranquil Boxwood"	Gladys
"Faeries in My Mother's Flower Garden"	Gladys
"Horehound Compound II"	The Hazelnuts
"A Fireside: A Pipe & a Pet"	O.B. Abbott, Gladys
"Edna Jones, The Elephant Girl"	Hazel, The Hazelnuts, O.B. Abbott
"Paging the Ether"	Hazel

ACT II

"Royal Radio"	America, Rennabelle, Mabel, Azilee
"Weather Song"	Rennabelle, America, Mabel, Azilee
"Buster, He's a Hot Dog Now"	Mabel, Azilee
(original dance by Mark Hardwick)	
"Why Did You Make Me Love You?"	O.B. Abbott
"Kittens in the Snow"	The Hazelnuts, O.B. Abbott
"Old Gals"	Hazel, Mabel, Azilee
"A Gal's Got to Do What a Gal's Got to Do"	Hazel
The NBC Broadcast	Hazel, The Hazelnuts
"Horehound Compound III," "Whispering Pines," "The Wedding of the Flowers" (Reprise), "Queenie Take Me Home"	
"Royal Radio" (Reprise)	Hazel, The Hazelnuts

Valiant Theater Company. Schedule of two revivals. **Rhinoceros** (22). By Eugene Ionesco; adapted by Theresa Rebeck. Opened October 2, 1996. (Closed October 20, 1996) **A Soldier's Play** (24). By Charles Fuller. Opened November 19, 1996. (Closed December 8, 1996) Pro-

WHEN PIGS FLY—Michael West *(left)* and David Pevsner wearing two of Howard Crabtree's Lucille Lortel, American Theater Wing, Drama Desk and Outer Critics Award-winning costumes for his musical

duced by Valiant Theater Company, Herbert Beigel producer, Michael Murray artistic director, Leon B. Denmark managing director, at Theater Four.

RHINOCEROS

Waitress	Heather Carnduff	Old Gentleman	Burt Edwards
Grocer's Wife	Debbie Lamedman	Bar Owner; Fireman	Cortez Nance Jr.
Grocer; Fireman	Michael Etheridge	Daisy	Erin J. O'Brien
Housewife; Mrs. Beef	Elizabeth Van Dyke	Bofford	J.R. Horne
Berenger	Peter Jacobson	Doddard	Geoffrey Owens
John	Zach Grenier	Flutterby	Fred Burrell
Logician	David Green		

Directed by Michael Murray; scenery, Karl Eigsti, Ted Simpson; costumes, Amela Baksic; lighting, Neil Peter Jampolis; sound. Aural Fixation; casting, Judy Henderson, Alycia Aumuller; production stage manager, Allison Sommers; stage manager, Shannon Ferguson; press, Springer/Chicoine Public Relations, Gary Springer, Susan Chicoine.

Act I, Scene 1: The square. Scene 2: The office. Act II, Scene 1: John's bedroom. Scene 2: Berenger's apartment.

The first major New York production of Ionesco's *Rhinoceros* took place on Broadway 1/9/61 for

240 performances (and was named a Best Play of its season), with a return engagement 9/18/61 for 16 performances. This is its first major New York revival.

A SOLDIER'S PLAY

Tech. Sgt. Vernon C. Walters	Albert Hall	Pvt. James Wilkie	Keith Randolph Smith
Capt. Charles Taylor	Jonathan Walker	Pvt. Tony Smalls	Cedric Harris
Corp. Bernard Cobb	Sean Squire	Capt. Richard Davenport	Geoffrey C. Ewing
Pvt. 1st Class Melvyn Peterson	Wood Harris	Pvt. C.J. Memphis	Danny Johnson
Corp. Ellis	Robb Leigh Davis	Lt. Byrd	P.J. Brown
Pvt. Louis Henson	Jonathan Earl Peck	Capt. Wilcox	Barton Tinapp

Directed by Clinton Turner Davis; scenery and costumes, Felix E. Cochren; lighting, Dennis Parichy; sound, Aural Fixation; casting, Judy Henderson, Alycia Aumuller; production stage manager, Daniel L. Bello; stage manager, Dwight R.B. Cook.

Time: 1944. Place: Ft. Neal, La. The play was presented in two parts.

A Soldier's Play was first produced off Broadway by Negro Ensemble Company 11/20/81 for 468 performances when it was named a Best Play of its season and won the Critics Award for best American play and the Pulitzer Prize. This is its first major New York revival.

*Late Nite Catechism** (272). By Vicki Quade and Maripat Donovan. Produced by Entertainment Events Inc. and Joe Corcoran Productions at St. Luke's Church. Opened October 3, 1996.

Sister .... Maripat Donovan
Father Martinez .... George Bass

Understudy: Miss Donovan—Jodi Capless.

Directed by Patrick Trettenero; production design, Marc Silvia; lighting, Tom Sturge; associate producer, Dan Corcoran; press, David Rothenberg Associates, David Gersten.

Time: 1966. Place: An adult Catechism class. The play was presented in two parts.

Interactive comedy, a nun lectures on Catholicism and the lives of many of its saints. Previously produced in Chicago (Live Bait Theater), Boston and Australia.

Political Animal (28). Solo performance by Douglas McGrath; written by Douglas McGrath. Produced by the Westside Theater, Marshall R. Purdy executive producer, at the Westside Theater. Opened October 7, 1966. (Closed November 3, 1996)

Directed by Peter Askin; scenery, Rob Odorisio; costumes, Candice Donnelly; lighting, Phil Monat; sound, Bruce Ellman; video, Dennis Diamond; asssociate producers, Terry Byrne, Michael Robin; production stage manager, Renee Lutz; press, Boneau/Bryan-Brown, Erin Dunn.

Comedy characterization of an opportunistic self-appointed Presidential candidate.

*Forbidden Broadway Strikes Back** (262). Musical revue created and written by Gerard Alessandrini. Produced by John Freedson, Harriet Yellin and Jon B. Platt at the Triad Theater. Opened October 17, 1996.

Bryan Batt   David Hibbard
Donna English   Christine Pedi

Understudies: Messrs. Batt, Hibbard—Phillip George; Misses English, Pedi—Whitney Allen.

Directed by Gerard Alessandrini; associate director and choreographer, Phillip George; musical direction, Matthew Ward; scenery, Bradley Kaye; costumes, Alvin Colt; wigs, Robert Fama; production consultant, Pete Blue; associate producers, Steve McGraw, Nancy McCall, Peter Martin, Masakazu Shibaoka; production stage manager, Alex Lyu Volckhausen; press, the Pete Sanders Group, Glenna Freedman.

Newest edition of the musical revue parodying the current New York theater scene. The play was presented in two parts.

Playwrights Horizons. Schedule of five programs. **Fit To Be Tied** (25). By Nicky Silver. Opened October 20, 1996. (Closed November 10, 1996) **Demonology** (9). By Kelly Stuart. Opened November 10, 1996. (Closed November 17, 1996) **Cloud Tectonics** (17). By Jose Rivera. Opened January 5, 1997. (Closed January 19, 1997) **Violet** (32). Musical based on *The Ugliest Pilgrim* by Doris Betts; book and lyrics by Brian Crawley; music by Jeanine Tesori; presented in association with AT&T:*OnStage*. Opened March 11, 1997. (Closed April 6, 1997) And *Baby Anger* by Peter Hedges scheduled to open 6/8/97. Produced by Playwrights Horizons, Tim Sanford artistic director, Leslie Marcus managing director, Lynn Landis general manager, at Playwrights Horizons.

FIT TO BE TIED

Arloc	T. Scott Cunningham	Carl	Dick Latessa
Nessa	Jean Smart	Boyd	Matt Keeslar

Directed by David Warren; scenery, James Youmans; costumes, Teresa Snider-Stein; lighting, Donald Holder; sound and original music, John Gromada; casting, Janet Foster; production stage manager, C.A. Clark; press, James L.L. Morrison, Tom D'Ambrosio, Kathy McAllen.

Act I: Mistakes & Amends, Thanksgiving Week in New York City. Act II: The New Year, three weeks later.

Comedy of emotional entanglements, as a young man mistakes an actor costumed as an angel in the Music Hall Christmas show for the real thing.

DEMONOLOGY

Gina	Marisa Tomei	Collins	Bray Poor
De Martini	Rocco Sisto	Child	Kathleen Glaudini

Directed by Jim Simpson; scenery, David Harwell; costumes, Therese Bruck; lighting, Anne M. Padien; sound, Michael Clark; music, Mike Nolan; production stage manager, Leila Knox.

Office boss harried by a demon in the person of a temporary worker. The play was presented in two parts.

CLOUD TECTONICS

Celestina del Sol	Camilia Sanes	Nelson de la Luna	Javi Mulero
Anibal de la Luna	John Ortiz		

Directed by Tina Landau; scenery, Riccardo Hernandez; costumes, Anita Yavich; lighting, Frances Aronson; sound, Mark Bennett, J.R. Conklin; original sound score, Mark Bennett; casting, James Calleri; production stage manager, Martha Donaldson.

Prologue: Los Angeles. *Cloud Tectonics*: The same, later that night. Epilogue: The same, 40 years later. The play was presented without intermission.

Love and metaphysics one stormy night in Los Angeles. Previously produced in regional theater in Louisville, Los Angeles and Chicago.

VIOLET

Young Vi	Amanda Posner	Creepy Guy; Bus Driver 2; Radio Singer; Billy Dean; Virgil	Kirk McDonald
Leroy Evans; Waiter; Mechanic; Lead Radio Singer; Bus Driver 3; Earl	Michael Medeiros	Woman With Fan; Music Hall Singer; Mabel	Paula Newsome
Violet	Lauren Ward	Woman Knitting; Landlady; Hotel Singer 2; Gospel Soloist	Roz Ryan
Father	Stephen Lee Anderson	Flick	Michael McElroy
Bus Driver 1; Preacher; Rufus; Radio Singer; Bus Driver 4	Robert Westenberg	Monty	Michael Park
Old Lady 1; Hotel Singer 1; Old Lady 2	Cass Morgan		

Orchestra: Michael Rafter conductor, keyboard 1; Gordon Twist associate conductor, keyboard 2; Steve Tyler keyboard 3; Jon Herrington guitar 1; Greg Utzig guitar 2; Kermit Driscoll bass; Clint DeGanon drums, percussion; Mary Whitaker violin; Anik Oulianine cello.

Directed by Susan H. Schulman; choreography, Kathleen Marshall; musical direction, Michael Rafter; scenery, Derek McLane; costumes, Catherine Zuber; lighting, Peter Kaczorowski; sound, Tony Meola; fight direction, Luis Perez; orchestrations, Joseph Joubert, Buryl Red; vocal arrangements, Jeanine Tesori; associate producer, Ira Weitzman; casting, James Calleri; production stage manager, Perry Kline; stage manager, Steve Zorthian.

Time: Early September 1964.

Badly scarred teenaged girl sets off in search of healing by a TV preacher and is befriended by two young soldiers. Developed at the O'Neill Music Theater Conference and winner of the 1996–97 New York Drama Critics Circle and Lucille Lortel Awards for best musical; see the Prizewinning Plays section of this volume.

ACT I

Spruce Pine, N.C. to Kingsport, Tenn.
Opening/"Surprised" .... Young Vi, Violet
"On My Way" .... Violet, Company
"Luck of the Draw" .... Father, Young Vi, Violet, Monty, Flick
Kingsport to Nashville, Tenn.
"Question & Answer" .... Monty, Violet
"All to Pieces" .... Violet, Monty, Flick
Nashville to Memphis, Tenn.
"Let It Sing" .... Flick
Memphis
"Who'll Be the One (If Not Me)" .... Radio Singers
"You're Different" .... Monty
"Lonely Stranger/Anyone Would Do" .... Music Hall & Hotel Singers
"Lay Down Your Head" .... Violet

ACT II

Memphis to Fort Smith, Ark.
"Lonely Stranger" .... Bus Driver 3
"Hard to Say Goodbye" .... Violet, Flick
"Promise Me, Violet" .... Violet, Monty, Flick
Tulsa, Okla.—Hope and Glory Building
"Raise Me Up" .... Gospel Soloist, Preacher, Gospel Choir
"Down the Mountain" .... Young Vi, Father
"Raise Me Up" (Reprise) .... Violet
"Look at Me" .... Violet, Young Vi
"That's What I Could Do" .... Father
Tulsa to Fort Smith, Ark.
"Promise Me, Violet" (Reprise) .... Flick, Violet
"Bring Me to Light" .... Flick, Violet, Young Vi, Company

The New Bozena (74). Clowning revue produced by Falstaff Presents, Michael Winter and Rachel Colbert at the Cherry Lane Theater. Opened October 31, 1996. (Closed January 5, 1997)

Ramon .... David Costabile   Revhanavaan
Spiv Westenberg .... Michael Dahlen   Sahaanahanadaan .... Kevin Isola

Directed by Rainn Wilson; scenery, Chris Muller; costumes, Melissa Toth; lighting, Adam Silverman; sound, Andrew S. Keister; music coordinator, Ray Bokhour; associate producer, Taylor Reinhart; production stage manager, J. Philip Bassett; press, Tony Origlio, Kevin Rehac, Michael Cullen.

Series of clowning skits and demonstrations in post-modern style. The show was presented without an intermission.

*Manhattan Theater Club. Schedule of eight programs. **The Blues Are Running** (25). By Michael Cristofer. Opened November 3, 1996. (Closed November 24, 1996) **Nine Armenians** (72). By Leslie Ayvazian. Opened November 12, 1996. (Closed January 12, 1997) **Neat** (35).

Solo performance by Charlayne Woodard; written by Charlayne Woodard; produced in association with Seattle Repertory Theater. Opened January 7, 1997. (Closed February 9, 1997) **Psychopathia Sexualis** (62). By John Patrick Shanley. Opened February 26, 1997. (Closed April 20, 1997) **Dealer's Choice** (32). By Patrick Marber. Opened April 8, 1997. (Closed May 4, 1997) **The Green Heart** (30). Musical based on the story by Jack Ritchie; book by Charles Busch; music and lyrics by Rusty Magee. Opened April 10, 1997. (Closed May 4, 1997) *Col-lected Stories (14). By Donald Margulies. Opened May 20, 1997. And *Seeking the Genesis* by Kia Korthron, schedule to open 6/17/97. Produced in its 25th season by Manhattan Theater Club, Lynne Meadow artistic director, Barry Grove executive producer, Michael Bush associate artistic director, Victoria Bailey general manager, *The Blues Are Running, Neat, Dealer's Choice* and *Seeking the Genesis* at Stage II, *Nine Armenians, Psychopathia Sexualis* and *Collected Stories* at Stage I, Manhattan Theater Club; *The Green Heart* at Variety Arts Theater.

THE BLUES ARE RUNNING

Pyle; Boo; Johnny .... Paul Giamatti
Stile; Mickey; JoJo .... Marcus Giamatti

Understudies: Paul Giamatti—Adam Dannheisser; Marcus Giamatti—John Sperekados.
Directed by Melvin Bernhardt; scenery, James Youmans; costumes, Jess Goldstein; lighting, Kenneth Posner; sound, Raymond D. Schilke; casting, Nancy Piccione; production stage manager, Mark Cole; press, Boneau/Bryan-Brown, Chris Boneau, Andy Shearer.
Act I: Pyle and Stile; Mickey and Boo. Act II: JoJo and Johnny; Pyle and Stile.
The paths of three pairs of men—tramps, old friends and hit men, played by two actors—cross on a Central Park bench at 2 a.m.

NINE ARMENIANS

Armine; Mom .... Linda Emond	Raffi .... Cameron Boyd
John; Dad .... Michael Countryman	Aunt Louise .... Sophie Hayden
Pop; Vartan .... Ed Setrakian	Uncle Garo .... Richard Council
Non; Marie .... Kathleen Chalfant	Ani .... Sevanne Martin
Virginia; Ginya .... Ellen Muth	

Musician: George Mgrdichian.
Directed by Lynne Meadow; scenery, Santo Loquasto; costumes, Tom Broecker; lighting, Kenneth Posner; sound, Aural Fixation; original music. George Mgrdichian; choreography, Michele Assaf; casting, Nancy Piccione; production stage manager, Diane DiVita; stage manager, Kirsten Mooney.
Time: Now. Place: An American suburb and Armenia over the course of four seasons. The play was presented without intermission.
Three generations of a close-knit family of Armenian descent disclose their loving unity along with their tragic past. Previously produced in regional theater at Intiman Theater, Seattle.

NEAT

Directed by Tazewell Thompson; scenery, Donald Eastman; costumes, Jane Greenwood; lighting, Brian Nason; original music and sound, Fabian Obispo; production stage manager, Lisa Iaccuci.
Portraits of members of her black family, especially a well remembered aunt, in the 1960s when the actress Charlayne Woodard was growing up; a companion piece to her *Pretty Fire* produced by Manhattan Theater Club 3/26/93 for 30 performances.

PSYCHOPATHIA SEXUALIS

Ellie .... Margaret Colin	Dr. Block .... Edward Herrmann
Howard .... Daniel Gerroll	Lucille .... Park Overall
Arthur .... Andrew McCarthy	

Directed by Daniel Sullivan; scenery, Derek McLane; costumes, Jane Greenwood; lighting, Pat Collins; sound, John Kilgore; casting, Ilene Starger; production stage manager, Michael Brunner.

A Fanfare of Playwriting
At Manhattan Theater Club

Above, Edward Herrn *top)* with Daniel Ge John Patrick Shanley *chopathia Sexualis*

Above, Kathleen Chalfant and Linda Emond in a scence from Leslie Ayvazian's *Nine Armenians*

Above, Paul Giamatti and Marcus Giamatti in Michael Cristofer's *The Blues Are Running*

Left, Maria Tucci and Debra Messing in *Collected Stories* by Donald Margulies

Time: Now. Place: New York City. The play was presented in two parts.

Comedy, a psychiatrist tries to rid a troubled husband-to-be of his fetish for a pair of argyle socks that belonged to his father. Previously produced in regional theater at Seattle Repertory Theater and the Mark Taper Forum.

THE GREEN HEART

Manager; Rutherford	Jay Russell	McPherson	John Ellison Conlee
William Graham	David Andrew Macdonald	Molly; Clara	Julie J. Hafner
Uta	Alison Fraser	Estelle	Karyn Quackenbush
Edith; Lydia	Elizabeth Ward	Mrs. Tragger	Ruth Williamson
Minister; Santiani	Tim Salamandyk	Ruby	Lovette George
Henrietta Lowell	Karen Trott	Dallas	Don Goodspeed
Harvey	Jeff Edgerton		

Tailors, Salespeople: Jeff Edgerton, Lovette George, Don Goodspeed, Julie J. Hafner, Karyn Quackenbush, Tim Salamandyk, Elizabeth Ward. Mourners: Jeff Edgerton, Lovette George, Don Goodspeed, Julie J. Hafner, Karyn Quackenbush, Jay Russell. Calypso Singers: Lovette George, Karyn Quackenbush, Elizabeth Ward. House Servants: Jeff Edgerton, Jay Russell, Elizabeth Ward. Guests: Jeff Edgerton, Lovette George, Don Goodspeed, Karyn Quackenbush, Tim Salamandyk. Birdwatchers: Jeff Edgerton, Lovette George, Don Goodspeed, Julie J. Hafner, Karyn Quackenbush, Jay Russell, Tim Salamandyk, Elizabeth Ward.

Orchestra: Joe Baker conductor, pianist; Steven Silverstein assistant conductor, keyboard; Robert DeBellis reeds; Gary Guzio trumpet, flugelhorn; Ray Grappone drums, percussion.

Understudies: Mr. Macdonald—Don Goodspeed; Miss Trott—Julie J. Hafner; Miss Williamson—Karyn Quackenbush; Mr. Conlee—Tim Salamandyk; Miss Fraser—Elizabeth Ward; Swings—Deborah Leamy, Robin Lewis.

Directed by Kenneth Elliott; musical staging, Joey McKneely; musical direction and arrangements, Joe Baker; scenery, James Noone; costumes, Robert Mackintosh; lighting, Kirk Bookman; sound, Tom Morse; orchestrations, Curtis McKonly; director of musical theater program, Clifford Lee Johnson III; casting, Nancy Piccione; production stage manager, Pamela Edington; stage manager, Andrew Bryant.

Time: The present. Place: New York City, Dutchess County and the Adirondacks.

Romance and melodrama in the relationship between a playboy and a wealthy botanist.

ACT I

"Our Finest Customer"	Manager, William, Ensemble
"I'm Poor"	William
"Picture Me"	Uta
"Henrietta's Elegy"	Henrietta
"I Can't Recall"	Henrietta
"Til Death Do They Part"	Ensemble
"Tropical Island Breezes"	Ensemble
"An Open Mind"	William
"The Easy Life"	Mrs. Tragger, Ensemble
"The Easy Life" (Reprise)	Mrs. Tragger
"Get Used to It"	McPherson
"Get Used to It" (Reprise)	Company

ACT II

"Why Can't We Turn Back the Clock?"	Henrietta, William, Ensemble
"Horns of an Immoral Dilemma"	William, Uta, Henrietta
"Ornithology"	Ensemble
"The Green Heart"	Henrietta
"The Green Heart" (Reprise)	William
"I'm the Victim Here"	Uta, Mrs. Tragger, McPherson
"I'm Poor" (Reprise)	William
"What's It Gonna Take (To Make It Clear Across the Lake)?"	William, Uta, Mrs. Tragger, McPherson, Henrietta
"The Green Heart" (Reprise)	William, Henrietta, Ensemble

DEALER'S CHOICE

Mugsy	Jamie Harris	Frankie	Dan Futterman
Sweeney	Ritchie Coster	Carl	Sam Trammell
Stephen	Dermot Crowley	Ash	Byron Jennings

Directed by John Tillinger; scenery, David Gallo; costumes, Laura Cunningham; lighting, Kenneth Posner; sound, Aural Fixation; dialect coach, Elizabeth Smith; production stage manager, James Fitzsimmons.

Time: Over one Sunday and Monday morning in winter. Place, Acts I and II: The kitchen area and dining room of a restaurant in London. Act III: The basement. The play was presented in two parts.

Eruptions of masculine character and emotion stimulated by a poker game. A foreign play previously produced at Royal National Theater in London.

COLLECTED STORIES

Ruth Steiner .... Maria Tucci
Lisa Morrison .... Debra Messing

Directed by Lisa Peterson; scenery, Thomas Lynch; costumes, Jess Goldstein; lighting, Kenneth Posner; sound, Mark Bennett; production stage manager, Jane E. Neufeld.

Time: Scene 1: September 1990. Scene 2: May 1991. Scene 3: August 1992. Scene 4: December 1994. Scene 5: October 1996. Scene 6: Later that night. Place: Ruth Steiner's apartment in Greenwich Village. The play was presented in two parts with the intermission following Scene 3.

Development of a relationship between an aging, successful writer and her young, ambitious student. Previously produced in regional theater at South Coast Repertory, Costa Mesa, Calif. The play was presented in two parts.

Cakewalk (71). By Peter Feibleman. Produced by Julian Schlossberg, Meyer Ackerman and Donna Knight at the Variety Arts Theater. Opened November 6, 1996. (Closed January 5, 1997)

Lilly	Linda Lavin	Women	Suzanne Grodner
Cuff	Michael Knight	Men	Kirby Mitchell

Understudies: Miss Lavin—Suzanne Grodner; Women—Deborah Jolly; Messrs. Knight, Mitchell—Erik Leeper.

Directed by Marshall W. Mason; incidental music, Carly Simon; scenery, Michael McGarty; costumes, Laura Crow; lighting, Tharon Musser; sound, Randy Freed; music produced and performed by Teese Gohl; associate producers, Georgia Frontiere, Michael Winter; casting, Stuart Howard, Amy Schecter; production stage manager, Denise Yaney; press, Boneau/Bryan-Brown, Chris Boneau, Jackie Green.

Time: Now and in the past. Place: Beginning and ending in Lilly's house on Martha's Vineyard. The play was presented without intermission.

Peter Feibleman's dramatization of his close and longstanding relationship with the late Lillian Hellman.

The Santaland Diaries (63). Adapted by Joe Mantello from David Sedaris's *Barrel Fever*. Produced by David Stone and Amy Nederlander-Case at the Atlantic Theater. Opened November 7, 1996. (Closed December 29, 1996)

With Karen Valentine, Timothy Olyphant.

Directed by Joe Mantello; scenery, Ian Falconer; costumes, Isaac Mizrahi; lighting, Jan Kroeze; sound, David Van Tieghem; associate producers, Lisa Goldsmith Productions, David Binder; production stage manager, Pamela Edington; press, Boneau/Bryan-Brown, Chris Boneau, Jackie Green.

Adaptations of two of Sedaris's stories: *Season's Greetings to Our Friends and Family*, with Miss Valentine as a housewife who encounters her husband's illegitimate daughter on her doorstep; and *The Santaland Diaries*, with Mr. Olyphant describing the experience of playing a Christmas elf at Macy's. The play was presented in two parts.

Family Values (109). By Carl Ritchie. Produced by Robert M. Cavallo at the Irish Arts Center. Opened November 8, 1996. (Closed February 23, 1997)

Barbara	Ellen Evans	Philip	James Hallett
Ed	Joel Fabiani	Lewis	Jeff P. Weiss
Christine	Patty Jamieson	Mark	Craig Addams

Directed by Norman Hall; scenery, Daniel Ettinger; lighting, Phil Hymes; technical direction, Matthew Katz; associate producer, Penny Ann Green; stage manager, Sarah Jane Runser; press, Springer/Chicoine Associates, Candi Adams.

Place: An apartment in New York City. Act I, Scene 1: Late winter. Scene 2: Indian summer, six months later. Act II, Scene 1: The same. Scene 2: Early spring, six months later.

Husband leaves his wife, then changes his mind.

The Queen of Bingo (33). By Jeanne Michaels and Phyllis Murphy. Produced by Rowan Joseph, Shane T. Partlow, Robert B. Shaffer and Eric N. Schwarz in association with Kevin Eberly and Neal Roberts at Greenwich House. Opened November 10, 1996. (Closed December 8, 1996)

Sis	Carmen Decker	Fr. Mack; The Caller	Tracy Davis
Babe	Nancy-Elizabeth Kammer		

Directed by Rowan Joseph; scenery, Robert B. Johnson; costumes, Charlotte Deardorff; lighting, F. Burris Jackes; casting, Sherie L. Seff; production stage manager, Steve Wildern; press, Shirley Herz Associates, Sam Rudy.

Time: Tuesday night. Place: St. Joseph's Catholic Church, Battle Creek, Mich. The play was performed without intermission.

Events at a church bingo soiree include audience participation in a bingo game.

The Waste Land (67). Solo performance by Fiona Shaw of the poem by T.S. Eliot. Produced by Jedediah Wheeler and En Garde Arts Inc. at the Liberty Theater. Opened November 14, 1996. (Closed January 5, 1997)

Directed by Deborah Warner; lighting, Jean Kalman; press, James L.L. Morrison.

A flow of images from the Eliot poem, presented without intermission.

*A Brief History of White Music (220). Musical revue conceived by DeeDee Thomas and David Tweedy; music and lyrics by various authors (see listing below). Produced by Gene Wolsk, RAD Productions Inc. and Art D'Lugoff at The Village Gate. Opened November 19, 1996.

James Alexander   Deborah Keeling
Wendy Edmead

Understudies: Catrice Joseph, Dwayne Grayman.

Trio: Alva Nelson piano; Konrad Adderley bass; Joeham Eric drums.

Directed and choreographed by Ken Roberson; musical direction, Alva Nelson; scenery, Felix E. Cochren; costumes, Debra Stein; lighting, Alan Keen; sound, Stan Wallace; musical arrangements, Nat Adderley Jr., Alva Nelson, Art Yelton; associate lighting designer, Matt Berman; casting, Stuart Howard, Amy Schecter; production stage manager, Femi Sarah Heggie; press, Shirley Herz Associates, Kevin McAnarney.

Black performers gently ribbing white pop music of the 1940s to 1970s. The show was performed without intermission.

MUSICAL NUMBERS: Overture; "Who Put the Bomp" (by Barry Mann and Gerry Coffin)—Company; "Bei Mir Bist Du Schoen" (by J. Jacobs, Sammy Cahn, S. Chaplin and S. Secunda)—Deborah Keeling, Company; "I Got a Gal in Kalamazoo" (by Mack Gordon and Harry Warren)—James Alexander, Company; "That'll Be the Day" (by Buddy Holly)—Company; "Teenager in Love" (by Doc

Pomus and Mort Shuman)—Company; "Where the Boys Are" (by Howard Greenfield and Neil Se-daka)—Wendy Edmead; "Leader of the Pack" (by J. Barry, E. Greenwich and G. Morton)—Edmead, Company; "Walk Like a Man" (by Bob Crewe and Bob Gaudio)—Alexander, Company; "Love Potion No. 9" (by Jerry Leiber and Mike Stoller)—Company; "Blue Suede Shoes" (by Carl Lee Perkins)—Keeling; "Love Me Tender Medley" (by Elvis Presley and P. Matson) —Company; "Jailhouse Rock" (by Jerry Leiber and Mike Stoller)—Company; "California Dreaming" (by J. Phillips and M. Gilliam)—Company; "Monday, Monday" (by J. Phillips)—Alexander, Company; "Surfin' USA" (by Brian Wilson and Chuck Berry)—Alexander, Company; "I Got You Babe" (by Sonny Bono)— Alexander, Keeling; "Itsy Bitsy Teeny Weenie Yellow Polkadot Bikini" (by Paul J. Vance and Lee Pockriss)—Edmead; "These Boots Are Made for Walking" (by Lee Hazelwood)—Company; "Do Wah Diddy Diddy" (by J. Barry and E. Greenwich)—Alexander; "Son of a Preacher Man"—Keeling; "To Sir With Love" (by Don Black and Mark London)—Edmead; "Downtown" (by Tony Hatch)— Keeling; "She Loves You" (by John Lennon and Paul McCartney)—Company; "I Wanna Hold Your Hand" (by John Lennon and Paul McCartney)—Alexander; "With a Little Help From My Friends" (by John Lennon and Paul McCartney)—Company; "Sgt. Pepper's Lonely Hearts Club Band" (by John Lennon and Paul Mc-Cartney)—Company; "Imagine" (by John Lennon)—Company; "We Can Work It Out" (Finale) (by John Lennon and Paul McCartney—Company.

The Joseph Papp Public Theater/New York Shakespeare Festival. Schedule of five programs. **Golden Child** (24). By David Henry Hwang; produced in association with South Coast Repertory, David Emmes producing artistic director, Martin Benson artistic director. Opened November 19, 1996; see note. (Closed December 8, 1996) **Insurrection: Holding History** (15). By Robert O'Hara. Opened December 11, 1996. (Closed December 22, 1996) **A Huey P. Newton Story** (26). Solo performance by Roger Guenveur Smith; written by Roger Guenveur Smith. Opened February 5, 1997; see note. (Closed March 9, 1997) **One Flea Spare** (39). By Naomi Wallace. Opened February 25, 1997; see note. (Closed March 29, 1997) **The Gypsy and the Yellow Canary** (34). Solo performance by Irene Worth; adapted by Irene Worth from a story by Prosper Mérimée. Opened April 16, 1997; see note. (Closed May 18, 1997) Produced by The Joseph Papp Public Theater/New York Shakespeare Festival, George C. Wolfe producer, Rosemarie Tichler artistic producer, at The Joseph Papp Public Theater (see note).

ALL PLAYS: Margaret M. Lioi senior director of external affairs; Kevin Kline and Brian Kulick artistic associates; Wiley Hausam and Bonnie Metzgar associate producers; casting, Jordan Thaler, Heidi Griffiths; press, Carol R. Fineman, Thomas V. Naro, Bill Coyle.

GOLDEN CHILD

Andrew Kwong; Eng Tieng-Bin	Stan Egi	Eng Luan	Jodi Long
Eng Ahn	Julyana Soelistyo	Eng Eling	Liana Pai
Eng Siu-Yong	Tsai Chin	Rev. Baines	John Christopher Jones

Directed by James Lapine; scenery, Tony Straiges; costumes, Martin Pakledinaz; lighting, Richard Nelson, David J. Lander; sound, Dan Moses Schreier; projection design, Wendall K. Harrington; production stage manager, Buzz Cohen.

Time: Act I, the present and winter of 1918. Act II, the spring of 1919 and the present. Place: A taxicab traveling between Manhattan and Kennedy Airport, as well as Eng Tieng-Bin's home village near Amoy in the province of Fukien in Southeast China.

Modern Chinese man is induced to reflect on his family background, specifically in the village home of his great grandfather with his three wives.

INSURRECTION: HOLDING HISTORY

Nat Turner; Ova' Seea' Jones	Bruce Beatty	Reporter; Cop; Clerk Husband; Buck Naked;	
Hammet	Jeremiah W. Birkett	Detective	T.J. Kenneally
Gertha; Clerk Wife; Mistress Motel	Ellen Cleghorne	Mutha Wit; Mutha	Vickilyn Reynolds
Ron	Robert Barry Fleming	Octavia; Katie Lynn	Heather Simms
TJ	Nathan Hinton	Izzie Mae; Clerk Son	Sybyl Walker

Above, Bruce Beatty, Robert Barry Fleming and Ellen Cleghorne in a scene from *Insurrection: Holding History,* written and directed by Robert O'Hara; *left,* Julyana Soelistyo and Tsai Chin in David Henry Hwang's *Golden Child,* directed by James Lapine

Family, Friends, Field Slaves: Company.

Directed by Robert O'Hara; scenery, James Schuette; costumes, Toni-Leslie James; lighting, David Weiner; sound, Red Ramona; composer, Zane Mark; choreographer, Ken Robinson; production stage manager, Lisa Gavaletz.

Time: Now and then. Place: Here and there. The play was presented without intermission.

1990s characters mingle with those of 1831, taking part in and reviewing the events of Nat Turner's slave rebellion.

A HUEY P. NEWTON STORY

Live sound design, Marc Anthony Thompson; scenery and lighting, David Welle; production coordinator, Erica Schwartz.

Smith in a stream-of consciousness characterization of the black activist in his rise and fall, killed in Oakland in 1989. Previously produced at the Magic and Oakland Ensemble Theaters.

ONE FLEA SPARE

Morse	Mischa Barton	Mrs. Darcy Snelgrave	Dianne Wiest
Bunce	Bill Camp	Kabe	Paul Kandel
Mr. William Snelgrave	Jon DeVries		

Directed by Ron Daniels; scenery, Riccardo Hernandez; costumes, Paul Tazewell; lighting, Scott Zielinski; sound, Stuart J. Allyn; original music, Michael Rasbury; production stage manager, C.A. Clark.

Time: 1665. Place: A comfortable house in Axe Yard, off King Street, Westminster, London. The play was presented in two parts.

Sailor and waif thrust into an abrasive relationship with an elderly upper-class couple, as they are confined together in quarantine because of the plague. An American play previously produced in London and in regional theater at the Actors Theater of Louisville.

THE GYPSY AND THE YELLOW CANARY

Scenery, Myung Hee Cho; lighting, Chad McArver; production dramaturge, Mervin P. Antonio; production coordinator, Lloyd Davis.

The drama of Carmen the gypsy and her lover Don Jose, with Miss Worth portraying both characters in a reading-style rendition.

Note: Press date for *Golden Child* was 10/29/96, for *A Huey P. Newton Story* was 2/12/97, for *One Flea Spare* was 3/9/97, for *The Gypsy and the Yellow Canary* was 5/4/97.

Note: In The Joseph Papp Public Theater there are many auditoria. *Golden Child* played the Estelle R. Newman Theater, *Insurrection: Holding History* and *A Huey P. Newton Story* played LuEsther Hall, *One Flea Spare* and *The Gypsy and the Yellow Canary* played Martinson Hall.

Beat (155). Solo performance by John DiResta; written by John DiResta; developed by Donna Daley. Produced by Abrams Gentile Entertainment, Inc. at the Martin Kaufman Theater. Opened November 20, 1996. (Closed May 25, 1997)

Directed by Donna Daley; *Beat* theme and incidental music, Albert Evans and Ron Kaehler; scenery, Thomas Baker; costumes, Anne-Marie Wright; lighting and sound, Matt Berman; associate producer, Steven Harris; production stage manager, Bonnie Boulanger; press, The Pete Sanders Group.

Subtitled A Subway Cop's Comedy, anecdotes and dramatizations of law enforcement underground. The play was presented without intermission.

Note: The schedule of *Beat* was adjusted over the December holiday season to accommodate the presentation of *On Deaf Ears* by Robin Rothstein; produced by Do Gooder Productions, Mark Robert Gordon artistic director; directed by John Ruocco, scenery by Bill Wood, costumes by Jeffrey Wallach, lighting by Chris Dallos, sound by Vincent Apollo; with Chevi Colton, Rosemary Prinz, Richard Sheinmel, Mark Robert Gordon, Susan Finch, Gil Rogers, Dana Smith; for 28 performances 12/18/96-1/12/97 for the benefit of the Museum of Jewish Heritage.

The Springhill Singing Disaster (31). Return engagement of the solo performance by Karen Trott; written by Karen Trott. Produced by Randall L. Wreghitt, Georgia Buchanan, Norma Langworthy and Richard & Peter Fitzgerald at the 47th Street Theater. Opened November 20, 1996. (Closed December 15, 1996)

Directed by Lonny Price; scenery, Derek McLane; costumes, Gail Brassard; lighting, Phil Monat; sound, Red Ramona; associate producers, James L. Simon, Keith Golke; production stage manager, Craig Palanker; press, James L.L. Morrison.

Vignettes and pitfalls of a life in the theater, first produced off Broadway by Playwrights Horizons 6/22/95 for 14 performances.

Sharps, Flats & Accidentals (40). Comedy and juggling revue written by The Flying Karamazov Brothers. Produced by The New 42nd Street Inc., Cora Cahan president, in The Flying Karamazov Brothers production at the New Victory Theater. Opened November 29, 1996. (Closed January 1, 1997)

The Flying Karamazov Brothers:

Dmitri	Paul Magid	Rakitin	Michael Preston
Ivan	Howard Jay Patterson	Smerdykov	Sam Williams

Others: Andrew Cormier, Peter Dansky, Tim Furst, Bliss Kolb, Barbara Karger, Doug Nelson, Randy Nelson, Robert Woodruff.

Directed by The Flying Karamazov Brothers; lighting, Stan Pressner; original music, Douglas Wieselman; ballet choreography, Doug Elkins; dance costumes, Susan Hilferty; stage manager, Shannon Rhodes; press, Lauren Daniluk.

Comic-acrobatic antics of the the troupe which calls itself The Flying Karamazov Brothers, whose last major appearance on the New York stage was in *The Flying Karamazov Brothers Do the Impossible* on Broadway 11/20/94 for 50 performances.

MUSICAL NUMBERS, ACT I: Concerto in B Flat for Bassoon, first movement, by Mozart, arranged by Douglas Wieselman; Hall of the Mountain King by Grieg; Percussion Quartet for Juggling Ensemble by Howard Jay Patterson; "Begin the Beguine" by Cole Porter; Taiko by Howard Jay Patterson; Fan Dance by Douglas Wieselman with Howard Jay Patterson; Minaret by The Flying Karamazov Brothers; Minuets From the Suites for Unaccompanied Cello by Bach; The Gamble by The Flying Karamazov Brothers.

ACT II: Suite in Three Movements for Diverse Juggling Instruments by Howard Jay Patterson, Anonymous and W.C. Handy; Sextette from *Lucia di Lammermoor* by Donizetti; Pas de Six from *Guillaume Tell* by Rossini; Two Part Invention in D Minor by Bach; Minimalament by Howard Jay Patterson; Jazz by The Flying Karamazov Brothers; Symphony Number 9, fourth movement excerpt, by Beethoven; B.P. II (Working Title) by Douglas Wieselman; Whole World by Howard Jay Patterson.

Warp (24). Conceived by Stuart Gordon; written by Lenny Kleinfeld; story by Stuart Gordon and Lenny Kleinfeld. Produced by Crystal Theater Productions at St. Clements Theater. Opened December 3, 1996. (Closed December 22, 1996)

Cast: Janitor, Faceless One, Prince Chaos—Todd Alan Johnson; David Carson, Lord Cumulus—Kane Schirmer; Mrs. O'Grady, Ego, Snurtle—Tanya Oesterling; Penny Smart, Sargon—Denise Thomas; Bank President, Dr. Victor Vivian Symax, Infinity, Faceless One—Scott Thomson; Mary Louise, Valerie, Snurtle—Darlene Mann; Bank Employee, Yggthion, Xander—Kofi; Psychiatric Director, Lugulbanda—Ed Criscimanni; Faceless One, Snurtle, He Who Dreams—Chris MacEwen.

Understudies: Male Roles—Chris MacEwen; Female Roles—Tanya Oesterling.

Directed by Philip Baloun; scenery, Cecile Bouchier; costumes, Jose M. Rivera; lighting, Peter L. Smith; sound, Bernard Fox; fight choreographer, Chris Harrison; original music and sound effects, Richard Dysinger; executive producer, Frederic B. Vogel; casting, Helyn Taylor; production stage manager, Rachel Stern; press, Jeffrey Richards Associates.

Multimedia production subtitled The Sci-Fi Epic Adventure Play, as a bank teller is catapulted into the Fifth Dimension.

Fyvush Finkel (16). Musical performance produced by Eric Krebs at the John Houseman Theater. Opened December 22, 1996. (Closed January 5, 1997)

With Fyvush Finkel, Ian Finkel.

The Finkel Orchestra: Byron Stripling trumpet, David Gross piano; Ralph Olson reeds; Louis Bruno bass; Bruce Uchitel guitar; Abbott Finkel drums.

Musical direction, orchestrations, arrangements, Ian Finkel; lighting, Robert Bessoir; production manager, Christine Catti; press, David Rothenberg Associates, David J. Gersten.

Subtitled From Second Avenue to Broadway, a Musical Comedy Gift, a Fyvush Finkel showcase of songs by various authors. The show was presented in two parts.

MUSICAL NUMBERS: Bie Mir Overture, "Bumble Bee Freilach," Yiddish Theater Kletzmer Medley, "Finkel & Son," Songs in My Mother Tongue and in English, "As Long as I'm With You" (by Elliot Finkel and Philip Nameworth), "Mambo Jambo," Gershwin Tribute, "In the Barrel House," "Not on the Top," "If I Were a Rich Man" (by Jerry Bock and Sheldon Harnick), "I'm Glad I'm Not Young Anymore" (by Frederick Loewe and Alan Jay Lerner), "L'Chaim to Life" (by Jerry Bock and Sheldon Harnick).

*Roundabout Theater Company. Schedule of two revivals. **Scapin** (85). By Molière; adapted by Bill Irwin and Mark O'Donnell. Opened January 9, 1997. (Closed March 23, 1997) ***All My Sons** (32). By Arthur Miller. Opened May 4, 1997. Produced by Roundabout Theater Company, Todd Haimes artistic director, Ellen Richard general manager, Gene Feist founding director, at the Criterion Center Laura Pels Theater.

SCAPIN

Octave	Maduka Steady	Argante	Count Stovall
Sylvestre	Christopher Evan Welch	Geronte	Gerry Vichi
Scapin	Bill Irwin	Leander	Jonathan Wade
Gendarmes; Porters	Hillel Meltzer,	Zerbinette	Marina Chapa
	Sean Rector	Nerine	Mary Bond Davis
Hyacinth	Kristin Chenoweth		

At the Keyboard: Bruce Hurlbut.

Understudies: Messrs Irwin, Wade—Michael Gannon; Messrs. Stovall, Vichi, Steady, Welch—Jason Antoon; Messrs. Meltzer, Rector—Amo Gulinello.

Directed by Bill Irwin; scenery, Douglas Stein; costumes, Victoria Petrovich; lighting, Nancy Schertler; sound, Tom Morse; composer and arranger, Bruce Hurlbut; dance historians, Richard Powers, Michelle Robinson; casting, Pat McCorkle; collaborator and production stage manager, Nancy Harrington; press, Boneau/Bryan-Brown, Erin Dunn.

Place: The street before the houses of Argante and Geronte. The play was presented in two parts.

The last major revivals of this Molière comedy took place in the season of 1973–74, as follows: as *Scapin* by City Center Acting Company on Broadway 12/28/73 for 1 performance and as *Scapino* with Jim Dale as Scapin in The Young Vic production off Broadway for 10 performances 3/12/74 and on Broadway 5/18/74 for 121 performances at Circle in the Square.

ALL MY SONS

Joe Keller	John Cullum	Dr. Jim Bayliss	Stephen Stout
Kate Keller	Linda Stephens	Sue Bayliss	Anne Lange
Chris Keller	Michael Hayden	Frank Lubey	Jed Diamond
Ann Deever	Angie Phillips	Lydia Lubey	Keira Naughton
George Deever	Steven Barker Turner	Bert	Sean Fredricks

Standbys: Mr. Cullum—Robert Stattel; Miss Stephens—Phyllis Somerville. Understudies: Mr. Diamond—Brian Keane; Messrs. Hayden, Turner—Ryan Shively; Miss Phillips—Keira Naughton; Mr. Stout—Jed Diamond; Misses Lange, Naughton—Kate Hampton; Mr. Fredricks—Jeffrey Stroming.

Directed by Barry Edelstein; scenery, Narelle Sissons; costumes, Angela Wendt; lighting, Donald Holder; sound, Kurt B. Kellenberger; casting, Jim Carnahan, Jay Binder; production stage manager, Leila Knox; press, Boneau/Bryan-Brown, Erin Dunn.

Act I: The backyard of the Keller home in the outskirts of an American town, August of 1946. Act II: The same evening, as twilight falls. Act III: Two o'clock the following morning. The play was presented in two parts.

The last major New York revival of *All My Sons* took place on Broadway 4/22/87 for 29 performances.

Theater for a New Audience. Schedule of two revivals. **The Two Gentlemen of Verona** (21). By William Shakespeare; produced in association with The International Shakespeare Globe Center, Mark Rylance artistic director, Greg Ripley-Duncan executive producer, Maralyn Sarrington general manager. Opened January 9, 1997. (Closed January 26, 1997) **The Changeling** (15). By Thomas Middleton and William Rowley. Opened March 1, 1997. (Closed March 15, 1997) Produced by Theater for a New Audience, Jeffrey Horowitz artistic/producing director, Michael Solomon general manager, *The Two Gentlemen of Verona* at the New Victory Theater, *The Changeling* at The Playhouse at St. Clement's Church.

THE TWO GENTLEMEN OF VERONA

Duke	Matthew Scurfield	Speed	Ben Walden
Valentine	Lennie James	Launce	Jim Bywater
Proteus	Mark Rylance	Julia	Stephanie Roth
Antonio	George Innes	Sylvia	Anastasia Hille
Thurio	Steven Alvey	Lucetta	Aicha Kossoko
Eglamour	Graham Brown	Stage Attendant	Amanda Orton
Host	Andrew Fielding		

Musicians: Lindsey Horner, Bill Ruyle, Claire van Kampen, Bruce Williamson.

Directed by Jack Shepherd; stage design, Jenny Tiramani, based on the design of Shakespeare's Globe by Jon Greenfield and Theo Crosby, Pentagram, London; costumes, Susan Coates; original music, Claire van Kampen; production stage manager, Mary Ellen Allison; stage manager, Chris Morrison; press, Springer/Chicoine Associates, Gary Springer, Susan Chicoine.

Jig (Elizabethan theater tradition whereupon at the end of the play the company presents a satirical sketch lampooning the issues of the day) written by Cindy Oswin; movement, Roddy Maude-Roxby.

Place: Verona, Milan and a forest. The play was presented in two parts.

The last major New York revival of *The Two Gentlemen of Verona* was in the New York Shakespeare Festival Shakespeare Marathon 8/9/94 for 22 performances.

THE CHANGELING

Antonio	Firdous Bamji	Diaphanta	Lee Lewis
Isabella	Melissa Bowen	De Flores	Christopher McCann
Pedro	Joel Carino	Alsemero	Chris McKinney
Lollio	Reg E. Cathey	Tomazo	Ntare Mwine
Vermandero	Thom Christopher	Alibius	Frederick Neumann
Jasperino	Glenn Fleshler	Alonzo	Trellis Stepter
Beatrice	Marin Hinkle		

Inmates of the Asylum: Amy Lee, David Matiano, Beverley Prentice, Nadia Tarr, Jennifer Tarrazi-Scully.

Directed by Robert Woodruff; scenery, Neil Patel, based on an original design by Miriam Gouretsky; costumes, Kasia Walicka Maimone; lighting, Donald Holder, based on an original design by Felice Ross; soundscape, Darron L. West, based on an original design by Eldad Lindor and Robert Woodruff; choreography, Sa'ar Magal; production stage manager, Elizabeth Burgess; stage manager, Jana Llynn.

Place: Alicant, Spain. The play was presented in two parts.

The last major New York revival of *The Changeling* was by Repertory Theater of Lincoln Center 10/29/64 for 32 performances. This production was created for the Beer Sheva Theater, Israel.

The Steward of Christendom (32). By Sebastian Barry. Produced by Brooklyn Academy of Music, Bruce C. Ratner chairman of the board, Harvey Lichtenstein president and executive producer, in the Out of Joint production, Max Stafford-Clark director, Sonia Friedman producer, at the Majestic Theater. Opened January 18, 1997. (Closed February 23, 1997)

Thomas Dunne	Donal McCann	Willie	Carl Brennan
Maud	Ali White	Matt; Recruit	Rory Murray
Annie	Tina Kellegher	Mrs. O'Dea	Maggie McCarthy
Dolly	Aislin McGuckin	Smith	Kieran Ahern

Directed by Max Stafford-Clark; scenery, Julian McGowan; costume supervisor, Jenny Cook; lighting, Johanna Town; music, Shaun Davey; sound, Paul Arditti; stage managers, Rob Young, Robert Bennett; press, Heidi Feldman, Cameron Duncan.

Time: About 1932. Place: The county home in Baltinglass, County Wicklow, Ireland.

75-year-old man recalls the events of a life troubled sometimes to the point of despair, in the troubled land of Ireland, the fifth in a cycle of plays drawn from the experiences of the author's family. A foreign play previously co-produced in London by the Royal Court Theater.

My Astonishing Self (54). Solo performance by Donal Donnelly; adapted by Michael Voysey from the writings of George Bernard Shaw. Produced by Irish Repertory Theater, Charlotte Moore artistic dirctor, Ciaran O'Reilly producing director, at the Irish Repertory Theater. Opened January 23, 1997. (Closed March 19, 1997)

Directed by Michael Voysey; lighting, Gregory Cohen; production stage manager, John Brophy; press, James L.L. Morrison.

Donnelly as Shaw in excerpts illustrating Shaw's rise to fame from humble beginnings. The play was presented without intermission.

Peter and Wendy (20). Adapted by Liza Lorwin from the novel by J.M. Barrie. Produced by The New 42nd Street Inc. in the Mabou Mines production, Liza Lorwin producer, at the New Victory Theater. Opened February 1, 1997. (Closed March 2, 1997)

Cast: Narrator—Karen Kandel; Puppeteers—Basil Twist, Jane Catherine Shaw, Sam Hack, Sarah Provost, Jessica Smith, Jenny Subjack, Lute Ramblin'.

Directed by Lee Breuer; puppetry direction, Jane Catherine Shaw, Basil Twist; music composed, arranged and directed by Johnny Cunningham; scenery, lighting and puppet design, Julie Archer; additional puppet design, Walter Stark, Stephen Kaplin, Basil Twist, Jane Catherine Shaw; costumes, Sally Thomas; sound, Edward Cosla; fights, B.H. Barry; stage manager, Jody Kuh; press, Lauren Daniluk.

Puppet version of the Peter Pan tale based on Barrie's 1911 novel adapted from his play, with a narrator speaking all the characters' lines. The play was presented in two parts.

Boychik (45). Solo performance by Richard Kline; written by Richard W. Krevolin. Produced by Michael Mann and Barrie & Lynn Wexler at Theater Four. Opened February 6, 1997. (Closed March 27, 1997)

Directed by Max Meyer; scenery, Thomas Lynch; costumes, Tommy Hilfiger; lighting, Jeff Croiter; sound, Guy Sherman, Aural Fixation; production stage manager, Laurie Ann Goldfelder; press, Peter Cromarty, Kate Cambridge.

A man's memories of his father with whom he was constantly in conflict. The play was presented without intermission.

*Capitol Steps (150). Musical revue conceived by Bill Strauss and Elaina Newport; written by Bill Strauss and Elaina Newport with contributions from the cast. Produced by Eric Krebs and Anne Strickland Squadron in association with Capitol Steps at the John Houseman Theater. Opened February 13, 1997.

Mike Carruthers	Bill Strauss
Janet Davidson Gordon	Mike Tilford
Ann Johnson	Brad Van Grack
Mike Loomis	Amy Felices Young
Tyjuana Morris	Jamie Zemarel
Elaina Newport	

Pianists: Bo Ayars, Howard Breitbart, Lenny Williams.

Directed by Bill Strauss and Elaina Newport; scenery, R.J. Matson; prop and costume design, Robyn Scott; lighting, Bob Bessoir; sound, Maryanne Mundy; press, David Rothenberg Associates, David J. Gersten.

Political satire with Congress as a principal target, with a cast of former Congressional staff members, and with five actors and one pianist at each performance. The show was presented in two parts. Previously produced in Washington.

Encores! Great American Musicals in Concert. Schedule of three musical revivals presented in limited concert engagements. **Sweet Adeline** (5). Musical with book and lyrics by Oscar Hammerstein II; music by Jerome Kern. Opened February 13, 1997. (Closed February 16, 1997) **Promises, Promises** (5). Musical based on the screen play *The Apartment* by Billy Wilder and I.A.L. Diamond; book by Neil Simon; music by Burt Bacharach; lyrics by Hal David. Opened March 20, 1997. (Closed March 23, 1997) **The Boys From Syracuse** (5). Musical based on *The Comedy of Errors* by William Shakespeare; book by George Abbott; music by Richard Rodgers; lyrics by Lorenz Hart. Opened May 1, 1997. (Closed May 4, 1997) Produced by City Center 55th Street Theater Foundation, Judith E. Daykin president and executive director, at City Center.

ALL PLAYS: Artistic director, Kathleen Marshall; musical director, Rob Fisher with The Coffee Club Orchestra; musical coordinator, Seymour Red Press; scenery, John Lee Beatty; sound, Bruce Cameron; casting, Jay Binder; press, Philip Rinaldi.

SWEET ADELINE

Dot	Kristi Lynes	James Day	Stephen Bogardus
Emil Schmidt	MacIntyre Dixon	Sid Barnett	Steven Goldstein
Addie	Patti Cohenour	The Sultan	Timothy Robert Blevins
Nellie	Jacquelyn Piro	Eddie	Timothy Breese
Lulu Ward	Dorothy Loudon	Hester Van Doren Day	Myra Carter
Dan Ward	Gary Beach	Willie Day	Tony Randall
Tom Martin	Hugh Panaro	Dancers	Shannon Lewis, Alexandre Proia
Ruppert Day	Patrick Breen		

1977 Encores! at the City Center

Participants in this season's Great American Musicals in Concert included *(above left)* Stephen Bogardus and Patti Cohenour in *Sweet Adeline, (above right)* Martin Short and Christine Baranski in *Promises, Promises* and *(below right)* Davis Gaines, Sarah Uriarte Berry, Rebecca Luker and Malcolm Gets in *The Boys From Syracuse*

Ensemble: Anne Allgood, Vanessa Ayers, Jamie Baer, Christopher Eaton Bailey, Timothy Robert Blevins, Timothy Breese, Kira Burke, Philip Chaffin, Lisa Ericksen, Peter Flynn, John Halmi, Marc Heller, Damon Kirschenmann, Robert Osborne, Alet Oury, Frank Ream, Margaret Shafer, Eric van Hoven.

The Coffee Club Orchestra for *Sweet Adeline*: Elizabeth Mann, Timothy Melosh flute, piccolo; Rob Ingliss oboe, English horn; William M. Blount, Albert Regni clarinet; Charles McCracken Jr. bassoon; Russell Rizner, Roger Wendt, French horn; Lowell Hershey, Lorraine Cohen-Moses trumpet; Jim Pugh trombone; Sue Evans drums, percussion; Lise Nadeau harp; Suzanne Ornstein, Mineko Yajima, Alicia Edelberg, Belinda Whitney-Barratt, Mary Rowell, Maura Giannini, Katherine Livolsi-Stern, Ashley Horne, Martin Agee, Lisa Matricardi violin; Jill Jaffe, Richard Brice viola; Clay Ruede, Lanny Paykin cello; John Beal acoustic bass; Tim Stella piano, celeste.

Directed by Eric D. Schaeffer; choreography, John DeLuca; apparel coordinator, Gregg Barnes; lighting, Howell Binkley; concert adaptation, Norman Allen; original orchestration, Robert Russell Bennett; production stage manager, Clayton Phillips; stage manager, Jane Neufeld; press, Philip Rinaldi.

Sweet Adeline was originally produced on Broadway 9/3/29 for 234 performances. Its only previous New York revival of record was in concert at Town Hall 5/20/85.

ACT I

Overture: "Fin de Siecle" .... Orchestra, Shannon Lewis, Alexandre Proia
    (based on melodies of the period)

Schmidt's Beer Garden, Hoboken, 1898
  "Play Us a Polka Dot" .... Kristi Lynes, Ensemble
  " 'Twas Not So Long Ago" .... Patti Cohenour, Ensemble
  "My Husband's First Wife" .... Dorothy Loudon
    (words by Irene Franklin)
  "Here Am I" .... Cohenour, Lynes
  "First Mate Martin" .... Hugh Panaro, Patrick Breen, Ensemble
  "Spring Is Here" .... Lynes, Breen
  "Here Am I" (Reprise) .... Panaro
Near San Juan Hill, Cuba, two months later
  "Out of the Blue" .... Stephen Bogardus, Panaro, Jacquelyn Piro, Ensemble
Olympic Burlesque Theater, the Bowery, one month later
  "Naughty Boy" .... Loudon, Female Ensemble
  "Oriental Moon" .... Timothy Robert Blevins, Frank Ream, Ensemble
  "Mollie O'Donahue" .... Gary Beach, Female Ensemble
  "Why Was I Born?" .... Cohenour
  Finale .... Ensemble

ACT II

Delmonico's, 18 months later
  " 'Twas Not So Long Ago" (Reprise) .... MacIntyre Dixon
  "I've Got a New Idea" .... Panaro, Piro
  "The Sun About to Rise" .... Steven Goldstein, Cohenour, Bogardus, Ensemble
Hoffman House Bar, a week later
  "Pretty Jennie Lee" .... Philip Chaffin
  "Some Girl Is on Your Mind" .... Bogardus, Goldstein, Panaro, Cohenour, Male Ensemble
  "Don't Ever Leave Me" .... Cohenour, Bogardus
Madison Square Garden Roof Theater, the next night
  "Here Am I" (Reprise) .... Lynes
  "Indestructible Kate" .... Loudon
    (words and music by Irene Franklin and Jerry Jarnagin)
  Finaletto .... Cohenour, Ensemble
A Broadway theater, the next month
  Finale .... Cohenour, Bogardus, Ensemble

PROMISES, PROMISES

Chuck Baxter	Martin Short	Dentist's Nurse	Kimberly Lyon
J.D. Sheldrake	Terrence Mann	Company Nurse	Jill Matson
Fran Kubelik	Kerry O'Malley	Company Doctor	Lloyd Culbreath
Bartender Eddie	Sean Martin Hingston	Peggy Olson	Jenifer Lewis
Mr. Dobitch	Eugene Levy	Lum Ding Hostess	Tara Nicole
Sylvia Gilhooley	Mary Ann Lamb	Waiter	Harrison Beal
Mr. Kirkeby	Samuel E. Wright	Madison Square Garden	
Ginger Wong	Cynthia Onrubia	Attendant	Vince Pesce
Mr. Eichelberger	Joe Grifasi	Bartender Eugene	Sergio Trujillo
Vivien Della Hoya	Carol Lee Meadows	Marge MacDougall	Christine Baranski
Dr. Dreyfuss	Dick Latessa	Karl Kubelik	Mike O'Malley
Mr. Vanderhof	Ralph Byers		

Employees and Bar Patrons: Harrison Beal, Lloyd Culbreath, Sean Martin Hingston, Mary Ann Lamb, Kimberly Lyon, Jill Matson, Carol Lee Meadows, Tara Nicole, Cynthia Onrubia, Vince Pesce, Raymond Rodriguez, Sergio Trujillo.
  Orchestra Voices: La Tanya Hall, Amy Jane London, Monica Pege, Kimberlee Wertz.
  The Coffee Club Orchestra for *Promises, Promises*: Seymour Red Press, Albert Regni, Edward Zuhlke, Roger M. Rosenberg woodwinds; Russell Rizner, French horn; John Frosk, Glenn Drewes, Kamau Adilifu trumpet; Jack Gale, Randall T. Andros trombone; Paul Pizzuti drums; Erik Charlston percussion; Lee Musiker piano; Jay Berliner, Andrew Schwartz guitar; John Beal bass; Suzanne Ornstein, Maura Giannini, Katherine Livolsi-Stern, Lisa Matricardi, Anthony Posk, Belinda Whitney-

Barratt, Mia Wu, Mineko Yajima violin; Clay C. Ruede, Jeanne Le Blanc, Lanny Paykin cello; Grace Paradise harp.

Directed by Rob Marshall; choreography, Rob Marshall; associate choreographer, Cynthia Onrubia; lighting, Peggy Eisenhauer; concert adaptation, Neil Simon; apparel coordinator, William Ivey Long; original orchestration, Jonathan Tunick; musical coordinator, Seymour Red Press; production stage manager, Peter Hanson; stage manager, Karen Moore.

Promises, Promises was first produced on Broadway by David Merrick 12/1/68 for 1,281 performances. This is its first New York revival of record.

ACT I

Overture .... Orchestra, Company
The Offices of Consolidated Life
"Half as Big as Life" .... Martin Short
First Avenue bar
"Grapes of Roth" .... Ensemble
Outside Chuck's apartment
"Upstairs" .... Short
Medical office
"You'll Think of Someone" .... Kerry O'Malley, Short
Mr. Sheldrake's Office
"Our Little Secret' .... Short, Terrence Mann
Lobby
"She Likes Basketball" .... Short
Lum Ding's Chinese Restaurant and Madison Square Garden
"Knowing When to Leave" .... O'Malley
Executive dining room and sun deck of Consolidated Life
"Where Can You Take a Girl?" .... Eugene Levy, Samuel E. Wright,
                                                           Joe Grifasi, Ralph Byers
"Wanting Things" .... Mann
At the Elevator
"You've Got It All Wrong" .... Jenifer Lewis, O'Malley
Nineteenth-Floor Christmas party
"Turkey Lurkey Time" .... Mary Ann Lamb, Carol Lee Meadows,
                                                       Cynthia Onrubia, Ensemble

ACT II

Entr'acte .... Orchestra
Clancy's Lounge
"A Fact Can Be a Beautiful Thing" .... Short, Christine Baranski, Ensemble
Chuck's apartment
"Whoever You Are" .... O'Malley
"Christmas Day" .... Orchestra Voices
"A Young Pretty Girl Like You" .... Short, Dick Latessa
"I'll Never Fall in Love Again" .... O'Malley, Short
Mr. Sheldrake's Office
Outside Lum Ding's Chinese Restaurant
"Promises, Promises" .... Short
Chuck's Apartment

THE BOYS FROM SYRACUSE

Police Sergeant	Patrick Quinn	Luce	Debbie Gravitte
Duke of Ephesus	Allen Fitzpatrick	Adriana	Rebecca Luker
Corporal	John Wilkerson	Luciana	Sarah Uriarte Berry
Dromio of Ephesus	Michael McGrath	Courtesan	Julie Halston
Antipholus of Ephesus	Malcolm Gets	Fatima	Rachel Jones
Tailor; Merchant of Ephesus	Danny Burstein	Angelo the Goldsmith	Mel Johnson Jr.
Antipholus of Syracuse	Davis Gaines	Seeress	Marian Seldes
Dromio of Syracuse	Mario Cantone	Aegeon	Tom Aldredge
Merchant of Syracuse; Sorcerer	Kevin Ligon		

Ladies of the Ensemble: Rebecca Eichenberger, Susan Emerson, Rachel Jones, Sheryl McCallum, Alet Oury. Dancers: Sean Grant, Sean Martin Hingston, Darren Lee, Lisa Mayer, Carol Lee Meadows, Amiee Turner.

The Coffee Club Orchestra for *The Boys From Syracuse*: Mort Silver, Harvey Estrin, Ralph Olsen clarinet, saxophone, flute, piccolo; Blair Tindall oboe, English horn; John Frosk, Bob Millikan trumpet; Jack Gale trombone; Russell Rizner, French horn; John Redsecker drums; Erik Charlston percussion; Lise Nadeau harp, celeste; Suzanne Ornstein, Belinda Whitney-Barratt, Maura Giannini, Robert Lawrence, Ashley Horne, Katherine Livolsi-Stern, Lisa Matricardi, Jon Kass violin; Masako Yanagita, Richard Brice viola; Clay Ruede, Lanny Paykin cello; John Beal, Dennis James acoustic bass; Janet Aycock piano.

Directed by Susan H. Schulman; choreography, Kathleen Marshall; concert adpatation, David Ives; apparel coordinator, Toni-Leslie James; lighting, Peter Kaczorowski; original orchestration, Hans Spialek; production stage manager, Pete Hanson.

Place: Ancient Greece.

The only previous major New York revival of *The Boys From Syracuse* took place off Broadway 4/15/63 for 500 performances.

ACT I

Overture .... Orchestra
A Square in Ephesus
   "I Had Twins" .... Patrick Quinn, Ladies, Men
   "Dear Old Syracuse" .... Davis Gaines, Mario Cantone
   "What Can You Do With a Man" .... Debbie Gravitte, Michael McGrath
Inside the House of Antipholus of Ephesus
   "Falling in Love With Love" .... Rebecca Luker, Sarah Uriarte Berry, Ladies
A Square in Ephesus
   "The Shortest Day of the Year" .... Malcolm Gets
Inside the House of Antipholus of Ephesus
   "The Shortest Day of the Year" (Reprise) .... Luker, Gets
   "This Can't Be Love" .... Gaines, Berry
Street Outside the House of Antipholus of Ephesus
   Finale, Act I: "Let Antipholus In" .... Gets, Company

ACT II

Entr'acte .... Orchestra
Outside the Courtesan's House
   "Ladies of the Evening" .... Julie Halston, Quinn, Ladies, Men
Street Outside the House of Antipholus of Ephesus
   "He and She" .... Gravitte, Cantone
   "You Have Cast Your Shadow on the Sea" .... Gaines, Berry
A Square in Ephesus
   "Come With Me" .... Quinn, Gets, Men
   "Big Brother" .... McGrath
The Twins Ballet .... Orchestra
Inside the House of Antipholus of Ephesus
   "Sing for Your Supper" .... Luker, Berry, Gravitte, Ladies
A Square in Ephesus
   "Oh, Diogenes" .... Gravitte, Ladies, Men
Street Outside the Temple
   Act II Finale: "This Can't Be Love" .... Company

Space Trek (28). Musical with book by Mark Lipitz; music and lyrics by Rick Crom. Produced by Joyce M. Sarner in association with Spectrum Stage at the Chelsea Playhouse. Opened February 16, 1997. (Closed March 9, 1997)

Ensign Bambi	Stephanie Jean	Mr. Schlock	Shawn Sears
Chief Engineer Sloshy	Billy Sharpe	Lt. Yomama	Michelle Merring
Ensign Chicks-Love	Adam Wald	Dr. Moans	Randy Lake
Capt. Slim Quirk	Jason Hayes	Capt. Christian Spike	Hank Jacobs

Musicians: John Bowen conductor, piano; Joe Guciard percussion.

Directed by Vincent Sassone; choreography, Karen Molnar; musical direction, John Bowen; scenery, William F. Moser; costumes, Carol Brys; lighting, Jason Livingston; sound, Kelly Dempsey; assistant director, Mic McCormack; stage manager, Tracy Jackson; press, Cromarty & Company.

Place: The space ship Merchandise.

Musical parody of space adventure, presented without intermission.

MUSICAL NUMBERS

Opening Sequence	Quirk, Crew
"Captain of the Ship"	Quirk, Crew
"Shoulda Been, Coulda Been Mine"	Spike
"The Ballad of Happy Planet"	Sloshy
"Hello Boys"	Spike, Quirk, Sloshy, Moans, Chicks-Love, Schlock
"Shoulda Been, Coulda Been Mine" (Reprise)	Spike
"The Problem With Us"	Quirk, Yomama
"Ensign's Lament"	Ensigns
"Picnic on a Planet"	Company
"Amour Time"	Company
"To Be a Captain"	Schlock
"Brain Drain"	Moans, Schlock
"To Be a Captain" (Continued)	Spike, Quirk
"Spike's Turn"	Spike, Crew
"Got to Get a Life"	Quirk, Crew
"Captain of the Ship" (Finale)	Company

In-Betweens (31). By Bryan Goluboff. Produced by Evangeline Morphos, Judith Resnick, Joan & Richard Firestone, Frederick M. Zollo and Mara Gibbs at the Cherry Lane Theater. Opened February 18, 1997. (Closed March 16, 1997)

Eddie	Tony Cucci	Ray	Mark Hutchinson
Peanut	Andrew Miller	Lolli	Carolyn Baeumler

Directed by Dante Albertie; scenery and costumes, Beowulf Boritt; lighting, Ken Moreland; sound, Hector Olivieri; associate producers, Peter Burtscher, Barbara Goldfarb, Richard Kornberg, William O'Boyle; production stage manager, David A. Winitsky; press, Richard Kornberg.

Love and violence in a group of assorted misfits. Previously produced off off Broadway at Belmont Italian American Playhouse.

*Stonewall Jackson's House (110). By Jonathan Reynolds. Produced by the American Place Theater, Wynn Handman artistic director, Susannah Halston executive director, at the American Place Theater. Opened February 19, 1997.

LaWanda	Lisa Louise Langford	Barney	Ron Faber
Junior	R.E. Rodgers	Del	Mimi Bensinger
Mag	Katherine Leask		

Directed by Jamie Richards; scenery, Henry S. Dunn; costumes, Barbara A. Bell; lighting, Chad McArver; sound, Kurt B. Kellenberger; casting, Rebecca Taichman; production stage manager, Joe Witt; stage manager, Peter Asplund; press, Susan Chicoine, Charlie Siedenberg.

Time: The present. Place: Stonewall Jackson's House, a historical restoration in Lexington, Va.

A black tour guide's future seems so bleak that she asks an Ohio couple to take her home to their farm as a slave, within a play about the theater people producing it and discussing its views of racism, U.S. society, etc.

Starla Benford replaced Lisa Louise Langford 3/26/97.

The Tokyo Shock Boys (63). Performance piece devised by The Tokyo Shock Boys. Produced by Arthur Cantor, executive producer, Murray Pope and Shuji Shibata at the Minetta Lane Theater. Opened February 19, 1997. (Closed April 14, 1997)

With Danna, Gyuzo, Nambu, Sango.

Directed by Murray Pope; music performed by Satoshi Nishikata; musical direction, Paul Jackson; arrangements, Satoshi Nishikata, Paul Jackson; props master, Chiyokichi; associate producers, Sonny Everett & William O'Boyle, Alan Schuster & Mitchell Maxwell, Tim Woods; production manager, Justin Reiter; press, James L.L. Morrison, Tom D'Ambrosio.

Program of sensational antics—such as pretending to drink a liquid detergent—performed by the four Japanese performers, "Samurai vaudevillians," named above, presented without intermission. A foreign show previously produced in Japan and in Australia, Europe and Canada.

Robbers (9). By Lyle Kessler. Produced by Scott Allyn and Richard L. Barovick at the American Place Theater. Opened February 23, 1997. (Closed March 2, 1997)

Ted	Michael Rapaport	Lucinda	Reiko Aylesworth
Pop	John Doman	Vinnie	Paul Ben-Victor
Feathers; Owner	Jonathan Hadary	Cleo	Elizabeth Rodriguez

Understudy: Messrs Rapaport, Ben-Victor—Myk Watford.

Directed by Marshall W. Mason; scenery, Loren S. Sherman; costumes, Laura Crow; lighting, Phil Monat; sound, Jim van Bergen; original music, Peter Kater; associate producer, Mary Lu Roffe; casting, Pat McCorkle, Tim Sutton; production stage manager, Tamlyn Freund; press, Cromarty & Co., Peter Cromarty, Hugh Hayes.

Time: The present. Place: Brooklyn. The play was presented in two parts.

An undercover agent investigates pilfering in a canning factory. Previously produced in regional theater at Seattle Repertory and Long Wharf Theater.

Minor Demons (33). By Bruce Graham. Produced by Playwrights Preview Productions, Blake Edwards, Tony Adams, Frances Hill, Sterling Productions with J.C. Compton and the Century Theater at the Century Theater. Opened March 16, 1997. (Closed April 13, 1997)

Deke Winters	Reed Birney	Vince DelGatto	Steve Ryan
Diane Gardner	Amelia Marshall	Mrs. Simmonds	Alexandra O'Karma
Kenny Simmonds	Charlie Hofheimer	Mr. Simmonds	Murphy Guyer
Carmella DelGatto	Susan Pellegrino	Mr. O'Brien	Robin Haynes

Directed by Richard Harden; scenery, Patrick Mann; costumes, Alan Michael Smith; lighting, Jeffrey McRoberts; musical composition and sound, Matt Balitsaris; associate producers, Endemol Theater Productions, Metropolitan Entertainment Group; production stage manager, Liz Reddick; press, Peter Cromarty, Hugh Hayes.

Discredited Mafia lawyer returns to the small town of his origin and finds himself involved in the defense of a brutal murderer.

*Tap Dogs (84). Dance revue choreographed by Dein Perry; music by Andrew Wilkie. Produced by Back Row Productions/Peter Holmes à Court and Columbia Artists Management Inc. in association with Richard Frankel and Mark Routh, by arrangement with Dein Perry and Nigel Triffitt. Opened March 16, 1997.

Billy Burke	Dein Perry
Darren Disney	Ben Read
Christopher Horsey	Nathan Sheens
Drew Kaluski	Gil Stroming
Jeremy Kiesman	

Scott Bruce guitar, keyboards, percussion; Jason Yudoff keyboards, percussion.

Directed by Nigel Triffitt; designed by Nigel Triffitt; lighting, David Murray; sound, Darryl Lewis; production stage manager, Arabella Powell; press, Boneau/Bryan-Brown, Adrian Bryan-Brown, John Wimbs.

Variations on the art of tap-dancing by the nine-member Australian cast, presented without intermission. A foreign show previously produced in Sydney, Australia and on tour in North America.

TAP DOGS—Members of the cast airborne in a scene under Nigel Triffitt's direction

Doctor Doctor (31). Musical revue with music and lyrics by Peter Ekstrom; additional lyrics and material by David DeBoy. Produced by Barter Theater, Richard Rose artistic director, at the Players Theater. Opened March 26, 1997. (Closed April 30, 1997)

Jay	Buddy Crutchfield	William	James Weatherstone
Audrey	Jill Geddes	Receptionist	Albert Ahronheim
Gloria	Nancy Johnston		

Directed by Richard Rose; musical direction and arrangements, Albert Ahronheim; scenery, Crystal Tiala; costumes, Amanda Aldridge; lighting, David G. Silver-Friedl; sound, Scott Koenig; production stage manager, Bill McComb; press, Jeffrey Richards Associates.

Revue about various aspects of modern medicine, based on a collection of songs originally commissioned and performed in 1979 by Actors Theater of Louisville and produced in 1996 in Abingdon, Va. at Barter Stage II, both times under the title *Doctors and Diseases*.

ACT I

"The Human Body" .... Company
"Oh, Boy! How I Love My Cigarettes!" .... Jay, Audrey
"The Consummate Picture" .... Gloria
"I'm a Well-Known, Respected Practitioner" .... William
"Tomorrow" .... Audrey
"A World of My Own" .... Gloria
"And Yet I Lived On" .... Company

"Willie" .... Gloria
"The Right Hand Song" .... Albert
"Please, Dr. Fletcher?" .... Audrey
"Take It Off, Tammy!" .... William
"It's My Fat!" .... Jay
"Nine Long Months Ago" .... Company

ACT II

"Hymn" .... Company
"Medicine Man Blues" .... Gloria
"Private Practice" .... William
"Nurse's Care" .... Audrey
"I'm Sure of It" .... Audrey, William
"I Loved My Father" .... Jay
"Jesus Is My Doctor" .... Gloria, Company
"Bing, Bang, Boom!" .... Audrey, Jay
"Eighty Thousand Orgasms" .... Gloria, William
"Good Ole Days (of Sex)" .... William, Audrey
"Do I Still Have You" .... William
"I Hope I Never Get" .... Jay, Company
"The Human Body" (Reprise) .... Company

Bunny Bunny (64). By Alan Zweibel. Produced by Bernie Brillstein, James D. Stern and Harriet Newman Leve by special arrangement with Lucille Lortel at the Lucille Lortel Theater. Opened April 1, 1997. (Closed May 2, 1997)

Alan .... Bruno Kirby
Gilda .... Paula Cale

Stagehand, Waiter, Stage Manager, Cameraman, Gilda's Date, Emery, Fishmonger, Moviegoer, Conductor, Richard Carlton, Andy Warhol, Gilda's Fans, Program Vendor, Office Boy, Judy, European Phone Operator, Taxi Driver, Alan's Bride, FTD Man, Bouncer, Movie Director, Butler, Federal Express Man, Another Stage Manager, Doug: Alan Tudyk.
Standbys: Miss Cale—Jennifer Naimo; Mr. Tudyk—Jamison Selby. Understudy: Mr. Kirby—Alan Tudyk.
Directed by Christopher Ashley; scenery, David Gallo; costumes, David C. Woolard; lighting, Michael Lincoln; projections, Jan Hartley; sound, Jim van Bergen; associate producer, Douglas Meyer; casting, Marion Levine; production stage manager, Kate Broderick; press, Merle Frimark Associates.
Time: July 1975–May 1989. Place: New York City and Los Angeles. The play was presented in two parts.
Subtitled Gilda Radner: A Sort of Romantic Comedy, the playwright's memories of his friendship with the gifted comedienne. Previously produced at Philadelphia Theater Company.

The Hairy Ape. (47). Revival of the play by Eugene O'Neill. Produced by The Wooster Group in association with Frederick Zollo, Ron Kastner, Hal Luftig and Nicholas Paleologos at the Selwyn Theater. Opened April 3, 1997. (Closed May 2, 1997)

Yank .... Willem Dafoe   Aunt .... Peyton Smith
Paddy .... Scott Renderer   Prisoner .... Roy Faudree
Long .... Dave Shelley   IWW Secretary .... Paul Lazar
Mildred Douglas .... Kate Valk

Directed by Elizabeth LeCompte; scenery, Jim Clayburgh; lighting, Jennifer Tipton; music, John Lurie; sound, James Johnson, John Collins; video, Christopher Kondeck, Philip Bussmann; producer for The Wooster Group, Peyton Smith; associate producer, William P. Suter; production manager, Jim Findlay; press, the Pete Sanders Group, Pete Sanders, Helene Davis.
The Hairy Ape was first produced in New York at the Provincetown Theater March 9, 1922. This, presented without intermission, is its first major revival of record, first offered off off Broadway by The Wooster Group in 1995 and 1996 at the Performing Garage.

God's Heart (57). By Craig Lucas. Produced by Lincoln Center Theater, under the direction of Andre Bishop and Bernard Gersten, at the Mitzi E. Newhouse Theater. Opened April 6, 1997. (Closed May 25, 1997)

Carlin	Ndehru Roberts	Ana	Lisa Leguillou
Janet	Amy Brenneman	Eleanor	Viola Davis
David	John Benjamin Hickey	Barbara	Julie Kavner
Angela	Kia Joy Goodwin	Cashmere; Dr. Farkas	Kevin Carroll

Ensemble: Kisha Howard, Kim Yancey Moore, Akili Prince, Peter Rini, Pamela Stewart.

Understudies: Messrs. Roberts, Carroll—Akili Prince; Misses Brenneman, Kavner—Pamela Stewart; Misses Goodwin, Leguillou—Kisha Howard; Miss Davis—Kim Yancey Moore; Mr. Hickey—Peter Rini.

Directed by Joe Mantello; scenery, Robert Brill; costumes, Toni-Leslie James; lighting, Brian MacDevitt; original music and sound, Dan Moses Schreier; video and projections, Batwin + Robin Productions; casting, Daniel Swee; stage manager, Thom Widmann; press, Philip Rinaldi, Miller Wright.

Time: The present, after dark. Place: New York City. The play was presented in two parts.

Drug-dealing, murder and computer wizardry, much of it in nightmares inspired by the Internet.

*How I Learned to Drive (31). Transfer from off off Broadway of the play by Paula Vogel. Produced by The Vineyard Theater, Douglas Aibel artistic director, Barbara Zinn Krieger founder and executive director, Jon Nakagawa managing director, in association with Daryl Roth and Roy Gabay at the Century Theater. Opened May 6, 1997.

Li'l Bit	Mary-Louise Parker	Female Greek Chorus	Johanna Day
Peck	David Morse	Teenage Greek Chorus	Kerry O'Malley
Male Greek Chorus	Michael Showalter		

Directed by Mark Brokaw; scenery, Narelle Sissons; costumes, Jess Goldstein; lighting, Mark McCullough; original sound, David Van Tieghem; production stage manager, Thea Bradshaw Gillies; press, Shirley Herz Associates, Sam Rudy.

Compassionate treatment of a middle-aged man's pedophiliac obsession with his wife's teen-aged niece. Previously presented 3/16/97 by the Vineyard Theater in this production, without intermission. Winner of the 1996–97 New York Drama Critics Circle and Lucille Lortel Awards for best play; see the Prizewinning Plays section of this volume.

*Bermuda Avenue Triangle (24). By Renée Taylor and Joe Bologna. Produced by Starhearts Productions Inc., Richard A. Rosen, Jerry Greenberg & Norman Pattiz, Nicholas Eliopoulos, Doc McGhee and Stephen Schnitzer at the Promenade Theater. Opened May 11, 1997.

Fannie	Renée Taylor	Angela	Ronnie Farer
Johnny	Joe Bologna	Rita	Priscilla Shanks
Tess	Nanette Fabray	Rabbi Levine	Manny Kleinmuntz

Directed by Danny Daniels; scenery, James Noone; costumes, Gail Cooper-Hecht; lighting, Tharon Musser; sound, Jon Gottlieb; production stage manager, Meredith J. Greenburg; press, Loving & Weintraub.

Time: The present. Place: Las Vegas.

The adventures of a Jewish mother and an Irish Catholic mother, exiled by their daughters to a retirement home.

*Men on the Verge of a His-Panic Breakdown (20). Solo performance by Felix A. Pire; written by Guillermo Reyes. Produced by Frances Hill & Associates with T.L. Reilly in the Playwrights' Preview Production at the 47th Street Theater. Opened May 13, 1997.

Directed by Joseph Megel; choreography, Annmaria Mazzini; scenery, George Xenos; costumes, Ramona Ponce; lighting, Jeff Nellis; sound, Johnna Doty; stage manager, Jen McGlashan; press, Keith Sherman & Associates, Kevin Rehac.

Portrayals of six characters in a study of Hispanic immigrants' experience in the gay community.

***As You Like It** (6). Revival of the play by William Shakespeare. Produced by The Acting Company, Margot Harley producing director, at St. Clements Theater. Opened May 18, 1997; see note.

Silvius	William Hulings	Le Beau; Jacques	Kevin Orton
Touchstone	Marc Damon Johnson	Audrey	Mary F. Randle
Rosalind	Felicity Jones	Celia	Heather Robison
Orlando	Kevin James Kelly	Phebe	Drew Richardson

Others: Carl Jay Cofield, Robert Alexander Owens, Andy Paterson Danny Swartz, Cheryl Turner.

Directed by Liviu Ciulei; scenery, Liviu Ciulei; costumes, Smaranda Branescu; lighting, Dennis Parichy; sound, Michael Creason; original music, Scott Killian; songs, Teodor Grigoriu; fight direction and choreography, Felix Ivanov; press, Boneau/Bryan-Brown, John Barlow.

The Acting Company's 1997 Touring Ensemble in a production that started its tour in January 1997. The last major New York revival of *As You Like It* was at Brooklyn Academy of Music 10/4/94 for 14 performances.

Note: Press date for *As You Like It* was 5/28/97.

CAST REPLACEMENTS AND TOURING COMPANIES

Compiled by Jeffrey A. Finn

The following is a list of the major cast replacements of record in productions which opened in previous years, but were still playing in New York during a substantial part of the 1996–97 season; or were on a first-class tour in 1996–97.

The name of each major role is listed in *italics* beneath the title of the play in the first column. In the second column directly opposite appears the name of the actor who created the role in the original New York production (whose opening date appears in *italics* at the top of the column). In shows of the past five years, indented immediately beneath the original actor's name are the names of subsequent New York replacements, together with the date of replacement when available. In shows that have run longer than five years, only this season's or the most recent cast replacements are listed under the names of the original cast members.

The third column gives information about first-class touring companies. When there is more than one roadshow company, #1, #2, etc., appear before the name of the performer who created the role in each company (and the city and date of each company's first performance appears in *italics* at the top of the column). Their subsequent replacements are also listed beneath their names in the same manner as the New York companies, with dates when available.

ANNIE

	New York 3/26/97	*Houston 11/29/96*
Annie	Brittny Kissinger	Joanna Pacitti
		Brittny Kissinger 2/25/97
Miss Hannigan	Nell Carter	Roz Ryan
		Nell Carter 1/3/97
Grace Farrell	Colleen Dunn	Colleen Dunn
Oliver Warbucks	John Schuck	John Schuck
Rooster Hannigan	Jim Ryan	Jim Ryan
Lily	Karen Byers Blackwell	Karen Byers Blackwell

BEAUTY AND THE BEAST

		#1 Los Angeles 4/12/95
	New York 4/18/94	*#2 Minneapolis 11/7/95*
Beast	Terrence Mann	#1 Terrence Mann
	Jeff McCarthy	James Barbour 8/1/95
	Chuck Wagner	#2 Frederick C. Inkley
Belle	Susan Egan	#1 Susan Egan
	Sarah Uriarte	Yvette Lawrence 3/27/96
	Christianne Tisdale	#2 Kim Huber
	Kerry Butler	

Lefou	Kenny Raskin	#1 Jaime Torcelinni
	Harrison Beal	#2 Dan Sklar
Gaston	Burke Moses	#1 Burke Moses
	Marc Kudisch	Stephen Bishop 12/26/96
		#2 Tony Lawson
Maurice	Tom Bosley	#1 Tom Bosley
	MacIntyre Dixon	#2 Grant Cowan
	Tom Bosley	
	Kurt Knudson	
	Tim Jerome	
Cogsworth	Heath Lamberts	#1 Fred Applegate
	Peter Bartlett	Gibby Brand 4/24/96
	Gibby Brand	#2 Jeff Brooks
Lumiere	Gary Beach	#1 Gary Beach
	Lee Roy Reams	#2 Patrick Page
	Patrick Quinn	
	Gary Beach	
Babette	Stacey Logan	#1 Heather Lee
	Pamela Winslow	#2 Leslie Castay
		Mindy Paige Davis 2/15/97
Mrs. Potts	Beth Fowler	#1 Beth Fowler
	Cass Morgan	Jeanne Lehman 9/26/95
	Beth Fowler	#2 Betsy Joslyn

BRING IN 'DA NOISE BRING IN 'DA FUNK

New York
Off Broadway 11/15/95
Broadway 4/25/96

Savion Glover

Baakari Wilder

Jimmy Tate

Vincent Bingham
Omar A. Edwards 2/4/97

Reg E. Gaines
Jeffrey Wright 4/25/96

Ann Duquesnay

Jared Crawford

Raymond King

Dulé Hill

CATS

	New York 10/7/82	*National tour 1/94*
Alonzo	Hector Jaime Mercado	William Patrick Dunne
	Hans Kriefall 4/24/95	Rudd Anderson 6/6/95
Bustopher	Stephan Hanan	Richard Poole
	Richard Poole 12/12/94	Brian Noonan 10/1/96
		Daniel Eli Friedman 4/14/97

Bombalurina	Donna King Marlene Danielle 1/9/84	Helen Frank Courtney Young 10/1/96
Cassandra	Rene Ceballos Meg Gillentine	Laura Quinn Izabela Lekic 5/16
Coricopat	Rene Clemente Steve Ochoa Billy Johnstone	(not in tour)
Demeter	Wendy Edmead Mamie Duncan-Gibbs Emily Hsu	N. Elaine Wiggins Jeanine Meyers 6/18/96
Grizabella	Betty Buckley Laurie Beechman	Mary Gutzi Natalie Toro 3/24/97
Jellylorum	Bonnie Simmons Nina Hennessey 6/22/92	Patty Goble Kris Koop 12/26/95
Jennyanydots	Anna McNeely Carol Dilley 8/22/94	Alice C. DeChant
Mistoffeles	Timothy Scott Jacob Brent	Christopher Gattelli Randy André Davis 3/12/96
Mungojerrie	Rene Clemente Roger Kachel 5/11/92	Gavan Palmer Gavan Palmer 5/28/96
Munkustrap	Harry Groener Michael Gruber Matt Farnsworth	Robert Amirante Michael Sangiovanni 6/18/96 James Patterson 12/17/96
Old Deuteronomy	Ken Page Ken Prymus	John Treacy Egan Doug Eskew
Plato/Macavity	Kenneth Ard Rick Gonzalez Jim T. Ruttman Jaymes Hodges Karl Wahl Philip Michael Baskerville	Steve Bertles Taylor Wicker
Pouncival	Herman W. Sebek Christopher Gattelli	Joey Gyondla Michael Barriskill 4/19/96
Rum Tum Tugger	Terrence Mann Stephen M. Reed Ron DeVito Abe Sylvia	Ron Seykell Robert Bartley 6/18/96 David Villella 12/17/97
Rumpleteazer	Christine Langner Maria Jo Ralabate 4/1/96	Jennifer Cody Amy Shure 4/28/97
Sillabub	Whitney Kershaw Alaine Kashian	Lanene Charters Carolyn J. Ockert 10/28/96
Skimbleshanks	Reed Jones Eric Scott Kincaid 6/3/94	Carmen Yurich Josh Prince 12/31/96
Tantomile	Janet L. Hubert Jill Nicklaus 12/19/94	(not in tour)
Tumblebrutus	Robert Hoshour Randy Bettis	Joseph Favolora Mark R. Moreau 10/28/96
Victoria	Cynthia Onrubia Nadine Isnegger 7/25/94	Tricia Mitchell Missy Lay Zimmer 10/15/96

Note: Only this season's or the most recent cast replacements are listed above under the names of the original cast members. For previous replacements, see previous volumes of *Best Plays*.

CATS—Ken Prymus as Old Deuteronomy and Laurie Beechman as Grizabella in the 1997 cast of the long-run musical

CHICAGO

	New York 11/14/96	*Washington, D.C. 4/16/97*
Velma Kelly	Bebe Neuwirth	Jasmine Guy
Roxie Hart	Ann Reinking Marilu Henner	Charlotte d'Amboise
Fred Casely	Michael Berresse	Rick Pessagno
Sergeant Fogarty	Michael Kubala	Eric Jordan Young
Amos Hart	Joel Grey	Ron Orbach
Liz	Denise Faye	Sharon Moore
Annie	Mamie Duncan-Gibbs	Deidre Goodwin
June	Mary Ann Lamb	Janine LaManna
Hunyak	Tina Paul	Belle Callaway
Mona	Caitlin Carter	Mary MacLeod

Matron "Mama" Morton	Marcia Lewis	Carol Woods
Billy Flynn	James Naughton	Obba Babatunde
Mary Sunshine	D. Sabella J. Loeffelholz	M.E. Spencer
Go-To-Hell-Kitty	Leigh Zimmerman	Angie L. Schworer

DEFENDING THE CAVEMAN

| *New York 3/26/95* | *Miami 1/14/97* |
| Rob Becker
Michael Chiklis 1/29/97 | Rob Becker |

THE FANTASTICKS

New York 5/3/60

El Gallo	Jerry Orbach Christopher Councill
Luisa	Rita Gardner Sara Schmidt
Matt	Kenneth Nelson Eric Meyersfield

Note: Only this season's or the most recent replacements are listed above under the names of the original cast members. For previous replacements, see previous volumes of *Best Plays*.

A FUNNY THING HAPPENED ON THE WAY TO THE FORUM

New York 4/18/96

Pseudolus	Nathan Lane Whoopi Goldberg 2/11/97
Hysterium	Mark Linn-Baker Ross Lehman
Senex	Lewis J. Stadlen Dick Latessa
Philia	Jessica Boevers
Hero	Jim Stanek
Domina	Mary Testa

GREASE

	New York 5/11/94	*Syracuse 9/19/94*
Vince Fontaine	Brian Bradley Mickey Dolenz Brian Bradley Joe Piscopo Brian Bradley Nick Santa Maria Brian Bradley Dave Konig Jeff Conaway	Davy Jones Mickey Dolenz Don Most 8/95 Nick Santa Maria 11/95 Joe Piscopo 1/96 Brian Bradley 1/96 Nick Santa Maria 4/96 Peter Scolari 11/96 Brian Bradley 1/97

Miss Lynch	Marcia Lewis	Sally Struthers
	Mimi Hines	Dody Goodman 6/95
	JoAnne Worley	Sally Struthers 9/95
	Dody Goodman	Mimi Hines 9/24/95
	Marcia Lewis	Sally Struthers 8/20/96
	Mimi Hines	
	Sally Struthers	
	Mimi Hines	
	Marilyn Cooper	
Betty Rizzo	Rosie O'Donnell	Angela Pupello
	Maureen McCormick	Wendy Springer 8/95
	Brooke Shields	Angela Pupello 10/95
	Joely Fisher	Debbie Gibson 11/95
	Tia Riebling	Mackenzie Phillips 3/96
	Susan Moniz	Sheena Easton 8/20/96
	Jody Watley	Mackenzie Phillips
	Debby Boone	Jasmine Guy 11/19/96
	Sheena Easton	Tracy Nelson 1/7/97
	Tracy Nelson	
	Mackenzie Phillips	
	Jasmine Guy	
	Angela Pupello	
Doody	Sam Harris	Scott Beck
	Ray Walker	Ric Ryder 7/95
	Ty Taylor	Roy Chicas 4/96
	Ric Ryder	
Kenickie	Jason Opsahl	Douglas Crawford
	Douglas Crawford	Steve Geyer 10/95
	Steve Geyer	Douglas Crawford 10/8/95
		Christopher Carothers 1/14/97
		Douglas Crawford 4/9/97
Frenchy	Jessica Stone	Beth Lipari
	Monica Lee Gradischek	Jennifer Naimo 1/96
	Beth Lipari	Megan Lawrence 8/6/96
	Alisa Klein	Beth Lipari 10/8/96
Danny Zuko	Ricky Paull Goldin	Rex Smith
	Adrian Zmed	Jon Secada 6/95
	Ricky Paull Goldin	Adrian Zmed 7/95
	Jon Secada	Joseph Barbara 12/3/95
	Jeff Trachta	Adrian Zmed 9/20/96
	Joseph Barbara	
	Vincent Tumeo	
	Sean McDermott	
Sandy Dumbrowski	Susan Wood	Trisha M. Gorman
	Susan Moniz	Sutton Foster 11/95
	Lacey Hornkohl	Kelli Severson 1/7/97
	Kelli Severson	Lacey Hornkohl 3/25/97
	Melissa Dye	Kelli Severson 4/29/97
Patty Simcox	Michelle Blakely	Melissa Papp
	Christine Toy	Lesley Jennings 9/95
	Carrie Ellen Austin	Leanna Polk 2/96
	Dominique Dawes	Stephanie Seely 9/5/96

Teen Angel

Billy Porter
Mary Bond Davis
Charles Gray
Jennifer Holliday
Charles Gray
Al Jarreau
Chubby Checker
Kevin-Anthony
Lee Truesdale
Darlene Love

Kevin-Anthony
Lee Truesdale 9/5/96
Kevin-Anthony 10/15/96

HAVING OUR SAY

	New York 4/6/95	*Galveston 10/17/96*
Miss Sadie Delany	Gloria Foster Frances Foster 10/95	Micki Grant
Dr. Bessie Delany	Mary Alice Novella Nelson 10/95	Lizan Mitchell

HOW TO SUCCEED IN BUSINESS WITHOUT REALLY TRYING

	New York 3/23/95	*Baltimore 5/28/96*
J. Pierrepont Finch	Matthew Broderick John Stamos 11/13/95 Matthew Broderick 3/19/96	Ralph Macchio
Rosemary Pilkington	Megan Mullaly Jessica Stone 1/30/96 Sarah Jessica Parker 3/12/96	Shauna Hicks
J.B. Biggley	Ronn Carroll	Richard Thomsen
Bud Frump	Jeff Blumenkrantz Brooks Ashmanskas 2/19/96	Roger Bart Todd Weeks 1/19/97
Hedy LaRue	Luba Mason	Pamela Blair
Twimble/Wally Womper	Gerry Vicchi	Michael Cone
Smitty	Victoria Clark	Susann Fletcher
Miss Jones	Lillias White	Tina Fabrique

THE KING AND I

	New York 4/11/96	*Minneapolis 4/1/97*
Anna Leonowens	Donna Murphy Faith Prince 3/17/97	Hayley Mills
Royal Dance Soloists	Lainie Sakakura Kristine Bendul 8/5/96	Hsin-Ping Chang Youn Kim
The King of Siam	Lou Diamond Phillips	Vee Talmadge
Lun Tha	Jose Llana	Timothy Ford Murphy
Tuptim	Joohee Choi Cornilla Luna Joohee Choi 3/24/97	Luzviminda Lor
Lady Thiang	Taewon Kim	Naomi Itami

LES MISERABLES

	New York 3/12/87	*Tampa 11/18/88*
Jean Valjean	Colm Wilkinson Robert Evan 9/10/96 Ivan Rutherford 9/24/96 Robert Marien 3/12/97	Gary Barker Craig Schulman 9/9/96 Robert Evan 9/30/96 Gregory Calvin Stone 3/3/97
Javert	Terrence Mann Christopher Innvar 10/15/96	Peter Samuel David Jordan 11/18/96 David Masenheimer 1/27/97 Todd Alan Johnson 3/31/97
Fantine	Randy Graff Florence Lacey 9/10/96 Juliet Lambert 3/12/97	Hollis Resnik Laurie Beechman 12/16/96 Lisa Capps 1/27/97 Catherine Hickland 3/10/97 Lisa Capps 3/24/97
Enjolras	Michael Maguire Paul Avedisian 10/29/96 Stephen R. Buntrock 3/12/97	Greg Zerkle Brian Herriott 9/30/96
Marius	David Bryant Ricky Martin 6/24/96 Tom Donoghue 9/10/96 Peter Lockyer 3/12/97	Matthew Porretta Rich Affannato 8/12/96
Cosette	Judy Kuhn Jennifer Lee Andrews 11/19/96 Christeena Michelle Riggs 3/12/97	Jacquelyn Piro Kate Fisher 9/9/96
Eponine	Frances Ruffelle Sarah Uriarte Berry 3/12/97	Michele Maika Lea Salonga 9/9/96 Dawn Younker 9/30/96 Andrea McArdle 12/16/96 Dawn Younker 1/27/97 Rona Figueroa 3/31/97

Note: Only this season's or the most recent replacements are listed above under the names of the original cast members. For previous replacements, see previous volumes of *Best Plays*.

MASTER CLASS

	New York 11/5/95	*Boston 11/96*
Maria Callas	Zoe Caldwell Patti LuPone 7/2/96 Dixie Carter 1/31/97	Faye Dunaway
Manny	David Loud Gary Green 7/2/96 David Loud 8/20/96 Gerald Steichen 12/31/97	Gary Green
Sharon	Audra McDonald Helen Goldsby 7/2/96 Alaine Rodin-Lo 12/10/96	Suzan Hanson
Sophie	Karen Kay Cody Theodora Fried 7/2/96	Melinda Klump

Callas in Triplicate

Appearing in the *Master Class* role created by Zoe Caldwell were Patti LuPone (*above,* with Helen Goldsby) and Dixie Carter (*left*) in New York, and Faye Dunaway (*below*) on tour

Tony	Jay Hunter Morris Matthew Walley 4/15/97	Kevin Paul Anderson
Stagehand	Michael Friel Wally Dunn 12/31/97	Scott Davidson

MISS SAIGON

		#1 *Chicago 10/12/93*
	New York 4/11/91	#2 *Seattle 3/16/95*
The Engineer	Jonathan Pryce Joseph Anthony Foronda 11/11/96 Luoyong Wang 12/11/97	#1 Raul Aranas Joseph Anthony Foronda #2 Thom Sesma Joseph Anthony Foronda
Kim	Lea Salonga Joan Almedilla Roxanne Taga (alt.) Elizabeth Paw (alt.)	#1 Jennie Kwan Jennifer C. Paz Hazel Raymundo (alt.) Melanie Mariko Tojio (alt.) Cristina Paras #2 Deedee Lynn Magno Cristina Paras (alt.) Alex Lee Tano (alt.) 10/3/95
Chris	Willy Falk Matt Bogart 12/20/97	#1 Jarrod Emick Pat McRoberts #2 Matt Bogart Will Chase 4/16/96

Note: Only this season's or the most recent cast replacements are listed above under the names of the original cast members. For previous replacements, see previous volumes of *Best Plays*.

THE PHANTOM OF THE OPERA

		#1 *Los Angeles 5/31/90*
		#2 *Chicago 5/24/90*
	New York 1/26/88	#3 *Seattle 12/13/92*
The Phantom	Michael Crawford Thomas James O'Leary 11/96	#1 Michael Crawford Frank D'Ambrosio 3/28/94 #2 Mark Jacoby Craig Schulman 1/30/97 #3 Frank D'Ambrosio Brad Little 9/28/96
Christine Daae	Sarah Brightman Tracy Shayne Laurie Gayle Stephenson (alt.) Teri Bibb (alt.)	#1 Dale Kristien Lisa Vroman 12/2/93 Cristin Mortenson (alt.) #2 Karen Culliver Sandra Joseph 3/26/96 Susan Owen (alt.) 9/24/96 #3 Tracy Shayne Adrienne McEwan 7/30/96 Kimilee Bryant 11/1/96 Susan Facer (alt.) Kimilee Bryant (alt.) 8/28/96 Tamra Hayden (alt.) 11/1/96 Kate Suber 3/26/96

Raoul	Steve Barton
	Gary Mauer 11/96
		#1 Reece Holland
		    Aloysius Gigl 5/2/95
		#2 Keith Buterbaugh
		    Nat Chandler
		#3 Ciaran Sheehan
		    Jason Pebworth 1/29/97

Note: Only this season's or the most recent cast replacements are listed above under the names of the original cast members. For previous replacements, see previous volumes of *Best Plays*.

RENT

	New York Off Broadway 2/13/96 Broadway 4/29/96	Boston 11/18/96
Roger Davis	Adam Pascal	Sean Keller Manley Pope 3/14/97
Mark Cohen	Anthony Rapp	Luther Creek
Tom Collins	Jesse L. Martin	C.C. Brown
Benjamin Coffin III	Taye Diggs	James Rich
Joanne Jefferson	Fredi Walker	Sylvia MacCalla
Angel Schunard	Wilson Jermaine Heredia	Stephan Alexander
Mimi Marquez	Daphne Rubin-Vega Marcy Harriell 4/5/97	Simone
Maureen Johnson	Idina Menzel	Carrie Hamilton Amy Spanger 6/5/97

SHOW BOAT

	New York 10/2/94	#1 Los Angeles 11/12/96 #2 Chicago 3/24/96

Cap'n Andy	John McMartin
	John Cullum 1/30/96
	John McMartin 11/5/96
		#1 George Grizzard
		    Ned Beatty 1/22/96
		    Len Cariou 5/97
		    Tom Bosley 2/97
		#2 John McMartin
		    Dick Van Patten 12/96
		    Pat Harrington 6/97

Parthy	Elaine Stritch
	Carole Shelley 9/12/95
		#1 Cloris Leachman
		    Karen Marrow 2/97
		#2 Dorothy Loudon
		    Joyce Van Patten 2/97
		    Anita Gillette 6/97

Magnolia	Rebecca Luker Sarah Pfisterer 2/96	#1 Teri Hansen #2 Gay Willis

Gaylord Ravenal	Mark Jacoby
	Hugh Panaro 11/95
		#1 J. Mark McVey
		#2 Mark Jacoby
		    Kevin Gray 9/96
		    J. Mark McVey 12/96
		    Doug LaBrecque 2/97
		    Keith Buterbaugh 6/97

Julie	Lonette McKee Marilyn McCoo 9/26/95 Lonette McKee 2/13/96	#1 Valarie Pettiford Karen-Angela Bishop 5/97 #2 Marilyn McCoo Terry Burrell 2/97
Frank	Joel Blum	#1 Keith Savage #2 Eddie Korbich
Ellie	Dorothy Stanley Beth Leavel 11/95	#1 Jacquey Maltby #2 Clare Leach Ann Van Cleave 6/97
Queenie	Gretha Boston	#1 Anita Berry #2 Jo Ann Hawkins Whige
Steve	Doug LaBrecque Fred Love 9/26/95	#1 Todd Noel Kip Wilborn 3/29/96 Ross Neill 5/97 #2 Todd Noel
Joe	Michel Bell André Solomon Glover 2/13/96	#1 Dan Tullis, Jr. #2 Michel Bell Kenneth Nichols 2/97

SMOKEY JOE'S CAFE

New York 3/2/95	*Minneapolis 8/16/96*
Ken Ard	Eugene Fleming
Adrian Bailey	Trent Kendall Dwayne Clark 4/14/97
Brenda Braxton	Reva Rice
Victor Trent Cook	Darrian C. Ford
B.J. Crosby D'Atra Hicks B.J. Crosby	Alltrinna Grayson
Pattie Darcy Jones	Kim Cea
DeLee Lively Natasha Rennalls Paige Price DeLee Lively	Mary Ann Hermansen
Michael Park	Jerry Tellier
Frederick B. Owens	Ashley Howard Wilkinson

SUNSET BOULEVARD

	New York 11/17/94	*Denver 12/28/96*
Norma Desmond	Glenn Close Betty Buckley 7/4/95 Elaine Page 8/26/96	Linda Balgord
Joe Gillis	Alan Campbell	Ron Rohmer
Max von Mayerling	George Hearn	Ed Dixon
Betty Schaefer	Alice Ripley	Lauren Kennedy

Cecil B. DeMille	Alan Oppenheimer	William Chapman
	Rod Loomis	
Artie Green	Vincent Tumeo	James Clow
	Jordan Leeds	

VICTOR/VICTORIA

	New York 10/25/95
Carroll Todd	Tony Roberts
Victoria Grant	Julie Andrews
	Liza Minnelli 1/7/97
	Julie Andrews 2/2/97
	Raquel Welch 6/10/97
Norma Cassidy	Rachel York
King Marchan	Michael Nouri

OTHER SHOWS
ON FIRST CLASS TOURS IN 1996–97

CAROUSEL

	Houston 2/2/96
Billy Bigelow	Patrick Wilson
Julie Jordan	Sarah Uriarte
	Jennifer Laura Thompson
	11/13/96
Carrie Pipperidge	Sherry D. Boone
	Katie Hugo 2/18/97
Enoch Snow	Sean Palmer
	Jessie Means III 2/18/97
Nettie Fowler	Rebecca Eichenberger
	Patricia Phillips 12/25/96
Jigger Craigin	Brett Rickaby

A CHORUS LINE

	Minneapolis 9/25/96
Sheila	Michelle Bruckner
Maggie	Charlene Carr
Zach	Mark Martino
Val	Kimberly Dawn Neumann

Cassie	Jill Slyter
Paul	Luis Villabon

DAMN YANKEES

Baltimore 9/25/95

Applegate	Jerry Lewis
Lola	Valerie Wright
	April Nixon
Joe Hardy	David Elder
	John-Michael Flate
Joe Boyd	Dennis Kelly
Gloria Thorpe	Linda Gabler
	Ellen Grosso
Meg Boyd	Susan Bigelow
	Joy Franz
Sister	Amy Ryder
	Julie Prosser 3/26/96
Benny Van Buren	Joseph R. Sicari

DEATHTRAP

Stamford 9/17/96

Sidney Bruhl	Elliot Gould
Myra Bruhl	Mariette Hartley
	Alexandra O'Karma 12/24/96
	Cindy Williams 1/27/97
Clifford Anderson	Douglas Wert
Helga Ten Dorp	Marilyn Cooper
Porter Milgrim	Doug Stender

AN INSPECTOR CALLS

Baltimore 10/17/95

Sybil Birling	Susan Kellerman
Edna	Kaye Kingston
Arthur Birling	Philip LeStrange
	Stacy Keach 5/7/96
Gerald Croft	David Andrew Macdonald
Sheila Birling	Jane Fleiss
Eric Birling	Harry Carnahan
Inspector Goole	Sam Tsoutsouvas
	John Lantz 1/16/96
	Curt Hostetter 4/30/96
	Kenneth Cranham 5/7/96

| *Boy* | Jeffrey Force |
| | Zachary Freed 2/13/96 |

JOSEPH AND THE AMAZING TECHNICOLOR DREAMCOAT

	#1 West Point, NY 1/13/95
	#2 Toronto 5/31/95
Joseph	#1 Sam Harris
	Brian Lane Green 2/26/96
	#2 Donny Osmond
Narrator	#1 Kristine Fraelich
	Jodie Langel
	#2 Kelli James Chase
	Donna Kane 11/12/95
Jacob/Potiphar/Guru	#1 Russell Leib
	Steve Pudenz 2/25/96
	#2 James Harms
	Gary Krawford 11/29/95
	James Harms 3/31/96
Pharoah	#1 John Ganun
	Jeffrey Scott Watkins 1/12/96
	#2 Johnny Seaton
Butler	#1 Glenn Sneed
	Jon Carver
	#2 J.C. Montgomery
Baker	#1 Paul J. Gallagher
	Max Perlman
	#2 Erich McMillan-McCall
Mrs. Potiphar	#1 Justine DiCostanzo
	Mindy Franzese
	Jennifer Werner
	#2 Carole Mackereth
	Julia Alicia Fowler 3/31/96

MAN OF LA MANCHA

	Chattanooga 8/96
Don Quixote	Robert Goulet
Aldonza	Susan Hoffman
Sancho Panza	Darryl Ferrer
The Padre	David Wasson
Dr. Carrasco	Ian Sullivan
The Innkeeper	William Parcher
	Jack Dabdoub 2/97
Antonia	Linda Cameron
Captain of the Inquisition	Michael Licata

WEST SIDE STORY

	Detroit 9/5/95
Tony	H.E. Greer
	Scott Carollo 11/95
	Jeremy Koch 9/96
Maria	Marcy Harriell
	Sharen Camille 9/96
Anita	Natascia A. Diaz
	Michelle DeJean 4/97
Riff	Jamie Gustis
	Christian Borle 9/96
Bernardo	Vincent Zamora
	Kevin Bernardo 9/96

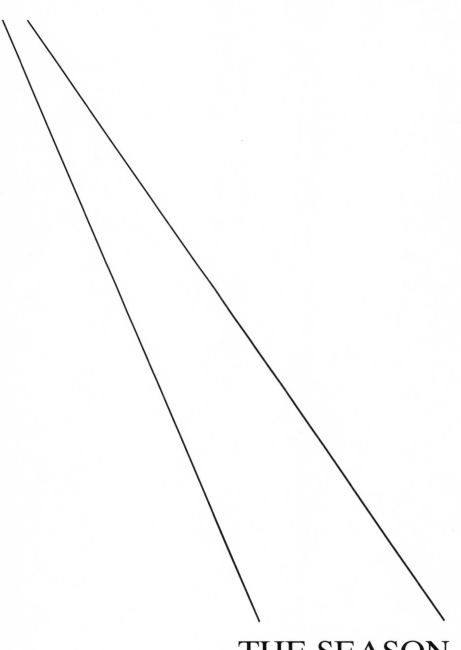

THE SEASON
OFF OFF BROADWAY

○
○
○

OFF OFF BROADWAY

○ *By Mel Gussow*
○
○

IN THE 1996–97 season, the aridity of Broadway straight plays was offset by the vitality off off Broadway. Adventurous work came from unfamiliar as well as familiar sources, and, as usual, some of the most striking work derived from other countries. This year, five plays are cited as outstanding OOB productions. New companies continued to have an impact, in particular the New Group, the Drama Dept. and the Blue Light Theater Company. Although playwrights and directors are also involved in the creation of these troupes, the primary impetus came from actors, banding together in order to challenge themselves and to expand their opportunities in New York theater. These three and others are nomadic, free-floating from stage to stage. The emphasis is not on any kind of institutionalization but on the work process itself. In a very short space of time, each has achieved a unity and an identity, and theatergoers have learned to look forward to the next production, wherever it happens to surface.

Under the artistic direction of Scott Elliott, the New Group specializes in new plays, often from England, in previous seasons with Mike Leigh's *Ecstasy* and Stephen Bill's *Curtains*. This year, the company offered the world premiere of Kenneth Lonergan's *This Is Our Youth*, a sharply ironic play about two dedicated dropouts of the 1980s. This very promising American playwright has a keen ear for the problems and the special pleading of young people. The play boasted fine performances by Josh Hamilton (as a poseur) and Mark Ruffalo (as an inept thief). The director, Mark Brokaw, went on to direct Paula Vogel's *How I Learned to Drive*, while Elliott was on Broadway staging *Present Laughter* with Frank Langella. At the end of the season, the New Group presented the New York premiere of Kevin Elyot's prize-winning British play, *My Night With Reg*, about the interwoven lives of six gay men in London.

The Drama Dept., a collective of actors, writers, directors and others, opened its doors in 1996 with a revival of Tennessee Williams's *Kingdom of Earth* and followed it this year with a fresh and funny revival of *June Moon* by Ring Lardner and George S. Kaufman. This 1929 comedy about the aspirations of Tin Pan Alley tunesters was reinvigorated in Mark Nelson's production, which featured sparkling performances by Robert Joy, Cynthia Nixon, Geoffrey Nauffts (as a naive songwriter trying to

311

break into the music business), and, especially, Albert Macklin as a pianist with a dry wit and a sense of humanity, otherwise lacking in most of his colleagues. The spontaneity of the cast obliterated any concern that the play might seem dated. Late in the season, the Drama Dept. turned its attention to a new play, Douglas Carter Beane's *As Bees in Honey Drown*, an arch, sporadically amusing spoof of the wages of success (in this case, a first novelist, played by the busy Josh Hamilton, was seduced and abandoned). Beane is also the company's artistic director. Elevating the play and Brokaw's production was J. Smith-Cameron's captivating performance as a con-woman with self-parodying panache. Mimicking Audrey Hepburn and Liza Minnelli, among others, the actress once again revealed her comic virtuosity.

Blue Light is an actors' theater "founded on the principal of reinvestment," allying established professionals with younger artists. Last season the company revived Clifford Odets's *Golden Boy*, directed by Joanne Woodward and starring Greg Naughton (the actor-manager of the troupe) in the title role. This year, Woodward took on the daunting task of directing *Waiting for Lefty*, about a strike of taxi drivers. Although the Odets play is mired in its time, it has an historic significance, particularly in the way that it approached theater as a platform for social improvement. Wisely, the director began the evening with a collage of labor songs, setting the atmosphere for this hortatory drama, which was then given a rousing rendition by an energetic ensemble. Watching *Waiting for Lefty*, one had a semblance of how the original audience might have reacted, joining the actors in protesting unfair labor practices. Blue Light also offered a Tex-Mex cowboy version of *The Two Gentlemen of Verona*. Led by Greg Naughton and Joe Grifasi, this was a lowdown, breezy variation on Shakespeare, a considerable improvement over the tepid Anglo-American Globe Theater *Two Gentlemen* that played at the New Victory Theater on 42d Street.

Other established OOB troupes, like the Vineyard Theater and New York Theater Workshop, had strong seasons. Tisa Chang's Pan Asian Repertory Theater celebrated its 20th anniversary with a musical, *Shanghai Lil's*. Though homeless, Everett Quinton's Ridiculous Theatrical Company remained firmly dedicated to the lunatic Ludlam brand of comedy on which it is based. The Brooklyn Academy of Music (some of whose offerings straddle the line between OOB and off Broadway) and La Mama continued to be prime metropolitan locations for impressive theater from other countries. This year BAM earned two citations for outstanding production: for Sebastian Barry's *The Steward of Christendom* and Robert Lepage's *The Seven Streams of the River Ota*. In Barry's play, an old man looks back ruefully on his life as the last head of the Irish police under British rule. In love with the Crown, he is reviled by his countrymen even as he makes way for the rule of Michael Collins. In the course of the play, his children move in and out of his memory. Torn between family and political loyalty, he is pushed further into a state of dementia. This is a strange, poetic drama, acted with eloquence by Donal McCann as the anguished protagonist, one of the most memorable performances of the season. The splendid direction was by Max Stafford-Clark.

In contrast to the intense, interior *Steward*, *The Seven Streams of the River Ota* was a prismatic epic, a marathon in two parts, eight hours, dealing with Hiroshima, the Holocaust, AIDS and more. There are other diverse strands in this stream: two brothers, one Japanese, one American; a *Madame Butterfly* story; suicide in a death camp; a survivor who becomes a celebrated Zen poet. Too much? Of course, but what unites everything is the fervid imagination of Lepage, a masterly visualist and conceptualist. Individual scenes were stunning: an interlude about concentration camps, done with mirrors projecting the past against the present. Late in the second part, there is an eye-defying switch with different personages seeming to emerge from the same wraparound kimono. There were a few excisable scenes, but many that lodge in one's memory, including a tableau of life in a New York rooming house. Through walls and windows we see characters moving from room to room, and interacting. *The Seven Streams* was a movie on stage, illusionary magic from this Canadian wizard.

For variety, BAM sponsored *Chimere*, an equestrian evening in a tent in Battery Park. The horses in this French company were impeccably trained and disciplined, but the show was bathed in a pool of pretension.

As its centerpiece, Lincoln Center Festival presented Dublin's Gate Theater in all Samuel Beckett's stage plays. A monumental achievement, the series was highlighted by the Gate production of *Endgame* (starring Barry McGovern) and by its recovery of lesser known shorter pieces like *Rough for Theater II*. The festival also featured *The Three Lives of Lucie Cabrol*, an earthy environmental epic about the brutish life of a French peasant, from London's Théâtre de Complicité. Among the other offerings was *Brain Opera*, a walk-through, mall-style electronic musical, in which the audience participated in programming the dramatic events.

En Garde Arts, Anne Hamburger's site-specific company, welcomed the innovative English director Deborah Warner to New York, where she and Fiona Shaw made their debut with their dramatization of *The Waste Land*, cited as an outstanding OOB production. This closely collaborative team had previously presented their interpretation of T.S. Eliot's seminal poem in widely disparate locations (from Paris to Toronto). Alone on stage in an unrenovated Times Square theater, Ms. Shaw acted as the voice of the poet and also played all the characters, unearthing drama and dialogue in and between the lines, richly populating a complex canvas. "Hurry up please, it's time," wrote Eliot, and indeed it was, as Ms. Shaw and Ms. Warner endowed the poem with a visceral theatrical life.

Among homegrown experimentalists, Anne Bogart looked to the early days of the movies in *American Silents* and Elizabeth LeCompte reinterpreted *The Hairy Ape*, keeping O'Neill's words while submerging them in her own clanging, expressionistic landscape. Led by Willem Dafoe in the title role, the play represented the Wooster Group's move into a more popular arena. Resident in Times Square theaters in open-ended off-Broadway-type runs, *The Hairy Ape* and *The Waste Land* offered alternatives to the merchandise-minded Disneyfication of the area.

The Vineyard Theater presented Paula Vogel's *How I Learned to Drive*, a sensitive play about sexual abuse and a breakthrough work, winner of major awards and soon elevated to off-Broadway status. Earlier, the Vineyard was also a home for Lisa Loomer's *The Waiting Room*. An outstanding OOB production, *The Waiting Room* was a deeply probing comic look at the plight of women through the ages.

Mel Gussow Citations

Scenes from BAM's two programs
as outstanding OOB productions a
*at left (The Seven Streams of the
Ota*—"a movie on stage, illusi
magic from the Canadian wizard
rector Robert Lepage) and *d
below* (Sebastian Barry's *The St*
of Christendom—"a strange, p
drama, acted with eloquence by I
McCann")

Right, June Kyoko Lu, Michele Shay
and Veanne Cox in a scene from Lisa
Loomer's *The Waiting Room* at the
Vineyard Theater—"a deeply probing comic look at the plight of
women through the ages"

Above, Fiona Shaw in her solo performance of T.S. Eliot's poem *The Waste Land* under Deborah Warner's direction at En Garde Arts—"Ms. Shaw and Ms. Warner endowed the poem with a visceral theatrical life." *Left,* Michael Emerson as Oscar Wilde in *Gross Indecency: The Three Trials of Oscar Wilde* written and directed by Moises Kaufman at Tectonic Theater Project—"a potent play about hypocrisy and the law, art and the price of integrity."

In 1995, the play earned an American Theater Critics Association Citation. After playing at several regional theaters, it finally made its way to New York. Freely mixing past and present in a style somewhat akin to that in Caryl Churchill's *Top Girls,* the playwright proved that misogyny—or at least subjugation of women by men—is endemic to various cultures through the ages.

The New York Theater Workshop, which discovered *Rent,* presented David Rabe's *A Question of Mercy,* a thoughtful, moving exploration of assisted suicide. Based on a Richard Selzer essay, the play focused on a man dying of AIDS (Juan Carlos Hernandez) and a doctor (Zach Grenier) who is drawn into the patient's life while trying to maintain a cool objectivity. The astute direction was by Douglas Hughes. This was an unusual change of pace for a playwright more often concerned with writing about men at war (in battle and at home).

Richard Foreman continued to explore his signature images, ideas and intricate stage techniques in *Permanent Brain Damage*. On tap here were "empty husks of memory." *Paved Paradise* represented a return engagement of John Kelly's eerily entertaining impersonation of Joni Mitchell. With *Peter and Wendy*, Lee Breuer, a founder of Mabou Mines, created one of his most imaginative and accessible works: a look behind the storybook facade of Peter Pan. With adaptation by Liza Lorwin, music by Johnny Cunningham and inspiration by Breuer, this was a puppet musical, with Julie Archer and her team of puppeteers pulling the strings behind the scenes (there were also hand, shadow and Bunraku puppets). The versatile Karen Kandel was the narrator and supplied the voices for Wendy and all the other characters. *Peter and Wendy* was the high point of the annual International Festival of Puppet Theater (at the Public Theater), and returned later for a longer engagement at the New Victory on 42d Street. The low point of the puppet festival was *Soup Talk I*, the excruciatingly self-indulgent work of Warner Blake, a Seattle puppeteer. In the same festival, Eric Bass's version of *The Caucasian Chalk Circle* was pedestrian, but *Ubu Roi*, from the Hystopolis Puppet Theater, was a bawdy, inventive trip through Jarry-land.

A disappointment came from a surprising source. The Signature Theater, which made such an important contribution in past years (devoting individual seasons to the work of Romulus Linney, Lee Blessing, Horton Foote, Edward Albee and Adrienne Kennedy) focused on Sam Shepard. The results were scattershot, both in terms of the plays chosen and the productions. *When the World Was Green (A Chef's Fable)*, a new mystery play written in collaboration with Joseph Chaikin (who also directed), offered Alvin Epstein an opportunity to overact as a man in prison for murder. That play was paired with a revival of *Chicago*, Shepard's vintage bathtub monologue. An ill-conceived off-Broadway revision of *The Tooth of Crime* lacked both intensity and humor. The series reached its modest high point with a triple bill of revivals, *The Sad Lament of Pecos Bill on the Eve of Killing His Wife* (a mini-musical about homicide), *Killer's Head* (a confession before an execution) and *Action* (about varieties of disaffected youth). The season ended with still another production of *Curse of the Starving Class*. In the Shepard season, there was no sense of discovery, as there was with all previous Signature playwrights.

David Mamet returned with a revival of his grim, compelling *Edmond*, with a powerful performance by David Rasche as the Wozzeck-like protagonist. *Edmond* was at the Atlantic Theater, as was Tom Donaghy's *Minutes From the Blue Route*, diminishing returns in a play about a woefully dysfunctional family, a step back for the still promising playwright. At Primary Stages, Gen LeRoy was introduced with *Not Waving*, a mother-daughter play, in which the younger woman succumbs to mental illness as the parent becomes the carekeeper. Sloane Shelton and Kyra Sedgwick were touching in the central roles.

The prolific Romulus Linney presented *Mock Trial*, a provocative reinvention of an historic trial (of Adolf Hitler) as a case in Montana in the near future. The play was short on drama, but it was instructive and informative. David Ives, the master of the one-act comedy, was represented at Primary Stages by another anthology, *Mere Mortals and Others*. The funniest was the title play, originally performed at the Ensemble Studio Theater in 1990, about three construction workers with intellectual illusions. There was also a malicious spoof of Mamet, but the Ives sextet was not in a class with his previous collection *All in the Timing*. The annual Marathon of one-acts at the Ensemble Studio freely mixed plays by newcomers with ones by house favorites like Linney, Frank D. Gilroy and Michael Weller. The Weller, *Mistresses*, was a particular pleasure, a late night street colloquy between two guys (Bob Balaban and Roscoe Born). Around a dumpster, they talked wryly about the women running through their lives. Julie McKee's *A Backward Glance* was a neat little dialogue about missed opportunity.

Archie Rice, the aging vaudevillian in John Osborne's *The Entertainer*, was given a resonant performance (and a certain poignance) by Brian Murray at the CSC. The enterprising Irish Repertory Theater offered Tony Walton a chance to combine designing with directing, with a production of *The Importance of Being Earnest*. As it turned out, Walton's elegant setting was the choicest part of the evening, although there were artful performances by Daniel Gerroll and Melissa Errico.

Oscar Wilde, himself, was the subject of one of the season's triumphs. The playwright's life has been told in countless books, plays and movies, but Moises Kaufman discovered a vivid new theatricality in a play called *Gross Indecency: The Three Trials of Oscar Wilde*, cited as an outstanding OOB production. As written and directed by Kaufman, this docu-drama skillfully mingled trial testimony with news events and literary commentary to create a potent play about hypocrisy and the law, art and the price of integrity. With clearsighted objectivity, the work did not overlook Wilde's own penchant for self-entrapment. Michael Emerson made an astonishing New York debut as Wilde. Although he does not bear a physical resemblance to his character, the actor conveyed an emotional and intellectual connection. In common with *How I Learned to Drive* and several other plays, *Gross Indecency* will move into an extended off-Broadway run, broadening the audience for experimental drama.

PLAYS PRODUCED
OFF OFF BROADWAY

AND ADDITIONAL N.Y.C. PRODUCTIONS

Compiled by Camille Dee

Here is a comprehensive sampling of off-off-Broadway and other experimental or peripheral 1996–97 productions in New York. There is no definitive "off-off-Broadway" area or qualification. To try to define or regiment it would be untrue to its fluid, exploratory purpose. The listing below of hundreds of works produced by more than 100 OOB groups and others is as inclusive as reliable sources will allow, however, and takes in all leading Manhattan-based, new-play producing, English-language organizations.

The more active and established producing groups are identified in **bold face type,** in alphabetical order, with artistic policies and the names of the managing directors given whenever these are a matter of record. Each group's 1996–97 schedule, with emphasis on new plays and with revivals of classics usually omitted, is listed with play titles in CAPITAL LETTERS. Often these are works-in-progress with changing scripts, casts and directors, sometimes without an engagement of record (but an opening or early performance date is included when available).

Many of these off-off-Broadway groups have long since outgrown a merely experimental status and are offering programs which are the equal in professionalism and quality (and in some cases the superior) of anything in the New York theater, with special contractual arrangements like the showcase code, letters of agreement (allowing for longer runs and higher admission prices than usual) and, closer to the edge of the commercial theater, a so-called "mini-contract." In the list below, all available data on opening dates, performance numbers and major production and acting credits (almost all for Equity members) is included in the entries of these special-arrangement offerings.

A large selection of lesser-known groups and other shows that made appearances off off Broadway during the season appears under the "Miscellaneous" heading at the end of this listing.

American Jewish Theater. Produces plays reflecting the Jewish experience. Stanley Brechner artistic director.

ANNE AND FRANK AND ME. Written and directed by Cherie Bennett. December 7, 1996. Scenery, James Wolk; lighting, Susan White; costumes, Pamela Scofield; sound, Bruce Ellman. With Abigail Hardin, Rachel Ulanet, Janan Raouf, Careena Melia, Richard H. Blake, Christopher Cook, Greta Storace, John Simeon Sloan, Mandy Siegfried, Karen Shallo, David Winton.

VILNA'S GOT A GOLEM. By Ernest Joselovitz. January 4, 1997. Director, Lou Jacob; scenery, David F. Gordon; lighting, Thomas C. Hase; costumes, Greco; music, Jeff Warschauer. With David Ingram, Richard Topol, Stan Lachow, Thomas Pasley, Jason Kravits, Susan Blackwell.

NAMES. Written and directed by Mark Kemble. March 1, 1997. Scenery, William Barclay; lighting, Phil Monat; costumes, Gail Cooper Hecht; sound, Red Ramona. With Gordon Greenberg, John C. Mooney, Robert Ari, Joel Polis, Lee Wilkof, Clayton Landey, Tovah Feldshuh, Paul Lieber.

YIDDLE WITH A FIDDLE. Book, based on the Yiddish film *Yidl Mtn Fidl,* and lyrics, Isaiah Sheffer; music, Abraham Ellstein. April 19, 1997. Director, Lori Steinberg. With Aileen Quinn, Sean McCourt, Mark Lotito.

American Theater of Actors. Dedicated to providing a creative atmosphere for new American playwrights, actors and directors. James Jennings artistic director.

Schedule included:

THE DRY BRANCH. By Travis Baker. June 19, 1996. Director, James Jennings. With Bob Crafford, Deirdre MacNamara, Allan Pollack, Renatta Rodriguez, Christopher Jennings.

PLANET OF JEWS. By Michael S. Lazan. June 19, 1996. Director, Keith T. Fadelici. With Jefferson Arca, Antoinette Gallo, Melanie Robichaux, Graig Slivka.

SLICES. By Gus Edwards. July 18, 1996. Director, O.L. Duke. With Michael Wright, Inga Ballard, Ramon Beedles, Ron Brice, Curtis McClarin, Marcus Naylor, Anton Pagan, Sherrima, Jeffrey V. Thompson, Sharon Washington.

THE CRIME OF ANNY SEGAL. By Bobby Wittenberg. July 31, 1996. Director, Janet O'Hair. With Jeff Pucillo, Antoinette Gallo, Joe Iacona, Abigail Walker, Nessa Wolfe-Baum, Alexandra Cremer, Nancy Moss, Morgan Demel.

JOHN AND ELLEN, COMMENT and GAIL (one-act plays). By Alex Menza. August 7, 1996. Directors, Judith Caporale, Barbara Pitcher. With Barbara Friend, Joe Iacona, William Greville, Judith Caporale.

MOVEMENT BETWEEN CELLS. By Madelyn Kent. August 14, 1996. Director, Jeff Lynn Miller. With Page Gravely, David Kring, Todd Woodard.

THE GOOD LIFE. By Jim Barden. August 21, 1996. Director, Jeff S. Dailey. With Tracie Black, Morgan Demel, David Davita, John P. Lavin, Dean Negri, Irene Woods.

ANTI-SEMI-(O)TICS. By Andrew Case. August 21, 1996. Director, Hayley Finn. With Mort Forrest, Joshua Feinstein, Jefferson Arca, Amanda Margulies.

FULL CIRCLE. By Jean E. Singer. September 6, 1996. Director, Jane Culley. With Julie Zimmerman, Tracy Grinnell, Jessica Jennings, Ivy Lehner.

FORCING PUSSY WILLOWS. By George J.R. Sauer. September 11, 1996. Director, Kelly Moore. With Jeanne Pearson, Joan Porter Holland, Tine Firmin, Elizabeth Stearn.

ALTERED STATES. Written and directed by James Jennings. September 18, 1996. With James Kosior, Ahri Birnbaum, Stephanie Kelly.

LETTERS FROM MOTHER AND DAUGHTER. Written and directed by James Jennings. September 18, 1996. With Victoria Agresti, Nessa Wolfe-Baum.

WHEN THE LAUGHTER DIES. By David Lessoff. October 9, 1996. Director, James Jennings. With Mark Neveldine, Dean Negri, Melanie Bean, Shannondoah Sorin, Christopher Morgan.

THE KITCHEN LOVERS. By Roger Kristian Jones. November 13, 1996. Director, Jamie Marcu. With Veronica Bero, David Gravens, Jeff Pucillo, DeLora Whitney.

RUNNING. By Richard Silver. November 20, 1996. Director, Rosemary Andress. With Ken Coughlin, Cliff Diamond, Bert Gurin, Peter Jaskowiak, Alison Karayanes, Pamela Nicholson, Bruce Ross, Ben Tolefson.

COUNTENANCE. By Norman Rhodes. November 20, 1996. Director, Barbara Pitcher. With Antoinette Gallo, William Greville, Kathryn Hahn, Laura LeBlanc, Marianne Mueller, David Tillistrand.

SOUTHERN BELLES FROM HELL. By C.C. Henley. November 27, 1996. Director, Jane Culley. With Melanie Robichaux, Julie Zimmerman, Teresa Fischer, Brenda Smiley, Ginger Masoud.

ATLANTIC THEATER COMPANY—Jordan Lage, J.R. Horne and Guy Boyd in the world premiere of Quincy Long's comedy *The Joy of Going Somewhere Definite* under the direction of William H. Macy

STONES FROM HEAVEN. Written and directed by James Jennings. December 4, 1996. With James Kosior, Cindy Owens, Carl Battles.

SANCTIMONIOUS MONDAY. Written and directed by Louis LaRusso II. December 4, 1996. With Robert Capelli Jr., Richard D'Alessandro, Joshua Feinstein, Nicholas J. Giangiulio, Joe Maruzzo, Dan McCormick, Vincent Pastore, George Palermo Jr., Tom Patti, Harvey Perr, George Pollack, Max Raven, Anthony J. Ribustello.

THAT'S AMORE, TRUTHS ONLY LOVERS CAN TELL and A CINDERELLA STORY (one-act plays). By Joseph P. Simone. December 11, 1996. Directors, John Koprowski, Dori Hertzberg. With Michelle Aragon, Erin Hamilton, William Greville, Ruth Heyman, Angela Shuford, Curtis Deveraux, Adrian Lee.

ASHES TO ASHES and SWEETWATER. Written and directed by James Jennings. January 29, 1997. With Dean Negri, Adam R. Brown, Cynthia Pierce, Carl Bradford, Michelle McKiernan.

HEARTS SOUNDS. By Alex Menza. February 5, 1997. Director, Barbara Pitcher. With William Greville, Judith Caporale, Joe Iacona.

THE WIND DOGS. Written and directed by James Jennings. February 12, 1997. With Mark Schmetterer, Marie Thomas, Jinn S. Kim.

STORIES FROM A TRAIL DOG written, directed and performed by James Jennings; LETTERS FROM MOTHER AND DAUGHTER written and directed by James Jennings. February 19, 1997. With Veronica Bero, Antoinette Gallo.

ICE CUBES. Written and directed by Vincent Apollo. March 5, 1997. With Christopher Batyr, Robert Capici, William DePaolo, Alice Gold, Seth Greenblatt, Joseph Riccobene, Hilit Shifman.

COYOTE REBEL. Written and directed by James Jennings. March 26, 1997. With Tom Bruce, Mark Neveldine.

LETTERS FROM MOTHER AND DAUGHTER. Written and directed by James Jennings. March 26, 1997. With Jane Culley, Jennifer Jennings.

THE WAY RAIN LIKES GRASS. By Peter Spiro. April 9, 1997. Director, Jeff Dailey. With Derrick Begin, Adam Brown, Richard Collie, Dennis Kaiser, Sharon Laughlin, Jason Margolies, Keong Sim.

IN MAMA'S HOUSE. By Mara Dresner. April 23, 1997. Director, Sue Winik. With Robert Capici, Tracy Grinnell, Dean Negri, Michael Colombo, Marianne Mueller, Mark Schmetterer.

RAIL DOGS. Written and directed by James Jennings. May 28, 1997. With Michael Mora, Kelly Atkins, Courtney Everett.

DEN OF THIEVES. By Carl Ross. May 28, 1997. Director, Robert Mulligan. With Tom Reid, Will Buchanan, Renae Plant, Morton Hall Millen, Paul Empson, Alexandra Cremer, Randy Ehrmann.

Atlantic Theater Company. Produces new plays or reinterpretations of classics that speak to audiences in a contemporary voice on issues reflecting today's society. Neil Pepe artistic director, Hilary Hinckle managing director.

EDMOND (47). By David Mamet. October 1, 1996. Director, Clark Gregg; scenery, Kevin Rigdon; lighting, Howard Werner; costumes, Kaye Voyce. With David Rasche, Leslie Silva, Kevin Thigpen, Rod McLachlan, Maryann Urbano, Isiah Whitlock Jr., Jordan Lage, Mary McCann, Neil Pepe.

MINUTES FROM THE BLUE ROUTE (47). By Tom Donaghy. January 30, 1997. Director, David Warren; scenery, Derek McLane; lighting, Donald Holder; costumes, Mark Wendland; sound and music, John Gromada. With Elizabeth Franz, Stephen Mendillo, Catherine Kellner, Matt McGrath.

THE JOY OF GOING SOMEWHERE DEFINITE (41). By Quincy Long. April 7, 1997. Director, William H. Macy; scenery, Kyle Chepulis, lighting, Howard Werner; costumes, David Zinn. With Guy Boyd, J. R. Horne, Jordan Lage, Neil Pepe, Dale Soules, Felicity Huffman.

CLEAN (40). By Edwin Sanchez. June 9, 1997. Director, Neil Pepe; scenery, Todd Rosenthal; lighting, Howard Werner; costumes, David Zinn. With Victor Anthony, Victor Argo, Ron Butler, Paula Pizzi, Rod McLachlan, Nelson Vasquez.

Brooklyn Academy of Music Next Wave Festival. Since 1981, this annual three-month festival has presented over 200 events, including more than 50 world premieres. Featuring leading international artists, it is one of the world's largest festivals of contemporary performing arts. Harvey Lichtenstein president and executive producer.

CHIMERE (42). Conceived and directed by Bartabas. September 17, 1996. Costumes, Marie-Laurence Schakmundes; musical direction, Jean-Pierre Drouet. With Zingaro Equestrian Theater (Bartabas, Manuel Bigarnet, Shantih Breikers, Arnaud Gillette, Laure Guillaume, Claire Leroy, Brigitte Marty, Patrick Labasque, Pierrick Moreau, Jocelyn Petot, Pascal Petot, Bernard Quental, Etienne Regnier, Eva Schakmundes, Shantala Shivalingappa, Max Soulignac).

THE BEATIFICATION OF AREA BOY (5). By Wole Soyinka. October 9, 1996. Director, Jude Kelly; scenery and costumes, Niki Turner; lighting, Mark Pritchard; sound, Mic Pool, Roman Kung; musical direction, Tunji Oyelana, Juwon Ogungbe. With The West Yorkshire Playhouse (Femi Elufowoju Jr., Denise Orita, Janice Acquah, Marcia Hewitt, Wale Ogunyemi, Ombo Gogo Ombo, Makinde Adeniran, Yomi A. Michaels, David Webber). Co-produced by the Solomon R. Guggenheim Foundation, in collaboration with Works and Process.

THE SEVEN STREAMS OF THE RIVER OTA (7). Conceived by Eric Bernier, Normand Bissonnette, Rebecca Blankenship, Marie Brassard, Anne-Marie Cadieux, Normand Daneau, Richard Frechette, Marie Gignac, Patrick Goyette, Ghislaine Vincent, Macha Limonchik, Gerard Bibeau and Robert Lepage. December 1, 1996. Director, Robert Lepage; scenery, Carl Fillion; lighting, Sonoyo Nishikawa; costumes, Marie-Chantale Vaillancourt, Yvan Gaudin, assisted by Sylvie Courbron; music, Michael F. Cote. With Patrick Goyette, Rebecca Blankenship, Marie Brassard, Normand Daneau, Richard Frechette, Marie Gignac, Anne-Marie Cadieux, Eric Bernier, Ghislaine Vincent. (Performed in two parts.)

Classic Stage Company. Reinventing and revitalizing the classics for contemporary audiences. David Esbjornson artistic director, Mary Esbjornson executive director.

THE ENTERTAINER (34). By John Osborne. November 13, 1996. Director, David Esbjornson; choreography, Ted Pappas; scenery, Hugh Landwehr; lighting, Frances Aronson; costumes, Elizabeth Hope Clancy; sound, Mark Bennett; music, John Addison. With Brian Murray, Jean Stapleton, Douglas Seale, Kate Forbes, Barry McEvoy, Birgit Darby, Adrianna Dufay, Gia Forakis.

ANOTHER PART OF THE HOUSE (33). By Migdalia Cruz. March 12, 1997. Director, David Esbjornson; scenery, Chris Muller; lighting, Michael Krass; costumes, Ken Posner; sound, John Kilgore. With Irma St. Paule, Doris Difarnecio, Sarah Erde, Kadina Halliday, Mercedes Herrero, Seth Kanor, Paula Pizzi, Adriana Sevan, Patricia Triana.

En Garde Arts. Dedicated to developing the concept of "site-specific theater" in the streets, parks and buildings of the city. Anne Hamburger founder and producer.

THE TROJAN WOMEN: A LOVE STORY (14). By Charles L. Mee Jr., based on Euripides's and Hector Berlioz's works. June 27, 1996. Director, Tina Landau; scenery, James Schuette; lighting, Blake Burba; costumes, Anita Yavich; sound, Christopher Todd. With Marin Mazzie, Steven Skybell, Tom Nelis, Jane Nichols, Nancy Hume, Sharon Scruggs, Jason Danieley.

THE WASTE LAND (67) Solo performance by Fiona Shaw of the poem by T.S. Eliot. November 14, 1996. Directed by Deborah Warner. See its entry in the Plays Produced Off Broadway section of this volume.

Ensemble Studio Theater. Membership organization of playwrights, actors, directors and designers dedicated to supporting individual theater artists and developing new works for the stage. Over 200 projects each season, ranging from readings to fully-mounted productions. Curt Dempster artistic director, Evangeline Morphos executive director.

OCTOBERFEST. Festival of over 20 new works by members. October 1–31, 1996.

MARATHON '97 (festival of one-act plays). TENNESSEE AND ME by Will Scheffer, directed by Bob Balaban; MAFIA ON PROZAC by Edward Allan Baker, directed by Ron Stetson; SISTERS by Cherie Vogelstein, directed by Kirsten Sanderson; THE POTATO CREEK CHAIR OF DEATH by Robert Kerr, directed by Richard Caliban; MISTRESSES by Michael Weller, directed by Susann Brinkley; A BACKWARD GLANCE by Julie McKee, directed by Julie Boyd; PATRONAGE by Romulus Linney, directed by Tom Bullard; REAL REAL GONE by Michael Louis Wells, directed by Jamie Richards; GETTING IN by Frank D. Gilroy, directed by Christopher A. Smith; WHAT I MEANT WAS by Craig Lucas, directed by Peg Denithorne; SPARROW by Vicki Mooney, directed by Curt Dempster; WHEN IT COMES EARLY by John Ford Noonan, directed by Daniel Selznick. May 6–June 15, 1997.

INTAR. Mission is to identify, develop and present the talents of gifted Hispanic American theater artists and multicultural visual artists. Max Ferra artistic director.

TERRA INCOGNITA. Libretto, lyrics and direction, Maria Irene Fornes; music, Roberto Sierra. March 26, 1997. Scenery, Van Santvoord; lighting, Philip Widmer; costumes, Willa Kim. With Jennifer Alagna, Lawrence Craig, John Muriello, Candace Rogers O'Connor, Matthew Perri. Co-produced by The Women's Project and Productions.

UNDER A WESTERN SKY. By Amparo Garcia. May 1, 1997. Co-produced by The Women's Project and Productions; see its entry in this section.

Irish Repertory Theater. Aims to bring works by Irish and Irish American masters and contemporary playwrights to a wider audience and to develop new works focusing on a wide range of cultural experiences. Charlotte Moore artistic director, Ciaran O'Reilly producing director.

DA (52). By Hugh Leonard. July 18, 1996. Director, Charlotte Moore; scenery, Shelley Barclay; lighting, Gregory Cohen; costumes, David Toser. With Brian Murray, Malcolm Adams, Paddy Croft, Julia Gibson, John Leighton, Paul Mc Grane, Aideen O'Kelly, Ciaran O'Reilly.

THE IMPORTANCE OF BEING EARNEST (61). By Oscar Wilde. October 24, 1996. Direction, scenery and costumes, Tony Walton; lighting, Kirk Bookman; sound, Randy Freed. With Thomas Carson, Melissa Errico, John Fiedler, Daniel Gerroll, Schuyler Grant, Nancy Marchand, Sloane Shelton, Eric Stoltz.

MY ASTONISHING SELF (54). Solo performance by Donal Donnelly; created by Michael Voysey from George Bernard Shaw's writings. January 23, 1997. See its entry in the Plays Produced Off Broadway section of this volume.

YEATS ON STAGE: THE PLAYS. Readings of the full canon of W.B. Yeats's plays. January 30–February 16, 1997.

THE PLOUGH AND THE STARS (40). By Sean O'Casey. April 3, 1997. Director, Charlotte Moore; scenery, Akira Yoshimura; lighting, A.C. Hickox; costumes, Mirena Rada; sound, George Zarr. With Blythe Baten, Dara Coleman, Terry Donnelly, Louise Favier, Rosemary Fine, Pauline Flanagan, Con Horgan, Des Keogh, John Keating, John Leighton, Paul Mc Grane, Tim Smallwood.

THE NIGHTINGALE AND NOT THE LARK and THE INVISIBLE MAN (one-act plays) (29). By Jennifer Johnston. April 13, 1997. Director, Ciaran O'Reilly; scenery, David Raphel; lighting, Ken Davis; costumes, Victor Whitehurst. With W.B. Brydon, Tony Coleman, Paddy Croft, Betty Whyte.

The Joseph Papp Public Theater/New York Shakespeare Festival. Schedule of special projects, in addition to its regular off-Broadway productions. George C. Wolfe producer, Rosemarie Tichler artistic producer, Wiley Hausam, Bonnie Metzgar, Steve Tabakin associate producers, Kevin Kline, Brian Kulick artistic associates.

INTERNATIONAL FESTIVAL OF PUPPET THEATER. September 10–22, 1996. See its entry under Miscellaneous in this section.

NEW WORK NOW! (festival of staged readings). Schedule included LILLIAN by and with David Cale, directed by Joe Mantello; ONLY BEAUTY written and directed by David Greenspan; SWEET HOME by Keith Josef Adkins. directed by Jo Bonney; THE LESSER MAGOO by Mac Wellman, directed by Jim Simpson; MIDDLE FINGER by Han Ong, adapted from Frank Wedekind's *Spring Awakening,* directed by Brian Kulick; TRUEBLINKA by Adam Rapp, directed by Richard Caliban; CENTAUR BATTLE OF SAN JACINTO by Ruth Margraff, directed by Liz Diamond; PERSONAL HISTORY by Dominic A. Taylor, directed by Donald Douglass; SANTA CONCEPCION by Anne Garcia-Romero, directed by Leah Gardiner; (U)NDER (F)RANK (O)BSERVATION by Jake-Ann Jones, directed by Peter Francis James; MYTHS AND HYMNS music and lyrics by Adam Guettel, directed by Tina Landau, musical direction by Ted Sperling. May 5–19, 1997.

La Mama (a.k.a. LaMama) Experimental Theater Club (ETC). A busy workshop for experimental theater of all kinds. Ellen Stewart founder and artistic director.

Schedule included:

THE WILD. By Andy Tierstein. June 6, 1996.

SNOWMAN SERENADE. Written and directed by Charles Allcroft. June 13, 1996. With Bill Rice, Jim Neu, Ron Jones, Joe Munley, Carol Mullins, David Nunemaker, Terrell Robinson, Agosto Machado, Ron Jones, Silver Saunders, Lavinia Co-op.

GERANOS: DANCE WITHIN THE LABYRINTH. By Andrea Paciotto and Mia Yoo. June 20, 1996. Director, Andrea Paciotto; music, Genji Ito, Alexandros. With the Great Jones Repertory Company.

TIMES SQUARE MOTEL: GHOSTWRITER, THE HUSTLER AND THE BUSINESSMAN, LUCILLE PEANUTS, DEMENTIA SUITE (one-act plays). By Charles E. Drew. June 20, 1996. Director, Susan Huffaker.

RUBY AND THE REDNECKS: SINGIN' IN THE ISLANDS. Written and directed by Ruby Lynn Reyner; music, John Madera, Susan Lampert; lyrics, Tom Murrin, Jackie Curtis, John Vaccaro. June 27, 1996. With Ruby Lynn Reyner and The Rednecks.

MYTHOS OEDIPUS. Written and directed by Ellen Stewart; music, Elizabeth Swados. July 2, 1996. With the Great Jones Repertory Company.

RED LUNA (work-in-progress). By Rocelia Fung. July 30, 1996.

INTERNATIONAL FESTIVAL OF PUPPET THEATER. September 10–22, 1996. See its entry under Miscellaneous in this section.

FESTIVAL OF POLISH THEATER ARTS. Schedule included: HELENA—THE IMMIGRANT QUEEN (one-woman show) by Kazimierz Braun, directed by Joseph Kutrezeba. October 15–27, 1996. With Nina Polan.

MISSIONARIES. Written, composed and directed by Elizabeth Swados. October 18, 1996.

MASKED MEN. By Ilan Hatsor, translated by Miriam Schlessinger, Michael Taub and Kira Goldstein. October 31, 1996. Directed by Geula Jeffet Attar and Victor Attar; music, Tim Schellenbaum. With Victor Attar, Ernest Abuba, Hussein Fassa.

BODY OF CRIME. Written, directed and designed by Theodora Skipitares. November 7, 1996. With Michael P. Moran, Jennie Giering.

ALICE POINT LOVE. Conceived and directed by Peter Todorov. November 14, 1996. Music, Mary Oliver. With New Forms Theater Shtrich.

SERIES CANADA: THE NIGHT ROOM by Primus Theater of Winnipeg; directed by Richard Fowler; LA COMPAGNIE by Oren Safdie, directed by Frank Licato; BY A THREAD by and with Diane Flacks, directed by Richard Greenblatt; DRY LIPS by Tomson Highway, directed by Paul Leishman; THE STONE DIARIES (staged reading) by Carol Shields, directed by Eduardo Machado. November 20–December 1, 1996.

HAPPY END. By Igor Bojovic. November 21, 1996. Director, Ivana Vujic.

THE SECOND CUM-ING. By and with SLANT (Richard Ebihara, Wayland Quintero and Perry Yung). December 5, 1996.

JOAN OF HOLLYWOOD. Written and directed by Edward Kinchley Evans. December 5, 1996. With the Acting Company of the Laurel Highlands Regional Theater, Pittsburgh.

THE TROJAN WOMEN. Based on the play by Euripides; created by Great Jones Repertory Company. December 12, 1996. Director, Andrei Serban; scenery, David Adams, Jun Maeda, Mark Tambella; lighting, Howard Thies; costumes, Sandra Muir; music, Elizabeth Swados. With Natalie Gray, Joanna Peled, Onni Johnson, Valois Mickins, Daniel Raphael Katz, Charles Hayward.

A FUNNY OLD BIRD. Written and directed by Mike Gorman. January 2, 1997. With the Fabulous Giggin' Brothers (Mike Gorman, Will Gorman, Bill Meyer).

VIRTUAL SOULS. By and with Yara Arts Group. January 16, 1997. Director, Virlana Tkacz; scenery, Watoku Ueno; music, Genji Ito and Vladilen Pantaev.

THREE SISTERS. By Anton Chekhov, translated by Michele Minnick. January 16, 1997. Director, Richard Schechner; scenery, Chris Muller; lighting, Russell H. Champa; costumes, Linette Del Monico; musical direction, Ralph Denzer. With East Coast Artists (Rebecca Ortese, Shaula Chambliss, John Schmerling, David Letwein, Jeff Ricketts, Maria Vail Guevara, Michele Minnick, Ronobir Lahiri, Frank Wood, Lars Hanson, Robin Weigert, Sudipto Chatterjee).

APNEA (performance art). By Aida M. Croal. January 23, 1997. With Massimo Monacelli.

AFTER SORROW. By Muna Tseng, Ping Chong and Josef Fung. January 31, 1997. Director, Ping Chong; choreography, Muna Tseng; music, Josef Fung.

WARD NUMBER SIX AND . . . Adapted from Anton Chekhov's novel and directed by Damyan Popchristov. February 6, 1997.

CHIMERA. By Allen Lang. February 6, 1997. Director, Kevin Confoy.

KANADEHON HAMLET. By Harue Tsutsumi. February 18, 1997. Director, Toshifumi Sueki.

NIGHT STALKERS. Written and directed by Ernest Abuba. February 20, 1997. Choreography, Shigeko Suga; music, Erin Kambler.

IRISH REPERTORY THEATER—*Above,* Nancy Marchand, Melisa Errico, Daniel Gerroll and Eric Stoltz in a revival production of Oscar Wilde's *The Importance of Being Earnest* designed and directed by Tony Walton; *right,* Donal Donnelly in a solo portrayal of George Bernard Shaw in *My Astonishing Self,* devised by Michael Voysey.

THE QUADROON BALL: AN AMERICAN TRAGEDY. By Damon Wright. February 20, 1997. Direction and choreography, Terrell W. Robinson; scenery, Mark Tambella; music, Fred Carl. With Yvette Ganier, Charmaine Lord, Perri Gaffney, Stanley Earl Harrison.

OUT OF THE SOUTH: SUPPER FOR THE DEAD, WHITE DRESSES and QUARE MEDICINE (one-act plays). By Paul Green. March 6, 1997. Director, Barbara Montgomery.

THE GOLEM. Written and directed by Vit Horejs. March 13, 1997. Choreography, Yoshiko Chuma; scenery, Roman Hladik; costumes, Boris Caksiran. With Czechoslovak American Marionette Theater.

METEOR GIRL. By Sidra Rausch. March 27, 1997. Direction and choreography, Ken Roberson; music, Herbert G. Draesel Jr.

MONKEY KING IN NEW YORK. By Ben Wang and Lu Yu, adapted from Wu Cheng-En's novel, *Journey to the West.* March 30, 1997. Director, Lu Yu; choreography, Yung-Yung Tsuai. With Lu Yu, Ben Wang, Yung Yung Tsuai, Malina Yung, Cui Shu Min, Tyson Hwee, Doug Hwee.

DESIRE AND DEATH: THE KING OF BABYLON. By Dionysis Maravegias. April 17, 1997. Director, Olga Zissi.

I COUNT THE HOURS. By Stig Dalager, translated by Lone Thygesen Bleeher and Jane Mushabac. April 17, 1997. Director, Roger Hendricks Simon; music, David J. Simons.

AGAMEMNON. By Aeschylus, translated by Richmond Lattimore, adapted by John Allman and Alexander Harrington. April 24, 1997. Director, Alexander Harrington; music, John Allman.

THE REALISM OF SIMPLE MACHINES. Conceived and directed by Kevin Cunningham, Mike Taylor and Jill Schutzmacher. May 1, 1997.

EVERYDAY NEWT BURMAN (THE TRILOGY OF CYCLIC EXISTENCE). By John Moran. May 9, 1997. Director, Bob McGrath. With The Ridge Theater.

THE FEVER. By Wallace Shawn. May 15, 1997. Director, Joann Shapiro. With David Shapiro.

WOYZECK '97. By Georg Buchner, translated by John MacKendrick, adapted and performed by the Todd Theater Troupe. May 15, 1997. Director, Mervyn Willis; scenery, John Folbrook III.

THROWIN' BONES. By Matthew Maguire. May 29, 1997. Director, Joumana Rizk; scenery, Chris Doyle; lighting, Howard Thies; costumes, Quina Fonesca. With the Creation Company.

The Club

FUZE. Written and directed by Caryl Glaab and Gary Chiappa. October 7, 1996. With ORLOU (Gary Chiappa, Jodi Lennon, Christine Knight, Ned Malouf).

A HALLOWEEN EXTRAVAGANZA. By Edgar Oliver. October 31, 1996.

I THINK IT'S GONNA WORK OUT FINE, THE LEGEND OF LILY OVERSTREET and BIG BUTT GIRLS, HARD-HEADED WOMEN. By Rhodessa Jones and Idris Ackamoor. November 14–25, 1996.

MOON OVER ALABAMA (songs from THE THREEPENNY OPERA). December 5, 1996. Director, Petar Selem. With Bozidar Alic, Edita Majic.

RUBY AND THE REDNECKS: CHRISTMAS IN THE ISLANDS. Written and directed by Ruby Lynn Reyner; music, John Madera and Susan Lampert. December 12, 1996. Scenery, Tony Zanetta; costumes, Sage. With Ruby Lynn Reyner, Christopher Cook, John Madera, Susan Lampert, Mike Garner, Gary Adamson, Emma Channing, Melanie Mastro, Bianca Smith.

SLEEP. By Jack Gelber. January 9, 1997. Director, Ted Lambert.

TELETHON. By and with Ken Bullock and David Ilku. January 23, 1997.

THE LITTLE FREIDA MYSTERIES. By The Talent Family (Amy and David Sedaris). February 6, 1997. Director, Tom Aulino; scenery, Hugh Hamrick; lighting, Howard Thies. With Penny Boyer, Chuck Coggins, David Rakoff, Amy Sedaris. Reopened April 3, 1997.

MONDO BEYONDO. By Jim Neu; music, Neal Kirkwood and Harry Mann. March 30, 1997. Director, Keith McDermott. With Bill Rice, Mary Shultz, Jim Neu, Black-Eyed Susan.

FAITH AND DANCING: MAPPING FEMININITY AND OTHER NATURAL DISASTERS. By and with Lois Weaver. May 8, 1997.

Lincoln Center Festival. An annual international summer arts festival offering classic and contemporary works. For Lincoln Center for the Performing Arts, Beverly Sills Chairman, Nathan Leventhal President, John Rockwell festival director.

Schedule included:

THANG LONG WATER PUPPET THEATER (11). July 22, 1996.

THE BECKETT FESTIVAL (Samuel Beckett's complete stage works): WAITING FOR GODOT, HAPPY DAYS, OHIO IMPROMPTU, ROUGH FOR THEATER I, ROUGH FOR THEATER II, CATASTROPHE, ENDGAME, FOOTFALLS, ROCKABY, NOT I, WHAT WHERE, ACT WITHOUT WORDS I, ACT WITHOUT WORDS II, KRAPP'S LAST TAPE, COME AND GO, PLAY, BREATH, THAT TIME, A PIECE OF MONOLOGUE. July 29–August 11, 1996. With The Gate Theater of Dublin.

FOUR SAINTS IN THREE ACTS (4). Concept, direction and scenery, Robert Wilson; libretto, Gertrude Stein; music, Virgil Thomson. August 1, 1996. Lighting, Jennifer Tipton, Robert Wilson; costumes, Francesco Clemente. With Ashley Putnam, Suzanna Guzman, Marietta Simpson, Wilbur Pauley, Sanford Sylvan. Co-produced by Houston Grand Opera.

THE THREE LIVES OF LUCIE CABROL (5). By Simon McBurney and Mark Wheatley, adapted from John Berger's story, devised by Théâtre de Complicité. August 7, 1996. Director, Simon McBurney; scenery and costumes, Tim Hatley; lighting, Paule Constable; sound, Christopher Shutt. With Lilo Baur, Simon McBurney, Hannes Flaschberger, Helene Patarot, Stefan Metz, Tim McMullan, Mick Barnfather.

Mabou Mines. Theater collaborative whose work is a synthesis of motivational acting, narrative acting and mixed-media performance. Collective artistic leadership. Frederick Neumann, Terry O'Reilly, Ruth Maleczech, Lee Breuer artistic directors.

PETER AND WENDY (20). By Liza Lorwin, adapted from J.M. Barrie's novel. February 1, 1997. See its entry in the Plays Produced Off Broadway section of this volume.

HAJJ (24). Written and directed by Lee Breuer. May 6, 1997. Scenery and lighting, Julie Archer; masks, Linda Hartinian; live sound mix, Mio Morales; video, Craig Jones; music, Chris Abajian. With Ruth Maleczech.

PRELUDE TO A DEATH IN VENICE (6). Written and directed by Lee Breuer. May 16, 1997. With Stephen Peabody.

MCC Theater. Dedicated to the promotion of emerging writers, actors, directors and theatrical designers. Robert LuPone and Bernard Telsey executive directors.

THE GRAVITY OF MEANS (16). By John Kolvenbach. November 3, 1996. Director, Russ Jolly; scenery, Russell Parkman; lighting, Karen Spahn; costumes, Erik Bruce; music and sound, David Van Tieghem. With Christopher Collet, Chris Eigeman, Susan Floyd, Lenny Venito.

GOOD AS NEW (24). By Peter Hedges. March 2, 1997. Director, Brian Mertes; scenery, Rob Odorisio; lighting, Blake Burba; costumes, Sharon Sprague; music and sound, David Van Tieghem. With Laura Esterman, John Spencer, Jennifer Dundas, Chelsea Altman.

Music-Theater Group. Pioneering in the development of new music-theater. Lyn Austin producing director, Diane Wondisford general director.

THREE OF HEARTS: THE SONGS OF MARY RODGERS. Music, Mary Rodgers; lyrics, Marshall Barer, Martin Charnin, John Forster, Richard Maltby Jr., Mary Rodgers, William Shakespeare, Stephen Sondheim and Mark Waldrop. September 3, 1996. Director, Mark Waldrop. With Faith Prince, Mark Waldrop, Jason Workman.

MOBY DICK IN VENICE (6). Co-produced by Roman Paska's Theater for the Birds; see its entry under International Festival of Puppet Theater in the Miscellaneous section.

JUAN DARIEN. By Julie Taymor and Elliot Goldenthal. November 24, 1996. See its entry in the Plays Produced on Broadway section of this volume.

YOU DON'T MISS THE WATER (25). Text, Cornelius Eady; music, Diedre Murray. June 6, 1997. Director, Evan Yionoulis; scenery, G.W. Mercier; lighting, David Weiner. With Mike Hodge, Robert Jason Jackson, Brenda Pressley, Andrea Frierson Toney. Produced in association with the Vineyard Theater.

New Dramatists. An organization devoted to playwrights; member writers may use the facilities for anything from private cold readings of their material to public script-in-hand readings. Todd London director of artistic programming, Jana Jevnikar director of finance, Paul A. Slee executive director.

Readings:
THE KISSING WAS ALWAYS THE BEST. By Robert Anderson. June 6, 1996. Director, David Dorwart.
THE FAREWELL CONCERT OF IRENE AND VERNON PALAZZO. By Frank Gagliano. June 11, 1996. Director, Michael Montel.
DEMOCRACY. Book and lyrics, Joe Sutton; music, Lewis Flinn. June 24, 1996. Director, Jean Wagner.
HEART LAND. Book and lyrics, Darrah Cloud; music, Kim D. Sherman. July 1, 1996. Director, Jonathan Moscone.
NEW MEMBER EVENT: RAPID CITY by Sander Hicks, directed by Richard Nash-Siedlecki; SEVERITY'S MISTRESS by Gordon Dahlquist, directed by Ivan Talijancic; TRAFFICKING IN BROKEN HEARTS written and directed by Edwin Sanchez; FISHES written and directed by Diana Son. September 4, 1996.
IMAGINARY LOVER. By Silvia Gonzalez S. September 5, 1996. Director, Gail Lerner.
LOS MATADORES. By Silvia Gonzalez S. September 10, 1996. Director, Melanie White.
STRAIGHT AS A LINE. By Luis Alfaro. September 16, 1996. Director, Peter Brosius.

PENETRATE THE KING. By Gordon Dahlquist. September 20, 1996. Director, James Peck.
SOUL PSYCHEDELICIDE. Written and directed by Steven Sapp. October 7, 1996.
CASH COW. By Sander Hicks. October 9, 1996. Director, Frank Licato.
SCHOOLGIRL FIGURE. By Wendy MacLeod. October 21, 1996. Directed by David Petrarca.
MACHINES CRY WOLF. By Wendy MacLeod. October 21, 1996. Directed by David Petrarca.
KING OF COONS. By Michael Henry Brown. October 24, 1996. Director, Gordon Edelstein.
THE HOLE. By Wendy Hammond. October 28, 1996. Director, Vincent Murphy.
RAPID CITY. By Sander Hicks. November 11, 1996. Director, Frank Licato.
WAKING. By Darrah Cloud. November 12, 1996. Director, Stephen Haff.
SEALOVE, MANAGER. By Sander Hicks. November 21, 1996. Director, Richard Eoin Nash-Siedlecki.
IN THE DARK. By Lynne Alvarez. December 4, 1996. Director, Jim Simpson.
THE SECRET MACHINE. By Gordon Dahlquist. December 10, 1996. Director, James Peck.
CHOP SUZIED! Written and directed by Diana Son. January 13, 1997.
TWO GOOD BOYS. By Barry Jay Kaplan. January 13, 1997. Director, Clinton Turner Davis.
THE RIDDLES OF BAMBOO. By Kipp Cheng. January 30, 1997. Director, Rebecca Holderness.
BEDFELLOWS. By Herman Daniel Farrell III. February 3, 1997. Director, Jim Simpson.
DEAD DAY AT CONEY. By Martin McDonagh. February 12, 1997. Director, Gregory Mosher.
THE WORGELT STUDY. By Kate Ryan. March 4, 1997. Director, Stephen Haff.
GIVEN AWAY. By Kate Robin. March 7, 1997. Director, Eduardo Machado.
THE NEXT STOP. By Carmen Rivera. March 13, 1997. Director, Michael John Garces.
THE INTERNET TRILOGY. By Kipp Cheng. March 17, 1997. Director, Damon Kiely.
LES TROIS DUMAS. By Charles Smith. March 24, 1997. Director, Tazewell Thompson.
WHEN NIGHT TURNS DAY. By Edgar Nkosi White. April 11, 1997. Director, Clinton Turner Davis.
SPIRIT DANCING. By Jose Cruz Gonzalez. May 8, 1997. Director, George Ferencz.
EDEN. Book and lyrics, Edgar Nkosi White; music, Gregory Pliska. May 9, 1997. Director, George Ferencz.
BEAUTY IS A RARE THING. By Marion McClinton. May 22, 1997. Director, Keith Glover.
THE APOSTLE'S CREED. By Marion McClinton. May 23, 1997. Director, Clinton Turner Davis.

New Federal Theater. Dedicated to presenting playwrights and plays dealing with the minority and Third World experience. Woodie King Jr. producing director.

JOE TURNER'S COME AND GONE (39). By August Wilson. October 16, 1996. Director, Clinton Turner Davis; scenery, Felix E. Cochren; lighting, Shirley Prendergast; costumes, Vassie Welbeck-Browne; music, Todd Barton. With Peggy Alston, Jerome Preston Bates, Aaron Beener, Chad L. Coleman, Arthur French, Mike Hodge, Joyce Lee, Ron Riley, Kim Yancey Moore.

DO LORD REMEMBER ME (29). By James de Jongh. January 15, 1997. Director, Regge Life; scenery, Kent Hoffman; lighting, Shirley Prendergast; costumes, Vassie Welbeck-Browne. With Barbara Montgomery, Glynn Turman, Chuck Patterson, Roscoe Orman, Ebony Jo-Ann.

THE LAST STREET PLAY (30). By Richard Wesley. April 9, 1997. Director, Thomas Bullard; scenery, Rob Odorisio; lighting, Shirley Prendergast; costumes, Edmond Felix; sound, Tim Schellenbaum. With Chad L. Coleman, Arthur French, Kenn Green, Ella Joyce, Ramon Moses, Gordon T. Skinner, Brian Spivey.

The New Victory Theater. Goal is to introduce young people and families, reflective of New York City's diverse communities, to live performances. Cora Cahan president.

Schedule included:

INTERNATIONAL FESTIVAL OF PUPPET THEATER. September 10–22, 1996. See its entry under Miscellaneous in this section.

THE CROWN OF DESTINY. By Henriette Major, translated by Linda Gaboriau. October 14, 1996. Director, Andre Viens; visual conception, Michel Demers; image design, Marc Mongeau; lighting, Claude Accolas. Puppeteers: Louis Ayotte, Serge Des Lauriers, Pier Dufour, Alain Lavallee, Denise Leprohon, Jacques Trudeau.

On OOB Stages

Above, Stephen Spinella, Juan Carlos Hernandez, Veanne Cox and Zach Grenier in the world premiere of David Rabe's *A Question of Mercy* at New York Theater Workshop; *below,* Shannon Burkett and Michael O'Keefe in the Playwrights Horizons New Theater Wing production of *The Young Girl and the Monsoon* by James Ryan

Left, Everett Quinton in his solo performance of his own adaptation of *Phaedra* at Ridiculous Theater Company

SHARPS, FLATS & ACCIDENTALS. By and with the Flying Karamazov Brothers. December 5, 1996. See its entry in the Plays Produced Off Broadway section of this volume.

THE TWO GENTLEMEN OF VERONA. By William Shakespeare. January 12, 1997. Director, Jack Shepherd; scenery, Jenny Tiramani; costumes, Susan Coates; music, Claire van Kampen. With Mark Rylance, Lennie James, Anastasia Hille, Stephanie Roth, Matthew Scurfield, Jim Bywater, Aicha Kossoko, Ben Walden. Co-produced by Theater for a New Audience and the International Shakespeare Globe Center.

SOFRITO! By David Gonzalez. March 21, 1997. With David Gonzalez, Larry Harlow and the Latin Legends Band.

OLD MAN RIVER (5). By and with Cynthia Gates Fujikawa. April 3, 1997. Director, Beth Schachter.

EXCEPTIONS TO GRAVITY. By and with Avner the Eccentric (Avner Eisenberg). April 17, 1997.

New York Theater Workshop. Produces new theater by American and international artists and encourages risk and stimulates experimentation in theatrical form. James C. Nicola artistic director, Nancy Kassak Diekmann managing director.

VIEW OF THE DOME (38). By Theresa Rybeck. September 13, 1996. Director, Michael Mayer; scenery, Neil Patel; lighting, Frances Aronson; costumes, Michael Krass; sound, Darron L. West. With Jim Abele, Patrick Breen, Candy Buckley, Tom Riis Farrell, Julia Gibson, Dion Graham, Richard Poe.

O SOLO MIO FESTIVAL: SO ... IT'S COME TO THIS and EMMETT: A ONE-MORMON SHOW (monologues) by and with Emmett Foster, directed by Kirk Jackson; MONSTER by and with Dael Orlandersmith, directed by Peter Askin. October 31, 1996-January 19, 1997. Scenery, Mark Wendland; lighting, Matthew Frey; costumes, Paul Tazewell; sound, Red Ramona.

A QUESTION OF MERCY (51). By David Rabe, based on Richard Selzer's essay. February 7, 1997. Director, Douglas Hughes; scenery, Neil Patel; lighting, Michael Chybowski; costumes, Jess Goldstein; music and sound, David Van Tieghem. With Zach Grenier, Stephen Spinella, Juan Carlos Hernandez, Michael Kell, Veanne Cox, Doc Dougherty, Christopher Burns.

THE DEVILS (38). By Elizabeth Egloff, adapted from Dostoyevsky's novel. May 2, 1997, Director, Garland Wright; scenery, Douglas Stein; lighting, James F. Ingalls; costumes, Susan Hilferty; sound, David Van Tieghem. With Michael Arkin, Bill Camp, Lynn Cohen, James Colby, Randy Danson, Patrice Johnson, Patrick Kerr, Christopher McCann, Boris McGiver, Denis O'Hare, Daniel Oreskes, Nathalie Paulding, Frank Raiter, Kali Rocha, Ray Anthony Thomas.

Pan Asian Repertory Theater. Celebrates and provides opportunities for Asian American artists to perform under the highest professional standards and to create and promote plays by and about Asians and Asian Americans. Tisa Chang artistic/producing director.

THE INNOCENCE OF GHOSTS (28). By Rosanna Staffa. October 18, 1996. Director, Peter C. Brosius; scenery, Myung Hee Cho; lighting, Victor En Yu Tan; costumes, Sang-Jin Lee; sound, Peter Griggs. With Anney Giobbe, Tina Chen, Mel Duane Gionson, Emi Kikuchi.

SLANT PERFORMANCE GROUP (14). By and with Richard Ebihara, Wayland Quintero, Perry Yung. November 13, 1996. Lighting, Richard Schaefer.

SHANGHAI LIL'S (22). Book and lyrics, Lilah Kan; music, Louis Stewart. April 25, 1997. Direction and choreography, Tisa Chang; scenery, Robert Klingelhoefer; lighting, Stephen Petrill; costumes, Terry Leong. With Steven Eng, Jeanne Sakata, Mimosa, Timothy Huang, Emy Coligado, Maria E. Aggabado, Susan Ancheta, Matt Hyland.

Playwrights Horizons New Theater Wing. Full productions of new works, in addition to the regular off-Broadway productions. Tim Sanford artistic director.

DEMONOLOGY (9). By Kelly Stuart. November 10, 1996. Director, Jim Simpson; scenery, David Harwell; lighting, Anne M. Padien; costumes, Therese Bruck; sound, Michael Clark; music, Mike Nolan. With Marisa Tomei, Rocco Sisto, Bray Poor, Kathleen Glaudini.

THE YOUNG GIRL AND THE MONSOON (9). By James Ryan. April 27, 1997. Director, William Carden; scenery, David Harwell; lighting Chris Dallos; costumes, Therese Bruck; sound, Bruce Ellman. With Michael O'Keefe, Shannon Burkett, Susan Floyd, Saundra Santiago, Todd Gearhart, Marilyn Chris.

Staged Readings:

BLACK INK (plays from the African-American Playwrights Unit): LOST CREEK TOWNSHIP by Charlotte A. Gibson, directed by Liz Diamond; EASTVILLE by Ellen Lewis, directed by Benny Sato Ambush; LAS MENINAS by Lynn Nottage, directed by Daniela Varon; SUGAR book inspired by Jean Toomer's novel, *Cane,* lyrics and direction, Ed DuRante; music, Miriam Daly. March 3–17, 1997.

Primary Stages Company. Dedicated to new American plays by new American playwrights. Casey Childs artistic director, Margaret Chandler general manager, Janet Reed associate artistic director, Seth Gordon associate producer.

MISSING/KISSING: MISSING MARISA and KISSING CHRISTINE (one-act plays) (41). Written and directed by John Patrick Shanley. October 17, 1996. Scenery, Brad Stokes; lighting, Brian Nason; costumes, Laura Cunningham; music and sound, David Van Tieghem. With Daniel Oreskes, Jake Weber, Laura Hughes, Reiko Aylesworth.

NIGHTMARE ALLEY (15). Based on William Gresham's novel; book, music and lyrics, Jonathan Brielle; additional conceptualization, Larry Kornfeld. November 16, 1996. Direction and choreography, Danny Herman; scenery, Michael Hotopp; lighting, Gene Lenahan; costumes, Catherine Zuber; musical direction, Phil Reno. With Willy Falk, Silvia Aruj, Carolyn Campbell, Victoria Cave, Vicki Frederick, Nick Jolley, Nancy Lemenager, Sarah Litzsinger, Jonas Moscartolo, Ken Prymus, Evan Thompson. Co-produced by The Directors Company.

SECOND-HAND SMOKE (34). By Mac Wellman. January 16, 1997. Director, Richard Caliban; scenery, Kyle Chepulis; lighting, Brian Aldous; costumes, Anita Yavich; sound, Mike Nolan. With Joanna Adler, Frank Deal, Kristen Dispaltro, Vera Farmiga, David Greenspan, David Patrick Kelly, Kristine Nielsen, Matt Servitto.

NOT WAVING (34). By Gen LeRoy. March 5, 1997. Director, Chris Smith; scenery, Tony Walton; lighting, Michael Lincoln; costumes, Sharon Sprague; sound, Randy Freed. With Kyra Sedgwick, Sloane Shelton, Nancy Jo Carpenter, Tim Michael.

HATE MAIL (34). By Bill Corbett and Kira Obolensky. April 2, 1997. Director, Seth Gordon; scenery, Brian Whitehill; lighting, Deborah Constantine; music and sound, David Van Tieghem. With Joanna Adler, Nathan Smith.

MERE MORTALS AND OTHERS: FOREPLAY OR: THE ART OF THE FUGUE, MERE MORTALS, TIME FLIES, SPEED-THE-PLAY, DR. FRITZ OR: THE FORCES OF LIGHT and DEGAS, C'EST MOI (short plays) (75 +). By David Ives. May 6, 1997. Director, John Rando; scenery, Russell Metheny; lighting, Phil Monat; costumes, Anita Yavich; sound, Aural Fixation. With Arnie Burton, Jessalyn Gilsig, Nancy Opel, Anne O'Sullivan, Willis Sparks, Danton Stone.

Puerto Rican Traveling Theater. Professional company presenting bilingual productions primarily of Puerto Rican and Hispanic playwrights, emphasizing subjects of relevance today. Miriam Colon founder and producer.

Schedule included:

THE BLACKOUT. By Jose Luis Gonzalez, adapted and directed by Rosario Rolon. August 1, 1996.

TO CATCH THE LIGHTNING. By Carmen Rivera. May 22, 1997. Director, Max Ferra. With Johnny Sanchez, Marilyn Seri.

The Ridiculous Theatrical Company. The late Charles Ludlam's comedic troupe devoted to productions of his original scripts and new works in his style. Everett Quinton artistic director, Adele Bove managing director.

PHAEDRA (39). Adapted from Jean Racine's play and performed by Everett Quinton. July 28, 1996. Director, Bill Nobes; scenery, Rue Catorz; lighting, Cordelia Aitkin; costumes, Larry McLeon.

CORN (40). Book, Charles Ludlam; music and lyrics, Virgil Young. April 15, 1997. Director, Everett Quinton; scenery, Garry Hayes; lighting, Richard Currie; costumes, Ramona Ponce; musical direction, Lance Cruce. With Eureka, Everett Quinton, Lisa Herbold, Christa Kirby, Randy Lake, Stephen Pell, Lenys Sama, Jimmy Szczepanek, Charlie Schroeder.

Signature Theater Company. Dedicated to the exploration of a playwright's body of work. James Houghton artistic director, Thomas C. Proehl managing director.

WHEN THE WORLD WAS GREEN (A CHEF'S FABLE). By Sam Shepard and Joseph Chaikin; director, Joseph Chaikin; scenery, Christine Jones; lighting, Beverly Emmons; costumes, Mary Brecht; music, Woody Regan. With Alvin Epstein, Amie Quigley, Woody Regan. CHICAGO. By Sam Shepard; director, Joseph Chaikin; scenery, E. David Cosier; lighting, Beverly Emmons; costumes, Teresa Snider-Stein; sound, Red Ramona. With Wayne Maugans, Leslie Silva. (one-act plays) (39). November 7, 1996.

TOOTH OF CRIME (SECOND DANCE). By Sam Shepard. December 23, 1996. Co-produced with Second Stage Theater; see its entry in the Plays Produced Off Broadway section of this volume.

THE SAD LAMENT OF PECOS BILL ON THE EVE OF KILLING HIS WIFE, KILLER'S HEAD and ACTION (one-act plays) (42). By Sam Shepard. February 9, 1997. Director, Darrell Larson; scenery, E. David Cosier; lighting, Jeffrey S. Koger; costumes, Teresa Snider-Stein; sound, Red Ramona; music, Loren Toolajian. With Debbon Ayer, Julie Christensen, John Diehl, Romain Frugé, Tanya Gingerich, Bruce MacVittie, Jamey Sheridan, Scott Glenn, Dermot Mulroney, Bill Pullman.

CURSE OF THE STARVING CLASS (35). By Sam Shepard. April 27, 1997. Director, James Houghton; scenery, E. David Cosier; lighting, Jeffrey S. Koger; costumes, Teresa Snider-Stein; sound, Red Ramona. With Paul Dawson, Deborah Hedwall, Gretchen Cleevely, Darrell Larson, Jude Ciccolella, Jack R. Marks, Kevin Carrigan, Clark Middleton, Joe Caruso.

Soho Rep. Dedicated to new and avant-garde American playwrights. Julian Webber artistic director, Lisa Portes associate director.

A DEVIL INSIDE (19). By David Lindsay Abaire. January 8, 1997. Director, Julian Webber; scenery, Molly Hughes. With Larry Block, Marylouise Burke, Bill Dawes, Heather Goldenhirsh, John McAdams, Pamela Nyberg.

2.5 MINUTE RIDE (12). By and with Lisa Kron. April 2, 1997.

Theater for the New City. Developmental theater and new American experimental works. Crystal Field executive director.

Schedule included:

WERK (2). Conceived and directed by Joanna Sherman; written by Joanna Sherman and Luanne Dietrich, Michael McGuigan, Carvell Wallace, Bruce Williamson, Sima Wolf. July 27, 1996. Choreography, Mayra Carrion, Blake Montgomery; scenery, Joanna Sherman, Michael McGuigan; lighting, Theresa Gonzalez; costumes, Gabriella Simon, Anna Kiraly; sound, Michael McGuigan; music, Bruce Williamson, Sima Wolf. With Bond Street Theater.

PHAEDRA. Adapted from Racine's play and performed by Everett Quinton. July 28, 1996. See its entry under Ridiculous Theatrical Company in this section.

IT'S TOAST (13). Book, lyrics and direction, Crystal Field; music, Christopher Cherney. August 3, 1996. Scenery, Anthony Angel; costumes, Seth Hanson; masks, Pamela Mayo; sound, Paul Garrity.

With Joseph C. Davies, Crystal Field, Jerry Jaffe, Terry Lee King, Mark Marcante, Craig Meade, Cheryl Gadsden, Michael-David Gordon.

AMEENA SHUNDARI (9). Adaptation, music and direction, S.M. Solaiman. August 9, 1996. Scenery, A.K. Babul Chowdhury; lighting, Jude Domski, Ben Clemens, Faisal; costumes, Mirazi Abed. With Tanveer Alam Sajeeb, S.M. Solaiman, Lizi Rahman, Swapna Kawsar, Shamsoddoula Shiplu, Jharna Choudhury, Mohammed Fazlul Kabir, Sultan Mahmud, Homaira Khandakar, Shamim Mamun.

BEATA, THE POPE'S DAUGHTER. By Mario Fratti. September 5, 1996. Director, Vera Beren; scenery, Mark Symczak; lighting, Stewart Wagner. With Dominic Chianese, Seana Kofoed, Gene Silvers, Mary Carol Johnson, Peter Johl, James Kohli, Peter Lucas.

ON THE BLOCK (musical revue). Book, Donald Arrington and Camille Tibaldeo; music and lyrics, Donald Arrington. September 12, 1996. Directed and performed by Donald Arrington and Camille Tibaldeo.

MATTERS OF LOVE, LIFE AND DEATH: COASTAL COMPLEXES by Richard West; BILL'S WINDOW by Jon Spano; THE STREET KAT'S SONG by Susan Mitchell; TIME IT IS by Lissa Moira (one-act plays). September 26, 1996. Director, Lissa Moira. With Steven Field, Jon Spano, Richard West, Susan Mitchell, Mark Hamlet, Lissa Moira.

FLIPZOIDS. By Ralph Pena. September 30, 1996. Director, Loy Arcenas; lighting, Blake Burba; sound and music, Fabian Obispo. With Mia Katigbak, Ken Leung, Ching Valdes-Aran.

SPICE OF BENGAL (12). By Bina Sharif. October 3, 1996. Director, Franco M. D'Alessandro; lighting, Chris Lee. With Kevin Mitchell Martin, Samia Shoaib, Bina Sharif.

MOVERS AND SHAKERS. Written and directed by Frank Biancamano. November 7, 1996. Lighting, Ian Gordon; costumes, Mary Marsicano. With Kathleen Gates, Jess Hanks, David Ige, Jerry Jaffe, Martin Rudy, Antonia Stout, Ari Tomais, T.D. White.

G.A.F.F. (GATHERING AUTOMOTIVE FACTS FOR THE FUTURE). By Faisal Aneem. November 14, 1996. Director, Jean-Paul Mulero. With Faisal Aneem, Jenifer Bass, Fazlul Kabir, Alex Lyres, Bud Courtney, Tom Belluci, Aks Khan, Jean-Paul Mulero.

MONOGRAMS. By Susan Mach. December 12, 1996. Director, Crystal Field; scenery, Donald L. Brooks; lighting, Ian Gordon; costumes, Seth Hanson; sound, Paul Garrity; music, David Tice. With Kitty Lunn, Mark Marcante, Andy Reynolds, Laura Wickens.

DIG OR FLY. By The Pig Iron Theater Company (Gabriel Quinn Bauriedel, Solveig Holum, Julia Humphreys, Dan Rothenberg, Dito van Reigersberg, Telory Williamson). January 2, 1997. Director, Dan Rothenberg; scenery, Gabriel Quinn Bauriedel; lighting, Jeffrey Sugg; costumes, Cory Lippiello. With Gabriel Quinn Bauriedel, Solveig Holum, Dito van Reigersberg, Telory Williamson.

MOCK TRIAL. Written and directed by Romulus Linney. January 16, 1997. Scenery, Mark Marcante; lighting, Arjan Smook; costumes, Allison Ronis. With Heather Robinson, Christopher Cappiello, Nancy Joyce Simmons, John-Martin Green, Christopher Roberts, Dave Johnson, Anthony Pick.

HALF OFF. By Harry Kondoleon. January 23, 1997. Director, Tom Gladwell; scenery, Donald L. Brooks. With Crystal Field, Larry Fleischman, Melissa Hurst, Andy Reynolds, Stephen Sinclair, Laura Wickens.

PIPE DREAMS by Ira L. Jeffries, directed by David Sheppard; QUEEN OF CARNIVAL and FATHER NEW ORLEANS by Robert Kornfeld, directed by James DePaul (one-act plays). January 23, 1997. Lighting, Ian Gordon; sound, J.M. Wilson. With Robert Hatcher, Dominic Marcus, Cheryl McClendon, Primy Rivera, Molly Hayner, Daniel Rappaport.

THE BEST SEX OF THE XX CENTURY SALE. By Lissa Moira and Richard West. February 6, 1997. Director, Lissa Moira. With Colleen Crawford, Cynthia DeMoss, Patrick Duran, Glenn Healey, Ivy Levinson, Lissa Moira, Honor Moor, Eric R. Moreland, Tracey Rooney, David Salper, Stephen Singer, Jason Watkins, Pamela G. Weis, Richard West.

WHITHER THOU GOEST. Written and directed by Barbara Kahn. February 27, 1997. Scenery, Beverly Bronson; lighting, D.M. Wood; costumes, Andy Wallach. With Jolie Dechev, Jackie S. Freeman, Karen Klebbe, Gary Lamadore.

POET IN NEW YORK. By and with Dito van Reigersberg. March 6, 1997. Director, Dan Rothenberg; scenery, lighting and video, Jeffrey Sugg.

LIFE KNOCKS. By Tom Attea. March 20, 1997. Director, Mark Marcante; scenery, Tony Angel; lighting, Arjan Smook. With Amy de Lucia, Mark Marcante, Craig Meade, E.J. Morrison, Jocelyn Ruggiero.

THE INFERNO (A DETECTIVE STORY). Written and directed by Pavol Liska. March 20, 1997. Choreography, D.D. Dorvillier, Victoria Lepori and Julie Atlas Muz; lighting, Peter Nigrini; costumes, Jocelyn Worrall; sound, Scott Mascena. With Marcia Stephanie Blake, Kelly Copper, Marc Dale, D.D. Dorvillier, Bent Kite, Victoria Lepori, Julie Atlas Muz, Holden Toplin.

THE AMERICAN SLEEP (WITH WAKE-UP SERVICE). By and with Bread and Puppet Theater. March 28, 1997.

OUT ON THE EDGE FESTIVAL OF LESBIAN AND GAY THEATER: OF THAT WHICH MAKES HORSE RACINGS by Suzanne Zuckerman, directed by Melanie Sutherland; MOTHER FATHER GAY SON by Mike Teele, directed by Sue Lawless; RITE OF PASSAGE by Paul MacWhorter, directed by Jim Dowd; MY NAME IS . . . by Dasha Snyder, directed by Nela Wagman (one-act plays); HENRY'S BRIDGE by Benjamin Marshall, directed by Randy Gener; ALREADY SEEN by Jannett Bailey, directed by Clinton Turner Davis. April 16–27, 1997. With Peggy Allston, Debbon Ayer, Michael Babin, Brad Beyer, Jennifer Bill, Kathleen Butler, Lee Dobson, Wendi Franklyn, John Holt, Michael Latshaw, Joyce Lee, Dominic Marcos, Andreas Neidermeier, Stephen Nisbet, Maxine Prescott, Paola Renzi, Ron Riley, Cheryl Rogers, Rebecca Waxman.

CAPRICHOS. Conceived and directed by David Willinger. May 1, 1997. Choreography, Michael Vazquez; scenery, Ron Burns; lighting, Joe Saint; costumes, Paula Inocent. With Marianne Bailey, Nisha Beech, Amanda Hargrove, Mikael Huuska, Aixa Kendrick, Yeara Milton, Kimberley Myles, Magnus Percinthe, Matthew Reese, Luz Vallejo, Irma Vasquez, Khary Senghor Wilson.

LOTION written and directed by Liana Rosario; INSTANT CASH written and directed by Peter Arbour (one-act plays). May 1, 1997.

WE ARE PATRIOTS WITH DARK FACES. By and with Jose Torres Tama. May 1, 1997.

POSTMODERN MIRACLE PLAYS. By Walter Corwin. May 10, 1997. Director, Yuji Takematsu.

Ubu Repertory Theater. Committed to acquainting American audiences with new works by contemporary French-speaking playwrights from around the world in English translations. Francoise Kourilsky artistic director.

ALWAYS TOGETHER by Anca Visdei reopened June 11, 1996.

LADY STRASS (21). By Eduardo Manet, translated by Phyllis Zatlin. October 1, 1996. Director, Andre Ernotte; scenery, Watoku Ueno; lighting, Greg MacPherson; costumes, Carol Ann Pelletier; sound, Robert Gould. With Susanne Wasson, Robert Jimenez, Paul Albe.

CROSSCURRENTS (21). By Gerty Dambury, translated by Richard Philcox. March 4, 1997. Director, Francoise Kourilsky; scenery, Watoku Ueno; lighting, Greg MacPherson; costumes, Carol Ann Pelletier. With La Tonya Borsay, Assif Mandvi, Bryan Hicks, Bina Sharif, Kavitha Ramachandran, Jay Palit.

The Vineyard Theater. Multi-art chamber theater dedicated to the development of new plays and musicals, music-theater collaborations and innovative revivals. Douglas Aibel artistic director, Barbara Zinn Krieger executive director, Jon Nakagawa managing director.

THE WAITING ROOM (40). By Lisa Loomer. October 31, 1996. Director, David Schweizer; scenery, G.W. Mercier; lighting, Peter Kaczorowski; costumes, Gail Brassard; sound, Darron L. West. With Veanne Cox, June Kyoko Lu, Chloe Webb, Byron Jennings, Damian Young, Lou Liberatore, William Langan, James Saito, Michele Shay, Dylan Grewan, Mike Toto.

HOW I LEARNED TO DRIVE (48). By Paula Vogel. March 16, 1997. Director, Mark Brokaw; scenery, Narelle Sissons; lighting, Mark McCullough; costumes, Jess Goldstein; sound, David Van Tieghem. With Mary-Louise Parker, David Morse, Michael Showalter, Johanna Day, Kerry O'Malley. Also see its entry in the Plays Produced Off Broadway section of this volume.

...IATURE THEATER COMPANY—Per-
...rs in a season of works by Sam Shepard in-
...d *(above)* Julie Christensen and Romain
... in a scene from the musical *The Sad Lament*
...*cos Bill on the Eve of Killing His Wife* (with
... by Loren Toolajian) and *(at right)* Alvin Ep-
...in the New York premiere of *When the World*
...*Green (A Chef's Fable)* co-authored and di-
...d by Joseph Chaikin

YOU DON'T MISS THE WATER (25). Text, Cornelius Eady; music, Deidre Murray. June 6, 1997. Produced in association with Music-Theater Group; see its entry in that listing in this section.

Lab production:
MY MARRIAGE TO ERNEST BORGNINE (25). By Nicky Silver. April 24, 1997. Director, David Warren. With J. Smith-Cameron, Mary McCormack, Mark Blum, Adam LeFevre, James Van Der Beek.

The Women's Project and Productions. Nurtures, develops and produces plays written and directed by women. Julia Miles founder and artistic director.

TERRA INCOGNITA. Libretto, lyrics and direction, Maria Irene Fornes; music, Roberto Sierra. March 26, 1997. Co-produced by INTAR; see its entry in that listing in this section.

UNDER A WESTERN SKY. By Amparo Garcia. May 1, 1997. Director, Loretta Greco; scenery, Christine Jones; lighting, Kevin Adams; costumes, Kaye Voyce; music and sound, David Van Tieghem. With Irma Bello, Gilbert Cruz, Sol Miranda, Felix Solis.

WPA Theater. Produces new American plays and neglected American classics in the realistic idiom. Kyle Renick artistic director, Lori Sherman managing director.

THE RED DEVIL BATTERY SIGN (38). By Tennessee Williams. November 13, 1996. Director, Michael Wilson; scenery, Jeff Cowie; lighting, Michael Lincoln; costumes, David C. Woolard; music and sound, John Gromada. With Elizabeth Ashley, James Victor, William Devine, Annette Cardona, Stephen Mendillo, Angelica Torn.

FLIPPING MY WIG (48). By and with Charles Busch. December 19, 1996. Director, Kenneth Elliott; scenery, B.T. Whitehill; lighting, Michael Lincoln; costumes, Robert Legere; sound, John Kilgore.

ON HOUSE (35). By Kevin Heelan. April 2, 1997. Director, Constance Grappo; scenery, Anne C. Patterson; lighting, Jack Mehler; costumes, Angelina Avallone; music and sound, Robert C. Cotnoir. With Ron Domingo, Christopher Duva, Ken Garito, Tristine Skyler, Trish McCall, Lance Reddick, Lewis Merkin.

FAIRY TALES (musical revue) (40). Music and lyrics, Eric Lane Barnes. June 3, 1997. Director, Mark Cannistraro; choreography, Jackson McDorman; scenery, Hugh Walton; lighting, Jack Mehler; costumes, Jennifer Kenyon; musical direction, Daniel Harris. With Keith Anderson, Valerie Hill, Stephen Hope, Rob Maitner, Stephanie McClaine.

York Theater Company. Specializing in producing new works, as well as in reviving unusual, forgotten or avant-garde musicals. Janet Hayes Walker founding artistic director, James Morgan artistic director.

NO WAY TO TREAT A LADY (42). Book, music and lyrics, Douglas J. Cohen, based on William Goldman's novel. December 22, 1996. Director, Scott Schwartz; choreography, Daniel Stewart; scenery, James Morgan; lighting, Mary Jo Dondlinger; costumes, Yvonne De Moravia; sound, Jim van Bergen; musical direction, Wendy Bobbitt. With Adam Grupper, Alix Korey, Marguerite MacIntyre, Paul Schoeffler.

THE LAST SWEET DAYS (15). Book and lyrics, Gretchen Cryer; music, Nancy Ford. April 6, 1997. Director, Worth Gardner; scenery, James Morgan; lighting, Kirk Bookman; costumes, Jonathan Bixby; sound, David Gotwald. With Willy Falk, Ellen Foley, Ellen Sowney, Romain Fruge.

Miscellaneous

In the additional listing of 1996–97 off-off-Broadway productions below, the names of the producing groups or theaters appear in CAPITAL LETTERS and the titles of the works in *italics*. This list consists largely of new or reconstituted works. It includes a few productions staged by groups which rented space from the more established organizations listed previously.

THE ACTORS COMPANY THEATER. *Heartbreak House* by George Bernard Shaw. October 7, 1996. Directed by Scott Alan Evans; with Larry Keith, Delphi Harrington, Lynn Vogt, Tari Signor, John Cunningham, James Murtaugh, David Staller, Gregory Salata, Nora Chester, Charles Antalosky, Jason Culp. *Three Men on a Horse* by John Cecil Holm and George Abbott. November 18, 1996. Directed by Scott Alan Evans; with Lyn Wright, Greg McFadden, Gregory Salata, James Murtaugh, Cynthia Darlow, Michael Goz, Harry Murphy, John Plumpis, Bradford Cover, Jo-Ann Salata, Eric Martin Brown, Tom Stewart. *The Cocktail Party* by T.S. Eliot. January 27, 1997. Directed by Scott Alan Evans; with Simon Jones, Paul Hecht, Cynthia Harris, Francesca Di Mauro, Larry Keith, Maia Danziger, Simon Billig, Jo-Ann Salata, Scott Schafer, Gregory Salata. *Tiger at the Gates* by Jean Giraudoux. March 17, 1997. Directed by Amy Saltz; with Gregory Salata, Francesca Di Mauro, Laura Hughes, Joan Buddenhagen, Delphi Harrington, Bradford Cover, Joseph Bova, Paul Hecht, James Murtaugh, Richard Adrian Dorr, Jackie Angelescu, Todd Kozan, Scott Schafer, William Wise, Scott Robinowitz, Greg McFadden. *The Matchmaker* by Thornton Wilder. May 5, 1997. Directed by Scott Alan Evans; with Cynthia Harris, James Murtaugh, David Staller, Scott Schafer, Maia Danziger, Eve Michelson, Lyn Wright, Kevin Isola, Gregory Salata, Delphi Harrington, Greg McFadden, Ivar Brogger, Joyce Reehling, Jo-Ann Salata, David Edward Jones.

ACTORS STUDIO FREE THEATER. *Major Crimes* by Jay Presson Allen. February 26, 1997.

ADOBE THEATER COMPANY. *Possible Worlds* by John Mighton. August 7, 1996. Directed by Jeremy Dobrish; with Arthur Aulisi, Kathryn Langwell. *Notions in Motion* adapted from Luigi Pirandello's *Each in His Own Way* and directed by Jeremy Dobrish. May 28, 1997. With Arthur Aulisi, Kathryn Langwell, Adam Nelson, Henry Caplan, Stacy Leigh Ivey, Gregory Jackson, Erin Quinn Purcell, Josh Manson, Beau Ruland, Jay Rosenbloom.

AFRICA ARTS THEATER COMPANY. *Paradise Is Closing Down* by Pieter-Dirk Uys. November 11, 1996. Directed by George Ferencz; with Margie Rynn, Jacqueline Pennington, Louise Martin, Kevin Mambo.

ALL SOULS PLAYERS. *On the Road to Victory!* (musical revue) written and directed by Michael Tester. March 7, 1997.

ALTERED STAGES THEATER. *Earth, Wind* and *Fire* (one-act plays) written and directed by John Ganci. July 18, 1996. *Eating Crow* by Jack Groverland. January 9, 1997. *Seeing Things* by Michael Boodro. February 5, 1997. Directed by John Norris; with John Himmel, Robert Zaleski, Peter Calandra.

ARC LIGHT THEATER. *Miss Julie* by August Strindberg, adapted by Ingmar Bergman. April 30, 1997. Directed by John Strasberg.

THE BARROW GROUP. *Good* by C.P. Taylor. June 9, 1996. Directed by Seth Barrish; with Aaron Goodwin, Vera Farmiga, Jen Jones, Stephen Singer, Ava-Maria Carnevale, Peter Eldridge.

BEACON THEATER. *Your Arms Too Short to Box With God* adapted from the Gospel of St. Matthew and directed by Vinnette Carroll; music and lyrics by Alex Bradford and Micki Grant. June, 1996. With Stephanie Mills, Teddy Pendergrass, BeBe Winans, Raquelle Chavis, Aubrey Lynch, Derrock Minter. *The Sequel—It Ain't Over* by Doug Smith and Helen Smith. January 28, 1997. Directed by Douglas Knyght-Smith; with Millie Jackson, Douglas Knyght-Smith, Al Goodman, Antonio Fargas, Keisha Jackson.

BILLIE HOLIDAY THEATER. *In My Father's House* by Samm-Art Williams. July 1, 1996. Directed by Walter Dallas; with Peggy Alston, Charles Weldon, Kim Sullivan, Amani Gethers.

BLUE LIGHT THEATER COMPANY. *The Two Gentlemen of Verona* by William Shakespeare. February 23, 1997. Directed by Dylan Baker; with Greg Naughton, Talmadge Lowe, Camilia Sanes, Vivienne Benesch, Molly Regan, Joe Grifasi, Larry Nathanson, Matthew Saldivar. *Waiting for Lefty* by Clifford Odets. April 27, 1997. Directed by Joanne Woodward; with Marisa Tomei, Greg Naughton, Alex Draper, Lee Wilkof, P.J. Brown.

CENTER STAGE. *Come in From the Rain* by David Mauriello. June 9, 1996. Directed by Mark Harborth; with Eric Martin Brown, John Gasdaska, Russell Elder. Reopened October 9, 1996 with Joe Heffernan, Russell Elder.

CHAIN LIGHTNING THEATER. *To Moscow* by Karen Sunde. October 6, 1996. Directed by Steve Deighan; with Carol Emshoff, Ginger Grace, Brandee Graff, Kricker James, Blainie Logan, Gregory Seel.

CHELSEA PLAYHOUSE. *Senseless* by and with Gilgamesh Theater Group. October 12, 1996. Directed by Ralph Buckley.

CREATIVE PLACE. *It Begins With a Kiss . . .* (one-act plays) written and directed by Sammy Busby. September 13, 1996. With Elena Aaron, Jodi Barmash, Tom Berdik, Sammy Busby, Jenna Kellard, Luke Sabis. Reopened March 7, 1997 with Sammy Busby, Marilyn Torres.

CURRICAN THEATER. *Recreation* by Penn Jillette. October 17, 1996. *Hunting Humans* by Richard Thompson. November 22, 1996. Directed by Mike Wills; with Dean Bradshaw, Todd Butera, Jeffrey Dewhurst, Andrew Miller, Rob Leo Roy. *Hysterical Blindness* by Laura Cahill. February 11, 1997. Directed by Jared Harris; with Jill Larson, Jenny Robertson, Amy Ryan, Bill Sage, Tim Williams, William Wise. *The Last Session* book by Jim Brochu; music and lyrics by Steve Schalchlin. May 8, 1997. Directed by Mike Wills; with Bob Stillman, Grace Garland, Amy Coleman, Stephen Bienskie.

DIXON PLACE. *So . . . It's Come to This* by and with Emmett Foster. June 7, 1996. *The Tall Blonde Woman in the Short Puerto Rican Body* by and with Alba Sanchez. September 21, 1996. *Coyotes in Hell's Kitchen* by and with Seth Jones. January 10, 1997. Directed by Rob Barron. *Animal Instincts, Tales of Flesh and Tales of Blood* by and with Rae C. Wright. April 3, 1997.

DO GOODER PRODUCTIONS. *On Deaf Ears* by Robin Rothstein. December 18, 1996. Directed by John Ruocco; with Rosemary Prinz, Chevi Colton, Gil Rogers, Susan Finch, Dana Smith, Richard Sheinmel, Mark Robert Gordon.

THE DRAMA DEPT. *Kingdom of Earth* by Tennessee Williams. June 15, 1996. Directed by John Cameron Mitchell; with Cynthia Nixon, Tom Lacy, Scott Lawrence, Peter Sarsgaard, Allen Durgin, D. Scott Eads. *June Moon* by Ring Lardner and George S. Kaufman; music and lyrics by Ring Lardner. January 8, 1997. Directed by Mark Nelson; with Cynthia Nixon, Becky Ann Baker, Albert Macklin, Robert Joy, Geoffrey Nauffts, Stacy Highsmith, Amy Hohn, Robert Lamont, Peter Jacobson, Robert Ari. *As Bees in Honey Drown* by Douglas Carter Beane. June 5, 1997. Directed by Mark Brokaw. With Josh Hamilton, J. Smith-Cameron.

EXPANDED ARTS. *Beirut* by Alan Bowne. February 5, 1997. Directed by Deloss Brown; with Michael Laurence, Jenny Maguire, Jeremy Johnson.

FOUNDRY THEATER. *You Say What I Mean but What You Mean Is Not What I Said* conceived and composed by Grisha Coleman. January 19, 1997. Directed by Talvin Wilks; with Helga Davis, Ching Gonzalez, Ezra Knight, David Thomson, Grisha Coleman.

FOURTH STREET THEATER. *Touch My Face* written and directed by Jan Jalenak. May 15, 1997. With Nancy McDoniel, Matthew Rauch, Amy Hart Redford, Timothi-Jane Graham, Charle Landry, Deirdre Lewis.

FREESTYLE REPERTORY THEATER. *Innovations, Theatersports, Chameleons, Emilio Buckett's Traveling Tarot Review.* March 7, 1997.

GALATEA. *The Husband's Revenge* by Ashley Smith and *How He Lied to Her Husband* by George Bernard Shaw. September 27, 1996.

GREENWICH ST. THEATER. *Nellie* book by Bernice Lee; music by Jaz Dorsey; lyrics by Bernice Lee and Jaz Dorsey. May 22, 1997. Directed by Scott Pegg; with Jeanine Serralles, Garrison Phillips.

GROVE ST. PLAYHOUSE. *Heavenly Days* by John Glines. June 12, 1996. Directed by Peter Pope. *Death in a Landslide* by Jay Martel. October 6, 1996. Directed by Kirk Jackson; with Joseph McKenna, Chuck Montgomery. *Whiplash: A Tale of a Tomboy* by and with Shelly Mars. January 15, 1997. Directed by Janice Deaner.

HAMLET OF BANK ST. THEATER. *Origin of the Species* by Robert Weston Ackerman. December 4, 1996.

HERE. *The Vagina Monologues* by and with Eve Ensler. October 16, 1996. *Ourselves Alone* by Anne Devlin. April 26, 1997. Directed by Veronica Young; with Sasha Durcan, Jacqueline Kealy, Gilli Foss, James Hanlon, Edward Tully, Michael Reilly, Tim Mitchell, Greg O'Donovan.

HOMEGROWN THEATER. *Sun Flower* by and with Elizabeth Perry. September 26, 1996.

INTERART THEATER. *O Wholly Night and Other Jewish Solecisms* by and with Deb Margolin. August 12, 1996. Directed by Margot Lewitin.

INTERBOROUGH REPERTORY THEATER. *Noises Off!* by Michael Frayn. December 28, 1996. Directed by Tim Chamberlain.

INTERNATIONAL FESTIVAL OF PUPPET THEATER. Schedule included *Gesell Chamber* by El Periferico de Objetos; *Twin Houses* conceived and performed by Nicole Mossoux, directed by Patrick Bonte; *Moby Dick in Venice* by Roman Paska and Theater for the Birds, co-produced by Music-Theater Group; *Peter and Wendy* by Liza Lurwin, adapted from J.M. Barrie's novel, directed by Lee Breuer, music by Johnny Cunningham, lighting and puppets by Julie Archer; *The Araneidae Show* by Basil Twist; *Soup Talk I: Voice of the Turtledove* and *Soup Talk II: Voice of the Hollow Man* by Warner Blake; *The Caucasian Chalk Circle* by Eric Bass, adapted from Bertolt Brecht's play, with the Sandglass Theater; *Erotec: The Human Life of Machines* by Alice Farley and Henry Threadgill; *The Repugnant Story of Clotario Demoniax* by Hugo Hiriart, directed by Pablo Cueto, puppets by Mireya Cueto and Pablo Cueto, with Teatro Tinglado; *The Baroque Opera* by the Forman Brothers (Matej and Petr Forman); *Ubu Roi* by Alfred Jarry, adapted and performed by Hystopolis Productions; *Piskanderdula* by Frantisek and Vera (Ricarova); *Evidence of Floods* by Janie Geiser and Company; *Nightingale* conceived by John Farrell and Carol Farrell, music by Andrea Goodman, with Figures of Speech Theater; *Sunjata* by Amoros and Augustin and Ki-Yi Mbock Theater; *Frank Einstein* by Green Ginger; *Puppets, Music*

JUDITH ANDERSON THEATER—Francie Swift and Maria Tucci in a scene from the world premiere of *Marking* by Patrick Breen

and the Unexpected by Bernd Ogrodnik and Alchemilla Puppetworks; *A Rare Performance* by Michael Lindsay Simpson and Evolve Productions; *Rapunzel* by Gunter Staniewski and Theater Laku Paka; *Frog Prince* by John McDonough and Pumpernickel Puppets. September 10–22, 1996.

IRISH ARTS CENTER. *Family Values* by Carl Ritchie. November 8, 1996. Directed by Norman Hall; with Ellen Evans, Joel Fabiani, Craig Addams, James Hallett, Patty Jamieson, Jeff P. Weiss. *Secrets of the Celtic Heart* by and with Brian Mallon. April 17, 1997. Directed by Brian Mallon and Ellen Burstyn. *Translations* by Brian Friel. May 29, 1997.

IRONDALE ENSEMBLE PROJECT. *Andrew Carnegie Presents the Jew of Malta* by the Irondale Ensemble Project, adapted from Christopher Marlowe's *The Jew of Malta.* Directed by Jim Niesen; with Joe Fuer, Michael-David Gordon, Terry Greiss, Rana Kazkaz, Patrena Murray, John Silvers, Brigitte Viellieu-Davis, Patrice Wilson. *The Seagull* by Anton Chekhov. May 31, 1997. Directed by Jim Niesen; with Yvonne Brechbuhler, Joe Fuer, Michael-David Gordon, Terry Greiss, Rana Kazkaz, Barbara Mackenzie-Wood, Patrena Murray, John Silvers, Brigitte Viellieu-Davis.

JEAN COCTEAU REPERTORY. *What the Butler Saw* by Joe Orton. August 25, 1996. Directed by Scott Shattuck; with Joseph J. Menino, Craig Smith, Molly Pietz, Kennedy Brown, Elise Stone, Christopher Black. *Six Characters in Search of an Author* by Luigi Pirandello. October 13, 1996. Directed by Eve Adamson; with Harris Berlinsky, Elise Stone. *The Lucky Chance* by Aphra Behn. November 24, 1996. With Craig Smith, Molly Pietz. *Mother Courage and Her Children* by Bertolt Brecht, translated by Eric Bentley; music by Darius Milhaud. January 19, 1997. Directed by Robert Hupp; with Elise Stone, Harris Berlinsky, Will Leckie, Kennedy Brown, Molly Pietz. *Othello* by William Shakespeare. March 16, 1997. Directed by Scott Shattuck.

JEWISH REPERTORY THEATER. *The Shawl* by Cynthia Ozick. June 20, 1996. Directed by Sidney Lumet; with Dianne Wiest, Wendy Makkena, Dina Spybey, Bob Dishy, Boyd Gaines, Salem Ludwig. *431 of My Closest Friends* by Miriam Kouzel Billington, Peter Goldman and David Presby. October 20, 1996. Directed by Peter Goldman; with Miriam Kouzel Billington, David Presby. *Concert Pianist* by and with Barry Neikrug. January 19, 1997. Directed by Joe Cacaci. *The Disputation* by Hyam Maccoby. May 4, 1997. Directed by Robert Kalfin; with George Morfogen, David Edwards, Larry Pine.

JOHN HOUSEMAN THEATER. *Gunnin' for Jesus* by James Oakes, Tammy Lang and Charlie Schulman. February 23, 1997. Directed by Charlie Schulman; with James Oakes, Tammy Lang.

JOHN MONTGOMERY THEATER. *The Doll* by Patricia Minskoff, directed by Jessie Ericson Onuf; *Seduction* by Joe Borini, directed by Richard Kuranda; *Birthday* by Suzanne Bachner, directed by Patricia Minskoff (one-act plays). May 31, 1997.

JUDITH ANDERSON THEATER. *Dorian Gray* book by Allan Reiser and Don Price, based on Oscar Wilde's novella; music by Gary Levinson; lyrics by Allan Reiser. September 17, 1996. Directed by Don Price. *Code of the West* by Mark R. Giesser. October 12, 1996. *Cybele: A Love Story* adapted from Bernard Eschasseriaux's book, *Les Dimanches de Ville D'Avray,* music and lyrics by Paul Dick. November 8, 1996. *Three by Beckett '96: Not I, Nach und Traume, Quad I and II* by Samuel Beckett. December 7, 1996. Directed by Joseph Chaikin and Luly Santangelo; with Wendy vanden Heuvel, Peter Nichols Davis, Mary Forcade, Carolyn Lucas, Will Hare, Mark Isaac Epstein. *Marking* by Patrick Breen. January 21, 1997. Directed by Elizabeth Gottlieb; with Maria Tucci, Brian F. O'Byrne, Amy Ryan, Francie Swift, Peter Dinklage, Adina Porter. *The Most Important Playwright Since Tennessee Williams* by William Shuman. April 9, 1997. Directed by Elaine Smith.

LAMB'S LITTLE THEATER. *Genesis* (adapted from the Book of Genesis). March 17, 1997. Directed by John Pietrowski; with Max McLean.

LOST TRIBE THEATER COMPANY. *Returner* written and directed by Stephen F. Kelleher. March 23, 1997.

MARTIN R. KAUFMAN THEATER. *Mrs. Cage* by Nancy Barr. February 3, 1997. Directed by Alberta Handelman; with Heath C.A. Stanwhyck, Alberta Handelman.

MINT THEATER COMPANY. *The Spirit of Man* by Peter Barnes. May 16, 1997.

MUSICAL THEATER WORKS. *The Last Wedding* by Joan McHale. October 24, 1996. Directed by Dan Metelitz.

NADA. *Igloo Tales* conceived from Eskimo, Inuit and other myths and folk tales and directed by Mark Greenfield. January 26, 1997.

NAKED ANGELS. *Easter* by Will Scheffer. March 12, 1997. Directed by Richard Caliban; with Ken Marks, Jodie Markel, Sean Runnette, Kenneth P. Strong.

NEGRO ENSEMBLE COMPANY. *Boy X Man* by Ed Bullins. May 22, 1997. Directed by Clinton Turner Davis; with Janine Carter, Ghana-Lee Fickling, Rynel Johnson, Johnny Kitt, Gregory Prather, Sean Allen Rector, Michele Rashida Turner.

THE NEW GROUP. *This Is Our Youth* by Kenneth Lonergan. October 30, 1996. Directed by Mark Brokaw; with Josh Hamilton, Mark Ruffalo, Missy Yager. *The Flatted Fifth* by Seth Zvi Rosenfeld. February 10, 1997. Directed by Jo Bonney; with Danny Hoch, David Deblinger, Nicole Ari Parker, Rebecca Cohen Alpert, Jose Joaquin Garcia, Sarita Choudry. *My Night With Reg* by Kevin Elyot. June 3, 1997. Directed by Jack Hofsiss.

NEW PERSPECTIVES THEATER COMPANY. *Richard III* by William Shakespeare. February 14, 1997. Directed by Carol Kastendieck; with Austin Pendleton, Joseph W. Rodriguez, Dawn A. Greenidge, Mark Ehrlich.

NEW YORK GILBERT AND SULLIVAN PLAYERS. *The Gondoliers.* December 27, 1996. Directed by Albert Bergeret and Jan Holland; with Andrew MacPhail, Edward Prostak, Ana Rojas, Nancy Maria Balach, Philip Reilly, Stephen O'Brien, Jocelyn Wilkes, Susan Case, Brandon Jovanovich. *The Pirates of Penzance.* January 9, 1997. Directed by Albert Bergeret.

NEW YORK PUBLIC LIBRARY FOR THE PERFORMING ARTS READING ROOM READINGS. *Dreading Thekla* by Albert Innaurato. October 21, 1996. Directed by Nicholas Martin; with Leslie Lyles, John Benjamin Hickey, Sloane Shelton. *Ancient Lights* by Darci Picoult. November 18, 1996. Directed by Liz Diamond; with Oni Faida Lampley, Nancy Giles, Josie Chavez, Suzanne Shepherd, Randy Danson, Novella Nelson, Tony Ward, John Nesci, Akili Prince. *Old Men* by Charles Fuller. December 16, 1996. Directed by Clinton Turner Davis; with Larry Block, Carl Gordon, Ed Wheeler,

Paula Pizzi, Leland Gantt, Gordon Skinner, Tom Mardirosian, Caroline Clay, Barbara Montgomery. *The Beach* by Anthony Giardina. January 13, 1997. Directed by Itamar Kubovy; with John Benjamin Hickey, Scott Sherman, Kirk Jackson, Lisa Benavides, Julie Dretzin, Patricia Dunnock, Anne Lange, Rufus Reed, Mary Van Vamvoukakis. *A Classic Misunderstanding* by Regina M. Porter. February 10, 1997. Directed by Seret Scott; with Michele Shay, Rony Clanton, Jacinto Taras Riddick, Ruben Santiago Hudson, Natalia Harris. *Dreaming Through History* by Lizzie Olesker. March 10, 1997. Directed by Beth Schachter; with Joanna Adler, Lynn Cohen, Stephanie Mnookin, David Letwein, Andrew Dolan, Randy Danson. *Last Lists of My Mad Mother* by Julie Jensen. April 7, 1997. Directed by Holly Becker; with Ellen McElduff, Lois Smith, Ellen McLaughlin. *The Guest Lecturer* by A.R. Gurney. June 16, 1997. Directed by John Tillinger.

THE NEXT STAGE. *To the Hand: The Further Adventures of Gussie Mae in America* by and with Letitia Guillory and *Whatever the Matter May Be* by and with Misi Lopez Lecube. February 6 and 7, 1997 (in repertory).

NUYORICAN POETS CAFE. *Jason and Medea* by Dennis Moritz. September 15, 1996. Directed by Michael Leland. *Jack Pot Melting: A Commercial, General Hag's Skeezag* and *The Election Machine Warehouse* (one-act plays) by Amiri Baraka. October 17, 1996. Directed by Rome Neal. *Primitive World: An Anti-Nuclear Jazz Musical* by Amiri Baraka. January, 1997. Directed by Rome Neal; with Rocqueford Allen, Inger Tudor, Theo Polites, Stephen O'Brien, Robert Turner. *The C Above C Above High C* by Ishmael Reed. May 23, 1997. Directed by Rome Neal; with David D. Wright, Ron Bladel.

OHIO THEATER. *King Gordogan* by Radovan Ivsic. February 13, 1997. Directed by Andrew Frank; with Neil Maffin, Christy Baron, Mitchell Riggs, John Gould Rubin.

ONE DREAM THEATER. *Orestes: "I Murdered My Mother"* adapted from Euripides's play and directed by Jeff Cohen. July 28, 1996. With Paul Whitthorne, Corinna Lyons, John L. Damon, Peter Appel, Christine Cowin, Milo Bernstein, Kathryn Hahn. *Nothing Exists* by and with Copernicus. October 31, 1996. Directed by Christopher Sanderson.

ONTOLOGICAL-HYSTERIC THEATER. *Permanent Brain Damage* written, directed and designed by Richard Foreman. November 28, 1996. With D J Mendel, Robert Cucuzza, Stephen Jordan, Jennifer Krasinski, Claude Wampler, Cradeaux Alexander.

ONYX THEATER COMPANY. *A Not So Quiet Nocturne* written and directed by Jaye Austin Williams. January 15, 1997. With Michelle Banks.

PEARL THEATER COMPANY. *Misalliance* by George Bernard Shaw. September 8, 1996. Directed by Robert Williams; with Robert Stattel, Bradford Cover, Carol Schultz, Kathleen McNenny, Janet Zarish, Greg McFadden. *Cymbeline* by William Shakespeare. October 31, 1996. Directed by Shepard Sobel; with Kathleen McNenny, Jack Koenig, Brian G. Kurlander. *The Barber of Seville* by Beaumarchais, translated by Michael Feingold; music by Thomas Cabaniss. December 15, 1996. Directed by John Rando. *Venice Preserv'd* by Thomas Otway. February 2, 1997. Directed by Rich Cole; with David Adkins, Joey Collins, Hope Chernov, Robin Leslie Brown, Robert Hock, John Wylie. *The Guardsman* by Ferenc Molnar. March 23, 1997. Directed by Russell Treyz; with Tom Bloom, Joanne Camp, Helmar Augustus Cooper. *The Chairs* by Eugene Ionesco. May 11, 1997. Directed by John Morrison; with Robert Hock, Marylouise Burke, Christopher Graham.

PERFORMANCE SPACE 122. *Everybody Goes 2 Disco From Moscow to San Francisco* by Borut Separovic. September 26, 1996. With Montazstroj (Srecko Borse, Bernarda Pesa, Damir Klemenic). *Joking the Chicken* by and with Marga Gomez. October 18, 1996. *Go Go Go* by and with Juliana Francis. November 3, 1996. Directed by Anne Bogart. *1969 Terminal 1996* by Susan Yankowitz; music by Ellen Maddow. November 6, 1996. Directed by Joseph Chaikin; with Scott Blumenthal, Shami Chaikin, Hyun Yup Lee, Nkenge Scott, Tina Shepard, Paul Zimet. *Critical Mass* by Deb Margolin. February 27, 1997. Directed by Jamie Leo; with Deb Margolin, Andy Davis, Rae C. Wright, Nicole J. Adelman. *East of Eadie* by Ray Dobbins. May 8, 1997. With Bette Bourne, Ron Jones, Gerardo Espinosa.

PHIL BOSAKOWSKI THEATER. *Jasper in Gramercy Park* by Mary Mitchell. June 11, 1996. Directed by John James Hickey; with James Hallett, Cordis Heard. *The London Cuckolds* by Edward Ravenscroft, adapted by John Byrne. December 9, 1996. Directed by Owen Thompson; with Tricia Paoluccio, Elizabeth Richmond, Jeff Gurner, Michael Daly.

PLAYWRIGHTS' COLLECTIVE. *Bride Stripped Bare* by Kate Robin. June 22, 1996. Directed by Tim Cunningham; with Rob Campbell, Susan Floyd, Leslie Lyles.

PURGATORIO INK. *Othello and the Circumcised Turk* adapted from William Shakespeare's play and directed by Assurbanipal Babilla. September 5, 1996. With Bill Martin, Jennie Crotero.

QUAIGH THEATER COMPANY. *The Wild Guys* by Andrew Wreggitt and Rebecca Shaw. September 6, 1996. With David M. Pincus, Bill Bartlett, Derek LeDain, Charlie O'Hara.

RATTLESTICK PRODUCTIONS. *Volunteer Man* by Dan Clancy. September 8, 1996. Directed by Tracy Brigden; with Reed Birney, Ray Anthony Thomas, Elizabeth Bove. *Message to Michael* by Tim Pinckney. December 15, 1996. Directed by Michael Scheman; with David Beach, Michael Malone, Kevin Cristaldi, Eric Paeper, Tony Meindl, Rich Hammerly. *Heart of Man* by Jennifer Christman. February 16, 1997. With Elizabeth Hanly Rice, Jordan Lage, Kathryn Hahn. *Winning* by David Van Asselt. April 6, 1997. Directed by Laura Josepher; with Maura Russo, Sam Guncler, Jennifer Regan. *Suburban Motel: Problem Child* and other plays by George F. Walker. May 13, 1997. Directed by Daniel De Raey; with Christopher Burns, Tasha Lawrence, Mark Hammer, Kathleen Goldpaugh.

RAW SPACE. *Alone at the Beach* by Richard Dresser. November 1, 1996. *American Silents* conceived and directed by Anne Bogart. May 2, 1997.

ROSE'S TURN. *Impaled on a Magnolia* by Beth Glover and Randy Buck. February 16, 1997. Directed by Randy Buck; with Beth Glover.

SAMUEL BECKETT THEATER. *The All-Nude College Girl Revue* by Faith Phillips. September 3, 1996. Directed by Todd Stuart Phillips. *Dreamstuff* book and direction by John Pantozzi; music and lyrics by Sal Lombarde. February 17, 1997. With Carol Woods, Louise DuArt, Aileen Quinn, Evan Ferrante. *The Godsend* by Richard Willett. April 8, 1997. Directed by Charles Loffredo; with Cindy Chesler, Jamie Heinlein, Peggy R. Johnson, Judy Stone, James Sutton, Wendell Ward, Glen Williamson.

78TH STREET THEATER LAB. *The Packwood Papers* by Karen Houppert and Stephen Nunns. September 29, 1996. Directed by Eric Nightengale; with Toby Wherry, Katherine Heasley. *Reincarnation* by Jessica Litwak. November 15, 1996.

SYNCHRONICITY SPACE. *Keats* by David Shepard. August 14, 1996. Directed by Douglas Hall; with Austin Pendleton. *Love Letters to Adolf Hitler* adapted and directed by Tuvia Tenenbom. January 4, 1997. With Catherine Curtin, Samme Johnston Spolan, Susanna Schmitz, Mary F. Unser, Dana White, Ellen David.

TARGET MARGIN THEATER. *South* by Julian Green. January 12, 1997. Directed by David Herskovits; with Thomas Jay Ryan, Yuri Skujins, Will Badgett, Lenore Pemberton, Marissa Chibas.

TECTONIC THEATER PROJECT. *Gross Indecency: The Three Trials of Oscar Wilde* written and directed by Moises Kaufman. March 2, 1997. With Michael Emerson, William D. Dawes, Robert Blumenfeld, Trevor Anthony, John McAdams, Andy Paris, Greg Pierotti, Troy Sostillio, Greg Steinbruner.

THEATER AT ST. CLEMENT'S. *Tokyo Can Can* written and directed by Yutaka Okada; music by Saburo Iwakawa. June 12, 1996. With Reggie Lee. *Nijinsky—Death of a Faun* by David Pownall. April 2, 1997. Directed by Jennie Buckman; with Nicholas Johnson.

THEATER AT ST. PETER'S CHURCH. *Acts of Providence: Dolores* and *Dead Man's Apartment* by Edward Allan Baker. July 17, 1996. Directed by Ron Stetson; with David McConeghey, Ilene Kristen, Alexandra Lee, Michael Cambden Richards, Fiona Gallagher.

THEATER BY THE BLIND. *Blind Spots: Cathedral* by Scott Klavan, adapted from Raymond Carver's story; *Gus* by Ike Schambelan; *The Test* by Peter Mikochik; *The Convert* by Lynn Manning. June 7, 1996. Directed and performed by Theater by the Blind.

THEATER EAST. *Americana* written and directed by Sharon Hillegas. September 27, 1996.

THEATER OF THE RIVERSIDE CHURCH. *The Portable Pioneer and Prairie Show* book by David Chambers; music by Mel Marvin; lyrics by David Chambers and Mel Marvin. February 7, 1997. Directed by Lori Steinberg; with Melting Pot Theater Company.

THEATER ROW THEATER. *The Sleeping Hippo* written and directed by Max Mayer. September 9, 1996. With Rebecca Creskoff, Phyllis Somerville, Bill Camp, Douglas Weston. *The Last Manhattan* by Doug Dunlop. January 19, 1997. Directed by Darren Lee Cole; with Kelly Curtis, Herschel Sparber, Owen Hollander, Patrick Tull, Brett Lafield, Joan Porter Hollander. *The Beekeeper's Daughter* by Karen Malpede. March 3, 1997. Directed by Ivica Boban; with Beth Dixon, Myriam Cyr, George Bartenieff, Christen Clifford, Michael Louden.

THEATER-STUDIO. *Rod of Iron* (one-act play) written and directed by Norman Chaitin. January 10, 1997.

THEATER THREE. *Helmut Sees America* by George Malko. September 9, 1996. Directed by John Stewart; with Pamela Nyberg, Maduka Steady, Dan Daily.

TRIBECA LAB. *Fassbinder in the Frying Pan: The Bitter Tears of Petra von Kant* and *Bremen Freedom* by Rainer Werner Fassbinder, translated by Denis Calandra. March 10, 1997. Directed by Stuart Rudin and Deborah Stoll; with Maia Kretser, Tony Glazer, Bo Corre, Florence Cabre Andrews, Jacqueline Bowman.

28TH STREET THEATER. *Paradise Is Closing Down* by Pieter-Dirk Uys. November 11, 1996. With Jacqueline Pennington, Kevin Mambo. *Leopold and Loeb* by George Singer. May 27, 1997. Directed by Renee Philippi; with Brian Weiss, Marc Palmieri.

29TH STREET REPERTORY THEATER. *Pick Up Ax* by Anthony Clarvoe. June 19, 1996. Directed by James Abar; with Thomas Wehrle, Neil Necastro, David Mogentale. *The Pig* by Tammy Ryan. September 19, 1996. Directed by Tim Corcoran. *Night of Nave* (one-act plays) by Bill Nave. December 6, 1996. With Paula Ewin, Leo Farley. *Buffalo Kill: The Killer and the Comic* and *Never the Same Rhyme Twice* by Rooster Mitchell. May 15, 1997. Directed by Tim Corcoran and Michael Hillyer; with Paula Ewin, Elizabeth Elkins, Ruby Hondros, Susan Barrett, David Mogentale, Paul Zegler.

VIA THEATER. *Censored!!!* by Brian Jucha. April 3, 1997. With Leah Gray, Will Keenan, Kristen Lee Kelly, Sheryl Dold, Megan Spooner, Matthew Mohr.

VILLAGE GATE. *Big City Rhythm (The Songs of Barry Kleinbort).* March 23, 1997. Directed by Barry Kleinbort; with Marcia Lewis, Lewis Cleale, Eric Michael Gillett, Melanie Vaughan.

WESTBETH THEATER CENTER. *Paved Paradise: The Songs of Joni Mitchell.* September 10, 1996. With John Kelly. *Hedwig and the Angry Inch* by John Cameron Mitchell; music by Stephen Trask. March 9, 1997. Directed by Peter Askin; with John Cameron Mitchell.

WILLOW CABIN THEATER. *Street Scene* by Elmer Rice. October 28, 1996. Directed by Edward Berkeley; with Zachary Ansley, John Bolger, Mary Cushman, Angela Nevard, Linda Powell, Jed Sexton, Andre Ware, Ken Forman. *Don Juan Comes Back From the War* by Odon von Horvath, translated by Christopher Hampton. March 3, 1997. Directed by Edward Berkeley; with Kenneth Favre, Cynthia Besteman, Sarah Lively Clarke, Tasha Lawrence, Verna Lowe, Jacqueline Brookes.

WINGS THEATER. *Death in a Landslide* by Jay Martel. October 6, 1996.

WORKHOUSE THEATER. *Poor Folk's Pleasure* by Len Jenkin. September 13, 1996. Directed by David Karl Lee.

WORKING THEATER. *A Drop in the Bucket* by Edward Belling. May 28, 1997. Directed by Mark Plesent; with Dolores Sutton, Carol Morley, William Wise, Randy Frazier.

WORTH STREET THEATER. *Snapshots: Duck Pond* by Ara Watson, *Life Under Water* by Richard Greenberg, *You Belong to Me* by Keith Reddin, *Loft* (work-in-progress) by Jeff Cohen. April, 1997. Directed by Jeff Cohen; with Corinna Lyons, Abby Royle, Kathryn Hahn, Ethan Sandler, Heather Melton, David Stamper.

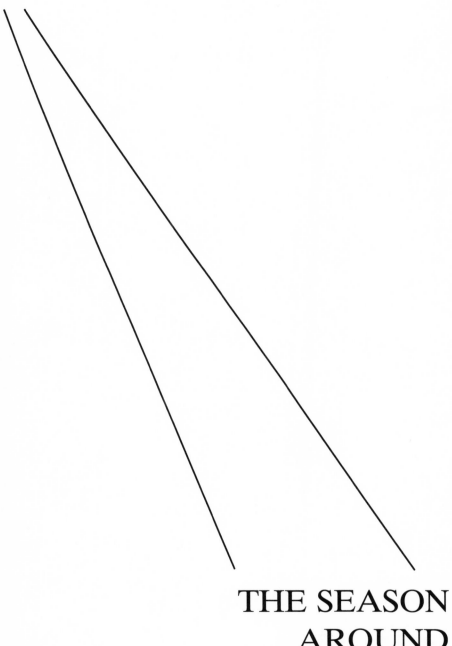

THE SEASON
AROUND
THE UNITED STATES

O
O
O

OUTSTANDING NEW PLAYS CITED BY AMERICAN THEATER CRITICS ASSOCIATION
and
A DIRECTORY OF NEW-PLAY PRODUCTIONS

O
O
O

THE American Theater Critics Association (ATCA) is the organization of over 250 leading drama critics in all media in all sections of the United States. One of the group's stated purposes is "To increase public awareness of the theater as a *national* resource" (italics ours). To this end, beginning in 1977 ATCA has annually cited outstanding new plays produced around the U.S., to be represented in our coverage by excerpts from each of their scripts demonstrating literary style and quality. This year one of these—*Jack and Jill* by Jane Martin, presented at the Actors Theater of Louisville's 1996 Humana Festival (Jon Jory producing director)—has been designated 1996's 21st annual principal citation and 12th annual ATCA New Play Award winner of $1,000.

Two other 1996 ATCA new play citations went to *The Last Night of Ballyhoo* by Alfred Uhry at Atlanta's Alliance Theater Company and the revised version of *The Ride Down Mount Morgan* by Arthur Miller at the Williamstown Theater Festival. And the third annual Elizabeth Osborn Award for an emerging playwright

347

THUNDER KNOCKING ON THE DOOR: A BLUSICAL TALE OF RHYTHM AND THE BLUES—Shawana Kemp and Lester Purry in the Alabama Shakespeare Festival production of the play by Keith Glover, the 1996 Elizabeth Osborn Award winner

was voted to Keith Glover for his musical *Thunder Knocking on the Door: A Blusical Tale of Rhythm and the Blues,* a co-production of Alabama Shakespeare Festival, Baltimore's Center Stage and the Dallas Theater Center.

Other plays nominated by individual ATCA members for the attention of the awards committee this year were *Lifeidreamof* by Stephen Daly, October 19, 1995 at Chicago's Center Theater; *An Asian Jockey in Our Midst* by Carter Lewis, January 4, 1996 at Cincinnati's Playhouse in the Park; *And Neither Have I Wings to Fly* by Ann Noble, January 28, 1996 at San Leandro's California Conservatory Theater; *Greensboro (a Requiem)* by Emily Mann, February 6, 1996 at Princeton's McCarter

Theater; and *The Cider House Rules, Part I*, adapted by Peter Parnell from John Irving's novel, March 2, 1996 at Seattle Repertory Theater. *The Diva Classification System* by Jeff Resta and *One on One* by Adam Goldberg were additional Osborn Award nominees.

The process of selection of these outstanding plays is as follows: any ATCA member may nominate a play which has been given a production in a professional house. It must be the first full professional production of a finished play (not a reading or an airing as a play-in-progress) during the calendar year. Nominated scripts were studied and discussed by an ATCA play-reading committee chaired by Michael Grossberg of the Columbus *Dispatch* and comprising Michael Barnes of the Austin *American-Statesman*, Misha Berson of the Seattle *Times*, Lawrence Bommer of the Chicago *Reader, Tribune* and Windy City *Times*, Michael Phillips of the San Diego *Union-Tribune*, Michael Sommers of the Newhouse Papers, Catherine Stadem of the Anchorage *Daily News* and alternates Beatrice MacLeod of the Ithaca *Journal* and Alec Harvey of the Birmingham *News*..

These committee members made their choices on the basis of script rather than production. If the timing of nominations and openings prevents some works from being considered in any given year, they will be eligible for consideration the following year if they haven't since moved to New York.

We offer our sincerest thanks and admiration to the ATCA members and their committee for the valuable insights into the 1996 theater year around the United States which their selections provide for this *Best Plays* record, in the form of excerpts from the outstanding scripts, and most particularly in the introductory reviews by Michael Grossberg *(Jack and Jill)* Michael Sommers *(The Last Night of Ballyhoo)* and Ed Siegel of the Boston *Globe (The Ride Down Mount Morgan)*.

1996 ATCA New Play Award

○○○
○○○
○○○
○○○
○○○
○○○ **JACK AND JILL**

A Play in Two Acts

BY JANE MARTIN

Cast and credits appear on page 441 of *The Best Plays of 1995–96*

JANE MARTIN was born like Athena full-grown from the brain of the creator of the 11 monologues in her 1982 program Talking With. *In other words, it's a pen name for an author or authors who want to keep her/his/their identity secret for one reason or another and have been doing so for a number of years. We presume that Jon Jory, producing director of Actors Theater of Louisville, and probably some other members of that group's staff, know who "Jane Martin" really is, but they're not telling.*

Talking With *brought its author to everyone's attention by winning a 1981–82 ATCA Citation after its production in Actors Theater's 6th annual Festival of New American Plays February 24–April 4, 1982. Here's what the Louisville playbill had to say about Jane Martin on that occasion:*

"Jane Martin is a Louisvillian. Her play Twirler *was produced in last spring's Festival of New American Plays and then went on to critically-acclaimed productions at the Toronto and Dublin international festivals. Her* 15 Minutes *and* Rodeo *received their world premieres at the Dublin Theater Festival this past fall. Ms. Martin's play* The Boy Who Ate the Moon, *her only two-character play, was originally produced as part of the Apprentice Showcase entitled* Stages. *Also seen again during '81* Shorts *were her monologues* 15 Minutes, Twirler, Rodeo, Marks, Handler, Lamps, Clear Glass Marbles *and* Cul de Sac."

The Actors Theater production of Talking With *was brought to New York by Manhattan Theater Club September 21, 1982 for 56 performances, and on November 14 of that year Martin's 8-character plays* Coup *and* Clucks *opened in Louisville, which has also seen this author's* Shasta Rue *(1983),* Summer *(1984),* Vital Signs *(1990),* Cementville *(1991),* Keely and Du *(1993, winner of that year's ATCA New Play Award and reportedly a runner-up for the Pulitzer) and* Middle-Aged White Guys *(1995). Her* Criminal Hearts *appeared in the GeVa Theater, Rochester, 1993 New Plays Festival. Her third ATCA citation and second New Play Award winner,* Jack and Jill, *had been previously offered as* Jack and Jill Go Up the Hill *at the Unicorn Theater in Kansas City before being presented in its prizewinning production at Louisville's Humana Festival March 14, 1996. And two in its lengthening string of subsequent productions are contemplated in the review below.*

INTRODUCTION: America's most famous anonymous playwright is a regional-theater staple. One can see why in *Jack and Jill*, which ranks with Jane Martin's best.

For Martin, the thirtysomethings' romance breaks new ground by offering equal time to both sexes. Past works focused exclusively on women *(Talking With* and *Vital Signs)*, primarily on men *(Middle-Aged White Guys)* or predominantly women *(Keely and Du)*. Arguably Martin's best balance of femininity and masculinity, comedy and drama, *Jack and Jill* explores the ups and downs of a contemporary couple with rueful insight, seductive wit and poignant feeling. Martin breaks through to a new level of realism, compassionate insight and painfully self-aware humor. Anyone who has dated, married or divorced will identify with Jack and Jill, from their first meeting and first date to the not-so-final divorce.

Some two-character pieces seem small; this update of the war between the sexes is a marvel of dramatic compression. Jack and Jill meet cute, date hot, get engaged, grow nervous, get married, get sunburned on honeymoon, get confused about career priorities and get divorced—and that's just the first act! Martin offers fresh takes on everything from the awkward first encounter, tricky first date and role-reversed marriage proposal to the inevitable conflicts.

Jill is wary; Jack needy. She is aggressive and controlling; he, passive and wimpy. He wants intimacy; she, independence. Both have been hurt before—and have just about had it with the frustrations and negotiations of dating.

Jack is a nice guy—too "nice," self deprecating and apologetic about his gender. Yet, Jack grows during the multi-year relationship, revealing a dogged loyalty, fierce tenderness and deep capacity for love. Jill is the trickier role. While more than a castrating bitch (as actress Pamela Stewart at times appeared under Jon Jory's direction in Louisville's arena-style premiere), Jill shouldn't seem too nice (as at the Pope Theater in Florida). The Ohio premiere at Columbus's Red Herring Theater Company achieved a middle ground, with actress Lori Cannon sometimes harsh, but always human.

Together, Jack and Jill bravely walk the tightrope of that crazy, hazy, out-ofphase, in-the-maze thing called love. The surprising thing is not that Jack and Jill fall, but that they keep getting back on the nervous high-wire act of today's romantic relationships.

Most refreshing is the canny treatment of such well-covered territory in American theater. The author avoids most cliches of courtship by focusing on the events between the traditional "big moments" with charming ambiguity and honesty. We see the groom's last-minute qualms, not the wedding. We see the dish-breaking prelude and book-packing aftermath, not the decision to divorce. The dialogue is fashionably current but naturalistic, with jerks, overlaps and dead-end pauses that puncture traditional romantic expectations. One character often answers the other's question in amusingly delayed sequence—while Martin's deepest questions about falling in love and letting go of fear stare the unconscious in the face.

Four nonspeaking dressers help the actors change clothes, props, locations and years. (While the Pope Theater's proscenium-style production milked transitions for laughs, Red Herring Theater's two dressers maintained a more discreet aura of infinite patience.) By adopting such a theatrical device, Martin maintains the love story's pellmell pace. While the nursery rhyme ends with a fall, the play's ending is hesitant but hopeful: Jack and Jill may fall down the hill, but they don't have to stay down. Even in the gender-confused, relationship-anxious, rules-questioning 1990s, Martin suggests, men and women can work things out—maybe.

Much of the suspense involves guessing whether the couple's feelings for each other will triumph over their considerable difficulties. An additional layer of suspense is generated for longtime Martin fans, who can appreciate the play as a mystery offering more tantalizing clues about the playwright's identity. Some suspect "she" is a man (most likely Jory, Actors Theater's producing director) or a man collaborating with a woman. If some men view *Middle-Aged White Guys* as male-bashing, some women view *Jack and Jill* as misogyny—and proof that Martin is a male.

Others aren't so sure. Good playwrights can create plausible characters of both sexes, and Martin is a wiser playwright today than a decade ago. Like *Keely and Du* or David Mamet's similarly spare, power-obsessed *Oleanna, Jack and Jill* arouses controversy and sparks discussions—one sign of a powerful play. Whatever one's view of the characters and issues, reasonable women and men should be able to agree that *Jack and Jill* represents the most balanced exploration yet of Martin's favorite themes: femininity, masculinity and male-female relationships

Who is Jane Martin? Theatergoers already know the best answer: a good playwright who keeps getting better.

—MICHAEL GROSSBERG

Excerpts From *Jack and Jill*

JACK: This is a marriage, what you do . . .
JILL: You want to fix it, right?

JACK: Don't start with that, Jill . . .

JILL: It's like having a plumber for my feelings.

JACK: And I . . .

JILL: You can't fix me, do you understand?
     Crash.

JACK: This is stress because of the residency.

JILL: My God, I can't shut you out, you're like the ocean, you're all-enveloping.

JACK: I am your companion, I love you, this is our house.

JILL: I am your companion. This has nothing to do with you. I'm not mad at you. I don't mean to hurt your feelings. I don't need to be placated. I just want to break these dishes.

JACK: Let's go out and grab a beer.

JILL: I don't want a beer.

JACK: Coffee, tea, cheesecake, a movie . . .

JILL: I was enjoying breaking the dishes . . .

JACK: It doesn't make any sense . . .

JILL: I'm not making sense, Jack, I'm breaking the dishes.
     Jill shoves a stack of bowls onto the floor.

JACK: Goddamnit, stop that!

JILL: Don't worry, I'll pay you for them.

JACK: That is really cheap, Jill.

JILL: Oh, it wasn't in your mind?

JACK: It was in my mind that it's wasteful.

JILL: Well, you can make a big point of replacing them.
     Crash.

JACK: You mean I'm financially brutalizing you?

JILL: Tell me you don't trade on my dependence?

JACK: I don't even think about it.

JILL: Bullshit.

JACK: Don't tell me what I think.

JILL: You know you like it.

JACK: It is incredibly temporary . . .

JILL: But it's a hold.

JACK: As a physician, you'll make . . .

JILL: So it's not merely supportive.

JACK: I'm not supportive?

JILL: Financially, yes.

JACK: That's the only way you find me supportive?

JILL: Don't give me the martyred look.

JACK: If that's your perception, I can fix it.

JILL: Fix it?

JACK: What is it that's wanted here, anger?

JILL: Will you . . . Jack . . . listen to yourself, "What is it that's wanted here." Jesus!

JACK: Yes?

JILL: That's not an emotion, that's a preface.

JACK: The question, damnit, precedes the answer.

JILL: Jack, you start with a question and then, worse, worse, you immediately try . . .

JACK: Fix it. I try to fix it. Yes, right, I know my sins. God forbid we should try to do anything about anything . . . *(Smash.)* . . . we should, we should *experience* it . . . or something, imbibe it, embody it, swim in it or some goddam . . .

JILL: I want you to leave the room.

JACK: What?

JILL: You asked what I want, I want you to leave the room.

JACK: This room . . .

JILL: Is your room . . .

JACK: I never said . . .

JILL: Your room, your apartment . . .

JACK: Goddamnit!

JILL: . . . your life, your agenda, your wife.
        Smash.

JACK: You are my wife, yes, and I . . .

JILL: Jesus, I wish I was out of here . . .

JACK: You are in the middle of a residency . . .

JILL: Why did I ever think . . .

JACK: The hours are horrendous, the sleep deprivation is brutal, you have no time to yourself . . .

JILL: Because every second I have, you're there.

JACK: *We* have no time . . .

JILL: I don't need "we" time, I need . . .

JACK: I need "we" time.

JILL: I don't.

JACK: How can you say . . .

JILL: I want to be alone, Jack. I know . . . believe me . . . it's a terrible failing . . . I'm . . . anti-social or something . . . there are times . . . yesterday, all day, I thought about you, but you never tell me I irritate you . . . don't I irritate you? You irritate me. For one thing, you can't *do* anything, Jack . . . don't get martyred . . . it's just the way you were raised, but it's . . . oppressive, so . . . what, what are you doing?

        Jack begins pushing plate fragments into piles with his feet.

JACK: It is very indulgent.

JILL: What?

JACK: Breaking things. Being anti-social. Showing off your emotions. Pretending who has what money or whatever is the point here. It is very, very, very indulgent. Now, let's stick with one problem and fix it.

JILL: Jack, you can't fix a toilet, you can't cope with . . .

JACK: Here we go.

JILL: Okay, it's not easy . . . the insurance . . .

JACK: I can cope with . . .

JILL: Canceled.

JACK AND JILL—Pamela Stewart and John Leonard Thompson in the Actors Theater of Louisville production of Jane Martin's ATCA Award-winning play

JACK: One time.

JILL: They turned off the phone.

JACK: One time.

JILL: The car registration.

JACK: Alright, Jesus, I get the point.

JILL: And I'm not saying . . .

JACK: And they didn't turn off the phone.

JILL: That you're not generous, because you are, you are so generous it's like water torture.

JACK: Jill, I love you. My heart . . . this life, it's richer, more . . . more various, just better.

JILL: Wait . . .

JACK: No. You give value . . . you change me.

JILL: It's sweet, it's . . . vague. I don't recognize . . . I wish, I really do . . . recognize me, Jill, as that person, Jack . . . that value-adding person . . . you are making up, and that's generous, too, this person who . . . I am selfish, I am ambitious, I am . . . oh, yes, unpleasant, angry, I-don't-know-what person . . . it's a burden . . . really . . . I'm sorry it's this way . . . but, Jesus, feeling like a shit all the time because I'm not . . . *that!* That stuff you make up to sustain this. Honestly say to me you don't see . . .

JACK: I want connection, and you . . .

JILL: I want . . .

JACK: To be, see . . . one with you and . . .

JILL: Baloney.

JACK: To be one . . .

JILL: This is nice, Jack.

JACK: Nice?

JILL: Nice, yes, this is something somebody would want to hear . . .

JACK: But I mean it.

JILL: Which is nice, which is your specialty.

JACK: Nice is?

JILL: Yes.

JACK: I want this central, but . . .

JILL: But disingenuous.

JACK: I am not . . .

JILL: Disingenuous. You obsess on my stimulus . . .

JACK: I wouldn't . . . wait . . .

JILL: Stir things up . . . keep you . . .

JACK: No, I want to share . . .

JILL: But you don't share. I don't know what you're feeling . . .

JACK: What?

JILL: Right now, now I don't . . . you just . . . Jack, you say a bunch of stuff just to . . . to restore order . . . to reduce people to calm . . . you don't care what you say . . . you'd say anything.

JACK: Right now?

JILL: Yes.

JACK: I am pissed off.

JILL: At what?

JACK: At what?

JILL: At what?

JACK: This conversation. The . . . the dishes, you know, to mention one . . . the tone . . . all of it.

JILL: And your feelings?

JACK: My feelings?

JILL: Yes, Jack, your feelings.

JACK: My feelings are . . . damn, Jill . . . what are these endless . . . endless feelings . . . c'mon Jill, these goddamn whatevers . . . right? . . . that you say I'm not having?

JILL: You want me to tell you your feelings?

JACK: No, as a matter of fact, I know my feelings, actually, I'm having them.

JILL: And?

JACK: And what?

JILL: They are?

JACK: This is ridiculous, you know my feelings!

JILL: Say them!

JACK: I'm upset, this is upsetting.

JILL: What is?

JACK: You say you're leaving.

JILL: When in this conversation did I . . .

JACK: About being alone . . . treating you . . . wanting to be alone.

JILL: I only want to be alone because I'm already alone with you.

JACK: How can you say that? How dare you say that?

JILL: What-are-you-feeling-Jack?!

JACK: I don't give a shit what I'm feeling!

JILL: And that's why I'm alone!

> *Jill starts out.*

JACK: Don't walk out on this!

JILL *(simply):* What are you feeling, Jack?

> *Jill waits. Jack is at a complete impasse. She goes and adds a vest and uses scarf to tie ponytail.*

JACK *(another moment):* Goddamnit! Goddamnit!!

> *He shoves the rest of the dishes and bowls to the floor. Lights change. During monologue, Jack removes sports coat and tosses it offstage. Later, he removes shirt and tosses it offstage. Also during monologue, two Dressers sweep broken dishes into a large circle, inside which the last scene is played. Other Dressers strike the table and spread books and empty boxes on the floor within the circle.*

Nice, right? Nice. Okay. One second. One second. This nice we are talking about here . . . "don't be nice, Jack." This "nice" has a bad name . . . to say the goddamn least. Women, to generalize, hate nice . . . no, no, they like it in clerks, they like it in auto mechanics . . . but . . . nice guys finish last, right? Why? Because "nice" is essentially thought to lack complexity, mystery, "Nice" just . . . has no sex appeal . . . it just doesn't understand the situation. Women distrust "nice" because, given the cultural context, they themselves can't possibly be nice. How can the powerless be "nice"? What good is nice to the "exploited"? So women loathe nice because they see, they know what a phony mask it is in their own lives, so when they perceive it in a man, it just pisses them off. What they prefer are abusive qualities moderated by charm, because they are already abused personalities, given the culture. I'm not kidding. Hey, I don't buy it because there is another "nice," a hard-won, complex, covered-with-blood-and-gore "nice." An existential, steel-willed, utterly crucial and necessary "nice" that says to the skags in the motorcycle gang, "Fuck you and the hogs you rode in on. I exemplify hope and reason and concern." See, I raise the fallen banner high, Jill, so satirize me, shoot me, stab me, dismiss me, go screw the Four Horsemen of the Apocalypse if that's what turns you on, *I'm nice!!*

> *He slowly turns back into himself. Jill enters and sits by stack of books.*

Sorry, I didn't, uh . . . don't know how I got into that . . . just "nice," you know . . . well, anyway, sorry.

> *Lights change. New scene. Jack turns back and is now involved in dividing books with Jill.*

JILL: Are all the Joyce Carol Oates . . .

JACK: All yours.

JILL: Not all.

JACK: Just take them!

JILL: We can't divide them if you won't divide.

JACK: Goddamnit, you divide them!

JILL: So you can criticize how I do it?

JACK *(looking away):* Bitch.

JILL: God, Jack . . .

JACK: Let's just do the books.

JILL: You called me a "bitch."

JACK: I did, yes.

JILL: You don't think that's sad?

JACK: Get off it!

JILL *(calm, not sarcastic):* Do you mean "bitch" in the sense that I told you something you didn't want to hear? Or that I'm "uppity" and don't do what I'm told . . .

JACK: Just shut up, okay?

JILL: . . . or remind you of Bette Davis or have assumed the male role . . .

JACK: I'm warning you . . .

JILL: Warning me?

JACK: Do the books, Jill.

JILL: Or is it just a lot simpler, and you mean "bitch" as a kind of catch-all general category for a woman who is truly, really sick of trying to laugh off your endlessly passive-aggressive behavior?

JACK: I want you out of here! Out of this space. Out of my life. Out of my nervous system. Out of here!

JILL: Why can't we . . .

JACK: Because we can't.

JILL: Close this out with some sense we were right to try.

JACK *(packing):* Because we obviously weren't.

JILL: Since it's a failure, why can't it be a useful failure?

JACK: Dostoevski, mine. Dr. Doolittle, mine. Toni Morrison, yours.

JILL: This is just another version of you walking out of the room.

JACK: Don't start with me. Goddamnit! What I would like is to finish this up and walk out of here without punching you out!

JILL: Whoa??

JACK: You want to know what I think? I think you can't feel anything but an extreme. I think the middle ground is without sensation for you. You drive too fast, you love the unknown, you need extremes, I think I was your last experiment in the ordinary, and it didn't have enough tingle, so you blew it off.

JILL: You don't think punching me out would be an extreme?

JACK: I think punching people out is the final, frustrated expression of the ordinary mind. I think you would like me to hit you so this would all be my fault. It is the only stupid, vulgar, debasing male idiocy you haven't been able to pry out of me, but you uh . . . you'll never know how . . . do you have any sense how close . . . this close . . . to nailing you . . . yes, there . . . happy now?

JILL: I'm supposed to feel sorry for you because you wanted to hit me?

JACK: I was making . . .

JILL: Well, I do. I am sorry.

JACK: You are, huh?

JILL: Really sorry.

JACK: Have I ever hit you?

JILL: Not the point.

JACK: Then why are we talking about this?

JILL: Jack . . .

JACK: No.

JILL: Jack. *(A moment.)* I think marriage is like the cockpit of a commercial airliner . . . you know . . . all those switches . . . and they all . . . all two hundred . . . have to be in . . . the right positions, only in aviation they know what those are, and in marriage you never do, so the odds . . . the odds are astronomical you won't . . . stay in the air. So I don't think we're a bad people, Jack, I think we're disgruntled victims . . . of the odds.

The production for which Jack and Jill *won the 1996 ATCA New Play Award premiered at the Actors Theater of Louisville March 14, 1996 during the 20th annual Humana Festival of New American Plays, under the direction of Jon Jory.*

ATCA New Play Citation

○ ○ ○
○ ○ ○
○ ○ ○
○ ○ ○
○ ○ ○
○ ○ ○

THE LAST NIGHT OF BALLYHOO

A Play in Two Acts

BY ALFRED UHRY

Cast and credits appear on page 376

ALFRED UHRY'S The Last Night of Ballyhoo *won not only this ATCA citation as an outstanding play in cross-country theater but also, in its later New York production, the Tony Award for the best play of the 1996-97 Broadway season. A biographical sketch of its author and a synopsis of the script appear in the Prizewinning Plays section of this volume. A review by Michael Sommers of its 1996 Atlanta production appears below.*

THE LAST NIGHT OF BALLYHOO: The happy ending that closes Alfred Uhry's *The Last Night of Ballyhoo* with a crowd-pleasing coda does not trivialize the dark central issue the play so winningly illuminates.

For all of its warm-hearted humor and Southern charm, *The Last Night of Ballyhoo* is an old-fashioned romatic comedy that's grounded in a thoughtful theme about prejudice of an unexpected kind. Plentiful details of place and nostalgic period—Atlanta ablaze with the *Gone With the Wind* movie premiere hoopla of 60 years ago—present an audience with a pleasurable historic background, while providing the play with a suitable dramatic frame.

Even as the *GWTW* hubbub crowds out the bleak headlines of Hitler's invasion of Poland, members of the well-to-do Freitag family debate more pressing concerns—like the upcoming Ballyhoo social season. These long-Americanized Ger-

THE LAST NIGHT OF BALLY-HOO—Mary Bacon as Lala Levy in the Alliance Theater, Atlanta production of Alfred Uhry's ATCA-cited play

man Jews are conspicuous Southerners who decorate a Christmas tree, dismiss traditional Passover ritual as "ish-kabibble" and belong to clubby social organizations that shun more recently arrived Jews of less-assimilated standing. "The other kind," the Freitags casually term their east-of-the-Elbe brethren.

Back in 1939, Ballyhoo was a week-long calendar of festivities for young folks in smart Jewish society. "A lot of Jews in expensive clothes dancing around the country club wishing they could kiss their elbows and turn into Episcopalians," an insider describes it.

No doubt neighbors of Uhry's celebrated Miss Daisy, the Freitag family traces its Atlanta roots back before the Civil War. Adolph, a middle-aged bachelor of means, shares a big, overstuffed house with his sharp-tongued sister, Boo, and their sister-in-law, Reba, both widowed ladies, and their respective daughters, Lala and Sunny.

Urged along by her domineering mother, Boo, the awkward, if spirited Lala—whose debutante days are fast-fading—has been scouting around for an eligible Ballyhoo escort. Her prettier cousin Sunny, home for the holidays from Wellesley, attracts the interest of Joe, her Uncle Adolph's bright new right-hand man from New York. But Boo quickly takes a dislike to the John Garfield-ish Joe, who is obviously not as white bread a gentleman caller as she'd like for her niece. "That kike you hired has no manners," Boo complains to her brother, who encourages the growing relationship between Joe and Sunny.

Boo's casual anti-Semitic remark usually raises something of a gasp from the audience, who until then have been happily eating up the comedy's flavorful curli-cues of roundabout Southern chit-chat. The family's appropriation of quasi-gentile manners appears dubious, of course, but witnessing such expressed bigotry towards one's own people becomes especially thought-provoking within these oh-so-pleasant circumstances. The uneasy issues of class prejudice and self-hatred provide conflict for the budding romance while lending contrast to the comedy. And let's mention that there's a great deal of humor in Uhry's authentic Southern stories about the ugly Feigenbaum sisters, DeWald Levy's table manners, the scandalous Nachman wedding, and from which side of his esteemed family Peachy Weil got his red hair.

Even when he sounds darker notes, Uhry's delineation of quirky character and sense of irony brightens his underlying topic with comical glints. Raging at Adolph, who retreats from domestic squabbles behind his newspaper, Boo snaps, "Stop worryin' about Poland so much and give a thought to your own flesh and blood for a change!"

Dana Ivey, the wonderful Atlanta-born actress who originated the role of Miss Daisy for Uhry and his director Ron Lagomarsino nearly a decade ago, portrayed Boo with flinty authority in both the premiere production at Atlanta's Alliance Theater Company July 20, 1996, and in the play's subsequent Broadway staging in early 1997. Features puckering into a scowl, dark eyes flashing malignantly, Ivey's iron-spined Boo is at once tart about the world and tender towards her child.

With all of its tasty regional talk, seriocomic situations, and well-crafted realistic form, *The Last Night of Ballyhoo* looks like a deliberate throwback to the 1950s theater of Inge and Anderson. Uhry deploys this comfortable style of American drama to seduce an audience into contemplating the disturbing nature of his family portrait. Although the work's harmonious conclusion at a Seder dinner may register as rather facile to some, Uhry and director Ron Lagomarsino nevertheless offer their wishful ending with grace.

—MICHAEL SOMMERS

The Last Night of Ballyhoo *was first produced at the Alliance Theater, Atlanta, July 20, 1996 under the direction of Ron Lagomarsino.*

ATCA New Play Citation

THE RIDE DOWN
MOUNT MORGAN

A Play in Two Acts

BY ARTHUR MILLER

Cast and credits appear on page 414

ARTHUR MILLER is a patriarch of world theater whose career, works and honors are so extensive that they are very difficult to abbreviate on an occasion such as this, his winning of a 1996 ATCA New Play citation for his newly revised version of The Ride Down Mount Morgan. *He was born in New York City October 17, 1915 and grew up there, attending James Madison and Abraham Lincoln High Schools, then working for two years in an auto parts warehouse before going to college at the University of Michigan. At Michigan he studied playwriting, wrote two plays that won awards (*Honors at Dawn *and* No Villain: They Too Arise*) and received his B.A. in 1938. Returning to New York, he worked in the Federal Theater Project and the CBS and NBC radio workshops. His first Broadway play,* The Man Who Had All the Luck *(1944, Theater Guild Award), lasted for only 4 performances, but it was followed by* That They May Win *(1944),* All My Sons *(1947, Miller's first hit, Drama Critics,*

Tony, Best Play and Donaldson winner) and Death of a Salesman *(1949, Drama Critics, Tony, Best Play, Donaldson and Pulitzer winner), which has electrified theater audiences the world around and stands out as one of the 20th century's major works of art in any language, in any medium.*

Here is the list of Miller's subsequent works for the theater and major honors, based on his entries in Who's Who in America *and the* Best Plays *yearbooks:* The Crucible *(1953, Tony, Best Play, Donaldson, Obie),* A View From the Bridge *(1955, Best Play),* A Memory of Two Mondays *(1955),* After the Fall *(1964, Best Play),* Incident at Vichy *(1964, Best Play),* The Price *(1968, Best Play),* Fame *(1970),* The Reason Why *(1970),* The Creation of the World and Other Business *(1972, Best Play),* Up From Paradise *(1974),* The Archbishop's Ceiling *(1976),* The American Clock *(1980),* Some Kind of Love Story *(1983),* Elegy for a Lady *(1983),* Playing for Time *(1986),* Danger: Memory! *(1986),* The Last Yankee *(1990),* The Ride Down Mount Morgan *(1991, revised 1996),* Broken Glass *(1994) and* The Ryan Interview *(1995).*

Miller has also written a number of screen plays (including The Story of G.I. Joe *and* The Misfits*), TV plays (winning Peabody and Emmy Awards) and books of fiction and non-fiction. He is the recipient of a National Institute of Arts and Letters Gold Medal for Drama (1959) and a John F. Kennedy Lifetime Achievement Award (1984). Miller has been married three times (the second time to the late Marilyn Monroe), with four children. He now lives in Connecticut with his third wife, the photographer Inge Morath.*

INTRODUCTION: Willy Loman gets into his car to kill himself in *Death of a Salesman* because the myths of his time have come apart. Willy lived under the illusion that if you played the game you would eventually win the trophy.

Lyman Felt gets into his car to kill himself because the myths of his time have come apart, too. "Socialism is dead," says his wife, Theodora, "and Christianity is finished." With neither Marx nor Jesus to help formulate a moral code, what's a guy to do? Lyman Felt, a character born of the who-says-you-can't-have-it-all 1980s, decides to take a second wife, Leah, without going to the trouble of divorcing Theo.

How far have we, and Miller, come from the deluded Loman to the deregulated Lyman? In *The Ride Down Mount Morgan* (in a newly revised version which received its American premiere July 17, 1996 at the Williamstown Theater Festival), Miller still has his eyes keenly focused on the American dream and the nightmares that result from blindly following that dream.

The Ride Down Mount Morgan isn't as good or powerful a play as *Salesman*, but it may be a wiser one. It's certainly a funnier one. Miller surprised even his harshest critics with the sense of humor here. In one of the many flashbacks in the play, Theodora remembers a vacation right around the time her husband met Leah. Theo wonders, as she recalls the incident, whether he tried to kill her when she was attacked by a shark. He did call for help, but was it a real cry for help? The scene is played twice with Lyman yelling at the top of his lungs and then barely uttering a very meek "Help!" The difference in how F. Murray Abraham played the two scenes in Williamstown is the stuff of very affecting comedy. (Michael Learned as Theo and Patricia Clarkson as Leah were also right on target under Scott Elliott's direction. Michael Blakemore directed the world premiere in London with Tom Conti, Gemma Jones and Clare Higgins.)

If Miller isn't the dour moralist/realist he is often thought to be, neither is he a farceur. *The Ride Down Mount Morgan* is not *Three's Company*. If, as Theo says, the twin gods of Marx and Jesus are dead, there is nothing left to guide us. And is this not the root of today's alienation, despite protestations to the contrary about the importance of religion in everyday life? If there is no moral code, then Lyman Felt, who has run one of the most socially conscious businesses in the country, is free to follow his own Darwinian personal mandate. Surprisingly, given the playwright's uncompromised left-of-liberal politics, Felt's moral code, or lack of one, has been misconstrued as Miller's own dirty old musings.

That Felt winds up "an endless string attached to nothing" is clear evidence to the contrary. Like all of us, Miller may fantasize about crossing moral boundaries and in *The Ride Down Mount Morgan*, he lets Lyman run wild with those fantasies. As Miller said in a speech, Lyman has integrity but no morals. "He's very intent on living a truthful life—truthful meaning that his own impulses are expressed and not suppressed . . . " But if Felt has lost his moral code, Miller hasn't. The palpable harm he has done to others, which leads to both his personal and spiritual isolation, leaves us with a moral without moralism.

The Ride Down Mount Morgan, which was written before *Broken Glass*, shares other similarities with *Salesman* and other Miller plays. People tend to forget, particularly if they've seen the Hal Holbrook revival of *Salesman*, that *Salesman* was not a beacon of dramatic realism. Miller was after what he called in *Timebends* a "superconsciousness" in *Salesman*, which resulted in "emergency speech of an unashamedly open kind, rather than . . . the crabbed dramatic hints and pretexts of the 'natural'."

Lyman and Loman share similar speech patterns, and much of the action takes place in the two men's minds where the deceased, Felt's father and Loman's brother, make frequent cameos. There are also hints of *All My Sons*—Felt has let his partner take the fall for something nefarious in the past, and the sins of Felt's greed will reverberate in the next generation, although not as clearly or dramatically.

Critics tend to see Miller's later plays as a breed apart from his early successes. For all its humor and jauntiness, *The Ride Down Mount Morgan* is surely a kissing cousin of his earlier work.

—ED SIEGEL

Excerpts From *The Ride Down Mount Morgan*

The following scene takes place early in Act I, after Leah Felt visits her husband, Lyman Felt, in the hospital. Lyman had told her he had divorced his first wife, Theo, but the two Mrs. Felts meet at the hospital and discover they're married to a biga-mist. (A staging note from the playwright: *"The play veers from the farcical to the tragic and back again and should be performed all-out in both directions as the situation demands, without attempting to mitigate the extremes."* It also veers from the present to the past.)

> *A couch and a chair. Leah is seated facing Tom Wilson, a middle-aged but very fit lawyer who is reading a will and sipping coffee. After a moment, she gets up and moves to a point and stares, eyes filled with fear. Then, dialing a phone, turns to him.*

LEAH: Sorry I'm not being much of a hostess. Sure you wouldn't like some toast?

TOM *(immersed):* Thanks. I'm just about done here.

LEAH *(dialing):* God, I dread it—my boy'll be home from school any minute . . . *(To phone.)* Put my brother on, Tina . . . Lou?—I don't know, they won't let me see him yet. What'd Uniroyal say? *What?* Well, call L.A. this minute! I want that business!—But we discussed all this yesterday! Jetlag doesn't last this long. *(Hangs up.)* I don't know what it is; there's no sense of continuity from one day to another any more. *(Tom closes the file.)*—I know you're her lawyer, but I'm not really asking advice, am I?

TOM: I can discuss this. *(Returning her the file.)* The will does recognize the boy as his son, but you are not his wife.

LEAH *(lifting the file):* But this refers to me as his wife . . .

TOM: That's meaningless—he never divorced. However . . . *(Breaks off, pressing his eyes.)* I'm just stunned, I can't absorb it.

LEAH: I'm still in midair someplace.

TOM: What'd you ask me? Oh, yes—provided the legal wife gets a minimum of one-third of the estate, he can leave you as much as he likes. So you're very well taken care of. *(Sighs. Leans forward gripping his head.)* He actually flies a plane, you say?

LEAH: Oh, yes, soaring planes too. We own one.

TOM: You know, for years he never got off the ground unless it was unavoidable.

LEAH: Oh, he's wonderful in the air. *(Pause.)* I'm not here. I'm simply . . . not here. Can he be insane?

TOM: . . . May I ask you . . . ?

LEAH: Please . . . Incidentally, have you known him long?

TOM: Sixteen, seventeen years . . . When you decided to marry, I assume he told you he'd gotten a divorce . . .

LEAH: Of course. We went to Reno together.

TOM: No kidding! And what happened?

LEAH: God, I'd forgotten all about this . . . *(Breaks off.)* How could I have been so *stupid!*—You see, it was July, a hundred and ten on the street, so he had me stay in the hotel with the baby while he went to the court to pick up his divorce decree . . . *(She goes silent.)*

TOM: Yes?

LEAH *(shaking her head):* It's incredible . . . I was curious to see what a decree looked like . . .

Lyman enters, wearing a short-sleeved summer shirt.

. . . no particular reason, but I'd never seen one . . .

LYMAN: I threw it away.

LEAH *(a surprised laugh):* Why!

LYMAN: I don't want to look back. Darling, I feel twenty-five! *(Laughs.)* You look stunned!

LEAH *(kisses him lightly):* I never really believed you'd do it, darling.

LYMAN: I know. It's a miracle. *(He draws her to him: Tom is a few feet away.)* I feel you flowing round me like I'm a rock in the river.—I have a car and driver downstairs; come to your wedding. Leah, my darling!

LEAH: But can I tell you the wedding vow I wish we could make?—it's going to sound strange, but . . .

LYMAN: No!—say it!

LEAH: I'm embarrassed but I will: "Dearly beloved, I promise everything good, but I might have to lie to you sometime." Could one say that and still love someone? Because it's the truth . . . nobody knows what can happen, right?

LYMAN *(slight, amazed pause):* What balls you have to say that! Yes, it's the truth and I love you for it *(He kisses her then seems distracted.)*

LEAH: You seem drained—are you sorry you divorced her?

LYMAN: I'm . . . a little scared, that's all, but it's natural. Tell you what. I'm going to learn to fly a plane . . .

LEAH: But you hate flying!

LYMAN *(lifts her to her feet):* Yes. But no more fear. Ever! Of any kind.

Lyman exits without lowering his arm. She turns to Tom.

LEAH: . . . And it was all lies! How is it possible! Why did he do it? What did he want?

TOM: Actually . . . *(Tries to recall.)* . . . You know . . . I think we did have a discussion about a divorce . . .

LEAH: You did? When?

TOM: About nine years ago . . . although at the time I didn't take it all that seriously. He suddenly popped into my office one day with this "research" he said he'd done . . .

Lyman enters in a business suit.

LYMAN: . . . I've been looking into bigamy, Tom.

TOM *(laughs, surprised):* Bigamy!—What are you talking about?

LYMAN: There was a piece in the paper a few weeks ago. There's an enormous amount of bigamy in the United States now.

TOM: Oh? But what's the point . . . ?

LYMAN: I've been wondering—how about bigamy insurance? Might call it the Desertion Protection Plan.

TOM *(laughs):* It's a great name for a policy . . . but you're kidding.

LYMAN: I mean this. We could set the premiums very low, like a few cents a week. Be great, especially for minority women.

TOM: Say now! *(Greatly admiring.)* Where the hell do you get these ideas?

LYMAN: I don't think they're ideas, I just try to put myself in other people's places. *(Laughs, enjoying his immodesty.)* It's what's made me what I am today! Incidentally, how frequently do they prosecute for bigamy anymore, you have any idea?

TOM: No. But it's a victimless crime, so it can't be often.

LYMAN: That's my impression, too. Get somebody to research it, will you, I want to be sure.—I'll be in Elmira till Friday. *(Starts to leave but dawdles.)*

TOM: Why do I think you're depressed?

LYMAN: Slightly, maybe. *(The self-deprecating grin.)* I'm turning fifty-four this July.

TOM: Fifty's much tougher, I think.

LYMAN: My father died at fifty-three.

TOM: Well, you're over the hump. Anyway, you're in better shape than anybody I know.

LYMAN: Famous last words.

TOM: —Something wrong, Lyman?

LYMAN *(slight pause; he decides to tell):* I was having lunch today at the Four Seasons, and just as I'm getting up, this woman—beautifully dressed, smile on her face—leans over me and says, "I hope you drop dead, you son of a bitch." You know what she was talking about.

TOM: I can't believe that's still happening.

LYMAN: Oh, three or four times a year; they don't always come out with it but a lot of people still think I turned in my partner to keep myself out of jail.—Which maybe I did, but I don't think so; I think Raoul paid for his crookedness, period. *(Smiles.)* But I can't help it, I still love that little bastard. We had some great years building the firm.

TOM: Well, it's over the dam and out to sea.

LYMAN: I did the right thing; it's just the imputation of cowardice that . . . *(Breaks off.)* Well, fuck it, I've lived my life, and I refuse to be ashamed of it! Talk to you soon. *(Stands, but hesitates to leave.)*

TOM: —Is there something else?

LYMAN: I don't think I have the balls.

> A pause. Lyman stands perfectly still, controlled; then, facing his challenge, turns rather abruptly to Tom.

It's funny about you, Tom—I've been a lot closer to other men, but there's nobody I trust like you. *(A grin.)* I guess you know I've cheated on Theodora, don't you.

TOM: Well, I've had my suspicions, yes–ever since I walked in on you humping that Pakistani typist on your desk.

LYMAN *(laughs):* "Humping!"—I love that Presbyterian jive of yours, haven't heard that in years.

TOM: Quaker.

LYMAN *(confessionally, quietly):* I don't want to be that way any more. It's kind of ridiculous at my age, for one thing. *(With difficulty.)* I think I've fallen in love.

TOM: Oh, don't tell me!

LYMAN *(pointing at him and laughing):* Look at you! God, you really love Theodora, don't you!

TOM: Of course I do! You're not thinking of divorce, are you?

LYMAN: I don't know what I'm thinking. It's years since anything like this has happened to me. But I probably won't do anything . . . maybe I just wanted to say it out loud to somebody.

TOM: I have a feeling it'll pass.

LYMAN: I've been waiting for it to, but it keeps getting worse.—I've frankly never believed monogamous guys like you are honestly happy, but with her I can almost see it for myself. And that can't ever be with Theodora. With her I'll be on the run till I croak, and that's the truth.

TOM: You know she loves you deeply. Profoundly, Lyman.

LYMAN: Tom, I love her too, but our neuroses just don't match.

TOM: Frankly, I can't imagine you apart from each other—you seem so dependent.

LYMAN: I know. I've always relied on her sense of reality, especially her insights into this country. But I just don't want to cheat anymore—it's gotten hateful to me, all deception has. It's become my Nazi, my worst horror—I want to wear my own face on my face every day till I die. Or do you think that kind of honesty is possible?

TOM: I don't have to tell you, the problem is not honesty but how much you hurt others with it.

LYMAN: Right. What about your religion? But there's no solution there either, I guess.

TOM: I somehow can't imagine you praying, Lyman.

> *Short pause.*

LYMAN: Is there an answer?

TOM: I don't know, maybe all one can do is hope to end up with the right regrets.

LYMAN: *(silent a moment):* You ever cheated, Tom?

TOM: No.

LYMAN: Honest to God?—I've seen you eye the girls around here.

TOM: It's the truth.

LYMAN: Is that the regret you end up with?

> *Tom laughs bashfully. Then Lyman joins him. And suddenly, Lyman's suffering is on his face.*

. . . Shit, that was cruel, Tom, forgive me, will you?—Dammit, why do I let myself get depressed? It's all pointless guilt, that's all! Here I start from nothing, create forty-two hundred jobs for people and raise over sixty ghetto blacks to office positions when that was not easy to do—I should be proud of myself, son of a bitch! And I am! I am!

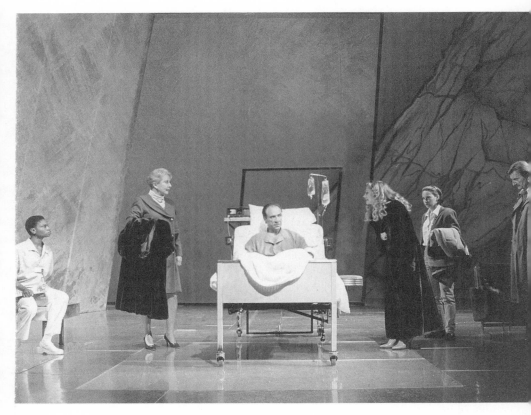

THE RIDE DOWN MOUNT MORGAN—Adina Porter, Michael Learned, F. Murray Abraham, Patricia Clarkson, Amy Ryan and Larry Bryggman in the Williamstown, Mass. Theater Festival production of Arthur Miller's revised play, winner of a 1996 ATCA Citation

> *He bangs on the desk, then subsides, looks front and downward.*

I love your view. That red river of taillights gliding down Park Avenue on a winter's night—and all those silky white thighs crossing inside those heated limousines ... Christ, can there be a sexier vision in the world? *(Turning back to Tom.)* I keep thinking of my father—how connected he was to his life; couldn't wait to open the store every morning and happily count the pickles, rearrange the olive barrels. People like that knew the main thing. Which is what? What's the main thing, do you know?

> *Tom is silent.*

—Look, don't worry, I really can't imagine myself without Theodora, she's a great, great wife! ... I love that woman! It's always good talking to you, Tom.

> *Lyman starts to go; halts.*

Maybe it's simply that if you try to live according to your real desires, you have to end up looking like a shit.

He exits. Leah covers her face, and there is a pause as Tom observes her.

TOM: I'm sorry.

LEAH: He had it all carefully worked out from the very beginning.

TOM: I'd say it was more like . . . a continuous improvisation.

LEAH: What's so bewildering is that he was the one who was pushing to get married, not me. It was the baby, you see—once I was pregnant, he simply wouldn't listen to reason . . .

Lyman hurries on in a winter overcoat, claps a hand over her mouth.

LYMAN: Don't tell me it's too late. *(Kisses her.)* Did you do it?

LEAH: I was just walking out the door for the hospital.

LYMAN: Oh, thank God.

Draws her to a seat and pulls her down.

Please, dear, give me one full minute and then you can do as you like.

LEAH: Don't, Lyme, it's impossible. *(Obviously changing the subject—with pain.)* Listen, up here they're all saying Reagan's just about won it.

LYMAN: Well, he'll probably be good for business. The knuckleheads usually are.—You know if you do this it's going to change it between us.

LEAH: Darling, it comes down to being a single parent, and I just don't want that.

LYMAN: I've already named him.

LEAH *(amused, touching his face):* How do you know it's a him?

LYMAN: I'm never wrong. I have a very intimate relationship with ladies' bellies. His name is Benjamin after my father, and Alexander after my mother's mother who I loved a lot. *(Grins at his own egoism.)* You can put in a middle name.

LEAH *(with an unhappy laugh):* Well, thanks so much! *(She tries to stand up, but he holds her.)* He asked me not to be late.

LYMAN: The Russians—this is an ancient custom—before an important parting, they sit for a moment, in silence. Give Benjamin this moment.

LEAH: He is not Benjamin, now stop it!

LYMAN: Believe in your feelings, Leah, the rest is nonsense. What do you really and truly want?

Silence for a moment.

I would drive him to school in the mornings, take him to ball games.

LEAH: Twice a month?

LYMAN: With the new office set up here, I could easily be with you more than half the time.

LEAH: And Theodora?

LYMAN: It's difficult to talk about her.

LEAH: With me, you mean.

LYMAN: I can't lie to myself, darling, she's been a tremendous wife. It would be too unjust.

LEAH: But keeping it secret—where does that leave me? It's hard enough to identify myself as it is. And I can't believe she won't find out sooner or later, and then what?

LYMAN: If I actually have to choose, it'll be you. But she doesn't know a soul in this whole area; it'd be a million-to-one shot for her ever to find out. I'm practically with you half the time now, and it's been pretty good, hasn't it?

LEAH *(touching her belly):* . . . But what do we tell this . . . ?

LYMAN: . . . Benjamin.

LEAH: Oh, stop calling him Benjamin! It's not even three weeks!

LYMAN: That's long enough to be Benjamin—he has a horoscope, stars and planets; he has a *future!*

LEAH: There's something . . . why do I feel we're circling around something? There's something I don't believe here—what is it?

LYMAN: Maybe that I'm this desperate. *(Kisses her belly.)*

LEAH: Are you?—I can't express it . . . there's just something about this baby that doesn't seem . . . I don't know—*inevitable.*

LYMAN: Darling, I haven't wanted anything this much since my twenties, when I was struggling to be a poet and make something of my own that would last.

LEAH: Really.

LYMAN: It's the truth.

LEAH: That's touching, Lyman . . . I'm very moved.

So it is up in the air for the moment.

But I can't, I won't, it's the story of my life, I always end up with all the responsibility; I'd have to be in total charge of your child and I know I'd resent it finally—and maybe even you as well. You're putting me back to being twelve or thirteen and my parents asking *me* where to go on vacations, or what kind of car to buy or what color drapes. I hate that position! One of the most sensuous things about you was that I could lie back and let you drive, and now you're putting me behind the wheel again. It's just all wrong.

LYMAN: But when you're thirty-six, I'll be sixty.

LEAH: Doesn't mean a thing to me.

LYMAN: Dummy, you're not listening; when you're forty-six, I'll be *seventy.*

LEAH: Well, it's not eighty.—I've made up my mind, dear.

LYMAN: I thought if we lived together, let's say ten years, you'd still be in the prime, and pretty rich, and I'd . . .

LEAH: . . . Walk away into the sunset?

LYMAN: I'm trying to be as cruelly realistic as life, darling. Have you ever loved a man the way you love me?

LEAH: No.

LYMAN: Well? That's the only reality.

LEAH: You can drive me to the hospital, if you like realism so much. *(She stands. He does.)* You look so sad! You poor man.

She kisses him; a silent farewell is in this kiss; she gets her coat and turns to him.

I won't weaken on this, dear, so make up your mind.

LYMAN: We're going to lose each other if you do this. I feel it.

LEAH: Well, there's a very simple way not to lose me, dear, I guess that's why they invented it.—Come, wait in the hospital if you want to. If not, I'll be back tomorrow.

She draws him on, but he halts.

LYMAN: Will you give me a week to tell her? It's still early for you, isn't it?

LEAH: Tell her what?

LYMAN: . . . That I'm going to marry you.

TOM: I see.

The Ride Down Mount Morgan *had its American premiere at the Williamstown, Mass. Theater Festival July 17, 1996 under the direction of Scott Elliott.*

A DIRECTORY
OF NEW-PLAY PRODUCTIONS

Professional productions June 1, 1996–May 31, 1997 of new plays by leading companies around the United States who supplied information on casts and credits at Camille Croce Dee's request, plus a few reported by other reliable sources, are listed here in alphabetical order of the locations of more than 70 producing organizations. Date given is opening date, included whenever such information was available. Most League of Resident Theaters (LORT) and other regularly-producing Equity groups were queried for this comprehensive Directory, and all ATCA-nominated productions which opened within the above time frame are included, with their citations noted. Theater companies not listed here either did not offer new or newly-revised scripts during the period under review or had not responded to our query by press time. Most productions listed below are world premieres; a few are American premieres, new revisions, second looks or scripts produced previously but not previously reported in *Best Plays*.

Abingdon, Va.: Barter Theater

(Richard Rose producing artistic director)

DOCTORS AND DISEASES. Musical revue with music and lyrics by Peter Ekstrom; additional material and lyrics by David DeBoy. June 19, 1996. Director, Don Stephenson; musical staging, Emily Loesser, Don Stephenson; musical direction and arrangements, Albert Ahronheim; scenery, Crystal Tiala; costumes and additional choreography, Amanda Aldridge; lighting, David G. Silver-Friedl; pianist, Elizabeth Falcone.

Woman #2 .... Linda Libby
Man #1 .... Alan Souza
Woman #1 .... Christianne Tisdale
Man #2 .... Todd Gearhart

MUSICAL NUMBERS, ACT I: "The Human Body Is a Most Amazing Thing," "Oh Boy! How I Love My Cigarettes," "The Consummate Picture," "I'm a Well-Known, Respected Practitioner," "Tomorrow," "A World of My Own," "And Yet, I Lived On," "Willie," "Please, Dr. Fletcher," "Take It Off, Tammy," "It's My Fat," "I Hope I Never Get . . . ".

ACT II: "Song," "Medicine Man Blues," "Private Practice," "There's Nothing Wrong," "Ballade a la Stephen Foster," "I'm Sure of It," "I Loved My Father," "Jesus Is My Doctor," "Bing Bang Boom," "Eighty Thousand Orgasms," "In the Good Old Days," "Do I Still Have You?", "Hymn," Finale: "The Human Body Is a Most Amazing Thing" (Reprise).

GIRL OF MY DREAMS. Musical with book and additional lyrics by David DeBoy; music by Peter Ekstrom; lyrics by Steven Hayes and Peter Ekstrom. June 27, 1996. Director, Richard Rose; choreography, Pamela Sousa; musical direction, Elizabeth Falcone; orchestrations and arrangements, Barry Levitt; scenery and lighting, Dale F. Jordan; costumes, Amanda Aldridge; sound, Scott Koenig.

Granddad .... Ed Sala
Ben Piper .... Ted Levy
Effie Lawrence .... Linda Libby
Cindy Hawthorne .... Michele Ragusa
Phil Gold .... Alan Souza
Luke Wheeler .... Todd Gearhart
Laurie; Liz .... Christianne Tisdale
Freddy Gillette .... Michael Malone
    Time: 1996 and 1944. Place: Granddad's attic.

MUSICAL NUMBERS, ACT I: "Wonderful Memories of You," "We're Here to Volunteer," "Boogie Back to Forty-Four," "The Volunteer March," "How Lucky Can a Person Hope To Be?", same (Reprise), "Girl of My Dreams," same (Reprise), "Pin Up Girls," "When It's Over There in Dover," "An Army Song," "Nocturne," "The Ladies Always Go for the Brass."

ACT II: "Coffee and Donuts," "We've Got a Lot in Common," "Look at Me," "A Nice Home," "We've Got a Lot in Common" (Reprise), "God Bless a Boy That I Love," "Close Your Eyes," "What Can I Do for My Country?", "Give Me a

OREGON SHAKESPEARE FESTIVAL, ASHLAND—Tamu Gray, Gina Daniels and BW Gonzalez in a scene from *The Darker Face of the Earth* by former U.S. Poet Laureate Rita Dove

Chance," "I'll Be Waitin'," "Freddy's Ready," "What Can I Do for My Country?" (Reprise), "Girl of My Dreams" (Reprise), "Wonderful Memories of You" (Reprise), "A Nice Home" (Reprise), "Wonderful Memories of You" (Reprise).

MIRACLES. By Frank Higgins. April 9, 1997. Director, Susanne Boulle; scenery, Bob Ordorsio; costumes, Pat Kealy; lighting, John McLain; sound, Scott Koenig.

Kate Kingsley	Cynthia Hood
Tom Hudson	Larry Cahn
Eve Hudson	Jenifer Rau

Place: Kate's classroom. Act I, Scene 1: A day in autumn of this year. Scene 2: That evening. Scene 3: The next day. Act II, Scene 1: A few minutes later. Scene 2: A short time later. Scene 3: A short time later.

Early Stages Staged Readings:
THE BETTINGER PRIZE. By Edwin Wilson. July 8, 1996.
ALMOST EDEN. By Frank Higgins. July 22, 1996.
SILE'S MIRACLE. By Sean O'Sullivan. August 5, 1996.
THE DEVIL IN DISPUTANTA. By Johnny Payne and Williams Underwood. August 19, 1996.
THE BEAR FACTS. By Jo Carson. August 26, 1996.

Ashland, Ore.: Oregon Shakespeare Festival

(Libby Appel artistic director; Paul Nicholson executive director)

THE DARKER FACE OF THE EARTH. By Rita Dove. July 24, 1996. Director, Ricardo Khan; scenery, Richard L. Hay; costumes, Karen Lim; lighting, James Sale; composer, Olu Dara; choreography, Dianne McIntyre; presented in association with Crossroads Theater Company,

New Brunswick, N.J., Ricardo Khan artistic director.
The Slaves:
Phebe .... BW Gonzalez
Psyche .... Gina Daniels
Hector .... Thomas Byrd
Alexander .... J.P. Phillips
Scylla .... Tamu Gray
Ticey .... Debra Lynne Wicks
Old Woman;
  Narrator .... Johanna Jackson
Diana .... Nadine Griffith
Scipio .... Davon Russell
Augustus Newcastle .... Ezra Knight
The Whites:
Amalia Jennings
  LaFarge .... Elizabeth Norment
Louis LaFarge .... Mark Murphey

Doctor .... Dennis Robertson
The Conspirators:
Ned .... Tyrone Wilson
Benjamin Skeene .... August Gabriel
Henry Blake .... Kevin Kenerly
  Chorus, Dancers—Ensemble. Drummers—
Russ Appleyard, Craig Goodmond.
  Time: Prologue, the early 1820s; play, the early 1840s. Place: The Jennings plantation and environs in South Carolina. One intermission.

Unstaged Readings:

PIECES OF THE QUILT. By Lanford Wilson, Tony Kushner, Migdalia Cruz, Octavio Solis, others; compiled by Sean San Jose Blackman. August 12, 1996.
SAILING TO BYZANTIUM. By Sandra Deer. September 13, 1996.

Atlanta: Alliance Theater Company

(Kenny Leon artistic director; Edith H. Love managing director)

THE LAST NIGHT OF BALLYHOO. By Alfred Uhry. July 20, 1996. Director, Ron Lagomarsino; scenery, John Lee Beatty; costumes, Susan E. Mickey; lighting, Kenneth Posner; music, Robert Waldman; sound, Brian Kettler.
Lala Levy .... Mary Bacon
Reba Freitag .... Valerie J. Curtin
Boo Levy .... Dana Ivey
Adolph Freitag .... Terry Beaver

Joe Farkas .... Stephen Mailer
Sunny Freitag .... Jessalyn Gilsig
Peachy Weil .... Stephen Largay
  Time: December 1939. Place: Atlanta, Ga., in Adolph Freitag's house, at the Standard Club and aboard the Crescent Limited. One intermission.
  An ATCA citation; see introduction to this section.

Baltimore: Center Stage

(Irene Lewis artistic director; Peter W. Culman managing director)

TRIUMPH OF LOVE. Musical based on the play by Marivaux; book by James Magruder; music by Jeffrey Stock; lyrics by Susan Birkenhead. November 21, 1996. Director, Michael Mayer; choreography, Doug Varone; musical direction, Bradley Vieth; scenery, Heidi Landesman; costumes, Catherine Zuber; lighting, Brian MacDevitt; sound, David Budries; orchestrations, Peter Matz; co-produced with Yale Repertory Theater, Stan Wojewodski Jr. artistic director.
Princess Leonide .... Susan Egan
Corine .... Denny Dillon
Agis .... Christopher Sieber
Hermocrates .... Robert LuPone
Hesione .... Mary Beth Peil
Harlequin .... Kenny Raskin
Dimas .... Daniel Marcus
  Place: The garden retreat of the philosopher Hermocrates. One intermission.
  MUSICAL NUMBERS, ACT I: "Anything,"

"The Bond That Can't Be Broken," "You May Call Me Phocion," "The Mysteries of Criticism," "Us," "The Ballad of Cecile," "Serenity," "Issue in Question," "Teach Me Not to Love You."
  ACT II: "Three Great Minds," "The Tree," "What Have I Done?", "Henchmen Are Forgotten," "Love Won't Take No for an Answer," Finale.

THUNDER KNOCKING ON THE DOOR: A BLUSICAL TALE OF RHYTHM AND THE BLUES. Musical by Keith Glover; music by various authors. December 13, 1996. Produced in association with Alabama Shakespeare Festival, Kent Thompson artistic director; see its entry in the Montgomery listing in this section; and Dallas Theater Center, Richard Hamburger artistic director.
  Elizabeth Osborn Award winner; see introduction to this section.

Berkeley, Calif.: Berkeley Repertory Theater

(Sharon Ott artistic director through 11/6/96; Tony Taccone 1997 artistic director)

MAUVAIS TEMPS. Solo performance by Anne Galjour; written by Anne Galjour. June 5, 1996. Director, Sharon Ott; scenery, John Mayne; costumes, Laura Hazlett; lighting, Novella Smith; sound, Stephen LeGrand.

Presented without intermission on a program with another Galjour one-acter, *Hurricane*.

Buffalo: Studio Arena Theater

(Gavin Cameron-Webb artistic director; Brian J. Wyatt executive director)

MUD, RIVER, STONE. By Lynn Nottage. October 20, 1996. Director, Seret Scott; scenery, Hugh Landwehr; costumes, Martha Hally; lighting, Dennis Parichy; sound, Rick Menke; original music composition, Lorna Zelt, Corey Kertzie; produced in association with The Acting Company.

David .... Marc Damon Johnson
Sarah .... Cheryl Turner
Joaquim .... Marcel Braithwaite
Neibert .... Kevin Orton
Blake .... Ross Bickell
Ama .... Mary F. Randle
Simone .... Drew Richardson
    Place: The lobby and veranda of a once grand colonial hotel in Western Africa—perhaps a former Portuguese colony. One intermission.

DEAD GUILTY. By Richard Harris. January 5, 1997 (American premiere). Director, Jane Page; scenery and costumes, G.W. Mercier; lighting, Jim Sale; sound, Rick Menke; composer, Bob Volkman.

Julia .... Patricia Dalen
Anne .... Suzanna Hay
Gary .... Peter Friedrich

Margaret .... Darrie Lawrence
    Time: The present. Place: London, in the late Victorian home of graphic designer Julia Darrow. One intermission.

TWELVE ANGRY MEN. By Reginald Rose. February 9, 1997 (American premiere of revised version). Director, Gavin Cameron-Webb; scenery and costumes, G. W. Mercier; lighting, Brian Nason; sound, Rick Menke.

Foreman .... Jack Hunter
Juror #2 .... Richard Wesp
Jurur #3 .... Ross Bickell
Juror #4 .... Terry Layman
Juror #5 .... Kevin Barwell
Juror #6 .... Tony Ward
Juror #7 .... Tracy Griswold
Juror #8 .... Anthony Fusco
Juror #9 .... Emanuel Fried
Juror #10 .... Michael Cullen
Juror #11 .... Saul Elkin
Juror #12 .... Richard Shoberg
Guard .... Dominic Telesco
Voice of the Judge .... Michael Baranski
    Time: 1956. Place: Lower Manhattan. One intermission.

Cambridge, Mass.: American Repertory Theater

(Robert Brustein artistic director)

THE CABINET OF DR. CALIGARI. Multimedia production; libretto, music and sound by John Moran. February 26, 1997. Director, Bob McGrath; scenery, Laurie Olinder, Fred Tietz; slides, Laurie Olinder; costumes, Catherine Zuber; lighting, Howard S. Thies; film, Anthony Chase; presented in conjunction with the American Music Theater Festival, Philadelphia.

With Alvin Epstein, Remo Airaldi, Benjamin Evett, Jeremy Geidt, Charles Levin, Karen MacDonald, Scott Ripley, Jack Willis, Kevin Bergen, Jay Boyer, Jada Galan, Steve Harper, Phoebe Jonas, Cheryl Kenan, Kwana Martinez.
No intermission.

Cambridge, Mass.: Cambridge Theater Company

(Andreas Teuber producing director)

CRY ME A RIVER. By Joyce Carol Oates; revised version of play formerly entitled *Black*. January 10, 1997. Director, Gordon Edelstein; scenery, Karl Eigsti; costumes, Paul Tazewell; lighting, Beverly Emmons; composer and sound, Johnna Doty; produced in association with Louise Westergaard, Mark S. Schwartz and William J. Condren.

Debra O'Donnell	Julia Gibson
Victor Slezak	Jonathan Boyd
Tony Todd	Lew Claybrook

No intermission.

Chicago: Goodman Theater

(Robert Falls artistic director; Roche Schulfer executive director)

THE HOUSE OF MARTIN GUERRE. Musical with book by Leslie Arden and Anna Theresa Cascio; music and lyrics by Leslie Arden. June 21, 1996. Director, David Petrarca; choreography, David Marques; musical direction, Jeffrey Klitz; scenery, Robert Brill; costumes, Susan Hilferty; lighting, James F. Ingalls; sound, Rob Milburn; orchestrations, Bruce Coughlin.

Young Bertrande	Cecily Strong
Bernarde de Rols	Hollis Resnik
Pierre Guerre	Kevin Gudahl
Martin Guerre	Guy Adkins
Father Boeri	John W. Eskola
Antoine	Norman Moses
Phillippe	Jeff Dumas
Guilhaume	Jeff Parker
Jehannot	Craig Bennett
Sanxi Guerre; Judge Francois de Ferriere	David Girolmo
Wise Woman	Cheryl Sylvester
Jeannette	Kelly Anne Clarke
Marie	Marnie Nicolella
Marguerite	Tina Gluschenko
Bertrande	Julain Molnar
Catherine	Frances Limoncelli
Little Sanxi	Willie Malnati
Jean Peghula	Allan Chambers
Arnaud du Tilh	Anthony Crivello
Suzanne	Genevieve VenJohnson
Suzanne's Husband; Judge Jean de Coras	Kingsley Leggs
Jehannot's Wife	Mary Ernster
Soldier; Carbon Barrau	Tim Rezash

Other Villagers, Soldiers and Townspeople of Toulouse: Bryan P. Brems, Stephanie Swanson, Company.

Time: 1538-1560. Place: Artigat, a remote farming village in southwestern France and the nearby city of Toulouse. One intermission.

MUSICAL NUMBERS, ACT I: "The House of the Guerres," "The Wedding Night," "Eight Years," "Lullaby," "Seasons Pass," "It Isn't That Easy for Me," "Martin's Home," "The House of the Guerres" (Reprise), "Devils and Doubts," "The World Is Changing," "Something Isn't Right," "Martin Couldn't Be Happier/Nothing Can Prepare You," "I've Had Enough," "Lullaby"/Act I Finale.

ACT II: "Nothing to Do But Wait," "Toulouse," "Nothing to Do But Wait" (Reprise), "Why Are You Still Crossing Me?", "The Way of the World," "No Life at All," "Every Word Is True," "Lullaby" (Reprise), "It Isn't That Easy for Me" (Reprise), "That Night I Won't Forget," "Monsieur Coras," "A Shred of Doubt," "Beautiful Day for a Hanging," "Arnaud's Apology," "The Way of the World/The World Is Changing."

The Studio

SEEKING THE GENESIS. By Kia Corthron. October 1, 1996. Director, Walter Dallas; scenery, Robert C. Martin; costumes, Karin Kopischke; lighting, Kathy A. Perkins; sound, Rob Milburn.

Kite	Raphael Vargas Chestang
Justin	Demetrius D. Thornton
Teacher	Kava Stewartson
C Ana	Ora Jones
Kandal	Rachel Robinson
Cheryl	Kim Leigh Smith
Mitch	Christopher Brown
Sac	Tim Edward Rhoze
Pizzaman; Professor	Rick Sandoval

Pizza Customers: Christopher Brown, Tim Edward Rhoze, Kim Leigh Smith, Kava Stewartson.

Time: Now. Place: In and around a big-city housing project. One intermission.

Chicago: Next Theater Company

(Steve Pickering artistic director; Peter Rybolt managing director)

THE HISTORY OF THE DEVIL, OR SCENES FROM A PRETENDED LIFE. By Clive Barker. November 8, 1996 (American premiere). Director, Steve Pickering; scenery, Rebecca Hamlin; costumes, Linda Roethke; lighting, Andrew Meyers; sound, Barry G. Funderburg.

Judge Popper .... William J. Norris
Pia Shim; Woman; Dante;
  Madeleine; Therese;
  Mrs. Mendoza .... Naama Potok
Nancy; Polyxene; Mary Ann Clarke;
  Macready .... Catherine O'Connor
Sam Kyle; George
  Keipenhauer .... Michael Grant

Verrier; Nicholas Vidal;
  Jack Easter .... Michael Park Ingram
Belial; Callimachus;
  Duke of York .... David Silvis
Araziel; Barbara .... Anne Dudek
Catherine Lamb .... Amy Galper
Jane Beck .... Kipleigh Brown
Milo Milo; Yapshi; Daniel Mendoza;
  Jesus Christ .... Timothy Thilleman
Devil .... Lusia Strus
Ulla Shim; Alette; Isobel Nider;
  Lilith .... Mary Chaisson
  Place: London and Lake Turkana, Africa. One intermission.

Chicago: Steppenwolf Theater Company

(Martha Lavey artistic director; Michael Gennaro managing director)

SLAUGHTERHOUSE-FIVE, OR THE CHILDREN'S CRUSADE. Adapted from Kurt Vonnegut by Eric Simonson. September 29, 1996. Director, Eric Simonson; scenery, Neil Patel; costumes, Kärin Simonson Kopischke; lighting, Scott Zielinski; sound design and composition, Michael Bodeen, Rob Milburn; projections, John Boesche; fight choreography, Nick Offerman.

Soldier .... Orion Barnes
Man .... Robert Breuler
Rosewater; Ensemble .... Matt DeCaro
Weary; Ensemble .... Matt Doherty
Mother; Grandmother;
  German Woman .... Deanna Dunagan
Lazzaro; Barbershop Quartet;
  Ensemble .... Raul E. Esparza
Soldier; Barbershop Quartet .... Tom Farnan
Young Billy .... Nicholas Jay Friedman
Englishman; Voice;
  Barbershop Quartet .... Jeffrey Hutchinson
Soldier .... Romanos Isaac
Montana; Ensemble .... Soseh Kevorkian
Derby; Ensemble .... Rich Komenich
Soldier .... Phillip J. Lee
Reg; Campbell; Barbershop
  Quartet .... David New
Soldier .... Paul Pierro
Soldier; Caddy .... David Perry
Barbara; Lily .... Jennifer Erin Roberts
Valencia; Ensemble .... Sharon Sachs
Soldier .... Gabriel Sigal
Soldier .... Chris Simpson

Billy Pilgrim .... Rick Snyder
Soldier .... Chas Vrba
Kilgore Trout; Ensemble .... Will Zahrn
  Time: Past, present and future. Place: Ilium, N.Y. and various parts of Germany.

THE VIEWING ROOM. By Daniel J. Rubin. October 27, 1996. Director, Anna D. Shapiro; scenery, Todd Rosenthal; costumes, Mara Blumenfeld; lighting, Kevin Snow; sound design and composition, Max Shapiro.

Brian .... Paul Adelstein
Gab .... Heidi Mokrycki
Kyle .... Darryl Alan Reed
  Time: The not-too-distant future. Place: The suburb of a large city. No intermission.

TIME TO BURN. By Charles L. Mee; inspired by Maxim Gorky's The Lower Depths. February 23, 1997. Director, Tina Landau; scenery, James Schuette; costumes, Mara Blumenfeld; lighting, Scott Zielinski; sound design and composition, Michael Bodeen, Rob Milburn; fight choreography, Robin McFarquhar.

Billy .... Jeb Brown
Jessie .... Irma P. Hall
Miroslav Varnenski .... Yasen Peyankov
Alessandra .... Alexandra Billings
Kadira .... Mariann Mayberry
Anna Varnenski .... Marilyn Dodds Frank
Raul .... Frankie Davila
Vinnie Pazzi .... Larry Russo

VICTORY GARDENS, CHICAGO—John Judd and Kate Goehring in a scene from *Drowning Sorrows* by Douglas Post

Tertius	Paul Mullins	Trang	Tonray Ho
Nikos	Romanos Isaac	Policemen	Michael Dailey, John Sierros
Nguyen	Manao DeMuth	Time: Nighttime in America. Place: An aban-	
Schlomo	Mike Nussbaum	doned factory. No intermission.	

Chicago: Victory Gardens Theater

(Dennis Zacek artistic director; John Walker managing director)

DROWNING SORROWS. By Douglas Post. November 8, 1996. Director, Curt Columbus; scenery, Bill Bartelt; costumes, Margaret Morettini; lighting, David Gipson; sound, Lindsay Jones.

Cole Rucker	Kenn E. Head
Duncan Crawford	John Judd
Gina Frances	Keli Garrett
Raymond Miles	Andrew Leman
Emily Miles	Kate Goehring

Time: Summer. Place: A bar on the east end of the island of St. John. No intermission.

THE WASHINGTON-SARAJEVO TALKS: A PLAY FOR THE NEXT MILLENNIUM. By

Carla Seaquist. November 21, 1996. Director, Sandy Shinner; scenery, Elizabeth McGeehan; costumes, Alexandra Sargent; lighting, Andrew Meyers; sound, Ray Nardelli.

Carla .... Deanna Dunagan
Vlado .... Raul E. Esparza
    Time: December 1994 to December 1995, when the siege of Sarajevo entered into its fourth year. Place: On the phone and in the mind. One intermission.

SIDNEY BECHET KILLED A MAN. By Stuart Flack. January 17, 1997. Director, Sandy Shinner; scenery, Jeff Bauer; costumes, Claudia Boddy; lighting, Rita Pietraszek; sound, Lindsay Jones.

Philip Litwin .... Jack McLaughlin-Gray
Marcel Freed .... John Judd
Emily Litwin .... Deanna Dunagan
Man; Broker; Policeman; Pilot .... A.C. Smith
Waitress; Nurse; Isabelle;
    Ticket Agent .... Kirsten Daurelio
Jerry ...... Reid Godshaw, Jordan M. Loperena
    Time: The present. Place: Chicago. One intermission.

ROOT CAUSES. By Steve Carter. March 14, 1997. Director, Dennis Zacek; scenery, Mary Griswold; costumes, Claudia Boddy; lighting, Todd Hensley; sound, Lindsay Jones; projections and video design, Stephan Mazurek.

Eunice Bell; Young Black Female;
    Black Woman .... Velma Austin
Young Black Male; Ice Heart .. T-Shaun Barrett
Ed Gaines .... Craig Boyd
Voiceovers .... Aaron Carter
Mrs. Gussie Harrison .... Laura Collins
Judge Caroline Weitzler .... Gail Curry
Lady Bresson .... Kelley Hazen
Tina Yu; Guard .... Jeany Park
"Princess" Dante; Foreperson ...... Bob Romeo
Revs. Andy and Lindsay Lightfoot .. A.C. Smith
Herman Oberstein .... Richard Shavzin
Black Male; Bailiff;
    Blood Black .... Ray Thompson
August "Happy Cat"
Harrison .... Philip Edward VanLear
    Time: The very recent past. Place: An American city.

Cincinnati: Cincinnati Playhouse in the Park

(Edward Stern producing artistic director; Buzz Ward executive director)

THE NOTEBOOK OF TRIGORIN. By Tennessee Williams; adapted from Ann Dunnigan's translation of *The Seagull* by Anton Chekhov. September 3, 1996 (American premiere). Director, Stephen Hollis; scenery, Ming Cho Lee; costumes, Candice Donnelly; lighting, Brian Nason; sound, David B. Smith.

Medvedenko .... Jack Cirillo
Masha .... Natacha Roi
Constantine .... Timothy Altmeyer
Yakov .... Jed Davis
Sorin .... Donald Christopher
Trigorin .... Jeff Woodman
Nina .... Stina Nielsen
Paulina .... Sonja Lanzener
Dorn .... Philip Pleasants
Shamrayev .... Alan Mixon
Arkadina .... Lynn Redgrave
Cook .... John Sharp
Old Woman .... Eleanor B. Shepherd
Maid .... Poppi Kramer
Workers .... Jack Marshall,
                                  Bruce Pilkenton
    Act I: Sorin's estate, early evening. Act II: The same, two days later. Act III: The same, two weeks later. Act IV: The same, two years later. One intermission following Act II.

SONGPLAY: THE SONGS AND MUSIC OF KURT WEILL. Musical conceived and adapted by Jonathan Eaton; music by Kurt Weill; lyrics by Ira Gershwin, Maxwell Anderson, Alan Jay Lerner, Bertolt Brecht, Paul Green, Langston Hughes, Ogden Nash, Jacques Deval, Roger Fernay, Lion Feuchtwanger, H.R. Hays, A. Pen, Nathan Alterman and Kurt Weill. September 24, 1996. Director, Jonathan Eaton; choreography, Daniel Pelzig; musical direction and arrangements, David Seaman; scenery, Paul Shortt; costumes, David Kay Mickelson; lighting, James Sale; sound, David B. Smith.

With Michael Brian, Herb Downer, Kim Lindsay, Karen Murphy, Pedro Porro, Craig Priebe.
    Place: Journeys to the dream island Youkali. One intermission.
    MUSICAL NUMBERS, ACT I: "Youkali," "My Ship," "The Song of the Brown Islands," "How Can You Tell an American?", "I'm Your Man," "Bilbao-Song," "Barbara Song," "It's a Miracle of Nature," "Apple Jack," "The Sailors' Tango," "Song of the Rhineland," "Havu I'venim," "Mon Ami, My Friend," "This Time Next Year," "Alabama Song," "J'Attends un Navire," "Song of the Big Shot," "Surabaya-Johnny," "Economics," "Youkali" (Reprise).

ACT II: "Lonely House," "Nanna's Song," "Love Song," "Trouble Man," "Song of Mandalay," "Mack the Knife," "High Wind in Jamaica," "The Girl of the Moment," "How Much I Love You," "Speak Low," "Lost in the Stars," "Voici le Train du Ciel," "Baa M'nucha," "Stay Well," "This Time Next Year" (Reprise), "September Song," "Here I'll Stay," "Youkali" (Reprise).

IN WALKS ED. By Keith Glover. February 11, 1997. Director, Keith Glover; scenery, David Gallo; costumes, Michael Alan Stein; lighting, Kevin Adams; sound, David B. Smith; choreography, Ken Roberson; fight direction, David Leong.

Pete Baez .... Joe Quintero
Sky .... Anthony Chisholm
Eddie Paladin .... Keith Randolph Smith
Darlene .... Kim Brockington
Bennie "The Jet" .... Leland Gantt
    Time: Circa nineteen-now. Place: A Harlem bar—Prologue, a blaque mystic groove; Scene 1, the invocation of the dark before dawn; Scene 2, the pursuance of a one and only love; Scene 3, the jungle Watusi and the twenty-five-cent blues. One intermission following Scene 1.

Cleveland: The Cleveland Play House

(Peter Hackett artistic director)

Next Stage Festival
Of New Play Readings

MACHINES CRY WOLF. By Wendy MacLeod. November 12, 1996. Director, Scott Kanoff.
SMOKING LESSON. By Julia Jordan. November 13, 1996. Director, William Hoffman.

AMBITION FACING WEST. By Anthony Clarvoe. November 13, 1996. Director, Melia Bensussen.
THE GENUINE ARTICLE. By Aubrey Wertheim. November 14, 1996. Director, Scott Kanoff.
A RUSSIAN ROMANCE. By Murphy Guyer. Novobmer 14, 1996. Directed by Murphy Guyer.

Costa Mesa, Calif: South Coast Repertory

(David Emmes producing artistic director; Martin Benson artistic director)

COLLECTED STORIES. By Donald Margulies. October 29, 1996. Director, Lisa Peterson; scenery, Neil Patel; costumes, Candice Cain; lighting, Tom Ruzika; sound, Mitchell Greenhill.
Ruth Steiner .... Kandis Chappell
Lisa Morrison .... Suzanne Cryer
    Time: 1990 to the present. Place: Ruth's apartment in Greenwich Village. One intermission.

BAFO (BEST AND FINAL OFFER). By Tom Strelich. January 21, 1997. Director, Martin Benson; scenery, John Iacovelli; costumes, Todd Roerhman; lighting, Lonnie Alcaraz; sound, Garth Hemphill.
Willie Peet .... Hal Landon Jr.
Clay .... Richard Doyle
Sayles .... Ron Boussom
Ashe .... Art Koustik
Shokanje .... Susan Patterson
P.K. .... Don Took
    Time: The present. Place: The conference room in the offices of a small defense contractor

in the declining Southern California Defense/Aerospace industry. No intermission.

THE TRIUMPH OF LOVE. By Marivaux; adapted by Richard Greenberg from a literal translation by John Glore. February 14, 1997. Director, Mark Rucker; scenery, Karen Teneyck; costumes, Katherine Beatrice Roth; lighting, Tom Ruzika; original music and sound, Michael Roth.
Phocion (aka Princess Leonide,
    aka Aspasie) .... Rene Augesen
Hermidas (aka Corine) .... Colette Kilroy
Harlequin .... Tom Beckett
Dimas .... Patrick Kerr
Agis .... Joshua Farrell
Leontine .... Jeanne Paulsen
Hermocrate ..,................ Patrick O'Connell
    Place: The gardens of the philosopher Hermocrate. One intermission.

THREE DAYS OF RAIN. By Richard Greenberg. March 4, 1997. Director, Evan Yionoulis; scenery, Christopher Barreca; costumes, Candice

CINCINNATI PLAYHOUSE IN THE PARK—Lynn Redgrave and Jeff Woodman in *The Notebook of Trigorin,* the U.S. premiere of Tennessee Williams's interpretation of Anton Chekhov's *The Seagull*

Cain; lighting, Donald Holder; sound, Garth Hemphill.

Walker; Ned .... John Slattery

Nan; Lina .... Patricia Clarkson

Pip; Theo .... Jon Tenney

Pia .... Julia Pearlstein

Time: Act I, 1995. Act II, 1960. Place: An apartment in downtown Manhattan.

Dallas: Dallas Theater Center

(Richard Hamburger artistic director; Robert Yesselman managing director)

THUNDER KNOCKING ON THE DOOR: A BLUSICAL TALE OF RHYTHM AND THE BLUES. Musical by Keith Glover; music by various authors. Produced in association with Alabama Shakespeare Festival (see its entry in the Montgomery listing in this section), Kent Thompson artistic director, and Center Stage, Irene Lewis artistic director.

Elizabeth Osborn Award winner; see introduction to this section.

Denver: The Changing Scene

(Al Brooks and Maxine Munt executive producers)

OH, YOU LITTLE WOMEN! By Frederick Vaughan. June 14, 1996. Director, Trace Oakley; scenery, Patricia Robertson; costumes, Mary Randolph; sound and music, Chuck Rhodes.

Jo March .... Julie Taylor
Amy March; Mrs. Clearchest ... Christy Kruzick
Beth March .... Kendra Wiig
Meg March .... Erika Elliott
Marmie .... Betsy Grisard
Hannah .... Diann Chapman
"Laurie" Lawrence .... Zeke Bielby
Mr. Brooks .... Nicholas Webb
Grandfather Lawrence .... John P. Tretbar
Aunt March; Prof. Bhaer;
   Chaplain .... Steven Divide

GIVEN BY OUR HAND. By Diane Ney. October 17, 1996. Director, Patricia Ann Madsen; scenery, Patricia Ann Madsen, Marshall Brodsky; lighting, Michael Krzyzek; sound, Cindy Ergenbright.

Advance Man .... Larry Bailey
Lynette .... Hylla Sue Fisher
Nigel .... Tomas Giles
Eleanor .... Anna Hadzi
Hank .... Vermont Smith
Gus Aldon .... Ken Witt

Summerplay '96 Festival of New Works
Series I, July 11-28

MUSING EVE. By Patricia Ann Madsen. Director, Patricia Ann Madsen.

Melpomene .... Jack Baker
Eve .... Gail Kessler
Attendant .... Catherine diBella

THE WHITTLING PLACE. By Pat Gabridge. Director, Pamela Clifton.

Talcum .... Nelson Embleton

Dusty .... Nick Webb
Odessa .... Mary Ann Amari
GINGERBREADCRUMBS. By Christopher Younggren. Director, Trace Oakley.

Bedilia Woods .... Karen Krause
Timmy .... Luke Eberl
Van Helsing .... John P. Tretbar
Hans .... Zeke Bielby
Greta .... Megan Wallace
   Series I designers: scenery, Eric Pruett; lighting, Carol Lyn McDowell; sound, Jay Shaffer.
   One intermission following *The Whittling Place.*

Series II, August 1-18

FIVESQUARE. By Mark Ogle. Director, Ken Crost.

With Stan Sawicki, Louniece SanFilippo.

OH, HELL! By Warren Ryan. Director, Liz Jury.

Jim .... Dan Carpenter
Rob .... Mateo Solano
June .... Mary Ann Amari
Bill .... Paul Blomquist
John .... John P. Tretbar
DO OR DIE. By John Ashton. Director, Dwayne Carrington.

Voice .... Dwayne Carrington
Bobby McMasters .... Damon Lindenberger
Damon Carruthers .... Stephen Remund
Ida Scribbons .... Pavlina Emily Morris
Ms. Skipper Beaumont .... Alexandra Leeper
Jake Jasperson .... James Mills
Nettie .... Amber Leigh Florest
Jake Jasperson III .... Nick Webb
   Music: Janet Feder.
   Series II designers: scenery, Eric Pruett; lighting, Carol Lyn McDowell.
   One intermission following *Oh, Hell!*

Denver: Denver Center Theater Company

(Donovan Marley artistic director)

ONE FOOT ON THE FLOOR. Adapted from Georges Feydeau's *Le Dindon* by Jeffrey Hatcher. Opened March 27, 1997. Conceived and directed by Marcia Milgrom Dodge; scenery, Vicki Smith; costumes, David Kay Mickelson; lighting, Don Darnutzer; sound, David R. White.

Betty Johnson .... Dee Ann Newkirk
Rod Larue .... Anthony Dodge
John Thomas Johnson .... Mark Shanahan
Miss Pritt; Muffin Foy .... Deborah LaCoy

Larry Fontayne .... Walter Hudson
Mayo LaRue .... Jacqueline Antaramian
L.B. Merkin .... Paul Stolarsky
Snivels .... Mark Rubald
LaVita Terrafamilia .... Isabel Keating
Bellboy .... Patrick Goss
Mr. Kilroy .... Farnham Scott
Congressman Clitterhouse;
   Sully .... Noble Shropshire
Mrs. Clitterhouse .... Christiane McKenna

Maid .... Rachel K. Taylor
Lt. O'Toole .... Tupper Cullum
Sergeant .... Keith L. Hatten
    Others: Gabriella Cavallero, Charlie Chiv,

Richard Lyons, Michael Rahhal, Kate Richard-son, Michael Scarsella.
    Time: 1939. Place: Hollywood. One inter-mission.

East Farmingdale, N.Y.: The Arena Players

    (Frederic DeFeis producer/director)

TUESDAYS. By John Thompson. February 13, 1997. Director, Frederic DeFeis; scenery, Fred Sprauer; costumes, Lois Lockwood; lighting, Al Davis; music, David DeFeis.

Willodean Emberson .... Jan Anderson
Sara Byers .... Sunny Taylor
Kevin .... Brian Schwimmer
Robert Emberson .... Don Frame
Linda Emberson .... Dawn DeMaio
Joseph Leisher .... John Anderson
Sharon Emberson .... Cyndy Casey
    Act I, Scene 1: Sara's home, Tuesday. Scene 2:

One week later. Scene 3: One week later. Scene 4: Several weeks later. Scene 5: A couple of weeks have passed. Act II, Scene 1: A couple of weeks have passed. Scene 2: Early morning. Scene 3: Several hours later. Scene 4: A sunny spring morning.

Second Stage:

THE SERPENT'S SERMON. Solo performance by Ron Stroman; written by Ron Stroman. May 8, 1997. Director, Frederic DeFeis; scenery, Fred Sprauer; costumes, Lois Lockwood; lighting, Al Davis; sound, David Dion.
    One intermission.

East Haddam and Chester, Conn.: Goodspeed Opera House

    (Michael P. Price producer)

PAPER MOON. Musical based on the novel *Addie Pray* by Joe David Brown and the Paramount Pictures film *Paper Moon*; book by Martin Casella; music by Larry Grossman; lyrics by Ellen Fitzhugh. June 26, 1996. Director, Matt Casella; choreography, John Carrafa; musical direction, Michael O'Flaherty; scenery, James Youmans; costumes, David C. Woolard; lighting, Kenneth Posner; orchestrations, Ned Ginsburg; produced in association with Walnut Street Theater, Bernard Havard executive director.
    Cast: Addie Loggins—Lindsay Cummings, Joanna Pacitti; Pastor, Station Master, Carnival Manager, Col. Culpepper—J.B. Adams; Minister, Sheriff, Chauffeur—Ken Triwush; Minister's Wife, Mrs. Stanley—Catherine Fries; Moses (Moze) Pray—Mark Zimmerman; Mr. Thompson—Craig Zehms; Ola Thompson, Mrs. Huff, Carnival Customer, Mrs. Kleehorn—Lynn Eldredge; Mechanic, Carnival Photographer—Larry Alexander; Waitress, Mrs. Cates—Natalie Blalock; Mrs. Morgan, Miss Brownell—Sandy Rosenberg; Carnival Barker, Floyd—Roy Leake Jr.; Trixie Delight—Julie Johnson; Imogene—Ariel Harris; Aunt Billie Roy Loggins—Blair Ross.
    Trixie's Girls: Lynn Eldredge, Natalie Blalock, Catherine Fries.
    Ensemble: J.B. Adams, Larry Alexander, Natalie Blalock, Brett Cramp, Lynn Eldredge, Cath-

erine Fries, Roy Leake Jr., Sandy Rosenberg, Ken Triwush, Schele Williams, Craig Zehms.
    Time: Smack in the middle of the Great Depression. Place: Alabama, Arkansas and Missouri.
    MUSICAL NUMBERS, ACT I: "Another Little Child," "I Recollect Him," "The Wida' Waltz," "Pretty Like Your Mama," "Goin' Along," "I Do What I Can (With What I Got)," "Boy-Oh-Boy," "I Do What I Can" (Reprise), "How Many Times."
    ACT II: "Doin' Business," "Someday, Baby," "Rabbity Stew," "Another Little Child" (Reprise), "Who Belongs to Who?", "You With Me?", "Girls Like Us."

Goodspeed Musicals at Chester

MIRETTE. Musical based on the book *Mirette on the High Wire* by Emily Arnold McCully; book by Elizabeth Diggs; music by Harvey Schmidt; lyrics by Tom Jones. August 1, 1996. Director, Drew Scott Harris; choreography, Janet Watson; musical direction, vocal and dance arrangements, Gary Adler; scenery, James Morgan; costumes, Suzy Benzinger; lighting, Phil Monat; associate producer, Sue Frost; casting director, Warren Pincus; resident musical director, Michael O'Flaherty.

Mirette .... Kelly Mady
Tabac .... David Duffield
Mme. Rouspenskaya .... Marsha Bagwell
Clouk .... Tony Sicuso

GOODSPEED-AT-CHESTER, CONN.—Richard Kline, John Scherer and Donna Lynne Champlin in the American premiere of the Alan Ayckbourn-Andrew Lloyd Webber musical *By Jeeves*

Claire .... Carol Schuberg
Gaby .... Kelly Swaim
Camembert .... MichaelJohn McGann
Madame Gateau .... Barbara Tirrell
Bellini .... Steve Barton
Max .... Gerry Vichi

Time: The 1890s. Place: Madame Gateau's hotel in Paris.

MUSICAL NUMBERS, ACT I: "Madame Gateau's Colorful Hotel," "I Like It Here," "Someone in the Mirror," "Irkutsk," "Practicing," "Learning Who You Are," "Keep Your Feet Upon the Ground," "Learning Who You Are" (Reprise), "If You Choose to Walk Upon the Wire," "She Isn't You."

ACT II: "The Great Bellini," "Sometimes You Just Need Someone," "Madame Gateau's Desolate Hotel" (Reprise), Finale: "The Great Bellini," "Practicing," "Sometimes You Just Need Someone," "The Show Goes On."

BY JEEVES. Musical based on the Jeeves stories by P.G. Wodehouse; book and lyrics by Alan Ayckbourn; music by Andrew Lloyd Webber. October 17, 1996 (American premiere). Director, Alan Ayckbourn; choreography, Sheila Carter, musical direction, Michael O'Flaherty; scenery,

Roger Glossop; costumes, Louise Belson; lighting, Mick Hughes; sound, Richard Ryan; arrangements, David Cullen, Andrew Lloyd Webber.

Bertie Wooster .... John Scherer
Jeeves .... Richard Kline
Honoria Glossop ...... Donna Lynne Champlin
Bingo Little .... Randy Redd
Gussie Fink-Nottle .... Kevin Ligon
Sir Watkyn Bassett .... Merwin Goldsmith
Madeline Bassett .... Nancy Anderson
Stiffy Byng .... Emily Loesser
Harold "Stinker" Pinker .... Ian Knauer
Cyrus Budge III .... Jonathan Stewart
Ozzie Nutledge .... Michael O'Flaherty

Others: Tom Ford, Molly Renfroe, Court Whisman.

Time: This very evening. Place: A church hall, later to represent a London flat and the house and grounds of Totleigh Towers.

MUSICAL NUMBERS, ACT I: "A False Start," "Wooster Will Entertain You," "Travel Hopefully," "That Was Nearly Us," "Love's Maze," "The Hallo Song."

ACT II: "By Jeeves," "When Love Arrives," "What Have You Got to Say, Jeeves?", "Half a Moment," "It's a Pig!", "Banjo Boy," "The Wizard Rainbow Finale."

Fort Worth, Tex.: Stage West Theater

(Gerald Russell artistic director; Diane Anglim executive director; James Covault associate director)

AND FAT FREDDY'S BLUES. By P.J. Barry. June 7, 1996. Director, P.J. Barry; scenery and costumes, Jim Covault; lighting, Michael O'Brien.

Russ Calhoun .... Peter Dobbins
Diane Caputo .... Jennifer Hester
Fat Freddy Caputo .... Jerry Russell
Jeannie Brown Calhoun ..... Deborah Sammons

Place: Russ Calhoun's bungalow in Jericho, R.I. Act I, Scene 1: A February night, 1952, about 8 p.m. Scene 2: Three days later, about midnight. Scene 3: 2 a.m. Act II, Scene 1: Three days later, afternoon. Scene 2: The same day, midnight. Scene 3: Two days later, late afternoon.

Gloucester, Mass.: Gloucester Stage Company

(Israel Horovitz artistic director; Ian McColl managing director)

MY OLD LADY. By Israel Horovitz. August 11, 1996. Director, David Wheeler; scenery and costumes, Lisa Pegnato; lighting, Ian McColl; sound, Michael Sielewics.

Mathilde Giffard .... Miriam Varon
Mathias "Jim" Gold .... Paul O'Brien
Chloe Giffard .... Lisa Richards
One intermission.

Hartford, Conn.: Hartford Stage

(Mark Lamos artistic director; Stephen J. Albert managing director; Greg Leaming producing director)

PEARLS FOR PIGS. By Richard Foreman. April 4, 1997. Director, Richard Foreman; scenery, costumes and sound, Richard Foreman; lighting, Heather Carson; presented in association with Top Shows Inc.

Maestro .... David Patrick Kelly

Pierrot .... Peter Jacobs
Colombine .... Jan Leslie Harding
Doctor .... Tom Nelis
Others: David Callahan, David Cote, Yehuda Duenyas, John Oglevee.
No intermission.

Houston: A.D. Players

(Jeannette Clift George artistic director)

CHRISTMAS PARTY OF ONE. Musical with book and lyrics by Ken Bailey; music by Gerry Poland. November 29, 1996. Director, Don Hollenbeck Jr.; choreography and assistant director, Deborah Chumley; scenery, Don Hollenbeck Jr.; costumes, Donna Southern; lighting, Lee Walker; sound, John Scott Chumley.

Chrissy .... Carrie Zochol, Kara Greenberg
Joseph; Joe .... Stephen Baldwin
Cariot .... Gerry Poland
Gabe .... Rowdy Stovall
Rachel; Shepherd's
   Wife 2 .... Luisa Amaral-Smith
Helen; Shepherd's Wife 1 .... Brenda Fager

Mary; Harriet .... Rebekah Dahl
Horace; Balthesar .... Marion Arthur Kirby
Melchior; Chad .... Tom Prior
Gasper; Dustin .... Ric Hodgin
Innkeeper .... Whitney Presley
   Ensemble: Lawrence Rife, Anna Maria Roselli.
   MUSICAL NUMBERS, ACT I: Prelude, "What Have You Done?", "Cariot," "Picture Yourself With Jesus," "Shouldn't I?", "Bright Star," "The Merriweathers Are Coming," "O Little Town of Bethlehem," "This Promise of Hope."
   ACT II: "Where Are the Men?", "Dysfunctionality," "The Future Knows Our Name," "Shouldn't I?" (Reprise).

Indianapolis: Indiana Repertory Theater

(Janet Allen artistic director; Brian Payne managing director)

THE MAGNIFICENT AMBERSONS. Adapted by James Fesuk-Geisel from the novel by Booth Tarkington. September 10, 1996. Director, Scott Wentworth; scenery, William Bloodgood; costumes, Gail Brassard; lighting, Ashley York Kennedy; composer, Gerardo Dirie; dance staging, David Hochoy.

George Amberson Minafer ...... Sean Arbuckle

Eugene Morgan .... Tim Grimm
Aunt Fanny .... Priscilla Lindsay
Lucy Morgan .... Nicole Marcks
Maj. Amberson .... Frank Raiter
Isabel Amberson Minafer .... Kate Levy
George Amberson .... Paul Mullins
    Time: The turn of the century. Place: In and around the city of Midland. One intermission.

Kansas City, Mo.: Unicorn Theater

(Cynthia Levin producing artistic director)

AT THE FEET OF DOVES. By Ron Simonian. October 25, 1996. Director, Cynthia Levin; scenery, Atif Rome; costumes, Paula Pearson; lighting, Shane Rowse; sound, Roger Stoddard.
Kevin .... T. Max Graham
Al .... Matthew Rapport
Stage Manager .... Aileen Antoni
    Time: Now. Place: Somewhere. No intermission.

MERCY KILLING. By Stephanie Keys. April 25, 1997. Director, Cynthia Levin; scenery, Atif Rome; costumes, Mary Traylor; lighting, Shane Rowse; sound, Roger Stoddard.
Mercy Rush .... Kathryn Hays
Lanie Rush .... Peggy Friesen
    Time: The present. Place: Act I, Lanie's living room in New York City; Mercy's den in the Midwest. Act II, Mercy's living room. Act III, Mercy's living room.

Key West, Fla.: Key West Theater Festival

(Charles A. Munroe executive producer; Joan McGillis artistic director; Elaine Chinnis general manager)

5th Annual Key West Theater Festival
Oct. 3-13, 1966

WATER BOY. By Rich Orloff. Director, Bruce Peterson; sound, Private Ear.
Victor Burlington .... Mike Alpern
Norman Waterbury .... John B. Good
    Time: The present. Place: Victor's office. One intermission.

EXPLODING LOVE. By Joseph Coyne; director, Mike Rutenberg; scenery and lighting, Gary McDonald; costumes, Jessica Steele.
Policeman .... Sam Trophin
Court Officer .... Ronnie Goldstein
Skeeter .... Tom Luna
Rory .... Joe DeLuca
Zeke .... Jed Sloe
Fran .... Vanessa McCaffrey
Winnona .... Mira Negron
Fiance .... Bill Carpenter
    Time: The present. Place: The public men's room, City Hall, New York City. One intermission.

IRIS FIELDS. By Sharr White. Director, Joan McGillis; costumes, Beverly Lindsay; sound, Private Ear.
Esther .... Conni Atkins
Sebastian .... Guiesseppe Jones
Lillian .... Katie Tierney
Johnny Reb .... Dale Kittle
Billy Yank .... Mark Hayes
Rudy .... Bob Smith
Sonya .... Amber McDonald
Maximillian .... Jack Ryland
Cassandra .... Sinéad Mylalsingh
    Time: Autumn 1865. Place: Athens, Ill. One intermission.

DENNY'S CHRONICLES. By Alana Macias. Director, Patrice M. Bailey; lighting, David Miller.
Clara .... Kei Berlin
John .... Doug Diamond
Bren .... Alexandra Chitty
Paco .... Enrique Hecker
Greta .... Erica Boynton
Sandra .... Christie Strong
    Time: Now. Place: Denny's Restaurant.

Festival Play Readings
Oct. 7-11, 1996

OH DANNY BOY THE PIPES HAVE PLAYED. By Patrick A. Lennon.
INCIDENT AT THE GETTYSBURG WELL. By Nick Bartos.

ROGER CASEMENT. By John Barrow.
SOMEWHERE IN BETWEEN. By Craig Pospisil.
THE GLORY OF LIVING. By Rebecca Gilman.
REMEMBERING HELOISE. By Carson Becker.

La Jolla, Calif.: La Jolla Playhouse

(Michael Greif artistic director; Terrence Dwyer managing director; Robert Blacker associate artistic director; Des McAnuff director-in-residence)

BOY. By Diana Son. June 11, 1996. Director, Michael Greif; scenery and costumes, Mark Wendland; lighting, James F. Ingalls; sound, Darron L. West.

Boy .... Michi Barall
Mama; Jessie .... Cynthia Martells
Papa .... Robert Dorfman
Their Daughters:
Vulva .... Alyssa Lupo
Labia .... Amy Elizabeth McKenna
Hymen .... Melody Butiu
Mr. Stickey .... James Saba
Weiner .... Damen Scranton
Dickie .... Mike Ryan
Woody .... Kevin Berntson
Shermie .... Todd Cerveris
Charlotte .... Andrea Renee Portes
Act I: Now. Act II: Seven years later. One intermission.

2.5 MINUTE RIDE. Solo performance by Lisa Kron; written by Lisa Kron. September 24, 1996. Director, Lowry Marshall; scenery, Richard Ortenblad Jr.; lighting, Trevor Norton; original music and sound, Dan Froot.
No intermission.

Lansing, Mich.: BoarsHead Michigan Public Theater

(John Peakes founding artistic director; Judith Gentry Peakes managing director)

DIVA DAYS. By Kate Hawley. January 9, 1997. Director, Larry Thelen; scenery, Peter Bathum; costumes, Edith Leavis Bookstein; lighting, Tina Newhauser.
Jane .... Jennifer Chudy
Margaret .... Roxanne Wellington
Henry .... John Peakes
Maggie .... Betsy Fast
Time: 1967-1987. Place: A student apartment, Berkeley, Calif. One intermission.

Staged Readings:
PASSAGES. By Debbie Patrick. October 28, 1996.
THE BALKAN WOMAN. By Jules Tosca. November 20, 1996.
TELLING TIME. By Sally Netzel. February 12, 1997.
APPARITIONS. By Christine Thatcher. March 18, 1997.
10 DAYS IN PARADISE. By Barbara Carlisle. April 23, 1997.

Lenox, Mass.: Shakespeare & Company

(Tina Packer artistic director; Christopher Sink managing director)

WOMEN OF WILL. Written and conceived by Tina Packer; with scenes from 20 plays by William Shakespeare. May 24, 1996. Costumes, John Pennoyer; lighting, Steve Ball.

Part I, The Warrior Women From Violence to Negotiation: Director, Gary Mitchell; sound, Gabriel Lloyd; with Tina Packer, Jonathan Epstein. Scenes: Kate and Petruchio from *The Taming of the Shrew*; Joan & the Dauphin and Joan & Duke of York from *Henry VI, Part 1*; Margaret & Duke of York and Elizabeth & Edward IV from *Henry VI, Part 3*; Elizabeth and Richard III from *Richard III*; Princess of France & King of Navarre from *Love's Labor's Lost*; Romeo and Juliet.

Part II, Going Underground or Dying to Tell the Truth: Director, Jonathan Epstein; sound, Carey Upton; with Tina Packer, Johnny Lee Davenport. Scenes: Constance & The Cardinal from *King John*; Rosalind & the bad Duke and Rosalind & Orlando from *As You Like It*; Desdemona & Othello; Gertrude/Ophelia & Hamlet; Lady Macbeth & Macbeth; Orsino & Viola from *Twelfth Night*; Antony & Cleopatra.

Part III, The Maiden Phoenix or the Daughter

LA JOLLA, CALIF. PLAYHOUSE—Michi Barall and Andrea Renee Portes in Diana Son's comedy *Boy* under the direction of Michael Greif

Redeems the Father: Director, Johnny Lee Davenport; scenery, John Pennoyer; sound, Carey Upton; with Tina Packer, Jonathan Epstein. Scenes: Goneril, Regan, Cordelia & King Lear; Pericles & the Oracle, Marina & Boult, Marina & Pericles; the blessing of the Baby Elizabeth from *Henry VIII*; Ariel/Miranda & Prospero from *The Tempest*; Hermione, Leontes, Polixenes, Paulina Florizel & Perdita from *The Winter's Tale*.

One intermission.

FAITH AND HOPE: EDITH AT WAR. By Gary Mitchell; inspired by Edith Wharton. June 8, 1996. Director, Gary Mitchell; costumes, Alison Ragland; lighting, Steve Ball; sound, Gabriel Lloyd; producer, Robin Hynek.

Edith Wharton .... Normi Noel

James Haverill Compton .... Bob Lohbauer
Percy Compton .... Jeffrey Pierce
Harvey Boyalston .... Max Vogler
Adele St. Jean .... Ann Podlozny
    Time: 1914-1916. Place: Paris. One intermission.

WHARTON ONE ACTS: MADAME DE TREYMES by Gary Mitchell; adapted from Edith Wharton; director, Eleanor Holdridge; and A LOVE $TORY by Dennis Krausnick; adapted from Edith Wharton's *Les Metteurs en Scene*; director, Dennis Krausnick. June 28, 1996. Costumes, Ted Ciro Giammona; lighting, Steve Ball; sound, Gabriel Lloyd; producer, Robin Hynek.
Madame de Treymes
John Durham .... Max Vogler

Mme. Fanny Malrive .... Karen Torbjornsen
Mrs. Boykin .... Christine Linkie
Mme. de Treymes .... Diane Prusha
    Time: The spring of 1907. Place: Various hotels, gardens, drawing rooms and salons throughout Paris.

A Love $tory
Jean Le Fanois .... Jeffrey Pierce
Blanche Lambart .... Ann Podlozny
    Place: One of the many public sitting rooms that flank the main lobby of the sumptuous Hotel Nouveau Luxe, an establishment in Paris catering to the wealthy international set. Scene 1: A late spring morning in l905. Scene 2: Late that same evening. Scene 3: Ten days later. Scene 4: Six weeks later. Scene 5: Two months later.

MERCY. By Laura Harrington. July 26, 1996. Directors, Gary Mitchell, Normi Noel; scenery, Gary Mitchell; costumes, Alison Ragland; lighting, Steve Ball; sound, Carey Upton, Gary Mitchell.
Faith Morning .... Annette Miller
Steven Morning .... Dennis Krausnick
Liz Morning .... Corinna May
Annie Morning .... Elizabeth Aspenlieder

Daniel Morning .... Walton Wilson
Foster Dade .... Jason Asprey
    Time: The end of summer, 1993. Place: Many locations along Cape Ann, Mass. One intermission.

THE DEATH OF THE FATHER OF PSYCHO-ANALYSIS (& ANNA). By Bridget Carpenter. August 20, 1996. Director, Cecil MacKinnon.
Anna .... Robin Hynek
Dr. Freud .... Bob Lohbauer
Nurse .... Sarah Cathcart

ETHAN FROME. By Dennis Krausnick; based on the novel by Edith Wharton. September 21, 1996. Director, Dennis Krausnick; scenery, Jim Youngerman; costumes, Govane Lohbauer; lighting, Gabriel Lloyd, Steve Ball; sound, Gabriel Lloyd, Chris Sigrist.
Homer Winterson; Townspeople ... Josef Hansen
Ethan Frome .... Kevin G. Coleman
Zenobia Frome .... Annette Miller
Mattie Silver .... Elizabeth Aspenlieder
    Time: Winter 1860 and winter 1884. Place: The Frome family farm and environs of Starkfield in Berkshire County, Mass. No intermission.

Los Angeles: East West Players

(Tim Dang artistic director)

IKEBANA. By Alice Tuan. November 21, 1996. Director, Lisa Peterson; scenery, Rachek Hauck; costumes, Joyce Kim Lee; lighting, Geoff Korf; sound, Joel Iwataki.
Bo .... Reg E. Cathey
Violet .... Lauren Tom
Rose .... Beulah Quo
Ester .... Emily Kuroda
Lily .... Natsuko Ohama
Woodman .... Ping Wu

Iris .... Deborah Nishimura
Ellison .... John Cho
    Prologue: Joyous play. Scene 1: Clouds. Scene 2: Tumbling. Scene 3: Resilience. Scene 4: Capricious. Scene 5: Winding Line. Scene 6: Bold strokes. Intermission. Scene 7: Midsummer sun. Scene 8: Organic form. Scene 9: Sensual. Scene 10: Spring bursts. Scene 11: Gracefulness. Scene 12: Sunbathing. Scene 13: Natural discard. Scene 14: Living contrast. Scene 15: Quietude.

Los Angeles: Mark Taper Forum

(Gordon Davidson artistic director)

THE STREET OF THE SUN. By Jose Rivera. May 27, 1997. Director, David Esbjornson; scenery, Christopher Barreca; costumes, Elizabeth Hope Clancy; lighting, Geoff Korf; sound, Jon Gottlieb; music, Dave Ossmann.

With Bertila Damas, Catherine Dent, Robert Dorfman, Dawnn Lewis, Vanessa Marquez, Jeanne Mori, Javi Mulero, John Ortiz, Victor Raider-Wexler, Herschel Sparber.
    One intermission.

Louisville, Ky.: Actors Theater of Louisville

(Jon Jory producing director)

EAST OF EDEN, PART I: PILLARS OF FIRE and EAST OF EDEN, PART II: BREAKING THE CHAIN. Both plays adapted for the stage by Alan Cook from the novel by John Steinbeck. *Part*

I October 23, 1996; *Part II* November 7, 1996. Directors, Jon Jory and Frazier W. Marsh; scenery, Paul Owen; costumes, Marcia Dixcy Jory; lighting, Greg Sullivan; sound, Martin R. Desjardins; original music, Charles Ellis, Vince Emmett; fight director, Steve Rankin.

PART I

Cyrus; Sam Hamilton's
  Friend .... Tom Stechschulte
Adam 1; Joe Hamilton .... Tommy Schrider
Adam 2 .... Richard Kuhlman
Lucille; Liza .... Cordis Heard
Abe; Mr. Ames; Minister ...... Craig Bockhorn
Wendell; Sexton; Luis .... Bob Burrus
Alice; Cathy 2 .... Jenna Stern
Charles 1 .... Justin Hagan
Charles 2 .... Robert Montano
Doctor 1; Mr. Edwards;
  Doc Tilson .... Fred Major
Mrs. Ames .... Peggy Cowles
Cathy 1 .... Anne Marie Nest
James Grew; Tom Hamilton .... Rick Galiher
Sam Hamilton; Captain; War Offices Clerk;
  Postmaster .... Jonathan Bolt
Mrs. Edwards; Faye .... Sarah Burke
Stationmaster; Cathy's Doctor; Lee .. Donald Li
Hotel Desk Clerk; Sam Hamilton's
  Friend .... Everette Ruby
Soldiers .... Briton Green, David Ray
  Ensemble: James Edward Quinn, Jared Randolph, Company.
  Time: 1862-1901. Place: Connecticut to California. One intermission.

PART II

Sam Hamilton; Dodson .... Jonathan Bolt
Adam 2; Aron 2 .... Richard Kuhlman
Lee .... Donald Li
Adam 3 .... Tom Stechschulte
Liza .... Cordis Heard
Tom Hamilton; Martin Hobbes .... Rick Galiher
Aron 1; Joe Hamilton .... Tommy Schrider
Cal 1 .... Justin Hagan
Will Hamilton .... Craig Bockhorn
Abra .... Twyla Hafermann
Kate .... Peggy Cowles
Cathy 2; Olive .... Jenna Stern
Eva; Sunday Whore .... Missy Thomas
Jake .... Clint Vaught
Mechanic; Brit .... Briton Green
Mr. Bacon; Luiz; Rabbit;
  Hans Fenchel .... Bob Burrus
Mrs. Bacon .... Sarah Burke
Cal 2 .... Robert Montano
Horace; Pierre .... Fred Major
Businessman .... Everette Ruby
Liberty Belle .... Martha Sorrentino
  Schoolboys: James Quinn, Jared Randolph, David Ray. Ensemble: Company.
  Time: 1901-1917. Place: California. One intermission.

ONLY A BIRD IN A GILDED CAGE. Conceived and written by Jon Jory in collaboration

with Karma Camp and Scott Kasbaum; music by Scott Kasbaum. January 1, 1997. Director, Jon Jory; scenery, Paul Owen; costumes, Delmar L. Rinehart; lighting, Ed McCarthy; sound, Christopher R. Hermanson; choreography, Karma Camp; arrangements, Scott Kasbaum.

Elizabeth Stuart Phelps ...... Twyla Hafermann
Polly Phelps .... Claire Anne Longest
Josef Ladislaus Pilsudski .... Scott Kasbaum
Dinwiddy Carrington ...... V Craig Heidenreich
Emmanual Bones .... Fred Major
Cithoneria Bulkhorn .... Adale O'Brien
Chastity Masticate .... Kathleen Early
Kaimo T. Stephanopoulos .... William McNulty
Calla Corliss Delahew Mayfair Aubergine
Titwillow Tennyson .... Deanna Lorette
Seamus Cantrell "Hot Pipes"
  Harrigan .... Bart Shatto
Joebobwillie "Slingsaddle" Smith .. Bob Burrus
  Time: Winter, mid-1890s. Place: A parlor in Dayton, Ohio. One intermission.

21st Annual Humana Festival
of New American Plays
March 4–April 13, 1997

PRIVATE EYES. By Steven Dietz. March 4, 1997. Director, Steven Dietz; premiered by Arizona Theater Company, David Ira Goldstein artistic director.

Matthew .... Lee Sellars
Lisa .... Kate Goehring
Adrian .... V Craig Heidenreich
Cory .... Twyla Hafermann
Frank .... Adale O'Brien
  Time: The present. Place: Various rooms in an American city. One intermission.

LIGHTING UP THE TWO-YEAR OLD. By Benjie Aerenson. March 8, 1997. Director, Lazlo Marton.

Carl .... Bob Burrus
Bud .... Lou Sumrall
George .... Allen Fitzpatrick
Junior .... George Kisslinger
  Time: The present. Place: Act I, a horse farm in north central Florida. Act II, George's house on the Miami waterway.

ICARUS. By Edwin Sanchez. March 12, 1997. Director, Melia Bensussen.

Altagracia .... Denise Casano
Primitivo .... Nelson Vasquez
The Gloria .... Julie Halston
Mr. Ellis .... Ray Fry
Beau .... Ross Gibby
  Time: The present. Place: On a beach. No intermission.

GUNSHY. By Richard Dresser. March 15, 1997. Director, Gloria Muzio.

Evie .... Maryann Urbano
Carter .... V Craig Heidenreich
Duncan .... William McNulty
Caitlin .... Twyla Hafermann
Others .... Lee Sellars
    Place: Act I, Various locations in the Pacific
Northwest, New England and Washington, D.C.
Act II, Duncan's house outside of Boston.

IN HER SIGHT. By Carol K. Mack. March 21,
1997. Director, Robert Scanlan.
Maria Theresa Paradies .... Angela Reed
Franz Anton Mesmer .... Jonathan Epstein
Karl .... Tommy Schrider
Ben Franklin; Baron Anton
    von Storck .... Fred Major
Dr. Jan Ingenhousze;
    Josef Paradies .... Allen Fitzpatrick
Frau Mesmer; Ensemble .... Toni Gorman
Stroller; Ensemble .... Dianne Archer
Street Entertainers .... Brian Carter,
                                   Christine Carroll
    Time and place: Beginning and ending at a
concert in the Tuileries Garden, Paris, 1784; re-
maining action takes place during four months in
Vienna, 1777. One intermission.

POLAROID STORIES. By Naomi Iizuka. March
28, 1997. Director, Jon Jory.
D (Dionysus) .... Scot Anthony Robinson
Philomel .... Monica Bueno
Eurydice .... Kim Gainer

Persephone (also Semele) .... Denise Casano
Orpheus .... Bruce McKenzie
Narcissus .... Michael Ray Escamilla
Echo .... Miriam Brown
G (Zeus, Hades) .... Nelson Vasquez
Lydian Sailor (also Theseus,
    Pentheus) .... Danny Seckel
Ariadne .... Caitlin Miller
    Time: The late 1990s, night. Place: A pier at
the edge of the city. One intermission.

    Humana Festival Designers: scenery, Paul
Owen; costumes, David Zinn, Marcia Dixcy Jory;
lighting, Ed McCarthy, Greg Sullivan; sound,
Robert Murphy, Martin R. Desjardins.

Humana Festival Ten-Minute Plays
April 4 & 6, 1997

MISREADINGS. By Neena Beber. Director, Jen-
nifer Hubbard.
Ruth .... Maryann Urbano
Simone .... Jennifer London
WATERBABIES. By Adam LeFevre. Director,
Simon Ha.
Emma .... Kate Goehring
Liz .... Jennifer Hubbard
STARS. By Romulus Linney. Director, Frazier W.
Marsh.
He .... William McNulty
She .... Karen Grassle

    Ten-Minute Play Designers: Scenery, Paul
Owen; costumes, Kevin R. McLeod; lighting, Ed
McCarthy; sound, Martin R. Desjardins.

Madison, N.J.: Playwrights Theater of New Jersey

(John Pietrowski producing artistic director; Buzz McLaughlin founding director; Joseph
Megel associate artistic director)

Rowing to America:
The Immigrant Project, May 1–18, 1997

DEAD BOLIVIANS ON A RAFT. By Guillermo
Reyes. Director, Joseph Giardina.
Gulliver .... Isaiah Cazares
Manuel .... Miles Grose
Rigoberta .... Divina Cook.
    Place: Watts, South Central neighborhood of
Los Angeles.

THE APRON. By Meg Griffith. Director, Brian
Platt.
Maire McMahon .... Millie Chow
Peig McMahon .... Tiffany Marshall
    Time: 1870. Place: On the western shore of
County Clare, Ireland.

ROWING TO AMERICA. By Kitty Chen. Di-
rector, John Pietrowski.
Girl .... Millie Chow
Sister .... Felicia Wilson

SLAVE COFFLE/WITH OBSERVER. By J. Ru-
fus Caleb. Director, John Pietrowski.
Clara .... Felicia Wilson
Charles .... Eddie Aldridge
Observer .... Tiffany Marshall
Interviewer .... Miles Grose

HOMELAND. By Sachi Oyama. Director, Joseph
Giardina.
Keiko .... Millie Chow
Neighbor Lomeli; Student .... Tamir
High Tech Neighbor; Student ..... Rizwan Manji
Storekeeper; Student .... Jay Palit
    Other Students: Divina Cook, Felicia Wilson,
Isaiah Cazares, Tiffany Marshall, Miles Grose.

FAMOUS ALL. By Robert Clyman. Director,
John Pietrowski.
Harris .... Eddie Aldridge
Ali .... Rizwan Manji
Latoya .... Felicia Wilson

Place: A customs office.

A MULE IN J.F.K. By Keith Glover. Director, Joseph Megel.

Guard .... Eddie Aldridge
Ramon .... Miles Grose
Place: An airport detaining room.

LET US GO THEN. By Akhil Sharma. Director, Joseph Megel.

Arjun .... Jay Palit
Swati .... Tamir
Vijay .... Rizwan Manji

OH WILD WEST WIND. By Karen Sunde. Director, Joseph Megel.

Eda .... Divina Cook

Dawn .... Millie Chow
Red .... Isaiah Cazares
Designers: Scenery, James A. Bazewicz; lighting and costumes, Bruce Goodrich.
One intermission following *Homeland*.

Concert Readings:

GOD'S FIELD. By Meg Griffith. October 11, 1996.

DADDY'S GONE A-HUNTING. By Karen Sunde. November 1, 1996.

FATHERS AND SONS. By Rufus Caleb. February 21, 1997.

MISS CONSUELO. By Guillermo Reyes. March 14, 1997.

Madison, Wis.: Broom Street Theater

(Joel Gersmann artistic director)

COOKIES FOR MY PRESIDENT, OR BUNNY WUNNY GOES TO WASHINGTON. By Joel Gersmann. June 14, 1996. Director, Joel Gersmann; scenery, Richard Swaback; costumes, Ron Fischer, Jessica Callahan; lighting, D.W. Wanberg; sound, Luke T. Delwiche.

Cast: Jackie Langenbach, Bill Jones, Barbara Hendricks, Artistic Dancer, Debbie—Jennie Capellaro; Elizabeth Sparks—Nora Cassidy; Video and Other Voices, Waiter—Luke T. Delwiche; Aaron Scouby, Hippolytus Aristopoulos, Convention Entertainer, Sewerslime—Daniel Konar; Alvin Sparks—Robert J. Moccero; Babs Blake, Rondine Roth—Amy Solberg; Ronald Reagan, Gladys Hooper, Laser Tornado Voice, Judge Edward McDowell—Phil Strowman; Elmer Gonzalez, Thor, Phil Woods, Garbage Man, Jacques Extayrier, Prison Guard, Tom, Comic Demon—Joe Wiener; Ambassadors, Cabinet Members, Delegates, Security Officers, Jury Members, Waiters, Children, Advisors, Old Film Stars—Company.

Theme song "Cookies for My President" music by Brian Wild, lyrics by Joel Gersmann, performed by Brian Wild.

Time: The early 21st Century.

PLEASE PLEASE PLEASE LOVE ME. By Rick Vorndran. August 2, 1996. Director, Rick Vorndran; scenery, Jason Kaiser, Rebecca Toft, Rick Vorndran; costumes, Amanda Jones; lighting, Ron Collins.

Atlas Apple; Drunk Man .... Luke T. Delwiche
Lillouise Chiquita .... Natalia Gakovich
Isabelle Chiquita .... Jennifer Grabow
Blanche Anderson .... Amanda Jones
Artemis Apple; Maria Tillman;
Tennis Referee .... Julie Levinson
Steven Chiquita; Bruno
the Thug .... Lenny Maki
John Kaufman .... Rob Matsushita

Janis Anderson;
Tennis Player .... Laura S. Newport
Sen. Bob Chiquita .... Rick Vorndran
Joey Anderson; Pro Wrestler;
Caterer .... Joe Wiener
Chiquita Campaign Workers, Coffee Zombies—Company.

IRISH LESBIAN VAMPIRE. By Joel Gersmann; based in part on *The Truth About Dracula* by Gabriel Ronay and *Carmilla* by Joseph Sheridan Le Fanu. September 27, 1996. Director, Joel Gersmann; scenery, Richard Swaback; costumes, Ron Fisher; lighting, Ron Collins; original folk song lyrics, Joel Gersmann.

Cast: Squaredance Caller, Soldier, Count Mircea Radescu, King of Romania, Jeffrey Farnsworth—Doug Banasky; Jester, Nicu, Soldier, Siszu, 2d Nun, Hunchbacked Peddlar—David Capen; Funeral Leader, Old Peasant, Madge—Lauri Harty; Mrs. Peridont, Mary Beth, Tara—Amanda Jones; Dorga Darvulia, Countess, Doreen—Betsy McNeely; Cornelia, Dana,1st Nun—Isa Norwood; Janet Farnsworth, Kathleen O'Farnsworth—Clare M. Sorman; Mitach Florescu, Soldier, Old Peasant, Doctor, General Harrison, Father Time—Philip Strowman; Fiddler, Mrs. Fontaine, Peasant, Dog, Lizzie—Cindy Toth; and Jessica L. Callahan.

Servants, Peasants, Aristocrats, Townspeople, Trees, Actors, Lesbians, etc.—Company.

Time and place: 17th century Romania, mid-19th century Ireland, Ireland during World War II, Ireland in 1996.

NAZI BOY. By Joel Gersmann. November 15, 1996. Director, Joel Gersmann; scenery, Richard Swaback, Laura Heiple; lighting, D.W. Wanberg; music, Doug Banasky.

Cast: Gen. Paul von Hindenberg, Siegfried, Max Jambrowski, Angel With Shofar—Doug

GEORGE STREET PLAYHOUSE, NEW BRUNSWICK, N.J.—Michael A. Shepperd (Jim), Stacey Todd Holt (Huck), the King (Tom Brennan) and the Duke (Reathel Bean) in *The Adventures of Huckleberry Finn,* adapted from Mark Twain by Randal Myler and directed by Gregory S. Hurst

Banasky; Horst Wessel, Mathias Erzberger—Nate T. Beyer; Werner Wessel, Frau Salm, Prostitute—Alissa M. Farrens; Martha, Erna Jaenichen, Prostitute, Rhinemaiden—Shelley Johnson; Heinz, Hagen—Rob Matsushita; Joseph Goebbels, Rhinemaiden—Robert J. Moccero; Margarete Wessel, Rhinemaiden, Prostitute—Isa Norwood; Ingeborg Wessel, Prostitute, Anne Frank—Megan Ryan; Ludwig Wessel, Albrecht Holer—Daniel Stevens; Irmengaard, Schiller, General Foch, God—Rick (Richard Wilhelm) Vorndran.

Street People, Soldiers, Students, Storm Troopers, German Citizens, etc.—Company.

Time: 1914 through 1933. Place: Berlin, Germany.

MY FAVORITE ALIEN. By Doug Banasky. January 10, 1997. Director, Doug Banasky; scenery, Christopher X. Burant; costumes, Geri Ager; lighting, D.W. Wanberg; choreography, Paul Schoeneman; song "Lynora's Theme" by Doug Banasky.

Cast: Doomsayer, Sarah Goldman, Lynora—Tracy Wieczorek; Man in Black, Penelope, TV Studio Assistant—Trisan Vincent; Doomsayer, Manfred Kranz, UFO Debunker—Philip Strowman; Major General, Keith Salverson—Jamie McCanless; Man in Black, Bob Costas, Bobby—Dan Jacobson; Agent Fitz, Man in Black, Hillary Clinton—Sam Butzer; Daniel Salverson—Kevin M. Bosley; Man in Black, Alien Messenger—Doug Banasky; piano and guitar—Tracy Wieczorek, Doug Banasky, Chet Toni.

Street People, Cameramen, Aliens, Webpage Hypertext, Hirelings, Patients, Reporters, etc.—Company.

Time: 1999. One intermission.

MUFFY THE BITCH. By Callen Harty. February 28, 1997. Director, Callen Harty; scenery, Steve Conroy; costumes, Ron Fischer; lighting, Luke T. Delwiche, Ron Collins, Chet Toni; music, Brian Wild.

Cast: Mrs. Drucker, Old Woman—Jackie Baker; Mr. Gardener, Judge—Alan Bickley; Sister Sue, Angela, 2d Policeman—Maritza Bryant; Father, Daddy —Ron Collins; Radio Announcer, Bob Two, 1st Policeman, Leroy, Man, Reporter— Luke T. Delwiche; Limo Driver, Bob One, Singer, Jeremy, Attorney—Mark Edwards; Mr. Bates, Mr. Drucker—Buck Hakes; Miss Deeds, Sister Pam, Telephone Operator—Lauri Harty; Mother—Shelley Johnson; Muffy—Amanda Jones; Professor Doctor, 2d Man, Jury Foreman— Jamie McCanless; Mrs. Lovejoy—Isa Norwood.

SEX, DRUGS, ROCK & ROLL: THE REAL WORLD. Musical with book and lyrics by John Sable; music by Brian Wild. April 18, 1997. Director, John Sable; choreography, Lauri Harty, John

Ferguson; costumes, Ron Fischer; lighting, Ron Collins.

Mary-Ellis Bunim	Betsy McNeely
Tuesday Springs	Cindy Toth
Amy Rockerfeller	Amanda Jones
Devon Clegg	John Ferguson
Mr. Moony	Toribio Baeza III
Clark Jones	Rob Matsushita
Heather Snappenduggle	Julie Levinson
Joan Smith "Latwanda"	Tracy Wieczorek
Ellen McDuffy	Lauri Harty
Mortimer Applebee	Dan Jacobson
Oscar Applebee	Aaron Oberman
Terry Bard	Chet Toni
Sachel the Donkey	Himself

No intermission.

Miami: Coconut Grove Playhouse

(Arnold Mittelman artistic director)

DON'T STOP THE CARNIVAL. Musical with book by Herman Wouk based on his novel; music and lyrics by Jimmy Buffett. April 19, 1997. Director, David H. Bell; choreography, David H. Bell; musical direction, Jack Gaughan; scenery, Dex Edwards; costumes, Susan E. Mickey; lighting, Diane Ferry Williams; sound, Steve Shapiro.

Norman Paperman	Michael Rupert
Sheila	Avery Sommers
Iris Tramm	Sandy Edgerton
Lester Atlas	Josh Mostel
Henny Paperman	Susan Dawn Carson
Governor	LaParee Young
Esme	Roz White
Senator	C.E. Smith
Mr. Tilson	Christopher Bishop
Mrs. Tilson	Tricia Matthews
Amy Ball	Megan McFarland
Hyppolyte	Aaron Cimadevilla
Gilbert	Charles E. Bullock
Millard	Karl E. Atkins
Ted Akers	Barry J. Tarallo

Lorna	Louisa Kendrick
Church Wagner	Brad Musgrove

Others: Lori Alexander, Leo Alvarez, Roxanne Barlow, Sue Delano, Jason Gillman, Aurelio Hurtado de Mendoza, Salome Mazard, Glenn Douglas Packard, Victor B. Pellegrino, Lainie Sakakura, Samuel N. Thiam.

One intermission.

MUSICAL NUMBERS: "The Legend of Norman Paperman," "Calaloo," "Sheila Says," "Public Relations," "Just an Old Truth Teller," "Smartest Man in New York," "Starting Life Over," "All About de Watah," "The Key to My Man," "Kinja Rules," "A Thousand Steps to Nowhere," "Champagne Si, Agua No," "Goodbye to Public Relations," "Handiest Frenchman in da Caribbean," "Hyppolyte's Habitat (Qui Mon Qui)," "Cutlash Dance," "Merci Monsieur Lamartine," "No Romancing," "Green Flash at Sunset," "Who Are We Trying to Fool," "Fot Person Mon," "Up on the Hill," "Reactionary Can-Can," "Separate Ways," "Carnival Day/Jungle Drums," "Tax Heaven," "Time to Go Home."

Milford, N.H.: American Stage Festival

(Matthew Parent producing director; Troy Siebels managing director)

THE DRAGON AND THE PEARL. Solo performance by Valerie Harper; written by Marty Martin; based on Peter Conn's biography Pearl S. Buck. July 18, 1996. Director, Pamela Berlin; scenery, James Noone; costume, Michael Krass; lighting, Ken Billington; sound, B.C. Keller; incidental

music, Albert Acosta; produced in association with Tony Cacciotti, executive producer.

Pearl Sydenstricker Buck .... Valerie Harper

Time: A spring day in the late 1960s. Place: Green Hills Farm, Bucks County, Pa.

Millburn, N.J.: Paper Mill Playhouse

(Angelo Del Rossi executive producer; Robert Johanson artistic director)

OUT OF ORDER. By Ray Cooney; based on the original play *Whose Wife Is It Anyway?* January 1, 1997. Directed by David Warwick; scenery, Douglas Heap; costumes, Ellis Tillman; lighting, Martin Aronstein; sound, Steven Shapiro; presented in the Coconut Grove Playhouse production, Arnold Mittelman artistic director.

Richard Willey .... Paxton Whitehead
Manager .... Burt Edwards
Waiter .... Vince O'Brien
Jane Worthington .... Kay Walbye
A Body .... John Seidman
George Pigden .... Reno Roop
Ronnie .... Timothy Wheeler
Pamela .... Delphi Harrington
Gladys .... Christine McMurdo-Wallis
    Time: About 8:30 on a September evening. Place: Suite 648 of the Westminster Hotel in London. No intermission.

JANE EYRE. By Robert Johanson; based on the novel by Charlotte Bronte. February 19, 1997. Director, Robert Johanson; scenery, Michael Anania; costumes, Gregg Barnes; lighting, Timothy Hunter; sound, David R. Paterson; music, Albert Evans; fight direction, Rick Sordelet.

Adult Jane Eyre .... Elizabeth Roby
Young Jane Eyre .... Blythe Auffarth
At Gateshead:
Mrs. Sarah Reed .... Nancy McDoniel
John Reed .... Justin M. Restivo
Young Georgiana Reed .... Grace Ann Pisani
Adult Georgiana Reed .... Laura Benanti
Young Eliza Reed .... Lauren A. Wanko
Adult Eliza Reed .... Julie Georgia Thomas
Bessie .... Ruth Moore
Miss Abbott .... Mikel Sarah Lambert
Mr. Reed .... Ronald H. Siebert
At Lowood:
Brocklehurst .... William Ryall
Miss Miller .... Nancy Auffarth
Miss Scatcherd .... Maureen Sadusk

Mme. Pierrot .... Mikel Sarah Lambert
Helen Burns .... Natalie Van Kleef
Miss Maria Temple .... Glory Crampton.
Mrs. Brocklehurst .... Nancy McDoniel
Augusta Brocklehurst .... Amanda White
At Thornfield:
Mrs. Fairfax .... Mikel Sarah Lambert
John .... John A. Andrews
Leah .... Julie Georgia Thomas
Adele Varens .... Amanda White
Grace Poole .... J. Petitchamps
Mr. Edward Rochester .... Tom Hewitt
Blanche Ingram; Bertha ...... Glory Crampton
Lady Ingram .... Maureen Sadusk
Mary Ingram .... Laura Benanti
Louisa Eshton .... Julie-Anne Liechty
Amy Eshton .... Karen Phillips
Sir George Lynn; Mr. Woods ... William Ryall
Lady Lynn .... Nancy McDoniel
Henry Lynn;
    Mr. Briggs .... Edward Staudenmayer
Frederick Lynn .... Nancy Auffarth
Richard Mason .... Ronald H. Siebert
Bertha .... Glory Crampton
At Marsh End:
Woman on the Road .... Ruth Moore
Woman at the Door .... Nancy McDoniel
Hannah .... Maureen Sadusk
Diana Rivers .... Karen Phillips
Mary Rivers .... Laura Benanti
St. John Rivers .... John Littlefield
At Morton:
Rosamund Oliver .... Julie-Anne Liechty
Fight Captain .... Ronald H. Siebert
    Schoolgirls at Lowood and Morton: Blythe Auffarth, Laura Benanti, Rahale Berman, Courtney Blaine Dunn, Anne Hathaway, Julie-Anne Liechty, Jacqueline Macri, Jennifer Lynne Margulis, Grace Ann Pisani, Karen Phillips, Julie Georgia Thomas, Natalie Van Kleef, Lauren A. Wanko, Jessica Waxman, Amanda White.
    One intermission.

Minneapolis: The Guthrie Theater

(Joe Dowling artistic director; David Hawkanson managing director)

Guthrie, Too at The Lab

MANY COLORS MAKE THE THUNDER KING. By Femi Osofisan; music and lyrics by Femi Osofisan and Tunji Oyelana. February 22, 1997. Director, Bartlett Sher; scenery, Nanya Ramey; costumes, Devon Painter; lighting, Michael Klaers; sound, Peter Still; choreography, Folabo

Ajayi; fight direction, John Stead; musical direction, Sowah Mensah.

Igunnun; Alagemo .... Omari Shakir
Shango .... T. Mychael Rambo
Gbonka; Alapandede;
    Ant .... Shawn Hamilton
Timi; Turtle; Ant .... James Austin Williams

WALNUT STREET THEATER, PHILADELPHIA—Callum Keith-King, William M. Whitehead and William McCauley in a scene from John W. Lowell's *Autumn Canticle*

Oya .... Melinda Lopez
Ireti; Ant .... Mary Easter
Egret; Porter; Ant .... Togba Norris
Aroni; Elder; Porter; Ant .... Terry Bellamy
Osun; Song Leader .... Marvette Knight
Yeye Iroko .... Kim Hines
Drummer; Porter; Ant .... Ahanti Young

Lead Drummer .... Sowah Mensah
Villagers, Birds, Dancers, Spirits, Tree Sprites: Alecia Carter, Tokunbo Okanla, Scholastica Simbi.

Act I, Scene 1: The public square of a village. Scene 2: Princess Oya's aquatic palace. Scene 3: Shango's palace. Scene 4: A clearing. Scene 5: Ceremonial courtroom in Shango's palace. Scene 6: A path leading to the mountain. Scene 7: Dinner at Shango's palace. Scene 8: A forest grove. Scene 9: Shango's palace. Scene 10: Outside the palace. Act II, Scene 11: A cave. Scene 12: Shango's palace. Scene 13: A forest grove. Scene 14: Shango's palace. Scene 15: Somewhere in the forest. Scene 16: By the iroko tree.

Minneapolis: Ordway Music Theater

(Kevin McCollum artistic director)

THE WIZARD OF OZ. Musical adapted by Worth Gardner from the book by L. Frank Baum; music by Harold Arlen; lyrics by E.Y. Harburg. July 23, 1996. Director and choreographer, Worth Gardner; scenery, Paul Shortt; costumes, Eduardo Sicangco; lighting, Kirk Bookman; sound, David B. Smith; orchestra design, Frederick Bianchi, David B. Smith; background music, Herbert Stothart.

L. Frank Baum	William Brown
Dorothy	Suzanne Bedford
Nemesis; Wicked Witch of the West	Darren Mathias
Scarecrow	John Schiappa
Tin Man	Howard Kaye
Lion	Bob Arnold

Others: Paul Blankenship, Brenda Braye, Desmond Zachary Dent, Don Farrell, Judy Fitzgerald, Brad Hamilton, Rebecca Hirsch, Tim Johnson, Soomi Kim, Billy Miller, Catherine Moore, Michael Pappa, Teri Parker-Brown, Bradley Reynolds, Lisa Rock, Peter Vitale.

One intermission.

MUSICAL NUMBERS: "Over the Rainbow," "Munchkin Land," "Come Out, Wherever You Are," "The Wind Began to Switch," "Ding, Dong, the Witch Is Dead," "The Lullabye League," "The Lollipop Guild," "We Welcome You to Munchkin Land," "Follow the Yellow Brick Road," "We're Off to See the Wizard," "If I Only Had a Brain," "If I Only Had a Heart," "If I Only Had the Nerve," "Emerald City," "Ozee Zoo Zah," "Optimistic Voices," "You're Out of the Woods," "If I Were King of the Forest," "I Want Those Ruby Shoes."

Minneapolis: Théâtre de la Jeune Lune

(Robert Rosen, Dominique Serrand, Vincent Gracieux, Barbara Berlovitz-Desbois artistic directors)

THE THREE MUSKETEERS. Adapted by Dominique Serrand from the novel by Alexandre Dumas. November 27, 1996. Director, Dominique Serrand; scenery, Dominique Serrand, Vincent Gracieux; costumes, Sonya Berlovitz; lighting, Dominique Serrand; original music, Eric Jensen.

Porthos	Joel Spence
Aramis	Steven Epp
Athos	Vincent Gracieux
Planchet	Sarah Agnew
Constance	Patricia Buckley
d'Artagnan	Luverne Seifert
Buckingham	Michael Lenz
Cardinal Richelieu	Rob Rosen
Milady	Barbra Berlovitz Desbois
Rochefort	Stephen Cartmell
Queen of France	Karin Rosen
Louis XIII	Ethan Angelica

One intermission.

Montgomery, Ala.: Alabama Shakespeare Festival

(Kent Thompson artistic director; Kevin Maifeld managing director)

THUNDER KNOCKING ON THE DOOR: A BLUSICAL TALE OF RHYTHM AND THE BLUES. Musical by Keith Glover; music by various authors, see listing below. October 1, 1996. Director, Marion McClinton; choreography, Ken Roberson; musical direction, Olu Dara; scenery, Neil Patel; costumes, Alvin Perry; lighting, William H. Grant III; sound, Thom Jenkins. Produced in association with Center Stage, Irene Lewis artistic director, and Dallas Theater Center, Richard Hamburger artistic director.

Good Sister Dupree	Harriett D. Foy
Dregster Dupree	Charles Weldon
Glory Dupree	Shawana Kemp
Jaguar Dupree	Victor Mack
Marrvel Thunder	Lester Purry

One intermission.

Elizabeth Osborn Award winner; see introduction to this section.

MUSICAL NUMBERS: "All Around the World" by Titus Turner, "Good, Good Lovin' " by James Brown and Albert Shubert, "Evil (Is

Going On)" and "I Just Want to Make Love to You" by Willie Dixon, "The Sky Is Crying" by Elmore James, "Tell Me" by Chester Burnett, "Three O'Clock Blues" by B.B. King and Jules Traub, "Suffering With the Blues" by Theodore Conyers and Lloyd Pemberton; "Someday After a While" by Sonny Thompson and Freddie King, "I Need Your Love So Bad" by Willie John.

Southern Writers' Project
1996 Workshop

BABY SHOWERS. By Heather McCutchen. July 16, 1996. Director, Susan Willis.
The LaDean Sisters:

Josephine (Pheenie)	Greta Lambert
Monty Louise	Trish McCall
Rachel Catherine Anne	Kim Ders
Danny S. (Dallas)	Camille Troy
Miss Floydd	Jill Tanner

Southern Writers' Project
Readings:

FAIR AND TENDER LADIES. Musical with book adapted by Eric Schmiedl from the novel by Lee Smith; music and lyrics by Karren Pell, Tommy Goldsmith and Tom House. January 18, 1997.

THE COMING OF RAIN. By Richard Marius. January 25, 1997.

New Brunswick, N.J.: Crossroads Theater Company

(Ricardo Khan artistic director)

WEDDING DANCE. By Dominic Taylor. March 4, 1997. Director, Donald Douglass; scenery, Myung Hee Cho; costumes, Loyce L. Arthur; lighting, Jan Kroeze; sound, Lloyd E. Vaughan Jr.; produced in association with AT&T:*OnStage*.

Bessie	Latonya Holmes
Milton	Ramon Melindez Moses
Rashad	Jacinto Taras Riddick
Ab	Kevin Thigpen
Gayle	Theara Ward

One intermission.

THE DARKER FACE OF THE EARTH. By Rita Dove. July 24, 1996. Director, Ricardo Khan. Produced in association with Oregon Shakespeare Festival, Libby Appel artistic director (see its entry in the Ashland listing in this section).

New Brunswick, N.J.: George Street Playhouse

(Gregory S. Hurst producing artistic director; Wendy Liscow associate artistic director; Diane Claussen managing director)

AVOW. By Bill C. Davis. October 4, 1996. Director, Gillian Lynne; scenery, Stephan Olson; costumes, James Scott; lighting, Donald Holder; sound, Shawn Deiger; composer, Marvin Laird; produced in association with Anita Howe-Waxman and Craig Anderson.

Brian	Peter Gantenbein
Tom	Michael Booth
Father Raymond	Michael Rupert
Irene	Christina Haag
Julie	Suzanne Inman
Rose	Rosemary Prinz
Father Nash	Richard Russell Ramos

One intermission.

SING A CHRISTMAS SONG. Musical based on *A Christmas Carol* by Charles Dickens; libretto and lyrics by Peter Udell; music by Garry Sherman. December 6, 1996. Director, Gregory S. Hurst; choreography, Deborah Roshe; co-musical directors, Garry Sherman, Andrew Wilder; scenery, Atkin Pace; costumes, Kim Krumm Sorenson; lighting, F. Mitchell Dana; sound, Leonard Manchess, Kaizad Bhabha; orchestrations, Garry Sherman; produced in association with Amy Buske.

Cast: Man From the Mayor, Christmas Past, Company—Philip Anthony; Marley, Cratchit, Company—Clent Bowers; Tiny Tim, Company—Jessica Dillan; Mary, Christmas Present, Company—Kim Hawthorne; Preacher, Christmas Future, Company—Erich McMillian-McCall; Scrooge—Rudy Roberson; Gospel Soloist, Company—Sharon Wilkins.

One intermission.

MUSICAL NUMBERS, ACT I: "Celebration Time," "Somebody's Gotta Be the Heavy," same (Reprise), "Now I Lay Me Down to Sleep," "There Oughta Be a Law," "Give It Up," "Now I Lay Me Down to Sleep" (Reprise), "Lifeline," "What Better Time for Love," "Lifeline" (Reprise), "Born Again."

ACT II: "Sing a Christmas Song," "What Goes Around, Comes Around," "Sing a Christmas Song" (Reprise), "What Better Time for Love" (Reprise), "Have I Finally Found My Heart," "Goin' Goin' Gone," "Get Down Brother," Finale.

ADVENTURES OF HUCKLEBERRY FINN. Adapted from Mark Twain's novel by Randal My-

Above, Rene Augesen as Princess Leonide with Patrick Kerr and Tom Beckett in *The Triumph of Love,* as adapted by Richard Greenberg, at South Coast Repertory, Costa Mesa, Calif.; *left,* Susan Egan as Princess Leonide with Mary Beth Peil in the musical version, *Triumph of Love,* with book by James Magruder, music by Jeffrey Stock and lyrics by Susan Birkenhead, at Baltimore's Center Stage

ight, Francesca Faridany and eil Maffin in *The Game of Love d Chance,* translated, adapted d directed by Stephen Wads-orth at the McCarter Theater, inceton, N.J.

ler. March 8, 1997 (revised version). Director, Gregory S. Hurst; scenery, Rob Odorisio; costumes, Deirdre Sturges Burke; lighting, Joshua Starbuck; sound, Michael Shawn Deiger.

Cast: Huck—Stacey Todd Holt; Widow Douglas, Mrs. Loftus, Aunt Sally, Ensemble—Amelia White; Miss Watson, Mrs. Grangerford, Widow Bartley, Aunt Polly, Ensemble—Donna Davis; Jim, Professor Ingram—Michael A. Shepperd; Tom Sawyer, Buck Grangerford, Ensemble—Shannon Stoeke; Ben Rogers, Sophia Grangerford, Mary Jane Wilkes, Ensemble—Debra Funkhouser; Joe Harper, Joanna Wilkes, Ensemble—Tami Dixon; Tommy Barnes, Bob Grangerford, Boy Fishing, Ensemble—Joseph Abel; Pap, King—Tom Brennan; Judge Thatcher, Bounty Hunter, Old Man Shepardson, Judge, Undertaker, Uncle Silas, Ensemble—David S. Howard; Bounty Hunter, Big Shepardson, Hank, Dr. Robinson, The Doctor, Ensemble—Ed Sala; Bounty Hunter, Shepardson, Bill, Fool, Hired Hand, Ensemble—Chris Lowry; Col. Grangerford, Duke—Reathel Bean; Shepardson, Lafe, Hired Hand, Ensemble—Len Duckman.

Time: Somewhere in the late 1840s. Place: Along the Mississippi River Valley. One intermission.

AND THEN THEY CAME FOR ME: REMEMBERING THE WORLD OF ANNE FRANK. By James Still. April 19, 1997. Director, Susan Kerner; scenery, Robert Koharchick; costumes, Barbara Forbes; lighting, Brenda Veltre; produced in association with Young Audiences of New Jersey.

Cast: Hitler Youth, Ed's Father, Heinz Geiringer—John Socas; Ed Silberberg, Eva's Father—Ron Scott; Eva Geiringer, Ed's Mother—Karen Zippler; German Citizens, Eva's Mother, Anne Frank—Michelle Spires.

Time: 1938-1945. Place: Europe. No intermission.

New Haven, Conn.: Long Wharf Theater

(Arvin Brown artistic director; M. Edgar Rosenblum executive director)

DEALER'S CHOICE. By Patrick Marber. October 16, 1996 (first full American production). Director, David Esbjornson; scenery, Hugh Landwehr; costumes, Elizabeth Hope Clancy; lighting, Frances Aronson; presented by special arrangement with Elizabeth I. McCann and the Royal National Theater.

Sweeney .... Ritchie Coster
Mugsy .... Reg Rogers
Carl .... Mark H. Dold
Frankie .... Alec Phoenix
Stephen .... Dermot Crowley
Ash .... Tom Spackman
One intermission.

THE OLD SETTLER. By John Henry Redwood. February 4, 1997. Produced in association with the McCarter Theater, Emily Mann artistic director; see its entry in the Princeton listing in this section.

New Haven, Conn: Yale Repertory Theater

(Stan Wojewodski Jr. artistic director; Victoria Nolan managing director)

TRIUMPH OF LOVE. Musical based on the play by Marivaux; book by James Magruder; music by Jeffrey Stock; lyrics by Susan Birkenhead. January 16, 1997. Produced in association with Center Stage, Irene Lewis artistic director; see its entry in the Baltimore section of this listing.

THE ADVENTURES OF AMY BOCK. By Julie McKee. March 27, 1997. Director, Stan Wojewodski Jr.; scenery, Scott Pask; costumes, Suttirat Larlarb; lighting, Les Dickert; sound, David Budries.

Cast: Amy—Enid Graham; Justice New Zealand, Swimmer, Accuser #3, Superintendent Kettle, Percy—Alec Phoenix; Mother, Nessie—Blair Sams; Mrs. Hookham, Accuser #2, Mrs. Ottaway—Sandra Shipley; Mrs. Finch, Mrs. Parnell, 50% Mad, Old Lady—Audrie Neenan; Robson, Father, Policeman, Mr. Ottaway—Reno Roop; Justice Australia, Mr. Parnell, Kenneth—Frank Deal; Ruby a.k.a. Opal, Accuser #1, Child (Edna)—Kristine Nielsen.

Time: Between 1870 and 1893, Place: Australia and New Zealand. One intermission.

Nyack, N.Y.: Helen Hayes Performing Arts Center

(Pam Klappas artistic director; Tony Stimac executive producer; Marilyn Stimac associate producer)

SONGS FOR A NEW WORLD. Revue with music and lyrics by Jason Robert Brown. March 7, 1997. Director, Michael Schiralli; choreography, Bernard Monroe; musical direction, Jason Robert Brown; scenery, Evelyn Sakash; costumes, Gail Brassard; lighting, Richard Latta; sound, Tim Brady; orchestrations, Brian Besterman, Jason Robert Brown.

With Scott Beck, Jessica Hendy, Beth Leavel, Don Corey Washington.

SCENES AND MUSICAL NUMBERS,

Act I: Opening Sequence: The New World; On the Deck of a Spanish Sailing Ship, 1492; "Just One Step," "I'm Not Afraid of Anything," "The River Won't Flow," Transition I, "Stars and the Moon," "She Cries," "The Steam Train."

Act II: "The World Was Dancing," "Surabaya-Santa," "Christmas Lullaby," "King of the World," "I'd Give It All for You," Transition II; The Flagmaker, 1775; "Flying Home," Final Transition, "Hear My Song."

Philadelphia: American Music Theater Festival

(Marjorie Sarnoff producing director; Ben Levit artistic director)

BLACK WATER. Opera with libretto by Joyce Carol Oates based on her novel; music by John Duffy. April 27, 1997. Director, Gordon Edelstein; musical direction, Alan Johnson; scenery, Douglas Stein; costumes, Candice Donnelly; lighting, Scott Zielinski; sound, David Meschter/Applied Audio Technologies.

Kelly Kelleher .... Karen Burlingame
Sarah Connor .... Erin Langston
Buffy St. John .... Stephanie Buckley
Roy Annick .... Wilbur Pauley
Lucius Smith .... David Lee Brewer
The Senator .... Patrick Mason
Dwight Murphy .... Kent Smith
Michelle Ravel .... Tara Venditti
Jenny O'Brien .... Kimberly Graham
Graeme Winthrop .... John Savarese
One intermission.

Philadelphia: Philadelphia Festival Theater for New Plays

(Sally de Sousa producing director)

BARE-KNUCKLE. By Art Becker. January 26, 1997. Director, Eugene Nesmith; scenery, Felix E. Cochren; costumes, Loyce L. Arthur; lighting, William H. Grant III; sound, Eileen Tague; music, Susan L. Merrill.

L'il Arthur .... Michael Broughton
Joe .... Chance Kelly
Guard .... David Sitler
Harry .... Steve Zettler
One intermission.

Philadelphia: Walnut Street Theater

(Bernard Havard executive director)

PAPER MOON. Musical based on the novel *Addie Pray* by Joe David Brown and the Paramount Pictures film *Paper Moon*; book by Martin Casella; music by Larry Grossman; lyrics by Ellen Fitzhugh. June 26, 1996. Produced in association with the Goodspeed Opera House, Michael P. Price producer; see its entry in the East Haddam listing in this section.

Studio Three

CHRONICLES OF A COMIC MULATTA. Solo performance by Josslyn Luckett; written by Jos-

slyn Luckett. January 21, 1997. Director, David G. Armstrong; scenery, Bernadette Brennan; costumes, Kevin E. Ross; lighting, Peter J. Jakubowski; sound, Pete Rydberg.

AUTUMN CANTICLE. By John W. Lowell. February 18, 1997. Director, David Ogden Stiers; scenery, Thom Bumblauskas; costumes, Melissa Wayne; lighting, Troy A. Martin-O'Shia; sound, William Rathbone.

David Williams .... William M. Whitehead
Peter Billings .... William McCauley
Walker Dennison .... Callum Keith-King

Time: Act I: An afternoon in late October 1972. Act II: Two weeks later, afternoon. Act III: One week later, late evening. Place: The atelier of a sizeable Tudor house located near the shores of the Hudson River in Croton, N.Y. One intermission following Act II.

KEMBLE VS. BUTLER. By Will Stutts. May 13, 1997. Director, Will Stutts; scenery, Andrew Thompson; costumes, Melissa Wayne; lighting, Peter Jakubowski; sound, Scott Smith.

Frances Anne (Fanny)
Kemble .... Elizabeth Roby
Pierce Butler Mease (Butler) .... Allyn Burrows
    Time: Perhaps four years in the period from 1832 through 1849. Place: The Butler Mansion, Philadelphia; a parlor and a theater dressing room in New York City; a wayside tavern near Valley Forge, Pa.; the Butler Plantation in Southern Georgia; a Common Pleas courtroom in Philadelphia. One intermission.

Pittsburgh: Pittsburgh Public Theater

(Edward Gilbert artistic director; Stephen Klein managing director)

JITNEY. By August Wilson; revised and expanded version. June 14, 1996. Director, Marion Isaac McClinton; scenery, Allen Moyer; costumes, Paul Tazewell; lighting, Phil Monat; sound, James Capenos.
Youngblood .... Russell Andrews
Turnbo .... Stephen McKinley Henderson
Fielding .... Anthony Chisholm
Doub .... Cortez Nance Jr.

Shealy .... Willis Burks II
Man .... Alan Burrell
Becker .... Paul Butler
Rena .... Yvette Ganier
Booster .... Leland Gantt
Woman .... Crystal Bates
    Time: 1971. Place: Pittsburgh's Hill District. One intermission.

Princeton, N.J.: McCarter Theater

(Emily Mann artistic director; Jeffrey Woodward managing director)

THE MAI. By Marina Carr. November 8, 1996 (American premiere). Director, Emily Mann; scenery, Thomas Lynch; costumes, Candice Donnelly; lighting, Peter Kaczorowski; composer, Baikida Carroll.
Millie .... Kali Rocha
Robert .... James Morrison
The Mai .... Katherine Borowitz
Connie .... Miriam Healy-Louie
Grandmother Fraochlan .... Myra Carter
Beck .... Colleen Quinn
Julie .... Isa Thomas
Agnes .... Barbara Lester
    Others: Jonathan Headley, Lizzy Osborn, Christopher J. Rzasa.
    Time: Act I, summer 1979 and the present; Act II, one year later and the present. Place: The Midlands, Ireland.

THE OLD SETTLER. By John Henry Redwood. February 7, 1997. Director, Walter Dallas; scenery, Loren Sherman; costumes, David Murin; lighting, Frances Aronson; sound, Stephen G. Smith; produced in association with the Long Wharf Theater, Arvin Brown artistic director.
Elizabeth Borny .... Brenda Pressley
Quilly McGrath .... Myra Lucretia Taylor
Husband Witherspoon .... Tico Wells

Lou Bessie Preston ...... Caroline Stefanie Clay
    Time: Spring, 1943. Place: A tenement apartment belonging to Elizabeth Borny in Harlem, New York. Act I, Scene 1: Thursday, late afternoon. Scene 2: Friday, 2:25 a.m. Scene 3: The same day, 8:20 a.m. Scene 4: The same day, late afternoon. Act II, Scene 1: Saturday, two weeks later, mid afternoon. Scene 2: Sunday, 9:30 a.m. Scene 3: Friday, 12 days later, afternoon. Scene 4: The same day, early evening.

THE GAME OF LOVE AND CHANCE. By Pierre Carlet de Chamblain de Marivaux; translated and adapted by Stephen Wadsworth. May 9, 1997. Director, Stephen Wadsworth; scenery, Thomas Lynch; costumes, Martin Pakledinaz; lighting, Peter Kaczorowski.
Silvia .... Francesca Faridany
Lisette .... Margaret Welsh
Orgon .... Laurence O'Dwyer
Mario .... Jared Reed
Valet .... Reid Armbruster
Dorante .... Neil Maffin
Harlequin .... John Michael Higgins
    Others: Kathleen Heenan, Ed Mahler.
    Place: Monsieur Orgon's house near Paris. Two intermissions.

Providence, R.I.: Trinity Repertory Company

(Oskar Eustis artistic director; Patricia Egan managing director)

Providence New Play Festival

THE MINEOLA TWINS. By Paula Vogel. March 5, 1997. Director, Molly D. Smith; scenery, Judy Gailen; costumes, William Lane; lighting, Christien Methot; sound, Andrew Keister.

Myra; Myrna .... Anne Scurria
Jim; Sarah .... Phyllis Kay
Kenny; Ben .... Dan Welch
Psychiatric Aides;
    F.B.I. Agents .... Algernon D'Ammassa,
                                        Mauro Hantman
Announcer .... Amanda Dehnert
    Time: Scenes 1 & 2, during the Eisenhower administration. Scenes 3 & 4, at the beginning of the Nixon administration. Scenes 5 & 6, during the Bush administration. One intermission following Scene 3.

AMBITION FACING WEST. By Anthony Clarvoe. April 23, 1997. Director, Oskar Eustis; scenery, Christine Jones; costumes, William Lane; lighting, Geoff Korf.

Stefan; Joey; Jim .... Mauro Hantman

Father Luke .... William Damkoehler
Miss Adamic; Young Alma ... Elizabeth Quincy
Yovan; Old Stefan .... Timothy Crowe
Mrs. Adamic; Josefina .... Phyllis Kay
Marya; Older Alma .... Anne Scurria
    One intermission.

Workshops and Staged Readings,
June 1, 1996–May 31, 1997:

OH WHAT A WONDER! By Leslie Lee.
TYPHOID MARY. By Bridget Carpenter.
A GIRL'S LIFE. By Kathleen Tolan.
IKEBANA and MALL. By Alice Tuan.
GOLDEN CHILD and FACE VALUE. By David Henry Hwang.
THE DEVILS. By Elizabeth Egloff.
BRIAR ROSE. By Gina Gionfriddo.
DEATH OF A HO. By Jake-Ann Jones.
BIRTH OF A MOON. By Suzanne Maynard.
LUNATIC GRACE. By Elana Greenfield.
THE BRIDE WHO BECAME FRIGHTENED WHEN SHE SAW LIFE OPEN. By Alva Rogers.
PASSION PLAY. By Sarah Ruhl.
THE LEAVE TAKER. By Edward Bok Lee.

Purchase, N.Y.: Phoenix Theater Company

(Bram Lewis producing director; Robert Bennett general manager)

SONYA. By Leon Katz. July 5, 1996. Director, Bram Lewis; scenery, Campbell Baird; costumes, Amela Baksic; lighting, Dennis Parichy, Shawn K. Kaufman; sound, Aural Fixation.
Countess Tolstoy .... Julie Harris
Chertkov .... Philip Baker Hall
Sasha .... Miriam Healy-Louie
Audrey .... Jud Meyers
Tatiana .... Jennifer Harmon
Sergey .... Reno Roop

Dushan .... Timothy Jerome
Alexis .... Peter Smith
Nikitin .... Van Cockroft
Stationmaster .... Banislav Tomich
Priest .... Daniel Marcus
Nurse .... Eileen MacMahon
Cameraman .... Anthony O'Donoghue
    Others: Jonathan Turner, Chris Ries.
    One intermission.

Richmond: TheaterVirginia

(George Black producing artistic director; Donna E. Coghill, *New Voices* project director)

New Voices for the Theater
Staged Readings, July 10-13, 1996

CAGED RAT. By Charles Frick Jr. Director, Adam W. Nixon.
CONCERNING ELLA, MERLE, AND THEIR GRANDCHILD CAITLIN. By Cara M. Nalle. Director, Adam W. Nixon.
LITTLE HENRY AND THE TENT SHOW. By Clay McLeod Chapman. Director, George Black.
HERITAGE. By Elizabeth Turner. Director, George Black.

NOBODY LIKES A QUITTER. By Rob Remington. Director, Steve Riedel.
WAITING FOR HARRY. By David C. White. Director, Anna Senechal.
THE GAME. By Antonio F. Straight. Director, Steve Carr.
THE WATERBABIES. By Michal Leamer. Director, Donna E. Coghill.
NO EXITWAY: THE ROAD TRIP FROM HELL. By Clay McLeod Chapman. Director, Harry McEnerney.

OLD GLOBE THEATER, SAN DIEGO—Cherry Jones, Jeffrey Hayenga and Marceline Hugot in a scene from *Pride's Crossing* by Tina Howe, directed by Jack O'Brien

St. Louis: Repertory Theater of St. Louis

(Steven Woolf artistic director; Mark D. Bernstein managing director)

Imaginary Theater Company

CHANTICLEER! Adapted by Brian Hohlfeld; music by Brian Hohlfeld. Tour October 21, 1996; mainstage March 22, 1997. Director, Jeffery Matthews; scenery and costumes, J. Bruce Summers.

Chanticleer .... Joel Gray
Scooter .... Eric J. Conners
Henrietta .... Gretchen Gamble
Fox .... Laura McConnell

BAH! HUMBUG! Adapted by Jack Herrick from Charles Dickens's *A Christmas Carol*. Tour December 2, 1996; mainstage December 14, 1996. Director, Bruce Longworth; scenery, Nichelle Kramlich; costumes, J. Bruce Summers.

Cast: Man, Cratchit, Marley's Ghost, Ghost of Christmas Past, Young Scrooge, Announcer—Eric J. Conners; Little Beggar Girl, Mama, Ma Cratchit, Ghost of Christmas Present—Gretchen Gamble; Scrooge—Joel Gray; Woman, Little Polly, Tiny Tim, Ghost of Christmas Future—Laurie McConnell.

San Diego: Old Globe Theater

(Jack O'Brien artistic director; Thomas Hall, managing director; Craig Noel executive director)

PLAY ON! Musical conceived by Sheldon Epps; book by Cheryl L. West; with the songs of Duke Ellington. September 14, 1996. Director, Sheldon Epps; choreography, Mercedes Ellington; musical direction, Leonard Oxley; scenery, James Leonard Joy; costumes, Marianna Elliott; lighting, Jeff Davis; sound, Jeff Ladman; musical supervision, orchestrations and arrangements, Luther Henderson.

Vy .... Cheryl Freeman
Jester .... Andre De Shields
Sweets .... Larry Marshall
Miss Mary .... Yvette Cason
Duke .... Carl Anderson
Rev .... Lawrence Hamilton

Lady Liv .... Tonya Pinkins
Denizens of Harlem: Crystal Allen, Wendee Lee Curtis, Frantz G. Hall, Bryan Haynes, Kimberly Hester, Derrick Demetrius Parker, Stacie Precia, Lisa Scialabba, William Wesley, Darius Keith Williams.

Time: The swingin' 40s. Place: The magical kingdom of Harlem.

MUSICAL NUMBERS (music and lyrics by Duke Ellington unless otherwise noted), ACT I: "Take the A Train" (music and lyrics by Billy Strayhorn), "Drop Me Off in Harlem" (lyrics by Nick Kenny), "Jester's Snake Song" (music by Luther Henderson), "I've Got To Be a Rug Cutter," "I Let a Song Go Out of My Heart" (music and lyrics by Duke Ellington, Irving Mills, Henry Nemo, John Redmond), "C Jam Blues," "Mood Indigo" (music and lyrics by Duke Ellington, Irving Mills, Albany Bigard), "Don't Get Around Much Anymore" (lyrics by Bob Russell), "Don't You Know I Care" (lyrics by Mack David), "It Don't Mean a Thing if It Ain't Got That Swing" (lyrics by Irving Mills), "I Got It Bad and That Ain't Good" (lyrics by Paul Francis Webster), "Hit Me With a Hot Note" (lyrics by Don George), "I'm Just a Lucky So and So" (lyrics by Mack David), "Everything But You" (music and lyrics by Duke Ellington, Don George, Harry James), "Solitude" (music and lyrics by Duke Ellington, Eddie DeLange, Irving Mills).

ACT II: "Perdido" (music and lyrics by Juan Tizol, H.J. Lengsfelder, Ervin Drake), "Black Butterfly" (music and lyrics by Duke Ellington, Ben Carruthers, Irving Mills), "I Ain't Got Nothin' But the Blues" (lyrics by Don George),

"I'm Beginning to See the Light" (music and lyrics by Duke Ellington, Don George, Harry James, Don Hodges), "I Got It Bad and That Ain't Good" (Reprise), "Rocks in My Bed," "Something to Live For" (lyrics by Billy Strayhorn), "Love You Madly," "Prelude to a Kiss" (music and lyrics by Duke Ellington, Irving Gordon, Irving Mills), "In a Mellow Tone" (lyrics by Milt Gabler).

PRIDE'S CROSSING. By Tina Howe. January 25, 1997. Director, Jack O'Brien; scenery, Ralph Funicello; costumes, Robert Morgan; lighting, Michael Gilliam; sound, Jeff Ladman.

Cast: Mabel Tidings Bigelow—Cherry Jones; Vita Bright, Pru O'Neill, Kitty Lowell—Marceline Hugot; Chandler Coffin, Phinney Tidings, Mary O'Neill —Jeffrey Hayenga; West Bright, Frazier Tidings, Pinky Wheelock, David Bloom— Robert Knepper; Gus Tidings, Anton Gurevitch, Porter Bigelow, Wheels Wheelock—William Anton; Maud Tidings, Julia Renoir—Monique Fowler; Minty Renoir, Emma Bigelow—Hilary Elizabeth Clarke, Nichole Danielle Givans.

Place: Pride's Crossing, Mass. and *in Mabel's memory*. Act I, Scene 1: Mabel's bedroom, the end of June, the present. Scene 2: *The Tidings dining room, summer 1915*. Scene 3: Mabel's living room, the next day. Scene 4: *The Tidings kitchen, summer 1920* . Scene 5: Mabel's living room, later that afternoon. Scene 6: *The Tidings living room, summer 1927*. Act II, Scene 1: Mabel's living room, four days later. Scene 2: *Mabel and Porter Bigelow's living room, Boston, summer 1937*. Scene 3: Mabel's lawn, the Fourth of July. Scene 4: *The Cliffs of Dover, England 1928*.

San Francisco: Magic Theater

(Mame Hunt artistic director)

WAITING AT THE WATER'S EDGE. By Lucinda Coxon. June 4, 1996 (American premiere). Director, Julie Hebert; scenery, Giulio Cesare Perrone; costumes, Allison Connor; lighting, Jeff Rowlings; sound, J.A. Deane.

Violet .... Francesca Faridany

Susie .... Nicola Frances
Therese .... Lynne Soffer
Will .... Michael Oosterom
Davie .... Craig Dickerson
One intermission.

San Francisco: Theater Rhinoceros

(Adele Prandini artistic director)

BRIDES OF THE MOON. By the Five Lesbian Brothers. November 9, 1996. Director, Kate Stafford; scenery, Nancy Bardawil; costumes, Kristine Woods; lighting, Lori E. Seid; sound, Carmen Borgia, Peg Healey.

Cast: Lynn Stone, Gabrielle Bichon-Frisse—

Maureen Angelos; Bridget MacKinney, Ken Powers—Babs Davy; Tylie Holway—Dominique Dibbell; Mrs. Steve Powers, Dal Dal—Peg Healey; Carmen Powers, Slotya Rimjobovich—Lisa Kron.
One intermission.

THE STAND-IN. By Keith Curran. January 11, 1997. Director, Danny Scheie; scenery, Iva Walton; costumes, Kim Curtis; lighting, Michael Romero; music, Don Seaver; assistant director and choreographer, Ian Michael Enriquez.

With Stephen Bowman, Eric Carillo, P.A. Cooley, Matt Cornwall, David Eppel, Adam Gavzner, Alexis Lezin, Carmen Elena Sosa, Liam Vincent, Michelle Wolff.
One intermission.

San José, Calif.: San José Repertory Theater

(Timothy Near artistic director; Alexandra Urbanowski managing director)

New American Playwright Festival
October 26-27, 1997
SONG OF THE RICE, SONG OF LIFE: TALES OF JAPAN. By Karen Yamamoto Hackler. Director, John McCluggage; original music composed and played by Kenny Endo.

With Karen Amano, Michael Ching, David Furumoto, Dian Kobayashi, Del Pedagat, Yumi Sumida, Randal Leigh Wung, Karen Piemme.

MISS CONSUELO. By Guillermo Reyes. Director, Octavio Solis.

With Suzy Berger, George Castillo, Bruce Elsperger, Alma Martinez, Dena Martinez, Ed Rob-

ledo, Monica Sanchez, Michael A. Torres, Rebecca Wink.

COMING OF AGE: THE STORY OF OUR CENTURY BY THOSE WHO'VE LIVED IT. Adapted for the stage by Ronnie Gilbert from Studs Terkel. Director, Timothy Near.

With Ronnie Gilbert, Ken Ruta.

THE SWORD OF KAZARAN. Written and directed by Keith Glover.

With Buddy Butler, L. Peter Callendar, Gina Marie Fields, Norman Gee, Wendi Hodgen, Michael McFall, Mack Miles, James Tyrone Wallace II.

Sarasota: Asolo Theater Company

(Howard J. Millman producing artistic director; Bruce E. Rodgers, Brant Pope associate artistic directors; Linda M. DiGabriele managing director)

OVER MY DEAD BODY. By Michael Sutton and Anthony Fingleton; suggested by the novel *The Murder League* by Robert L. Fish. December 21, 1996. Director, Walton Jones; scenery, Jeffrey Dean; costumes, David M. Covach; lighting, Victor Parker; sound, Matthew Parker.

Trevor Foyle .... Robert Murch
Dora Winslow .... Sharon Spelman
Bartie Cruikshank .... Bradford Wallace

Charters .... James Lawson
Simon Vale .... Jim Iorio
Leo Sharp .... William Pitts
Chief Inspector Smith .... Douglas Jones
Sgt. Trask .... Jonathan Robinson
Time: Act I, an autumn afternoon and after midnight the following day. Act II, later that same day. Place: The Reading Room of The Murder League, London.

Seattle: Intiman Theater

(Warner Shook artistic director; Laura Penn managing director; Victor Pappas associate artistic director)

SMASH. By Jeffrey Hatcher; adapted from the novel *An Unsocial Socialist* by George Bernard Shaw. August 14, 1996. Director, Victor Pappas; scenery, Robert A. Dahlstrom; costumes, David Zinn; lighting, Mary Louise Geiger; sound, Steven M. Klein.

Sir Charles Brandon .... Mark Anders
Mr. Jansenius .... Wayne Ballantyne
Henrietta Jansenius .... Suzanne Bouchard
Miss Wilson .... Susan Browning
Lumpkin .... William Denis
Agatha Wylie .... Megan Dodds

Jane Carpenter .... Anne McAdams
Gertrude Lindsay .... Kari McGee
Sidney Trefusis .... John Leonard Thompson
Photographer .... Todd Tressler
Chichester Erskine .... R. Hamilton Wright
New Voices Playreading Series
HALF LIVES. By Chay Yew. August 19, 1996. Director, Victor Pappas.
TONGUE OF A BIRD. By Ellen McLaughlin. October 28, 1996.

ASOLO THEATER COMPANY, SARASOTA—Jim Iorio and Douglas Jones in *Over My Dead Body* by Michael Sutton and Anthony Fingleton

Seattle: Seattle Repertory Theater

(Daniel Sullivan artistic director)

THE CIDER HOUSE RULES, PART II. By Peter Parnell; adapted from the novel by John Irving. January 15, 1997. Production on the same program with *The Cider House Rules, Part I*; conceived and directed by Tom Hulce and Jane Jones; scenery, Christine Jones; costumes David Zinn; lighting, Greg Sullivan; sound and musical direction, Jim Ragland; original music, Dan Wheetman.

Melony	Jillian Armenante
Fuzzy Stone; Mary Agnes	Tom Beyer
Nurse Edna; Squeeze Louise	Sarah Brooke
Rose Rose; Peaches	Brienin Bryant
Debra; Nurse Caroline	Rebecca Chace
Herb Fowler; Stationmaster	James Chesnutt
Wally; Young Larch	Christopher Collet
Homer Wells	Neal Huff
Dr. Gingrich; Walter	A. Bryan Humphrey
Jack	Reginald A. Jackson
Mr. Rose	Anthony Lee
Nurse Angela; Muddy	Novella Nelson
Ray; Bob	Dougald Park
Candy	Myra Platt
Musician	Jim Ragland
Grace; Lorna	Stephanie Shine
Angel	Todd Sibble
Wednesday; David Copperfield	Ron Simons
Mrs. Grogan; Big Dot	Jayne Taini
Olive; Mrs. Goodall	Lauren Tewes
Curly Day; Hero	David-Paul Wichert
Dr. Wilbur Larch	Michael Winters

Place: St Cloud's, Maine, and other parts of the world. One intermission.

NEAT. Solo performance by Charlayne Woodard; written by Charlayne Woodard. March 19, 1997; a two-coast world premiere. Director, Tazewell Thompson; scenery, Donald Eastman; costumes, Jane Greenwood; lighting, Brian Nason; original music and sound, Fabian Obispo; produced in association with Manhattan Theater Club, Lynne Meadow artistic director.
One intermission.

AN AMERICAN DAUGHTER. By Wendy Wasserstein. April 30, 1997; a two-coast world premiere. Director, David Saint; scenery, John Lee Beatty; costumes, David Murin; lighting, Pat Collins; sound, Steven M. Klein; also produced in New York under the direction of Daniel Sullivan by Lincoln Center Theater, Andre Bishop and Bernard Gersten directors.

Lyssa Dent Hughes	Barbara Dirickson
Quincy Quince	Mari Nelson
Judith B. Kaufman	Shona Tucker

Walter Abrahmson	John Procaccino
Morrow McCarthy	Henri Lubatti
Timber Tucker	Mark Chamberlin
Sen. Alan Hughes	Rex Robbins
Charlotte "Chubby" Hughes	Luce Ennis
Jimmy	James Garver
Billy Robbins	James Chesnutt

Television Crew: Peggy Gannon, Demene E. Hall, Peter Lohnes, Ryland Merkey.

Time: Act I, the present; Act II, one week later. Place: A Georgetown living room, Washington, D.C.

New Play Workshop Series

HOMECOMING. Solo performance by Lauren Weedman; written by Lauren Weedman. May 9, 1997. Director, Ted Sod; choreography, Amii LeGendre.

A LONG, DEAD SORROW; A DEATH PENALTY IN AMERICA PROJECT. Solo performance by Todd Jefferson Moore; written by Todd Jefferson Moore. May 30, 1997. Director, John Kazanjian.

Sharon, Conn.: Sharon Stage

(Michael Gill managing director; David Colfer general manager)

DREAMLAND. Musical with conception and story by Leonard Foglia; music by Harold Arlen; lyrics by Truman Capote, Ira Gershwin, E.Y. Harburg, Ted Koehler, Johnny Mercer, Leo Robin and Jack Yellen. August 20, 1996. Director, Leonard Foglia; choreography, David Marques; musical direction, vocal arrangements and orchestrations, Peter Matz; scenery, Michael McGarty;

costumes, David Woolard; lighting, Russell H. Champa; sound, David Gotwald.

With Colette Hawley, Thos Shipley, Jason Opsahl, Natalie Venetia Belcon, Deborah Leamy, Jim Osorno, Kele Baker, Harry L. Colley II.

Conductor, Bruce W. Coyle.
One intermission.

Skokie, Ill.: Northlight Theater

(Russell Vandenbrouke artistic director; Richard Friedman managing director)

ATOMIC BOMBERS. By Russell Vandenbrouke. March 19, 1997. Director, Alan MacVey; scenery and lighting, John Culbert; costumes, Nan Zabriskie.

Enrico Fermi	David Alan Novak
Laura Fermi	Lusia Strus
Richard Feynman	Jeffrey Hutchinson
Leo Szilard	William J. Norris
Arline Greenbaum Feynman	Debbie Bisno
Robert Wilson	John Guzzardo
Arthur Compton	Glen Allen Pruett
J. Robert Oppenheimer	Karm Kerwell
Gen. Leslie Groves	Matt Penn
Hans Bethe	Aaron H. Alpern

Leona Woods; Railroad Clerk;

W.A.C. Secretary	Maryke Huyding

Student Helpers, Members of Special Engineering Detachment: Kevin Kalinsky, Joe Gold, Bru Miller, Jason G. Wilson.

Other Voices, Officials, Scientists, Townspeople: Company.

Time: December 1938-September 1945, but encompassed by Feynman's hindsight of the 1960s. Place: A stage, Stockholm concert hall; the campuses of Columbia University, Princeton and the University of Chicago; a secret laboratory in New Mexico and the surrounding desert; a sanitarium in Albuquerque. One intermission.

Stockbridge, Mass.: Berkshire Theater Festival

(Arthur Storch artistic director; Kate Maguire managing director)

VISITING MR. GREEN. By Jeff Baron. June 20, 1996. Director, John Rando; scenery, Patrick Fahey; costumes, Murell Horton; lighting, Phil Monat; sound, James Wildman.

Ross Gardiner .... Neal Huff
Mr. Green .... Eli Wallach
    Time: The present. Place: The Upper West Side of Manhattan, Mr. Green's apartment. One intermission.

JITTA'S ATONEMENT. By Siegfried Trebitsch; translated and adapted by George Bernard Shaw. July 30, 1996 (second American production; first was in 1923). Director, Harris Yulin; scenery, Miguel Romero; costumes, Pamela Scofield; lighting, Dan Kotlowitz; sound, James Wildman.

Jitta Lenkheim .... Dianne Wiest
Alfred Lenkheim .... Jon DeVries
Agnes Haldenstedt .... Elizabeth Franz
Edith Haldenstedt .... Calista Flockhart
Bruno Haldenstedt .... Harris Yulin
Dr. Fessler .... Scott Cohen
Mrs. Billiter .... Avril Gentles
    Others: Jennifer Hammontree, Dafna Kapshud.
    One intermission.

FREE FALL. By Sandy Duncan and Marc Alan Zagoren. August 13, 1996. Director, Guy Stroman; choreography, Thommie Walsh; musical concept and direction, Jack Lee; scenery, Edward Gianfrancesco; costumes, Jef Billings; lighting, Phil Monat; sound, James Wildman.
    With Sandy Duncan, Don Correia, Diana Rice. No intermission.

L-PLAY. By Beth Henley. August 21, 1996 (opening of New Unicorn Theater). Director, Eric Hill; scenery, Gary M. English; costumes, Pamela Scofield; lighting, Phil Monat; sound, James Wildman.

Cast: Actress A (Monica, Lunatic)—Allyn Rose; Actress B (Joan, Granddaughter, Small One, Lucheca)—Jennifer Thomas; Actress C (Gertrude, Grandmother, Shelly, Middle One)—Nicole Bradin; Actor A (Price, Malcolm, Ben, Big One)—John Lenartz; Actor B (Jay, Wes, Shoe)—Duane Noch; Actor C (Learner, Narrator, Others)—Jonathan Uffelman.
    Scene 1: Loneliness. Scene 2: Linked. Scene 3: Loser. Scene 4: Lunatic, Part 1. Scene 5: Learner, Part 1. Scene 6: Leaving. Scene 7: Lunatic, Part 2. Scene 8: Lost. Scene 9: Learner, Part 2. Scene 10: Life. Scene 11: Lunatic, Part 3. Scene 12: Learner, Part 3. No intermission.

Reading:

THE HOUSEWIVES OF MANNHEIM. By Alan Brody. July 19, 1996. Director, Jolyn Unruh. With Lillo Way, Gretchen Egolf, Kate Maguire, Miriam Varon, Tanny Jones.

Tucson and Phoenix: Arizona Theater Company

(David Ira Goldstein artistic director; Jessica L. Andrews managing director)

LA MALINCHE. By Carlos Morton. January 17, 1997 (Tucson), February 8, 1997 (Phoenix). Director, Abel Lopez; scenery, Monica Raya; costumes, Rose Pederson; lighting, Tracy Odishaw; composer and sound design, David Maddox.

La Llorona .... Yolande Bavan
Ciuacoatl .... Dawnnie Mercado
La Malinche .... Karmin Murcelo
Sanchez .... Steve Ramshur
Bishop Lizarraga .... Richard Russell Ramos
Hernan Cortez ..... Christopher Michael Bauer
Dona Catalina .... Annabelle Nunez
Martin .... Joseph P. Concannon
                              Patrick B. Concannon
    Time: The 16th century, seven years after the Spanish conquest. Place: Mexico City.

Waterbury, Conn.: Seven Angels Theater

(Semina De Laurentis artistic director)

TEDDY AND ALICE. Musical with book by Jerome Alden; music by John Philip Sousa; lyrics by Hal Hackady; adaptations and original music by Richard Knapp. October 19, 1996 (revised version). Director, Richard Sabellico; choreography, Richard Sabellico, Don Johanson; musical direction, Richard DeRosa; scenery, Robert John Andrusko; costumes, Theoni V. Aldredge; lighting, Peter Petrino; sound, Eric Talorico.

Teddy Roosevelt .... John Davidson
Alice Roosevelt .... Jennifer Lee Andrews
Edith Roosevelt .... Roxann Parker
Nick Longworth .... Dan Sharkey
Henry Cabot Lodge .... Richard Bell
William Howard Taft .... Stephen Carter-Hicks
Elihu Root .... Bob Freschi
Wheeler .... Tom Cochrane
Rose Schneiderman .... Andrea Drobish
Eleanor Roosevelt .... Stephanie Fredricks
Admiral Murphy; Reporter .... Scott Kealey
Tarbell .... Robin Manning
Mame .... Pamela Peach
Franklin Roosevelt; Reporter .. Shannon Stoeke
The Children:
Ethel Roosevelt .... Ashleigh Davidson
Archie Roosevelt .... Regan Flynn
Agnes O'Davis .... Marissa Follo
Quentin Roosevelt .... Richard Guisti Jr.
Ted Roosevelt .... Matthew Johnston
Kermit Roosevelt .... Bryan Rosengrant
    Ensemble: Tom Cochrane, Andrea Drobish, Scott Kealey, Robin Manning, Pamela Peach, Shannon Stoeke.
    Time: Between 1901 and 1905. Place: In and around the White House.
    MUSICAL NUMBERS, ACT I: "This House," "But Not Right Now," "She's Got to Go," "A Girl Made of Lace," "Battle Lines," "Leg-O-Mutton," "Cronies Conspiracy," "She's Got to Go" (Reprise), "4th of July," "He's Got to Go," "Perfect for Each Other," "Her Father's Daughter," "Can I Let Her Go?"
    ACT II: "4th of July" (two Reprises), "You've Nothing to Lose," "I Told You So," "You Must Let Her Go," "Private Thoughts," "Wave the Flag."

MORE ACHES AND PAINS: A GERIATRIC VAUDEVILLE. Musical revue with book and lyrics by Dan Calabrese, music by Richard DeRosa. December 28, 1996. Directors, Kevin Thompson, Barry Finkel; choreography, Barry Finkel; musical direction, Richard DeRosa; scenery, Peter Petrino; costumes, Judith E. Davis; lighting, Kirk Matson; sound, Eric Talorico.

Emyline Lacey .... Andrea Drobish
Josie Gaudiosi .... Joyce Follo
Mavis Marchand .... Julie Kiley
Ziggy Weinbaum .... Michael Greenwood
"Phil" Gaudiosi .... Donald Leona
Elmo Cahill .... Gabor Morea
Angela Delvecchio .... Jan Neuberger

Bruno .... Jon Vandertholen
Zeena .... Linda Thompson Williams
    Place: The Geri-Care Health Pavilion
    MUSICAL NUMBERS, ACT I: "Sign of the Times," "Depend on Me," "Home Away From Home," "You Shoulda Seen Me," "Bubbles and Bingo," "I Forget," "Youth Is Wasted on the Young," "The Gaudiosi Girls," "Happy Endings," "That's Just the Way I Am," "Things Were Better Back Then."
    ACT II: "Over the Hill," "Home Away From Home" (Reprise), "Middleclass Blues," "Where Are You Tonight?", "You Shoulda Seen Me" (Reprise), "Momma," "Smell the Roses," "Amanda's Lullaby," Finale.

THE SINGING WEATHERMAN. Musical with book by Jim McGinn; music by Keith Herrmann; lyrics by Jim McGinn and Larry Goodsight. March 8, 1997. Director, Bill Castellino; choreography, Bill Castellino; scenery, Robert John Andrusko; costumes, Judith E. Davis; lighting, Peter Petrino; sound, Amy Lester.

Charlie Gibbs .... Ron Holgate
Stanley Crane .... Tom Chute
Larry; Juan .... O.V. Daniels
Mary; Gina; Rose .... Andrea Drobish
May Tam .... Fay Ann Lee
Kathleen Calder .... Robin Skye
Herb Taylor .... Vince Trani
Lurice Powell .... Gayle Turner
    One intermission.
    MUSICAL NUMBERS: "Sunshine! Sunshine!", "Charlie!", "His Ratings Are Down," "Springtime Blues," "Amazing Grace," "Chinese Folk Song," "Safe in Here," "All Sorts o' Services," "Early Mornin'," "They See Me on TV," "God's World," "A Long, Long Way," "He Made the Trees," "Have You Ever."

HEART AND SOUL: THE LIFE AND TIMES OF FRANK LOESSER (IN HIS OWN WORDS). Musical revue conceived by Richard Sabellico; book by Susan Loesser; songs by Frank Loesser. April 19, 1997. Director and choreographer, Richard Sabellico; musical direction, Richard DeRosa; scenery, Tom Hooper; costumes, Jonathan Bixby; lighting, Brian Nason; sound, Bernard Fox; presented in association with the Frank Loesser Library and Musical Trust.
    With James Darrah, Laura Kenyon, Laurie Gamache, Rebecca Baxter, Patrick Ryan Sullivan, James Beaman.
    One intermission.

Reading:

THE BACCALA CODICIL. By Lou Cutell. December 11, 1996. With John LaMotta, Mary Tahmin, Angelo Vacco.

SEVEN ANGELS THEATER, WATERBURY, CONN.—*Center,* John David-son as Teddy Roosevelt and Jennifer Lee Andrews as Alice Roosevelt, with members of the press (Robin Manning, Tom Cochrane and Shannon Stoeke) in a scene from the Jerome Alden-Hal Hackady-Richard Knapp musical *Teddy and Alice,* set to the music of John Philip Sousa

Waterford, Conn.: Eugene O'Neill Theater Center

(George C. White president; Lloyd Richards artistic director, National Playwrights Conference; Paulette Haupt artistic director, National Music Theater Conference)

National Playwrights Conference
June 30–July 27, 1996
Staged Readings
UNDEAD. By Mary Lathrop.
SWIMMING ON THE MOON. By John Richards Soster.
GHOSTS IN THE COTTONWOODS. By Adam Rapp.
MOTHERS by I.E. Issak and THE MISSIONARY OF LOVE by Lennart Lidstrom.
WE MISS YOU, STINK. By Karen L.B. Evans.
THE ADVENTURES OF HERCULINA. By Kira Obolensky.
BLACK RUSSIAN. By Thomas Gibbons.

HOTEL DESPERADO. By Will Dunne.
THE YOUNG GIRL AND THE MONSOON. By James Ryan.
MOST WANTED. By Peter Sagal.
BANISHMENT FROM HELL. By Anton Markov.
GOING TO ST. IVES. By Lee Blessing.
    Directors: Casey Childs, Walter Dallas, William Partlan, Amy Saltz.

National Music Theater Conference
July 29–August 10, 1996
Staged Concert Readings
HURRICANE! Musical with book, lyrics and co-music by Cheryl Hawkins; music and co-lyrics by

Jay Gaither. Director, Kent Gash; musical direction, James Laev.

PARAMOUR. Musical with book and lyrics by Joe Masteroff; music by Howard Marren. Director, Robert Kalfin; musical direction, Rob Bowman.

THE CAPTAIN'S DAUGHTER. Musical based on the novella by Pushkin; book and lyrics by Adele Ahronheim; some songs based on original Russian lyrics by Albina Shulgina and Vitaly Gordienko; music by Andrei Petrov. Director, Elise Thoron; musical direction, Thomas Maurice.

THE BOSWELL SISTERS. Musical by Stuart Ross and Mark Hampton. Director, Stuart Ross; musical direction, Joseph Baker.

Westport, Conn.: Westport Country Playhouse

(James B. McKenzie executive producer; Eric Friedheim associate producer)

MEN IN SUITS. By Jason Milligan. August 5, 1996. Director, Joe Cacaci; scenery and projections, Richard Ellis; costumes, Kathryn Morrison; lighting. Susan Roth; sound, Charles Dayton.

Max .... James Handy
Bobby .... Dan Lauria
The Boss .... Charles Durning
    Time: The present. Place: Various locations in New York, on Long Island and on the road to Vermont. One intermission.

SNAPSHOTS. Musical conceived by Michael Scheman and David Stern; book by David Stern; music and lyrics by Stephen Schwartz; additional music and lyrics by David Crane, Seth Friedman, Marta Kauffman, Alan Menken and Charles Strouse. September 3, 1996. Director, Michael Scheman; musical direction and vocal arrangements, Andrew Lippa; associate director, Kathryn Kendall; scenery, Richard Ellis; costumes, David Murin; lighting, Susan Roth.

Sue .... Cass Morgan
Dan .... William Parry
Susie; Others .... Erin Leigh Peck
Danny; Others .... Ric Ryder
Susan; Others .... Julia K. Murney
Daniel; Others .... Don Goodspeed
    Time: Autumn of this year. Place: The attic of a suburban home. One intermission.
    MUSICAL NUMBERS, ACT I: "Snapshots," "New Kid in the Neighborhood," "Neat To Be a Newsboy," "Lion Tamer," "Extraordinary/Corner of the Sky," "With You," "Proud Lady," "Cold Enough to Snow/Where Did the Magic Go?", "Morning Glow," "If We Never Meet Again/Nothing to Do With Love/West End Avenue," "Endless Delights," "Meadowlark."
    ACT II: "Moving In With Susan," "Chanson," "A World Without You/With You," "Beside You," "Spark of Creation," "All Good Gifts," "Parents' Day/I Remember," "The Hardest Part of Love/Father and Sons," "Code of Silence," "If We Never Meet Again" (Reprise), Finale.

Williamstown, Mass.: Williamstown Theater Festival

(Michael Ritchie producer; Deborah Fehr general manager; Jenny C. Gersten associate producer)

MACS (A MACARONI REQUIEM). By David Simpatico. June 26, 1996. Director, Jenny Sullivan; scenery, Stephen G. Judd; costumes, Mattie Ullrich; lighting, Jeff Nellis; sound, Kurt B. Kellenberger; fight director, Rick Sordelet.

Tony Madrifina .... Tony Amendola
Rosie Madrifina .... Randy Danson
Tonse Madrifina .... Scott Sowers
Bernie Madrifina .... Keira Naughton
Dominic Madrifina .... Adam Stein
Tillie Campanella .... Mary Fogarty
Nornie Campanella .... Dominic Chianese
Mikey Rourke .... Stephen Harrison
    Time: Sunday afternoon. Place: The Madrifina household, Palisades Park, N.J. One intermission.

THE RIDE DOWN MOUNT MORGAN. By Arthur Miller. July 17, 1996 (American premiere of revised version). Director, Scott Elliott; scenery, Derek McLane; costumes, Eric Becker; lighting, Brian MacDevitt; sound, Eileen Tague; composer, Tom Kochan.

Lyman .... F. Murray Abraham
Nurse .... Adina Porter
Father .... Ben Hammer
Theodora .... Michael Learned
Bessie .... Amy Ryan
Leah .... Patricia Clarkson
Tom .... Larry Bryggman
    Time: The 1980s. One intermission.
    An ATCA citation; see introduction to this section.

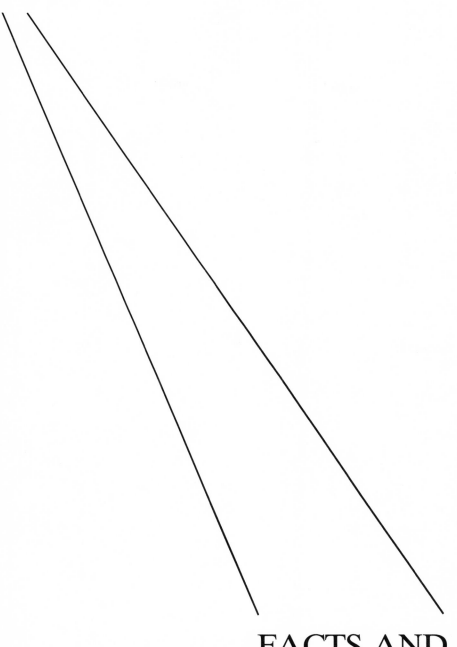

FACTS AND
FIGURES

LONG RUNS ON BROADWAY

The following shows have run 500 or more continuous performances in a single production, usually the first, not including previews or extra non-profit performances, allowing for vacation layoffs and special one-booking engagements, but not including return engagements after a show has gone on tour. In all cases, the numbers were obtained directly from the show's production offices. Where there are title similarities, the production is identified as follows: (p) straight play version, (m) musical version, (r) revival, (tr) transfer.

THROUGH MAY 31, 1997

(PLAYS MARKED WITH ASTERISK WERE STILL PLAYING JUNE 1, 1997)

Plays	Number Performances	Plays	Number Performances
A Chorus Line	6,137	Ain't Misbehavin'	1,604
†*Cats	6,116	Mary, Mary	1,572
Oh! Calcutta! (r)	5,959	Evita	1,567
*Les Misérables	4,195	The Voice of the Turtle	1,557
*The Phantom of the Opera	3,902	Barefoot in the Park	1,530
42nd Street	3,486	Brighton Beach Memoirs	1,530
Grease	3,388	Dreamgirls	1,522
Fiddler on the Roof	3,242	Mame (m)	1,508
Life With Father	3,224	Same Time, Next Year	1,453
Tobacco Road	3,182	Arsenic and Old Lace	1,444
Hello, Dolly!	2,844	The Sound of Music	1,443
My Fair Lady	2,717	Me and My Girl	1,420
*Miss Saigon	2,556	How to Succeed in Business Without	
Annie	2,377	Really Trying	1,417
Man of La Mancha	2,328	Hellzapoppin	1,404
Abie's Irish Rose	2,327	The Music Man	1,375
Oklahoma!	2,212	Funny Girl	1,348
Pippin	1,944	Mummenschanz	1,326
South Pacific	1,925	*Beauty and the Beast	1,312
The Magic Show	1,920	Angel Street	1,295
Deathtrap	1,793	Lightnin'	1,291
Gemini	1,788	Promises, Promises	1,281
Harvey	1,775	The King and I	1,246
Dancin'	1,774	Cactus Flower	1,234
La Cage aux Folles	1,761	Sleuth	1,222
Hair	1,750	Torch Song Trilogy	1,222
The Wiz	1,672	1776	1,217
Born Yesterday	1,642	*Grease (r)	1,213
The Best Little Whorehouse in		Equus	1,209
Texas	1,639	Sugar Babies	1,208
Crazy for You	1,622	Guys and Dolls	1,200
		Amadeus	1,181
		Cabaret	1,165
		Mister Roberts	1,157
		Annie Get Your Gun	1,147

† On 6/19/97 *Cats* is to become the longest running show in Broadway history with 6,138 performances

417

Plays	Number Performances	Plays	Number Performances
Guys and Dolls (r)	1,144	Chapter Two	857
The Seven Year Itch	1,141	A Streetcar Named Desire	855
Butterflies Are Free	1,128	Barnum	854
Pins and Needles	1,108	Comedy in Music	849
Plaza Suite	1,097	Raisin	847
They're Playing Our Song	1,082	Blood Brothers	839
Grand Hotel (m)	1,077	You Can't Take It With You	837
Kiss Me, Kate	1,070	La Plume de Ma Tante	835
Don't Bother Me, I Can't Cope	1,065	Three Men on a Horse	835
The Pajama Game	1,063	The Subject Was Roses	832
Shenandoah	1,050	Black and Blue	824
The Teahouse of the August Moon	1,027	Inherit the Wind	806
Damn Yankees	1,019	Anything Goes (r)	804
Never Too Late	1,007	No Time for Sergeants	796
Big River	1,005	Fiorello!	795
The Will Rogers Follies	983	Where's Charley?	792
Any Wednesday	982	The Ladder	789
Sunset Boulevard	977	Forty Carats	780
A Funny Thing Happened on the Way to the Forum	964	Lost in Yonkers	780
The Odd Couple	964	The Prisoner of Second Avenue	780
Anna Lucasta	957	M. Butterfly	777
Kiss and Tell	956	Oliver!	774
Show Boat (r)	949	The Pirates of Penzance (1980 r)	772
*Smokey Joe's Cafe	932	Woman of the Year	770
Dracula (r)	925	My One and Only	767
Bells Are Ringing	924	Sophisticated Ladies	767
The Moon Is Blue	924	Bubbling Brown Sugar	766
Beatlemania	920	Into the Woods	765
The Elephant Man	916	State of the Union	765
Kiss of the Spider Woman	906	Starlight Express	761
Luv	901	The First Year	760
The Who's Tommy	900	Broadway Bound	756
Chicago (m)	898	You Know I Can't Hear You When the Water's Running	755
Applause	896	Two for the Seesaw	750
Can-Can	892	Joseph and the Amazing Technicolor Dreamcoat (r)	747
Carousel	890	Death of a Salesman	742
I'm Not Rappaport	890	For Colored Girls, etc.	742
Hats Off to Ice	889	Sons o' Fun	742
Fanny	888	Candide (m, r)	740
Children of a Lesser God	887	Gentlemen Prefer Blondes	740
Follow the Girls	882	The Man Who Came to Dinner	739
City of Angels	878	Nine	739
Camelot	873	Call Me Mister	734
I Love My Wife	872	West Side Story	732
The Bat	867	High Button Shoes	727
My Sister Eileen	864	Finian's Rainbow	725
No, No, Nanette (r)	861	Claudia	722
Song of Norway	860	The Gold Diggers	720

Plays	*Number Performances*	*Plays*	*Number Performances*
Jesus Christ Superstar	720	Two Gentlemen of Verona (m)	627
Carnival	719	The Tenth Man	623
The Diary of Anne Frank	717	The Heidi Chronicles	621
I Remember Mama	714	Is Zat So?	618
Tea and Sympathy	712	Anniversary Waltz	615
Junior Miss	710	The Happy Time (p)	614
Last of the Red Hot Lovers	706	Separate Rooms	613
The Secret Garden	706	Affairs of State	610
Company	705	Oh! Calcutta! (tr)	610
Seventh Heaven	704	Star and Garter	609
Gypsy (m)	702	The Mystery of Edwin Drood	608
The Miracle Worker	700	The Student Prince	608
That Championship Season	700	Sweet Charity	608
Da	697	Bye Bye Birdie	607
The King and I (r)	696	Irene (r)	604
Cat on a Hot Tin Roof	694	Sunday in the Park With George	604
Li'l Abner	693	Adonis	603
The Children's Hour	691	Broadway	603
Purlie	688	Peg o' My Heart	603
Dead End	687	Street Scene (p)	601
The Lion and the Mouse	686	Flower Drum Song	600
White Cargo	686	Kiki	600
Dear Ruth	683	A Little Night Music	600
East Is West	680	Agnes of God	599
Come Blow Your Horn	677	Don't Drink the Water	598
The Most Happy Fella	676	Wish You Were Here	598
The Doughgirls	671	Sarafina!	597
The Impossible Years	670	A Society Circus	596
Irene	670	Absurd Person Singular	592
Boy Meets Girl	669	A Day in Hollywood/A Night in the	
The Tap Dance Kid	669	Ukraine	588
*Victor/Victoria	669	The Me Nobody Knows	586
Beyond the Fringe	667	The Two Mrs. Carrolls	585
Who's Afraid of Virginia Woolf?	664	Kismet (m)	583
Blithe Spirit	657	Gypsy (m, r)	582
A Trip to Chinatown	657	Brigadoon	581
The Women	657	Detective Story	581
Bloomer Girl	654	No Strings	580
The Fifth Season	654	Brother Rat	577
*Defending the Caveman	653	Blossom Time	576
Rain	648	*Master Class	573
Witness for the Prosecution	645	Pump Boys and Dinettes	573
Call Me Madam	644	Show Boat	572
Janie	642	The Show-Off	571
The Green Pastures	640	Sally	570
Auntie Mame (p)	639	Jelly's Last Jam	569
A Man for All Seasons	637	.Golden Boy (m)	568
Jerome Robbins' Broadway	634	One Touch of Venus	567
The Fourposter	632	The Real Thing	566
The Music Master	627	Happy Birthday	564

Plays	Number Performances	Plays	Number Performances
Look Homeward, Angel	564	Rumors	531
Morning's at Seven (r)	564	A Raisin in the Sun	530
The Glass Menagerie	561	Godspell (tr)	527
I Do! I Do!	560	Fences	526
Wonderful Town	559	The Solid Gold Cadillac	526
Rose Marie	557	Biloxi Blues	524
Strictly Dishonorable	557	Irma La Douce	524
Sweeney Todd, the Demon Barber of		The Boomerang	522
Fleet Street	557	Follies	521
The Great White Hope	556	Rosalinda	521
A Majority of One	556	The Best Man	520
The Sisters Rosensweig	556	Chauve-Souris	520
Sunrise at Campobello	556	Blackbirds of 1928	518
Toys in the Attic	556	The Gin Game	517
Jamaica	555	Sunny	517
Stop the World—I Want to Get Off	555	Victoria Regina	517
Florodora	553	Fifth of July	511
Noises Off	553	Half a Sixpence	511
Ziegfeld Follies (1943)	553	The Vagabond King	511
Dial "M" for Murder	552	The New Moon	509
Good News	551	The World of Suzie Wong	508
Peter Pan (r)	551	The Rothschilds	507
How to Succeed in Business Without		On Your Toes (r)	505
Really Trying (r)	548	Sugar	505
Let's Face It	547	Shuffle Along	504
Milk and Honey	543	Up in Central Park	504
Within the Law	541	Carmen Jones	503
Pal Joey (r)	540	The Member of the Wedding	501
What Makes Sammy Run?	540	Panama Hattie	501
The Sunshine Boys	538	Personal Appearance	501
What a Life	538	Bird in Hand	500
Crimes of the Heart	535	Room Service	500
Damn Yankees (r)	533	Sailor, Beware!	500
The Unsinkable Molly Brown	532	Tomorrow the World	500
The Red Mill (r)	531		

LONG RUNS OFF BROADWAY

Plays	Number Performances	Plays	Number Performances
*The Fantasticks	15,356	Vampire Lesbians of Sodom	2,024
*Perfect Crime	4,169	Jacques Brel	1,847
Nunsense	3,672	Forever Plaid	1,811
*Tony 'n' Tina's Wedding	3,281	Vanities	1,785
The Threepenny Opera	2,611	You're a Good Man Charlie	
*Tubes	2,478	Brown	1,597
Forbidden Broadway 1982–87	2,332	The Blacks	1,408
Little Shop of Horrors	2,209	One Mo' Time	1,372
Godspell	2,124	*Stomp	1,362

Plays	*Number Performances*	*Plays*	*Number Performances*
Let My People Come	1,327	Adaptation & Next	707
Driving Miss Daisy	1,195	Oh! Calcutta!	704
The Hot l Baltimore	1,166	Scuba Duba	692
I'm Getting My Act Together and		The Foreigner	686
Taking It on the Road	1,165	The Knack	685
Little Mary Sunshine	1,143	The Club	674
Steel Magnolias	1,126	The Balcony	672
El Grande de Coca-Cola	1,114	Penn & Teller	666
The Proposition	1,109	America Hurrah	634
Beau Jest	1,069	Oil City Symphony	626
Tamara	1,036	Hogan's Goat	607
One Flew Over the Cuckoo's Nest		Beehive	600
(r)	1,025	The Trojan Women	600
The Boys in the Band	1,000	The Dining Room	583
Fool for Love	1,000	Krapp's Last Tape & The Zoo Story	582
Other People's Money	990	Three Tall Women	582
Cloud 9	971	The Dumbwaiter & The Collection	578
Sister Mary Ignatius Explains It All for		Forbidden Broadway 1990	576
You & The Actor's Nightmare	947	Dames at Sea	575
Your Own Thing	933	The Crucible (r)	571
Curley McDimple	931	The Iceman Cometh (r)	565
Leave It to Jane (r)	928	The Hostage (r)	545
*Grandma Sylvia's Funeral	902	What's a Nice Country Like You	
The Mad Show	871	Doing in a State Like This?	543
Scrambled Feet	831	Forbidden Broadway 1988	534
The Effect of Gamma Rays on Man-in-		Frankie and Johnny in the Clair de	
the-Moon Marigolds	819	Lune	533
A View From the Bridge (r)	780	Six Characters in Search of an Author	
The Boy Friend (r)	763	(r)	529
True West	762	All in the Timing	526
Isn't It Romantic	733	Oleanna	513
Dime a Dozen	728	The Dirtiest Show in Town	509
The Pocket Watch	725	Happy Ending & Day of Absence	504
The Connection	722	Greater Tuna	501
The Passion of Dracula	714	A Shayna Maidel	501
		The Boys From Syracuse (r)	500

NEW YORK DRAMA CRITICS CIRCLE AWARDS, 1935–36 TO 1996–97

Listed below are the New York Drama Critics Circle Awards from 1935–36 through 1996–97 classified as follows: (1) Best American Play, (2) Best Foreign Play, (3) Best Musical, (4) Best, regardless of category (this category was established by new voting rules in 1962–63 and did not exist prior to that year).

1935–36—(1) Winterset

1936–37—(1) High Tor

1937–38—(1) Of Mice and Men, (2) Shadow and Substance

1938–39—(1) No award, (2) The White Steed

1939–40—(1) The Time of Your Life

1940–41—(1) Watch on the Rhine, (2) The Corn Is Green

1941–42—(1) No award, (2) Blithe Spirit

1942–43—(1) The Patriots

1943–44—(2) Jacobowsky and the Colonel

1944–45—(1) The Glass Menagerie

1945–46—(3) Carousel

1946–47—(1) All My Sons, (2) No Exit, (3) Brigadoon

1947–48—(1) A Streetcar Named Desire, (2) The Winslow Boy

1948–49—(1) Death of a Salesman, (2) The Madwoman of Chaillot, (3) South Pacific

1949–50—(1) The Member of the Wedding, (2) The Cocktail Party, (3) The Consul

1950–51—(1) Darkness at Noon, (2) The Lady's Not for Burning, (3) Guys and Dolls

1951–52—(1) I Am a Camera, (2) Venus Observed, (3) Pal Joey (Special citation to Don Juan in Hell)

1952–53—(1) Picnic, (2) The Love of Four Colonels, (3) Wonderful Town

1953–54—(1) The Teahouse of the August Moon, (2) Ondine, (3) The Golden Apple

1954–55—(1) Cat on a Hot Tin Roof, (2) Witness for the Prosecution, (3) The Saint of Bleecker Street

1955–56—(1) The Diary of Anne Frank, (2) Tiger at the Gates, (3) My Fair Lady

1956–57—(1) Long Day's Journey Into Night, (2) The Waltz of the Toreadors, (3) The Most Happy Fella

1957–58—(1) Look Homeward, Angel, (2) Look Back in Anger, (3) The Music Man

1958–59—(1) A Raisin in the Sun, (2) The Visit, (3) La Plume de Ma Tante

1959–60—(1) Toys in the Attic, (2) Five Finger Exercise, (3) Fiorello!

1960–61—(1) All the Way Home, (2) A Taste of Honey, (3) Carnival

1961–62—(1) The Night of the Iguana, (2) A Man for All Seasons, (3) How to Succeed in Business Without Really Trying

1962–63—(4) Who's Afraid of Virginia Woolf? (Special citation to Beyond the Fringe)

1963–64—(4) Luther, (3) Hello, Dolly! (Special citation to The Trojan Women)

1964–65—(4) The Subject Was Roses, (3) Fiddler on the Roof

1965–66—(4) The Persecution and Assassination of Marat as Performed by the Inmates of the Asylum of Charenton Under the Direction of the Marquis de Sade, (3) Man of La Mancha

1966–67—(4) The Homecoming, (3) Cabaret

1967–68—(4) Rosencrantz and Guildenstern Are Dead, (3) Your Own Thing

1968–69—(4) The Great White Hope, (3) 1776

1969–70—(4) Borstal Boy, (1) The Effect of Gamma Rays on Man-in-the-Moon Marigolds, (3) Company

1970–71—(4) Home, (1) The House of Blue Leaves, (3) Follies

1971–72—(4) That Championship Season, (2) The Screens (3) Two Gentlemen of Verona (Special citations to Sticks and Bones and Old Times)

1972–73—(4) The Changing Room, (1) The Hot l Baltimore, (3) A Little Night Music

1973–74—(4) The Contractor, (1) Short Eyes, (3) Candide

1974–75—(4) Equus (1) The Taking of Miss Janie, (3) A Chorus Line

1975–76—(4) Travesties, (1) Streamers, (3) Pacific Overtures

1976–77—(4) Otherwise Engaged, (1) American Buffalo, (3) Annie

1977–78—(4) Da, (3) Ain't Misbehavin'

1978–79—(4) The Elephant Man, (3) Sweeney Todd, the Demon Barber of Fleet Street

1979–80—(4) Talley's Folly, (2) Betrayal, (3) Evita (Special citation to Peter Brook's Le Centre International de Créations Théâtrales for its repertory)

1980–81—(4) A Lesson From Aloes, (1) Crimes of the Heart (Special citations to Lena

Horne: The Lady and Her Music and the New York Shakespeare Festival production of The Pirates of Penzance)

1981–82—(4) The Life & Adventures of Nicholas Nickleby, (1) A Soldier's Play

1982–83—(4) Brighton Beach Memoirs, (2) Plenty, (3) Little Shop of Horrors (Special citation to Young Playwrights Festival)

1983–84—(4) The Real Thing, (1) Glengarry Glen Ross, (3) Sunday in the Park With George (Special citation to Samuel Beckett for the body of his work)

1984–85—(4) Ma Rainey's Black Bottom

1985–86—(4) A Lie of the Mind, (2) Benefactors (Special citation to The Search for Signs of Intelligent Life in the Universe)

1986–87—(4) Fences, (2) Les Liaisons Dangereuses, (3) Les Misérables

1987–88—(4) Joe Turner's Come and Gone, (2) The Road to Mecca, (3) Into the Woods

1988–89—(4) The Heidi Chronicles, (2) Aristocrats (Special citation to Bill Irwin for Largely New York)

1989–90—(4) The Piano Lesson, (2) Privates on Parade, (3) City of Angels

1990–91—(4) Six Degrees of Separation, (2) Our Country's Good, (3) The Will Rogers Follies (Special citation to Eileen Atkins for her portrayal of Virginia Woolf in A Room of One's Own)

1991–92—(4) Dancing at Lughnasa, (1) Two Trains Running

1992–93—(4) Angels in America: Millennium Approaches, (2) Someone Who'll Watch Over Me, (3) Kiss of the Spider Woman

1993–94—(4) Three Tall Women (Special citation to Anna Deavere Smith for her unique contribution to theatrical form)

1994–95—(4) Arcadia, (1) Love! Valour! Compassion! (Special citation to Signature Theater Company for outstanding artistic achievement)

1995–96—(4) Seven Guitars, (2) Molly Sweeney, (3) Rent

1996–97—(4) How I Learned to Drive, (2) Skylight, (3) Violet (Special citation to Chicago)

NEW YORK DRAMA CRITICS CIRCLE VOTING 1996–97

The smaller venue carried the day in this year's New York Drama Critics Circle voting, as the critics named Paula Vogel's off-Broadway play *How I Learned to Drive* the best of the season regardless of category on the second ballot of point-weighted voting and off Broadway's *Violet* by Brian Crawley and Jeanine Tesori the best musical of the season, also on the second ballot.

Having chosen an American play best-of-bests, the critics went on to name David Hare's *Skylight* the year's best foreign play on the first ballot by a large majority of 14 first-choices among the 25 members (including the New York *Times* critics, who resumed voting membership this year) of the Circle voting in person or by proxy, as follows: *Skylight* 14 (Clive Barnes, Ben Brantley, Greg Evans, Robert Feldberg, Jeremy Gerard, John Heilpern, Howard Kissel, Michael Kuchwara, Jacques le Sourd, Peter Marks, Frank Scheck, John Simon, Sydney Weinberg, Linda Winer), *The Skriker* 4 (Alexis Greene, David Sheward, Michael Sommers, David Patrick Stearns), *Stanley* 3 (Mary Campbell, Ken Mandelbaum, Richard Zoglin) and 1 each for *The Lucky Chance* (Michael Feingold), *The Steward of Christendom* (Jack Kroll), *The Waste Land* (Donald Lyons) and *Dealer's Choice* (Jan Stuart).

The Critics also awarded a special citation to the cast and creative team of the revival of the musical *Chicago* for "its distinguished contribution to the Broadway season."

How I Learned to Drive ran a close race with *Skylight* on the critics' first ballot for best-of-bests, ending up with a plurality of the 25 first choices (the Circle's rules require a majority for a first-ballot victory), as follows: *How I Learned to Drive* 9

(Brantley, Feingold, Greene, Kuchwara, Lyons, Mandelbaum, Sheward, Sommers, Stearns), *Skylight* 8 (Barnes, Evans, Feldberg, Gerard, Heilpern, Marks, Scheck, Weinberg), 2 each for *An American Daughter* (Campbell, Winer) and *Stonewall Jackson's House* (le Sourd, Kroll) and 1 each for *This Is Your Youth* (Kissel), *Sympathetic Magic* (Simon), *Gross Indecency: The Three Trials of Oscar Wilde* (Stuart) and *The Last Night of Ballyhoo* (Zoglin).

Violet led narrowly on the first-choice ballot for musicals, recorded as follows: *Violet* 8 (Campbell, Evans, Kissel, Kuchwara, Lyons, Stuart, Weinberg. Winer), *The Life* 7 (Barnes, Brantley, Heilpern, Kroll, Scheck, le Sourd, Zoglin), *When Pigs Fly* 4 (Feingold, Sheward, Simon, Sommers) *Steel Pier* 2 (Feldberg, Stearns), *Titanic* 1 (Mandelbaum) and 3 abstentions (Gerard, Greene, Marks).

After no entry received a majority of votes on the first ballot for best play and best musical, the critics proceeded to a second, point-weighted (first choice 3 points, second 2 points, third 1 point) ballot on which, to win, an entry must collect a number of points equal to or higher than three times the number of Circle members voting (24 in the ballot for best play, 22 for best musical) divided by two, plus one—37 for best play, 34 for best musical this year. In the play category, 19 plays figured in the balloting, but it was again a contest between the two front-runners, *How I Learned to Drive* winning with 38 points to 32 for *Skylight*. In the second ballot for best musical, *Violet* won easily with 45 points. Another off-Broadway musical, *When Pigs Fly,* was the runner-up with 27 points. The leading Broadway musicals were *The Life* with 20 points and *Steel Pier* with 18.

Here is how the critics voted on the second point-weighted ballots for best play regardless of category and best musical.

SECOND BALLOT FOR BEST PLAY REGARDLESS OF CATEGORY

Critic	1st Choice (3 pts.)	2d Choice (2 pts.)	3d Choice (1 pt.)
Clive Barnes *Post*	How I Learned to Drive	Skylight	The Last Night of Ballyhoo
Ben Brantley *Times*	How I Learned to Drive	Gross Indecency: The Three Trials of Oscar Wilde	A Question of Mercy
Mary Campbell AP	How I Learned to Drive	An American Daughter	Neat
Greg Evans *Variety*	Skylight	How I Learned to Drive	The Last Night of Ballyhoo
Michael Feingold *Village Voice*	How I Learned to Drive	Sympathetic Magic	Good As New
Robert Feldberg Bergen *Record*	Skylight	The Last Night of Ballyhoo	Dealer's Choice
Jeremy Gerard *New York*	Skylight	An American Daughter	The Last Night of Ballyhoo
John Heilpern *Observer*	Skylight	Dealer's Choice	The Skriker
Howard Kissel *Daily News*	Skylight	This Is Our Youth	Stonewall Jackson's House

Jack Kroll *Newsweek*	Stonewall Jackson's House	The Steward of Christendom	Stanley
Michael Kuchwara AP	How I Learned to Drive	Gross Indecency	Stanley
Jacques le Sourd Gannett Papers	Stonewall Jackson's House	Skylight	Dealer's Choice
Donald Lyons *Wall St. Journal*	· How I Learned to Drive	Cloud Tectonics	The Red Address
Ken Mandelbaum *Playbill*-on-Line	How I Learned to Drive	The Last Night of Ballyhoo	Stanley
Peter Marks *Times*	Skylight	This Is Our Youth	The Seven Streams of the River Ota
Frank Scheck *Christian Science Monitor*	Skylight	This Is Our Youth	The Last Night of Ballyhoo
David Sheward *Back Stage*	How I Learned to Drive	The Skriker	This Is Our Youth
John Simon *New York*	Skylight	Sympathetic Magic	Psychopathia Sexualis
Michael Sommers Newhouse Papers	How I Learned to Drive	The Skriker	This Is Our Youth
David Patrick Stearns *USA Today*	How I Learned to Drive	An American Daughter	Gross Indecency
Jan Stuart *Newsday*	Gross Indecency	How I Learned to Drive	Dealer's Choice
Sydney Weinberg *Time Out New York*	Skylight	This Is Our Youth	Dealer's Choice
Linda Winer *Newsday*	An American Daughter	How I Learned to Drive	Skylight
Richard Zoglin *Time*	The Last Night of Ballyhoo	How I Learned to Drive	A Question of Mercy

SECOND BALLOT FOR BEST MUSICAL

Critic	1st Choice (3 pts)	2d Choice (2 pts)	3d Choice (1 pt)
Clive Barnes	The Life	Violet	Play On
Mary Campbell	Violet	Titanic	Play On
Greg Evans	Violet	Steel Pier	When Pigs Fly
Michael Feingold	When Pigs Fly	Violet	The Life
Robert Feldberg	Violet	When Pigs Fly	Steel Pier
John Heilpern	The Life	When Pigs Fly	Violet
Howard Kissel	Violet	Titanic	Steel Pier
Jack Kroll	The Life	Violet	Steel Pier
Michael Kuchwara	Violet	Titanic	When Pigs Fly
Jacques le Sourd	The Life	Violet	The Green Heart
Donald Lyons	Violet	Steel Pier	Dream
Ken Mandelbaum	Titanic	Steel Pier	When Pigs Fly
Peter Marks	When Pigs Fly	Peter and Wendy	Hedwig and the Angry Inch

Frank Scheck	The Life	Steel Pier	Violet
David Sheward	When Pigs Fly	The Life	The Green Heart
John Simon	When Pigs Fly	Violet	Steel Pier
Michael Sommers	When Pigs Fly	Violet	Steel Pier
David Patrick Stearns	Steel Pier	Violet	When Pigs Fly
Jan Stuart	Violet	Violet	Titanic
Sydney Weinberg	Violet	When Pigs Fly	The Life
Linda Winer	Violet	When Pigs Fly	The Green Heart
Richard Zoglin	The Life	Steel Pier	Play On
		Violet	

CHOICES OF SOME OTHER CRITICS

Critic	Best Play	Best Musical
Joy Browne WOR	Barrymore	I Love You, You're Perfect, Now Change
Casper Citron Casper Citron Program	Barrymore	Chicago
Sherry Eaker *Backstage*	How I Learned to Drive	Titanic
Martin Gottfried *N.Y. Law Journal*	Collected Stories	Violet
Ralph Howard WINS Radio	How I Learned to Drive	Violet
Alvin Klein *Times* Suburban	How I Learned to Drive	Abstain
Joel Siegel WABC-TV	Gross Indecency: The Three Trials of Oscar Wilde	Abstain
Liz Smith *Tribune-News* Syndicate	How I Learned to Drive	The Life
Roma Torre NY 1 News	Stanley	The Life
Ross Wetzsteon *Village Voice*	One Flea Spare	Peter and Wendy
John Willis *Theater World*	The Last Night of Ballyhoo	I Love You, You're Perfect, Now Change

PULITZER PRIZE WINNERS 1916–17 TO 1996–97

1916–17—No award
1917–18—Why Marry?, by Jesse Lynch Williams
1918–19—No award
1919–20—Beyond the Horizon, by Eugene O'Neill
1920–21—Miss Lulu Bett, by Zona Gale
1921–22—Anna Christie, by Eugene O'Neill
1922–23—Icebound, by Owen Davis
1923–24—Hell-Bent fer Heaven, by Hatcher Hughes
1924–25—They Knew What They Wanted, by Sidney Howard

1925–26—Craig's Wife, by George Kelly
1926–27—In Abraham's Bosom, by Paul Green
1927–28—Strange Interlude, by Eugene O'Neill
1928–29—Street Scene, by Elmer Rice
1929–30—The Green Pastures, by Marc Connelly
1930–31—Alison's House, by Susan Glaspell
1931–32—Of Thee I Sing, by George S. Kaufman, Morrie Ryskind, Ira and George Gershwin
1932–33—Both Your Houses, by Maxwell Anderson
1933–34—Men in White, by Sidney Kingsley

1934–35—The Old Maid, by Zoe Akins
1935–36—Idiot's Delight, by Robert E. Sherwood
1936–37—You Can't Take It With You, by Moss Hart and George S. Kaufman
1937–38—Our Town, by Thornton Wilder
1938–39—Abe Lincoln in Illinois, by Robert E. Sherwood
1939–40—The Time of Your Life, by William Saroyan
1940–41—There Shall Be No Night, by Robert E. Sherwood
1941–42—No award
1942–43—The Skin of Our Teeth, by Thornton Wilder
1943–44—No award
1944–45—Harvey, by Mary Chase
1945–46—State of the Union, by Howard Lindsay and Russel Crouse
1946–47—No award
1947–48—A Streetcar Named Desire, by Tennessee Williams
1948–49—Death of a Salesman, by Arthur Miller
1949–50—South Pacific, by Richard Rodgers, Oscar Hammerstein II and Joshua Logan
1950–51—No award
1951–52—The Shrike, by Joseph Kramm
1952–53—Picnic, by William Inge
1953–54—The Teahouse of the August Moon, by John Patrick
1954–55—Cat on a Hot Tin Roof, by Tennessee Williams
1955–56—The Diary of Anne Frank, by Frances Goodrich and Albert Hackett
1956–57—Long Day's Journey Into Night, by Eugene O'Neill
1957–58—Look Homeward, Angel, by Ketti Frings
1958–59—J.B., by Archibald MacLeish
1959–60—Fiorello!, by Jerome Weidman, George Abbott, Sheldon Harnick and Jerry Bock
1960–61—All the Way Home, by Tad Mosel
1961–62—How to Succeed in Business Without Really Trying, by Abe Burrows, Willie Gilbert, Jack Weinstock and Frank Loesser

1962–63—No award
1963–64—No award
1964–65—The Subject Was Roses, by Frank D. Gilroy
1965–66—No award
1966–67—A Delicate Balance, by Edward Albee
1967–68—No award
1968–69—The Great White Hope, by Howard Sackler
1969–70—No Place To Be Somebody, by Charles Gordone
1970–71—The Effect of Gamma Rays on Man-in-the-Moon Marigolds, by Paul Zindel
1971–72—No award
1972–73—That Championship Season, by Jason Miller
1973–74—No award
1974–75—Seascape, by Edward Albee
1975–76—A Chorus Line, by Michael Bennett, James Kirkwood, Nicholas Dante, Marvin Hamlisch and Edward Kleban
1976–77—The Shadow Box, by Michael Cristofer
1977–78—The Gin Game, by D.L. Coburn
1978–79—Buried Child, by Sam Shepard
1979–80—Talley's Folly, by Lanford Wilson
1980–81—Crimes of the Heart, by Beth Henley
1981–82—A Soldier's Play, by Charles Fuller
1982–83—'night, Mother, by Marsha Norman
1983–84—Glengarry Glen Ross, by David Mamet
1984–85—Sunday in the Park With George, by James Lapine and Stephen Sondheim
1985–86—No award
1986–87—Fences, by August Wilson
1987–88—Driving Miss Daisy, by Alfred Uhry
1988–89—The Heidi Chronicles, by Wendy Wasserstein
1989–90—The Piano Lesson, by August Wilson
1990–91—Lost in Yonkers, by Neil Simon
1991–92—The Kentucky Cycle, by Robert Schenkkan
1992–93—Angels in America: Millennium Approaches, by Tony Kushner
1993–94—Three Tall Women, by Edward Albee
1994–95—The Young Man From Atlanta, by Horton Foote
1995–96—Rent, by Jonathan Larson
1996–97—No award

TONY AWARDS 1996–1997

The American Theater Wing's Antoinette Perry (Tony) Awards are presented annually in recognition of distingushed artistic achievement in the Broadway theater. The League of American Theaters and Producers and the American Theater Wing present the Tony Awards, founded by the Wing in 1947. Legitimate theater productions opening in the 36 eligible Broadway theaters during the eligibility season of the year—May 2, 1996 to April 30, 1997—were considered for Tony nominations.

The Tony Awards Administration Committee appoints the Tony Awards Nominating Committee which makes the actual nominations. The 1996–97 Nominating Committee consisted of Jon Robin Baitz, playwright; Price Berkley, publisher; Donald Brooks, costume designer; Mary Schmidt Campbell, educator; Marge Champion, choreographer; Betty L. Corwin, theater archivist; Gretchen Cryer, composer; Merle Debuskey, press agent; Thomas Dillon, administrator; Mallory Factor, entrepreneur; Robert Fitzpatrick, educator; Brendan Gill, historian; Jay Harnick, artistic director; Sheldon Harnick, lyricist; Geoffrey Holder, director; Charles Hollerith Jr., producer; Barnard Hughes, actor; David Ives, playwright; Robert Kamlot, general manager; Ming Cho Lee, set designer; Robert McDonald, union administrator; Peter Neufeld, general manager; Dorothy Olim, theatrical administrator; David Richards, writer; Douglas Watt, critic; Franklin R. Weissberg, judge; George White, administrator; and Edwin Wilson, writer.

A new category, Best Orchestrations, was added this season, bringing the total to 21 categories. For the fourth time, because of the large number of revivals that opened on Broadway, the category of Best Revival was split in two (for play and for musical).

The Tony Awards are voted from the list of nominees by the members of the governing boards of the five theater artists' organizations: Actors' Equity Association, the Dramatists Guild, the Society of Stage Directors and Choreographers, the United Scenic Artists and the Casting Society of America, plus the members of the designated first night theater press, the board of directors of the American Theater Wing and the membership of the League of American Theaters and Producers. Because of the fluctuation within these boards, the size of the Tony electorate varies from year to year. In the 1996–97 season, there were 763 qualified Tony voters.

The list of 1996–97 nominees follows, with winners in each category listed in **bold face type.**

BEST PLAY (award goes to both author and producer). *Skylight* by David Hare, produced by Robert Fox, Roger Berlind, Joan Cullman, Scott Rudin, The Shubert Organization, Capital Cities/ABC, The Royal National Theater; *Stanley* by Pam Gems, produced by Circle in the Square, Gregory Mosher, M. Edgar Rosenblum; *The Last Night of Ballyhoo* by **Alfred Uhry**, produced by **Jane Harmon, Nina Keneally, Liz Oliver**; *The Young Man From Atlanta* by Horton Foote, produced by David Richenthal, Anita Waxman, Jujamcyn Theaters, The Goodman Theater, Robert Cole.

BEST MUSICAL (award goes to the producer). *Juan Darién* produced by Lincoln Center Theater, Andre Bishop, Bernard Gersten, Music-Theater Group; *Steel Pier,* produced by Roger Berlind; *The Life,* produced by Roger Berlind, Martin Richards, Cy Coleman, Sam Crothers; *Titanic,* produced by **Dodger Endemol Theatricals, Richard S. Pechter, The John F. Kennedy Center for the Performing Arts**.

BEST BOOK OF A MUSICAL. *Jekyll & Hyde* by Leslie Bricusse; *Steel Pier* by David Thompson; *The Life* by David Newman, Ira Gasman, Cy Coleman; *Titanic* by **Peter Stone**.

BEST ORIGINAL SCORE (music & lyrics) WRITTEN FOR THE THEATER. *Juan Darién,* music and lyrics by Elliot Goldenthal;

A DOLL'S HOUSE—Tony-winning performers Owen Teale (best featured actor in a play) and Janet McTeer (best leading actress in a play) in a new version of Ibsen's *A Doll's House* (best revival of a play) by Frank McGuinness under the direction of Anthony Page (best direction of a play)

Steel Pier, music by John Kander, lyrics by Fred Ebb; *The Life,* music by Cy Coleman, lyrics by Ira Gasman; ***Titanic,*** music and lyrics by **Maury Yeston**.

BEST ORCHESTRATIONS. Michael Gibson for *Steel Pier,* Luther Henderson for *Play On!,* Don Sebesky and Harold Wheeler for *The Life,* **Jonathan Tunick** for *Titanic.*

BEST LEADING ACTOR IN A PLAY. Brian Bedford in *London Assurance,* Michael Gambon in *Skylight,* **Christopher Plummer** in *Barrymore,* Antony Sher in *Stanley.*

BEST LEADING ACTRESS IN A PLAY. Julie Harris in *The Gin Game,* Shirley Knight in *The Young Man From Atlanta,* **Janet McTeer** in *A Doll's House,* Lia Williams in *Skylight.*

BEST LEADING ACTOR IN A MUSICAL. Robert Cuccioli in *Jekyll & Hyde,* Jim Dale in *Candide,* Daniel McDonald in *Steel Pier,* **James Naughton** in *Chicago.*

BEST LEADING ACTRESS IN A MUSICAL. Pamela Isaacs in *The Life,* **Bebe Neuwirth** in *Chicago,* Tonya Pinkins in *Play On!,* Karen Ziemba in *Steel Pier.*

BEST FEATURED ACTOR IN A PLAY. Terry Beaver in *The Last Night of Ballyhoo,* William Biff McGuire in *The Young Man From Atlanta,* Brian Murray in *The Little Foxes,* **Owen Teale** in *A Doll's House.*

BEST FEATURED ACTRESS IN A PLAY. Helen Carey in *London Assurance,* Dana Ivey in *The Last Night of Ballyhoo,* **Lynne Thigpen** in *An American Daughter,* Celia Weston in *The Last Night of Ballyhoo.*

BEST FEATURED ACTOR IN A MUSICAL. Joel Blum in *Steel Pier,* **Chuck Cooper** in *The Life,* Andre De Shields in *Play On!,* Sam Harris in *The Life.*

BEST FEATURED ACTRESS IN A MUSICAL. Marcia Lewis in *Chicago,* Andrea Martin in *Candide,* Debra Monk in *Steel Pier,* **Lillias White** in *The Life.*

BEST DIRECTION OF A PLAY. John Caird for *Stanley,* Richard Eyre for *Skylight,* **Anthony Page** for *A Doll's House,* Charles Nelson Reilly for *The Gin Game.*

BEST DIRECTION OF A MUSICAL. Michael Blakemore for *The Life,* **Walter Bobbie** for *Chicago,* Scott Ellis for *Steel Pier,* Julie Taymor for *Juan Darién.*

BEST SCENIC DESIGN. John Lee Beatty for *The Little Foxes,* **Stewart Laing** for *Titanic,* G.W. Mercier and Julie Taymor for *Juan Darién,* Tony Walton for *Steel Pier.*

BEST COSTUME DESIGN. Ann Curtis for *Jekyll & Hyde,* **Judith Dolan** for *Candide,* William Ivey Long for *Chicago,* Martin Pakledinaz for *The Life.*

BEST LIGHTING DESIGN. **Ken Billington** for *Chicago,* Beverly Emmons for *Jekyll & Hyde,* Donald Holder for *Juan Darién,* Richard Pilbrow for *The Life.*

BEST CHOREOGRAPHY. Wayne Cilento for *Dream,* Joey McKneely for *The Life,* **Ann Reinking** for *Chicago,* Susan Stroman for *Steel Pier.*

BEST REVIVAL OF A PLAY (award goes to the producer). *A Doll's House* produced by **Bill Kenwright, Thelma Holt**; *London Assurance* produced by Roundabout Theater Company, Todd Haimes, Ellen Richard; *Present Laughter* produced by David Richenthal, Anita Waxman, Jujamcyn Theaters; *The Gin Game* produced by National Actors Theater, Tony Randall.

BEST REVIVAL OF A MUSICAL (award goes to the producer). *Annie* produced by Timothy Childs, Rodger Hess, Jujamcyn Theaters, Terri B. Childs, Al Nocciolino; *Candide* produced by Livent (U.S.) Inc.; *Chicago* produced by **Barry Weissler, Fran Weissler, Kardana Productions Inc.**; *Once Upon a Mattress* produced by Dodger Productions, Joop van den Ende.

SPECIAL TONY AWARDS. Lifetime Achievement Award to **Bernard B. Jacobs,** the late President of The Shubert Organization; Regional Theater Award to **Berkeley Repertory Theater,** Berkeley, Calif.

TONY AWARD WINNERS, 1947–1997

Listed below are the Antoinette Perry (Tony) Award winners in the categories of Best Play and Best Musical from the time these awards were established until the present.

1947—No play or musical award
1948—Mister Roberts; no musical award
1949—Death of a Salesman; Kiss Me, Kate
1950—The Cocktail Party; South Pacific
1951—The Rose Tattoo; Guys and Dolls
1952—The Fourposter; The King and I
1953—The Crucible; Wonderful Town
1954—The Teahouse of the August Moon; Kismet
1955—The Desperate Hours; The Pajama Game
1956—The Diary of Anne Frank; Damn Yankees

1957—Long Day's Journey Into Night; My Fair Lady
1958—Sunrise at Campobello; The Music Man
1959—J.B.; Redhead
1960—The Miracle Worker; Fiorello! and The Sound of Music (tie)
1961—Becket; Bye Bye Birdie
1962—A Man for All Seasons; How to Succeed in Business Without Really Trying
1963—Who's Afraid of Virginia Woolf?; A Funny Thing Happened on the Way to the Forum

1964—Luther; Hello, Dolly!
1965—The Subject Was Roses; Fiddler on the Roof
1966—The Persecution and Assassination of Marat as Performed by the Inmates of the Asylum of Charenton Under the Direction of the Marquis de Sade; Man of La Mancha
1967—The Homecoming; Cabaret
1968—Rosencrantz and Guildenstern Are Dead; Hallelujah, Baby!
1969—The Great White Hope; 1776
1970—Borstal Boy; Applause
1971—Sleuth; Company
1972—Sticks and Bones; Two Gentlemen of Verona
1973—That Championship Season; A Little Night Music
1974—The River Niger; Raisin
1975—Equus; The Wiz
1976—Travesties; A Chorus Line
1977—The Shadow Box; Annie
1978—Da; Ain't Misbehavin'
1979—The Elephant Man; Sweeney Todd, the Demon Barber of Fleet Street

1980—Children of a Lesser God; Evita
1981—Amadeus; 42nd Street
1982—The Life & Adventures of Nicholas Nickleby; Nine
1983—Torch Song Trilogy; Cats
1984—The Real Thing; La Cage aux Folles
1985—Biloxi Blues; Big River
1986—I'm Not Rappaport; The Mystery of Edwin Drood
1987—Fences; Les Misérables
1988—M. Butterfly; The Phantom of the Opera
1989—The Heidi Chronicles; Jerome Robbins' Broadway
1990—The Grapes of Wrath; City of Angels
1991—Lost in Yonkers; The Will Rogers Follies
1992—Dancing at Lughnasa; Crazy for You
1993—Angels in America, Part I: Millennium Approaches; Kiss of the Spider Woman
1994—Angels in America, Part II: Perestroika; Passion
1995—Love! Valour! Compassion!; Sunset Boulevard
1996—Master Class; Rent
1997—The Last Night of Ballyhoo; Titanic

LUCILLE LORTEL AWARDS

The Lucille Lortel Awards were established in 1985 by a resolution of the League of Off-Broadway Theaters and Producers, which administers them and has presented them annually since 1986 for outstanding off-Broadway achievement. Eligible for the 12th annual awards in 1997 were all off-Broadway productions which opened between March 1, 1996 and March 31, 1997 except any which had moved from an off-Broadway to a Broadway theater. The 1996–97 selection committee comprised Clive Barnes, Peter Filichia, Howard Kissel, Alvin Klein, Jack Kroll, Michael Kuchwara, Jacques le Sourd, John Simon, Linda Winer, Edith Oliver and Miss Lortel.

PLAY. *How I Learned to Drive* by Paula Vogel.

MUSICAL. *Violet* book and lyrics by Brian Crawley, music by Jeanine Tesori, based on *The Ugliest Pilgrim* by Doris Betts.

REVIVAL. *June Moon* produced by The Drama Dept.

ACTOR IN A PLAY OR MUSICAL. **David Morse** in *How I Learned to Drive*.

ACTRESS IN A PLAY OR MUSICAL. **Mary-Louise Parker** in *How I Learned to Drive*.

DIRECTOR. **Mark Brokaw** for *How I Learned to Drive* and *This Is Our Youth*.

SCENERY. **David Gallo** for *Bunny Bunny*.

COSTUMES. **Howard Crabtree** for *When Pigs Fly*.

LIGHTING. **Brian MacDevitt** for *By the Sea by the Sea by the Beautiful Sea*.

BODY OF WORK. **Gerard Alessandrini**.

ACHIEVEMENT. **Rob Fisher** for the Encores! series.

LORTEL AWARD WINNERS, 1986–1997

Listed below are the Lucille Lortel Award winners in the categories of Outstanding Play and Outstanding Musical from the time these awards were established until the present.

1986—Woza Africa!; no musical award
1987—The Common Pursuit; no musical award
1988—No play or musical award
1989—The Cocktail Hour; no musical award
1990—No play or musical award
1991—Aristocrats; Falsettoland

1992—Lips Together, Teeth Apart; And the World Goes 'Round
1993—The Destiny of Me; Forbidden Broadway
1994—Three Tall Women; Wings
1995—Camping With Henry & Tom; Jelly Roll!
1996—Molly Sweeney; Floyd Collins
1997—How I Learned to Drive; Violet

ATCA PRINCIPAL CITATIONS AND NEW PLAY AWARD WINNERS, 1976–1996

Beginning with the season of 1976–77, the American Theater Critics Association (ATCA) has cited one or more outstanding new plays in cross-country theater, the principal ones, listed below, to be presented in script excerpts in *Best Plays* and—since 1985—to receive the ATCA New Play Award (see the complete 1996 ATCA citations in The Season Around the United States section of this volume).

1976—And the Soul Shall Dance, by Wakako Yamauchi
1977—Getting Out, by Marsha Norman
1978—Loose Ends, by Michael Weller
1979—Custer, by Robert E. Ingham
1980—Chekhov in Yalta, by John Driver and Jeffrey Haddow
1981—Talking With, by Jane Martin
1982—Closely Related, by Bruce MacDonald
1983—Wasted, by Fred Gamel
1984—Scheherazade, by Marisha Chamberlain
1985—Fences, by August Wilson
1986—A Walk in the Woods, by Lee Blessing
1987—Heathen Valley, by Romulus Linney

1988—The Piano Lesson, by August Wilson
1989—2, by Romulus Linney
1990—Two Trains Running, by August Wilson
1991—Could I Have This Dance?, by Doug Haverty
1992—Children of Paradise: Shooting a Dream, by Steven Epp, Felicity Jones, Dominique Serrand and Paul Walsh
1993—Keely and Du, by Jane Martin
1994—The Nanjing Race, by Reggie Cheong-Leen
1995—Amazing Grace, by Michael Cristofer
1996—Jack and Jill, by Jane Martin

ADDITIONAL PRIZES AND AWARDS, 1996–97

The following is a list of major prizes and awards for achievement in the theater this season. In all cases the names of winners appear in **bold face type** and the titles of winners in ***bold face italics***.

16th ANNUAL WILLIAM INGE FESTIVAL AWARD. For distinguished achievement in American Theater. **Neil Simon**.

1996 THEATER HALL OF FAME FOUNDERS AWARD. For outstanding contribution to the theater. **Henry Hewes**.

19th ANNUAL KENNEDY CENTER HONORS. For distinguished achievement by individuals who have made significant contributions to American culture through the arts. **Edward Albee, Benny Carter, Johnny Cash, Jack Lemmon, Maria Tallchief.**

NATIONAL MEDAL OF THE ARTS. Presented by President Clinton on recommendation by the National Council on the Arts. **Edward Albee** and **Stephen Sondheim.**

19th ANNUAL SUSAN SMITH BLACKBURN PRIZES. For women who deserve recognition for having written works of outstanding quality for the English-speaking theater, selected by a committee comprising JoAnne Akalaitis, Jude Kelly, Sian Thomas, Michael White, Robert Whitehead and George C. Wolfe. lst prize—**Marina Carr** for *Portia Coughlin.* 2d prize—**Pam Gems** for *Stanley.* Other finalists—**Katherine Burger** for *Morphic Resonance,* **Migdalia Cruz** for *Salt,* **Elizabeth Egloff** for *The Devils,* **Susan Flakes** for *To Take Arms,* **Jennifer Johnston** for *The Desert Lullaby,* **Julia Jordan** for *Tatjana in Color,* **Emily Mann** for *Greensboro,* **Suzan-Lori Parks** for *Venus,* **Kate Moira Ryan** for *Hadley's Mistake,* **Hanan Al-Shaykh** for *The Paper Husband.*

1996 ELIZABETH HULL-KATE WARRINER AWARD. To the playwright whose work dealt with controversial subjects involving the fields of political, religious or social mores of the time, selected by the Dramatists Guild Council. **August Wilson** for *Seven Guitars.*

AMERICAN ACADEMY OF ARTS AND LETTERS. Award for distinguished service to the arts: **Kitty Carlisle Hart**. Richard Rodgers Award in Musical Theater: *Violet* by Brian Crawley and Jeanine Tesori.

12th ANNUAL MR. ABBOTT AWARD. For lifetime achievement, presented by the Stage Directors and Choreographers Foundation. **Lloyd Richards**. President's Award for contribution to the theater: **Philip Morris Companies Inc**.

GEORGE JEAN NATHAN AWARD. For dramatic criticism, administered by the Cornell University English Department. **Michael Feingold**.

1996 GEORGE OPPENHEIMER AWARD. To the best new American playwright, presented by *Newsday.* **Tim Blake Nelson** for *The Grey Zone.*

1996 KESSELRING PRIZES. Presented by the National Arts Club to playwrights nominated by qualified production companies and selected by a panel of judges comprising Anne Cattaneo, John Guare and John Lahr. First prize, **Naomi Wallace** for *One Flea Spare,* nominated by Actors Theater of Louisville. Second prize, **Nilo Cruz** for *A Park in Our House,* nominated by the McCarter Theater.

RICHARD RODGERS AWARD. For distinguished service to the performing arts. **Bob Avian**.

16th ANNUAL ASTAIRE AWARDS. For excellence in dance and choreography, administered by the Theater Development Fund. Dancers: **Ann Reinking, Bebe Neuwirth**. Choreography: **Ann Reinking** for *Chicago.*

1997 AMERICAN THEATER WING DESIGN AWARDS. For design originating in the U.S., voted by a committee comprising Tish Dace (chair), Alexis Greene, Mel Gussow, Henry Hewes, Jeffrey Sweet and Joan Ungaro. Scenic design: **Robin Phillips, James Noone** and **Christina Poddubiuk** for *Jekyll & Hyde.* Costume design: **Howard Crabtree** for *When Pigs Fly.* Lighting design: **Beverly Emmons** for *Jekyll & Hyde* and *When the World Was Green.* Noteworthy unusual effects: **Julie Archer** for the puppets, set and lighting for *Peter and Wendy.*

LA MAMA 35th ANNIVERSARY SILVER BELL AWARD. For distinguished contribultion to the survival of off off Broadway. **Jerry Tallmer** of the *Village Voice;* **Henry Hewes** of *The Saturday Review.*

12th ANNUAL DANCE AND PERFORMANCE BESSIE AWARDS. For achievement in dance and performance art, selected by a panel of writers, producers and dancers. Included Choreographer and Creator

Awards to **Culture Clash** for *Radio Mambo* at INTAR; **Savion Glover, Reg E. Gaines** and **George C. Wolfe** for *Bring in 'da Noise Bring in 'da Funk* at the Joseph Papp Public Theater; **Cynthia Oliver** for *Death's Door* at Performance Space 122.

7th ANNUAL SUSAN STEIN SHIVA AWARD. For an artist who, having started a career in the theater and gone on to subsequent acclaim and popularity in film and television, remains committed to working on the stage, presented by The Joseph Papp Public Theater/New York Shakespeare Festival. **Christopher Walken.**

42d ANNUAL DRAMA DESK AWARDS. For outstanding achievement in the 1996–97 season, voted by an association of New York drama reporters, editors and critics from nominations made by Alexis Greene, Frank Scheck, David Sheward, Michael Sommers, David Patrick Stearns, Jan Stuart and Sydney Weinberg. New play: *How I Learned to Drive*. New musical: *The Life*. Revival of a play: *A Doll's House*. Revival of a musical: *Chicago*. Actor in a play: **David Morse** in *How I Learned to Drive* and **Christopher Plummer** in *Barrymore*. Actress in a play: **Janet McTeer** in *A Doll's House*. Actor in a musical: **Robert Cuccioli** in *Jekyll & Hyde*. Actress in a musical: **Bebe Neuwirth** in *Chicago*. Featured actor in a play: **Brian Murray** in *The Little Foxes*. Featured actress in a play: **Dana Ivey** in *The Last Night of Ballyhoo* and *Sex and Longing*. Featured actor in a musical: **Joel Grey** in *Chicago*. Featured actress in a musical: **Lillias White** in *The Life*. One-person show: **Fiona Shaw** in *The Waste Land*. Music: **Cy Coleman** for *The Life*. Lyrics: **Gerard Alessandrini** for *Forbidden Broadway Strikes Back*. Direction of a play: **Mark Brokaw** for *How I Learned to Drive*. Direction of a musical: **Walter Bobbie** for *Chicago*. Choreography: **Ann Reinking** for *Chicago*. Scenery of a play: **David Gallo** and **Jan Hartley** for *Bunny Bunny*. Scenery of a musical: **Robin Phillips, James Noone** and **Christina Poddubiuk** for *Jekyll & Hyde*. Costumes: **Howard Crabtree** for *When Pigs Fly*. Lighting: **Ken Billington** for *Chicago*. Sound: **John Gromada** for *The Skriker*. Orchestrations: **Jonathan Tunick** for *Titanic*. Musical revue:

When Pigs Fly. Unique theatrical experience: *The Waste Land*.

Special award: **Moscow Theater Sovremennik** for its repertory of *Three Sisters* and *Into the Whirlwind*.

53d ANNUAL THEATER WORLD AWARDS. For outstanding new talent in Broadway and off-Broadway productions during the 1996–97 season, selected by a committee comprising Clive Barnes, Peter Filichia, Frank Scheck, Michael Sommers, Douglas Watt and John Willis. **Terry Beaver** in *The Last Night of Ballyhoo*, **Helen Carey** in *London Assurance*, **Kristin Chenoweth** and **Daniel McDonald** in *Steel Pier*, **Jason Danieley** in *Candide*, **Linda Eder** in *Jekyll & Hyde*, **Allison Janney** in *Present Laughter*, **Janet McTeer** in *A Doll's House*, **Mark Ruffalo** in *This Is Our Youth*, **Fiona Shaw** in *The Waste Land*, **Antony Sher** in *Stanley*, **Alan Tudyk** in *Bunny Bunny*. Special award: **Ensemble** of *Skylight*: **Michael Gambon, Lia Williams, Christian Camargo.**

63d ANNUAL DRAMA LEAGUE AWARDS. For distinguished achievement in theater. Production of a play: *The Last Night of Ballyhoo*. Production of a musical: *The Life*. Production of a revival: *Chicago*. Performance: **Bebe Neuwirth** in *Chicago*; **Charles Durning** in *The Gin Game*. Unique contribution to the theater: **Jason Robards** for his 50 years in the American theater. Distinguished achievement in musical theater: **Gerard Alessandrini** for his *Forbidden Broadway* revues.

47th ANNUAL OUTER CRITICS CIRCLE AWARDS. For outstanding achievement in the 1996–97 season, voted by critics on out-of-town periodicals and media from nominations made by a committee comprising Marjorie Gunner, Mario Fratti, Glenn Loney, Joan T. Nourse, Barbara Siegel, Ros Lipps, Aubrey Reuben and Simon Saltzman. Broadway play: *The Last Night of Ballyhoo*. Off-Broadway play: *How I Learned to Drive*. Revival of a play: *A Doll's House*. Broadway musical: *The Life*. Off-Broadway musical: *When Pigs Fly*. Revival of a musical: *Chicago*. Actor in a play: **Christopher Plummer** in *Barrymore*. Actor in a musical: **Robert Cuccioli** in *Jekyll & Hyde*. Actress in a play:

Janet McTeer in *A Doll's House*. Actress in a musical: **Bebe Neuwirth** in *Chicago*. Featured actor in a play: **Terry Beaver** in *The Last Night of Ballyhoo*. Featured actor in a musical: **Joel Grey** in *Chicago*. Featured actress in a play (tie): **Deborah Findlay** in *Stanley*, **Allison Janney** in *Present Laughter*, **Celia Weston** in *The Last Night of Ballyhoo*. Featured actress in a musical: **Lillias White** in *The Life*. Solo performance: **Felix A. Pire** in *Men on the Verge of a His-Panic Breakdown*. Director of a play: **John Caird** for *Stanley*. Director of a musical: **Walter Bobbie** for *Chicago*. Choreography: **Ann Reinking** for *Chicago*. Scene design (tie): **David Gallo** for *Bunny Bunny*, **Stewart Laing** for *Titanic*. Costume design: **Howard Crabtree** for *When Pigs Fly*. Lighting design (tie): **Paul Gallo** for *Titanic*, **Peter Kaczorowski** for *Steel Pier*.

John Gassner Playwriting Award: **Leslie Ayvazian** for *Nine Armenians*.

42d ANNUAL *VILLAGE VOICE* OBIE AWARDS. For outstanding achievement in off- and off-off-Broadway theater, chosen by a panel of judges chaired by Ross Wetzsteon. Playwriting: **Naomi Wallace** for *One Flea Spare* (designated best play), **Eve Ensler** for *The Vagina Monologues*, **Paula Vogel** for *How I Learned to Drive*, **Lanford Wilson** for *Sympathetic Magic*. Distinguished performance: **Andre Braugher** in *Henry V*, **Tsai Chin** in *Golden Child*, **Jennifer Dundas** in *Good as New*, **David Greenspan** in *The Boys in the Band*, **Karen Kandel** in *Peter and Wendy*, **Albert Macklin** in *June Moon*, **David Morse** and **Mary-Louise Parker** in *How I Learned to Drive*, **Sharon Scruggs** in *The Trojan Women: A Love Story*, **Ray Anthony Thomas** in *Volunteer Man*, **Ching Valdes-Aran** in *Flipzoids*. Distinguished direction: **Mark Brokaw** for *How I Learned to Drive*. Distinguished contribution to off Broadway: **James Hatch** and **Camille Billops**; **Dona Ann McAdams**; *Tap Dogs*; the music of *Violet* (by Jeanine Tesori). Sustained excellence: Performance, **Joanne Camp, Arthur French**; scene design, **Derek McLane**; costume design, **Catherine Zuber**; lighting design, **Shirley Prendergast**. Sustained achievement: **Woodie King Jr.** of the New Federal Theater.

Special citations: *Tap Dogs*; **Roger Guenveur Smith** in *A Huey P. Newton Story*; **Marc Anthony Thompson** for *A Huey P. Newton Story*; **Howard Crabtree** and **the creators of When Pigs Fly; the creators of Peter and Wendy** (designated best production). Special grants to **Great Small Works, St Paul's, Naomi Wallace** for *One Flea Spare*, **Woodie King Jr.**

7th ANNUAL CONNECTICUT CRITICS CIRCLE AWARDS. For outstanding achievement in Connecticut theater during the 1996–97 season. Production of a play: **Long Wharf Theater** for *Dealer's Choice*. Production of a musical: **Candlewood Playhouse** for *Tommy*. Actor in a play: **Ron Cephas Jones** in *Thunder Knocking on the Door*. Actress in a play: **Julie Harris** in *The Road to Mecca*. Actor in a musical: **Charles Dillon** in *Tommy*. Actress in a musical: **Erin Dilly** in *Finian's Rainbow*. Ensemble performance: **Ritchie Coster, Dermot Crowley, Mark H. Dold, Alec Phoenix, Reg Rogers** and **Tom Spackman** in *Dealer's Choice*. Direction of a play: **David Esbjornson** for *Dealer's Choice*. Direction of a musical: **Tom Ruggiero** for *Tommy*. Choreography: **Bob Durkin** and **Mitzi Hamilton** for *Seven Brides for Seven Brothers*. Set design: **Michael Boyer** for *Tommy*. Costume design: **Catherine Zuber** for *Triumph of Love*. Lighting design: **Christopher J. Landy** for *Tommy*. Sound design: **Mark Clark** and **Simon Mathews** for *Tommy*.

Lucille Lortel Debut Award: **Joey Adams** for *Dare Not Speak Its Name*. Tom Killen Memorial Award: **Steve Karp** of Stamford Theater Works.

15th ANNUAL ELLIOT NORTON AWARDS (formerly Boston Theater Awards). For outstanding contribution to the theater in Boston, voted by a Boston Theater Critics Association selection committee comprising Skip Ascheim, Terry Byrne, Carolyn Clay, Iris Fanger, Arthur Friedman, Joyce Kulhawik, Jon Lehman, Bill Marx, Ed Siegel and Caldwell Titcomb. Production—Visiting company: *Carousel* produced by the Royal National Theater. Large resident company: *Six Characters in Search of an Author* produced by American Repertory Theater. Small resident company: *Speed-the-Plow* produced by Lyric Stage. Local fringe company: *subUrbia* produced by SpeakEasy

Stage Company. Actor—Large resident company: **Bill Camp** and **Michael Stuhlbarg** in *Long Day's Journey Into Night*. Small resident company: **Stephen Largay** in *Equus*. Actress—Large resident company: **Gretchen Cleevely** in *Arcadia*. Small resident company: **Dee Nelson** in *The Scarlet Letter* and *Blithe Spirit*. Solo performance: **Spalding Gray** in *It's a Slippery Slope* and **Anna Deavere Smith** in *Twilight: Los Angeles 1992*. Director—Large resident company: **Oskar Eustis** for *Angels in America, Parts 1* and *2*. Small resident company: **Steve Maler** for *A Midsummer Night's Dream* and *subUrbia*. Designer—Large company: **Laurie Olinder** and **Fred Tietz** for *Alice in Bed* and *The Cabinet of Dr. Caligari*. Small company: **Janie Fliegel** for *The Scarlet Letter, American Buffalo, Speed-the-Plow* and *Blithe Spirit*. Script in its local premiere: *Arcadia* by Tom Stoppard.

Lifetime Achievement Award: **Zoe Caldwell** whose artistry on the world's stages, in works old and new, serious and comic, proclaims her "a lass unparallel'd." Norton Prize for Sustained Excellence: **Christopher Plummer** for a career of astonishing richness and bracing variety. Special citation: **Súgán Theater Company** for enriching Boston during the past five years with provocative productions of contemporary Irish and Celtic works.

13th ANNUAL HELEN HAYES AWARDS. In recognition of excellence in Washington, D.C. area theater, presented by the Washington Theater Awards Society. Resident productions—Play: *Two Trains Running*. Musical: *Passion*. Lead actor, play: **Floyd King** in *Quills*. Lead actress, play: **Nancy Robinette** in *Better Living*. Lead actor, musical: **Lewis Cleale** in *Passion*. Lead actress, musical: **Anne Kanengeiser** in *Passion*. Supporting actor, play: **Wallace Acton** in *Henry VI*. Supporting actress, play: **Helen Carey** in *Volpone*. Supporting performer, musical: **Lawrence Redmond** in *The Rink*. Director, play: **Michael Kahn** for *Henry VI*. Director, musical: **Eric D. Schaeffer** for *Passion*. Set design, play or musical: **John Conklin** for *Dance of Death*. Costume design, play or musical: **Martin Pakledinaz** for *Volpone*. Lighting design, play or musical: **Daniel Maclean Wagner** for *Passion*. Sound design, play or musical: **Bruce Odland** for *Dance of Death*.

Non-resident productions—Production: *A Midsummer Night's Dream*. Lead actress (tie): **Micki Grant** and **Lizan Mitchell** in *Having Our Say*. Lead actor: **Roger Guenveur Smith** in *A Huey P. Newton Story*. Supporting performer: **Desmond Barrit** in *A Midsummer Night's Dream*.

Charles MacArthur Award for Outstanding New Play: *Torn From the Headlines* by Jennifer L. Nelson. Special awards—American Express Tribute to an artist who has enriched our lives through theater: **Lynn Redgrave**. Marwick Award for distinguished service to the Washington professional theater community: **The Washington Post**. Washington Post Award for distinguished community service: **John F. Kennedy Center for the Performing Arts** for its Performing Arts for Everyone initiative.

28th ANNUAL JOSEPH JEFFERSON AWARDS. For achievement in Chicago Theater during the 1995–96 season, selected by a 40-member Jefferson Awards Committee from 120 Equity productions offered by 49 producing organizations. Resident productions—Play: *Having Our Say* produced by Camille O. Cosby and Judith Rutherford James in association with Michael Leavitt and Fox Theatricals. Musical: *The House of Martin Guerre* produced by the Goodman Theater. Revue: *Great Women in Gospel* produced by the Black Ensemble Theater and *Sophisticated Ladies* produced by the Drury Lane Theater. Actor in a principal role, play: **James Gammon** in *Buried Child*. Actress in a principal role, play: **Albena Dodeva** in *Beast on the Moon*. Actor in a principal role, musical: **Anthony Crivello** in *The House of Martin Guerre*. Actress in a principal role, musical: **Kelli Cramer** in *Annie Get Your Gun*, **Eartha Kitt** in *Lady Day at Emerson's Bar & Grill*. Actor in a supporting role, play: **Greg Vinkler** in *Twelfth Night*. Actress in a supporting role, play: **Tara Mallen** in *Wrens*, **Pamela Payton-Wright** in *A Touch of the Poet*. Actress in a cameo role, play: **Linda Stephens** in *Supple in Combat*. Actor in a supporting role, musical; **Kevin Gudahl** in *The House of Martin Guerre*. Actress in a supporting role, musical: **Sara Davis** in *The Secret Garden*, **Hollis Resnik** in *The House of Martin Guerre*. Actor in a cameo role, musical:

Kenny Ingram in *My One and Only*. Actor in a revue: **Larry Neumann Jr.** in *Hitting for the Cycle*. Actress in a revue: **Felicia Fields** in *Sophisticated Ladies*, **Lori Hammel** in *Forbidden Hollywood*, **Jenna Jolovitz** in *Citizen Gates* and **Alene Robertson** in *And the World Goes Round*. Ensemble: **Rivendell Theater Ensemble** in *Wrens*. Director, play: **Emily Mann** for *Having Our Say*, **Charles Newell** for *Celimene and the Cardinal* and **Gary Sinise** for *Buried Child*. Director, musical: **David Petrarca** for *The House of Martin Guerre*. Director, revue: **John Freedson** for *Forbidden Hollywood*, **Marc Robin** for *Sophisticated Ladies*, **Jackie Taylor** for *Great Women in Gospel*. Scenery: **Robert Brill** for *Buried Child*, **Linda Buchanan** for *I Hate Hamlet*. Costumes: **Karin Kopischke** for *Richard III*. Lighting: **Kenneth Posner** for *Richard III*. Sound: **Barry G. Funderburg** for *Macbeth*. New work: *Detachments* by Colleen Dodson, *Wrens* by Anne McGravie. New adaptation: *The Talisman Ring* by Christina Calvit, *WAS* by Paul Edwards. Original music: **Alaric Jens** for *Twelfth Night*. Choreography: **Marc Robin** for *42nd Street*. Musical direction: **Jeffrey Klitz** for *The House of Martin Guerre*, **Jimmy Tillman** for *Great Women in Gospel*.

Touring productions—Production: *Show Boat* produced by Livent (U.S.) Inc. Actor in a principal role: **Robert Cuccioli** in *Jekyll & Hyde*. Actress in a principal role: **Gay Willis** in *Show Boat*. Actor in a supporting role: **Michel Bell** in *Show Boat*. Actress in a supporting role: **Natascia A. Diaz** in *West Side Story*.

Special Awards: **Richard Christiansen** for his lifetime commitment to Chicagoland's theater community and for his unique contribution to fostering the reputation of theater in Chicago; **Fergus G. Currie** for his vision, devotion and commitment to the Chicago theater community and for establishing Season of Concern.

1996 JOSEPH JEFFERSON CITATION AWARDS. For achievement by non- Equity productions in Chicago theater during the 1995–96 season. Production: *A Piece of My Heart* produced by Circle Theater and *Tracers* produced by Mary—Arrchie Theater. Actor in a principal role: **Scott Cummins** in *Burn This*, **Andrew Rothenberg** and **Paul Zegler** in *The Killer and the Comic*. Actress in a principal role: **Cynthia Jackson** in *Three Ways Home*, **Eileen Niccolai** in *And a Nightingale Sang* and **Linda Reiter** in *Les Liaisons Dangereuses*. Actor in a supporting role: **Larry Grimm** in *The Glass Menagerie*. Actress in a supporting role: **Amy Bruneau** in *The Art of Dining*, **Maggie Carney** in *Bedroom Farce*, **Jaqueline Fleming** in *The Trial of One Short-Sighted Black Woman vs. Mammy Louise and Safreeta Mae*. Ensemble: **Circle Theater** in *A Piece of My Heart*, **Mary—Arrchie Theater** in *Tracers*. Director: **DADO** for *Tracers*, **Greg Kolak** for *A Piece of My Heart*, **Richard Shavzin** for *Burn This*, **Matt Tauber** for *American Divine—The Spirit*. Scenery: **Michael Menendian** for *The Glass Menagerie*, **Robert Whitaker** for *Agamemnon*. Costumes: **Ann Kessler** for *Les Liaisons Dangereuses*, **Michael Alan Stein** for *The Temple*. Lighting: **Kevin Geiger** for *Tracers*, **Christine A. Solger** for *Frankenstein*. Sound: **Chuck Sansone** for *Tracers*. Musical direction: **William Underwood** for *Into the Woods*. Original music: **Michael Zerang** for *Frankenstein*. New work/adaptation: *The Trial of One Short-Sighted Black Woman vs. Mammy Louise and Safreeta Mae* by Anne V. McGravie, Dwight Okita, Nicholas A. Patricca and David Zak, *If the Radiance of a Thousand Suns: The Hiroshima Project* by Bailiwick Repertory.

Special citations: **Redmoon Theater Company** for diverse puppet designs and imaginative uses of puppetry in the telling of the tale of *Frankenstein;* **Abena Joan Brown** for her lifetime of achievements in the Chicago theater community and for her unique contributions in establishing and sustaining the ETA Creative Arts Foundation.

28th ANNUAL LOS ANGELES DRAMA CRITICS AWARDS. For distinguished achievement in Los Angeles theater during 1996 (since they do not designate "bests," there can be multiple recipients, or none, in any category). Production: *Breaking the Code* produced by the Blank Theater Company, *Eleemosynary* produced by West Coast Ensemble, *Great Expectations* produced by A Noise Within. Writing: **Lee Blessing** for *Eleemosynary*, **Donald Margulies** for *Collected Stories*. Writing/Adaptation: **Barbara Field** for *Great Expectations* and *A Noise Within*. Lead Performance: **Meredith Bishop** in *Eleemosynary*, **Kandis Chappell** in *Collected Stories*, **Dennis Christopher** in *Breaking the Code*, **Cherry Jones** in *The Heiress*, **Donald Sage Mackay** in *Great Expectations*, **Julia Sweeney** in *God Said "Ha!"*. Featured performance: **Ellia English** in *dinah was*, **Tom Hillmann** in *She Loves Me*, **Deborah Strang** in *Great Expectations*, **Tamara Zook** in *Homefires*. Ensemble performance: **Matrix Theater Company** in *Mad Forest*. Direction: **Peter Grego** for *Eleemosynary*, **Mark Rucker** for *The Taming of the Shrew*. Choreography: **Kenneth Macmillan** for *Carousel*, **Chris Salmon** for *She Loves Me*. Musical direction: **Kevin Farrell** for *Carousel*, **Perry Hart** for *The All Night Strut*. Scenery: **John Arnone** for *How to Succeed in Business Without Really Trying*, **Yael Pardess** for *Blade to the Heat*. Costumes: **Jane Greenwood** for *The Heiress*, **Martin Pakledinaz** for *Changes of Heart*, **Shigeru Yaji** for *The Taming of the Shrew*. Lighting: **Rick Fisher** for *An Inspector Calls*. Sound: **Jon Gottlieb** for *Blade to the Heat*.

Special Awards—Lifetime achievement: **Jack Lemmon**. Ted Schmitt Award for an outstanding new play: *Collected Stories* by Donald Margulies. Angstrom Lighting Award for lifetime achievement in stage lighting by a lighting designer whose career was established in the small theaters of Los Angeles: **Martin Aronstein**. Bob Z Award for outstanding set design: **Deborah Raymond, Dorian Vernacchio**. Natalie Schafer Award for an emerging comic actress of exceptional promise: **Laurel Green**. Margaret Harford Award for sustained achievement in the smaller theater arena: **Actors Co-op**.

1996 LOS ANGELES OVATIONS. Year's bests, peer-judged by Theater LA, an association of more than 130 theater companies and producers. All theaters— World premiere of a play or musical: *The Ellis Jump* by Jim McGrath. New translation/adaptation: *Imaginary Invalid* by Beth Miles. Lead actor in a play: **Alec Mapa** in *Porcelain*. Lead actor in a musical: **Juan Chioran** in *Kiss of the Spider Woman*. Lead actress in a play: **Marian Seldes** in *Three Tall Women*. Lead actress in a musical: **Yvette Freeman** in *dina was*. Featured actor in a play: **Steven M. Porter** in *Imaginary Invalid*. Featured actress in a play: **Jane Kazmarek** in *Kindertransport*. Featured actor in a musical: **Lego Luis** in *City of Angels*. Featured actress in a musical: **Melody Garrett** in *dina was*. Ensemble performance: **The cast** of *Radio Mambo: Culture Clash Invades Miami*. Director of a play: **Ron Orbach** for *The Ellis Jump*. Director of a musical: **Nicholas Hytner** for *Carousel*. Choreographer: **Patti Colombo** for *Radio Gals*.

In a larger theater—Play: *Changes of Heart*. Musical: *Radio Gals*. Lighting: **Rick Fisher** for *An Inspector Calls*. Scenery: **James Leonard Joy** for *Camping With Henry and Tom*. Costumes: **Martin Pakledinaz** for *Changes of Heart*. Sound: **Steve Canyon Kennedy** for *Carousel*.

In a smaller theater—Play: *The Central Ave. Chalk Circle*. Franklin R. Levy Award for a musical: *City of Angels*. Lighting: **J. Kent Inasy** for *Mad Forest*. Scenery: **Deborah Raymond** and **Dorian Vernacchio** for *Mad Forest*. Costumes: **Alix Hester** for *Imaginary Invalid*. Sound: **Laurence O'Keefe** for *Imaginary Invalid*.

Board of Governors Award for lifetime achievement: **August Wilson**. James A. Doolittle Award for leadership in the Los Angeles theater: **Joseph Stern**.

THE THEATER HALL OF FAME

The Theater Hall of Fame was created in 1971 to honor those who have made outstanding contributions to the American theater in a career spanning at least 25 years, with at least five major credits. Members are elected annually by the nation's drama critics and editors (names of those so elected in 1996 and inducted February 3, 1997 appear in ***bold face italics***).

GEORGE ABBOTT	KERMIT BLOOMGARDEN	CHARLOTTE CUSHMAN
MAUDE ADAMS	JERRY BOCK	JEAN DALRYMPLE
VIOLA ADAMS	RAY BOLGER	AUGUSTIN DALY
STELLA ADLER	EDWIN BOOTH	E.L. DAVENPORT
EDWARD ALBEE	JUNIUS BRUTUS BOOTH	OSSIE DAVIS
THEONI V. ALDREDGE	SHIRLEY BOOTH	RUBY DEE
IRA ALDRIDGE	ALICE BRADY	ALFRED DE LIAGRE JR.
JANE ALEXANDER	FANNIE BRICE	AGNES DEMILLE
WINTHROP AMES	PETER BROOK	COLLEEN DEWHURST
JUDITH ANDERSON	JOHN MASON BROWN	HOWARD DIETZ
MAXWELL ANDERSON	BILLIE BURKE	DUDLEY DIGGES
ROBERT ANDERSON	ABE BURROWS	MELVYN DOUGLAS
JULIE ANDREWS	RICHARD BURTON	ALFRED DRAKE
MARGARET ANGLIN	MRS. PATRICK CAMPBELL	MARIE DRESSLER
HAROLD ARLEN	ZOE CALDWELL	JOHN DREW
GEORGE ARLISS	EDDIE CANTOR	MRS. JOHN DREW
BORIS ARONSON	MORRIS CARNOVSKY	WILLIAM DUNLAP
ADELE ASTAIRE	MRS. LESLIE CARTER	MILDRED DUNNOCK
FRED ASTAIRE	GOWER CHAMPION	ELEANORA DUSE
EILEEN ATKINS	FRANK CHANFRAU	JEANNE EAGELS
BROOKS ATKINSON	CAROL CHANNING	FRED EBB
PEARL BAILEY	RUTH CHATTERTON	FLORENCE ELDRIDGE
GEORGE BALANCHINE	PADDY CHAYEFSKY	LEHMAN ENGEL
WILLIAM BALL	INA CLAIRE	MAURICE EVANS
ANNE BANCROFT	BOBBY CLARK	ABE FEDER
TALLULAH BANKHEAD	HAROLD CLURMAN	JOSE FERRER
RICHARD BARR	LEE J. COBB	CY FEUER
PHILIP BARRY	***RICHARD L. COE***	DOROTHY FIELDS
ETHEL BARRYMORE	GEORGE M. COHAN	HERBERT FIELDS
JOHN BARRYMORE	JACK COLE	LEWIS FIELDS
LIONEL BARRYMORE	CY COLEMAN	W.C. FIELDS
NORA BAYES	CONSTANCE COLLIER	JULES FISHER
BRIAN BEDFORD	BETTY COMDEN	MINNIE MADDERN FISKE
S.N. BEHRMAN	MARC CONNELLY	CLYDE FITCH
NORMAN BEL GEDDES	BARBARA COOK	GERALDINE FITZGERALD
DAVID BELASCO	KATHARINE CORNELL	HENRY FONDA
MICHAEL BENNETT	NOEL COWARD	LYNN FONTANNE
RICHARD BENNETT	JANE COWL	HORTON FOOTE
IRVING BERLIN	LOTTA CRABTREE	EDWIN FORREST
SARAH BERNHARDT	CHERYL CRAWFORD	BOB FOSSE
LEONARD BERNSTEIN	HUME CRONYN	RUDOLF FRIML
EARL BLACKWELL	RUSSEL CROUSE	CHARLES FROHMAN

GRACE GEORGE
GEORGE GERSHWIN
IRA GERSHWIN
JOHN GIELGUD
JACK GILFORD
WILLIAM GILLETTE
CHARLES GILPIN
LILLIAN GISH
JOHN GOLDEN
MAX GORDON
RUTH GORDON
ADOLPH GREEN
PAUL GREEN
CHARLOTTE GREENWOOD
JOEL GREY
JOHN GUARE
TYRONE GUTHRIE
UTA HAGEN
LEWIS HALLAM
OSCAR HAMMERSTEIN II
WALTER HAMPDEN
OTTO HARBACH
E.Y. HARBURG
SHELDON HARNICK
EDWARD HARRIGAN
JED HARRIS
JULIE HARRIS
ROSEMARY HARRIS
SAM H. HARRIS
REX HARRISON
KITTY CARLISLE HART
LORENZ HART
MOSS HART
TONY HART
HELEN HAYES
LELAND HAYWARD
BEN HECHT
EILEEN HECKART
THERESA HELBURN
LILLIAN HELLMAN
KATHARINE HEPBURN
VICTOR HERBERT
JERRY HERMAN
JAMES A. HERNE
AL HIRSCHFELD
RAYMOND HITCHCOCK
CELESTE HOLM
HANYA HOLM
ARTHUR HOPKINS
DE WOLF HOPPER
JOHN HOUSEMAN
EUGENE HOWARD
LESLIE HOWARD

SIDNEY HOWARD
WILLIE HOWARD
BARNARD HUGHES
HENRY HULL
JOSEPHINE HULL
WALTER HUSTON
EARLE HYMAN
WILLIAM INGE
BERNARD B. JACOBS
ELSIE JANIS
JOSEPH JEFFERSON
AL JOLSON
JAMES EARL JONES
ROBERT EDMOND JONES
RAUL JULIA
JOHN KANDER
GARSON KANIN
GEORGE S. KAUFMAN
DANNY KAYE
ELIA KAZAN
GENE KELLY
GEORGE KELLY
FANNY KEMBLE
JEROME KERN
WALTER KERR
MICHAEL KIDD
SIDNEY KINGSLEY
FLORENCE KLOTZ
JOSEPH WOOD KRUTCH
BERT LAHR
BURTON LANE
LAWRENCE LANGNER
LILLIE LANGTRY
ANGELA LANSBURY
CHARLES LAUGHTON
ARTHUR LAURENTS
GERTRUDE LAWRENCE
JEROME LAWRENCE
EVA LE GALLIENNE
ROBERT E. LEE
LOTTE LENYA
ALAN JAY LERNER
SAM LEVENE
ROBERT LEWIS
BEATRICE LILLIE
HOWARD LINDSAY
FRANK LOESSER
FREDERICK LOEWE
JOSHUA LOGAN
PAULINE LORD
LUCILLE LORTEL
ALFRED LUNT
CHARLES MACARTHUR

STEELE MACKAYE
ROUBEN MAMOULIAN
RICHARD MANSFIELD
ROBERT B. MANTELL
FREDRIC MARCH
JULIA MARLOWE
ERNEST H. MARTIN
MARY MARTIN
RAYMOND MASSEY
SIOBHAN MCKENNA
TERRENCE MCNALLY
HELEN MENKEN
BURGESS MEREDITH
ETHEL MERMAN
DAVID MERRICK
JO MIELZINER
ARTHUR MILLER
MARILYN MILLER
HELENA MODJESKA
FERENC MOLNAR
LOLA MONTEZ
VICTOR MOORE
ZERO MOSTEL
ANNA CORA MOWATT
PAUL MUNI
THARON MUSSER
GEORGE JEAN NATHAN
MILDRED NATWICK
NAZIMOVA
JAMES M. NEDERLANDER
MIKE NICHOLS
ELLIOT NORTON
CLIFFORD ODETS
DONALD OENSLAGER
LAURENCE OLIVIER
EUGENE O'NEILL
GERALDINE PAGE
JOSEPH PAPP
OSGOOD PERKINS
BERNADETTE PETERS
MOLLY PICON
CHRISTOPHER PLUMMER
COLE PORTER
ROBERT PRESTON
HAROLD PRINCE
JOSE QUINTERO
JOHN RAITT
MICHAEL REDGRAVE
ADA REHAN
ELMER RICE
LLOYD RICHARDS
RALPH RICHARDSON
CHITA RIVERA

JASON ROBARDS
JEROME ROBBINS
PAUL ROBESON
RICHARD RODGERS
WILL ROGERS
SIGMUND ROMBERG
HAROLD ROME
LILLIAN RUSSELL
GENE SAKS
WILLIAM SAROYAN
JOSEPH SCHILDKRAUT
ALAN SCHNEIDER
GERALD SCHOENFELD
ARTHUR SCHWARTZ
GEORGE C. SCOTT
MARIAN SELDES
IRENE SHARAFF
SAM SHEPARD
ROBERT E. SHERWOOD
J.J. SHUBERT
LEE SHUBERT
HERMAN SHUMLIN
NEIL SIMON
LEE SIMONSON

EDMUND SIMPSON
OTIS SKINNER
MAGGIE SMITH
OLIVER SMITH
STEPHEN SONDHEIM
E.H. SOTHERN
KIM STANLEY
MAUREEN STAPLETON
ROGER L. STEVENS
ELLEN STEWART
DOROTHY STICKNEY
FRED STONE
LEE STRASBERG
ELAINE STRITCH
JULE STYNE
MARGARET SULLAVAN
JESSICA TANDY
LAURETTE TAYLOR
ELLEN TERRY
TOMMY TUNE
GWEN VERDON
NANCY WALKER
ELI WALLACH
JAMES WALLACK

LESTER WALLACK
TONY WALTON
DOUGLAS TURNER WARD
DAVID WARFIELD
ETHEL WATERS
CLIFTON WEBB
JOSEPH WEBER
MARGARET WEBSTER
KURT WEILL
ORSON WELLES
MAE WEST
ROBERT WHITEHEAD
THORNTON WILDER
BERT WILLIAMS
TENNESSEE WILLIAMS
LANFORD WILSON
P.G. WODEHOUSE
PEGGY WOOD
IRENE WORTH
ED WYNN
VINCENT YOUMANS
STARK YOUNG
FLORENZ ZIEGFELD

MUSICAL THEATER HALL OF FAME

This organization was established at New York University on November 10, 1993. Names of those elected in 1996 appear in ***bold face italics.***

HAROLD ARLEN
IRVING BERLIN
LEONARD BERNSTEIN
EUBIE BLAKE
ABE BURROWS
GEORGE M. COHAN
DOROTHY FIELDS
GEORGE GERSHWIN

IRA GERSHWIN
OSCAR HAMMERSTEIN II
E.Y. HARBURG
LARRY HART
JEROME KERN
BURTON LANE
ALAN JAY LERNER

FRANK LOESSER
FREDERICK LOEWE
COLE PORTER
ETHEL MERMAN
JEROME ROBBINS
RICHARD RODGERS
HAROLD ROME

MARGO JONES
CITIZEN OF THE THEATER
MEDAL

Presented annually to a citizen of the theater who has made a lifetime commitment to the encouragement of the living theater in the United States and has demonstrated an understanding and affirmation of the craft of playwriting.

1961 LUCILLE LORTEL	1968 DAVEY MARLIN-JONES	1982 ANDRE BISHOP
1962 MICHAEL ELLIS	ELLEN STEWART	1983 BILL BUSHNELL
1963 JUDITH RUTHERFORD	(Workshop Award)	1984 GREGORY MOSHER
MARECHAL	1969 ADRIAN HALL	1985 JOHN LION
GEORGE SAVAGE	EDWARD PARONE &	1986 LLOYD RICHARDS
(University Award)	GORDON DAVIDSON	1987 GERALD CHAPMAN
1964 RICHARD BARR,	(Workshop Award)	1988 NO AWARD
EDWARD ALBEE &	1970 JOSEPH PAPP	1989 MARGARET GOHEEN
CLINTON WILDER	1971 ZELDA FICHANDLER	1990 RICHARD COE
RICHARD A. DUPREY	1972 JULES IRVING	1991 OTIS L. GUERNSEY JR.
(University Award)	1973 DOUGLAS TURNER	1992 ABBOT VAN NOSTRAND
1965 WYNN HANDMAN	WARD	1993 HENRY HEWES
MARSTON BALCH	1974 PAUL WEIDNER	1994 JANE ALEXANDER
(University Award)	1975 ROBERT KALFIN	1995 ROBERT WHITEHEAD
1966 JON JORY	1976 GORDON DAVIDSON	1996 AL HIRSCHFELD
ARTHUR BALLET	1977 MARSHALL W. MASON	
(University Award)	1978 JON JORY	
1967 PAUL BAKER	1979 ELLEN STEWART	
GEORGE C. WHITE	1980 JOHN CLARK DONAHUE	
(Workshop Award)	1981 LYNNE MEADOW	

1996–97 PUBLICATION
OF RECENTLY-PRODUCED NEW PLAYS
AND NEW TRANSLATIONS/ADAPTATIONS

Amphitryon. Adapted by Eric Overmyer from *After Kleist.* Broadway Play Publishers. (paperback).

Arts & Leisure. Steve Tesich. Samuel French (acting edition).

Ashes to Ashes. Harold Pinter. Grove Press (paperback).

Ballad of Yachiyo. Philip Kan Gotanda. TCG (paperback).

Blinded by the Sun & Sweet Panic. Stephen Poliakoff. Methuen USA (paperback).

Blood Wedding. Federico Garcia Lorca, translated by Ted Hughes. Faber & Faber (paperback).

Blue Murder. Peter Nichols. Methuen. (paperback).

Brothers Karamazov, The. Anthony Clarvoe. Broadway Play Publishing (paperback).

Christmas Carol, A. Adapted by Romulus Linney from Charles Dickens's work. Dramatists (paperback).

Cyrano. Adapted by Jatinda Verma from Edmond Rostand's *Cyrano de Bergerac.* Absolute Press (paperback).

Designated Mourner, The. Wallace Shawn. Farrar Straus (also paperback).

Doll's House, A. Henrik Ibsen, translated by Frank McGuinness. Faber & Faber (paperback).

Dr. Jekyll & Mr. Hyde. David Edgar. Nick Hern (paperback).

Fair Country, A. Jon Robin Baitz. TCG (paperback).

Father, The. August Strindberg, adapted by Richard Nelson. Broadway Play Publishing (paperback).

Figaro/Figaro. Adapted by Eric Overmyer from works by Beaumarchais and von Horvath. Broadway Play Publishing (paperback).

General From America, The. Richard Nelson. Faber & Faber (paperback).

Handyman, The. Ronald Harwood. Faber & Faber (paperback).

Ivanov. Anton Chekhov, translated by David Hare. Methuen (paperback).

Jack and Jill: A Romance. Jane Martin. Samuel French (acting edition).

John Gabriel Borkman. Henrik Ibsen, translated by Nicholas Wright (paperback).

Kiss of the Spider Woman: Libretto, The. Terrence McNally, John Kander and Fred Ebb. Samuel French (acting edition).

Mad Forest. Caryl Churchill. TCG (paperback).

Mary Stuart. Friedrich Schiller, translated by Jeremy Sams. Nick Hern (paperback).

Mother Courage and Her Children. Bertolt Brecht, adapted by David Hare. Arcade (paperback).

Misanthrope, The. Molière, adapted by Martin Crimp. Faber & Faber (paperback).

Monogamist, The. Christopher Kyle. Dramatists (paperback).

Moon Over Buffalo. Ken Ludwig. Samuel French (acting edition).

Nixon's Nixon. Russell Lees. Dramatists (acting edition).

Northeast Local. Tom Donaghy. Dramatists (acting edition).

Old Wicked Songs. Jon Marans. Dramatists (acting edition).

Picasso at the Lapin Agile and Other Plays. Steve Martin. Grove.

Red Diaper Baby: 3 Comic Monologues. Josh Kornbluth. Mercury House (paperback).

Rent. Jonathan Larson. William Morrow. (libretto).

Scarlet Letter, The. Phyllis Nagy, adapted from the novel by Nathaniel Hawthorne. Samuel French (paperback).

Seven Guitars. August Wilson. Dutton.

Seven Streams of the River Ota, The. Robert Lepage and Ex Machina. Methuen (paperback).

Sex, Drugs, Rock & Roll. Eric Bogosian. HarperCollins (also paperback HarperCollins, Samuel French and TCG).

Simply Disconnected. Simon Gray. Faber & Faber (paperback).

Slaughter City. Naomi Wallace. Faber & Faber (paperback).

Slavs! Tony Kushner. Broadway Play Publishing (paperback).

Sleep Deprivation Chamber. Adam P. Kennedy and Adrienne Kennedy. TCG (paperback).

Splendid's. Jean Genet, translated by Neil Bartlett. Faber & Faber (paperback).

Stewart of Christendom, The. Sebastian Barry. Methuen USA (paperback).

Sweet Panic. Stephen Poliakoff. Methuen (paperback).

True Crimes. Romulus Linney. Dramatists (paperback).
Valley Song. Athol Fugard. TCG (paperback).
War and Peace. Helen Edmundson. Nich Hern (paperback).
Zombie Prom. John Dempsey and Dana P. Rowe. Samuel French (acting edition)

A SELECTED LIST OF OTHER PLAYS PUBLISHED IN 1996–97

Best American Short Plays: 1995–1996, The. Howard Stein and Glenn Young, editors. Applause (paperback).
Best of the West: An Anthology of Plays From the 1989–1990 Padua Hills Playwrights Festival. Bill Raden, Murray Mednick and Cheryl Slean, editors. Padua Hills Press (paperback).
Christopher Hampton: Plays I. Christopher Hampton. Faber & Faber, (paperback).
Colored Contradictions: An Anthology of Contemporary African-American Plays. Harry J. Elam and Robert Alexander, editors. New American Library (paperback).
Drama Contemporary: Germany. Carl Weber, editor. Johns Hopkins University (paperback).
Eight Interludes. Miguel De Cervantes. Translated and edited by Dawn Smith. Everyman's Classic Library/Charles Tuttle (paperback).
Fie! Fie! Fi-Fi! F. Scott Fitzgerald et al. University of South Carolina. (libretti).
Four Comedies. Plautus, translated by Erich Segal. Oxford (paperback).
Humana Festival '95: The Complete Plays. Marisa Smith, editor. Smith & Kraus (paperback).
Humana Festival '96: The Complete Plays. Michael Bigelow Dixon and Liz Engelman, editors. Smith & Kraus (paperback).
John Guare—Collected Works: Volume I. John Guare. Smith & Kraus (paperback).
John Osborne: Plays I. John Osborne. Faber & Faber (paperback).
Lanford Wilson: Collected Plays 1965–1970. Lanford Wilson. Smith & Kraus (paperback).
Latin American Plays: New Drama From Argentina, Cuba, Mexico and Peru. Sebastian Doggart, editor. Nick Hern (paperback).
Light Shining in Buckinghamshire. Caryl Churchill. TCG (paperback).
Lost Plays of the Harlem Renaissance 1920–1940. James V. Hatch and Leo Hamalian, editors. Wayne State University (paperback).
Nativity Scene, The. Eduardo de Filippo. Guernica (paperback).
New Plays From the Abbey Theater: 1993–1995. Christopher Fitz-Simon and Sanford Sternlicht, editors. Syracuse (paperback).
New York Musicals of Comden & Green, The. Betty Comden and Adolph Green. Applause (libretti).
Off-Off-Broadway Festival Plays–21st Series. Samuel French. Samuel French (acting edition).
On Stage, America! Walter J. Meserve, editor. Feedback Theaterbooks (paperback).
Plays of Anton Chekhov: A New Translation by Paul Schmidt, The. HarperCollins. (paperback).
Plays I: Willy Russell. Willy Russell. Methuen (paperback).
Plays 2: Tom Stoppard. Tom Stoppard. Faber & Faber (paperback).
Rusty Bugles. Sumner Locke-Elliott. Currency Press (paperback).
Tartuffe: Bilingual Edition. Translated by Richard Wilbur. Harcourt Brace.
Terrence McNally: Volume 2. Terrence McNally. Smith & Kraus (paperback).
Testimonies: Four Plays. Emily Mann. TCG (paperback).

NECROLOGY
MAY 1996–MAY 1997

PERFORMERS

Abbott, Bud Jr. (57)—January 19, 1997
Abbott, John (90)—May 24, 1996
Addy, Wesley (83)—December 31, 1996
Alvary, Lorenzo (87)—December 13, 1996
Ames, Eugene (73)—April 26, 1997
Amsterdam, Morey (87?)—October 27, 1996
Andrews, Norma (66)—June 29, 1996
Ayres, Lew (88)—December 30, 1996
Baker, LaVern (67)—March 10, 1997
Barnes, Mae (89)—December 13, 1996
Baxter, Jane (87)—September 13, 1996
Beal, John (87)—April 26, 1997
Belgrave, Cynthia (76)—February 1, 1997
Bernard, Jason (58)—October 18, 1996
Bessell, Ted (61?)—October 6, 1996
Bettger, Mary Rolfe (79)—October 28, 1996
Billig, Steve S. (66)—August 30, 1996
Bird, Dorothy (84)—November 12, 1996
Blackstone, Harry Jr. (62)—May 14, 1997
Blair, Joan (93)—January 9, 1997
Boatwright, Christopher (42)—March 2, 1997
Botto, Louis A. (45)—March 25, 1997
Bressler, Charles (70)—November 28, 1996
Brinkman, Ruth (62)—January 18, 1997
Bunin, Morey (86)—February 26, 1997
Cajafa, Gianni (82)—April 19, 1997
Campbell, Sylvester (59)—March 9, 1997
Carlson, June (72)—December 9, 1996
Carpenter, Thelma (77)—May 15, 1997
Casares, Maria (74)—November 22, 1996
Charpentier, Suzanne Georgette ("Annabella") (86)—September 18, 1996
Chiriaeff, Ludmilla (72)—September 22, 1996
Christine, Virginia (76)—July 24, 1996
Clark, Lillian (70)—August 20, 1996
Clarke, Alyce King (80)—August 21, 1996
Colbert, Claudette (92)—July 30, 1996
Collyer, David Soren (81)—May 9, 1996
Combs, Ray (40)—June 3, 1996
Cooper, Roy (88)—September 9, 1996
Cornett, Barbara (86)—January 16, 1997
Corteggiano, Joseph (49)—April 7, 1997
Danon, Jack (Bergal) (64)—August 12, 1996
Davis, Fred (74)—July 5, 1996
Dorste, Marguerite Ganser (48)—July 28, 1996
Downing, Virginia (92)—November 21, 1996
Doyle, David (67)—February 27, 1997
Draper, Paul (86)—September 20, 1996
Dru, Joanne (73?)—September 10, 1996
Duckworth, Dortha (91)—November 14, 1996

Duffy, John (62)—December 10, 1996
Edelman, Herb (62)—July 21, 1996
Eno, Terry (50)—April 20, 1997
Faye, Joey (87)—April 26, 1997
Field, Lisabeth (72)—April 13, 1997
Fitch, Louise (81)—September 11, 1996
Fitzgerald, Ella (79)—June 15, 1996
Forbes, Brenda (87)—September 11, 1996
Fox, Michael (75)—June 1, 1996
Frankel, Mark (34)—September 24, 1996
Fried, Howard (75)—July 10, 1996
Gates, Larry (81)—December 12, 1996
Glassgold, Sophia Delza (92)—June 27, 1996
Godreau, Miguel (49)—August 29, 1996
Goetz, Dana Hill (32)—July 15, 1996
Good, John (77)—December 19, 1996
Gorman, Fred (44)—September 12, 1996
Green, Chuck (78)—March 6, 1997
Green, Joseph (96)—June 20, 1996
Gross, Marjorie (40)—June 7, 1996
Guess, Alvaleta (36?)—September 2, 1996
Haley, Florence (90s?)—December 30, 1996
Hardy, Ethel Gilbert (96)—November 2, 1996
Harris, Paul E. (86)—November 2, 1996
Hemingway, Margaux (41)—July 1, 1996
Heppenstall, John Staunton (38)—June 11, 1996
Heyman, Barton (59)—May 15, 1996
Hill, Ralston (69)—October 19, 1996
Hobbs, Elsbeary (59)—May 31, 1996
Holloway, Robert (62)—December 9, 1996
Kennedy, Bill (88)—January 27, 1997
Khaury, Herbert ("Tiny Tim") (66?)—November 30, 1996
Kitchell, Alma (103)—November 13, 1996
Kneeland, Richard (68)—July 19, 1996
Komar, Chris (47)—July 17, 1996
Koremin, Walter Michael (69)—June 2, 1996
Kressyn, Miriam (84)—October 28, 1996
La Plante, Laura (92)—October 19, 1996
LaCentra, Peg (86)—June 1, 1996
Lambert, Paul (74)—April 27, 1997
Lamour, Dorothy (81)—September 22, 1996
LaRue, Lash (70s-80s?)—May 24, 1996
Leeds, Peter (79)—November 12, 1996
Lenard, Mark (68)—November 22, 1996
Leonard, Sheldon (89)—January 11, 1997
Levant, June Gilmartin (late 70s)—November 13, 1996
LoPresti, Lenore (69)—March 10, 1997
Marshall, Lois (72)—February 19, 1997
Martini, Virginia Cherrill (88)—November 14, 1996
Mason, Pamela (80)—June 29, 1996

445

Mastroianni, Marcello (72)—December 19, 1996
McCoy, Seth (68)—January 22, 1997
McLeod, Catherine (75)—May 11, 1997
Meisner, Sanford (91)—February 2, 1997
Melvin, Harold (57)—March 24, 1997
Moore, Alvy (75)—May 4, 1997
Morris, Greg (61)—August 27, 1996
Morton, Howard (71)—May 11, 1997
Muir, Jean (85)—July 23, 1996
Mulhare, Edward (74)—May 24, 1997
Nall, Adeline Mart (90)—November 19, 1996
Nance, Jack (53)—December 30, 1996
Neise, George N. (79)—April 14, 1997
Novack, Cynthia (49)—September 27, 1996
O'Neal, Charles (92)—August 29, 1996
Osborne, Seymour (93)—August 13, 1996
Ossorio, Robert (73)—November 27, 1996
Paulsen, Pat (69)—April 24, 1997
Pertwee, Jon (76)—May 20, 1996
Peterson, Arthur (83)—October 31, 1996
Porter, Don (84)—February 11, 1997
Prince, William (83)—October 8, 1996
Prowse, Juliet (59)—September 14, 1996
Reagon, Cordell Hull (53)—November 12, 1996
Reid, Beryl (76)—October 13, 1996
Reynolds, Marjorie (76)—February 1, 1997
Ridgely, Robert (65)—February 8, 1997
Ritz, Philip (47)—February 17, 1997
Rolfe, Mary (79)—October 28, 1996
Rollins, Howard (46)—December 8, 1996
Ross, Winston (84)—November 26, 1996
Rostova, Lubov (80)—January 13, 1997
Ruisinger, Thomas A.—March 11, 1997
Scotti, Vito (78)—June 5, 1996
Seneca, Joe (82)—August 15, 1996
Shakur, Tupac (25)—September 13, 1996
Shaw, Marian (80)—December 27, 1996
Slattery, Richard X. (72)—January 27, 1997
Stanley, Alvah H. Jr. (56)—August 6, 1996
Steiner, Arthur H. (82)—February 10, 1997
Stroka, Michael (58)—April 14, 1997
Terborgh, Bert (51)—June 21, 1996
Toumanova, Tamara (77)—May 29, 1996
Van Fleet, Jo (76)—June 10, 1996
Varno, Roland (88)—May 24, 1996
Vernon, Harvey (69)—October 9, 1996
Walker, Keith A. (61)—December 30, 1996
Welitsch, Ljuba (83)—September 2, 1996
White, Jesse (79)—January 8, 1997
Williams, Vince (39)—January 6, 1997
Wood, Forrest Benjamin (76)—July 22, 1996
Yoder, Alma Kitchell (103)—November 13, 1996
Young, Faron (64)—December 10, 1996
Youskevitch, Anna Scarpova (85)—May 15, 1997
Zuckert, Bill (76)—January 23, 1997

PLAYWRIGHTS

Alden, Jerome (76)—May 4, 1997
Cao, Yu (86)—December 13, 1996

Crabtree, Howard (41)—June 28, 1996
del Rio, Amelia Agostino (100)—December 11, 1996
DuBois, William (93)—March 16, 1997
Elder, Lonne III (69)—June 11, 1996
Essex, Harry (86)—February 6, 1997
Granger, Percy (51)—March 10, 1997
Lewin, Albert E. (79)—April 23, 1996
Marcus, Frank (68)—August 5, 1996
Neubauer, Christine (40)—February 9, 1997
Piper, Myfanwy (85)—January 18, 1997
Popplewell, Jack (87)—November 16, 1996
Stark, Sheldon H. (87)—February 6, 1997
Stockton, Richard (65)—April 5, 1997
Tesich, Steve (53)—July 1, 1996
Topor, Roland (59)—April 16, 1997
Valency, Maurice (93)—September 28, 1996
Wannous, Saadallah (56)—May 15, 1997

COMPOSERS, LYRICISTS, SONGWRITERS

Axton, Mae Boren (82)—April 9, 1997
Barati, George (83)—June 22, 1996
Berry, Richard (61)—January 23, 1997
Brittan, Robert (65)—October 4, 1996
Caesar, Irving (101)—December 17, 1996
Cunningham, Arthur (68)—March 31, 1997
Danzig, Evelyn (94)—July 26, 1996
de Carvalho, Eleazar (84)—September 12, 1996
DeForest, Charles (72)—July 6, 1996
Diamond, Keith (46)—January 18, 1997
Ewald, Mary T. (75)—February 5, 1997
Finney, Ross (90)—February 4, 1997
Gannon, Lee (36)—September 2, 1996
Gideon, Miriam (89)—June 18, 1996
Goeb, Roger (82)—January 3, 1997
Goldschmidt, Berthold (93)—October 17, 1996
Goodman, Miles (47)—August 16, 1996
Gordon, Irving (81)—December 1, 1996
Handy, George (76)—January 8, 1997
Lane, Burton (84)—January 5, 1997
Levine, Irwin (58)—January 21, 1997
Luening, Otto (96)—September 2, 1996
Marks, Gerald (96)—January 27, 1997
Nyro, Laura (49)—April 8, 1997
Raleigh, Ben (83)—February 26, 1997
Reid, Don (85)—September 16, 1996
Spielman, Fritz (90)—March 21, 1997
Stutz, Carl (80)—October 8, 1996
Talma, Louise (89)—August 13, 1996
Van Zandt, Townes (52)—January 1, 1997
Weisgall, Hugo (84)—March 11, 1997
Werle, Frederick (87)—May 15, 1997
Weston, Paul (84)—September 20, 1996
White, Augusta (91)—March 27, 1997
White, Eddie R. (77)—October 22, 1996
Wigglesworth, Frank (78)—March 19, 1997

CONDUCTORS

Baron, Samuel (72)—May 16, 1997
Behr, Jan (85)—November 21, 1996
Brown, Beatrice (79)—February 11, 1997
Deutsch, Emery (91)—April 16, 1997
Jenkins, Newell (81)—December 21, 1996
Kubelik, Rafael (82)—August 11, 1996
Mead, George B. (94)—September 2, 1996
Santiago, Al (64)—December 9, 1996
Siciliani, Francesco (85)—December 17, 1996
Sussman, Stanley B. (58)—July 29, 1996
Vegh, Sandor (91)—January 6, 1997
Weston, Paul (84)—September 20, 1996

MUSICIANS

Booth, Alan (71)—June 4, 1996
Breaux, Zachary (36)—February 20, 1997
Brodsky, Jascha (90)—March 3, 1997
Clarke, William (45)—November 2, 1996
Doggett, Bill (80)—November 13, 1996
Fenby, Eric (90)—February 18, 1997
Fuchs, Joseph (97)—March 14, 1997
Garbousova, Raya (87)—January 28, 1997
Glickman, Harry (86)—October 6, 1996
Grolnick, Don (48)—June 1, 1996
Harris, Eddie (62)—November 5, 1996
Lowe, Jack Warren (79)—June 2, 1996
Manson, Eddy (77)—July 12, 1996
Monroe, Bill (84)—September 9, 1996
Moore, Kenny (45)—March 24, 1997
Ormandy, Martin (95)—June 4, 1996
Panozzo, John (47)—July 16, 1996
Porter, Art (35)—November 23, 1996
Porter, Richard (83)—October 6, 1996
Rachell, Yank (87)—April 9, 1997
Rivers, Jerry (68)—October 4, 1996
Robbins, Carol (54)—December 12, 1996
Robinor, Genia (95)—October 22, 1996
Rose, Bernard (80)—November 21, 1996
Rowles, Jimmy (77)—May 28, 1996
Saidenberg, Daniel (90)—May 18, 1997
Scott, Ronnie (69)—December 23, 1996
Stephens, Phil (89)—May 29, 1996
Sucoff, Herbert (58)—December 17, 1996
Taylor, Mel (62)—August 11, 1996
Tudor, David (70)—August 13, 1996
Wallace, Burt (70)—March 12, 1997
Williams, John O. (91)—November 24, 1996
Williams, Tony (51)—February 23, 1997
Yepes, Narciso (69)—May 3, 1997

PRODUCERS, DIRECTORS, CHOREOGRAPHERS

Abrahams, Geulah (65)—August 17, 1996
Alvarez, Aida (78)—October 26, 1996
Beardon, Nanette (69)—August 10, 1996
Berman, Pandro S. (91)—July 13, 1996
Biracree, Thelma (93)—May 12, 1997
Bowden, Charles (83)—December 22, 1996
Brodsky, Stanley (45)—June 28, 1996
Carlin, Edward (64)—October 24, 1996
Carne, Marcel (90)—October 31, 1996
Clouse, Robert (68)—February 4, 1997
Cowles, Chandler (79)—February 1, 1997
Currie, Robert D. (62)—February 12, 1997
Cuyjet, Marion D. (76)—October 22, 1996
Danielian, Leon (75)—March 8, 1997
Donahue, Dorothea Phelan (90)—May 26, 1996
Doolittle, James Arnold (83)—February 1, 1997
Dunn, Robert Ellis (67)—July 5, 1996
Feld, Irving (76)—March 30, 1997
Galterio, Lou (53)—June 20, 1996
Glenville, Peter (82)—June 3, 1996
Gudde, Lynda (54)—August 5, 1996
Jacobs, Bernard B. (80)—August 27, 1996
Jerry, Philip (41)—August 2, 1996
Johnson, Tim (65)—March 14, 1997
Kahn, Jacques L. (76)—March 19, 1997
Krainik, Ardis (67)—January 18, 1997
Krezel, Kenneth J. (58)—February 24, 1997
Lammers, Paul (74)—July 16, 1996
Launder, Frank (91)—February 23, 1997
Leporska, Zoya (78)—December 16, 1996
Lewenstein, Oscar (80)—February 23, 1997
Mann, Burch (87)—June 25, 1996
Marchowsky, Marie (90)—March 8, 1997
Matthews, Billy (76)—December 15, 1996
Nelson, Gene (76)—September 16, 1996
Putterman, William Zev (67)—May 27, 1996
Racolin, Alexander (88)—June 6, 1996
Rene, Norman (45)—May 24, 1996
Roberts, Louise (85)—January 17, 1997
Salkind, Alexander (76)—March 8, 1997
Selznick, J. Jeffrey (64)—May 12, 1997
Septee, Moe (71)—April 1, 1997
Sieh, Theodore (71)—September 21, 1996
Stone, Jon (65)—March 29, 1997
Tanaka, Tomoyuki (86)—April 2, 1997
Tarloff, Milt (92)—April 16, 1997
Volbach, Walther R. (98)—August 5, 1996
Walker, Janet Hayes (71)—February 20, 1997
Wiener, Gabriel (26)—April 9, 1997
Zinnemann, Fred (89)—March 14, 1997

DESIGNERS

Clark, Margaret Bronson (80)—June 19, 1996
Feder, Abe (87)—April 24, 1997

Johnson, Bernard (60)—January 22, 1997
Nelson, Richard (57)—November 6, 1996
Rand, Paul (82)—November 26, 1996
Smith, Michael R. (39)—June 11, 1996
Wills, Mary Lillian (82)—February 7, 1997

CRITICS

Cassidy, Claudia (96)—July 21, 1996
Jacobs, Leslie (93)—February 11, 1997
Kerr, Walter F. (83)—October 9, 1996
Melani, Marco (48)—April 13, 1996
Schaeffer, Martin M. (50)—May 29, 1996
Short, Randall (41)—September 25, 1996
Sorell, Walter (91)—February 21, 1997
Tinker, Jack (58)—October 27, 1996
Winsten, Archer (92)—February 21, 1997

OTHERS

Albert, George (83)—March 18, 1997
  Cash Box
Armstrong, Lois (72)—September 30, 1996
  People
Austin, Laurence (70)—January 17, 1997
  Silent movie showman
Bain, Wilfred C. (89)—March 7, 1997
  Music educator
Bertino, Albert (84)—August 18, 1996
  Disney animator
Bigman, Rose (87)—April 23, 1997
  Winchell's secretary
Bradley, Bill (73)—March 17, 1997
  The Gypsy Robe
Chancellor, John (68)—July 12, 1996
  Commentator
Cox, Winston H. (55)—September 21, 1996
  Showtime/The Movie Channel
Coyte, Kenneth (64)—January 6, 1997
  TV reporter
Csida, Joseph (83)—June 18, 1996
  Billboard
Dawson, Thomas H. (82)—June 2, 1996
  CBS TV
Denis, Paul (86)—March 26, 1997
  Columnist
Diamond, Bernard (79)—April 6, 1997
  Theater executive
Dickey, James (73)—January 19, 1997
  Poet
Duschl, Mary Louise Stack (45)—November 20, 1996
  Pittsburgh Ballet Theater

Feist, Leonard (85)—November 18, 1996
  Century Music, Mercury Music
Fichandler, Thomas C. (81)—March 16, 1997
  Arena Stage
Franey, Pierre (75)—October 15, 1996
  Pavillon
Gabor, Jolie (97)—April 1, 1997
  Mother of Eva, Zsa Zsa
Gillespie, Dennis (64)—December 19, 1996
  Viacom Enterprises
Ginsberg, Allen (70)—April 5, 1997
  Poet
Gough, Hugh Percival Henry (81)—April 14, 1997
  Musicologist
Haberthur-Williams, Kathleen (41)—June 19, 1996
  Press Agent
Heckscher, August—Spring 1997
  Theater Development Fund
Hift, Fred (74)—July 6, 1996
  Journalist
Kalmus, Allan H. (79)—March 12, 1997
  Press agent
Kent, Arthur (74)—February 9, 1997
  Union leader
Kroll, Lucy (87)—March 14, 1997
  Agent
Lejwa, Madeleine Chalette (81)—June 7, 1996
  Metropolitan Opera patron
Lyon, Peter (81)—October 14, 1996
  Radio Writers Guild
Mazel, Vera (90)—January 4, 1997
  Voice teacher
Miller, Philip Lieson (90)—November 23, 1996
  Musicologist
Royko, Mike (65)—April 29, 1997
  Columnist
Sarnoff, Robert W. (78)—February 22, 1997
  NBC, RCA
Saudek, Robert (85)—March 13, 1997
  Omnibus
Schönberg, Bessie (90)—May 14, 1997
  Dance teacher
Simon, Louis M. (90)—October 28, 1996
  Theater executive
Starin, Abe (85)—June 15, 1996
  Barnum & Bailey Circus
Stewart, Larry (67)—February 26, 1997
  TV Academy
Weeks, Clair (84)—August 26, 1996
  Disney animator
Wiener, George (96)—April 8, 1997
  Music publisher
Zabelin, Leo (82)—January 9, 1997
  Variety
Zipper, Herbert (92)—April 21, 1997
  Secret Orchestra at Dachau

THE BEST PLAYS, 1894–1996

Listed in alphabetical order below are all those works selected as Best Plays in previous volumes of the *Best Plays* series. Opposite each title is given the volume in which the play appears, its opening date and its total number of performances. Two separate opening-date and performance-number entries signify two separate engagements off Broadway and on Broadway when the original production was transferred from one area to the other, usually in an off-to-on direction. Those plays marked with an asterisk (*) were still playing on June 1, 1997 and their number of performances was figured through May 31, 1997. Adaptors and translators are indicated by (ad) and (tr), the symbols (b), (m) and (l) stand for the author of the book, music and lyrics in the case of musicals and (c) signifies the credit for the show's conception, (i) for its inspiration. Entries identified as 94–99 are 19th century plays from one of the retrospective volumes. 94–95 and 95–96 are 20th century plays.

PLAY	VOLUME	OPENED	PERFS
ABE LINCOLN IN ILLINOIS—Robert E. Sherwood	38–39	Oct. 15, 1938	472
ABRAHAM LINCOLN—John Drinkwater	19–20	Dec. 15, 1919	193
ACCENT ON YOUTH—Samson Raphaelson	34–35	Dec. 25, 1934	229
ADAM AND EVA—Guy Bolton, George Middleton	19–20	Sept. 13, 1919	312
ADAPTATION—Elaine May; and NEXT—Terrence McNally	68–69	Feb. 10, 1969	707
AFFAIRS OF STATE—Louis Verneuil	50–51	Sept. 25, 1950	610
AFTER THE FALL—Arthur Miller	63–64	Jan. 23, 1964	208
AFTER THE RAIN—John Bowen	67–68	Oct. 9, 1967	64
AFTER-PLAY—Anne Meara	94–95	Jan. 31, 1995	400
AGNES OF GOD—John Pielmeier	81–82	Mar. 30, 1982	599
AH, WILDERNESS!—Eugene O'Neill	33–34	Oct. 2, 1933	289
AIN'T SUPPOSED TO DIE A NATURAL DEATH—(b, m, l) Melvin Van Peebles	71–72	Oct. 20, 1971	325
ALIEN CORN—Sidney Howard	32–33	Feb. 20, 1933	98
ALISON'S HOUSE—Susan Glaspell	30–31	Dec. 1, 1930	41
ALL MY SONS—Arthur Miller	46–47	Jan. 29, 1947	328
ALL IN THE TIMING—David Ives	93–94	Feb. 17, 1994	526
ALL OVER TOWN—Murray Schisgal	74–75	Dec. 29, 1974	233
ALL THE WAY HOME—Tad Mosel, based on James Agee's novel *A Death in the Family*	60–61	Nov. 30, 1960	333
ALLEGRO—(b, l) Oscar Hammerstein II, (m) Richard Rodgers	47–48	Oct. 10, 1947	315
AMADEUS—Peter Shaffer	80–81	Dec. 17, 1980	1,181
AMBUSH—Arthur Richman	21–22	Oct. 10, 1921	98
AMERICA HURRAH—Jean-Claude van Itallie	66–67	Nov. 6, 1966	634
AMERICAN BUFFALO—David Mamet	76–77	Feb. 16, 1977	135
AMERICAN ENTERPRISE—Jeffrey Sweet (special citation)	93–94	Apr. 13, 1994	15
AMERICAN PLAN, THE—Richard Greenberg	90–91	Dec. 16, 1990	37
AMERICAN WAY, THE—George S. Kaufman, Moss Hart	38–39	Jan. 21, 1939	164
AMPHITRYON 38—Jean Giraudoux, (ad) S.N. Behrman	37–38	Nov. 1, 1937	153
AND A NIGHTINGALE SANG—C.P. Taylor	83–84	Nov. 27, 1983	177

PLAY	VOLUME	OPENED	PERFS
LEFT BANK, THE—Elmer Rice	31–32	Oct. 5, 1931	242
LEND ME A TENOR—Ken Ludwig	88–89	Mar. 2, 1989	481
LES LIAISONS DANGEREUSES—Christopher Hampton, based on Choderlos de Laclos's novel	86–87	Apr. 30, 1987	148
*LES MISERABLES—(b) Alain Boublil, Claude-Michel Schönberg, (m) Claude-Michel Schönberg, (l) Herbert Kretzmer, add'l material James Fenton, based on Victor Hugo's novel	86–87	Mar. 12, 1987	4,195
LESSON FROM ALOES, A—Athol Fugard	80–81	Nov. 17, 1980	96
LET US BE GAY—Rachel Crothers	28–29	Feb. 19, 1929	353
LETTERS TO LUCERNE—Fritz Rotter, Allen Vincent	41–42	Dec. 23, 1941	23
LIFE, A—Hugh Leonard	80–81	Nov. 2, 1980	72
LIFE & ADVENTURES OF NICHOLAS NICKLEBY, THE—(ad) David Edgar from Charles Dickens's novel	81–82	Oct. 4, 1981	49
LIFE IN THE THEATER, A—David Mamet	77–78	Oct. 20, 1977	288
LIFE WITH FATHER—Howard Lindsay, Russel Crouse, based on Clarence Day's book	39–40	Nov. 8, 1939	3,224
LIFE WITH MOTHER—Howard Lindsay, Russel Crouse, based on Clarence Day's book	48–49	Oct. 20, 1948	265
LIGHT UP THE SKY—Moss Hart	48–49	Nov. 18, 1948	216
LILIOM—Ferenc Molnar, (ad) Benjamin Glazer	20–21	Apr. 20, 1921	300
LION IN WINTER, THE—James Goldman	65–66	Mar. 3, 1966	92
LIPS TOGETHER, TEETH APART—Terrence McNally	91–92	June 25, 1991	406
LITTLE ACCIDENT—Floyd Dell, Thomas Mitchell	28–29	Oct. 9, 1928	303
LITTLE FOXES, THE—Lillian Hellman	38–39	Feb. 15, 1939	410
LITTLE MINISTER, THE—James M. Barrie	94–99	Sept. 27, 1897	300
LITTLE NIGHT MUSIC, A—(b) Hugh Wheeler, (m, l) Stephen Sondheim, suggested by Ingmar Bergman's film *Smiles of a Summer Night*	72–73	Feb. 25, 1973	600
LIVING ROOM, THE—Graham Greene	54–55	Nov. 17, 1954	22
LIVING TOGETHER—Alan Ayckbourn	75–76	Dec. 7, 1975	76
LOMAN FAMILY PICNIC, THE—Donald Margulies	89–90	June 20, 1989	16
LONG DAY'S JOURNEY INTO NIGHT—Eugene O'Neill	56–57	Nov. 7, 1956	390
LOOK BACK IN ANGER—John Osborne	57–58	Oct. 1, 1957	407
LOOK HOMEWARD, ANGEL—Ketti Frings, based on Thomas Wolfe's novel	57–58	Nov. 28, 1957	564
LOOSE ENDS—Michael Weller	79–80	June 6, 1979	284
LOST HORIZONS—Harry Segall, revised by John Hayden	34–35	Oct. 15, 1934	56
LOST IN THE STARS—(b, l) Maxwell Anderson, based on Alan Paton's novel *Cry, the Beloved Country,* (m) Kurt Weill	49–50	Oct. 30, 1949	273
LOST IN YONKERS—Neil Simon	90–91	Feb. 21, 1991	780
LOVE LETTERS—A.R. Gurney	89–90	Aug. 22, 1989	64
	89–90	Oct. 31, 1989	96
LOVE OF FOUR COLONELS, THE—Peter Ustinov	52–53	Jan. 15, 1953	141
LOVE! VALOUR! COMPASSION!—Terrence McNally	94–95	Nov. 1, 1994	72
	94–95	Feb. 14, 1995	249
LOVERS—Brian Friel	68–69	July 25, 1968	148
LOYALTIES—John Galsworthy	22–23	Sept. 27, 1922	220
LUNCH HOUR—Jean Kerr	80–81	Nov. 12, 1980	262
LUTE SONG—(b) Sidney Howard, Will Irwin from the Chinese classic *Pi-Pa-Ki,* (l) Bernard Hanighen, (m) Raymond Scott	45–46	Feb. 6, 1946	385

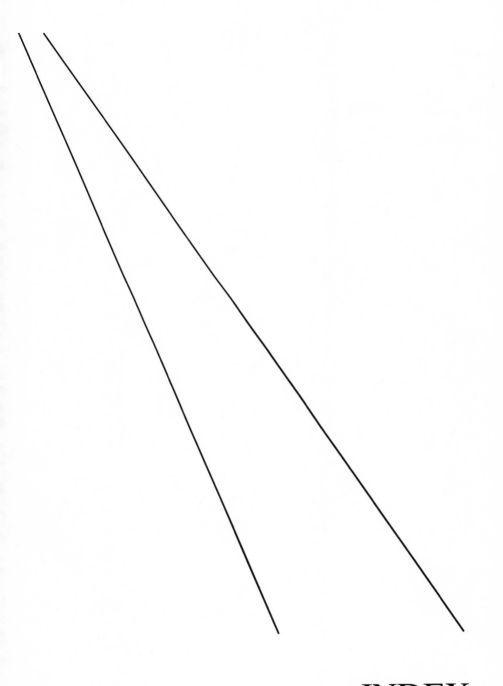

INDEX

INDEX

Play titles appear in **bold face**. *Bold face italic* page numbers refer to those pages where cast and credit listings may be found.

473